EARLY CHILDHOOD Special Education

Birth to Eight

FRANK G. BOWE

THOMSON
DELMAR LEARNING

Australia Canada Mexico Singapore Spain United Kingdom United States

KH

THOMSON
DELMAR LEARNING

Early Childhood Special Education: Birth to Eight, Fourth Edition
Frank G. Bowe, Ph.D., LL.D.

Vice President, Career Education Strategic Business Unit:
Dawn Gerrain

Director of Learning Solutions:
John Fedor

Managing Editor:
Robert L. Serenka, Jr.

Senior Acquisitions Editor:
Erin O'Connor

Product Manager:
Philio Mandl

Editorial Assistant:
Stephanie Kelly

Director of Production:
Wendy A. Troeger

Production Assistant:
Jeffrey Varecka

Compositor:
ICC Macmillan Inc.

Director of Marketing:
Wendy Mapstone

Channel Manager:
Kristin McNary

Cover Design:
Suzanne Nelson

Printed in United States of America
1 2 3 4 5 CK 10 09 08 07

For more information contact Delmar Learning,
5 Maxwell Drive, PO Box 8007, Clifton Park, NY 12065-2919.

Or you can visit our Internet site at
http://www.delmarlearning.com.

Library of Congress Cataloging-in-Publication Data

Bowe, Frank.
Early childhood special education, birth through eight / Frank Bowe.—4th ed.
p. cm.
Rev. ed. of: Birth to eight. 3rd ed. c2004.
Includes bibliographical references and index.
ISBN 978-1-4180-4810-5
ISBN 1-4180-4810-0 (alk. paper)
1. Children with disabilities—Education (Early childhood)—United States.
I. Bowe, Frank. Birth to eight. II. Title.
LC4019.3.B69 2007
371.9'0472—dc22

2006100132

NOTICE TO THE READER

Publisher does not warrant or guarantee any of the products described herein or perform any independent analysis in connection with any of the product information contained herein. Publisher does not assume, and expressly disclaims, any obligation to obtain and include information other than that provided to it by the manufacturer.

The reader is expressly warned to consider and adopt all safety precautions that might be indicated by the activities herein and to avoid all potential hazards. By following the instructions contained herein, the reader willingly assumes all risks in connection with such instructions.

The Publisher makes no representation or warranties of any kind, including but not limited to, the warranties of fitness for particular purpose or merchantability, nor are any such representations implied with respect to the material set forth herein, and the publisher takes no responsibility with respect to such material. The Publisher shall not be liable for any special, consequential, or exemplary damages resulting, in whole or part, from the readers' use of, or reliance upon, this material.

7/29/08

For Phyllis

Join us on the web at

EarlyChildEd.delmar.com

Contents

PREFACE xi
ABOUT THE AUTHOR xv

PART I

INTRODUCTION 1

1 Theory, Development, and Philosophy 5

Overview · 6
Theoretical Bases · 6
Developmental Approaches · 7
Behavioral Approaches · 10
Other Approaches · 11
Development · 12
Five Domains of Development · 13
Development: Birth to Eight · 15
Adaptive Development · 15
Self-Help Behaviors · 16
Social Behaviors · 16
Cognitive Development · 17
Communication Development · 19
Hearing · 20
Language · 21
Speech · 22
Vision · 22
Physical Development · 23
Social or Emotional Development · 27
Philosophy · 30
Differences · 31

2 Prelude: Overview of Early Childhood Special Education 39

Overview · 40
Early Intervention and Preschool/Primary Special Education · 40
Part C: Early Intervention · 41
Section 619, Part B: Preschool Special Education · 44
Primary Special Education · 47
Rationale for ECSE · 47
What is ECSE? · 48
Who Are the Children Being Served? · 49
Early Intervention · 49
Preschool Special Education · 52
Primary Special Education · 54
Cultural Diversity among Children · 55
Cultural Competence · 55
Who are the Workers in the Field? · 59
Roles and Responsibilities · 61
The Federal Role · 62
The State Role · 63
The Local Role · 64
The Parents' Role · 64

3 How Are We Doing? Research in ECSE 67

Overview · 68
Bird's-Eye View · 68
Research and Researchers · 71
Reading Research Reports · 72
Variables · 72
How Research Findings Are Reported · 72
Generalizability · 73
Subject Attrition · 74
Some Examples · 74

What Was Done? · 75
Randomization · 75
Long-Term Effects · 75
Validity · 76
Reliability · 76
Opinion · 76
Qualitative Versus Quantitative Research · 77
Problems in ECSE Research · 78
Within-Group Differences · 79
Sample Size · 79
Other Issues · 80
Research Findings · 80
Unanswered Questions and Unquestioned Answers · 80
The Role of Research in ECSE · 95

PART II

THE LAWS 97

4 The IDEA 99
Overview · 100
Historical Foundations · 101
Constitutional Foundations · 102
Laws and Regulations · 103
Beginnings · 104
HCEEP: Planting the Seeds · 105
Education of the Handicapped Act · 106
Education for all Handicapped Children Act · 107
The 1983 Amendments · 108
The 1986 Amendments · 109
Individuals with Disabilities Education Act · 112
PL 102–52 · 112
1991 IDEA Amendments · 112
The IDEA Amendments of 1997 · 114
No Child Left Behind · 114
IDEA 2004 · 115
The IDEA Today and Tomorrow · 115

5 Family Rights and Services 121
Overview · 122
Rights · 123
Section 504 · 123
Americans with Disabilities Act · 125
Procedural Safeguards · 128
IDEA Part B · 128
IDEA Part C · 129
Discussion · 130
In Brief · 133
Fair Housing Amendments Act (FHAA) · 133
Air Carriers Access Act · 134
Television Decoder Circuitry Act · 134
Telecommunications Act · 134
Services · 134
Supplemental Security Income · 135
Significance of SSI · 136
Definition · 136
Medicaid · 137
Significance of Medicaid · 137
Covered Services · 138
Family Opportunity Act · 139
Early and Periodic Screening Diagnosis and Treatment (EPSDT) · 139
State Children's Health Insurance Program (SCHIP) · 139
Maternal and Child Health · 140
Significance of MCH Block Grants · 140
Respite Care · 140
Significance of Respite Care · 140
Developmental Disabilities Assistance and Bill of Rights Act · 141
Definition · 141
Significance of the DD Act · 142
Head Start · 142
Early Head Start · 143
Significance of Head Start · 143
Assistive Technology Act · 144

PART III

ECSE PRACTICES 147

6 Methods 149
Overview · 150
Curriculum · 152
Curriculum and Individualization · 155
EC versus ECSE Curricula · 156
Curriculum and Structure · 157
Curriculum Choices · 157

Methods in Early Intervention · 159
Embedding · 159
Special Sessions · 163
Family Services · 166
Methods in Preschool · 166
Embedding · 166
Phonemic Awareness and Phonics · 168
Shared Reading · 169
Number Sense · 169
Behavior Modification · 169
Sign Language · 170
Special Sessions · 171
Methods in the Primary Grades · 172
Response to Intervention (RTI) · 172
Embedding · 174
Grouping · 174
Teaching Strategies · 174
Creating Advance Organizers · 175
Providing Community-Based Instruction · 175
Literacy · 175
Mathematics and Science · 176
Related Services · 177
The "Place" of Place · 177
Natural Environments · 178
Least Restrictive Environments · 179
Inclusion · 180
Indoor and Outdoor Environments: Accessibility · 182
Indoor Environments · 182
Outdoor Environments · 185
Practical Issues · 185

7 Evaluation and Assessment 189
Overview · 190
Child Find · 193
Screening · 194
Testing · 195
Legal Issues · 196
Variables in Children · 197
Variables in Examiners · 198
Variables in Instruments · 199
Test Interpretation · 200
Cultural Diversity Issues · 202
Evaluation · 203
The Federal Requirements · 203
Infants and Toddlers · 203
Children with Disabilities · 204
Evaluation Instruments · 204
Assessment · 206
Infants and Toddlers · 206
Families · 207
Children with Disabilities · 208
Communicating with Families · 209
Program Evaluation · 211

8 Individual Planning 217
Overview · 218
Using Assessment and Evaluation Findings · 219
Individualized Family Service Plans · 221
Assessment of Infants or Toddlers · 222
Family Assessment · 222
IFSP Team · 223
IFSP Review · 223
Timing of The IFSP · 223
IFSP Contents · 223
Natural Environment · 225
Start Date and Duration · 225
Service Coordinator · 225
Transition · 225
Informed Consent · 225
Individualized Education Programs · 226
IEP Meeting · 226
Educational Performance · 228
Goals and Objectives · 228
Services · 229
Districtwide Assessments · 229
Transition · 230
Date and Duration · 230
Progress Reports · 230
"Appropriate" · 230
Writing the Plans · 232
Transition · 234
Within Part C · 234
From Part C to Part B · 234
From Part C to Other Service Programs · 235
Parents and Transition from Part C · 236
From Preschool to Elementary School · 236

9 Technology 241
Overview · 242
"Low-Tech" · 243
Assistive Technology Devices · 244
In the Classroom · 246
Reaching the Potential? · 248
Broadband—An Exciting Technology · 249
Assistive Technology Services · 250

Financing Options · 252
ECSE Professionals and Technology · 254
Getting Started · 255
Television · 256
Multimedia · 257
Information Sources · 258
Not for Profit · 258
For Profit · 260

PART IV

DOMAINS OF DEVELOPMENT 263

10 Practical and Ethical Issues 267
Overview · 268
Introduction: Statistics and the IDEA · 269
The Families · 270
Children Being Served · 272
Infants and Toddlers · 272
Preschoolers · 275
Primary-Grade Children · 275
Labels · 277
Family Involvement · 280
Traditional Approaches · 282
A "Reconceptualization" · 283
Family-Focused Programs · 283
Family-Centered Programs · 285
Empowering Families · 286
Involving Fathers · 287
Siblings · 287
Teaming · 288
Ethical Issues · 290
Prenatal Services? · 290
Gene Therapy · 292
Surgical Interventions · 293
Program Issues · 295
Mission · 295
Inclusion · 296
Diversity · 297
Deafness Is Different · 297

11 Communication Development 301
Overview · 302
Prevalence · 303
Developmental Delays · 303
Established Conditions · 305
Speech and Language Impairments · 305
Deafness and Hearing Impairments · 305
Blindness and Low Vision · 306
Assessment · 308
Hearing · 308
Speech and Language · 310
Vision · 311
Intervention · 312
Speech and Language Impairments · 313
Deafness and Hearing Impairments · 314
Blindness and Low Vision · 318
Technology · 321
Working with Families · 322

12 Physical Development.................... 325
Overview · 326
Prevalence · 328
Developmental Delays · 328
Established Conditions · 329
Asthma and Cystic Fibrosis · 330
Back, Leg, and Side Impairments · 331
Cerebral Palsy · 332
Amputation · 334
Traumatic Brain Injury/Spinal Cord Injury · 334
Arthritis and Other Fingers/Hands Impairments · 336
Medically Fragile, Technology-Dependent Children · 336
Assessment · 337
Intervention · 338
Traumatic Brain Injury · 340
Spinal Cord Injury · 341
Asthma · 341
Muscular Dystrophy · 342
Spina Bifida · 342
Cerebral Palsy · 343
Amputation · 343
Medically Fragile, Technology-Dependent Children · 344
Working with Families · 344

13 Cognitive Development 349
Overview · 350
Prevalence · 350
Developmental Delays · 351
Established Conditions · 351
Learning Disabilities · 351

Mental Retardation · 353
Down Syndrome · 353
Fragile X Syndrome · 354
Assessment · 355
Intervention · 356
Prevention · 356
Stimulation · 358
Curriculum · 359
Mental Retardation · 359
Learning Disabilities · 360
Fragile X Syndrome · 361
Working with Families · 362

14 Social or Emotional Development 365
Overview · 366
Prevalence · 367
Developmental Delays · 368
Established Conditions · 369
Assessment · 372
Intervention · 375
Behavior Modification · 377
Other Interventions · 381
Interagency Coordination · 382
Working with Families · 382

15 Adaptive Development 385
Overview · 386
Prevalence · 387
Developmental Delays · 388
Established Conditions · 388
Fetal Alcohol Syndrome · 389
Vulnerable Child Syndrome · 389
AIDS · 390
Epilepsy · 391
Autism Spectrum Disorders · 392
Assessment · 393
Intervention · 395
Autism Spectrum Disorders · 398
Working with Families · 400

RESOURCES 405
Medical Information · 405
Books · 406
Journals · 409
Directories · 410
Information Sources · 410
GLOSSARY 423
REFERENCES 433
INDEX 465

Preface

Early intervention for infants and toddlers with disabilities and preschool/primary special education for children with disabilities are nationally mandated services now helping more than two million children under age nine in the United States. We use the term *early childhood special education* and the acronym *ECSE* to refer to the seamless system of services for infants and toddlers (birth through age two), preschoolers (ages three through five), and K–3 students (ages six through eight).

The Individuals with Disabilities Education Act (IDEA) has required all 50 states to provide early intervention since 1993, preschool special education since 1991, and primary-grade special education since 1977. The IDEA was most recently extended in 2004 by PL 108–446, which continues funding through 2010.

The first edition of this book appeared in 1995. It supported preparation at the preservice and inservice levels for early intervention specialists, related services personnel, and special educators as they sought to meet what then were new requirements. That edition, and the second, appearing in 2000, showed how a fast-growing ECSE field was seeking to discover "what works" and to extend nationwide the "best practices" of a few long-established "model programs." By the time of the third edition (2004), the pace of growth in ECSE was slowing, which gave professionals opportunities to study what they were doing, and how well.

This fourth edition finds ECSE maturing as a field. New, national studies show that families are very satisfied with ECSE programs and services. Other large research projects demonstrate that early intervention and special education are finding young children who need assistance and are giving them, and their families, services to meet those needs. At the same time, new challenges confront the field. No Child Left Behind, the federal law calling for greater accountability in K–12 academics and annual testing beginning in third grade, is challenging ECSE personnel to move beyond its strengths in developing children in all five domains so as to prepare students for success in literacy, numeracy, and science.

FEATURES OF THE BOOK

Early Childhood Special Education: Birth to Eight, fourth edition, documents what we now know about what works in ECSE and what we need to do in preacademics and early childhood academic instruction. The book and its Online Companion™

(www.delmarlearning.com/companions/) offer Web resources for up-to-date information. An *Instructor's Guide* by the author is also available for this edition. That ancillary supplies model test questions as well as chapter outlines, definitions of terms, and other material that should help professors.

The structure of the book remains largely the same as in past editions. Content has been updated throughout, notably about academic instruction in the primary grades, what research is telling us, how ECSE can coordinate better with Early Head Start and Head Start programs, and inclusion of children with and without disabilities. Of course, given its extreme pace of innovation, technology has also been updated for this edition.

Part I introduces ECSE by laying the theoretical groundwork in child development, by providing a bird's-eye view of the field, and by summarizing new findings from the National Early Intervention Longitudinal Study (NEILS), Head Start outcomes studies, and longitudinal research in early childhood (EC) generally.

Part II offers in-depth coverage of the IDEA and other laws that are important to ECSE and to the families it serves. Those other laws include the Americans with Disabilities Act, Supplemental Security Income, Medicaid, and Head Start, as well as No Child Left Behind. This section long has been a strength of *Early Childhood Special Education.*

Part III is the "methods and techniques" section of the book. It focuses on early intervention, special education, and related-services techniques used in the field. Because third graders are tested in math, English, and science, the fourth edition offers more coverage of preacademics and academics in these areas. This section of the book also shows readers how to write Individualized Family Service Plans (IFSPs) and Individualized Education Programs (IEPs).

Part IV discusses, in depth, the five domains of development (communication, physical, cognitive, social or emotional, and adaptive) and the various disabilities that are associated with each. This section of the book focuses on what early interventionists, special educators, and related-services personnel do differently to meet the diverse needs of young children with a wide range of needs.

Resources follow. These offer students jumping-off points for continued study, including books and on-line information sources. References, a glossary of terms, and an index conclude the book.

ACKNOWLEDGMENTS

I thank Thomson Delmar Learning acquisitions editor Erin J. O'Connor, developmental editor Philip I. Mandl, and editorial assistant Stephanie Kelly for their support and guidance. My graduate student Ioanna Louvi deserves appreciation for helping select the new photographs that illustrate this edition. I also thank the reviewers who offered helpful comments on the third edition and on drafts of the fourth edition:

Jacqualine Berger,
Empire State College,
Buffalo, New York

Marie Brand,
SUNY Empire State College,
New York, New York

Mary Cordell,
Navarro College,
Corsicana, Texas

Barbara Fiechtl,
Utah State University,
Logan, Utah

Marilyn Haller,
Oklahoma Baptist University,
Shawnee, Oklahoma

Susan Johnston,
University of Utah,
Salt Lake City, Utah

Andrea L. Rotzien,
Grand Valley State University,
Allendale, Michigan

Yolanda O. Touré,
Los Angeles Trade Technical College,
Los Angeles, California

Dina Vouis,
Santa Fe Community College,
Gainesville, Florida

ACRONYMS

Early Childhood Special Education: Birth to Eight contains several acronyms. The first time a frequently used technical term appears, the full term is used and its acronym is given. Thereafter, the acronym is used. The author hopes that this approach strikes a balance between the Scylla of irritating readers by using too many abbreviations and the Charybdis of annoying them by repeating lengthy phrases too often. Similarly, to avoid innumerable uses of the awkward phrases "he or she" and "him or her," this book adopts the convention of alternating "he/him" in even-numbered chapters and "she/her" in odd-numbered chapters.

The following list of acronyms may also help:

ADA Americans with Disabilities Act
ADHD Attention-deficit/hyperactivity disorder
AIDS Acquired immune deficiency syndrome
ASL American Sign Language
CDA Child development associate
CDC Centers for Disease Control and Prevention
CEC Council for Exceptional Children
CMV Cytomegalovirus infection
CP Cerebral palsy
CPS Current Population Survey
DAP Developmentally appropriate practice
DEC Division for Early Childhood
EC Early childhood
ECSE Early childhood special education
ED Emotional disturbance
EEPCD Early Education Program for Children with Disabilities
FAE Fetal alcohol effect
FAS Fetal alcohol syndrome
HCEEP Handicapped Children's Early Education Program
HHS Health and Human Services, U.S. Department of
HIV Human immunodeficiency virus
ICC Interagency Coordinating Council
ICU Intensive care unit
IDEA Individuals with Disabilities Education Act
IEP Individualized Education Program
IFSP Individualized Family Service Plan
IHDP Infant Health and Development Program
LBW Low birthweight
LD Learning disabilities
LRE Least restrictive environment
MD Muscular dystrophy
NAEYC National Association for the Education of Young Children
NE Natural environment
NEILS Natural Early Intervention Longitudinal Study
NICU Neonatal intensive care unit

NLTS	National Longitudinal Transition Study
ROP	Retinopathy of prematurity
SCI	Spinal cord injury
SES	Socioeconomic status
SIPP	Survey of Income and Program Participation
SSI	Supplemental Security Income
TBI	Traumatic brain injury
VCS	Vulnerable child syndrome

About the Author

Dr. Frank G. Bowe is the Dr. Mervin Livingston Schloss Distinguished Professor for the Study of Disabilities at Hofstra University, Long Island, New York. Hofstra University has the largest early childhood special education teacher and early-interventionist training program in the New York City metropolitan area. In addition to writing the three previous editions of this text, Dr. Bowe is also the author of *Making Inclusion Work* (Prentice Hall/Merrill Education) and other texts.

His Ph.D., from NYU, is in educational psychology (research). He earned a master's in education from the Gallaudet Graduate School and his B.A. in English from McDaniel College (then known as Western Maryland College).

Dr. Bowe and his wife Phyllis reside on the South Shore of Long Island.

Introduction

PART 1

1 Theory, Development, and Philosophy

2 Prelude: Overview of Early Childhood Special Education

3 How Are We Doing? Research in ECSE

Early childhood special education (ECSE) serves young children from birth through the age of eight (i.e., until they turn nine years of age). That is why the subtitle of this book is *Birth to Eight*.

The fourth edition of this text comes as our nation is giving unprecedented attention to the early childhood (EC) years. About half of all kindergartners now attend full-day kindergarten (Lee, Burkam, Ready, Honigman, & Meisels, 2006). Many thousands of American families now send their three- to five-year-olds for tutoring at for-profit institutes run by the likes of Kaplan Inc. and Sylvan Learning Centers. Some of this is in response to the heightened academic demands of the No Child Left Behind Act of 2001 (NCLB), notably high-stakes tests as early as third grade. Some of it, however, seems to reflect parental anxieties. One mother, explaining why she pays for extra help in academics for her five-year-old son, commented, "Kids can't only be little kids any more. I want him to go to the college he wants. As long as it's in the Ivy League" (quoted in Borja, 2005, p. 10).

Young children with disabilities, and the ECSE professionals who teach them, are confronted with ever-greater pressures as a result of all of this. The bar for these young children is much higher than it was just a few years ago. The greatly increased emphasis on academics also threatens to dwarf ECSE's traditional holistic focus on all five domains of development in young children (adaptive, cognitive, communication, physical, and social/emotional). How ECSE as a field is coping, and what directions it should now pursue, are topics for much discussion. An Online Companion helps readers to continue the debates (NCLB, for example, is being reauthorized as this edition goes to press). The site is www.earlychilded.delmar.com. Other updates are available at www.frankbowe.net.

Part I of this book lays the groundwork. Chapter 1 discusses child development. Educators need to know what young children are capable of learning and doing at different ages. This chapter outlines competing theories about child development, each of which has something to offer to enrich our understanding of young children. Chapter 2 then provides a bird's-eye view of the field we call ECSE. The three components of ECSE (early intervention, preschool special education, and primary-grade special education), the professionals who work in these fields, the key terms ("jargon") they use, and demographics about the children being served are introduced. Chapter 3 completes the introduction by highlighting what research has taught us about what ECSE is doing, how well it is doing these things, and how satisfied the families are.

The balance of this Part I introduction briefly describes the young children of interest to us in this book. We look first at their ages, then at the size of the population, and finally at rights and services.

AGE RANGES

Our coverage is divided into three three-year age ranges. These are illustrated in Figure I–1.

The first age range is birth to two inclusive. Very young children in this grouping are referred to, in the Individuals with Disabilities Education Act (IDEA), as *infants or toddlers with disabilities*. Early intervention services for them are authorized by IDEA Part C. Infants and toddlers are eligible for Part C services until they "age out" when they turn three years of age. Thus, the first age range spans 0 to 36 months of age. IDEA 2004,

Infants and toddlers with disabilities	Birth to 36 months of age	Part C
Preschoolers with disabilities	36 to 72 months of age	Part B, Section 619
Young children with disabilities	72 to 108 months of age	Part B

FIGURE I–1 Age ranges for ECSE.

PL 108–446, permits states to create agreements under which these very young children would continue under Part C through kindergarten.

The second age range is three to five inclusive (36 to 72 months of age). These children are called, in the IDEA, *children with disabilities*. Services for them are authorized by Section 619 of IDEA Part B or, as just noted, in some cases, Part C.

The third and final age range of interest to us in this book is six to eight inclusive (72 to 108 months). These students, too, are called *children with disabilities* in the IDEA. That law does not have a section specific to these children. Rather, the IDEA recognizes as "children with disabilities" those between the ages of three and when children depart high school (typically, age 18 to 21).

SIZE OF THE POPULATION

Disabilities may occur at any time in a person's life. Most disabilities, in fact, appear after birth. Relatively few are diagnosed at birth. It typically takes time before family members, doctors, and other professionals identify a child's disability. Even some conditions that occur at birth are not recognized as such until a year or more later. For these reasons, we would anticipate that the number of young children with disabilities would rise as we move through the three age ranges that are illustrated in Figure I–1.

In fact, that is what happens. Of the more than 2.2 million children with disabilities who are in the nine-year ECSE span, one in every eight are infants or toddlers (birth to two inclusive). IDEA Part C serves some 300,000 very young children. Another 3 in every 10 ECSE students (approximately 31 percent) are preschoolers (three to five inclusive). IDEA Part B, Section 619, serves more than 700,000 preschoolers. The bulk of the ECSE population, more than one out of every two (57 percent), are in the six-to-eight-inclusive age range. IDEA Part B serves about 1.2 million children in that span. In each instance, the numbers come from the U.S. Department of Education's *28th Annual Report to Congress on Implementation of the Individuals with Disabilities Education Act* (2006c). Figure I–2 summarizes the statistics.

To help place these figures into context, consider how they compare with the numbers of young children served by the well-known federally funded Head Start programs. Early Head Start provided services to 62,000 children under age three during 2004. That is about one-fifth as many as were helped by IDEA Part C that year. The older, better-known Head Start program had 900,000 young children enrolled that same year, the vast majority of whom were in the three to five age range. Thus, Head Start served somewhat more children than did IDEA Part B, Section 619 preschool programs. The figures on

Infants and toddlers with disabilities	300,000 children	14% of all ECSE children
Preschoolers with disabilities	700,000 children	32% of all ECSE children
Young children with disabilities	1,200,000 children	54% of all ECSE children

FIGURE 1–2 Statistics of ECSE.

Head Start appeared in the *Head Start Program Fact Sheet, Fiscal Year 2004* (U.S. Department of Health and Human Services, 2005).

PROMISES

The IDEA is an *entitlement* program. Infants and toddlers who meet Part C eligibility criteria, and their families, have a right to early intervention services. Similarly, young children with disabilities who satisfy Part B eligibility rules are entitled to special education and related services. No eligible young children may be denied service.

Teachers in training and others sometimes ask, "What happened in the years before IDEA entitlement became a nationwide reality?" (National mandates for early intervention took effect in 1993, those for preschool special education in 1991, and those for primary special education in 1977.) The short answer to the question is that, prior to entitlement, families often made private arrangements. Some families paid as much as $40,000 a year (in today's dollars) for special education and therapy services for their children. Other families were successful in convincing local school officials to enroll their children at public expense. Typically, however, tutoring and such "related services" as speech and language pathology, occupational therapy, and physical therapy were not offered by the public school system. Families had to hire specialists to help their young children in these areas, usually in after-school hours, or teach the children themselves.

Today, *all* young children with disabilities are entitled to services they need—special education and related services alike. The entitlement extends all the way through high school. That is one of our nation's promises to these children and their families. Other promises are important as well. The Americans with Disabilities Act (ADA) and Section 504 of the Rehabilitation Act, both of which will be described in Part II's Chapter 5, offer very significant civil rights for people with disabilities and for their families. Virtually every college and university in the United States must admit and educate students with disabilities on a nondiscriminatory basis. These postsecondary programs must provide, at no charge to students and families, such support services as sign language interpreters and note-taking assistance. Most large employers, too, are forbidden from discriminating on the basis of disabilities. These for-profit and not-for-profit organizations must offer reasonable accommodations for applicants and employees with disabilities.

For all of these reasons, the future for today's young children with disabilities appears quite bright. Our country has made, and will keep, promises to them. Families having young children with disabilities may be reassured by all of this. Their children will be given a chance at success in school and in life.

It all begins with ECSE.

CHAPTER

Theory, Development, and Philosophy

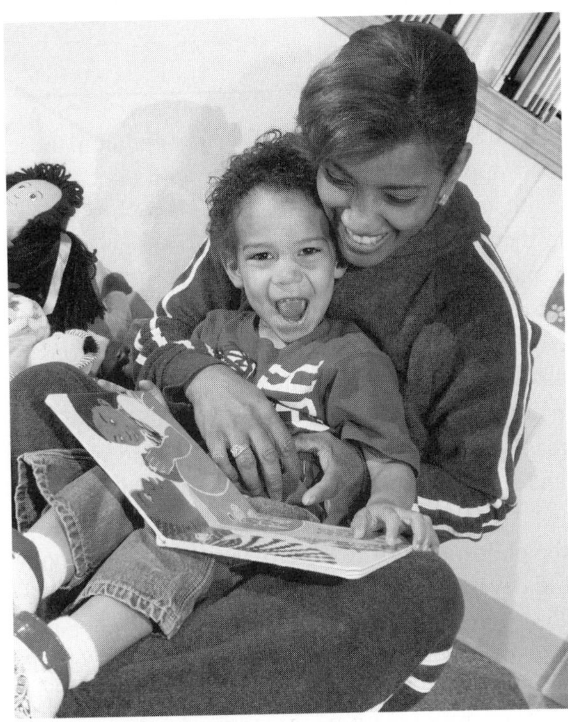

A primary goal of early childhood special education is to attempt to change children's developmental trajectories by intervening early with specialized instruction. We are attempting to remediate delays caused by the child's disabilities and prevent any secondary disabilities from developing. When we work with families to develop Individual Education Plans we are making an implicit contract with them to provide specialized instruction. What we have learned through inclusion and working closely with professionals in early childhood education is that specialized instruction generally does not require special places, special materials, or special activities. What it does require is special planning, special training, and special attention. (SANDALL, SCHWARTZ, & JOSEPH, 2001, PP. 3–4)

OBJECTIVES

After reading this chapter, you should be able to:

- Describe Piaget's stages of development for young children.
- Describe Erikson's developmental crises for young children.
- Describe Vygotsky's zone of proximal development.
- Identify the five domains of development.
- Describe how young children with disabilities or delays develop in these domains.

- Describe the guiding philosophy of early childhood education.
- Describe the guiding philosophy of early childhood special education.

CHAPTER OUTLINE

- OVERVIEW
- THEORETICAL BASES
  - Developmental Approaches
  - Behavioral Approaches
  - Other Approaches
- DEVELOPMENT
  - Five Domains of Development
  - Development: Birth to Eight
- PHILOSOPHY
  - Differences

OVERVIEW

Early childhood special education (ECSE)
is the term describing early intervention, preschool, and primary-grade services for young children who have disabilities or delays in development and with their families. It is a specialized form of the broader field of early childhood education.

Early childhood special education (ECSE)* works with very young children, those who are under the age of nine. It is appropriate for us to begin with the children being served; thus, the chapter opens with an overview of development theory. What are the major psychological and learning theories that inform our understanding of child development? For some readers, this material will be review; for others, it is essential background information. In fact, students who come to this book without any prior training in psychology may do well to read up on the major theories described in this section.

The chapter then considers domains of development in young children. How do maturation and learning occur in children during the birth-to-eight period? ECSE describes their development in terms of five areas, known as domains of development: physical, cognitive, adaptive, communication, and social or emotional. Each domain is introduced and briefly described in this chapter.

From development, we move to the philosophy of ECSE as a field. This philosophy derives from our understanding of child development. That is, our philosophy is a statement of what we as educators should do given what we know about development in young children. What are the broad and underlying beliefs that characterize early childhood special educators as a group? This section introduces the philosophy of ECSE as it relates to the philosophy of the broader field of **early childhood (EC) education.** As we will see, those philosophies have much in common, but they do differ on some key points. In general, the ideals of EC education envision the teacher as a guide and facilitator who helps children learn for themselves, while ECSE sees the teacher in a much more active and directive role.

Early childhood (EC) education
is the term referring to services for young children in the birth-to-eight-inclusive period. EC is a much larger field than is ECSE.

THEORETICAL BASES

Families are inherently vulnerable at the time of a child's birth. When that child has or appears to have a disability, the family is often even more susceptible to being hurt or divided by the experience. These vulnerabilities may lead families of young children

*__Note__: Terms appearing in boldface are defined in page margins. The terms and their definitions also are listed in alphabetical order in the glossary at the end of this text.

with disabilities to seek ECSE services. At other times, disability is not evident at birth but becomes apparent during a child's first few years of life. That is particularly the case with low-socioeconomic-status (SES) families. Craig Ramey and his associates launched what they called *The Abecedarian Project* for exactly this reason: Such factors as low SES, low parental education attainment levels, and single-parent households are associated, to unusual degrees, with at-risk status in young children, especially for mild to moderate mental retardation (Martin, Ramey, & Ramey, 1990). The Abecedarian Project offered early and intensive support for parents on infant stimulation, preacademic training, and other steps family members could take to accelerate cognitive development in young children. Without such interventions, Kaplan-Sanoff, Parker, and Zuckerman (1991) agreed, children in low-SES families are at considerable risk of delays in development. The **double jeopardy** they referred to arises because the children tend not only to have more accidents and illnesses than do children in higher-SES families but also to suffer more than other children and for longer periods of time from those illnesses or accidents that do occur.

Double jeopardy

is a term used by some researchers to help explain risks children face due to *both* biological and environmental risk factors acting together. Children from families of low socioeconomic status tend to have more illnesses and accidents *and* to suffer more long-lasting consequences from these than do children from families of high socioeconomic status.

The philosophy and theory behind such efforts as the Abecedarian Project stress the importance of early, effective intervention. Project Head Start began in 1964 because of a similar driving philosophy: Preschool services would give young children, especially children from lower-SES homes, a *head start* toward success in kindergarten and first grade. Early intervention and preschool programming both were founded on beliefs about **developmental plasticity:** Young children, to an extent not found in adolescents and adults, can change course if provided with timely, directed assistance.

Developmental plasticity

is the belief that young children in particular can develop rapidly, changing their behavior—and indeed their lives—if services are provided early in life.

Impressive new evidence indicates that educational services offered to young children can make major, long-lasting differences in their lives. We now know that quality preschool education is connected to success through K–12 and beyond and that it is cost-effective (e.g., Oppenheim & McGregor, 2002; Reynolds, 2005). As for the specialized field of ECSE, research shows that it does what it is intended to do. ECSE is effective in meeting the unique needs of infants, toddlers, preschoolers, and primary-grade children with disabilities (e.g., McCormick et al., 2006). The major issues about which questions remain are two: (1) Is ECSE cost-effective? and (2) How well is ECSE managing the sea changes launched by No Child Left Behind (2001) and IDEA 2004 that emphasize skills and knowledge in core academic areas, notably language arts and mathematics? We will review evidence on these issues in Chapter 3.

ECSE draws on a rich theoretical framework that undergirds early intervention and preschool services. Much of this theoretical work has been carried out in fields such as educational and developmental psychology (Kohlberg et al., 1987; Kohlberg & Mayer, 1972). Increasingly, however, the field is generating its own body of knowledge, its own theories, and its own philosophies. Three approaches are found in ECSE today: developmental, behavioral, and other, including work by Abraham Maslow (1954) and by Elizabeth Kübler-Ross (1969).

DEVELOPMENTAL APPROACHES

The American psychologist Arnold Gesell, working in the 1920s and 1930s, described children's behavior at different stages of development. He suggested that development, both physical and cognitive, progressed very rapidly through a series of stages, leveling off by about age six (Gesell, 1925). Nearly 40 years later, the Swiss psychologist Jean

Sensorimotor stage

is the Piagetian period in which young children perform goal-directed actions and acquire the idea of object permanence.

Preoperational stage,

for Piaget, is the stage in child development just before children acquire the ability to engage in symbolic mental actions. A preoperational child, for example, cannot grasp the concept of reversibility.

Concrete operational stage,

for Piaget, is the stage at which children can perform *operations* on ideas, specifically symbolic and logical thoughts. This stage begins at age 7 and concludes at age 11, according to Piaget.

Developmentally appropriate

services are designed to be suitable for children at particular stages of development. Thus, very short individual activities are developmentally appropriate for infants and toddlers, while lengthy large-group activities are not.

Discovery learning

(Jerome Bruner) is an approach in which children learn things themselves as teachers structure the environment to facilitate children's discovery.

Piaget described the **sensorimotor** and **preoperational stages** through which newborns to 36-month-olds typically pass. Sensorimotor stage tasks include performing goal-directed actions and acquiring the idea of object permanence. Preoperational stage tasks include pretend play and use of such symbols as words (Piaget, 1962). The preoperational stage ends at about age seven, at which point Piaget believed that young children entered a **concrete operational stage** in which they began to be capable of using symbolic and logical information. It is that ability that marks the end of the *early childhood* period. All these tasks are facilitated by intact senses, particularly vision and hearing.

Piaget's findings created a view of infants, toddlers, and preschool-age children as *active* agents. Young children, Piaget said, are little scientists, performing trial-and-error experiments on the world around them. Child care workers can help them to develop skills for which they are developmentally ready. Piaget's work set the stage for EC approaches in which program staff guide and facilitate young children in child-initiated and child-directed activities (Bredekamp, 1987; Gestwicki, 2007). These are aspects of a **developmentally appropriate** approach to EC services. Piaget did not believe that parents or professionals should attempt to teach young children abilities that are characteristic of later stages. Young children can, however, be guided in performing stage-appropriate activities (Piaget, 1962; Piaget & Inhelder, 1969).

The challenge in ECSE is to find ways to help children with special needs do the work Piaget believed to be appropriate for their stages (e.g., Allen & Marotz, 2007). How, for example, can child care workers help toddlers who are deaf learn language despite their inability to hear what is said around them? Piaget's theoretical framework helps us understand the task as being one of assisting children who are deaf to learn language as active participants in the task. That approach runs counter to traditional attempts to *teach* these children words and syntax, efforts that do not give the children as active a role to play. Psycholinguists have shown that language is best acquired when it is constructed anew, when children take in many thousands of discrete utterances and use them to generate rules (Chomsky, 1957, 1968).

Similar suggestions have been made by Jerome Bruner, who advanced the notion of **discovery learning.** Bruner (1966), a cognitive psychologist, stated, for example, "We teach a subject . . . to get a student to think . . . for himself, to consider matters as an historian does, to take part in the process of knowledge-getting. Knowing is a process, not a product" (p. 72).

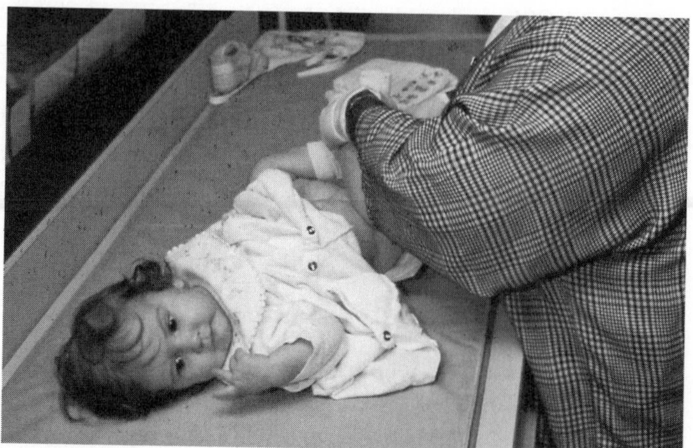

Very young children characteristically show fascination with their own bodies and enjoy watching their fingers move.

Erik Erikson (1963) added a psychosocial perspective to our understanding of early childhood. He proposed that each of us must pass through and successfully resolve "developmental crises" throughout life. Infants and toddlers, he suggested, must master the **trust versus mistrust** crisis, in which infants learn to trust their caregivers, particularly parents. Toddlers then confront the **autonomy versus shame and doubt** stage, during which they learn to assume some responsibilities for themselves, including self-feeding and toileting. They also gain confidence by exploring their environments without being dissuaded by parental limits or punishment. Erikson insisted that infants and toddlers who do not successfully resolve these crises are harmed for life, or at least until later resolution. The next stage, Erikson said, is that of **initiative versus guilt.** At this level, children learn to have confidence in their own explorations and inventions—that is, in taking the initiative. If they are thwarted at this stage, Erikson believed, they may become hesitant and lack self-confidence. Their curiosity and desire to strike out on their own may be suppressed and even replaced by a sense of guilt about "going too far" or "stepping outside the boundaries of approved behavior." Erikson's fourth stage, that of **industry versus inferiority,** stretches from age 6 to age 12. During this time, young children focus on personal achievements. If they succeed, they become industrious. If they fail, they develop a sense of inferiority.

Trust versus mistrust is the Eriksonian stage in which infants learn to trust their caregivers, particularly parents.

Autonomy versus shame and doubt is the Eriksonian stage in which toddlers learn to assume self-responsibility, including feeding and toileting activities.

Initiative versus guilt is the Eriksonian stage in which preschool-age children struggle between exploring for its own sake and feeling guilty for doing so.

Industry versus inferiority is Erikson's fourth stage. Industriousness, or achievement, is the successful outcome of this stage. Failure to achieve leads to a sense of inferiority.

Those insights are particularly helpful for EC specialists and for parents, because they warn against parental overprotection, which is a major concern of EC educators. Erikson taught us the importance of allowing young children to pass unhindered through these developmental stages and to resolve for themselves the crises they present. With respect to the *autonomy versus shame and doubt* stage, this approach means permitting children to explore their environments, to learn to trust themselves, and to take pride in their accomplishments. Erikson's insights are particularly valuable in warning parents and professionals about the dangers of **experiential deprivation.** When young children are not allowed to confront strange, even dangerous situations—as when parents protect them unnecessarily—the children do not resolve Erikson's autonomy stage successfully. They enter school still unsure of themselves, having internalized parental fears (Erikson, 1963).

Experiential deprivation occurs when young children are not allowed to confront strange, even dangerous, situations—as when parents overprotect them. According to Erikson, overprotected children may enter school still unsure of themselves, having internalized parental fears.

Urie Bronfenbrenner (1979, 1989) encouraged us to look at *context.* Bronfenbrenner was one of the founding fathers of Head Start. A longtime professor at Cornell University, he died on September 25, 2005. According to Bronfenbrenner, the child develops within the context of the family while the family, in turn, evolves within the context of the community. He called this *ecology.* Thus, in assessing the child's development, Bronfenbrenner urged us to examine the familial and community contexts as well as the child herself (e.g., contextual or ecological assessment). Similarly, in deciding how to enhance a child's development, Bronfenbrenner would have us use familial and community resources.

Lev Vygotsky also focuses attention on the social context. His sociohistorical theory urges us to develop strong support networks around the child and around the family. Vygotsky's main claim to fame, however, is his concept of the **zone of proximal development.** Oversimplified, this idea tells us that a child is ready, at any given moment, to learn some things but not others. Vygotsky urges us to identify exactly what the child is almost ready to learn and to teach it at that time. One good clue: If the child can do something in the presence of (and with a little help from) a teacher but is not able to do the same task independently, that task probably is within Vygotsky's zone. Tasks that are more challenging cognitively should not be introduced until the child has developed further. The teacher's support at the "zone" serves much the same purposes as it does in Bruner's theory of discovery learning—it provides "scaffolding," which structures the child's explorations (Bronfenbrenner & Morris, 1998).

Zone of proximal development (Lev Vygotsky) is the edge to which children's development has brought them—that is, what they can learn, if helped. Teachers should not attempt to introduce more cognitively challenging material, however, until children progress to higher levels of development.

Other work that is helpful in ECSE was carried out by Lawrence Kohlberg, who was a psychology professor at Harvard University. Kohlberg believed that children progress through stages of moral development. According to his theory, children begin with a *law of the jungle* mentality in which the operative questions are "Will I be punished or rewarded for doing this?" and "Can I manipulate my parents (caregiver) and get away with this?" He saw these as low-level stages of moral reasoning. Only later in childhood and in adolescence do people begin to recognize that rules are created by people for reasons and that a mature human being makes her own decisions, based on personal value systems, then faces the consequences (Kohlberg, 1984).

Kohlberg's work has attracted surprisingly little attention in disability-related fields of study. Gliedman and Roth (1980), writing in *The Unexpected Minority,* offer a brief but trenchant analysis of how Kohlberg's theory applies to children with disabilities, criticizing his theory of stages because they see it as applying only where children are confident that their worlds make sense. For many children with disabilities, particularly those with cognitive or sensory impairments, the world around them may not in fact be one inspiring a sense of justice and morality. Gliedman and Roth add that many caregivers may not permit young children with disabilities to make their own moral decisions and to act on those, thus interfering with the process through which Kohlberg believed children must progress to reach the higher levels of moral reasoning.

BEHAVIORAL APPROACHES

A very different stream of work in psychology gave us the principles of **behavior modification.** B. F. Skinner's approach of **operant conditioning** related behavior to its consequences, specifically to reinforcements (Skinner, 1953). As people "operate" on the environment, things happen. Actions that are followed by pleasant events tend to be repeated. Skinner called this process *positive reinforcement,* though a better term is **presentation reinforcement.** Actions that remove us from unpleasant circumstances likewise tend to be repeated. Skinner called this *negative reinforcement,* though a better term is **removal reinforcement.** Figure 1–1 illustrates the principles.

Behavior modification uses *presentation reinforcement, removal reinforcement,* and other techniques to increase the likelihood that children will display desired behaviors and will not produce undesired behaviors.

Operant conditioning is a process through which behavior is altered by manipulating its consequences.

Presentation reinforcement is the presentation of a consequence that increases the frequency of the behavior it follows. Also called *positive reinforcement,* it contrasts with negative reinforcement, in which a consequence is removed.

Removal reinforcement increases the frequency of the behavior it follows by removing on undesired consequence. Also called *negative reinforcement,* an example is when children are released from doing daily assigned household chores when they behave appropriately during dinner.

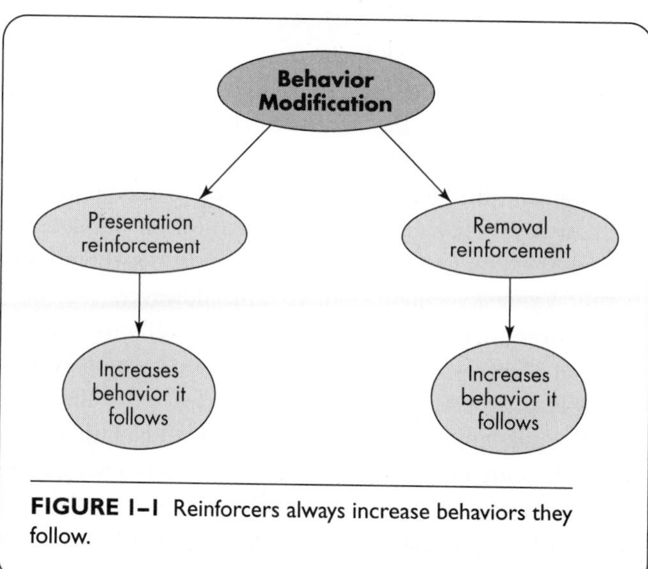

FIGURE 1–1 Reinforcers always increase behaviors they follow.

Skinner and the legions of behaviorists who followed him demonstrated that behavior modification works as long as the consequences immediately and consistently follow behavior. By contrast, by removing reinforcement altogether, eliminating some behaviors is possible. **Extinction** can help parents and professionals to remove undesirable habits and behavior patterns in young children. **Punishment,** to Skinner, makes behavior less likely; that behavior may, however, reappear in other contexts (displacement), for which reason Skinner preferred reinforcement to punishment.

Extinction

occurs when reinforcement is removed altogether so that behavior decreases and then ceases.

Punishment

is any consequence that decreases the frequency of the behavior it follows. One possible outcome, however, is displacement, in which some other behavior increases in frequency.

One of the most important ideas Skinner gave us is that of *shaping.* He was able to teach pigeons to play a toy piano by first reinforcing any movement by the pigeon toward the piano, then only those further movements bringing the pigeon even closer to the piano, and finally only direct pecks on piano keys. Also called the method of *successive approximations,* shaping is a key tool parents and early intervention specialists can use to help an infant or toddler learn new behaviors. This method is useful because young children with disabilities or developmental delays frequently are not able to do things just right the first time. Shaping is particularly useful in physical and occupational therapy, speech and language pathology, and other interventions requiring young children to develop new habits. Through successive approximations, parents and professionals can produce increasingly acceptable behavior (Skinner, 1953). A great deal of experimental evidence demonstrates that behavior modification helps children with disabilities (Wolery, Bailey, & Sugai, 1988).

OTHER APPROACHES

The psychologist Abraham Maslow (1953), in his influential *Motivation and Personality,* posits five levels of needs. The lowest two are for survival (shelter, food, sleep) and safety (physical and psychological). According to Maslow, until those needs are met, they dominate a person's interactions with the environment. Once they have been met, however, they are satiated and no longer drive behavior. Middle-level needs are for love and esteem, neither of which is ever completely satisfied. The highest-level needs, according to Maslow, are what he called self-actualization needs. These needs are, to quote a U.S. Army slogan, to "be all you can be"—to fulfill your potential. Maslow believes that self-actualization needs can never be satisfied; the more they are fulfilled, the more an individual intensifies the search for more ways to "self-actualize."

Maslow's work helps us understand both young children with disabilities and their families. For the families in particular, the birth of a child with a disability, especially a severe one, threatens safety and survival. The parents are driven to find safe havens in the form of competent and caring professionals who can cure or at least ameliorate the child's condition. Some parents persist in what an objective observer might regard as an unrealistic and unremitting pursuit of a cure, putting aside virtually everything else, including their own needs and the needs of other family members. Maslow's work helps us understand why these parents act as they do (see Figure 1–2).

Elizabeth Kübler-Ross (1969), in her powerful book *On Death and Dying,* suggests that families will cope with death (and, by extension, with the disability of a family member) first by denying the reality. Any early intervention or preschool special education program staff member who has worked with parents of newly diagnosed children knows that denial is a powerful impulse in these parents. Later, anger emerges, as they eventually face the reality. Parents may move to Kübler-Ross's third stage, that of bargaining with God: "If you cure my child, I promise to . . . ." Depression and, ultimately, acceptance complete the process. Other parents move directly to acceptance.

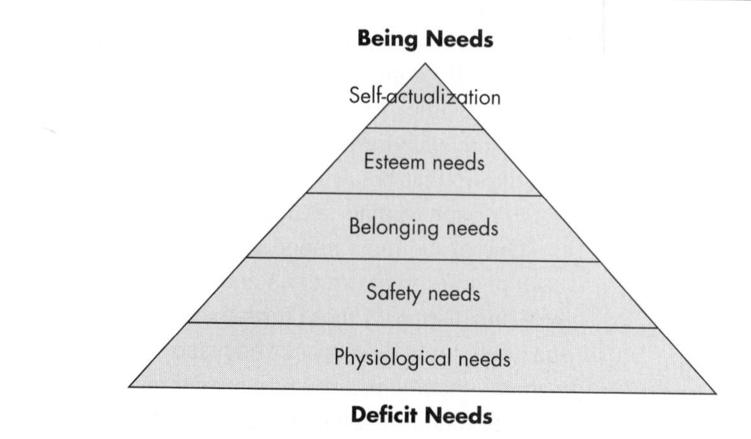

FIGURE 1–2 Maslow's Hierarchy of Needs. According to Maslow (1954), physiological needs (for food, water, etc.) and safety (for physical and psychological security) drive human beings until they are satisfied. Family members, particularly mothers of young children, may feel that their and the family's safety is at risk due to a child's disability. The mother may, accordingly, respond to that need, even if it means neglecting what are for Maslow higher needs, such as self-esteem.

Children with disabilities may themselves move through these five stages. However, experience suggests that children who are born with disabilities or who become disabled very early in life have no sense of a prior (nondisabled) self and therefore may not experience the kind of loss that is a premise of Kübler-Ross's theory. Rather, as Gliedman and Roth (1980) demonstrated, what anger these individuals feel tends to come from their perception (usually quite accurate) that the world into which they were born is not one they experience as being fair and just.

DEVELOPMENT

Development in young children is remarkable for its *diversity.* Although charts showing average developmental milestones are readily available, in both professional and lay literature, divergence from these averages is normal and to be expected. That is why the major issue in early childhood development is not so much the age at which a child does something but rather the *sequence* the child follows. Gross motor skills are usually displayed before fine motor skills appear. Babbling most often precedes articulate speech. Children generally sit before they stand. It is these patterns, or sequences, that signal "normal" development. Some young children proceed through one developmental phase faster than others do. By the time they enter kindergarten or first grade, however, most children have caught up with their peers in all major areas of development.

The age at which a young child first speaks, for example, is widely reported to be one year of age. But some children speak as early as 8 months, some as late as 18 months. Some children walk as early as 7 months, some as late as two years. There is a range of normal ages at which children reach developmental milestones. Walking, to continue

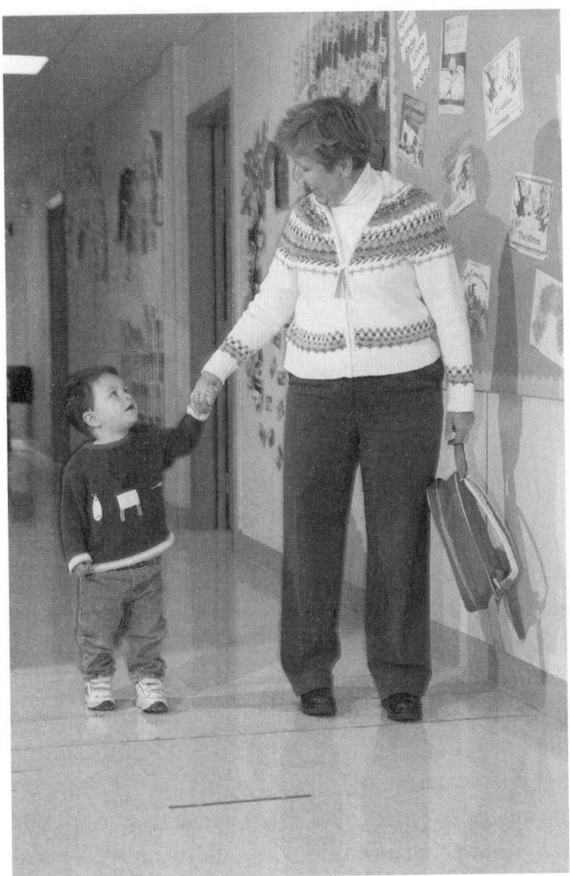

Abraham Maslow's theory of development helps us understand how critical survival and safety needs are in enabling children to feel free to satisfy higher-level needs.

with this example, usually occurs between 11 and 15 months of age; anything within that range is normal. In fact, first walking at 20 months is within a normal range, although somewhat late. A child who first walks at two years, however, is delayed.

The concept that the sequence matters more than the actual time periods is central in the field of child development. When young children proceed as expected from one level to another, even if some of those stages occur later than anticipated, development appears to be normal. The sequence is so critical that experts allow considerable leeway for achievement of milestones in development. To illustrate with a common measure, children's weight by 36 months is typically reported to average 30 pounds. However, weights as high as 35 pounds and as low as 28 pounds are still within a normal range. More important for a child's physical development is that a rapid weight increase during the first 12 months be followed by a somewhat slower, but also steadier, increase during the next two years. That sequence—very rapid growth followed by slower but smoother growth—matters much more than the specific weight attained at any given age.

Developmental delays and disabilities are most likely to occur when a child is exposed to *multiple risk factors.* Risk factors may be *biological*, *environmental*, or both. Biological risks include exposure to illegal drugs such as cocaine in utero. One effect of maternal use of cocaine during pregnancy is oxygen deprivation, as the supply of oxygen passing through the placenta is limited by vasoconstriction (Schneider & Chasnoff, 1987; Williams & Howard, 1993). The evidence at present seems to show that unless further problems emerge, many fetuses and infants can survive such oxygen debts with little or no developmental consequences. However, if environmental factors are added—as when a cocaine-abusing mother neglects her infant—delays may result. The point is that delays are often due not to one, or even two, risk factors but rather to multiple pre-, peri-, and postnatal stress factors *and* low family stability, often indicated by poverty and peripatetic lifestyles.

Development proceeds in spurts. Children may begin speaking, for example, and then seem to plateau at one- or two-word utterances while they master motor development—walking and balancing while walking, in particular—after which speech and language development seem to accelerate again. Other children do not show this pattern. Such alternations in development are yet another reason ECSE workers and parents alike should exercise caution when assessing whether apparent delays in development are serious enough to warrant extensive intervention (Allen & Marotz, 2007).

Domains

are areas of development. Part C of the Individuals with Disabilities Education Act recognizes five such domains: adaptive, cognitive, communication, physical, and social or emotional.

FIVE DOMAINS OF DEVELOPMENT

The Individuals with Disabilities Education Act (IDEA), through the 2004 reauthorization, recognizes five developmental **domains:** adaptive, cognitive, communication, physical, and social or emotional (Figure 1–3). Although this book considers each

Adaptive—development of age-appropriate self-care and other behaviors so as to adapt successfully to different circumstances

Cognitive—development of age-appropriate mental functions, especially those of perceiving, understanding, and knowing

Communication—development of abilities to express thoughts and feelings and to understand others' vocal, nonverbal, signed, gestural, and written expressions

Physical—development of age-appropriate abilities by controlling and coordinating gross motor and fine motor movements

Social or emotional—development of age- and situation-appropriate abilities to understand one's own feelings and those of others and to respond to both with behavior that is socially acceptable

FIGURE 1–3 The five developmental domains.

developmental domain in turn, such segmentation of development is artificial. Development in any one domain is affected by development in other domains. To illustrate, consider that the reported average age for a child's ability to stand alone is 13 months, compared with 12 months for the first word. Many parents begin to worry if the child does not walk or speak "on time." However, the two domains interact in predictable ways. Young children typically reach the one-word milestone on time and then seem to plateau for about a year. That second year of life appears to be devoted to mastering physical mobility. The need to move is characteristic of the toddler period. This imperative sweeps all before it. The child *must* move. Not until walking, balancing while standing, and related physical activities are mastered does the child return to discernible progress in verbal communication. At two years of age, the toddler says two or three words in sequence. Some children begin walking earlier than 13 months, and they may delay speaking first words until after they master physical mobility. Others may begin speaking earlier and walking later. Such divergences in development are very normal.

The domains are interrelated in other ways as well. To continue with the example of mobility and communication, a child typically begins using the pronoun *I* only after achieving independence in physical mobility. That is, the toddler's ability to move away from the caregiver appears to promote the cognitive development task of establishing a separate identity. The whole concept that the toddler is a different person from the primary caregiver is one that develops from experience. A young child with a severe physical disability who does not move about independently by the expected ages may also be delayed in use of the word *I*—and all that that implies. Such interconnections are natural given the relationships between physical and communication development.

Cognitive development refers to age-appropriate mental functions, especially in perceiving, understanding, and knowing—that is, becoming capable of doing intellectual tasks.

Cognitive development refers to the growing capability of the infant, toddler, or preschooler to perform intellectual tasks. Piaget (1962) demonstrated that the child's mind is able at a certain point to do things not previously possible. To illustrate this, he hid an object and distracted the child's attention. At a very young age, the child promptly forgot the hidden object; at a later age, the child refused to allow Piaget to distract her and persistently sought out the hidden object. Similarly, children become able to understand that they are distinct human beings, with their own experiences, only after long periods of time in which they believe that what their mothers or other caregivers see, hear, and feel is identical to what they themselves see, hear, and feel.

Social or emotional development

(sometimes called *psychosocial* or *affective* development) refers to young children's age-appropriate ability to understand their own feelings and those of others and to respond to both with behavior that is socially acceptable for children of that age. It also includes behavior children exhibit in play.

Adaptive development

(sometimes referred to as *self-help* development) refers to a child's ability to display age-appropriate self-care and other behaviors in such a way as to adapt meaningfully to different circumstances.

Physical development

(sometimes called *motor* or *coordination development*) is the display of age-appropriate fine motor control and gross motor control abilities.

Communication development

(sometimes referred to as *speech and language development*) refers to a young child's ability to express thoughts and feelings and to understand vocal, nonverbal, signed, or other communication by others.

Social or emotional development has to do with affective growth. Erikson (1963) was concerned with the infant's attachment to the caregiver and the development of a sense of trust enabling the young child to venture out into the immediate environment to explore and learn. The preschool-age child, he believed, confronts societal rules and expectations during such explorations and from those confrontations learns to balance personal desires against social constraints. **Adaptive development,** a related concept, looks more toward self-help capabilities. As young children grow, expectations rise that they will take care of themselves, with ever-dwindling needs for adult supervision. However, to the extent that exploration and other kinds of play are limited by worried adults, young children with disabilities may not acquire the self-reliance that developmental theories assume will emerge.

Physical development affects both social or emotional and adaptive development, as progress in these areas may depend on a child's physical ability to do such things as play, eat, dress, use the bathroom, and so on, independently. *Gross* motor development (large-scale muscle use) typically occurs prior to *fine* motor development (more precise muscle use, as in manipulation of small objects). **Communication development** is much more than simply speaking and listening. Children communicate needs, emotions, and other things nonverbally as well as verbally.

Although the five developmental domains are important, ECSE workers must not lose sight of the need to attend, first and foremost, to the whole child. Children have developmental needs in *all five* areas, not just those in which they have disabilities or delays. In addition, most young children with disabilities will have unique needs or express delays in more than one developmental domain. Take, for example, a preschooler with cerebral palsy. Are the primary needs in the domain of physical development (in which case physical and occupational therapy, braces and other mobility aids, etc., are indicated)? Or is the major issue the child's difficulty in expressive communication (in which case augmentative communication technologies and speech pathology might be more helpful)? Similarly, are the needs of a child who has autism best understood in terms of her social or emotional development or her physical development? Are the needs of the children best approached as intellectual, communication related, social and emotional, or adaptive? Experts have yet to agree (e.g., Heflin & Alaimo, 2007).

DEVELOPMENT: BIRTH TO EIGHT

In this section, development is traced in each of the five domains. The emphasis here is on expected ("normal") development. Much more information on developmental delays and deviations is offered in Part IV.

Adaptive Development

Infants first establish a rhythm with the primary caregiver, usually the mother. They behave differently with a responsive, low-activity-oriented parent than with a task-oriented, high-activity-level parent, for example (Allen & Marotz, 2007). As a parent who likes physical play approaches, the child visibly readies herself for physical activity. At the approach of a parent who likes to discern the infant's mood and respond accordingly, however, the child relaxes physically and smiles. These are early illustrations of adaptive behavior—the infant is adapting to different situations.

Self-Help Behaviors

While infants can do few things for themselves, toddlers can do much independently and, indeed, often insist on doing so. During the second year of life (12 to 24 months), toddlers indicate the need to use restroom facilities, demonstrate an ability to feed themselves with their fingers and to hold a cup for drinking, and remove clothing that has been unfastened. By the end of the third year, many young children can use bathrooms with little or no assistance, can feed themselves, and can both put on and take off many items of clothing. They can also put things away and assist others in cleaning a room.

Young children with disabilities or developmental delays increasingly are learning self-help skills at child care, nursery, or other ECSE programs, in addition to or rather than at home. This experience contrasts with that of many nondisabled young children. ECSE personnel teach self-help skills for several reasons. First, parents may tend to neglect these behaviors, excusing the child on the grounds that the child does, after all, have a disability. Second, parents may be unsure how to teach children with special needs, in particular how hard to push for developmentally appropriate achievements. Third, other developmental needs, including learning how to use adaptive equipment and how to cope with their limitations, often mean that many hours each week may be spent with ECSE personnel. Being young children, they will have self-help needs during these times and will need assistance from ECSE personnel in meeting those needs.

Social Behaviors

Children with disabilities learn to enter, gain status in, and remain members of groups in child care, nursery, and other EC and ECSE programs. The strategies these children use vary by age and situation. Children who are able to gain entry into preexisting groups rely not only on their personalities but also on their ability to read the group, its members, and its dynamics. These skills are rarely taught. Rather, children seem to learn them through trial and error. Children who are successful in entering infant and toddler, preschool, and kindergarten groups are those able to match their behavior to that of other group members (Ross, 1985). That is, they first observe what group members are doing. They display cooperative behaviors, seeking not to dictate or control activity but rather to join ongoing activities. Often, they bring to the group an interesting object and offer to share it. Success in using the object as an entry strategy appears to depend in part on the child's knowledge of the object and how it might be used (Kantor, Elgas, & Fernie, 1993).

Status in early childhood groups appears to depend in large part on the social history of a child within a particular group. While physical factors (height, weight, facial attractiveness) and personality variables (outgoing vs. withdrawn, adaptable vs. rigid, accommodating vs. aggressive) are important, social history (the group members' collective experiences with a child and the patterns of interaction group members have used with that child) matter as well (Kantor et al., 1993).

Maintaining membership in a group requires the ability to keep one's behavior, both physical and verbal, in tune with that of other group members. One study conducted in the mid-1970s suggested that children who introduce and elaborate on play themes (things to do), who take roles in play activities already in progress, and who consistently display situation-appropriate verbal and nonverbal behaviors will be most successful (McDermott & Church, 1976). By contrast, "rejects" or "loners" appear to offer poorly timed comments or actions and to depend exclusively upon a limited number of strategies, even when those approaches are not accepted by a group (Corsaro, 1985; Ross, 1985). Young children need to master **pragmatics,** the socially appropriate use of language. There are things one says while engaged in free play and other things one says during story time or other more supervised activities. There are things one says to other children but not to teachers or other ECSE personnel. Failure to master pragmatics may, by itself, limit a child's success in integrating with nondisabled children.

Pragmatics
is the use of language that is suitable to the occasion.

Although inappropriate behaviors—insisting on a new activity before the group completes the current one, saying things that are out of place, being physically aggressive—may lead to rejection or even make a child a social outcast, it is important for ECSE workers to remember that children *can* change their behaviors and gain or regain acceptance from peers. One study focused on how a child who was rejected one year was able to gain acceptance the following year with a different group after learning more appropriate play behaviors (Massoulos, 1988).

Cognitive Development

The infant's brain appears to develop in phases (Zigler, Finn-Stevenson, & Hall, 2004). Neurological imaging techniques, particularly magnetic resonance imaging (MRI) and computed tomography (CT), are helping us understand how that happens. The first phase, that of tissue differentiation and neural tube closure, occurs within the first few weeks of gestation. The second phase, which lasts from the fourth week to the middle of the third month of gestation, leads to formation of the face and head. Overlapping that phase and continuing until the fourth month of gestation, the third phase features neuronal migration to nearby brain areas. The fourth phase of mental development is characterized by neuronal migration to the farther reaches of the brain. Nickel (1992) calls the third and fourth phases *organization* and *myelination* and reports that both continue after birth; indeed, myelination lasts well into adulthood.

Infant cognitive development is heavily influenced by the environment. A debate has raged for years on the relative contributions to cognitive development of nature (heredity) versus nurture (environment). In fact, both appear to be essential. A stimulating play area with aural, visual, and tactile sensations is important. Just as critical is parental permissiveness, the need for primary caregivers to grant the infant unrestricted opportunities to explore. The infant further prods her own cognitive growth by completing the developmental imperative to walk. By freeing the hands, walking accelerates exploration of the environment—and with it, cognitive development.

A critical aspect of cognitive development, especially during the first two years of life, is the creation in the brain of structures or connections to handle language. During those years, neural connections, or synapses, are formed that prime the brain to learn the native language. After the age of two, synapses specialized in language that have not been tapped to perform those functions begin to be suppressed or even eliminated in the brain, a process that continues into adolescence. The key is for language as such—*any* language—to be laid down during the first two years. Thereafter, the brain's ability to acquire a first language gradually dissipates. By age 15 it disappears altogether.

The fact that language is best learned in early childhood has long been known. What is new is the understanding of how the brain does its work. The most recent theories suggest that language makes liberal use of many sections of the brain, with names of objects stored in one location and their attributes in others. While speech is centered in Broca's area in most people and language usually in Wernicke's, that is not always the case. Language is so central to brain function that the brain finds room for it virtually anywhere. Antonio and Hannah Damasio (1989) of the University of Iowa have developed a well-received theory of cognition and language that helps to explain the role language plays in cognition. Antonio Damasio illustrates the theory:

> *When I ask you to think about a styrofoam cup you do not go into a filing cabinet in your brain, and come up with a ready-made picture of a cup. Instead, you compose an internal image of a cup drawn from its features. The cup is part of a cone, white, crushable, three inches high, and can be manipulated. In reactivating the concept of this cup, you draw on distant clusters of neurons that separately store knowledge of cones, the color white, crushable objects and manipulated objects. (quoted in Blakeslee, 1991a, p. C10)*

This neuropsychological view of cognition is one in which the brain is active in generating syntheses or knowledge from information and in which language serves as an organizing mechanism that assists in this creative process. Cognition, then, is not so much a function of factual memory as it is of creation. The theory, advanced most forcefully by the Damasios, has consequences familiar to us all. Among many other things, it helps explain why eyewitnesses at crime scenes report such different versions of what happened and why people remember childhood experiences in ways that differ sharply from how others recall these same events. People do not store events or complex images as such; rather, they re-create them mentally.

Cognition is, of course, far broader than language use. The primary work of young children in the cognitive domain is to learn about themselves, their environments, and the basic laws of nature (gravity, cause and effect, etc.) that are essential to safety. They must also master preacademics, including readiness to read and basic computational skills. Additionally, children must learn adaptive behavior as they enter into and become skilled at responding to new and different situations. For children with disabilities, delays, or deviations in development in *any* domain, cognitive development is urgently important.

Attention

is the process through which a child acquires information through the senses. Learning cannot occur absent attention.

Perception

is a process in which information entering the sensory register takes on meaning—for example, is interpreted.

Processing

occurs when information that has been perceived is analyzed and used by an individual.

Assimilation,

for Piaget, occurs when new information is added to existing knowledge but does not change a child's view of the world.

To learn, children must first *attend* to information (Figure 1–4). In the early childhood years, much of that input is auditory and visual. Especially during play, children learn a great deal about the size, texture, and other properties of objects. When guided by a caregiver, they acquire words to describe what they are learning. When a building block falls off a tower, for example, the caregiver could introduce the word *gravity* and use this concept to explain why the block fell. Simpler words such as *big* and *small* or *hard* and *soft* may be taught in much the same manner. In each instance, the early childhood educator or other caregiver, such as a parent, is calling the child's **attention** to a property of physical objects. The child then attends to that aspect of the play experience.

However, much information that young children attend to makes no sense to them. This is especially true of things they hear, as when two adults converse about inflation or about politics. While the children may attend to these conversations, they are not able to *perceive* the information because it holds no meaning for them. Another illustration of the **perception** phenomenon is when two people at a bus stop converse in Portuguese. A child may pay attention, perhaps out of curiosity, but the words being spoken are not perceived in the brain because the child cannot relate them to her experience.

A third concept important in cognitive development is that of information **processing.** Piaget (1962) believed that young children **assimilate** information by fitting new facts into existing mental structures or accommodate information by altering those structures.

Attention Children must attend in order to learn. A common problem in autism, for example, is apparent overselection of what to attend to; the child may attend to some sensory variables, ignoring others. Children with Down syndrome may have hearing losses such that they cannot attend to unstressed parts of speech, such as conjunctions and prepositions, or to high-pitched sounds, such as consonants. In each instance, ECSE help is needed to facilitate attention to the entire stimulus, or learning will not occur. In attention, relevant information is found, while irrelevant information is ignored.

Perception Information must not merely enter the brain's sensory register but also be perceived. Perception is interpretation: Sensory information (sounds, smells, colors, etc.) takes on meaning to the child. Young children hear much dinner table conversation but fail to perceive it because it holds no meaning for them. A child with a learning disability may hear the word *bat* but perceive it to have been *tab*.

Processing Information that has been attended to and perceived is then analyzed and used. This stage is called *information processing*. In *assimilation*, Piaget said, new information is added to existing knowledge; in *accommodation*, new data alter existing knowledge, changing the child's view of reality.

Memory Information is retrieved from memory and used as needed. Many theorists hypothesize that data are reassembled, or re-created; in this view, retrieval is not just pulling information from memory but rather is an active process of reproducing knowledge.

FIGURE 1–4 Cognitive development: key terms.

Upon seeing a duck, for example, a child may assume that because it is a nonhuman that walks, it must be an animal. The whole concept that it might be a bird is a new one, requiring that the child accommodate by changing her idea of what constitutes "birdness." Once that **accommodation** is made, the child may, much later, use **memory** to retrieve the notion that ducks are birds.

Accommodation, for Piaget, is a process in which new information alters a child's understanding of reality.

Memory is retrieval of information. Recent studies suggest that data actually are re-created, not merely retrieved from storage.

What exactly, then, is learning? Behavioral theorists such as B. F. Skinner (1953) suggest that learning is a change in behavior. That is, we know a child has learned something when her behavior alters. Similarly, if she does not behave differently, we can safely conclude that she has not learned. Others, such as Albert Bandura (1977), assert that learning may in fact occur without being displayed in behavior. Such cognitive behaviorists believe that learning is a change in the *capacity* to behave but not necessarily in behavior itself. These theories underlie two approaches to instruction that are considered in later chapters. Behavior modification, which grew out of Skinner's work, holds that behavior itself must change for learning to occur. Cognitive behavior modification, which has its roots in Bandura's work, contends that learning may occur, and in fact be shown to have occurred, without a change in behavior.

Communication Development

Communication development relates to hearing, vision, speech, and language in particular. This section examines each, in turn. The reader is urged to attend to how speech differs from language. The key terms are defined in Figure 1–5.

The infant's communication development includes several abilities that typically emerge during the first year of life. One is the ability to use *multimodal* channels for communication. Infants learn to look at, as well as listen to, people and things that make sounds; they touch, smell, and even taste objects; and they find comfort in the caregiver's voice, touch, and smell. Infants and toddlers also learn to express their desires in not just

Speech is the oral expression of meaning, usually, but not always, with symbols (words).

Language is a formal symbol system in which words are ordered according to rules to express meaning. It may be spoken, written, or signed. It may be expressive or receptive. Most people have far larger receptive than expressive capabilities.

Communication is the expression and reception of meaning. It may occur through speech/hearing, reading/writing, signing/seeing, or gesturing/reading gestures.

Phonemes are units of sound that cannot further be divided. An example is "ph" in the term *phoneme,* expressed as /f/. The study of phonemes and the role they play in speech is *phonology.*

Morphemes are the smallest units of words that carry meaning. The word *morphemes,* for example, has three such units: "morph," "eme," and "s," meaning, in order, "form/substance," "part," and "plural."

Semantics is the system of meaning we give to words.

Syntax is a rule system for language governing the order of words or parts of sentences.

Pragmatics is the social use of language. People use different ways of communicating with a boss, for example, than with a spouse.

FIGURE 1–5 Communication-related terms: definitions.

one but rather several ways all at the same time, as when they grab their mother's dress while crying. A second, related skill is to use *sensory integration*—to bring together what is seen, heard, and felt so as to make sense of all available information. And a third is *habituation.* Infants and toddlers are exposed, as are all of us, to much more sensory information than is needed to comprehend what is happening. While very young infants attend to virtually every new sound and sight, they quickly learn, in effect, to ignore "old" sights and sounds and to attend to what is different, and new, in the environment. Habituation helps prevent sensory overload and expedite our response to changes in the environment.

Hearing

Infants are born with normal or near-normal hearing. They can hear virtually as well at birth as they can as adults, although the ability to hear quiet sounds appears still to be developing during infancy. Even neonates, however, can tell the difference between sounds; they demonstrate this by calming to sounds they like and responding to unexpected sounds by blinking, crying, stopping a movement, or making a startle response. By one or two months of age, infants have integrated their hearing to the point of being able to use it for directionality; they turn their heads correctly to the source of a sound.

From that point forward, the sense of hearing is used for two principal functions. First, it is the major means by which children acquire **language;** language, in turn, is the principal way children learn information from parents, caregivers, peers, and teachers. Second, hearing serves as a means of connection with the environment. Hearing has the characteristics of always being on, of functioning both at a distance and at close range, of being multidirectional, and of working around corners. Because of these features, hearing is an early warning system far superior to vision or touch. Vision, by contrast, is on only when the eyes are open, is unidirectional, and does not work around corners—eyes

Language
is a formal symbol system in which words are ordered according to rules to express meaning. It may be spoken, written, or signed and may be expressive or receptive.

take in light only from straight lines. It is the language acquisition function of hearing that is of most concern to ECSE professionals.

Language

By five to eight months, most infants demonstrate understanding of simple words and phrases ("bye-bye," "da-da," etc.). Language development is very rapid during the first year of life, even though the child often does not demonstrate her knowledge. By the time the first words are spoken, infants understand far more than they can produce in speech.

Bruner (1981) suggests that infants perform purposive communication even before they say their first words. He offers three categories of such purposive prelinguistic communication. One is to obtain others' assistance, a second is to get people's attention, and a third is to share attention with others. Children use a wide variety of gestures and vocalizations to accomplish these three purposes.

Language is acquired by very young children almost as if by osmosis. Children take in many thousands of utterances and from them learn what words mean, how they are formed, and how they work together. It is much more than that, of course. Children's minds are active in the language acquisition process, integrating discrete statements to extract the underlying rules, or structure, that produced them. Thus, each child "invents" anew the language of her community. This is why young children produce sentences no one around them ever said and why they make characteristic errors of grammar and **syntax.** Children say "go-ed" before they say "went," "outen" before "turn out," and "drived" before "drove." They will say "mans," "foots," and "womans"—all instances of correctly applying grammatical rules and all examples of how English sometimes disobeys its own rules.

Syntax
is a rule system for language governing the order of words or parts of sentences.

Development continues during the second and subsequent years, and the relative superiority of receptive to expressive language persists as well. During the second year, the child is putting together actual sentences—including subjects, verbs, and objects—and doing so quite successfully. This shows that the toddler has acquired an understanding of different parts of speech and has generated some rules for putting those together. From the age of three to five, young children demonstrate other syntactic structures as well, notably use of conjunctions to join two separate thoughts into one sentence. By the end of early childhood, most children can understand even compound-complex sentences, can differentiate declarative from interrogative questions, and can produce spoken language using these structures themselves. (The preceding sentence is an example of a compound-complex structure.) In addition, by age six most children know some 2,500 words (Wiig & Semel, 1984). Language development during early childhood, then, produces both mastery of the structure of language and knowledge of many hundreds of words.

Normal language development assumes intact hearing, normal or near-normal intelligence, and an environment rich in linguistic stimulation. These conditions are not always present. Children who are deaf do not hear the many thousands of sentences that children with normal hearing use as the raw materials with which to generate their own rules of language. Children with below-normal intelligence usually develop acceptable language in time, but they may have difficulty expressing it and may have problems with complex structures and with abstract words. Children raised in homes where language is not used expansively and where few opportunities for development of sophisticated language patterns exist may be delayed in language development even if hearing, intelligence, and motor control are all intact.

Phonemic awareness

is the ability to mentally separate utterances into phonemes, so that we can understand what we hear and so we can combine phonemes into spoken words.

Phonics instruction

is a method of teaching that assists children in connecting words on a page to the sounds of these words when spoken.

Phonemic awareness is an inborn capacity to isolate phonemes from words that are heard and to combine phonemes into spoken words. Early childhood educators can help young children develop these critical skills by asking them questions (e.g., "Tell me the sound that is the same in *bake* and *book*" [/b/]). Another teaching tool is **phonics instruction.** *Phonics* is the relationship between sounds and written symbols of sounds. Teachers can help young children spell phonetically as one step toward good spelling.

Speech

Vocal communication by the neonate is limited largely to crying. In the one-to-four-month period, however, infants babble or coo when spoken to or smiled at and may laugh out loud. The infant at this stage can make one-syllable sounds, and she delights in repeating them. Most communication, however, continues to be physical; the body itself, by being tense or relaxed, tells mothers and other caregivers how the infant feels and is a more useful yardstick at this stage than is vocalization for interpreting the infant's behavior. Infants typically begin babbling at three to six months of age. In babbling, simple sounds composed of two **phonemes,** a single consonant and a single vowel, are repeated again and again, sometimes combined with other one-syllable vocalizations.

Phonemes

are units of sound that cannot further be divided. An example is "ph" in *phoneme*, expressed as /f/. The study of phonemes and the role they play in speech is called *phonology*.

Morphemes

are the smallest units of words that carry meaning.

The much-awaited first word usually occurs between about 9 and 15 months of age. Parents can understand the infant's speech, but outsiders frequently cannot. Indeed, often it can be argued whether an actual word was or was not produced. Typically, these are repeated syllable sounds such as "da-da" or "ma-ma" and, as such, differ little from babbling. It is not clear that they are composed of **morphemes,** or units of meaning. A better indicator for "first word" would be something like "car" or "bottle" or some other word that is not composed of two identical sounds. Two- and three-word utterances typically appear just before the second year (18 to 24 months). However, children who continue to be very active physically may not speak several words in a string until later. The clarity of children's speech improves dramatically once they enter formal programs with other children. By necessity, they must articulate much better to make themselves understood.

All of this development assumes intact hearing in particular, as well as average or near-average intelligence. It assumes, additionally, good fine motor control of voluntary muscles. Cerebral palsy is an example of a condition that may delay speech production because the child has great difficulty controlling the many hundreds of small muscles used in speech.

Vision

Vision is still developing after birth. Neonates (infants from birth to 28 days) are sensitive to light; this is why many families keep an infant's room dim. They can see objects and shapes but cannot yet focus on distant objects. The eyes may at times seem not to work together and may even appear crossed. At one month, the eyes begin moving in unison and no longer appear crossed. Glass (1993) reports that neonates should be able to see as far as 2.5 feet. They also should be able to track a bright object. By two months, infants should alternate their gaze between objects and demonstrate a preference for a face over objects. Even at four months, though, infants often cannot tell the difference between the faces of the primary caregiver and others by vision alone but must rely on sound, touch, and other supplementary sensory information (Allen & Marotz, 2007). By five to eight months, depth perception is present; the infant will show signs of being afraid of falling off a tabletop, for example. The infant also by that time can recognize familiar faces by sight alone. The infant's vision continues developing throughout infancy and reaches near-adult levels shortly after six months of age.

Physical Development

By the time a child reaches five years of age, her height is already half that of an adult. To double height again—that is, to conclude her growth—will take another 10 years or so. The infant's weight triples during the first year of life, and body bulk increases 50 percent. These facts highlight the rapid physical development that characterizes the early childhood years.

Physical development usually proceeds from head to toe (cephalocaudal) and from the center out (proximodistal). The word *cephalocaudal* is from the Latin *cephalo,* meaning "head," and *caudal,* meaning "tail"; similarly, *proximodistal* joins *proximate,* or near, to *distal,* or remote from the center. Infants first lift, or rotate, the head; later, they also lift or move the shoulders, and yet later the trunk. The legs and feet are last, which developmentally has the important effect of making walking a task of the second year of life. Perhaps the most obvious illustration of center-out development is the sequence in which teeth appear: The infant's first teeth are in the center of the mouth; subsequent teeth appear on either side, moving from the center out. Or consider the infant's use of the arms. At first, arms are swung from the shoulder, and the entire arm is used to make gross, sweeping motions. Only later is the infant able to manipulate the arm independently of the shoulder; next the forearm by itself; and then the wrist, hand, and fingers. Thus, gross motor control precedes fine motor control.

The principles of cephalocaudal and proximodistal development provide guidelines for physical therapy and for early intervention. Infants lift the head before they voluntarily flex their legs. A neonate (newborn) will raise its head while prone (stomach down), stretching the legs out. Later, the infant will lie supine (stomach up) and pull its legs up against gravity. At about four months, the infant may position the legs in a diamond shape such that the feet touch while the knees are far apart. This results in enjoyable contact of one foot with the other. Similarly, infants will move the arms before manipulating fingers, the legs before wiggling toes. These center-out developments illustrate the proximodistal progression.

These patterns help therapists and teachers in two ways. First, they show what to look for. One anticipates emergence of movements by certain ages, and if they do not appear until long after they were expected, therapists and teachers are alerted to possible delays. Second, they provide *developmental guidelines* for intervention. The therapist knows what motions are essential precursors to other movements and can help the infant or toddler master these prerequisites in order to succeed in later developmental tasks. To illustrate, consider the seemingly simple matter of watching something interesting. To do this, the infant needs to hold up her head and adjust her neck so that her eyes may focus on the interesting object. She must maintain this posture over a continuous period of time, adjusting it as necessary to keep the interesting object in view. Knowing this, physical therapists focus on developing those body control capabilities as precursors to therapeutic and academic instruction (Kreutz, 1993). Similarly, as illustrated in the photographs of supports for young children, occupational therapists may use special supports to enable a child with a severe physical disability to maintain visual vigilance

Lekotek® and its affiliated Compuplay are local toy libraries. The main site is www.lekotek.org; you can also call (800) 366-PLAY. Lekotek recommends that early childhood special educators and parents consider multisensory appeal (sights, sounds, tactile features), method of activation (how does the child make the toy "work"?), and adjustability (can the toy be adjusted by speed, level of difficulty, etc.?), as well as safety and durability. Lekoteks are located at local United Cerebral Palsy Association schools/centers, at Easter Seals Society centers, and in local hospitals and schools. More than 50,000 toys, adaptive devices, and electronic play materials, as well as 5,000 software programs are available in the Lekotek system of libraries.

Toys 'R' Us at Amazon.com offers toys on-line. At the main site (www.amazon.com), select "Toys & Games." Toys are offered for birth to three, three and four, and five to seven years of age.

assistivetech.net℠ allows users to search by product name, manufacturer, key word, or function/disability. It is *not* limited to toys but rather covers the full range of assistive technologies for children, youth, and adults.

Kids on the Block® is an educational puppet program, providing puppet shows that answer children's questions about disabilities. It also has, at its Web site, curricula and other materials. The site is www.kotb.com, or you can call (800) 368-5437.

Alliance for Technology Access's Web site, www.ataccess.org, has a page on low-cost, low-tech products, including toys.

Abilitations (www.abilitations.com) offers therapy balls, scooter boards, and a variety of manipulatives, all described in its catalog.

Carolyn's Catalog (www.carolynscatalog.com) describes adapted board games for children who are blind or have low vision, among other products.

Crestwood Communication Aids (www.communicationaids.com) describes communication aids and switch-adapted toys in its 300-page catalog.

Different Roads to Learning (www.difflearn.com) has a variety of learning materials, flash cards, puzzles, and playthings for children with autism spectrum disorders. It also has other autism-related resources for teachers and parents.

Dragon Fly Toy Company Special Needs Store (www.dftoys.com) supplies adaptive and developmental toys. It also has a toy search service. The company is based in Winnipeg, Canada.

Flaghouse (www.flaghouse.com) has a wide variety of toys and educational materials related to physical education.

Quincy Toys and Games (www.quincyshop.com) has toys for infants/toddlers, preschoolers, and older children.

FIGURE 1–6 Adaptive toys: resources.

over a period of time, in a variety of positions. Until recently, such equipment was custom designed by rehabilitation engineers. Today, however, it is commercially available. In addition, "adaptive toys" are available from a variety of libraries (Figure 1–6). Again, until recently, such toys often had to be hand-made by rehabilitation engineers.

Both heredity and environment matter in physical development. In fact, development is affected not only by those two factors but also by the family's culture, SES, child-rearing practices, and other factors. The latter three may be grouped as *sociocultural influences.* They manifest themselves in physical development in the extent to which the infant, toddler, or preschooler is permitted to explore at will, free from artificial constraints, and in a safe environment. Generally, such permissiveness is associated with more rapid motor development, because the young child gains much more experience both with her body and with the surrounding environment. Overprotection, on the other hand, slows motor development. A physical disability may result in experiential deprivation similar in kind but more extreme in extent to that of an overprotected child: There is less exploration, less practice of physical activities and functions, and, often, less learning.

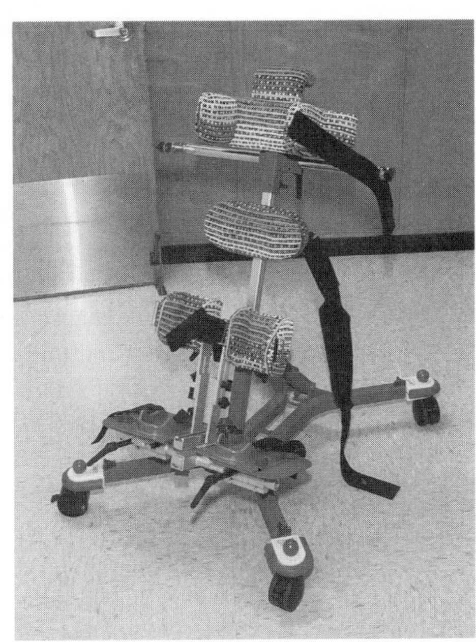

Supports for young children now are commercially available.

A great deal is known about the physical development of the under-nine child. Allen and Marotz (2007) and Malina (1982) are two excellent sources of information on developmental milestones in this domain. During the first 12 months of life, several important changes occur. The skeleton strengthens, cartilage yields to bone, and infants become able to support their weight when standing. At or about one month of age, infants can move their heads from side to side, make crawling movements while in a prone position, and hold their heads erect for a few seconds while being held. Within the first three months, infants can grasp objects placed into their hands, but this is largely an involuntary response rather than a purposive one.

The first evidence of voluntary motor control appears when the infant is able to lift or otherwise move her head at or about three months of age. As limbs strengthen, coordination improves, and at about six months, the infant can roll over and sit up without support. By this time, the infant can use the opposing thumb and other fingers in a pincer motion to pick up objects, this time purposively. Often, the objects are shaken in large arm/hand motions. She can transfer objects from hand to hand and, of course, into the mouth. Interestingly, at or about six months of age, the infant reaches for an object with the closer arm; prior to that, often the infant reaches across the body from the opposite side.

By 9 months of age, she can reach a standing position, holding on to something. Between 8 and 12 months, she stacks objects and can place a smaller one inside a larger one. The infant can pull the feet forward, putting one into the mouth, and can also pull herself up to a standing position. At 12 to 13 months, she can stand unaided and can walk while holding someone's hand; she might take a few steps unaided.

All of this does not just happen. The infant spends hour after hour practicing motor skills until they are mastered. Literally thousands of trials occur as the infant practices the same skill over and over again. Once one skill is habitual, the infant focuses with the same endless patience on the next.

Also important, as infants begin to move on their own, they become—and realize that they are—independent of the mother. They begin to grasp the concept that they are discrete beings, not merely extensions of the mother. This is an intellectual breakthrough, and it is due in very large part to independent mobility.

This stage is related to a second important idea: The more the infant can move, the more she learns. Kermoian and Campos (1988) examined two groups of eight-month-olds on the Piagetian object permanence test. In this test, the infant is shown an object, which is then hidden while she is being distracted. Infants who have attained object permanence know that the object still exists, and they look for it. Kermoian and Campos found that those who could move independently were much more likely to seek the hidden object than were those who could not.

By 18 months, most toddlers can walk alone; at two years, they can run. By the end of the second year, the toddler can build things with six or more blocks. Again, as in the first year, the toddler practices the same things over and over again. Even if a task takes days or weeks to accomplish—as might climbing onto countertops using chairs, stools, and so on—the toddler persists, seemingly without limits to her patience.

Toddlers do something infants seldom do: They practice and refine fine motor control, not only gross motor control. Hand and finger movements are coordinated with more and more precision. During this time, the toddler learns to eat independently, using utensils. The point is a central one: By the end of the second year, or by about age 2.5, the toddler is using gross and fine motor skills not for the sake of the activity itself but to *accomplish* something, in this case, eating.

Independent walking has one huge effect: It frees the hands. With the hands free, the child can engage in other motor tasks. In fact, walking is the indicator that infancy has ended and the toddler period has begun. Talking and functional use of objects (vs. exploration of them) begin at about the same time that walking does. Walking, by marking the completion of a long, strenuous period of learning, may spur cognitive development because so much attention need no longer be given over to walking.

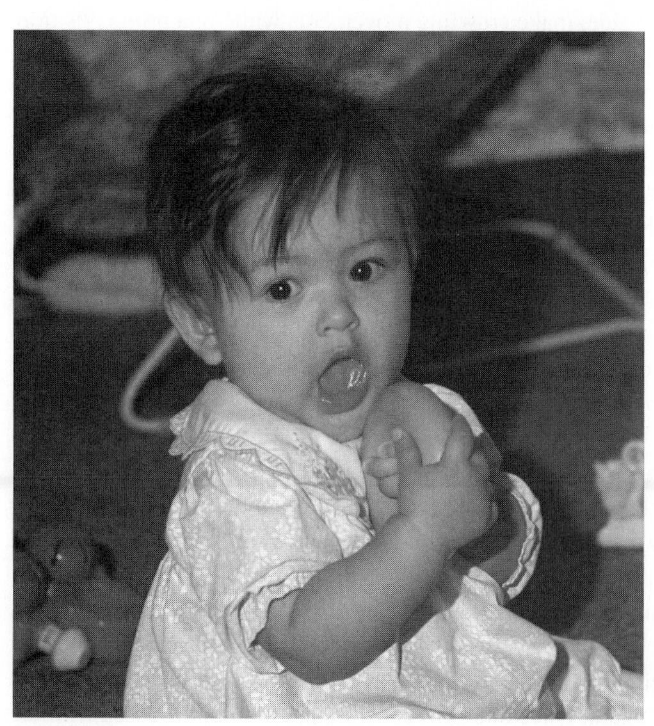

Infants use every sense to explore, including taste.

Movement appears to be central to self-awareness; for a child to differentiate herself from others, there must be a knowledge of the body and what it can do. Some children even learn better by moving and touching than they do by seeing. Motor behavior also integrates all the senses. As children move and pick things up, they taste them, smell them, touch them, and, if the things rattle, listen to them.

All of this assumes the coming together of maturational factors (neurological capabilities allowing the child to do something) with environmental facilitators (ways for the child to do those things, room to explore, permissive parents, the necessary equipment, etc.).

The critical time for motor skill development is 18 to 60 months of age. If the child has not developed key gross and fine motor control functions by age five, she needs help. At some point during the third year, the child can dress herself quite completely, including socks and shoes. She can throw an object a few feet, underhanded, and can catch a large ball, using both arms and body.

By the fourth year, the child can bounce a ball and catch it after it bounces, using just the arms and hands. She can jump down from a chair to the floor, landing smoothly on both feet. The child can push a wagon, steering it successfully. Hopping and skipping now are skillfully done, often in games. During the fifth year, the child can skip with alternating feet while maintaining balance, even while skipping rope. She can roller-skate and, for short periods, ice-skate. The child can roll a ball precisely to hit an object and can kick the ball even if it is rolling at the time.

Young children by age six are usually able to dress and feed themselves. They can also use restrooms independently. By ages seven to eight, they can play organized sports such as Little League Baseball™ as well as soccer and even football. They can also ride bikes. To do these things, they must have good control of their bodies, be able to maintain balance even while running and/or carrying objects, and be able to aim and throw or kick balls. As compared to what they could do just two years earlier, this is an impressive array of capabilities.

The domain of physical development is more important today than in years past for a simple reason: Obesity among young children has become a national concern. Children who are overweight are at risk for diabetes. Indeed, Type II diabetes used to be called "adult-onset" diabetes. It now occurs in children so frequently that the American Diabetes Association championed a name change. Some 10 percent of children under age five are obese, according to data collected by the Centers for Disease Control and Prevention (CDC). Pediatricians are seeing heart disease, chronic joint problems, high cholesterol, high blood pressure, and diabetes in young children. The CDC maintains several pages on its Web site just on obesity (www.cdc.gov). Body mass charts at CDC's Web site offer ECSE professionals and family members guidance on gender- and age-specific guidelines for what levels are considered to be "overweight" and which "obese."

Social or Emotional Development

The domain of social or emotional development is one in which definitions both of delays/disorders and assessments must be comparative. Infants and toddlers are expected to display behavior in only a limited number of areas, notably sleeping, eating, basic motor activity, and social relations with primary caregivers. This restricted range of normal behavior, combined with the natural variation from child to child (as well as from parent to parent), means that early indications of delays or other problems in this domain are difficult to discern.

Considerable research has been done on infant-adult relationships, attachment, rhythm and reciprocity, and temperament. Generally, infants begin interaction when they develop the ability to prolong attention to selected stimuli—that is, to maintain focus. Smiling, vocalizing, and using facial muscles are all means of initiating and then maintaining interaction with a caregiver. During the third and fourth months of life, the infant tests this new ability to control interactions. She looks to see how long she can keep an adult's attention or to get the adult to do something. At around four to five months of age, the infant begins to display autonomy in interactions, moving attention at will from one adult to another, from an object to an adult and back to the object. Infants between 6 and 10 months of age display increased intentional interaction with the mother or ECSE

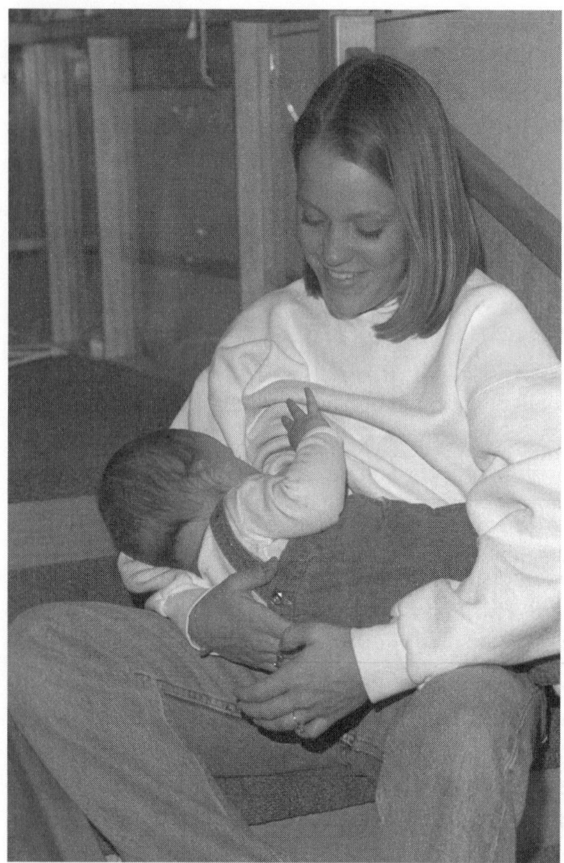

The mother-infant bonding process is essential for infant social and emotional development.

professionals. They coordinate their actions to comport with behavior of the other person, and they attempt to reinitiate play if that person disengages.

As the child begins speaking, she indicates her needs and expresses her feelings. By this time, she should display a range of emotions, from happiness to joy, discomfort to anger, and pride to shame. Especially during the second year of life, she demonstrates a strong sense of self, a sense of possession of treasured toys and objects ("mine!"), and a sense of wanting to do things for herself. She plays best at this stage in pairs; "three's a crowd" is very true with toddlers. By three years of age, many young children display a rather full range of emotions—including the more subtle ones of envy, guilt, and pride—and do so appropriately. They can moderate their expression of these emotions; a three- or four-year-old should show gradations of, say, anger (from annoyance to rage) or happiness (from pleasure to joy). She should be able to recover quickly from emotional extremes. The child should display feelings of pride and accomplishment when she does things well and regret when she does something wrong. When interactive play, as opposed to parallel play, becomes developmentally appropriate, social skills emerge as essential components of adaptive behavior. These skills do not lend themselves to being taught by adults as self-help skills do; rather, they must be learned with and from other children. By five to six years of age, the child should regulate her behavior according to the situations in which she finds herself. For example, she displays much more affection to a loved one in the privacy of her home than she does in a preschool or kindergarten setting where other people can see her. Increasingly, as she prepares to enter kindergarten or first grade, she demonstrates her ability to play not only by herself but also with other children in genuinely interactive and cooperative ways. She shows confidence in most age-appropriate behaviors and demonstrates pride in her abilities.

During the preschool years, what we consider to be "normal" behavior takes on more dimensions. Preschoolers are expected to engage in play with other children, to look to adults for clues on handling frustration, and to relate differently to familiar adults than to strangers. This increased variability has the effect of giving ECSE workers and parents more opportunities to discern what may be disabilities, delays, or deviations in behavior. However, unusual withdrawal or other displays of shyness, on the one hand, and unusual aggression or other acting-out behavior, on the other, do not necessarily signal problems in social or emotional development. They may, instead, be among the first clues that something else is wrong. Children who are deaf, for example, may respond to their condition by avoiding social interactions with other children. They may seem to ignore adult instructions or warnings. The problem here is not that the child has social or emotional limitations but that the inability to hear makes interpersonal communication very difficult for her. Mental retardation, autism, and even physical conditions may be confused during the preschool years with social or emotional conditions because the

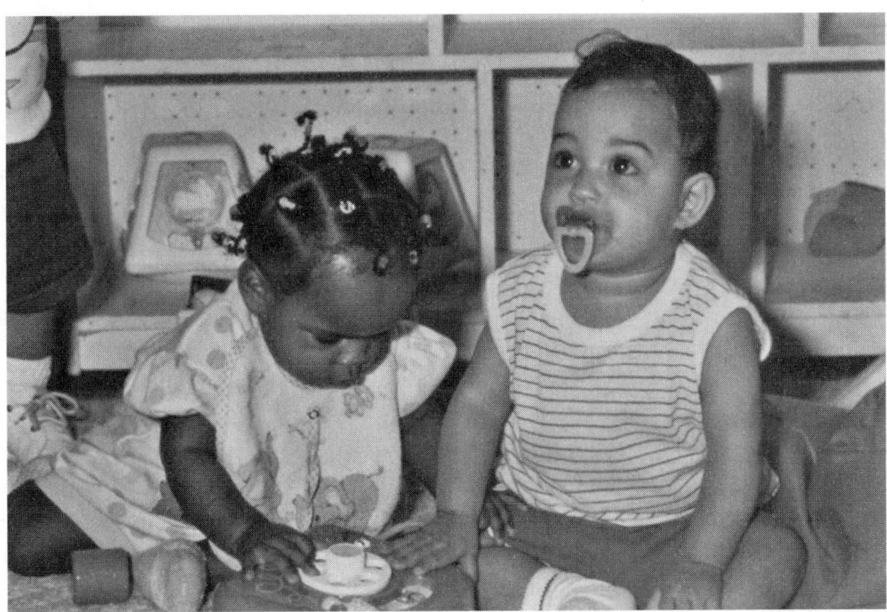

Learning to play with another infant or toddler—and to share—is a key step in social or emotional development.

"symptoms" are so similar. The challenge for ECSE workers confronting apparent delays or deviations in social or emotional development is to be aware that these symptoms may suggest some other concern. That is why assessment in this domain should begin by first ruling out other possible causes for observed behavior.

For these and other reasons, it is important for ECSE workers not to "blame the victim." Social and emotional behavior usually responds to environmental conditions or antecedents. Behavior, that is, serves a function. Rather than looking only at the child and labeling behavior she dislikes as "difficult" or "inappropriate," the ECSE worker should attempt instead to comprehend the conditions giving rise to the behavior. She might ask, "What function does this behavior serve for this child in this context?" Some behavior serves to obtain sensory feedback, other behavior to secure reinforcement, and yet other behavior to escape or avoid stimuli. Typical development includes many instances in which behavior plays communicative roles—that is, carries communication intent. Accordingly, the focus in ECSE is on the behavior itself rather than on the child. If we understand to what antecedents the child is reacting, we can change those, leading to more acceptable behavior. It is not necessary at any stage of that process to criticize or label the child for displaying "difficult behavior."

The point is a central one. Young children are limited in their ability to understand external stressors—and limited in how they can express their feelings about these events and incidents. The combination of not understanding what is happening and not being able to articulate her emotions may overwhelm a young child. Her behavior may be affected by changes other family members accept as necessary—the family moves to a new house or town, a new child care arrangement is made—or by changes that upset other family members as well—a parent loses a job or her mother and father are separated or divorced. That young children exhibit behavioral alterations after such external stressors is normal, not cause for diagnosing disability.

PHILOSOPHY

The philosophy guiding ECSE as a field draws from and contributes to the broader field of EC education. ECSE and EC education have more similarities than differences. Both are fields of direct service to young children and their families. There are, however, points of divergence between the guiding philosophies of the two fields. These differences become important when ECSE services are delivered in EC settings, as happens when young children with disabilities are integrated into preschool programs serving large numbers of children who have no disabilities. When a child with cerebral palsy is placed in a Head Start program, for example, the special educator and the general educator working with the child may approach the task of teaching that child very differently.

At the national level, two organizations have taken the lead in shaping the EC and ECSE philosophies. One is the National Association for the Education of Young Children (NAEYC), which issued "developmentally appropriate practice" (DAP) recommendations in 1987 (Bredekamp, 1987). This publication sparked intense interest in the general field of EC education, selling more than one-half million copies. It sparked more concern than interest, however, in the more specialized field of ECSE. Eventually, the Division for Early Childhood (DEC) of the Council for Exceptional Children (CEC) came out with its "recommended practices" (Sandall, McLean, & Smith, 2000). NAEYC issued a revised version of its DAP recommendations (Bredekamp & Copple, 1997).

In each of these published guidelines, the use of the word *practice* is somewhat curious. Both NAEYC and DEC have acknowledged that their recommendations are not as yet widely used in programs serving young children (Bredekamp, 1993b; Odom, McLean, Johnson, & LaMontagne, 1995). In actuality, the "practices" are recommendations from leaders in the two fields. In other words, the practices are aspects of a philosophy. They tell us more about the ideal than they do about the real.

Nevertheless, as statements of philosophy, NAEYC's DAP and DEC's recommended practices are very important documents. They contain a wealth of information that practitioners and students alike will find germane. (**Note:** The author strongly recommends that readers acquire their own copies from the publishers: NAEYC, 1509 16th Street NW, Washington, DC 20036, or www.naeyc.org; and DEC, c/o The Council for Exceptional Children, 1920 Association Drive, Reston, VA 22091, or www.dec-sped.org. The DEC publication is available at www.sopriswest.com. Also helpful is *Developmentally Appropriate Practice* [Delmar, 2007].)

Both sets of recommendations emphasize treating each child and each family as *unique.* Both express an aversion to *labels,* preferring to avoid terminology that might unnecessarily stigmatize a child. Both stress the need for *quality* in all aspects of programming. And both grant to *families* important roles in design and delivery of services.

The philosophical opposition to labeling extends to other kinds of invasion of the privacy of children and families. Thus, many ECSE programs will not identify which, if any, children attending the program have tested positive for the human immunodeficiency virus (HIV), for the hepatitis B virus (HBV), or for other communicable diseases. Rather, ECSE program administrators expect child care workers, early childhood special educators, and other professionals and paraprofessionals to follow universal precautions to avoid contamination. The American Academy of Pediatrics recommends universal immunization against HBV for all infants; child care workers should likewise be immunized as a routine precaution. No such preventive measure yet is available for HIV, the virus that can lead to acquired immune deficiency syndrome (AIDS). Because the virus is transmitted through bodily fluids, ECSE workers should wear gloves whenever blood may be spilled and should scrupulously avoid touching body fluids.

The increasing commonality in philosophy between EC and ECSE is a recent phenomenon. The 1987 version of NAEYC's DAP guidelines, for example, all but ignored children with disabilities. It included only one principle relating specifically to ECSE: "Modifications are made in the environment, when needed, for children with special needs" (Bredekamp, 1987, p. 11). In the years that followed, however, NAEYC recognized that EC programs throughout the nation served and would continue to serve many children with disabilities and delays in development. As Bredekamp (1993b) notes, much more specific information on serving children with disabilities was needed than appeared in the initial DAP guidelines. Taking one step in that direction, in an article for *Topics in Early Childhood Special Education,* Bredekamp (1993b) is at pains to emphasize that DAP builds on two core ideas, both of which are treasured by ECSE professionals—**age appropriateness** and **individual appropriateness:** "Developmentally appropriate practice is, by definition, individually appropriate as well as age appropriate. A program cannot possibly achieve individual appropriateness without assessing and planning for children's individual needs and interests" (p. 263).

Age appropriateness

is a philosophy in which activities are designed to match children's developmental stages. It is a key concept in NAEYC's developmentally appropriate practice (DAP) guidelines. DEC's Recommended Practice Task Force suggests that programs be *chronologically* age-appropriate as well, because otherwise some young children with disabilities might wrongly be placed in settings designed for far younger children.

Individual appropriateness

is an approach in which services are custom-designed and delivered to respond to a child's unique needs. Often, it is a concept more honored in theory than in practice, as child care workers often find it difficult to individualize services as much as they would like.

Developmentally appropriate practice (DAP)

is professional work that emphasizes activities with young children that are both age-appropriate and child-focused. In DAP approaches, children are encouraged to be active learners, while professionals guide and facilitate their activities.

ECSE today seeks, as much as does EC in general, to follow **developmentally appropriate practice (DAP)** guidelines. Early intervention personnel, preschool special education teachers, and support personnel—including therapists—attempt to "guide," "support," and "encourage" children and to structure the environment so that children can explore, interact, and learn on their own. (The quoted words appear in the NAEYC guidelines; see Bredekamp, 1987). Both fields are committed to ensuring that professionals follow the child, doing what the child wants to do, and using those activities to facilitate development of age-appropriate behaviors.

Another philosophy that ECSE shares with EC is that of valuing interdisciplinary approaches. As a whole, ECSE recognizes that many infants, toddlers, and preschoolers with disabilities have not one or even a few but rather many important needs. The expertise and ways of thinking of professionals from a wide variety of fields are needed to serve these children and their families effectively. As states pursue seamless systems of delivery for preschool-age children with disabilities, interdisciplinary approaches are increasingly seen in preschool special education programs as well.

Another area of increasing similarity between the two fields is that of the age ranges of children served. ECSE defines the word *early* to mean from birth, or from diagnosis of a disability or detection of a delay. EC, by contrast, tends to focus on serving a more traditional preschool-age population—that is, from three to five.

DIFFERENCES

While EC and ECSE are coming together philosophically, some differences remain. The most important difference between EC and ECSE may be one that few observers mention. ECSE programs are by law free to families with young children who have disabilities or delays; programs may charge only under special circumstances and then only in early intervention (birth to two). EC, by contrast, is rarely free to families.

Although Head Start and similar programs are free to qualifying (i.e., low-SES) families, most EC programs charge families for services. The difference becomes important when *choices must be made between cost and quality.* In ECSE much more than in EC programs, families and staff members alike press for higher standards, more options, and more family-friendly hours of service.

In EC, high costs constrain growth. PreKNow, an advocacy organization urging universal prekindergarten services, features on its Web site an interactive map showing which states offer preschool services, how many children are served, and with what level of quality (www.preknow.org). The sobering reality: Most states lack programs, help few young children, and/or have services that do not meet high standards. Even states that have laws "guaranteeing" prekindergarten services often have not appropriated sufficient funds to make the promise a reality.

New York and Florida are illustrative. The Empire State enacted a bill in 1997 assuring services for "all" four-year-olds by 2002. Today, several years past that year, New York has space only for about one-fourth of those young children. The situation is similar in Florida: the state legislature appropriated only enough to provide $2,500 per child, or roughly one-third what Head Start spends. Nationwide, some 750,000 young children attend prekindergarten programs, about the same number as are served by Head Start. According to the Brookings Institution, which launched a new Center on Children and Families in late 2005, and the Center for Law and Social Policy, it may cost as much as $50 billion a year to offer for all young children the kinds of early intervention and preschool services that IDEA provides to infants, toddlers, and preschoolers with disabilities (Schumacher, Ewen, Hart, & Lombardi, 2005).

A second area of difference is that ECSE measures and tracks development in children much more than is common in EC education. In ECSE, assessment is driven by the need to document progress in children's individualized plans (see Chapter 7). In EC, by contrast, there are no such plans and hence little formal year-to-year monitoring. Tracking of children's progress in Head Start programs has taken place throughout the 40-year history of Head Start. However, only since 1996 have Head Start Program Performance Standards called for teachers to conduct ongoing assessments of each child's progress. Beginning in 1998, the local programs were required to collect and analyze outcome data. In this area, then, Head Start is a good 20 years behind ECSE.

Directed discovery learning

is a variation on discovery learning in which teachers direct a student's inquiry. It is more structured than is guided discovery learning and more structured than discovery learning.

Guided discovery learning

is a variation on discovery learning in which teachers offer suggestions to a student in his or her discovery learning. It is more structured than discovery learning but less so than directed discovery learning.

A third difference relates to methods of teaching young children. ECSE has long relied on Direct Instruction and other didactic teaching approaches (see Chapter 6) and also on behavior modification (see Chapter 13). EC, by contrast, has championed constructivist (discovery) approaches to instruction and has shied away from using behavior modification. Head Start, similarly, has been more developmental than academic in its orientation. The 1998 reauthorization of the program, however, set new, more academically oriented, learning standards.

These differences are illustrated in Figures 1–7 and 1–8. The hypothetical mornings described show how ECSE and EC education philosophies "play out" in actual practice. These are not "ideal" classrooms. Rather, the portrait is intended to be realistic. The reader is encouraged to reflect on these scenarios. To what extent, for example, are the differences a function of the kinds of children being served in each setting?

A fourth area of difference is in the relative emphasis each field places on working with families. ECSE values family participation very highly, to the extent that many programs are moving to grant broad decision-making authority to parents. Such a

As her children arrive at about 8:30 A.M., Mrs. Madden and her aide, Terry, help them to take off their overcoats and then escort each, one at a time, to a nearby bathroom for toileting and wash-up. Each child must be attended to individually. Mrs. Madden and Terry take advantage of this one-to-one time to teach self-help skills such as unfastening pants, unzipping zippers, lowering underpants, using the toilets, redressing, and washing. The words associated with each of these activities are taught, as they have been for several months now.

The opening activity this morning is free play from 8:45 to 9:00. Each child selects and plays with a favorite toy or game. During this time, Mrs. Madden and Terry read the children's notebooks, most of which contain comments by the children's parents about what happened at home the previous evening and that morning. They have to read fast, however, because first one child then others require their attention. Two children with cerebral palsy need help picking up and holding toys. One child accidentally puts a jacket on backward and then screams in frustration; another tears a page in a favorite book and cries inconsolably; two others tug a toy between them, on the verge of a fight.

After free play, Mrs. Madden announces "circle time." This is a period when the children are asked to identify who came to school this morning, what the date is, which season it is, what the weather is, and so on. Even though it is three months into the school year, many of the children still do not know this information. Some lack the language to answer even simple questions, while others need constant prompting to be able to articulate their responses. Mrs. Madden has to adjust her questions to each child's level of functioning. She also has to interrupt the process repeatedly to regain one child's attention, to stop another child from turning away, and to prevent yet another from bothering a classmate. Mrs. Madden then surprises the children by opening a bag filled with colored objects. These allow her to teach, one by one, such concepts as "large," "yellow," "soft," "round," and "rough" and their opposites "small," "hard," "rectangular," and "smooth." The aide, Terry, reinforces the concepts with some of the children, reteaching the ideas and requesting appropriate responses. As with names and dates, these are things the children have worked on for several months. Mrs. Madden changes the objects frequently to keep the children's interest.

Art time follows from 9:30 to 10:00. The children need frequent one-to-one attention because they have difficulty handling the paper, triangles, paste, and crayons. Mrs. Madden and Terry move from table to table offering help. At each table, they focus on a different objective. That is because each child's individualized education program (IEP) has its own goals; these goals tell Mrs. Madden and Terry what the priorities are with each child.

Snack time is next. As with the morning arrival routine, this offers Mrs. Madden and Terry opportunities to teach each child self-help skills, in this case self-feeding competencies, as well as language (here, words to identify foods, how each is eaten, etc.). The children with cerebral palsy need constant, one-to-one assistance with feeding; however, the other children frequently call out for help or otherwise demand attention, so Mrs. Madden and Terry have to shuttle between children, briefly leaving the children with cerebral palsy.

After snack time, work time begins at 10:15. This is a period for concentrated activity on IEP goals and objectives. Some children work on letter and word identification, others on counting, and yet others on reading out loud. Errors are ignored by Mrs. Madden and Terry, but correct answers bring both praise and tokens. The tokens later will be exchanged by the child for candy or extra time with a favorite toy. Mrs. Madden prides herself on using discovery learning whenever possible. For children with severe disabilities, she uses **directed discovery learning** to provide structure. For others, whose needs are mild or moderate, Mrs. Madden adopts **guided discovery learning** in which she offers scaffolding for each child as needed. At every point, she makes sure that the learning is meaningful to and practical for the children. She also emphasizes pretend play, fantasy, and other activities designed to enhance their social and emotional development.

Moving time (gross motor skills) follows. Here, Mrs. Madden and Terry focus on helping children to meet age-appropriate developmental milestones such as walking without assistance, carrying objects while walking, jumping over objects, and throwing and catching a ball. Again, the IEP tells Mrs. Madden and Terry which competencies to work on with each child.

Finally, it is almost time for the children to leave. While Terry helps the children, one at a time, with toileting and dressing, Mrs. Madden writes notes in each child's journal, which she places in the children's bags. Then they accompany the children, who walk down the corridor in a procession, to the buses and help them onto the buses if necessary.

FIGURE 1–7 An ECSE preschool class.

As her children arrive at about 8:30 A.M., Miss Offerdahl and her aide, Judy, watch them take off their overcoats and go to the nearby bathroom. Miss Offerdahl and Judy assist the children only if asked or if something unexpected occurs. The children have long since mastered the basic self-help skills and want (indeed, insist!) on doing them independently.

Miss Offerdahl has arranged the room with different activity centers, each offering games or toys she thinks the children will find interesting. As they emerge from the bathroom, each child is allowed to go to whatever activity center appeals to her. Once the children have found their places, Miss Offerdahl and Judy walk unobtrusively from center to center, offering suggestions ("Why don't you try this?"), asking questions ("How many do you have?"), and supervising the occasional disturbance ("Susie, please, move your scissors to your side of the table").

After this free-play period, Miss Offerdahl and Judy assemble the group. The children are asked to describe what they were doing. Occasionally, Miss Offerdahl offers a new word or asks for a fuller explanation. Once the descriptions are over, she tells them that they can begin a new activity together, one of creating their own play about Thanksgiving. She asks for volunteers to make the scenery, create the costumes, and write the script. The children are allowed to do whichever part they prefer. They then assemble into smaller groups to plan what each child will do. Miss Offerdahl and Judy move from group to group, telling them what supplies are available, what additional supplies can be obtained, and the like, while encouraging the children to include all essential parts of their activity ("Don't forget—someone has to bring gravy!"). Finally, Miss Offerdahl and Judy volunteer to write out the group plans and each child's assignments. The children each get a short note to take home.

Story time follows. During this period, Judy moves unobtrusively from child to child to offer more information or to settle disputes. Miss Offerdahl has chosen an engaging story that features opportunities for the children to count, so from time to time she stops the story to ask for a new count total. She also stops occasionally to pose questions ("Why do you suppose Sandy did that?") designed to encourage the children to think about what they are hearing.

During snack time, Miss Offerdahl and Judy stand nearby, ready to assist if asked. From time to time, they comment ("What a nice snack your mother gave you this morning!") or ask questions ("How many chocolate chip cookies have you eaten this week?").

Play time gives the children a break from the sit-down routine of eating snacks. Miss Offerdahl and Judy encourage the children to engage in cooperative play, rather than just parallel (solitary) play. Scattered throughout the room are objects and activities that allow children to exercise both gross and fine motor muscles. Some of these are musical activities, while others are art or physical education activities.

After play time, Miss Offerdahl and Judy assemble the children again, this time to teach them several Thanksgiving-related songs. These songs, Miss Offerdahl explains, celebrate the holiday as a meaningful event in each of several different cultures. After they learn the songs, Miss Offerdahl asks them to comment on the cultural implications of each song ("What in this song talks about the importance of the spirit for Native Americans?").

Finally, it is almost time for the children to leave. Miss Offerdahl and Judy stand ready to help children with their overcoats if necessary, and they remind each child to give his or her parents the note about the play and what the child is expected to do to prepare for it. Then they watch as the children leave for the day.

FIGURE 1–8 An EC preschool class.

family-focused approach is not yet common in EC education. Bredekamp (1993b) concedes as much: "Partnerships with parents have long been a value of early childhood education, as reflected in the emphasis on parent involvement and decision making in Head Start. However, as children are perceived to be less 'at risk' and less vulnerable (i.e., older), the focus on families weakens" (p. 267).

A fifth and final area of difference is in transition planning. ECSE emphasizes the need to prepare young children with disabilities, delays, or deviations in development for success in the next environment. EC education, by contrast, tends to expect the next environment to conform to the needs of the child. Of course, because EC children typically

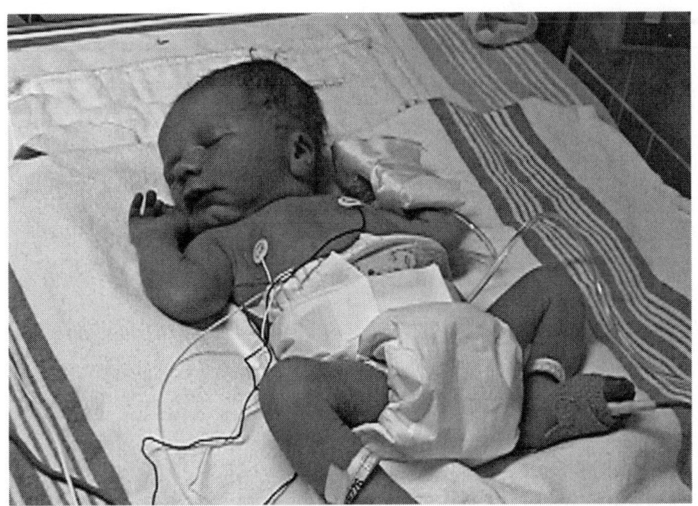

Premature infants usually develop with no lasting ill effects if early intervention services are provided on a timely basis.

have no disabilities, kindergarten and first-grade teachers and administrators can accomplish such steps much more readily than can their ECSE counterparts working with children who have severe needs.

The basic choice facing ECSE personnel is between preacademics and social development. Educators who believe that young children with special needs must receive intensive assistance in preacademics are almost compelled to use techniques from behavior modification to ensure that such instruction takes place. However, ECSE workers who determine that social skills are more important than academics could easily slow down and give children far more freedom to choose activities.

The heavy focus on academics that characterizes the No Child Left Behind (NCLB) Act of 2001 is causing many EC and ECSE professionals to increase their relative emphasis on preacademics. Some professionals worry that young children's social development may suffer as a result. The fourth edition of *Early Childhood Special Education* reflects this new orientation, because NCLB testing begins in third grade (i.e., at the end of the early childhood developmental period).

SUMMARY

The ways in which young children develop during the birth-to-eight period tell early childhood special educators how to work with them. A fundamental tenet of ECSE's philosophy is that of developmental plasticity. Research clearly shows that children can benefit significantly during the early childhood years when helpful therapies and instruction are offered to them and to their families. Similarly, ECSE workers believe that experiential deprivation is harmful to young children who have disabilities or delays in development. That is why these professionals seek to offer infants, toddlers, and young children with disabilities the full range of developmental and learning experiences that nondisabled young children get from birth to six years of age.

Child development in the birth-to-eight period is best understood as a sequence of maturational and learning steps, or stages. The exact age at which a child reaches a particular milestone is much less important than the sequence through which the child passes to come to and master that developmental task. Similarly, child development occurs in all five domains of development. These domains are not mutually independent. Rather, they interact with each other. For example, communication development speeds up once the physical domain task of walking has been achieved.

The guiding philosophy of ECSE is one that reflects these beliefs about child development. In general, ECSE professionals tend to emphasize the importance for each child to acquire developmentally important competencies, so much so, in fact, that these professionals often rely on the techniques of behavior modification to help children learn more rapidly. The broader field of EC education, not being faced as much with the challenges of disability or serious delays in development, tends to shy away from such techniques, preferring instead to play the more passive role of encouraging children to develop at their own pace. This difference between the ECSE and EC philosophies is entirely understandable given the different populations with which they work.

KEY TERMS

accommodation
adaptive development
age appropriateness
assimilation
attention
autonomy versus shame and doubt
behavior modification
cognitive development
communication development
concrete operational stage
developmental plasticity
developmentally appropriate
developmentally appropriate practice (DAP)
directed discovery learning
domains
double jeopardy
early childhood (EC) education
early childhood special education (ECSE)
experiential deprivation
extinction
guided discovery learning
individual appropriateness
industry versus inferiority
initiative versus guilt
language
memory
morphemes
operant conditioning
perception
phonemes
phonemic awareness
phonics instruction
physical development
pragmatics
preoperational stage
presentation reinforcement
processing
punishment
removal reinforcement
sensorimotor stage
social or emotional development
syntax
trust versus mistrust
zone of proximal development

QUESTIONS FOR REFLECTION

1. How does the work of Erikson help us understand development in the birth-to-eight period?
2. What did Maslow teach us that helps us understand why some parents persist, apparently beyond reason, in seeking "cures" for their children?
3. Reflect on your observations of young children. In what ways does development in one domain (say, communication) affect the child's development in another domain (say, cognition)? Have you seen, as well, ways in which a child's physical development (learning to walk, to stand, etc.) seems to delay that child's communication development? If so, describe your observations.
4. What "tricks" could you teach a young child to help that child gain entry into a group of children who are playing together?
5. How does "experiential deprivation" affect development of young children whose limitations of hearing or vision or physical mobility might cause their parents to be overly protective of them?
6. How is physical mobility related to the achievement by a young child of a sense of independent identity?
7. Thinking about the developmentally important role that physical movement plays in early childhood, what concerns might you have as a teacher about a three-year-old who has cerebral palsy or some other physical limitation?
8. In your own words, what concepts guide NAEYC's developmentally appropriate practice?
9. Again in your own words, what different beliefs seem to shape DEC's recommended practices?
10. Reflect on your observations of early childhood classes (Head Start, public or private preschool) and of early childhood special education classes (early intervention, preschool special education). In what ways did the children's behavior differ? How did the actions of the educators vary between the different kinds of programs? Did you observe the preference for behavior modification and for direct instruction that this chapter said was often characteristic of early childhood special education? If so, what were your reactions?

PRACTICAL EXERCISES

1. Visit a local early childhood program (e.g., a Head Start program) or an early childhood special education (ECSE) program (e.g., a special preschool or an early intervention program serving infants and toddlers). Observe for a morning or an afternoon. Talk with program staff members. Then describe, as best you can, the program's philosophy.

   Is it a typical early childhood philosophy (e.g., one that emphasizes discovery learning and has program staff supporting children more than teaching them)? Is it a typical ECSE philosophy (e.g., one that stresses direct instruction and has program staff teaching children more than supporting them)? Or is it a combination of the two?

2. Interview your own parents about your early childhood development. At about what age did you first walk? Talk? Did your parents take a "permissive" tact with you, allowing you to explore home and yard freely? Did they restrict you from any activities (experiential deprivation)? After your interview(s), reflect on what you learned as it relates to the philosophies described in this chapter.

WEB SITES OF INTEREST

www.naeyc.org National Association for the Education of Young Children—information on developmentally appropriate practice

www.dec-sped.org Division for Early Childhood, Council for Exceptional Children—information on special education for young children

www.nectac.org National Early Childhood Technical Assistance Center—information on Part C and Preschool Part B programs nationwide

www.frankbowe.net A site by the author, offering additional information of interest to readers of *Early Childhood Special Education*

Prelude: Overview of Early Childhood Special Education

CHAPTER

> Most alarming of all, the rates of obesity among children and teens have tripled in the past 25 years. Health-care providers say they are seeing something of an epidemic of potentially lethal Type 2 diabetes, once known as the adult-onset version of the disease, among children as young as 10 and 11. "Without some intervention, this is the first generation of young Americans, being born today, who are expected to have a shorter life span than their parents or grandparents," says Arkansas Governor Mike Huckabee. (Tumulty, 2006, p. 41)

OBJECTIVES

After reading this chapter, you should be able to:

- Describe IDEA's Part C services for infants and toddlers.
- Describe IDEA's Part B services for preschoolers with disabilities.
- Describe early primary special education (through age eight).
- Describe the population being served by ECSE programs.
- Identify key diversity/cultural issues in ECSE.
- Suggest ways that program staff may show cultural sensitivity.
- Identify the key professions represented in ECSE.

CHAPTER OUTLINE

- OVERVIEW
- EARLY INTERVENTION AND PRESCHOOL/PRIMARY SPECIAL EDUCATION
  - Part C: Early Intervention
  - Section 619, Part B: Preschool Special Education
  - Primary Special Education
- RATIONALE FOR ECSE
- WHAT IS ECSE?
- WHO ARE THE CHILDREN BEING SERVED?
  - Early Intervention
  - Preschool Special Education
  - Primary Special Education
  - Cultural Diversity Among Children
  - Cultural Competence
- WHO ARE THE WORKERS IN THE FIELD?
- ROLES AND RESPONSIBILITIES
  - The Federal Role
  - The State Role
  - The Local Role
  - The Parents' Role

OVERVIEW

Early childhood special education (ECSE) provides services for children under nine years of age and their families in response to disabilities or developmental delays in the children. These services usually are free of charge to the families, because federal and state governments fund ECSE programs in the hope that early assistance will alleviate the impact of disabilities, reduce developmental delays, and lessen children's needs for later services.

Chapter 2 introduces the ECSE field, explains the rationale for public support, outlines the services offered, sketches the demographics of the population served, discusses the different professions active in ECSE, and explores important issues of cultural diversity. The chapter concludes with a discussion of the roles played by federal, state, and local units of government, as well as by families.

EARLY INTERVENTION AND PRESCHOOL/ PRIMARY SPECIAL EDUCATION

Early intervention refers to services for infants and toddlers and their families to address the special needs of very young children who have disabilities, have developmental delays, or are at risk of developmental delays. The term is used in Part C of the Individuals with Disabilities Education Act.

Early intervention refers to services provided for **infants and toddlers** and their families to address the special needs of very young children who have disabilities, have developmental delays, or are at risk of developmental delays. All states are serving infants and toddlers in the birth-to-36-month age range, together with their families, under a federal program created in 1986. This program is **Part C** of the **Individuals with Disabilities Education Act (IDEA).** The IDEA is the nation's foundation law on special education. Although all states provide services for infants and toddlers, the scope and breadth of services offered vary greatly. **Preschool special education** is special education and related services for three- to five-year-old children with disabilities and,

Infants and toddlers
refers to children before they reach the age of three. Infancy begins at birth and ends with achievement of independent walking, while toddlers are young children who have begun walking but have not yet reached the age of three. Another commonly used way to refer to this population is "birth-to-two inclusive," which more directly incorporates the first 36 months of life.

Part C
is the state-operated program created in 1986 for infants and toddlers with disabilities and their families. It is an early intervention program for children under three years of age and (with family concurrence) their families.

Individuals with Disabilities Education Act (IDEA)
The IDEA is the landmark special education law in the United States. Formerly called the Education of the Handicapped Act, it includes (as Part B) PL 94–142, the Education for All Handicapped Children Act of 1975.

Preschool special education
refers to special education and related services to meet unique needs of three- to five-year-olds with disabilities and, in some states, developmental delays.

Preschool-age children
are children aged three-to-five inclusive. Most EC programs focus on this population.

Section 619
of Part B of the IDEA authorizes preschool special education and related services for children from three to five inclusive.

Part B
is the part of the IDEA describing how children with disabilities aged

The family is in the center of early childhood special education.

in some states, developmental delays. All 50 states serve **preschool-age children** under a mandate laid down in **Section 619** of **Part B** of the IDEA, also enacted in 1986. Primary special education is authorized under Part B as well.

Although participation in both Part C and Section 619 Part B programs is voluntary for states and other jurisdictions, all eligible jurisdictions have accepted the challenge. As they moved toward compliance, they tended to fashion a seamless system of services all the way from birth to age five, in effect meshing Part C and Section 619 Part B. This creative, single-system approach leads into primary education. The term *ECSE* covers this unified system of services for infants, toddlers, and preschool and primary children with disabilities, throughout the birth-to-eight age range.

PART C: EARLY INTERVENTION

Part C requires participating states to provide infants and toddlers who have **diagnosed conditions**—disabilities limiting or very likely to limit activities these young children can do—and their families with early intervention services. Such conditions as deafness (the inability to understand speech through the ear alone) are disabilities. The law also requires that infants and toddlers with **developmental delays** receive early intervention services as needed. Such children may include those who have not begun talking, walking, or reaching other milestones at expected developmental stages. Part C permits but does not require states to provide early intervention services for infants and toddlers who are **at risk** of developmental delays or disabilities but do not display any actual delays or activity limitations.

Figure 2–1 offers the statutory definition of infants and toddlers with disabilities. Part C uses the term ***infants and toddlers with disabilities*** in a way that grants the states considerable flexibility in deciding which young children with disabilities qualify for services. The states may define such key terms as *developmental delay, diagnosed conditions,* and *at risk.* To point out that states enjoy much flexibility in deciding what kinds of children to serve is notably not to say that state, county, local, and private Part C

3 to 18 shall receive a free appropriate public education.

Diagnosed conditions

(established conditions) are disabilities or other health conditions recognized by a state as limiting or very likely to limit activities young children can do. The term is used in Part C of the IDEA.

Developmental delays

are lags in child development in any one or more of the five domains (cognitive, communication, physical, adaptive, social or emotional). How much of a lag constitutes a "delay" is to be defined by each state. The term is used in both Part C and in Part B of the IDEA, for Section 619.

At risk

is a term used to refer to infants or toddlers who do not exhibit developmental delays but who for biological and/or environmental reasons are more likely than most to develop such delays. The concept is used only in Part C of the IDEA.

Infants and toddlers with disabilities

refers to those from birth to age two inclusive who need early intervention services because they are experiencing developmental delays in adaptive, cognitive, communication, physical, and/or social or emotional development; or because they have a diagnosed condition that has a high probability of resulting in developmental delay. The term may also include, at a state's discretion, at-risk children and preschool-age children.

Entitlement

means that infants and toddlers must receive early intervention services if they satisfy state criteria. Similarly, three- to five-year-old children must receive free preschool services to meet their unique needs

(1) The term "infant or toddler with a disability" (A) means an individual under 3 years of age who needs early intervention services because the individual (i) is experiencing developmental delays, as measured by appropriate diagnostic instruments and procedures in one or more of the areas of cognitive development, physical development, communication development, social or emotional development, and adaptive development; or (ii) has a diagnosed physical or mental condition which has a high probability of resulting in developmental delay; and (B) (i) may also include, at a State's discretion, at-risk infants and toddlers and (ii) children with disabilities who are eligible for services under section 619 and who previously received services under this part until such children enter, or are eligible under State law to enter, kindergarten or elementary school, as appropriate, provided that any programs under this part serving such children shall include—(I) an educational component that promotes school readiness and incorporates pre-literacy, language, and numeracy skills; and (II) a written notification to parents of their rights and responsibilities in determining whether their child will continue to receive services under this part or participate in preschool programs under section 619.
(Section 632[5]; 34 CFR 303.16)

FIGURE 2–1 Infants and toddlers with disabilities.

service providers may be selective in deciding which young children to serve. Federal law mandates that *all* infants and toddlers who meet state criteria must receive services: Part C is an **entitlement** program.

The age range covered, "under 3 years of age," means the first 36 months after birth. The definition emphasizes that *only* infants and toddlers "who need early intervention services" must be served. That qualification is not as self-evident as it may seem; infants and toddlers who have developmental delays or diagnosed conditions or are at risk may not require early intervention services. To take an obvious example, most at-risk infants, toddlers, and preschoolers develop normally without formal intervention. To take another example, a toddler may have epilepsy, but unless the condition has noticeable effects on the child's daily activities, there may be no discernible need for early intervention services.

Early intervention services are to be outlined in an **Individualized Family Service Plan (IFSP).** Figure 2–2 shows the contents of an IFSP. The plan is a written document

1. The infant or toddler's present levels of performance (e.g., needs) in five domains
2. The family's resources, priorities, and concerns
3. Outcomes to be achieved
4. Early intervention services to be provided, based on peer-reviewed research
5. Natural environment
6. Start date and duration of services
7. Service coordinator's name
8. Transition steps at about age three

FIGURE 2–2 Individualized Family Service Plan (based on IDEA Section 636).

if they satisfy federal and/or state eligibility standards. (The term *zero reject* expresses a similar idea—namely, that no child who meets eligibility criteria may be denied services.)

Individualized Family Service Plan (IFSP)

is a written document outlining services for infants and toddlers and (if the families concur) their families. IFSPs note the infant's or toddler's development in five domains, services the child (and family) will receive, and similar information, as well as the service coordinator's name.

Supports

are links to neighbors, friends, and community resources upon which the family may rely in times of need. Supports may empower the family so it functions more effectively on behalf of the infant or toddler.

that identifies the type of service coordination the family desires, any other early intervention services approved by the family, the name of the service coordinator, and a plan for transition from Part C to preschool Part B or other services. The law requires, in the words of the U.S. House of Representatives Committee on Education and Labor, that the parent or guardian "must be an integral member of the multidisciplinary team charged with developing the IFSP" (*House Report 102–198,* 1991, p. 18). The IFSP identifies the infant's or toddler's special needs, notes family resources and concerns, outlines services available, explains any fees (including sliding-fee scales), specifies the outcomes or results expected, and shows how the transition to preschool special education or to other programs and services will occur.

The plan is to be reviewed twice annually with the family and evaluated at least once each year. Its contents must, by law, be "fully explained to the parents," in their native language, if necessary. The family may decline any service and may refuse to participate in an assessment of family resources, priorities, and concerns without jeopardizing its right to other services for the child or for the family itself.

Families have the right to early intervention services that will meet an eligible infant's or toddler's unique needs in any of five areas of development: adaptive, cognitive, communication, physical, and social or emotional. Early intervention services feature assistance for both the infant or toddler and the family. Included by law are such direct services as special instruction for the infant or toddler; physical, occupational, or speech and language therapy; and psychological services, such as diagnosis, assessment, and mental health interventions. Services for the family include family counseling, training of family members in meeting the needs of the infant or toddler, psychological services, social work services, and service coordination (case management) services.

Most early intervention services are not instructional but rather are similar to what special educators call "related services." In education—whether preschool, elementary, or secondary—the emphasis is on special education, with related services playing an important but supportive role. Those roles are reversed in early intervention. That is, the stress in early intervention is on **supports** designed to empower the family so that it functions more effectively on behalf of the infant or toddler. Supports are links to community resources, neighbors, and friends to whom the family may turn when in need.

Interdisciplinary service delivery is essential to successful early intervention and preschool special education.

These services for infants or toddlers and their families must meet state standards, including the licensing or certification of the early intervention specialists providing the services, as well as the licensing or other approval of caregiver facilities and programs. The services are usually free to the parents, although sliding-scale and other fee-for-services arrangements are allowed under Part C where authorized by other federal or state laws. Third-party insurance companies, for example, may pay for ECSE-related services. Parents enjoy the right to choose among state-approved options for early intervention. As noted, parents may decline any particular early intervention service; they may even decline all services. Some parents do exactly that, much to the consternation of early intervention professionals (Minke & Scott, 1993). The law also grants to parents specific due process rights, including the right to appeal any adverse decision in case of disagreements between the family and the agency providing the services.

Special education is specially designed instruction to meet the unique needs of the child. The term is used in Part B of the IDEA.

Related services are noninstructional support services such as transportation, therapy, and counseling. The term is used in Part B of the IDEA.

Children with disabilities refers to children who meet the criteria in IDEA Section 602(3), notably that they have a recognized disability and for that reason need special education and related services.

The U.S. Department of Education's *Annual Reports* are a major source of information about special education in the United States. Each year, these reports provide statistical and other data about the field. According to the *Twenty-Seventh Annual Report*, most states served about 2 percent of their birth-to-two-inclusive populations under Part C, with some states serving more than 2 percent (U.S. Department of Education, 2005).

SECTION 619, PART B: PRESCHOOL SPECIAL EDUCATION

Another section of the IDEA authorizes **special education**—specially designed instruction—and **related services**—support services such as transportation, therapy, counseling, and the like—for **children with disabilities** who are in the three-to-five age range. A different definition is used for these preschoolers. As Figure 2–3 illustrates,

(A) "Child with a disability" means a child

(i) with

[1] mental retardation

[2] hearing impairments, including deafness

[3] speech or language impairments

[4] visual impairments, including blindness

[5] emotional disturbance

[6] orthopedic impairments

[7] autism

[8] traumatic brain injury

[9] other health impairments, or

[10] specific learning disabilities; and

(ii) who, by reason thereof, needs special education and related services.

(B) The term "child with a disability" for a child aged 3 through 9 may, at the discretion of the State and the local education agency, include a child

(i) experiencing developmental delays, as defined by the State and as measured by appropriate diagnostic instruments and procedures, in one or more of the following areas: physical development, cognitive development, communication development, social or emotional development, or adaptive development; and

(ii) who, by reason thereof, needs special education and related services. (Section 602[3]; 34 CFR 300.7)

FIGURE 2–3 Children with disabilities.

Art therapy can be a related service.

Part B makes no provision for services for at-risk children. Notice that children, to be eligible, must "need special education and related services."

Special education and related services are to be provided by local education agencies (LEAs) free of charge to the family, although LEAs may impose incidental fees that are also charged to families of nondisabled children. The families enjoy due process rights in any dispute with LEAs; these rights are very similar to those in Part C. Part B guarantees a free, appropriate public education regardless of the severity of a disability. In the classic case of *Timothy W. v. Rochester School District* (1989), a federal court of appeals affirmed the right of a young boy in New England to receive Part B services despite very severe and multiple disabilities that local education officials contended rendered him virtually uneducable. The IDEA is clear, the court ruled, in granting Timothy—and all other children with disabilities—an unequivocal right to an education (*Timothy W. v. Rochester [NH] School District,* 875 F.2d 954 [1st Cir. 1989] cert. denied 110 S. Ct. 519).

The term *special education* is defined in the IDEA using words that distinguish it from early intervention:

> 602(29) *"[S]pecial education" means specially designed instruction, at no cost to parents, to meet the unique needs of a child with a disability, including—(A) instruction conducted in the classroom, in the home, in hospitals and institutions, and in other settings; and (B) instruction in physical education.*

Special education contrasts with general, or regular, education in that it is "specially designed" to "meet the unique needs of a child with a disability." To stretch the point, special education could be compared to custom-designed production, general education to mass production manufacturing. Children with disabilities often receive general education along with children who have no disabilities in addition to special education.

The term *related services* is also defined in the IDEA. The term is used only with reference to Part B, not to Part C:

> 602(26)(A) *"[R]elated services" means transportation, and such developmental, corrective and other supportive services (including speech pathology and audiology services, interpreting services, psychological services, physical and occupational therapy, recreation, including therapeutic recreation, social work services, school nurse services designed to enable a child with a disability to receive a free appropriate public education as described in the individualized education program of the child, counseling services, including rehabilitation counseling, orientation and mobility services, and medical services (except that such medical services shall be for diagnostic and evaluation purposes only) as may be required to assist a child with a disability to benefit from special education, and includes*

the early identification and assessment of disabling conditions in children. Exception: The term does not include a medical device that is surgically implanted, or the replacement of such device.

That is, related services are supportive services that "may be required to assist a child with a disability to benefit from special education." Notable here is the word *benefit:* only those related services that are necessary for a child to benefit from special education need be provided. Related services that might help a child but are not necessary for the child to benefit from special education are not required. In addition, related services that might help a child excel in school are not required under Part B. Some examples of related services are speech and language pathology services, physical and occupational therapy, transportation between the child's home and the building in which preschool services are provided, and counseling.

This definition requires, as does Part C, that programs "meet the standards of the state" agency with jurisdiction, in this case, the state education agency. States retain authority to set personnel and program standards.

Individualized Education Program (IEP)

is a written document that identifies the unique needs of the child, the special education and related services needed to meet those unique needs, annual goals and short-term objectives, how the child's progress will be assessed, the date of initiation of services, and the projected duration of those services. The term is used in Part B of the IDEA.

Appropriate

is a term used in both Part C and in Part B of the IDEA, but it is not defined precisely in the statute. It appears to mean "meets the standards of the State" and "meets the unique needs of the child."

Special education and related services for preschool children appear in an **Individualized Education Program (IEP).** The IEP is a written document that identifies the unique needs of the child, the special education and related services to meet those unique needs, annual goals and short-term objectives, the way in which the child's progress will be assessed, the date of initiation of services, and the projected duration of those services. The contents of an IEP are given in Figure 2–4.

Section 619 of Part B guarantees the preschool child with a disability the provision of **appropriate** services designed to meet his unique needs. The law considers "appropriate" to mean that the services satisfy state standards and meet the child's needs. The statutory language in Section 602 is as follows:

"[F]ree appropriate public education" means special education and related services that—(A) have been provided at public expense, under public supervision and direction, and without charge; (B) meet the standards of the State education agency; (C) include an appropriate preschool, elementary, or secondary school education in the State involved; and (D) are provided in conformity with the individualized education program required under section 614(d).

1. The child's present levels of academic achievement and functional performance (e.g., needs), including how the child's disability affects participation in appropriate preschool activities
2. Annual goals for meeting all needs of the child
3. How the child's parents will be informed of progress
4. Services to be provided
5. Extent to which the child will participate with nondisabled children
6. Tests and test accommodations
7. Start date and duration of services; expected frequency and location of those services

FIGURE 2–4 Individualized Education Program (based on IDEA Section 614[(d]).

The term *appropriate* never has been statutorily defined, other than that an appropriate education meets state standards. A 1982 Supreme Court decision held that an "appropriate" education provides just enough to enable a child (in that case, Amy Rowley, a deaf student) to "benefit"—that is, to achieve passing marks and be promoted from grade to grade (*Board of Education, Hendrick Hudson School District v. Rowley,* 1982).

The *Twenty-Seventh Annual Report* (U.S. Department of Education, 2005) indicates that 679,212 preschool-age children with disabilities were served in the 50 states, Puerto Rico, and the District of Columbia during the 2003–2004 school year. Just over one out of every 20 (5.78 percent) children in this age range were being served (Table AA10). These numbers are much larger than those in the 1994–1995 school year, which is a benchmark year because it was the first year that preschool special education was made available throughout the United States.

PRIMARY SPECIAL EDUCATION

Services for children with disabilities who are six, seven, and eight years old are also authorized by Part B of the IDEA. The definition for "child with a disability" (Figure 2–3) applies. Notice that these children are within the age range for which "developmental delay" may be used in lieu of a label such as mental retardation. We often do not know what causes a child to have difficulty learning or reaching developmental milestones. The tests we use with children this young often are not sensitive enough to enable us to make definitive diagnoses of medical conditions. For these reasons, it may be helpful to use a "delay" label until we can do more observation and testing.

There are two significant differences between services for preschoolers and those for primary students with disabilities. First, special education and related services have been mandated for all six- to eight-year-old children with disabilities since 1977, nearly a decade longer than a mandate has been in place to serve three- to five-year-olds. Second, there is no optional or volitional aspect to special education for children with disabilities age six and over. Because all states have compulsory school attendance laws in place for children and youth between the ages of 6 and 16 (or, in some cases, 17), those states must offer a free public education for children with disabilities who are within that age range, as well.

The "early childhood" period ends when children begin to display symbolic and logical thinking abilities. This is generally accepted to occur, for most children, at about the age of eight. Stated differently, this time in Piaget's terms, children become capable of concrete operations (Wortham, 1998). There is another way to think about this six-to-eight-inclusive population: as children not yet expected to participate in the "high-stakes" assessments required by the No Child Left Behind Act of 2001. Those tests begin in third grade. Most eight-year-olds with disabilities are in second rather than third grade; some are still in first grade (Blackorby et al., 2005).

RATIONALE FOR ECSE

Why do we offer free services for young children with disabilities and their families? The rationale for federal and state investments has several parts.

We serve these young children and their families because we know that by intervening early we can often lessen the effects of disabilities. We can reduce delays in development.

Joint family-staff planning is a key element in the development of IFSPs and IEPs.

We can, that is, make a difference in the lives of these children. As is shown in detail in Chapter 3, the research evidence is quite impressive that ECSE does make a difference.

The second part of the rationale is that ECSE services help families. When young children have disabilities or developmental delays, it is often necessary for an adult in the home to reduce or even forgo employment so as to provide round-the-clock care for the child. By ameliorating the condition or lessening the delay, ECSE services may free family members to engage in other activities, including gainful employment.

The third reason we provide these services is that we hope thereby to lower costs later. Thus, money spent on young children may be an investment because these children may not require as many services when they are older. This part of the rationale has a logical basis. Free special education and related services are guaranteed to be provided to those children during the elementary and secondary years—if they need those services and to the extent they require them. The research evidence is not yet conclusive that money spent during the ECSE years actually saves money in later school years. We examine the evidence on this question in Chapter 3.

WHAT IS ECSE?

Seamless system

is a term referring to a set of services that has no gaps or delays between Part C early intervention and Part B services.

Interdisciplinary services

are services provided by specialists from different disciplines working together on a team (e.g., early childhood special educators and speech pathologists). The term contrasts with services that are provided by professionals representing only one discipline (unidisciplinary). The term *multidisciplinary* most often refers to a team (including family members) that plans and conducts assessments or evaluations. These

When states design a **seamless system** to serve the entire birth-to-eight range of children with disabilities, they usually adopt a *developmental* approach emphasizing services that help infants, toddlers, and young children with disabilities to achieve developmental milestones at the earliest possible age. A seamless system has no gaps or delays between Part C early intervention and Part B services. The developmental approach seeks to avoid labeling the infant, toddler, or young child. Rather, the child's strengths and needs are identified in the five developmental areas (cognitive, physical, communication, social or emotional, and adaptive). **Interdisciplinary services**—services offered by professionals from different disciplines working together on a team—are provided to meet the child's special needs and to promote the child's development. Other supports and services help families respond more effectively to their young child's unique needs. Extensive parental input helps in designing all these services.

These characteristics of ECSE reflect what model programs serving infants, toddlers, and preschool-age children with disabilities have demonstrated. Since 1969, the federal government has sponsored dozens of model programs, experimenting with a variety of child and family services. The federal mandates now in effect emerged only after more than 25 years of experience with model programs showed that services for very young children with disabilities could help not only the infant, toddler, or preschooler in question but the family and society as well.

terms are used most often in Part C of the IDEA. The term *transdisciplinary* refers to an approach in which the often artificial boundaries between disciplines or professions are transcended or ignored so as to deliver "holistic" services to a child and/or a family.

The IDEA allows states to use Part C to serve preschoolers and elements of Part B to serve infants and toddlers. These flexible statutory provisions have proven extremely helpful to states that wanted to create seamless systems of services. As you saw in Figure 2–1, the IDEA now defines "infant or toddler with a disability" to include, at a state's option, children up to and including kindergarten age. If states exercise this option, the IFSP is to note "educational" needs. Similarly, states may amend their definitions of the term "children with disabilities" to include three- to five-year-olds with developmental delays.

Taken together, these statutory provisions authorize states to make Part C and Part B services more similar and, thus, more seamless. That goal is clearly easiest to achieve in those states in which the state education agency (SEA) is also the Part C lead agency. Even states having other agencies as lead agencies for early intervention can use the law's flexibility to eliminate unnecessary barriers, gaps, and duplication of services.

WHO ARE THE CHILDREN BEING SERVED?

More than two million (2,220,000) young children in the birth-to-eight-inclusive age range are being served in ECSE programs nationwide. According to the U.S. Department of Education (2006c), the numbers served as of the 2004–2005 school year break down this way by age range: 279,154 infants and toddlers (12 percent of all ECSE children), 701,949 preschoolers (32 percent of all ECSE children), and 1,237,209 children in K–3 (56 percent of all ECSE children) (Tables 6–1 and 1–7, www.ideadata.org).

We know much more about these young children than we did in years past, thanks in large part to several major longitudinal studies. The **National Early Intervention Longitudinal Study (NEILS),** especially, has shed much light on infants and toddlers as well as their families. The **Pre-Elementary Education Longitudinal Study (PEELS)** has added to our understanding of preschool-age children with disabilities. Taken together, the new data suggest that ECSE may now shift, after decades of fast growth, into a new era of improving services for a more stable population of young children.

National Early Intervention Longitudinal Study (NEILS)

is a major, long-term examination of infants and toddlers and their families. A nationally representative sample of 5,668 families residing in 20 states is being followed. The study is important because so little information is available elsewhere about very young children with disabilities and their families.

Pre-Elementary Education Longitudinal Study (PEELS)

is another large-scale study, this one following 3,000 young children through their preschool and early elementary years. Data collection began in fall 2003, occurred again in winter 2005 and 2006, and will take place again in 2007 and 2009.

EARLY INTERVENTION

Three categories of infants and toddlers are recognized in Part C. The first is that of children with developmental delays. The law calls for these delays to be "measured by appropriate diagnostic instruments and procedures" and states that they may occur in one or more of five areas of development: cognitive, physical, communication, social or emotional, and adaptive.

The figures that follow illustrate several important points. First, infants and toddlers may have delays in development in any one, or several, of the five domains of development that are recognized in IDEA Part C. The NEILS study shows that children with such delays tend to be recognized later, rather than earlier (see Figure 2–5). That makes sense: it takes time for family members to notice delays and to consult pediatricians about them. Typically, physicians urge caution ("He will probably grow out of it"), thus further postponing the onset of services. NEILS reported an average age at first service at 27 months (late in the birth-to-36-month Part C range).

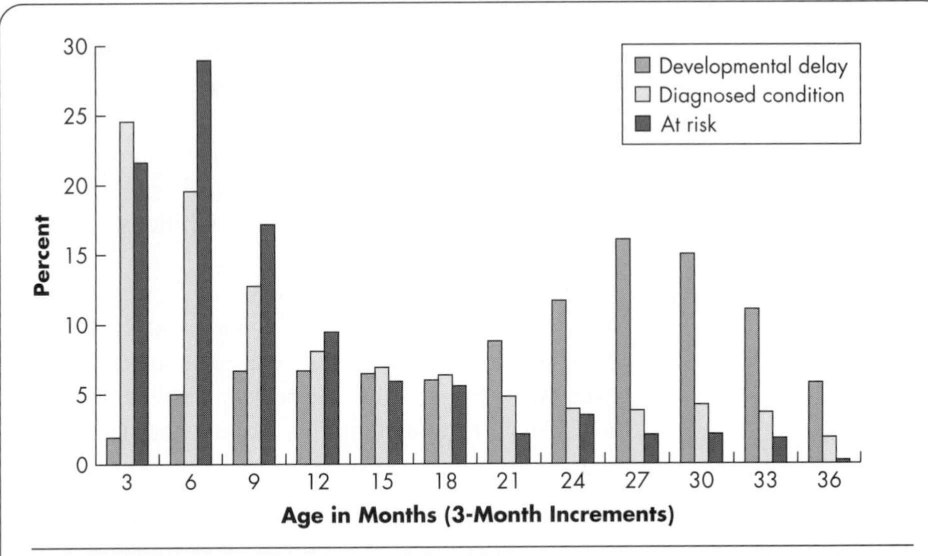

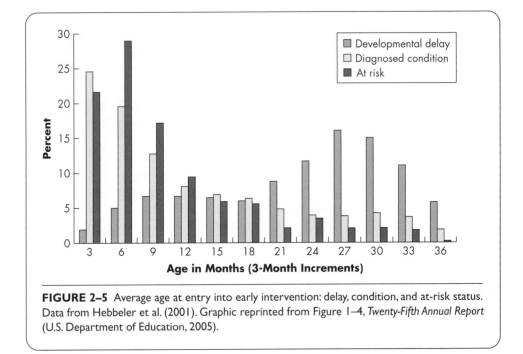

FIGURE 2–5 Average age at entry into early intervention: delay, condition, and at-risk status. Data from Hebbeler et al. (2001). Graphic reprinted from Figure 1–4, *Twenty-Fifth Annual Report* (U.S. Department of Education, 2005).

Second, these very young children may have "diagnosed conditions" (disabilities). Infants and toddlers with diagnosed conditions tend to be identified, and served, much earlier than is the case with those having delays.

Third, the IDEA allows states to serve "at-risk" infants and toddlers. Eight states (California, Hawaii, Indiana, Massachusetts, New Hampshire, New Mexico, North Carolina, and West Virginia) served a total of 7,250 at-risk infants and toddlers during the 2004–2005 school year. That was just 2.5 percent of all infants and toddlers served, so the category continues to be a small one (U.S. Department of Education, 2006c).

In Figures 2–6 and 2–7, the plateauing of the size of the population being served is evident. More than one-quarter million very young children are served now, and they represent about 2.5 percent of all infants and toddlers in the nation.

NEILS is a longitudinal study that is following more than 3,000 children with disabilities or at risk for disabilities and their families through their experiences in early intervention, plus follow-up through the preschool years and into the primary grades. The NEILS Data Report #3, *Demographic Characteristics of Children and Families Entering Early Intervention* (Hebbeler, Spiker, Mallik, Scarborough, & Simeonsson, 2004) tells us that infants and toddlers being served under IDEA Part C are more likely to come from poor families, to be African American, and to have mothers who never finished high school than is the case among infants and toddlers who do not have disabilities. Specifically, 27 percent of the Part C families studied had incomes of less than $15,000 a year, meaning that they lived in poverty. More than 25 percent were on welfare and food stamp programs. The children were one-third again as likely to be African American as are all infants and toddlers in the United States: 21 percent among those served by early intervention versus 14 percent in the general population. A high 16 percent of mothers of IDEA infants and toddlers lacked even a high-school diploma.

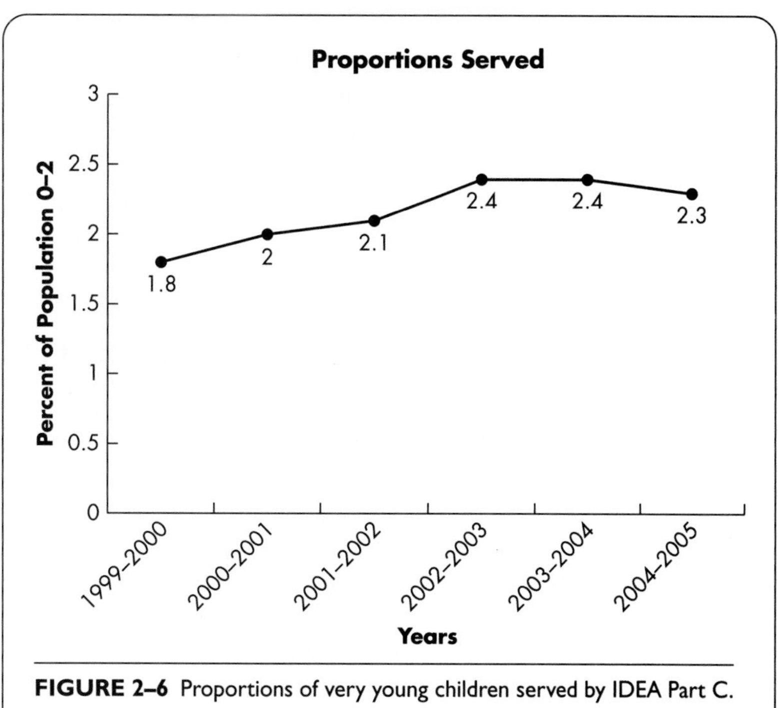

FIGURE 2–6 Proportions of very young children served by IDEA Part C.

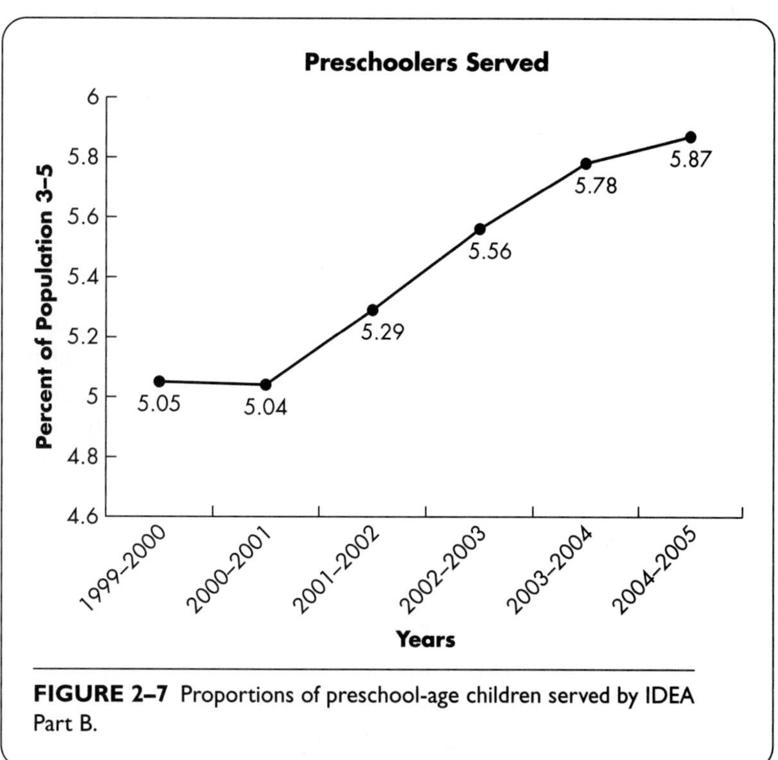

FIGURE 2–7 Proportions of preschool-age children served by IDEA Part B.

The NEILS staff used an index consisting of 10 indicators of demographic risk, such as family poverty, parental lack of education, and the like. Children in families with household income of less than $15,000 averaged 3.6 risk factors, compared with less than one risk factor for children in families earning more than $50,000. This illustrates the "double jeopardy" (Kaplan-Sanoff et al., 1991) idea that was introduced in Chapter 1. For example, familial poverty and low education attainment by parents are linked to limited access to preventive and restorative medical care. Those factors, in turn, exacerbate the effects of children's conditions.

PRESCHOOL SPECIAL EDUCATION

The IDEA states that three- to five-year-old children are eligible for services if they have one of the following 10 recognized disabilities: "mental retardation, hearing impairments including deafness, speech or language impairments, visual impairments including blindness, serious emotional disturbance, orthopedic impairments, autism, traumatic brain injury, other health impairments, and specific learning disabilities." Children having one or more of these conditions are eligible for preschool special education if they also "by reason thereof need special education and related services."

The IDEA allows states and other jurisdictions to amend their definitions for three- to nine-year-olds to encompass children who need special education and related services because of developmental delays in one or more of the five areas of development listed under Part C. This flexibility allows states to continue serving developmentally disabled children who remain in need of special services. Many states take advantage of this flexibility to create a catch-all category, **preschool child with a disability,** thus avoiding the need for labels with these young children. Children aged three to five who are at risk, however, are not eligible for services under Section 619.

Preschool child with a disability

is a three- to six-year-old child who has one of the disabilities recognized under the IDEA. The term is used in some states to avoid the need to label a child prior to elementary school. (Preschool age begins at three and ends when the child enters kindergarten or first grade, usually at about age six.)

As of the 2003–2004 school year, 679,212 preschool-age children with disabilities were being served under IDEA Part B. They represented 5.78 percent of all three- to five-year-olds in the United States. Most were five years of age (45 percent) or four (37 percent), with relatively few being three (22 percent) (U.S. Department of Education, 2005). Here, again, as with infants and toddlers, we see that some disabilities occur or are diagnosed well after birth. With respect to race and ethnicity, 15 percent were African American, or about the same proportion as exists in the general population. We do not see the same overrepresentation of African Americans here as we do in early intervention. One possible reason: Head Start, which serves preschool-age children, may be picking up many of these children. Early Head Start, which serves very young children under age three, is much smaller than is Head Start, so it helps far fewer children and families. We will discuss Head Start in detail later.

IDEA Part B uses disability labels, with developmental delay being one of 11 allowable classifications. Preschoolers were most often identified as having speech or language impairments (330,889 children, or 49 percent) or delays (239,161 children, or 35 percent). Few were given such labels as specific learning disabilities, mental retardation, or the like. One reason is the unease that many professionals in ECSE feel about labels. Another is the difficulty of diagnosing specific conditions when children are this young.

The number of preschoolers continues to grow (see Figures 2–8 and 2–9). During the five-year period between the 1999–2000 and the 2003–2004 school year, the number of three- to five-year-olds served under Section 619 of IDEA Part B increased by 16 percent, or about 3 percent per year. We do not yet see the plateauing here that we see among infants and toddlers.

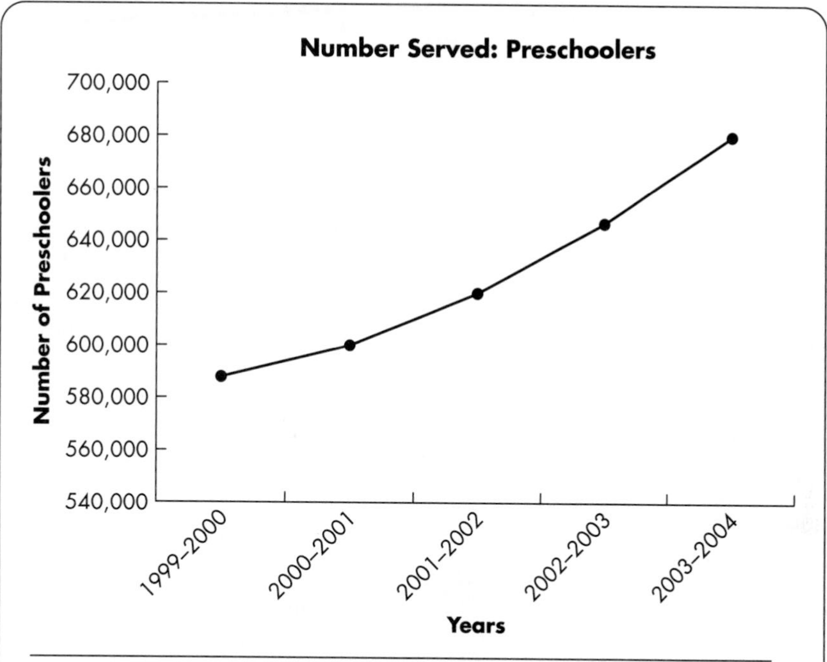

FIGURE 2–8 Numbers of preschoolers served each year, 1999–2000 through 2003–2004. Data sources: *Annual Reports,* U.S. Department of Education.

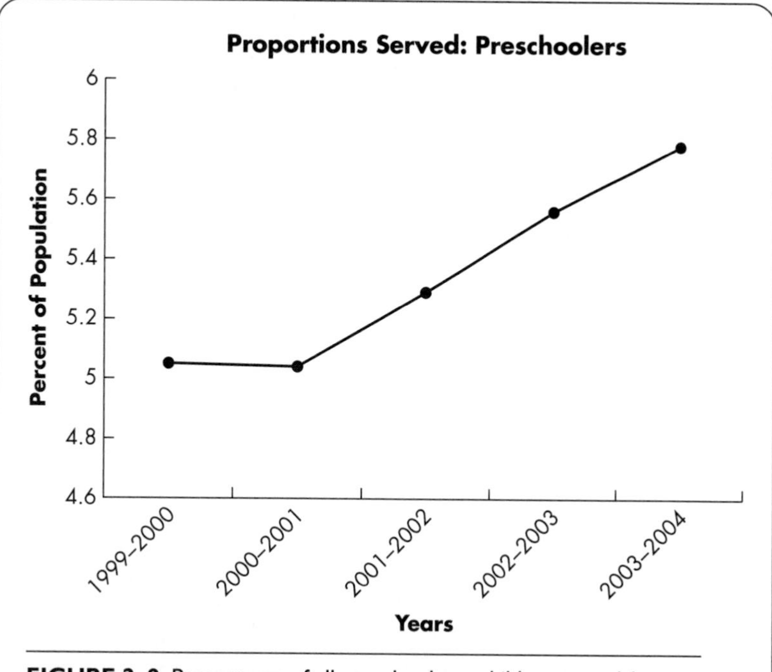

FIGURE 2–9 Percentages of all preschool-age children served, by year, 1999–2000 through 2003–2004. Data sources: Annual Reports, U.S. Department of Education.

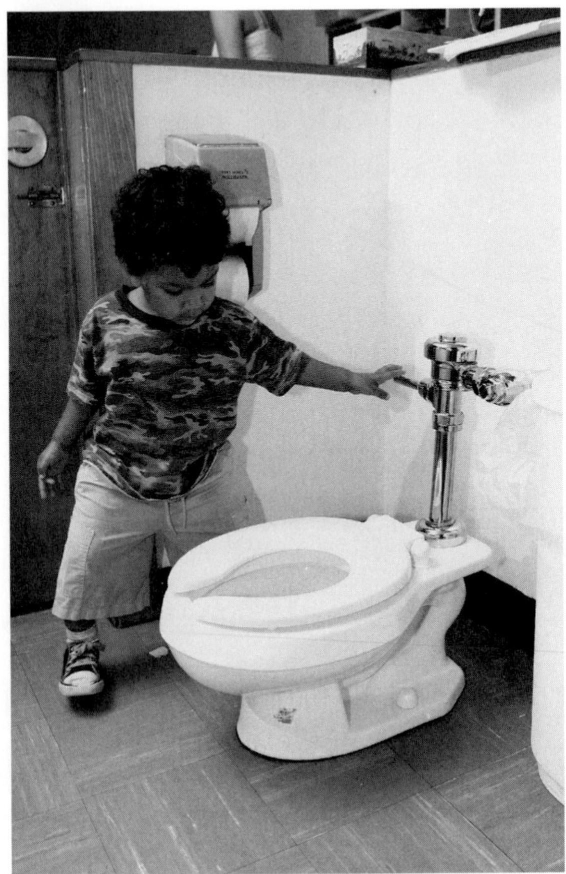

Learning to use a restroom is a key in adaptive development.

PRIMARY SPECIAL EDUCATION

The *Twenty-Second Annual Report* (U.S. Department of Education, 2000, Table AA9, p. A-45) reported that 326,260 six-year-olds, 396,406 seven-year-olds, and 477,527 eight-year-olds with disabilities were served in the public schools during the 1998–1999 school year. We know quite a bit more about these young children than we do about those under the age of six. Table AA8 of this report tells us that speech and language impairments are by far the most common disabilities, accounting for 65 percent of the conditions reported among six-year-olds, 54 percent among seven-year-olds, and 41 percent among eight-year-olds. Much less common were the second most prevalent (specific learning disabilities: 12 percent of the six-year-olds, 23 percent of the seven-year-olds, and 35 percent of the eight-year-olds) and third most prevalent (other health impairments: 3 percent of the six-year-olds, 3.5 percent of the seven-year-olds, and 4 percent of the eight-year-olds).

The 1,209,243 six- through eight-year-olds served under IDEA Part B during the 2003–2004 school year were about 11 percent of all six- to nine-year-olds. The year-to-year increase in number is more modest than we saw with younger age groups: 26 percent were 6, 33 percent were 7, and 38 percent were 8 years of age (U.S. Department of Education, 2005). Approximately 20 percent were African American, or slightly above the proportion in the general population. We again see speech or language impairments predominating, at 35 percent but we find as high a proportion (35 percent) being classified with specific learning disabilities. About one in every nine (11 percent) had the label mental retardation, and 6 percent were categorized as having emotional disturbance. Largely because many disabilities are diagnosed by this time, but also because elementary educators are accustomed to classifying students, and not using delay as a category, most of the primary-grade students have labels. Just 2 percent are categorized as developmentally delayed.

The number of six- through eight-year-olds with disabilities has remained stable over the past five years, at approximately 330,000 six-year-olds, 393,000 seven-year-olds, and 460,000 eight-year-olds. The growth in this age group that we had seen through the 1999–2000 school year has ceased. Services for children in this age range have been offered since 1977–1978. After nearly 30 years of child find outreach and nearly 20 years of mandated preschool services, it seems that we are serving virtually all eligible young children with disabilities.

While relatively few are categorized as in the autism spectrum disorder, nearly twice as many were served in 2003–2004 as compared with 1999–2000. By contrast, the number with specific learning disabilities remained fairly constant.

Special Education Elementary Longitudinal Study (SEELS)

is a research project funded by the U.S. Department of Education to track 11,000 young children with disabilities and their families. The children were aged 6 through 12, and were receiving special education services in first or higher grades on September 1, 1999. Parents were first interviewed in the summer of 2000.

The **Special Education Elementary Longitudinal Study (SEELS)** offers fresh insight into those with attention deficit hyperactivity disorders (ADHD). Because ADHD is not a separate classification, the U.S. Department of Education's *Annual Reports* have not reported data on this group. Interviewing family members, SEELS discovered that

27 percent of students with disabilities in elementary and middle-school grades had ADHD. Parents reported that 41 percent of those in elementary school (ages 6–11) were given the specific learning disability label, 15 percent were classified as having speech or language impairments, and 12 percent were in the Other Health Impaired (OHI) category. Others were served under Section 504, rather than under the IDEA. We will discuss Section 504 in Chapter 4.

CULTURAL DIVERSITY AMONG CHILDREN

Large numbers of young children with disabilities come from families that are "diverse" with respect to race, ethnicity, and socioeconomic status. NEILS, for example, reported that 22 percent of the 5,668 families it studied were African American and 15 percent were of Hispanic origin (Hebbeler et al., 2001). Both proportions were higher than national averages. Similarly, the 42 percent of the NEILS sample families received public assistance, again a much higher percentage than overall among American families (13 percent). Looking at preschool-age children and their families, PEELS has found much the same. As a result, sensitivity to and competence in working with diverse families is important in ECSE.

CULTURAL COMPETENCE

ECSE stresses close relations between professionals and parents. Those ties are most readily established and maintained when professionals are sensitive to cultural differences. Positioned on nearby pages are suggestions on cultural competence (Figure 2–10 to Figure 2–14). These offer ideas about cultural competence in general and with respect to particular minority groups. Although these figures may be helpful, the overriding principle in cultural sensitivity is to recognize that people are *individuals:* not all members of a racial or cultural minority will display all, or even many, of the beliefs or behaviors illustrated in these figures (Sciarra, 2004). Thus, being culturally sensitive is

General Principles

1. Program administrators, interventionists, teachers, and aides should reflect on their own cultural heritages and upon their beliefs about people of other cultures. Such self-awareness is a critical first step toward becoming culturally competent.
2. Program staff should make a priority of assessing every aspect of the program for possible cultural insensitivity. For example, do IFSP and IEP meetings always start at the scheduled time, or is flexibility allowed in respect for cultural differences about time? Advisory groups composed of family members might be asked to review all aspects of a program in order to suggest areas in need of improvement.
3. Programs should place emphasis on recruiting and retaining a culturally diverse staff. The "feeling" families get about programs often has its roots in the kinds of people family members see when they visit the program. Similarly, a culturally diverse staff is more capable than is a culturally monotonous staff of keeping everyone aware of cultural sensitivities.
4. Programs serving children with disabilities should recognize that disability is perhaps the key cultural variable. Do all staff members use sensitive language in talking about disabilities? Does the agency take affirmative steps to employ and retain staff members who themselves have disabilities?

FIGURE 2–10 Cultural competence I.

African Americans

1. Expressive communication for many African Americans is not exclusively verbal; rather, bodily movements convey considerable meaning. Many whites, by contrast, will "let the words speak for themselves."
   Professionals should be alert to nonverbal messages and respond appropriately to them.
2. Some African Americans consider time to begin when all expected people have arrived rather than on some preset schedule.
   Professionals in ECSE programs may show respect for this cultural tenet by beginning IFSP and IEP meetings when all invited individuals have assembled. At the same time, professionals might advise family members that agencies are under pressure from funding sources to adhere at times to a more strict sense of time (e.g., because staff members' time is billed by the hour).
3. In some African American families, government is seen as existing to serve citizens. Thus, there may be a readiness to refer children for services because the family feels entitled to them.
   If they believe underreferral is happening, as it often does, professionals should talk with family members to discover what is preventing referral. It may be that other pressures on the family (e.g., lack of available transportation, lack of available home child care, etc.) are causing the family not to refer a child for services.

FIGURE 2–11 Cultural competence II.

Latino and Hispanic Americans

1. Recognize that in many Latino and Hispanic American families, the family itself—not government agencies, or social service agencies, or "experts"—is the primary support system. Thus, Latino and Hispanic families may be reluctant to identify children for, and refer children to, agencies for services. This may help to account for the underrepresentation of disability among people of Hispanic origin that for so long has been reported (e.g., Bowe, 1985a, 1994). The family may regard disability as a private, personal matter, one not suitable for outside intervention.
   Early interventionists and preschool special educators may respect this cultural tenet by empowering the family to better serve its own members. This may mean offering information and teaching therapeutic techniques. Similarly, a professional may respond to this belief by spending the time necessary to get to know—and be known by—the family, thus becoming trusted as someone who will help the family, rather than someone who seeks to take the problem from the family. In time, this may make the family more amenable to referring the child for services.
2. Some Latino and Hispanic American families place more emphasis on interpersonal and intergroup cooperation than on competition.
   Professionals working in ECSE settings can show that they understand and accept this cultural belief. Certainly, early intervention and preschool programs, too, seek to foster cooperation and only rarely feature competition.
3. In many Latino and Hispanic American families, time is considered to begin when all expected people have arrived for the event.
   Early intervention and preschool special education professionals should demonstrate that they understand and value this belief by, for example, not starting a team meeting until all invited family members are present. Professionals should also help family members understand that organizations often have a different view of time (due, for example, to the fact that fees are billed on an hourly basis).
4. Some Latino and Hispanic American individuals view people as being more important than the tasks those people perform. Thus, they would not favor even temporary sacrifices to someone's well-being for the sake of timely completion of a task.
   This is not a belief that contradicts philosophical tenets characteristics of ECSE programs. While many early intervention and preschool special education staff members keep long hours on occasion, they usually agree quite readily that this should not be the case except during emergencies.

FIGURE 2–12 Cultural competence III.

Asian Americans

1. Aversion of eye gaze is a signal of respect for many Asian Americans. By keeping their eyes down, they convey modesty.
   The early interventionist or preschool special educator might say to the child, "Thank you for that indication of respect. I appreciate it. In my classroom, however, eye contact is important to me. It is not a sign of disrespect. Rather, it helps me by giving me clues as to how well you are understanding the lesson. So, while you are in my classroom, please do maintain eye contact with me."

2. In some Asian American families, especially those of Korean background, the family as a whole (which may well be an extended family) is the decision-making body.
   ECSE staff can show they respect this cultural value by not pressing parents for immediate decisions. Rather, accept as necessary a delay in decision making while the extended family is consulted.

3. Silence does not mean agreement for many Asian Americans. Rather, silence may indicate, "I understand your point, and at the appropriate time, I will respond to it."
   ECSE professionals need to avoid assuming that Asian American family members have consented to a course of action until an explicit statement to that effect is made by family members.

4. For some Asian American families, especially those of Japanese origin, stoic acceptance of fate may be important. Loss of face must be avoided whenever possible.
   For these reasons, some Asian American families may avoid referral of "problems" to agencies. ECSE workers should seek to convey an attitude of acceptance of disability (e.g., that no shame is associated with it).

FIGURE 2–13 Cultural competence IV.

Native Americans

1. Programs serving members of Native American (e.g., American Indian) populations need to recognize that disability occurs at very high rates on many reservations. Especially common are fetal alcohol syndrome (FAS) and fetal alcohol effect (FAE) due to heavy maternal drinking. This abuse of alcohol, in turn, may have its roots in the tendency of reservations to suppress native cultures and to devaluate residents of reservations.
   If FAS or FAE is suspected, professionals need to recognize that one or both parents may also have FAS or FAE. One common characteristics of FAS (and to some extent of FAE as well) is an inability to comprehend cause and effect. Parents may need to be trained (rather than taught) in key areas of child rearing.

2. Many Native Americans value what other Americans might call "nontraditional" intervention techniques, including "natural medicine" and religious rituals. Professionals should not disparage these methods. Rather, ECSE staff should explain that federal and state laws require them to use more objective and "traditional" intervention techniques.

3. In some Native American families, cooperation is emphasized over competition. Children learn through observation and imitation.
   ECSE programs, too, teach children to play with each other and to cooperate in other ways. While the deemphasis of competition in many Native American families may be a problem in K–12 settings, especially in high school, it is rarely a concern in early childhood.

4. Many Native Americans evince an unwillingness to criticize other people.
   Rather than assume that "absence implies consent," ECSE program staff should seek explicit expressions of consent before proceeding with interventions. Team members should also be alert to subtle signals that family members dislike or distrust a particular member of the team, rather than assuming that the family has no problems with any team member just because such concerns are not overtly voiced.

FIGURE 2–14 Cultural competence V.

not as easy as it may appear. Figures 2–10 through 2–14 summarize very basic themes. To translate those into effective practice, ECSE workers need to engage in open dialogue with representatives of the surrounding community—and be prepared to adjust as needed. Additional information is available in "Practitioner Briefs" that are posted on-line at the National Center for Culturally Responsive Educational Systems (www.nccrest.org) and other such sites.

Cultural competence (cultural sensitivity) refers to the skill and knowledge of ECSE workers in relating to family members from different ethnic, racial, and cultural groups.

The issue of **cultural competence** or cultural sensitivity is particularly pressing with respect to African American, Hispanic American, Asian American, and Native American children and their families. Outreach to and recruitment of families are more likely to be effective when program staff are members of the same ethnic and racial minority groups as the families and thus understand implicitly their cultural values and accepted norms of behavior. When ECSE program staff either are members of racial and ethnic minority groups or have been trained to exhibit culturally sensitive behavior, parents of minority children with disabilities are more likely to establish a rapport and cooperate with ECSE service programs over extended periods of time. Minority representation on program staff also provides the children with more suitable role models than otherwise would be the case. For all these reasons, recruitment and retention on program staff of professionals, paraprofessionals, support personnel, and clerical staff who are personally and/or professionally familiar with minority group dynamics are important.

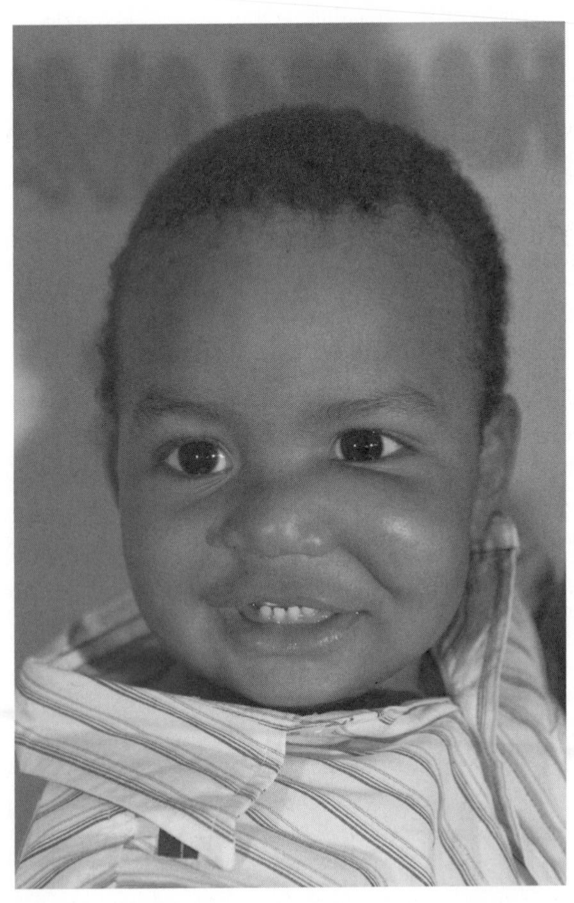

Many experts believe a disproportionate number of children in need of ECSE services are members of ethnic and/or racial minority groups.

Despite these benefits for programs, the reality is that the number of African American staff in the public school system, already low, is declining, which suggests serious ECSE shortages as well. Nationwide, just 9 percent of elementary teachers are male—a 40-year low—and only 2.4 percent are African American men (National Center for Education Statistics, 2005; National Education Association [NEA], 2003). According to NEA's report, *Status of the American Public School Teacher* (2003), teachers of color make up 16 percent of the teaching population, and some 42 percent of public schools have no minority teachers at all. That is why efforts such as the "Call Me Mister" program at Clemson University are so welcome. Named after the memorable line uttered by Sidney Poitier in the 1967 movie *In the Heat of the Night*, where he tells the southern white sheriff that, up North, "they call me *Mister* Tibbs," the program recruits young black males for the teaching profession (Richard, 2005). Also helpful is "Enlarging the Pool," a publication of the National Clearinghouse for Professions in Special Education (www.specialedcareers.org). It summarizes strategies developed by a wide variety of university-school partnerships. In part, these efforts are needed because of greater career opportunities for minority group members generally, as a result of which many pursue higher-paying, higher-status jobs than are offered by social service agencies, public schools, and family service organizations.

WHO ARE THE WORKERS IN THE FIELD?

Substantial demand continues to exist for ECSE workers. There is a great need for early intervention workers and special education teachers. In the area of preschool special education, to illustrate, for every six teachers employed, about one position is vacant or filled by someone less than fully qualified.

Early childhood special educators

are professionals trained in work with young children, methods of education, and other kinds of intervention for children with disabilities or developmental delays.

- **Early childhood special educators.** Trained in both work with young children and education methods, as well as other kinds of intervention, early childhood special educators perform a broad range of functions. They serve as team members in developing IFSPs and IEPs, contributing particularly to goal setting and objective writing. They work with psychologists and other specialists on eligibility and evaluation, as well as on both child and family assessment. Frequently, the early childhood special educator is the principal professional working day to day with the young child with a disability, performing instruction and assessing progress toward goals. He may also be the key team member in regular contact with the family, keeping them informed of the child's progress and providing family support services, including suggestions for at-home supplemental activities to enhance the child's progress toward goals.

Service coordinators

facilitate service delivery to families and represent the family in negotiations with public and private service providers.

- **Service coordinators.** Early intervention is, by federal mandate, an individualized service program. Everything revolves around a particular infant or toddler and his family. The service coordinator represents the family and guides it. This person may be an early childhood special educator, a social worker, a primary health care provider, a therapist, or other individual able to help the family—even a parent. The service coordinator's job is a challenging one. He must advocate for the family to an entire phalanx of local, county, state, and private service providers, cutting through red tape and ensuring that services are delivered.

  The name of the service coordinator appears in the IFSP. He is the family's contact with the entire social services system. In many states, the service coordinator also follows the child as the toddler moves to preschool special education to ensure a seamless transition from Part C to Part B. The service coordinator may be a member of the team assembling the IEP for the preschool Part B program in those states. In other states, the service coordinator plays a less formal role in smoothing the transition to preschool special education.

Social workers

are trained human services professionals who help the family qualify for and receive needed services for which the family and/or the infant or toddler is or are eligible. Social work services also are "related services" under Part B of the Individuals with Disabilities Education Act.

- **Social workers.** Early intervention is—and special education is increasingly becoming—an interdisciplinary program of services. Social workers may help the family identify and receive needed services for which the family and/or the infant or toddler are eligible. The profession of social work features knowledge and skills in negotiating the often confusing network of public and private service providers—and the myriad eligibility requirements. Social workers may also provide family, group, and individual counseling to help family members cope with their child's special needs.

  The IFSP includes written statements on the family's "resources, priorities, and concerns." While IEPs need not contain such statements, they may—and increasingly do, as states move toward more seamless service delivery. Those statements may guide the social worker's counseling role. As mentioned earlier, social workers may also fulfill the function of the service coordinator. Part B also recognizes the contributions of social workers and includes their services among allowed "related services."

Some On-line Resources on Diversity

Monarch Center

www.monarchcenter.org

This is the National Technical Assistance Center for Personnel Preparation in Special Education at Minority Institutions for Higher Education. It supports faculty at Traditionally black colleges in their efforts to recruit and prepare highly qualified K–12 teachers.

Project LASER

www.coedu.usf.edu

Project LASER seeks to help faculty and students at traditionally black colleges and universities engage in research about K–12 children.

National Center for Culturally Responsive Educational Systems

www.nccrest.org

This center focuses on children and youth from ethnic and racial minority groups, seeking to minimize inappropriate referrals and to reduce achievement gaps between minority and majority students.

Education World Diversity in Education Center

www.educationworld.com/a_diversity/

This site offers a wealth of resources for educators and families.

Therapists and other services personnel include speech and language pathologists, occupational therapists, and other professionals delivering related services to preschool-age children or early intervention services to infants and toddlers with disabilities.

- **Therapists and other services personnel.** Depending on the child's special needs, physical therapists, occupational therapists, speech and language therapists, psychotherapists, and others trained in providing specific services may work with the infant, toddler, or preschooler. Frequently, these specialists also train family members to perform therapeutic functions so as to reduce the number of formal therapy sessions required and thus contain costs.

  Physical and occupational therapists. These professionals help children with cerebral palsy and other physical disabilities learn to use orthotics and prostheses to feed and dress themselves and to get around independently at home, in school, and in the community. The principal difference between these two professions is that physical therapists work on developing the child's muscles and extremities and preventing atrophy, while occupational therapists concentrate on helping children perform daily tasks such as brushing teeth, holding a pen, and using an electronic device to "speak." A *prosthesis* is an artificial replacement, such as a mechanical arm; an *orthosis* is a device that enhances the function of a body part, such as a leg brace that helps a child walk. *Speech and language pathologists* help young children both learn language and produce intelligible speech to the best of their abilities. They may also work with children on feeding problems. Therapists from each of these disciplines are recognized by the IDEA under both Part C and Part B.

  Family therapists. These are professionals with degrees in such fields as marriage and family therapy. Family therapists may provide IDEA-reimbursed services only to the extent that their assistance directly affects family care of the child.

  Other services personnel. ECSE services may also be provided as needed by, among others, psychologists, sign language interpreters, orientation and mobility specialists, technology experts (who provide assistive technology devices and services),

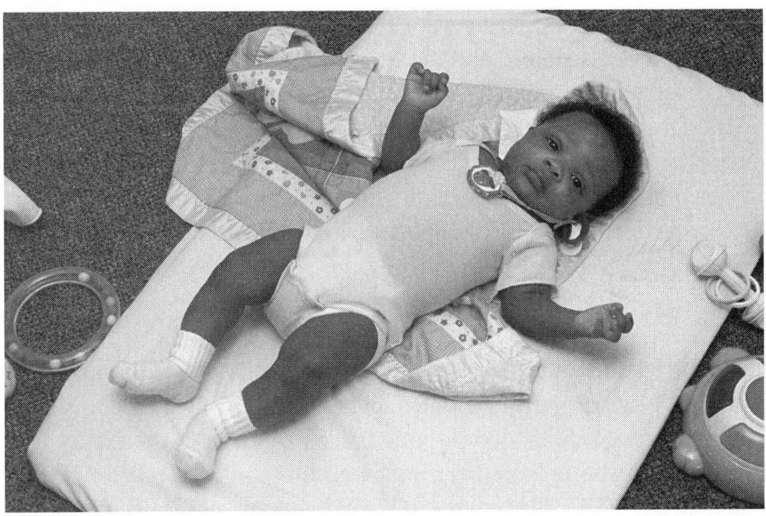

The IDEA allows but does not require states to service "at-risk" infants and toddlers.

and medical specialists. Psychologists play a wide range of roles in ECSE; some act as service coordinators, while others concentrate on assessment. Orientation and mobility specialists help children who are blind or have low vision learn to get around independently, use canes or guide dogs, and navigate in unfamiliar territory.

Of growing importance in ECSE are the services of technology experts. Assistive technology devices and services can dramatically enhance the quality of life of many infants, toddlers, and preschoolers with disabilities. Chapter 9 explores these products in detail.

Professionals who understand the potential of such products and services; who keep up with the rapidly changing computer-related technologies; and who are expert at selecting, integrating, and customizing such products and services for young children with disabilities play an increasingly important role in ECSE. The impact of technology can be as diverse as the needs of the children. Children with cerebral palsy may use laptop personal computers equipped with speech synthesizers to "talk," many for the first time in their lives. Technology specialists provide such devices and services.

Early childhood educators
are professionals trained in work with young children.

Elementary educators
are professionals trained at the BA or MA level in teaching K–6 children. They usually are state-certified as meeting state-set minimum requirements.

Child development associate (CDA) paraprofessionals
have a credential indicating postsecondary study in child development and child care. CDA-credentialed paraprofessionals often work in Head Start programs.

- **Early childhood educators.** Professionals trained in work with children under the age of nine whose training includes formal coursework in early childhood development and supervised practicum with young children. This preparation may occur at the BA level or at the MA level. Most are employed in EC settings that serve children in the three-to-five age range. Early childhood educators may have preservice (prior to employment) or inservice (while employed) training about disabilities, but not all EC educators have such knowledge and/or experience.
- **Elementary educators.** Preschool programs serving children with no disabilities that include some young children with disabilities often are staffed by teachers trained in elementary education. In large part, this is because many EC programs find it difficult to recruit professionals trained specifically in EC- and ECSE-related disciplines.
- **Child development associate (CDA) paraprofessionals.** In addition to the professional disciplines discussed in the preceding sections, paraprofessionals play important roles in ECSE. Prominent in Head Start programs and in some other EC settings are paraprofessionals credentialed as child development associates. Staff members with CDA degrees function as teacher aides in many mainstream programs serving children with and without disabilities.

ROLES AND RESPONSIBILITIES

The actors in ECSE are the federal and state levels of government, the local service providers, and the parents. The IDEA outlines specific roles and responsibilities for each. The federal role is actually limited, despite the fact that federal laws and regulations govern the entire activity; the U.S. Department of Education's responsibility is to disseminate funds, offer technical assistance, and monitor state compliance. The state role features decisions on personnel and program requirements, as well as the monitoring of local service providers. Despite state and federal dictates and oversight, local service providers enjoy considerable discretion in making day-to-day program decisions. Parents and other family members play a powerful role, reflecting the historic contributions parents have made to the development of ECSE over the past 40 years.

THE FEDERAL ROLE

The IDEA sets the requirements that programs receiving funds under the act must meet. Among these are the eligibility criteria states must meet to receive federal funds; the mandate that all appropriate services be provided free of charge to the family; the obligation that an IFSP or IEP be prepared for each child; the allowability of certain kinds of services (such as orientation and mobility and related vision services for blind or low-vision infants and toddlers) and disallowability of other types of services (such as surgery and other general medical interventions); and reporting requirements, including labels.

The U.S. secretary of education may approve state applications for funds and may conduct audits and other investigations to ensure that states comply with federal requirements. The secretary may also award personnel training, demonstration, and research grants to state agencies, universities, and service programs.

Because Part C in particular is an interagency program that envisions contributions from many discrete human services programs, the federal role also includes a heavy responsibility to remove as many barriers to interagency cooperation as possible consistent with other federal obligations. For example, the Developmentally Disabled Assistance and Bill of Rights Act (DD Act) of 1975 initially defined "developmental disabilities" in terms of four disabilities (autism, cerebral palsy, mental retardation, and epilepsy). The act authorized federal grants to states to coordinate education, health, welfare, and rehabilitation services—but *only* for children and adults with those four DD Act disabilities. Other gaps, duplications, contradictions, and barriers abounded. In recent years, many very significant changes have been made at the federal level, markedly easing long-standing strains in state and local cross-agency collaboration. To continue with the DD Act example, the federal definition of **developmental disabilities** now includes children with any condition of early onset requiring a multitude of services. Recently, the definition was again changed, after enactment of PL 99–457; the latest DD Act definition includes a clause (applying only to children under six) that comports with the Part C and preschool Part B definitions of infants, toddlers, and preschool-age children with disabilities. This change in definition makes interagency collaboration at the state and local levels much easier and ensures that young children will not fall between the cracks because of incompatible eligibility criteria.

Developmental disabilities
are conditions of early onset (occurring well in advance of adulthood) that require a range of diverse services or interventions. The term formerly referred to four disabilities (autism, cerebral palsy, mental retardation, and epilepsy).

Similarly, federal law now allows the Head Start program to use any recognized state definition of disability for the purpose of serving young children in Head Start programs. This change is very important, because states differ in their definitions of infants, toddlers, and children with disabilities. A third important change occurred in the Maternal and Child Health Services (MCH) block grant program. Federal law now specifically authorizes states to use these block grants for family-centered community programs.

THE STATE ROLE

Part C requires that states participating in the early intervention program meet 14 requirements. States must select a **lead agency** to carry out the state plan, coordinate the work of other public and private agencies, write policies for interagency contracts, and make other arrangements for service delivery throughout the state. By contrast, Part B permits little flexibility. The state education agency or a closely affiliated office must be the lead agency responsible for Section 619 preschool special education services. Part C adds the responsibility of creating a comprehensive directory of services available statewide and a statewide database containing the numbers of infants and toddlers with disabilities or delays. In many other respects, however, the state role is similar under both Part C and Part B. In both cases, for example, the state sets personnel qualifications. Both Part C and Part B require states to mount **child find** efforts and public awareness programs to identify potentially eligible infants, toddlers, preschoolers, and their families. States must arrange to conduct evaluations, prepare IFSPs or IEPs, ensure procedural safeguards, and serve all such children identified and their families. In addition, states must implement personnel preparation programs to ensure an adequate supply of service providers. Finally, states must define the term "developmental delay" as they will use it in Part C and, if the state so elects, in Section 619 Part B.

Lead agency

is the term used in Part C of the IDEA to refer to the state agency authorized to carry out the state Part C plan and to coordinate the work of other public and private agencies. In some states, the state education agency is the lead agency; in others, a health agency, social services agency, or child care agency serves as the lead agency. Up-to-date addresses for state lead agencies are available at www.nectac.org, the Web site of the National Early Childhood Technical Assistance Center, at the University of North Carolina.

Child find

is the term used in both Part C and Part B of the IDEA to refer to outreach and recruitment efforts by the state to identify, screen, and serve eligible children and families.

The law requires Part C and Part B lead agencies to work together, notably on outreach, transition, and other key tasks. It also assigns clear responsibility to the state lead agency for all in-state activities, including local service provider functions and local education agency programs. There are, for example, more than 15,000 LEAs (school districts) throughout the United States. Rather than attempt to monitor and ensure compliance from each of those local programs, the U.S. Department of Education holds the 50 state education agencies and their counterparts in other jurisdictions completely and solely responsible for the actions of these local bodies.

ECSE practitioners include early childhood special educators, speech and language pathologists, occupational therapists, and other service personnel working together on an interdisciplinary team.

THE LOCAL ROLE

While the federal and state actions are important, it is the local role that is paramount for infants, toddlers, and preschoolers with disabilities to receive services at the local level. The urgent need for family-focused services first emerged at the local level. Part C requires that services for infants, toddlers, and their families be provided, to the maximum extent appropriate, in **natural environments.** For very young children, that is usually the home. When services are given in other settings, the law prefers facilities that nondisabled young children also use. While the IDEA does not offer many more specifics, experience suggests that parental preference usually is a good guide in selecting the natural environment. This and other aspects of the parental role are examined in later chapters. Part B has a similar **least restrictive environment,** requiring that preschool special education students (as well as older students with disabilities) are to be educated together with nondisabled students to the maximum extent appropriate (i.e., without limiting the appropriateness of the education and related services they receive). Parents enjoy the right to offer input in this decision as well, but the local education agency retains the responsibility to make the selection in a way that complies with Part B requirements.

Natural environment is a philosophy emphasizing services for infants, toddlers, and their families in places that are typical or otherwise "natural." Early intervention services are to be delivered in such environments, to the extent that these are "appropriate" and meet the child's needs. The home is the usual such environment. The term is used in Part C of the IDEA.

Least restrictive environment is a philosophy stressing the placement of children with disabilities in appropriate settings closest (when compared with other appropriate settings) to settings used by nondisabled children. The term is used in Part B of the IDEA.

THE PARENTS' ROLE

Both Part C and Part B grant the parents of young children with disabilities extraordinary roles and rights. Parents may identify unique needs of their children and work with professionals to be sure that these needs appear in IFSPs or IEPs. They may see all records containing personally identifiable information about their children. They may also file complaints when they disagree with professional recommendations about services, placements, or other aspects of intervention and education. These remarkable parental powers come from a congressional determination that parents are in the best position of anyone to protect the rights of children with disabilities. Parents and, to a large degree, parents alone are responsible for the Part B and Part C mandates. In fact, what is now the IDEA was triggered by two federal district court cases in the early 1970s, *Pennsylvania Association for Retarded Children v. Commonwealth of Pennsylvania* (1972) and *Mills v. Board of Education of the District of Columbia* (1972). Both were brought by parents.

These powerful roles emerged first in PL 94–142's Part B in 1975. After a decade of experience with parental rights and roles in special education, Congress granted similar privileges and responsibilities to parents of infants and toddlers with disabilities in Part H (now Part C) in 1986. In many respects, the parental role under Part C is even larger than that under Part B. Family resources, priorities, and concerns appear in IFSPs only if the parents agree; similarly, a service agency may send information about an infant or toddler to another agency *only* with prior parental permission.

SUMMARY

ECSE is the coming together of early intervention and special education to form a seamless system for delivery of services to birth-to-eight children with disabilities or developmental delays. This field provides direct services to young children and their families under federal and state laws. These laws offer public financing for ECSE services and require states to serve all eligible young children. These laws also guarantee families with young children certain rights, including the right to be fully informed of the child's needs and of a program's intervention plans. Such plans are to be written in formal documents, called Individualized Family Service Plans (IFSPs) and Individualized Education Programs (IEPs).

The IDEA and corresponding state statutes are remarkable laws filled with very specific prescriptions (dictates) and proscriptions (prohibitions). They are as detailed as they are at the insistence of parents for their own and their children's protection. The U.S. Congress concurred with these parental requests, largely in the belief that early intervention and preschool special education programs offering appropriate services for birth-to-eight children with disabilities and delays would make important contributions to the national welfare. The rationale behind ECSE is that not only the children but that their families, neighborhoods, towns, and states, and, indeed, the nation as a whole would benefit. Congress also believed that ECSE programs could save society substantial sums of money by helping people with disabilities to become self-sufficient, gainfully employed, taxpaying citizens in adulthood.

The IDEA envisions specific roles for the federal, state, and local levels of government, as well as for parents. The federal role is a limited one. The U.S. Department of Education provides financial assistance to states, offers technical assistance to state lead agencies and to individual programs, and monitors implementation of the law. States add substantial financial resources for ECSE, define eligible populations under Part C, determine personnel standards, license or otherwise approve local delivery programs, and decide how the state will carry out the federal mandate. The most important roles, however, are reserved for parents and local government. The IDEA grants parents extraordinary rights and responsibilities. The local programs, despite federal and state regulation, make the key decisions. They decide, along with the parents, which children will receive what services, from what disciplines, from which personnel, and in what settings.

As it stands today, ECSE is a field facing tremendous challenges. Despite 40 years of serving birth-to-eight children with disabilities and developmental delays, the field continues to evolve rapidly. Perhaps the greatest current challenge is to meet the unique needs of children and families from lower-SES and racial and ethnic minority groups. How ECSE programs respond to this and other challenges is the subject of the next several chapters.

KEY TERMS

appropriate
at risk
child development associate (CDA) paraprofessionals
child find
children with disabilities
cultural competence
developmental delays
developmental disabilities
diagnosed conditions
early childhood educators
early childhood special educators
early intervention
elementary educators
entitlement
Individualized Education Program (IEP)
Individualized Family Service Plan (IFSP)
Individuals with Disabilities Education Act (IDEA)
infants and toddlers
infants and toddlers with disabilities
Interagency Coordinating Council (ICC)
interdisciplinary services
lead agency
least restrictive environment
National Early Intervention Longitudinal Study (NEILS)
natural environment
Part B
Part C
preschool child with a disability
preschool special education
preschool-age children
related services
seamless system
Section 619
service coordinators
social workers
special education
supports
therapists and other services personnel

QUESTIONS FOR REFLECTION

1. What do the terms *entitlement* and *zero reject* mean as these are used in ECSE? How does the case of *Timothy W. v. Rochester* (1989) help us understand these terms?
2. Compare "early intervention services" under Part C with "related services" under Part B. How are they similar—and different?

3. Compare the definitions for "infants and toddlers with disabilities" and "children with disabilities." How are they similar, and how are they different? Which unit of government defines the key terms in each case—federal or state? When might that matter to families?
4. In your own words, what are the major rationales for ECSE?
5. Differentiate "at risk" from "condition" and "delay." Why do few states recognize at-risk infants and toddlers as entitled to early intervention services? Are at-risk children age three and over entitled to Part B services?
6. What is in an IFSP that is not in an IEP? Vice versa?
7. Why is it so important for ECSE workers to reflect on the beliefs of their own cultural heritages before they focus on becoming more sensitive to other cultures?
8. Which cultural minority groups feature eye gaze aversion as an indication of respect? Which two tend to regard "time" as somewhat relative as compared with the more rigid view of time that characterizes the business world?
9. Why are disability prevalence rates more a function of socioeconomic status than of race or ethnic group membership?
10. What do service coordinators do? Why are they so important to many families that participate in early intervention?

PRACTICAL EXERCISES

1. Visit a local early childhood program (e.g., a Head Start program) or an early childhood special education program (e.g., a special preschool or an early intervention program serving infants and toddlers). Observe for a morning or an afternoon. Talk with program staff members. Then describe, as best you can, the program's population and its staff with respect to key demographic variables.

   Are the children and their families of similar backgrounds to those of program staff (e.g., socioeconomic status, race, ethnicity, etc.)? If not, how are the children/families different from the program staff? If differences are marked in any area(s), how has the program administration addressed those differences? For example, do staff receive training in cultural sensitivity and cultural competence? If so, do program staff regard that training as sufficient?
2. It is human nature for adults to consider themselves to be free of bias. That is why the Implicit Association Test can be so helpful. The test is on-line at www.implicit.harvard.edu. The "demonstration" site explains the test and gives you sample questions. The "research" part contains the actual assessment questions. The same tool, plus a posttest reflection page or tutorial, is at www.tolerance.org. Even experts in cultural sensitivity report being "humbled" by results indicating that they, too, harbor some unconscious associations that are contrary to their conscious beliefs.

WEB SITES OF INTEREST

www.ideadata.org IDEA Data—source of latest statistics in ECSE

www.nccrest.org NCCRES—the National Center for Culturally Responsive Educational Systems—offers technical support and training in cultural sensitivity and cultural competence.

www.sri.com/neils National Early Intervention Longitudinal Study—new data on how Part C is being implemented

CHAPTER

3

How Are We Doing? Research in ECSE

[P]articipation in early childhood programs is consistently associated with higher levels of cognitive development, early school achievement, and motivation in the short term, with lower rates of grade retention and special education services during the elementary grades, and, in the long-term, with higher rates of school completion and education attainment. . . . The most effective programs reported in the literature are those that began during the first 3 years of life, continue for multiple years, and/or provide support to children's school transitions. (Reynolds & Temple, 2005, p. 107)

OBJECTIVES

After reading this chapter, you should be able to:

- Explain why research is so important in ECSE.
- Discuss what to look for when reading a journal report on research.
- Describe problems that are often found in ECSE research.
- Describe what research tells us about the effectiveness and cost-effectiveness of ECSE.
- Explain how "earlier is better" may not necessarily be true in ECSE.
- Discuss why "more is better" may also not be accurate.

- Describe what research tells us about good ways to involve family members in ECSE.
- Discuss what ECSE programs should teach young children, according to research.

CHAPTER OUTLINE

- **OVERVIEW**
  - **Bird's-Eye View**
- **RESEARCH AND RESEARCHERS**
  - **Reading Research Reports**
- **PROBLEMS IN ECSE RESEARCH**
  - **Within-Group Differences**
  - **Sample Size**
  - **Other Issues**
- **RESEARCH FINDINGS**
  - **Unanswered Questions and Unquestioned Answers**
- **THE ROLE OF RESEARCH IN ECSE**

OVERVIEW

Chapter 1 and Chapter 2 introduced the field of early childhood special education (ECSE). In Chapter 1, we saw that ECSE draws on our knowledge about human development to serve children under the age of nine who have disabilities or delays in any one or more domains of development. The ways in which ECSE programs are supposed to deliver such services was outlined in Chapter 2. There we saw that services are to be individually selected and designed to respond to the unique needs of each child and family.

That is what *should* happen. In some respects, the information presented in Chapter 1 and Chapter 2 is more ideal than real. That is, the philosophy shaping ECSE and the custom-designed approaches of the field both feature rather lofty expectations. In this chapter, we explore what research is teaching us about what is actually happening in early childhood special education programs. Our intent is to understand how well the field is doing and thereby begin to understand how we as current and future interventionists and educators can improve the state of the art.

Over the years, I have come to appreciate that many students in personnel preparation programs in the areas of early intervention and special education have not taken courses in research methodology. Understandably, then, a lot of them are apprehensive when professors assign them readings in professional journals. That is why Chapter 3 is laid out the way it is. Following a "bird's-eye" summary of research on EC and ECSE, the chapter gives readers who lack a background in research design and statistics some tools with which to read journal articles reporting on research projects. The chapter then explains the factors that make research in early childhood special education especially challenging. A 10-point Q&A summary of research in ECSE concludes the chapter.

BIRD'S-EYE VIEW

The chapter-opening quote is by Arthur Reynolds, of the University of Wisconsin at Madison, and his colleague Judy Temple, of Northern Illinois University. I regard the longitudinal study that Reynolds led as being the gold standard of research in early childhood.

What Reynolds and his team did was to follow 1,400 young children enrolled in the Chicago Child and Parent Centers (CPCs) over a long period of time. The CPCs are high-quality public preschool programs that focus, much as do ECSE programs, on early language learning, intensive parent involvement, and health services. The Chicago Longitudinal Study (CLS) showed that effects traceable to early instructional services could be seen even decades later. Figure 3–1 summarizes the connections. We can see that the timing, duration and intensity of early childhood services led to greater motivation and achievement, as well as better adjustment during the early to middle childhood years and, later, to higher achievement, lower levels of grade retention, and even less delinquency and crime during adulthood. The CLS also showed that early services were cost-effective, returning about $7 per dollar invested (Reynolds, 2005; Reynolds & Temple, 2005).

The Chicago study compared young children who were enrolled in CPCs with similar children who were not admitted into those programs. Reynolds and his team were

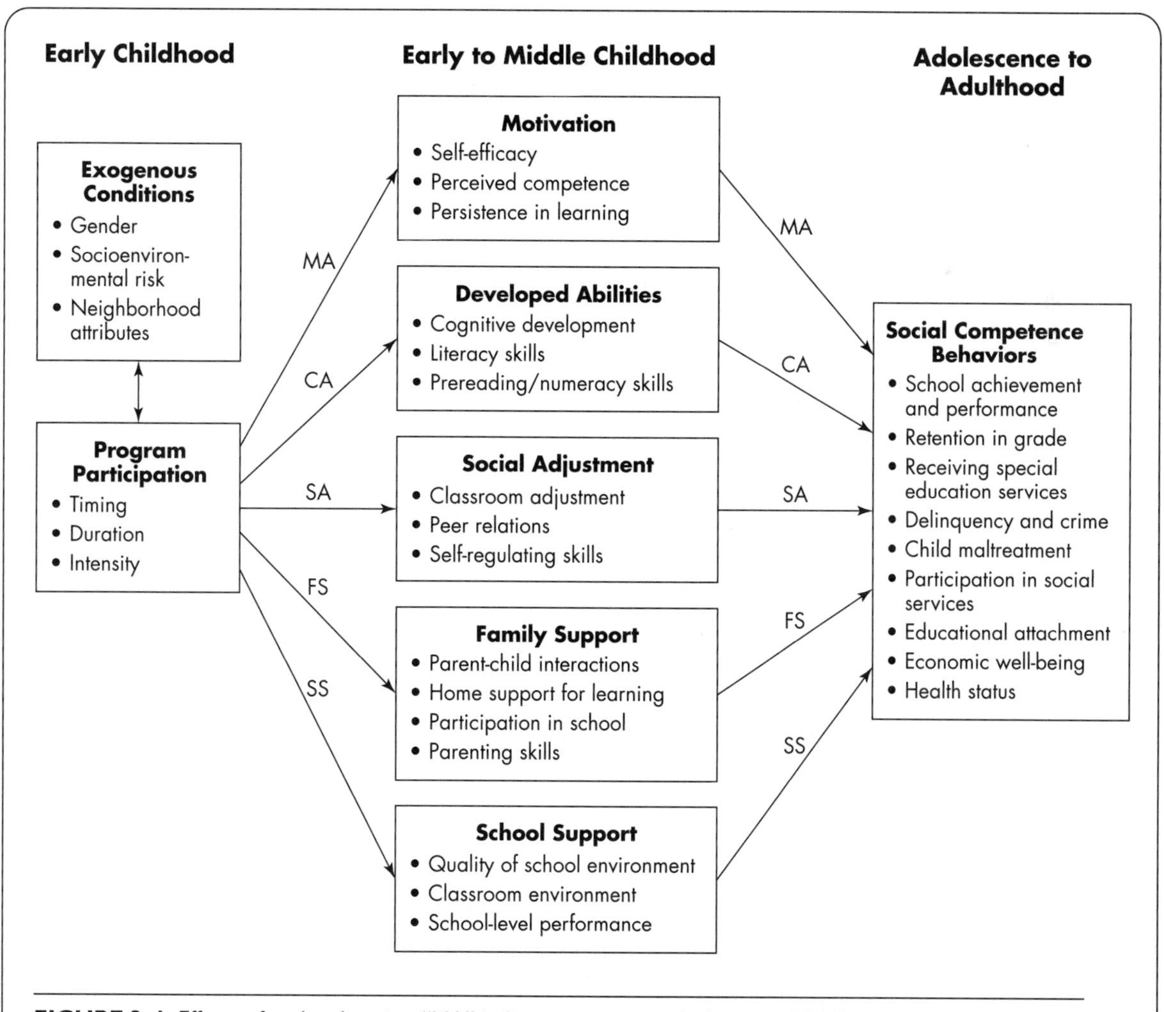

FIGURE 3–1 Effects of early education. "MA" indicates motivational advantage; "CA," cognitive advantage; "SA," social adjustment; "FS," family support; and "SS," school support. Source: Figure 2, page 109, in Reynolds and Temple (2005). Reprinted with permission.

able to do that because there was no entitlement guaranteeing the children the services they needed.

ECSE, by contrast, is an entitlement program. IDEA Part C serves all eligible infants and toddlers. Section 619 of IDEA Part B serves all eligible preschoolers with disabilities. Other sections of IDEA Part B provide free appropriate public education services to six- through eight-year-olds who have disabilities. For these reasons, it is not possible to carry out a Chicago-style study.

What we can do, and are doing, is longitudinal studies that track young children with disabilities and show how they, and their families, benefit from services. While we cannot reach the "gold standard" of truly comparative analyses (because there can be no comparable control group of children receiving no services), we can, nonetheless, show that early intervention, preschool special education, and primary special education do make a difference for children and for families. The closest we have come to date is research by McCormick and her team (2006). Their work is discussed later in this chapter (where we consider the question "Is more intensive better?").

NEILS is one of the major longitudinal studies now being sponsored by the federal government. (NEILS publications are available on-line at www.sri.com/neils.) It is following more than 3,000 families, both during the time when their very young children are served by IDEA Part C early intervention programs and afterward. The research demonstrates that family members are highly satisfied with services (Bailey, Palsha, & Simeonsson, 2003; Bailey, Scarborough, Hebberler, Spiker, & Mallik, 2004). It shows that the infants and toddlers are benefiting. Stated simply, NEILS is documenting that early intervention is doing what Congress intended when the program was launched in 1986. The study also reveals that the very young children who most need assistance are receiving the most help. For this reason, early intervention programs spend the most money on young children who show less progress than do other infants and toddlers (Levin, Perez, Lam, Chambers, & Hebbeler, 2004). Stated differently, according to NEILS, we do not see the simple cost-benefit relationships that some might have anticipated (i.e., that more money is associated with greater gains in achievement and adjustment) because of the very nature of IDEA Part C. While that is as it should be in an entitlement program designed to give very young children what they need, it does make the "sales" job of ECSE professionals and advocates a bit more difficult.

The Pre-Elementary Education Longitudinal Study (PEELS) is a second federally funded effort. PEELS is tracking more than 3,000 children from preschool through the elementary school years. Data tables began appearing in Spring 2006. (PEELS reports may be found on-line at www.peels.org and/or through the National Center for Special Education Research, Institute of Education Sciences, U.S. Department of Education, at www.ed.gov.)

A third effort is SEELS, the Special Education Elementary Longitudinal Study. SEELS is tracking more than 11,000 special education students who were ages 6 through 12 as of September 1, 1999. The SEELS reports already are shedding light on many questions. They show, for example, how elementary-age children with disabilities participate in extracurricular activities, how they spend their free time, and how their teachers and parents assess their skills in literacy, numeracy, and other academic areas. (SEELS Wave 1 and Wave 2 reports are on-line at http://www.sri.com/seels.)

To summarize: Impressive new evidence indicates that educational services offered to young children with no disabilities can make major, long-lasting differences in their lives. We now know that quality preschool education is connected to success through K–12 and beyond and that it is cost-effective (e.g., Oppenheim & McGregor, 2002; Reynolds, 2005). As for the specialized field of ECSE, research to date shows that it does what it is intended to do. ECSE is effective in meeting the unique needs of infants, toddlers, preschoolers and primary-grade children with disabilities (e.g., McCormick et al., 2006). The major issues about which questions remain are two: (1) Is ECSE cost-effective? and (2) How well is ECSE managing the sea changes launched by No Child Left Behind (2001) and the IDEA that emphasize skills and knowledge in core academic areas, notably language arts and mathematics? We will review evidence on these issues in this chapter.

RESEARCH AND RESEARCHERS

Why is research important in ECSE? The best way to answer this question is to consider what research does. First, in any field as new (relatively speaking) as ECSE, research helps administrators and practitioners to decide what we know and do not know. Much that appears to be obvious turns out, on closer inspection, to be not so self-evident. Second, research documents effectiveness and cost efficiency, thus enabling ECSE workers to make the case that programs deserve increased financial support in a time of tight federal, state, county, and local budgets. Third, it offers information about disabling conditions and treatments for them that helps parents and professionals alike set realistic outcomes for early intervention and special education. Research provides essential information about which techniques work best with what kinds of children at which stages of their development. Such data are fundamental for program design and for individual planning.

As important as research is, it is not the only, or even dominant, factor in policymaking in ECSE. Other considerations include the Constitution's equal protection and due process clauses, the availability of public financing, and the extent to which ECSE advocates are able to sustain political pressure for more services.

Some aspects of research are within the researcher's control. Experimenter bias is one of these. The element of researcher bias can never be eliminated completely (Creswell, 2002). Researchers in any field have their own beliefs and biases. Most are conscious of their own leanings, however, and try to remove bias from their experimental work. There are ways of doing that, among them double-blind designs in which those working with the experimental and control group subjects know neither the study's hypothesis nor which subject is in each group. However, designing a bias-free study is not always possible, nor is a bias-free review of other researchers' work. In ECSE, as in many other fields, beliefs are firmly held and emotions run strong—among researchers as among practitioners.

Inclusion

is an approach in which children with disabilities (including those with severe disabilities) are placed in room with, and receive services side by side with, children who have no disabilities.

As a reader of research reports, you should be alert to possible bias. On such issues as least restrictive environment or **inclusion,** for example, about which opinions are particularly strong, it makes sense to ask whether the writer of a study report has a record of advocacy on behalf of a particular point of view. This is not to say that researchers are unethical; it is simply to acknowledge that they are human—and that the research endeavor is therefore susceptible to bias. You should read both pro-inclusion and anti-inclusion articles with care, looking for any evidence of bias. Frequently, research is cited as supporting a point of advocacy; if you were to read those cited articles, however, you might find that they do not say what they were purported to say. There is evidence that some children may be harmed by placement in environments in which they are physically proximate with nondisabled children but are at the same time isolated from them in communication (as when the children are deaf) or in other ways. Frequently, such evidence is not included in literature reviews. Other evidence suggests that integration has differential effects on young children with mild versus those with severe disabilities. Again, such qualifications are often not made. This is one aspect of intelligent consumption of research reports, a subject to which the chapter now turns.

READING RESEARCH REPORTS

A quick glance at the references section of this book reveals that research reports are readily available to you. Such journals as *Exceptional Children, Infants and Young Children, Journal of Early Intervention, Journal of Special Education,* and others are available in public and university libraries; you may, of course, also subscribe to one or more of these. The question then becomes "How can one read research reports so as to gain the most from them?" Taking an introductory research course is a good way to learn how to read these articles. Creswell (2002) is a good text to use. Here, the intent is to skim the surface, noting important issues for ECSE professionals, issues that do not require you to have advanced training in research methodology and statistics.

Research reports in professional journals have usually been peer reviewed, or critiqued by other professionals, including researchers, prior to publication. This process certainly lessens the burden on the lay reader. However, peer review does not guarantee that all articles published are free from bias or even from error. Peer reviewers usually focus on research and design questions and on the relevance of the article to the journal's main readership. They do not even attempt to answer the lay reader's most important question—namely, "Is this study related to what I personally do every day?" Only you can answer that question.

Variables

Scientific inquiry is best described as the systematic pursuit of understanding how *variables* relate one to another (see Pedhazur & Schmelkin, 1991, for an extended discussion). A *variable* is anything that has at least two values—that is, that varies. People are male or female. Infants or toddlers with disabilities, under Part C, have established conditions or developmental delays or are at risk for such delays. Children are delayed or not delayed in development. Disabilities are deafness, blindness, cerebral palsy, mental retardation, learning disabilities, autism, traumatic brain injury, and so on. All of these are variables. Researchers seek to understand how variables vary with respect to other variables. Are infant boys more likely to have established conditions than are infant girls? To have delays? Are children with cerebral palsy always delayed in development? And, of more direct interest here, what interventions, treatments, or educational techniques best help young children with disabilities?

How Research Findings Are Reported

Most experimental research seeks to disprove a *null hypothesis.* A null hypothesis says that there is no relation between variables. By proving the null hypothesis to be incorrect, the researcher shows that there is in fact some kind of relation. Of course, one could alternatively hypothesize that there is in fact such a relation—and even what direction that

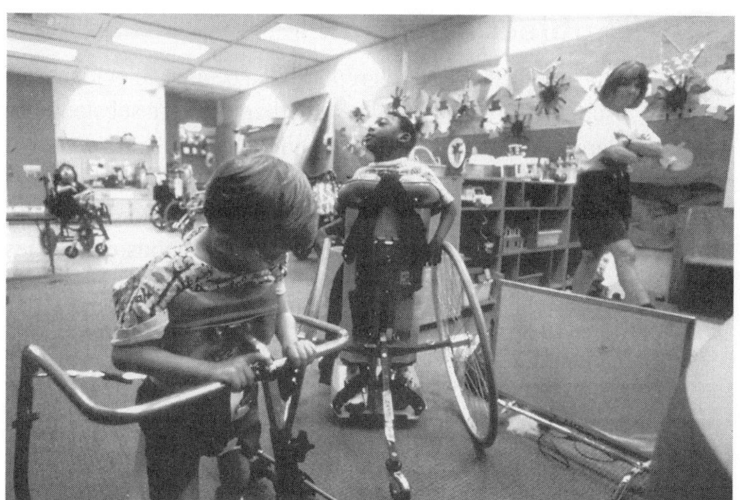

Qualitative research features an observer who reports on what happens but does not manipulate any variables.

relation has (positive, negative) and how strong it is. Most studies you will read use the null hypothesis, however, because statistical tests are readily available for use with such hypotheses.

Standard statistical tables are also readily available to help the researcher see whether a given finding is *statistically significant.* It is probably not going too far to say that the Holy Grail in behavioral research is a statistically significant finding. That being the case, it is important for you to understand that a statistically significant finding is one that is unlikely to have occurred purely by chance. Such findings are described using expressions such as "$p < .05$" and "$p < .01$." Those mean, respectively, that the finding was likely to have occurred strictly as a result of chance fewer than five times per hundred experiments like this one, or fewer than one time per hundred such experiments. Either level may be chosen to disprove the null hypothesis. Neither means that the result was not due to chance. No one can know that with absolute certainty. But a significant finding is one in which researcher and reader alike can have some confidence.

That a finding is statistically significant does not mean it is practically important. The difference is a central one. That a relation probably does exist does not mean that you should change your behavior because of it. Rather, the fact that a finding is statistically significant tells you that it probably is a real effect and that you may proceed to ask, "What does this effect mean to me?" It may mean little or nothing. If you are a preschool teacher of children with severe retardation and you read a study showing a relation between multisensory approaches and achievement by children with mild retardation, the fact that a multisensory approach produced significantly more learning than did a unisensory approach with those students should cause you to ask some critical questions. One might be the extent to which the students studied were like the children you teach. Are there enough similarities to cause you to believe that the study has implications for how you teach those children? None of these questions has anything to do with the statistical significance of the study's findings. Rather, they have to do with what the findings mean to *you.*

Generalizability

Accordingly, the first question to ask of any research report probably is "Are the families and children studied like the families and children with whom I work?" This is a question of *generalizability.* If, for example, you work with infants and toddlers, research on adolescents will probably be of little help. Perhaps not as obvious is the fact that much research draws upon programs that are geographically convenient to the researchers. It may be that families in rural South Carolina and their young children are described in a study; if you work with inner-city families in Philadelphia, the generalizability of the study's findings to your population may, in some respects, be problematic. The best advice is to read intelligently and critically. Ask questions as you read. Be especially alert to information that you can use.

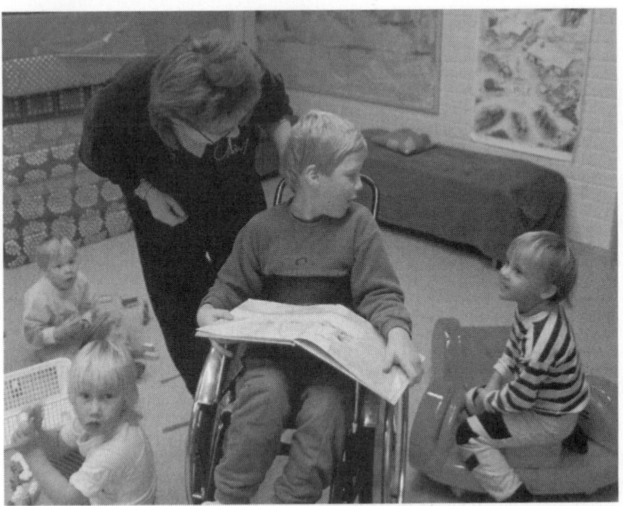

As you read reports on research, ask yourself, "Are the children studied like the children with whom I work?"

Subject Attrition

As you read a research report, also be alert to evidence of subject *attrition.* Did the study begin with a substantially larger number of subjects than were still being tested at its end? That problem is particularly evident in longitudinal studies, but it can affect short-term studies as well. The issue of attrition presents fairly obvious challenges for researchers. Consider, for example, a commercial weight loss or exercise program. People who do not receive benefits (or at least do not recognize any) tend to drop out; those who see benefits outweighing the inconvenience, cost, and so on, of participation tend to remain in the program. To study only long-term participants and conclude from their results that an exercise or diet program is effective is to ignore the fact that dropouts differ from persistent participants. So it is in ECSE. At the very least, researchers should compare a sample of families that dropped out of the program with families that remained in it. If there are no significant differences on such measures as education, family income, severity of disability of the child, and so on, you would have more confidence in the generalizability of the research findings.

Some Examples

Good examples of generalizability problems exist in the literature on cocaine exposure in infants and young children. The initial reports suggested that high proportions of women giving birth had used cocaine during pregnancy. For example, Chasnoff (1989) stated at a conference that 36 hospitals surveyed reported an average of 11 percent of new mothers studied admitted using some illegal drug while pregnant. Miller (1989) said at the same conference that hospitals testing the urine of newborns found evidence of cocaine in 10 to 15 percent of the infants. These proportions were disturbingly high. Do as many as 1 out of every 7, or even 1 out of every 10, women use cocaine during pregnancy? Only a careful reading of the data can answer that question. The hospitals that Chasnoff and Miller reported on may not have tested all, or even most, pregnant women and infants; rather, they may have tested only at-risk mothers and newborns, those whose behavior or backgrounds suggested possible use of illegal drugs.

Examining the literature on cocaine and pregnancy, Williams and Howard (1993) conclude, "In most current research, only highly select samples of women have been studied; those who have been referred to a drug treatment program. Prevalence and patterns of cocaine use during pregnancy have seldom been ascertained for a sample of women seeking routine prenatal care, not to mention those seeking no prenatal care" (p. 66). This immediately cautions the reader to ask, "Eleven percent of *what?*" The classic example of this kind of generalizability problem is the apocryphal case in which a researcher tests everyone in a mental hospital. Finding that 40 percent of these people are mentally ill tells us nothing about the prevalence of mental illness in the outside community. The study has no generalizability.

What Was Done?

If the study seems to be about the problems you deal with on an everyday basis, the next questions you should ask are about the study itself. What *exactly* was done in this experiment? With whom was it performed? Did everything actually occur as the researchers intended? One does not need a Ph.D. in behavioral research to realize that telling parents to spend 20 minutes daily doing physical therapy with their child does not mean that parents actually do that.

To continue with the parental involvement example, to say that parents were involved in a program is to beg the following question: What was the nature of the involvement? Did they attend parent group meetings? Were they instructed by staff in treatment methods? Were they provided with information about the child's disability or needs? Were they included in meetings to develop the individualized family service plan? All of these—and many others—are aspects of what might be called parent involvement. Unless an article clearly explains what was done with parents, you as the reader do not know the relevance of, let alone how to apply, the findings.

Equally important is finding out *with whom* these things were done. One could read an entire article summarizing previous research on age at start, for example, without recognizing that most of the studies being cited were done with children who have one disability, mental retardation.

Randomization

Experimental research should feature *random* selection of subjects from the universe of such individuals and the random assignment of subjects to treatments. Only if both kinds of randomization are performed can researchers have confidence that findings related to the subjects would probably have been seen to the same extent had the entire universe of such people been tested. That is, randomization ensures generalizability. Unfortunately, much research in ECSE features neither kind of randomization, let alone both.

Random numbers have some remarkable properties. One is that truly random assignment of subjects to treatments will wipe out many differences between groups. The variability of individuals is the bane of the behavioral researcher's professional life. For a controlled experiment to be useful, the two (or more) groups being compared need to be very similar. Randomization, fortunately, comes to the researcher's rescue. If subjects are chosen at random from the universe and assigned at random to treatments, both treatment groups will have about the same number of boys and girls as exist in the universe. Both will have about the same number of late developers, children with severe disabilities, or, for that matter, future Republicans. Randomization, thus, removes a great deal of variance between groups and helps to ensure that at the start of the experiment, the two groups are comparable on most measures. That, too, is an essential element. If two groups are comparable at the beginning of an experiment but different after it, there is increased confidence that the independent variable(s) really did have an effect.

Long-Term Effects

More difficult to ascertain (because it is less often reported) is another important question you should ask as you read research studies: "Were benefits maintained over time?" The fact that short-term benefits are observed does not mean that they will persist over time. Head Start is well known (see, e.g., Zigler & Valentine, 1979) for producing effects that for some children are transitory—that is, that wash out within a few years. In addition, young children are notoriously variable in growth patterns. This is yet another bane of the ECSE researcher's professional life, particularly because effects may need to be assessed as late as three years following intervention. The question of whether benefits occur, then, often has to be asked in longitudinal studies, which are much more costly to do than most other experiments.

Validity

As if these were not enough questions to ask about research studies, still others are important—for example, "Could any other factor(s) have accounted for the findings reported here?" This is a question of *validity.* When one speaks of a study's validity, what is meant is that the findings and implications of the project mean what they seem to mean. Stated differently, the study measures what its designers thought they were measuring. The IQ test, to illustrate, really does measure intelligence (and not the child's eyes, ears, or finger control). Perhaps most notable here is construct validity. What is an IQ? What is a delay? Those constructs must be understood before they can be measured in young children. Are the tests used valid with young children who have disabilities? That, as it turns out, is frequently a very serious problem. Many tests that are used in ECSE were never intended for use with children who have disabilities. Researchers, program administrators, and others use them (lacking anything better) but must always watch for evidence that they may not be valid in the ways in which they are being used.

Reliability

Yet another good question is that of *reliability.* Generally, reliability is a question of error. The more error in the measurements, the less reliability. Error may come from many sources, but errors of measurement are perhaps most significant. Examples include test instructions that are not identical for each subject or variations in the time of test (morning, afternoon, etc.) or in other aspects of the test administration. Another way of expressing the idea of reliability is that if one gave a "perfect" test and a "real" one, reliability is an expression of how close the real test scores come to the ideal ones. Because there are no perfect tests, one must turn to other methods to ascertain the reliability of a measure. One is to repeat the test to the same people over a period of time; in general, a reliable test will yield much the same scores each time. A second is to give two tests to a group of subjects, one known to be a reliable test and one about which there are questions. If the scores on both, or more precisely the *rank order* of the scores on both, are identical or close to it, the second test is probably also a reliable one. As a reader, you can look for such efforts. You can also ask whether the findings reported in a study have been replicated by the same or other investigators.

Opinion

Bear in mind that the discussion section, or interpretation of a study's findings, is opinion. Here the researcher gives a uniquely personal view of what the study means. Whereas the earlier parts of the article are objective by comparison, the implications section, by its very

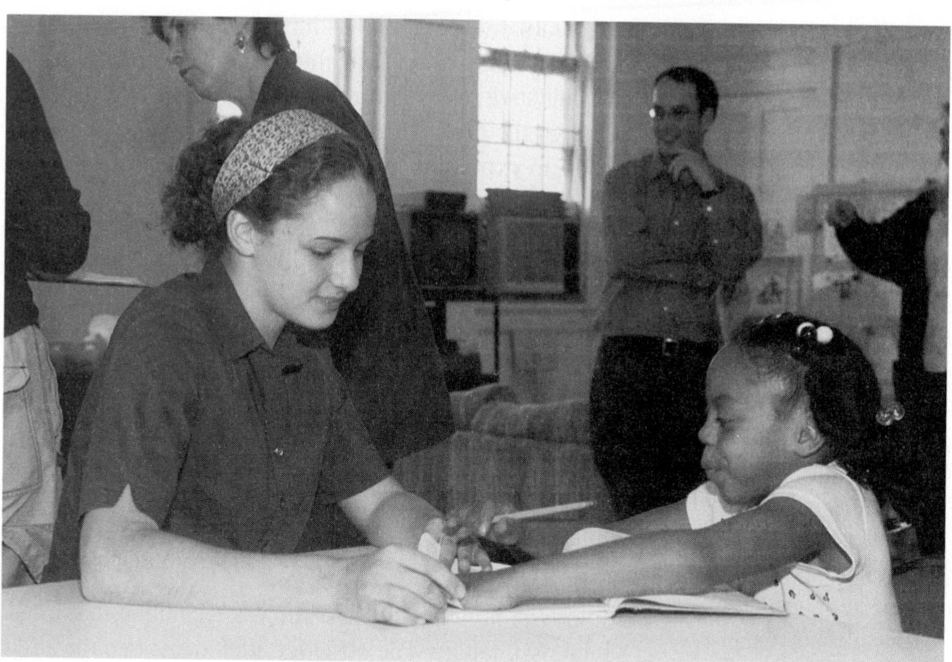

Tests should be valid, measuring what they are supposed to measure and not something else (e.g., the children's vision).

nature, is subjective. Both lay and professional readers may well have different points of view and alternative explanations for what the study findings say and mean.

Qualitative Versus Quantitative Research

There are two basic kinds of studies that you will read. The first is the experiment. In this case, a researcher manipulates one or more independent variables in order to observe the effect on a dependent variable. The controlled experiment is the best way to determine whether the independent variable(s) did in fact affect the dependent variable. This method is sometimes referred to as **quantitative research,** because it reports findings as numbers. Quantitative research is much in favor these days at the U.S. Department of Education. Its research arm, the Institute of Education Sciences, uses such terms as *scientifically valid research* in calling for randomized controlled trials, insisting that this is a critical factor in establishing "strong" evidence of an intervention's effectiveness. Similarly, the No Child Left Behind Act of 2001 uses the term *scientifically based research* more than 100 times. However, due in part to frustration with results to date from controlled experiments (see "Research Findings" later in the chapter), you will probably see an increasing number of naturalistic observation reports. These **qualitative research** articles draw on techniques from anthropology and social psychology in an effort to report information so that the reader fully understands it. In this second kind of study, nothing is manipulated. Rather, the researcher attempts to describe, in as objective a manner as possible, what occurred and what it seems to mean.

Quantitative research

usually manipulates one or more variables ("independent variables"), observing its or their effects on dependent variables. Such studies report findings as numbers, hence the name "quantitative."

Qualitative research

is observational study and report in which nothing is manipulated or controlled.

Qualitative research does not compare groups, nor does it use statistics to describe findings. Rather, in qualitative research a trained observer monitors what someone does and asks that person why she does those things. In qualitative research, the researcher's job is to describe, in rich detail, what happens in an intervention program or in a classroom.

Qualitative research has important limitations. First, perhaps most seriously, it cannot explain variance. If one thing happens in one setting and another in a second setting, all qualitative research can do is to describe what happened and perhaps add what participants in the two settings thought occurred. Quantitative research, by contrast, has the ability to explain to a level of confidence what happened and to rule out alternative explanations, again to a level of confidence. Second, qualitative research is as subject to researcher bias as is quantitative research. If, as qualitative researchers like to say, there is no such thing as an objective reality but only a participant's view of reality, this holds true of the researcher as well as the practitioner. A third concern is that the method, by its very nature, attempts to get into someone's mind and understand how and why people do things. That is a very ambitious goal, one few humans using any method are capable of achieving.

Qualitative research begins when the researcher attempts to enter the world of the practitioner. This process involves spending time in the classroom or program setting and asking questions about what is happening. It continues as the researcher attempts to understand the language of the practitioner—what words refer to which ideas and practices—so that the two can communicate. Much of what is done in qualitative research comprises participant observation, a technique that is widely used in anthropology and social psychology. The observer attempts to see the situation anew, with no preconceptions and no biases. She then tries to capture in words what is occurring in what are called *field notes*. Later, the researcher reads through these notes and attempts to compress them into a manageable summary, which becomes the journal article.

How does the reader evaluate such an article? Coleman (1993) suggests that the reader must trust the researcher. He comments that the situations being described cannot be replicated or revisited, so there is no independent way for the reader or for another researcher to find out whether what the article says happened really occurred: "The standard for establishing reliability is not replication of specific results; it is more general patterns of thought that are harmonious with the literature on the topic" (p. 27).

Another technique readers may use is *triangulation*—that is, seeing whether information from different aspects of the research hangs together into a coherent whole. A third is to compare the report with other reports on other professionals in similar situations.

PROBLEMS IN ECSE RESEARCH

Research in ECSE is difficult for many reasons. One is the basic fact that most intervention and preschool education is brief in duration. Experimental intervention may last just 20 minutes a day one day a week in the case of infants and toddlers under three, or three hours a day perhaps three days a week with preschoolers. Research means attempting to tease out what effects that assistance has, despite the fact that what goes on during the rest of the day has as much or more influence, and despite the fact that young children develop on their own at very different rates irrespective of intervention. This is particularly an issue in research on intensity (whether more intensive interventions are better than less intensive ones), because even the more intensive programs tend to offer modest levels of instruction, therapy, or other interventions. Establishing a difference between groups when both the more intensive and the less intensive treatments are rather mild can be problematic.

WITHIN-GROUP DIFFERENCES

The core of experimental research, of course, is establishing differences between groups. When that is done, the null hypothesis may be rejected and a significant difference reported. What happens, though, when there is as much variation, if not more, within one or more of the groups than there is between them? *Within-group differences* are, in experimental research, noise—unwanted variability. Yet the very nature of disability is that it varies tremendously. Even children who all have the same disability differ one from another, in fact more than do children with no disabilities. Accordingly, there is a great deal of noise in many experiments with children who have disabilities. That noise may drown out otherwise significant between-group differences. This factor of variation within groups often makes ECSE research difficult to do.

To illustrate, suppose a study reports on a group of children aged three to five who have cerebral palsy. This begs the question: How severe was the cerebral palsy? The condition varies tremendously; some children are able to speak, others are not; some are able to manipulate small objects with excellent fine motor control, others cannot; some are retarded, others are not. That is, a group of children with cerebral palsy probably has within it much greater variation of individual performance than generally is found in a group of nondisabled children in the same age range. For this reason, variance within groups is considerable—and may overwhelm variance between groups. Establishing a significant difference between groups is therefore a real challenge.

Bothersome differences within groups can be overcome in a number of ways. One is by restricting the differences within groups artificially by selecting only children with, in this case, mild cerebral palsy. That means that the children in each group are more like other children in the same group, thus reducing the "noise" within that group. While helpful to the researcher who wants to establish differences between groups, this strategy sharply limits the generalizability of the study. Any findings will be relevant only to the kinds of children studied—in this case, young children with mild cerebral palsy.

SAMPLE SIZE

Researchers can also deal with differences within groups by using large numbers of subjects. The law of large numbers is such that a given difference between groups will be significant with a large number of subjects, even when it is not significant with smaller groups (Bernoulli, 1956, cited in Kerlinger, 1986). But finding large numbers of children with disabilities—in this case, cerebral palsy—is difficult because most disabilities are low-incidence conditions. The researcher has little choice but to work with small numbers of subjects and hope that the treatment will be powerful enough to establish a difference between groups. Sometimes, the sampling problem is even more serious. The few children a researcher finds may already be in a preformed group. Suppose, for example, a preschool special education class contains three- to five-year-olds who are mildly to moderately retarded. If these children are in that class because experts referred them there as an appropriate placement to meet their unique needs, clearly they will differ from children with retardation who are not in that class. Using preformed groups, as in this example, may be convenient for the researcher, but it is dangerous. It is an example of *selection error,* and it represents yet another problem in ECSE research.

OTHER ISSUES

Sampling bias has another aspect, one that was mentioned earlier. In ECSE, by law, all children who are eligible for services must be served. One cannot legally (or morally) deny services to eligible children in order to create a control group for an experiment. Researchers are often limited, therefore, to comparing different kinds of interventions or educational programs. One might think that there is a simple solution to this problem: to compare children, some of whom have been referred for services and some of whom have not. The problem here is that children who come in for services differ from children who do not. Most obviously, the families themselves differ. This issue is explored in more detail later in this chapter, when research on age at start (the age of the child when services begin) is considered. For the present, suffice it to say that parental socioeconomic status (SES) influences age at start, meaning that family characteristics are confounded with age-at-start variables.

The interventions or education offered to young children with disabilities may have effects but not the ones researchers anticipated. To illustrate, young children in a preschool class may be given a language development curriculum that is not given to another class. Afterward, language competence is measured. That no significant differences emerge is, of course, disappointing. But there may have been changes in social or emotional development, with the children in the experimental group acquiring greater social competence than did the children in the control group. Yet because this was not measured, no one knows. The overdependence on IQ tests is especially relevant here. Some studies, oddly enough, have used IQ tests to measure effects in an experiment on social development. As a reader, you need to be alert to such inappropriate measures.

RESEARCH FINDINGS

Research in ECSE tends to follow more than lead practice. Infants, toddlers, and preschoolers with disabilities are receiving services in thousands of programs coast to coast. Parents and professionals alike in these programs are convinced that their efforts make a difference in the lives of the young children being served. An important task of the researcher is to document such effects.

UNANSWERED QUESTIONS AND UNQUESTIONED ANSWERS

The questions facing ECSE appear on their face to be simple enough. An example: "Does the age at which services begin matter?" Most parents and professionals would agree that it does. In fact, it is the major rationale for early intervention and for preschool special education. Another: "Is more better than less?" Again, the commonsense response would be yes.

The following section poses 10 questions and attempts to answer them. Note that this discussion focuses only on research evidence. There may well be experiential or anecdotal evidence in support of some of the issues on which research to date has not been able to document effectiveness. Our focus here is not on such material but, rather, on research itself.

1. "Is ECSE effective?" Let's start with the good news. Research to date demonstrates that ECSE does in fact lead to real, measurable benefits for young children with disabilities (Guralnick, 1997, 2001). The most convincing evidence on these kinds of questions comes from studies—such as the landmark Chicago CPC research of Reynolds et al.—comparing children who received services to those who did not receive services. I have only seen a few such studies. That is because early intervention, preschool special education, and K–12 special education are entitlement programs. All infants, toddlers, and children with disabilities have a right to these services. Researchers cannot deny such services to any eligible individual, no matter how worthy the research endeavor.

The only recent study of this kind that I have seen was done in Greece. At the time, that country had no entitlement program for young children with disabilities. The researchers were thus able to put together a comparison of 12 who received services and 12 who did not (Thomaidis, Kaderoglou, Stefou, Damianou, & Bakoula, 2000). The children ranged in age from eight months to five years. Most had medical conditions such as Down syndrome, fragile X syndrome, and brain damage due to prematurity. Over a two-year period, the researchers offered weekly home visits to the experimental children and their families. Control children and families received no intervention services. The visits taught parents how to use behavior modification with their young children. Children in both groups were tested after one year, after the second year, and finally eight months following the end of the program. Results showed "remarkable gains for the treatment group both in terms of overall functioning level and in terms of acceleration of different domains of development" (p. 17), while the control group actually regressed (fell farther behind) or displayed little progress.

ECSE was designed to offer *individualized* services that were *appropriate* in meeting the *unique needs* of infants, toddlers, preschoolers, and K–12 children and youth with disabilities. The question of effectiveness, then, is one of carrying out this mission. Have early intervention, preschool special education, and primary special education programs delivered services to meet those needs? That has been our question.

In early intervention, especially, families are important. IDEA Part C specifically charges early intervention programs with responding to the needs of infants and toddlers in all five domains: adaptive, cognitive, communication, physical, and social or emotional. The law also calls on early intervention programs to meet family needs, as distinct from those of infants and toddlers. If the question is "Has early intervention been effective in meeting family and infant/toddler needs?" the answer is yes. The NEILS longitudinal investigation conclusively shows that families are highly satisfied with the effectiveness of early intervention services provided under IDEA Part C (Bailey et al., 2004). Family members reported that their very young children received about the right amount of services. More than 7 out of

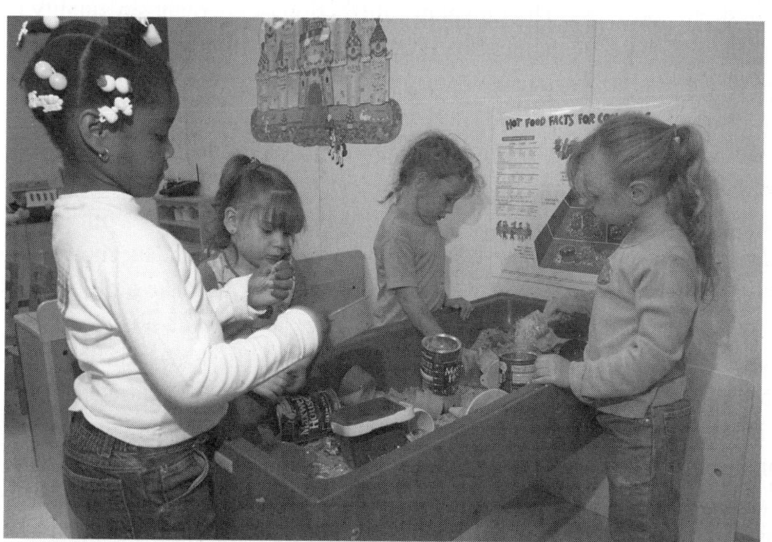

"What to teach" is a difficult issue. We should not allow academics to overwhelm development in all five domains.

every 10 of the 2,586 families interviewed said that. Asked whether the services made a difference in the lives of the children, 9 out of every 10 characterized the quality as excellent or good. For example, parents reported that their very young children were twice as likely to communicate well at the end of the Part C period (i.e., 36 months) than at the onset of early intervention. As for quality of services to the family itself (as distinct from child services), 90 percent said that those were excellent or good. Family members reported that their skills and knowledge in caring for their young child with a disability were much improved as a result of IDEA Part C services.

These findings are very gratifying for early childhood special educators. However, a few words of caution are in order. The NEILS study is not a comparison project. There is no control group. As a result, we cannot discern how much of the parent-reported improvement was likely due to simple maturation. Very young children do develop skills and knowledge over time. The parents, not being professionals in early childhood, may not have factored this into their assessments. In addition, because there was no comparison group, we cannot assess the effectiveness of the specific interventions that were used with these very young children vis-à-vis other kinds of interventions. In addition, because the types and intensities of services provided were chosen in response to the specific needs of individual infants and toddlers, we cannot readily evaluate the cost-effectiveness of services. To elaborate, if one child needs intensive language intervention, and a second child requires much less help in that area, it is not meaningful to ask about the cost-effectiveness of the intense services given to the first child.

PEELS, a second longitudinal effort, this one looking at preschool-age children with disabilities, is assessing quality of services, among other factors, in preschool special education. The project includes direct assessment of children's readiness for school, as well as rating scales and questionnaires completed by family members and by teachers. For example, PEELS has found that only 25 percent of preschoolers with disabilities can recognize all of the letters of the alphabet. Among the factors being explored are quality indicators of preschool programs, intensity of services, placement patterns, teacher characteristics, and children's outcomes. Initial data tables appearing in early 2006 show that family members and teachers of preschool-age children with disabilities tend to be pleased with the children's progress. Their level of satisfaction (49 percent say quality is "excellent" with another 40 percent characterizing it as "good") is almost as high as what NEILS found among early-intervention family members (90 percent calling it "excellent" or "good").

Other than PEELS, few research publications examine the effectiveness of preschool special education services. Most are rather narrow in scope, typically focusing on one disability. A good example is Corsello's (2005) review of different approaches with young children having autism spectrum disorders. Her examination of outcome data shows that when services are provided during the preschool age period, they do make a difference. Corsello also concludes that when young children receive services prior to about age four they do better than do those who are first served after that age (that is, "earlier is better" to preview a topic we will take up shortly). Sigman and McGovern (2005) concentrated, as did Corsello, on autism spectrum disorders. Their study is particularly significant because, as researchers affiliated with UCLA, they work in the shadows of the landmark Lovaas (1987, 1989) studies that demonstrated powerful outcomes from applied behavior analysis (ABA). Assessing persons with autism who are now adolescents and young adults, Sigman and McGovern found that their progress was dramatically slower than it was during their preschool and elementary years. The best predictors of later skills in language, they found, were functional play skills, responsiveness to others' bids for shared attention, and frequency of requesting behaviors during the early childhood period. The Sigman-McGovern longitudinal follow-up cautions us that effectiveness outcomes of preschool interventions, no matter how impressive initially, may not always be long-lasting.

SEELS, the third major longitudinal project funded by the U.S. Department of Education, includes direct assessment of children aged six and over, as well as other data. Recall that both IDEA 2004 and NCLB of 2001 stress the importance of literacy, numeracy, and other areas of academic performance. Reflecting that new emphasis, SEELS is looking at how well young children are performing academically in K–3, as well as in later years. The findings to date are sobering.

While 88 percent of six-year-old children with disabilities were, as expected, in first grade, SEELS found that large numbers of young children with disabilities are retained in grade ("held back") at least one year thereafter. Thus, while the typical seven-year-old child is in second grade, that was true only of 10 percent of children with disabilities in 2001. Fully 86 percent of those seven-year-olds were in first grade. Similarly, 60 percent of eight-year-olds with disabilities were in second grade, when one would expect them to be in third grade. By fourth grade, only 4 percent of nine-year-olds with disabilities were at expected grade level. Fully 61 percent were in the third grade, and another 31 percent were in second grade (Blackorby et al., 2005).

The SEELS-administered direct assessments (they gave Woodcock-Johnson III achievement tests in the areas of passage comprehension and mathematics computation) show significant lags in reading and math achievement among six- through eight-year-olds with disabilities as compared with national means. Those with disabilities often were one-half to three-quarters of a year behind their nondisabled peers.

To interpret these findings from the SEELS study, readers need to bear in mind that early intervention and preschool/primary special education traditionally have focused on the "whole child"—on the five domains of development (adaptive, cognitive, communication, physical, and social or emotional). The achievement tests, by contrast, are academic assessments that come out of a very different framework: the accountability demands of NCLB and IDEA 2004. We should not be surprised, then, to find that in 2005 some young children with disabilities are not performing well in standardized tests of language arts and math. Scores may rise in future years, after educators have altered the emphasis from "whole child" to "academics."

Also helping us place the SEELS findings into context are reports from the Early Childhood Longitudinal Study (ECLS), conducted by the National Center for Educational Statistics at the U.S. Department of Education. Rathbun and West (2004), for example, reported on reading and math achievements through third grade. The findings show strong, and steady, grade-to-grade improvements in basic literacy skills, vocabulary and comprehension (reading) and numeracy, shapes, patterns, mathematical operations, and problem-solving processes (math)—improvements that SEELS seldom found among children with disabilities.

The ECLS findings are sobering in light of the requirements of NCLB that virtually all young children with disabilities be tested in math and reading as early as third grade. Some may also be tested in science. The evidence in ECLS about the specific skills and knowledge of nondisabled young children is, at times, startling for anyone who has spent time in early intervention settings and in preschool and primary special education classrooms. The standard to be met if the goal is for young children with disabilities to achieve at parity with their nondisabled peers is a high one.

It may not all be about academic achievement, however. Readers of SEELS reports need to bear in mind that the "big tests" required by NCLB begin in third and fourth grades. Schools must report student scores, including those of children with disabilities. Those reports are made public, and are used by state and local officials, as well as by neighborhood families, in evaluating schools. These facts suggest that some schools may be holding back some young children with disabilities, so as to improve the schools' publicly supported performance. Because the National Assessment of Education Progress (NAEP) and other large-scale assessments are administered nationwide in fourth grade, the pressure to "look good" in fourth-grade tests may be particularly acute. This may help explain why SEELS found that only 4 percent of nine-year-olds with disabilities were, as would be expected, in fourth grade, and three out of every five nine-year-olds were still in third grade.

Finally, readers need to remind themselves that preschool/primary special education services—special education services, related services, and supplementary aids and services—are provided in response to the individual and unique needs of particular children. The new thrust on accountability from NCLB and IDEA 2004 is new at the primary-grade level. As educators work to respond to those new mandates, the SEELS findings of serious academic lags among young children with disabilities tell us that we need to examine the focus on preacademics and academics in preschool special education programs. Are those programs providing enough emphasis on these academics skills and knowledge? The SEELS study also alerts us to the need to look at preacademics and academics at the kindergarten and first-grade levels. Are we doing enough in those areas at those levels?

Age at start

is a child's age when early intervention or other services begin.

2. "Is earlier better?" The review continues with the commonsense statement that of course earlier intervention is better than later intervention—isn't it? This is a question of **age at start.** It is not a question of duration of services. Given that the belief that earlier is in fact better is one of the most central in all of ECSE, the paucity of research on the issue is discouraging (Boyce, Smith, Immel, Casto, & Escobar, 1993). A number of studies have included age at start as one of many variables, but whatever effects are due to age at start are confounded with influences from other variables, notably duration.

Another possible confounding factor is severity. Severe disabilities tend to be identified earlier and treatment begun earlier than is the case with mild disabilities. For this reason, children who begin services earlier may be more disabled than those who start later.

Age at onset

is a child's age when a condition begins.

A lesser problem in ECSE research, which is an important issue in other research, is the confounding of age at start with age at onset. **Age at onset** refers to the age of the child when the disability began. With some disabilities (deafness is a good example), the effect of the disability on the child's development varies strongly with age at onset; in deafness, to continue the example, children born deaf will experience speech, language, and academic difficulties that children who become deaf at, say, 10 years of age will not have.

The NEILS study convincingly shows that age at start varies greatly for good reasons. Very young children with disabilities, particularly severe ones, tend to begin services early. Their age at start is younger than is that of infants and toddlers with delays in development, but as yet no diagnosed disabilities. There is another factor at work, though. Some families, notably those headed by single parents of low SES, appear to seek services for their very young children with special needs later than do two-parent, middle- or high-SES families (see, e.g., Parish, Cloud, Huh, & Henning, 2005). In fact, those researchers found that family structure is a stronger predictive factor of use of out-of-home services than is the disability itself.

Parental motivation is confounded with age at start. As already mentioned, certain kinds of parents seek, and get, earlier services for their infants and toddlers than do other kinds of parents. Thus, effects on young children may reflect parental influence as much as, if not more than, programmatic effects due strictly to early age at start. In general, middle- and upper-class families tend to be better educated than lower-class families and they may notice delays in development earlier. Such families may also be more in control of their daily lives and have more time than lower-class families, especially large ones, to pursue diagnoses and treatment at earlier stages. Of course, middle- and upper-class families can also afford extensive medical care, including numerous referrals to specialists, until a condition is accurately diagnosed. In addition to other pressing concerns that may cause them to delay treatment, lower-class families may not have those financial resources; not even Medicaid covers all poor families. All of this leads to a sobering fact: The age at start of services is *confounded* with socioeconomic factors; it is not the only difference between groups. The task of separating out those socioeconomic factors from the age-at-start issue in and of itself may not be possible.

Bearing in mind these factors, which tend to complicate our efforts to answer the question of whether earlier is better, recent evidence does suggest that the answer is yes. One is Corsello's (2005) review of services for young children with autism. Another, this time on young children of low birth weight, comes from Boyce, Saylor, and Price (2004). In addition, research at Head Start programs shows that young children, including those with disabilities, tend to do better when services begin earlier rather than later (*Head Start Impact Study*, 2005).

3. "Is more intensive better?" This is another of those questions apparently "so obvious that one need not ask it." The question is not so self-evident, however. What is intensive? The question here is best understood as asking whether more frequent (e.g., thrice-weekly versus once-weekly sessions) or same-frequency, more lengthy services (twice-weekly, 60-minute vs. twice-weekly, 20-minute sessions) are superior. It is not quite that clear, however. If one is discussing home visits (a common method for serving infants and toddlers), is intensiveness best understood as how frequently or for how long a home visitor visits? What about parental use of techniques taught by the home visitor? Conceivably, less frequent home visits might be correlated with more intensive parental instruction of a child, making something of a mockery of measures of home visit intensity. One also needs to ask, "Intensive in what?"

However complex the construct, it has attracted considerable research interest, largely because it is so important in ECSE. How frequent and how lengthy sessions should be are questions that emerge every time an IFSP or IEP is written. With personnel salaries comprising some 70 percent to as much as 90 percent of program costs in special education (see, e.g., Levin et al., 2004), the issue of how much is enough obviously has major cost implications.

An important recent effort, and unfortunately one of only a few bearing directly on the "Is more intensive better?" question is that of Howard, Sparkman, Cohen, Green, and Sanislaw (2005). These researchers compared intensive (one-on-one, 25 to 40 hours/week) interventions for preschool age children with autism spectrum disorders against a less intensive (small groups, 15 hours/week) approach. The two groups appeared similar

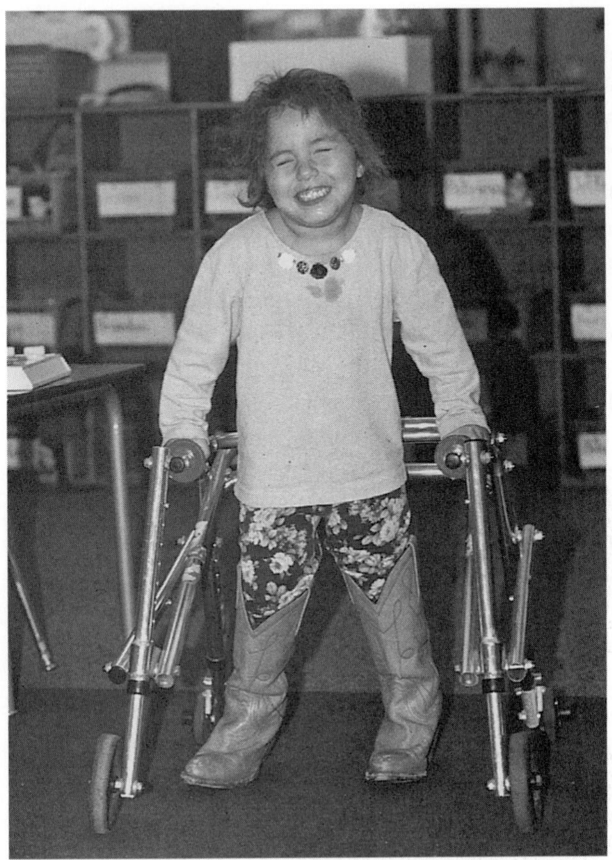

Is more intensive better? One would think so. But children with more severe needs tend to get more frequent service than children with more moderate needs, making research in this area difficult.

at onset of services. After the interventions, however, those receiving intensive services performed better in all skill domains. In addition, the speed with which these children picked up new skills was significantly greater than was the case with those children given less intensive services.

Even more important is another study, this one of young children with low birth weights. The work of McCormick and her colleagues (2006) is the closest we have come in ECSE research to the gold standard set by Reynolds and his team. McCormick et al. compared long-term outcomes achieved by infants and toddlers who had been in an intensive intervention program with those obtained by others who previously were in a less intensive program. Examining data on 636 individuals at age 18, they found that those who were given intensive services as infants or toddlers scored higher on the Woodcock-Johnson Tests of Achievement subscales on reading and mathematics and higher on the Peabody Picture Vocabulary Test. In addition, caregiver reports and self-reports by the young people showed fewer behavioral and social problems among those who, as very young children, had received intensive help as compared to those who had been given less intensive assistance. Thus, McCormick et al. demonstrated strong, sustained effects of intensive early intervention services. This follow-up on the historic Infant Health and Development Program (IHDP) (1990) is even more impressive because the subjects had been assigned to the differing levels of early intervention on a randomized basis as infants and toddlers.

These two efforts (i.e., Howard et al., 2005; McCormick et al., 2006) demonstrate that more intensive services are associated with higher outcomes. But is that always true? Hatton et al. (2000) point out that young children tend to receive more services as they become older. They found that boys with fragile X syndrome who were four years old were offered much more occupational therapy and speech pathology services than were those who were two years old. Thus, two-year-olds received an average of 10 hours of services per month, three-year-olds about 30 hours per month, and four-year-olds some 70 hours per month. This raises obvious questions about confounding of variables—in this case, age and intensity. Three- and four-year-olds received more intensive services simply because, being older than the two-year-olds, they were developmentally ready for it. And it may not just be the hours. Strain and Hoyson (2000) comment that intensity may "have little to do with hours that staff are paid to be with children. Rather . . . intensity is most meaningfully thought of in the context of large numbers of functional, developmentally relevant, and high-interest opportunities to respond actively" (p. 119). Put differently: what matters is not the amount of time but what is done with it.

Holahan and Costenbader (2000) caution us to look for unexpected benefits. They discovered that with respect to intensity of such related services as physical and occupational therapy, more minutes of service per week for preschool-age children with mild to moderate cognitive, physical, social, and language delays translated, unexpectedly, into faster progress in social/emotional skills and in self-help skills. That is, more time in physical and occupational therapy gave young children more opportunities to do things, helping them to learn those more rapidly.

Could it be that less intensive might actually be better? Suppose, for example, parents of children with severe disabilities benefit more by being given respite (a break from caring for the child) than they do by being taught how to develop their child's skills. In this case, more intensive services (or more "parental involvement," as it may also be called) might actually be detrimental to parents. Conceivably, they might also harm rather than help the child. It is also possible that the beneficial effects of education or other intervention may be subject to the law of diminishing returns—namely, that some therapy helps a lot, but subsequent therapy adds little to what the initial work contributed.

Hanft and Feinberg (1997), acknowledging that "[r]esearch has been equivocal, and there has been little documentation that specific frequencies of intervention yield particular results" (p. 29), sought to shift the debate from "How much is enough?" to "What exactly do the therapists do with their time?" They suggest that professionals should respond to family-set outcomes (desired results) in making decisions about frequency and intensity of services. "Intensity and frequency of services, then, are not the most important variables" (p. 34). Far more important, they insist, is "what professionals do with their time" (p. 34). What they should do is what is needed for a particular family and child to reach the goals they themselves have set.

4. "Does parental involvement help?" Part C of the IDEA requires that early intervention programs involve parents, notably in identifying family needs and priorities. Part B does not contain similar requirements but does encourage parents to become involved in preparing IEPs and in protecting their children's rights under the law. Parental involvement is a core concept of ECSE as it is practiced today. However, as is so often the case in this young field, what "parental involvement" means is not always clear. Parents may be involved in minor ways or in major ones. They may be consulted on program goals for their child and for the family as a whole, or they may just be given some printed materials about their child's disability and about community resources.

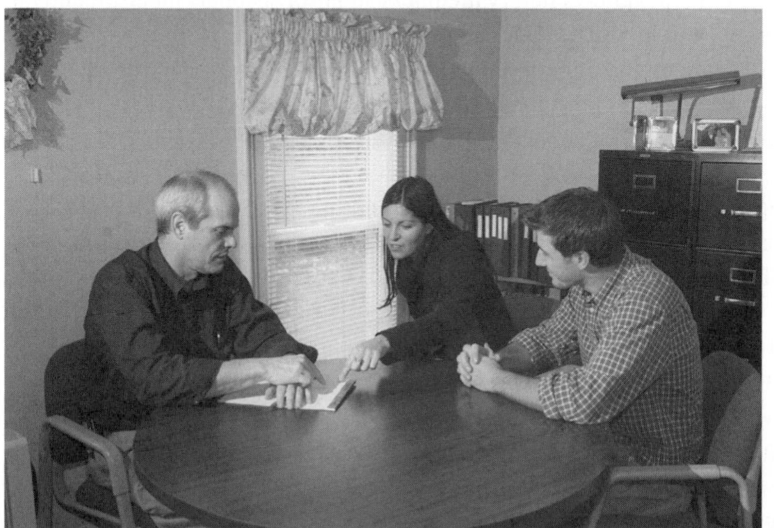

Whether parental involvement helps depends in part on how parents are involved. If they are just trained to care for the child, benefits may be minimal.

That parents should be involved in programs serving infants, toddlers, and preschoolers with disabilities is not in dispute. Parents are, after all, the most important people in these young children's lives. The law, particularly in Part C, is unequivocal in its insistence that parents be involved; and professional literature, too, has supported parental involvement.

Research dating back to the 1980s (e.g., Casto & Mastropieri, 1986a, 1986b) conclusively shows that more family involvement is better than less. That is why IDEA mandates family involvement in virtually all aspects of early intervention and special education. The new longitudinal studies, notably NEILS and SEELS, show that families typically are active in planning and monitoring services for their young children. The NEILS researchers asked parents about their involvement in, and satisfaction with, early intervention programs. Interviews with more than 2,500 families, performed when their very young children were about three years of age, revealed that family members were highly satisfied with the level and character of their involvement in early intervention services, and with the impact of those services on their family life as well as on their children's development (Bailey et al., 2004).

Previous editions of *Early Childhood Special Education* tracked efforts of early intervention and preschool special education programs to design and implement effective ways of involving family members. Early attempts featured family education and training for family members in carrying out professional-like services in the home. Research in the 1980s and early 1990s, notably at the Early Intervention Research Institute at Utah State University (e.g., White, Taylor, & Moss, 1992). showed that those types of family involvement practices were of limited value to families and children. Recent studies (e.g., Johnson, Ring, Anderson, & Marlow, 2005) continue to make the case that "turning family members into at-home paraprofessionals" is a low-value intervention.

As a result, the more recent patterns of family involvement feature meaningful participation in planning and monitoring services. They also seek to help family members identify community-based resources that can help family members cope with multiple demands on their time (Law et al., 2005; Heaton, Noyes, Sloper, & Shah, 2005). Professionals are also giving more attention to siblings of young children with disabilities (e.g., Stoneman, 2005). These steps help relieve family stress while also empowering family members to solve their own problems.

In addition, new scales and questionnaires have appeared which facilitate closer family-program communication and cooperation. An outstanding example of this is the "5 P's" scales developed by VCLC in Syosset, New York (www.vclc.org). The Preschool Performance Profile ("5 P's") allows family members and professionals independently to assess the functioning, and identify the needs, of children between six month of age and five years of age. Other such instruments include the Family-Professional Scales, one an 18-item scale and the other a 9-item scale, both of which appear to be valuable (Summers, Hoffman, Marquis, Turnbull, Poston, & Nelson, 2005).

5. "Is ECSE cost-effective? Cost-beneficial?" When one asks whether something is **cost-effective**, one is inquiring as to whether the costs incurred are less than costs for something else. If two programs are compared, both of which deliver the same services, yet the first does so at a lower cost than the second, it is possible to conclude that the first is cost-effective. Similarly, an evaluator might compare two programs, both costing about the same amount of money, but discover that one provides more services, greater benefits, and so on, and for that reason it is more cost-effective. **Cost-benefit** analysis, by contrast, examines the benefits accrued by the child, assigns them a (frequently arbitrary) dollar value, and compares these benefits with costs. That is, the monetary value of the benefits may exceed that of the services. Cost-benefit can be estimated for a single program, even for a single child, whereas cost-effectiveness usually requires that at least two programs be compared. Keilty (2001) outlines steps to follow in a cost-benefit analysis.

Cost-effective

analyses look to whether one approach, or one program, provides more benefits per dollar than another.

Cost-benefit

analyses look at benefits, assigning values to them, and compare those values with the costs of providing the benefits.

In ECSE, it is often difficult to perform either kind of analysis. One problem is identifying all relevant costs. Many studies neglect to include opportunity costs, where, for example, parents might give up income-generating opportunities in order to attend parent meetings. This chapter has suggested that more intensive services are not necessarily always better; for this reason, one cannot simply say, "Program A offers twice the number of hours of speech therapy for the same price as Program B does; therefore, Program A is more cost-effective." Quantifying costs and benefits of services is difficult. Cost studies may tilt the evidence in one way or another by, for example, not counting all relevant costs or by using very liberal definitions of benefits or other outcomes. Recent cost studies have attempted to avoid these problems.

A major new report, performed by the American Institutes for Research (AIR) at the request of SRI International, is the *NEILS Expenditure Study* (Levin et al., 2004). Looking at very young children who began early intervention services in late 1997 to late 1998, and at 160 early intervention service providers throughout the nation, Levin and colleagues found that, on average, infants and toddlers spend 17 months in early intervention, at a cost of $15,740 per child. Those who have delays in speech and language cost the least ($6,228 over 10 months), while those with diagnosed conditions (disabilities) cost more than $22,000 over 20 months of services.

A key finding was that "the highest expenditures are associated with the worst outcomes" (p. 4). In other words, the more that is spent, the less is the observable progress. At age 36 months, when they aged out of early intervention, the very young children with severe disabilities showed less improvement in health and/or in functioning as compared to those with less serious needs. This appears to cast into doubt the cost-benefit of early intervention. Infants and toddlers with diagnosed conditions who spent more than 30 months in early intervention cost, on average, $40,615. Those identified as having developmental delays who spent between 25 and 30 months in early intervention cost, on average, $38,077 per child. By contrast, infants and toddlers with speech impairments who spent 6 months or fewer in early intervention cost, on average, $3,314.

Although it may seem paradoxical to say this, the findings demonstrate that early intervention is in fact cost-effective. That is because the service is designed to provide individualized services that aim to meet the unique needs of each child. It offers more needed assistance per dollar spent than would less individualized offerings. The fact that the most money is being allocated to those most in need shows that, overall, IDEA Part C is fulfilling its mission. It is designed to allocate the most intensive and longest-duration services to those infants and toddlers who are most in need.

Tarr and Barnett (2001) found that early intervention costs were "substantial," averaging nearly $9,000 per child per year in New Jersey in 1996. Their review of the literature uncovered costs in other states (California, Florida, Massachusetts, Nebraska, and Pennsylvania) ranging from a low of $5,500 per child to a high of $12,000 per child per year. With respect to preschool special education services, a report by Odom et al. (2001) found, not surprisingly, that preschool services were even more costly, largely because each child receives more hours of service each week than is the case for early intervention. Generally, costs remain about double those of comparable services for young children with no disabilities, a proportion that has remained constant for more than a decade (e.g., Chaikind, Danielson, & Brauen, 1993; Moore, Strang, Schwartz, & Braddock, 1988). Clearly, services for young children with disabilities can be expensive. The question now is "Is the money well spent?"

To summarize the evidence on cost-effectiveness, if the question is whether early intervention, preschool special education, and primary-grade special education are cost-effective with respect to their traditional missions, the answer is yes. These programs are effectively targeting resources to meeting the unique needs of young children with disabilities. However, that mission, by its very nature, runs counter to standard economic analysis of the effectiveness in outcomes of each dollar invested. We have not been able to establish that ECSE is cost-effective in those terms. That would require us to compare outcomes of different programs (cost-effectiveness). Doing so is problematic because ECSE, by its essential nature, assigns children to programs according to their unique needs. With respect to cost-benefit analysis, which looks at whether the benefits attained are greater than the costs invested, for one child or for many, the answer seems to be No. ECSE invests more money into services for children who tend to achieve the fewest observable outcomes. Again, that traces to the traditional mission of ECSE.

Furthermore, as noted earlier (see "1. Is ECSE effective?"), IDEA 2004 and NCLB are redefining the mission. These new laws ask very different questions. The focus now is on how cost-effectively programs teach children literacy, numeracy, and other preacademic and academic skills and knowledge. Viewed from that perspective, we cannot now say that ECSE is cost-effective or that it is cost-beneficial. In part that is due to the newness of the academic focus. It is possible that in coming years we may be able to answer questions about the cost-effectiveness and cost-benefit of ECSE vis-à-vis this new emphasis on preacademic and academic instruction.

6. "Does inclusion help children with disabilities?" *Inclusion* is a term that people define differently. Most professionals in ECSE use this term to refer to integration of young children with and without disabilities. The IDEA does not contain the word *inclusion*, so there is no federal definition. Variations in definition, not surprisingly, compromise researchers' ability to answer the question of whether inclusion helps young children with disabilities. It has not stopped them from trying, however.

The effectiveness of inclusion with young children having disabilities may depend on what questions are asked. Kemp and Carter (2005), for example, combined measures of teacher perceptions about and child-demonstrated skills of 33 kindergartners with mental retardation. They discovered that teacher opinions varied sharply from student achievement. The kindergartners perceived by teachers to have better on-task behaviors and to respond more appropriately to teacher directions did not in fact perform better on direct assessments of those skills.

For some young children with disabilities, it may be that inclusion is less helpful than are other environments. Those who are blind or have low vision, for example, may benefit far more when helped by professionals trained as vision teachers, orientation and mobility specialists, and experts in technologies for people who have impairments of vision. That was the conclusion of Gray (2005) when she queried parents of preschool-age children in Northern Ireland.

Stahmer and Carter (2005) asked interesting questions about whether inclusion helps very young children with *no* disabilities. The importance of the issue is obvious: inclusive placements for children with disabilities may only be made if programs and parents alike perceive them to be helpful for nondisabled children. The researchers document "excellent gains in cognitive and language development and no detrimental behavioral effects of inclusion" (p. 321) for typically developing toddlers.

Stahmer and Ingersoll (2004) looked at infants and toddlers with autism spectrum disorders who were educated in inclusive settings. There are relatively few such programs, largely because the preferred methods of teaching these children emphasize one-on-one instruction. The researchers examined functioning in communication, social skills, and play behaviors. They found that the very young children with autism performed at much higher levels at age three than at entry into early intervention. That is an encouraging finding. What we do not know, because the study did not ask the question, is whether the children would have done as well, worse, or better in a different early intervention setting.

Much seems to depend on whether teachers of inclusive classrooms promote interactions between children with and without disabilities. Diamond (2001) explored the interactions of 45 preschoolers with no disabilities with classmates having disabilities over a six-week period. She discovered that 40 percent of the preschoolers with no disabilities had *no* such interaction at all. As for those who did have some interactions with classmates having disabilities, they devoted very little time to those interactions. Diamond concludes—as do Kohler, Anthony, Steighner, and Hoyson (2001) in their study of four boys with autism—that inclusion by itself does little to help young children with disabilities. Kohler and his colleagues observed that interactions occurred if, and only if, teachers intervened to make them happen. Stated differently, the physical proximity that comes with inclusion is meaningless, or nearly so, unless adults act to spur child-to-child interactions. When teachers do intervene, children with disabilities show, at best, slow and erratic gains in social skills, although Kohler et al. comment that better outcomes might have accompanied more teacher preparation.

One longtime observer, Diane Bricker (2000) of the University of Oregon, is not pleased with the state of the art in inclusionary practices in ECSE. She states, "An analysis of today's inclusion movement for young children leads me to, if not temper my optimism, at least recognize the many realities that surround the practice of inclusion" (p. 16). She is concerned that inclusion sometimes translates into lower levels of quality. This is particularly the case when young children require expert adult assistance with positioning, communication, and other specialized needs. Echoing her point, occupational therapists Hanft and Pilkington (2000) emphasize that *what* is done matters as much as, if not more than, *where* it is done.

As for whether inclusion saves money in ECSE programs, the evidence is mixed. Odom et al. (2001) examined inclusive preschool programs around the United States. They found that costs varied considerably, so no simple answer was possible. States differ in which program costs they will cover. Children differ in the amount and kinds of services they need. Some programs use team teaching, whereas others rely primarily upon one teacher.

As was shown in Chapter 2, many EC workers lack training on disabilities. Much the same is shown in Chapter 5: teachers in Head Start programs rarely have the training to teach children with cerebral palsy, deafness, blindness, or other disabilities effectively. This raises questions. Do families need to choose between quality and inclusion? Certainly, no one would argue that the choice should be that stark. The reality of present-day ECSE programs, sadly, is that well-trained teachers and other practitioners usually work in specialized programs.

The most accurate way to answer this question, at present, is probably yes, some young children will benefit from inclusion, especially in social development. Other children, whose needs are more severe, may not. The bottom line is not so much whether or not inclusion is offered as whether ECSE workers are trained in, and experienced at, supporting meaningful interactions between children with and children without disabilities. This is another way of saying what we just said: inclusion can help young children with disabilities *if* teachers and other ECSE workers are properly trained to deliver high-quality support services and, at the same time, to facilitate child-to-child interactions in an inclusive setting.

7. "Are we helping those most in need?" Earlier editions of this text summarized evidence suggesting that ECSE may be doing a better job with young children having mild or moderate disabilities than with those having more severe conditions. In part, this was traceable to the relative youth of the field. As with many other areas of human services, ECSE in the 1990s did better with less challenging children. In part, too, the evidence was limited. It is only recently that we have seen, thanks to the NEILS longitudinal study, that today early intervention is quickly finding, rapidly serving, and appropriately targeting resources to very young children with established conditions, including severe ones. NEILS, and to a lesser extent PEELS and SEELS as well, demonstrate that 21st-century ECSE programs do in fact help young children who are most in need.

8. "Does teaming work?" As is discussed in Chapter 7, Part C of the IDEA requires that multidisciplinary evaluations and assessments be done for each eligible infant or toddler and that IFSPs be written by multidisciplinary teams. As noted earlier, many preschool and primary programs are adopting similar teaming approaches, although Part B does not explicitly require them. The research question is "Are multidisciplinary teams effective?"

Perhaps the most interesting study on this issue is that of Garshelis and McConnell (1993). They examined how well individual practitioners identified family needs and priorities, compared with multidisciplinary teams. Their major finding is that teams were more accurate than individuals in such assessments. Even when the researchers examined the most perceptive professionals, they found that these experts did better as members of teams than they did individually. Evidently, different team members contribute bits and pieces of information about parent needs, concerns, and priorities—as well as about child strengths and weaknesses—that are, taken together, more comprehensive than those known to any one professional, even the most knowledgeable. If confirmed by further such studies, this investigation offers important support for the multidisciplinary team approach.

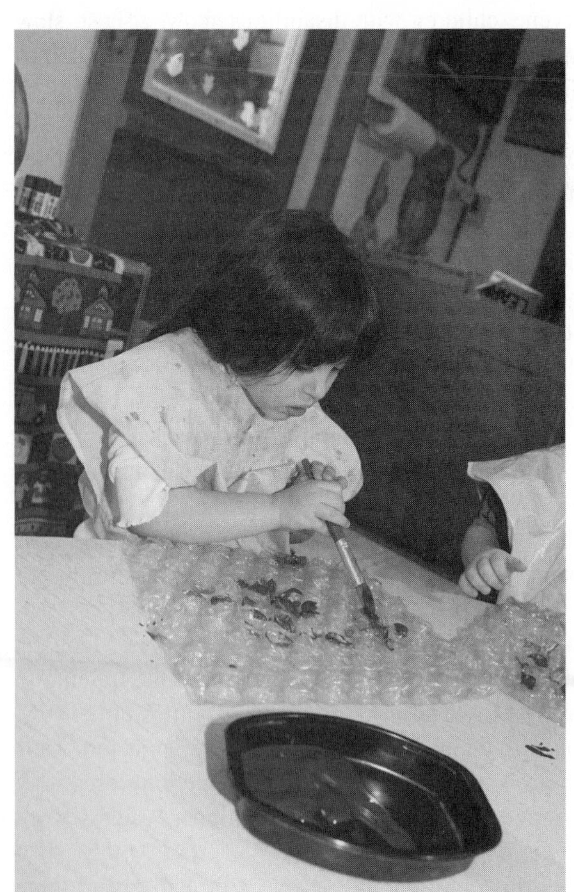

Academics, including science, are more prominent in ECSE today than in years past.

Minke and Scott (1993) used qualitative methods to study nine IFSP development meetings. They found parents playing an important, but not decisive, role as members of the multidisciplinary teams. They suggest that professionals sometimes have little appreciation of how much parents have to offer in identifying needs (particularly priorities) and in planning services. Some professional-parent tension was evident, as when staff withheld information or did not ask parents for their views. Bailey, McWilliam, and Winton (1992) suggest that these and other problems in parent-professional teaming may be due in part to the fact that many ECSE practitioners have not been trained in working with families; many, in fact, view themselves as experts on children rather than on family dynamics. Bailey et al. advance a decision-making model that stresses decision making at the team level (involvement of all team members) and training for professionals about ways of optimizing parental participation.

To summarize, multidisciplinary teams do seem to be better than individuals at doing what the law calls for them to do, notably evaluations and assessments. Balanced against those moderate but noticeable advantages is the fact that a multidisciplinary approach is more costly than an individual practitioner approach.

9. "What should we teach?" Recently, we have seen much more discussion in the professional literature about this very important question. Contributions have been made by Carl Dunst in North Carolina and colleagues at the Universities of Connecticut and Wisconsin (Dunst, Bruder, Trivette, Raab, & McLean, 2001), by Eva Horn at the University of Kansas and her colleagues at the Universities of Maryland and Washington (Horn, Lieber, Li, Sandall, & Schwartz, 2000), and by Susan Sandall and her colleagues at the University of Wisconsin (Sandall et al., 2001). Much of their work builds on the pioneering efforts of Diane Bricker, first at the University of Tennessee and later at the University of Oregon (Bricker 2000, 2001). It also arises from the theoretical work of Bronfenbrenner (1979, 1989), whose focus on the environment around a child was discussed in Chapter 1. Dunst and his colleagues are among those recognizing Bronfenbrenner's contributions.

Bricker (2000, 2001) demonstrates the importance of providing a variety of stimulating activities for young children with disabilities. She urges teachers to move beyond drill-and-practice routines. She also encourages ECSE workers to recognize that young children with disabilities will work for much more than just food and praise. Bricker also has led the way with a technique now gaining much favor: **embedding** of instruction into children's everyday play activities. The term *embedding* is defined as "a procedure in which children are given opportunities to practice individual goals and objectives that are included within an activity or event in a manner that expands, modifies, or adapts the activity/event while remaining meaningful and interesting to children" (Bricker, Pretti-Frontczak, & McComas, 1998, p. 13). Phillip Strain and Marilyn Hoyson (2000) are among the researchers acknowledging their debt to Bricker. Horn et al. (2000) also cite Bricker's leadership in embedding.

Embedding

is incorporating instruction or other support that helps young children with disabilities reach IEP/IFSP goals into activities that these young children and/or their families are engaging in on their own.

Dunst and his teams (Dunst, Bruder, Trivette, Raab, & McLean, 2001; Dunst, Herter, Shields, & Bennis, 2001) emphasize the need for early intervention personnel to study the everyday lives of infants and toddlers. They have identified a vast array of natural environments frequented by very young children with disabilities and their families. The key, they report, is to embed developmental and instructional support into those environments. Thus, such family routines as cooking, shopping, and doing errands in the community; such child routines as eating, dressing, and preparing for bed; such entertainment activities as watching television, going to the theater, and listening to music; such sports and athletic activities as taking walks, hiking, running, and playing ball; and such holiday activities as celebrating cultural and religious holidays all contain within them opportunities that may be mined by ECSE professionals. Family members may be instructed in how to embed literacy, numeracy, and other preacademic skills, as well as socialization skills, into these everyday activities.

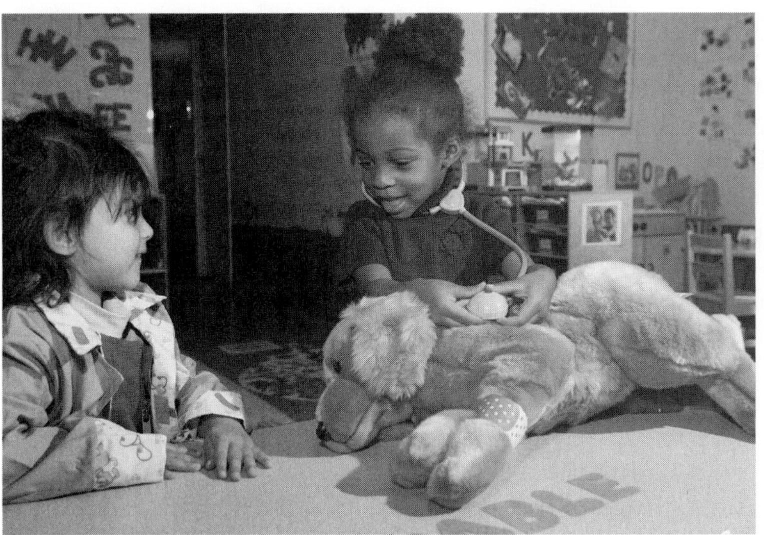

Career exploration, as here in "playing veterinarian," is an important component of ECSE.

Horn and her colleagues (2000) offer much the same guidance to teachers of preschool classrooms. Their work suggests that teachers adapt regular curricula and classroom activities rather than supplant them with special-needs activities. Teachers should set learning objectives that are individualized for each child. Horn et al. call this "activity-based intervention" (p. 209). They emphasize the importance of "child initiations" (p. 210). That is, they want teachers to take advantage of authentic activities—things young children want to do and do when they are freed from adult structure—to provide instruction. To illustrate, teachers might model, guide verbally, guide physically, and/or provide prompts for activities that young children themselves decided to do. Similarly, materials that young children want to play with may be modified so as to meet special needs. In both cases, the determining factor is the *child's* desire for a particular activity and/or material.

Kohler et al. (2001) also focus on "natural" activities and materials. In their work with young boys having autism, they found that communication could be elicited by teachers who joined child-selected activities; offered comments and questions; presented the boys with "novel materials, such as plastic eggs or letters and words hanging from the ceiling" (p. 101); and—perhaps most important—placed desired objects out of reach and pretended not to understand gestured requests for them. Building on what the children wanted, these teachers demanded verbal communication as a condition for granting children's wishes. Ideally, peers should also set communication preconditions for granting children with autism what they desire.

Once again, however, we note that IDEA 2004 and NCLB are challenging perceptions of the mission of ECSE. These federal laws call for instruction in, and direct assessment of child performance with, literacy, numeracy, and basic science. Thus, "what to teach" becomes much more narrowly focused. This troubles many professionals in ECSE. They were trained to identify the unique needs of young children having disabilities and to provide services targeted directly at those individual needs. Given the new mandates, the question becomes whether ECSE programs may continue to do that, while at the same time ramping up instruction in academics. To date, research has not yet given us solid answers.

10. "Are we reaching the target population?" The evidence seems to be that in the early years of the 21st century, ECSE finally is achieving this long-sought goal. According to the U.S. Bureau of the Census (www.census.gov), about 2 percent of infants and toddlers and some 5 percent to 6 percent of preschool-age children have disabilities. The U.S. Department of Education's *Annual Reports* (www.ideadata.org) show the same proportions of young children actually being served by the IDEA. This is strong evidence for the proposition that we are, indeed, reaching the target population, at least in the birth-to-five-inclusive age range. Neither the Census Bureau nor the Department of Education report population data specifically for children in the six-to-eight age range, but special education over the years has done better with child find in that group than in the younger age groups.

THE ROLE OF RESEARCH IN ECSE

IDEA 2004 and NCLB are shifting the focus not only of early interventionists and special educators but also of researchers. That is because the outcomes desired are shifting. The emphasis now is upon preacademics and academic skills and knowledge. Accordingly, researchers need to look at how effectively early intervention, preschool special education, and primary-grade special education are preparing young children with disabilities to meet state learning standards. What methods work, with which young children?

To offer one illustration of a promising line of research, consider that classroom preparation for the high-stakes tests that begin in third grade typically takes place in general/inclusive classrooms. Because young children with disabilities must take those tests, we may see more and more being taught in inclusive settings.

The SEELS longitudinal study raises troubling questions about how well-prepared young children with disabilities are for demands of IDEA 2004 and NCLB. The direct assessments given by the SEELS researchers, as well as the surveys of teachers and parents, suggest that, on the whole, primary-grade children with disabilities tend to lag well behind their peers in academic skills and knowledge. It is clear that educators face major challenges. We need research to help us identify promising techniques. And we need it now.

Guralnick (1993) proposes a model for what he called "second generation" research. That model continues to guide us. It tells us to recognize that what works in ECSE depends not only on child and family characteristics but also on program features. We now know that we need to look at interactions between child and family characteristics, on the one hand, and program features, on the other, relating both to goals and outcomes. We likely will continue to see that program and instructional features need to be selected so as to meet the unique needs of children. It is unlikely that one size will fit all.

SUMMARY

Research in ECSE has tended to lag, rather than lead, the field. At no time is that more apparent than now. The reason is that the game has changed. In years past, we asked questions about how best to meet the unique needs of young children in all five domains of development (adaptive, cognitive, communication, physical, and social or emotional), whether ECSE as a field was finding and serving its target population, and other questions arising out of the traditional mission of ECSE.

Now, quite suddenly, researchers are being asked to assess how well ECSE is doing in preparing young children for the high-stakes tests in reading, math, and science that they will take in the third, fourth, and later grades. If, as the early signs suggest (e.g., SEELS), children with disabilities are lagging behind nondisabled students in these areas, we need the assistance of researchers to discover and document new and better methods of instruction, and to tell us with whom those techniques work best.

We continue to seek, perhaps in vain, for a "gold standard" study analogous to the work in Chicago of Reynolds (2005) and his colleagues. While we cannot duplicate that work—there is no comparable population of young American children who are not receiving services they need—it should be possible, nonetheless, to design a longitudinal investigation that will demonstrate the value of ECSE services and, at the same time, connect those services to monetary and other savings for society as a whole.

KEY TERMS

age at onset
age at start
cost-benefit
cost-effective
embedding
inclusion
qualitative research
quantitative research

QUESTIONS FOR REFLECTION

1. What, in your view, are the pros and cons of quantitative versus qualitative research methods?
2. How do statistically significant and practically significant findings differ?
3. Explain, in your own words, the concept of generalizability.
4. In your own words, what is validity in research?
5. What different activities might a researcher be discussing when she uses the term *parental involvement?*
6. In what ways might less intensive professional intervention actually help young children more?
7. How might a journal author's personal beliefs about inclusion influence the research she reports on and the meaning she attributes to her findings?
8. Why is research evidence about the efficacy of teams so important with respect to public funding for ECSE programs? How might a lack of such evidence affect funding?
9. Is curriculum an appropriate subject for research? If so, is more-directive versus less-directive instruction a good way to approach the subject? Would it help you as a teacher to have clear information on this topic?
10. Why does it matter whether the field of ECSE is or is not reaching most of its target population? What differences in policy, program, or funding decisions might result from data showing that the vast bulk of the need is being met?

PRACTICAL EXERCISES

1. Ask your professor to recommend an article that describes a quantitative research study with young children. Read the article. Then write an analysis in which you note the extent to which it shows or does not show problems described in this chapter (e.g., subject attrition, lack of generalizability beyond the sample studied, validity, reliability, etc.).
2. Do the same for an article describing a qualitative study with young children. Do the authors make a convincing case that they successfully removed themselves from the project (that is, that they did not "see what they wanted to see")? Does the program have staff teaching children more than supporting them? Or is it a combination of the two?

WEB SITES OF INTEREST

www.sri.com/neils National Early Intervention Longitudinal Study—important demographic research on early intervention

www.census.gov The Census Bureau's main page on disability

www.nectac.org National Early Childhood Technical Assistance Center—links to new studies in ECSE

The Laws

PART 2

4 The IDEA

5 Family Rights and Services

While a free, appropriate public education for children from age 6 to 18 or 21 has been the law of the land for 30 years, wide availability of services for children under school age is much more recent. It was not until the early 1990s that most states, the District of Columbia, Puerto Rico, and other jurisdictions provided, under law, child and family services for the birth-to-five population of children with disabilities.

These chapters are important ones for use in preservice and inservice training. The federal laws discussed in Chapters 4 and 5 govern the everyday work of early interventionists, special educators, speech-language pathologists, and others in ECSE. They also offer vital rights and services for families having young children with disabilities.

Chapter 4 focuses on the landmark Individuals with Disabilities Education Act (IDEA) and the newer, much more controversial, No Child Left Behind Act (NCLB). As written in 2001 (NCLB) and amended in 2004 (PL 108–446, IDEA 2004), these laws shake ECSE to its foundations. That is because they change our goals. Throughout the last quarter of the 20th century, ECSE pursued a consistent mission: to offer individualized and appropriate services designed to meet the unique needs of children with disabilities. That mission continues. Now, however, interventionists and educators are challenged also to provide the preacademics and academic instruction that these young children require so as to perform well on high-stakes tests of language arts, math, and science. Those tests begin in third grade.

Chapter 5 opens by exploring a wide range of other laws that guide the work of service coordinators and that enhance the out-of-school lives of persons with disabilities. This chapter also features a discussion of topics frequently raised by family members when they talk with interventionists and educators. These include difficult ethical issues. Disabilities, by their nature, are medical conditions. Many are genetic. Family members may be confused and troubled by the unexpected appearance of disability in the family. At times, especially when the condition(s) is/are severe or even life-threatening, families may seek professional support as they grapple with life-and-death decisions. While answers to profound ethical questions are, as they must be, personal and unique, there is factual information that professionals may draw upon in giving families the guidance they seek. Chapter 5 aims to offer that knowledge.

CHAPTER

4

The IDEA

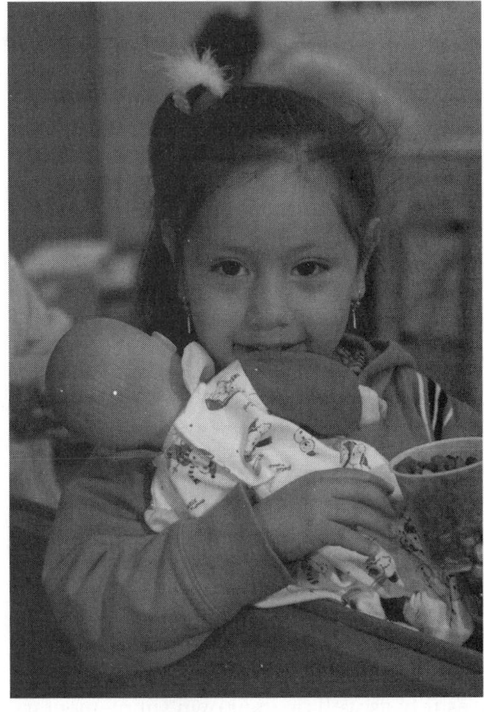

All persons born or naturalized in the United States, and subject to the jurisdiction thereof, are citizens of the United States and of the state wherein they reside. No state shall make or enforce any law which shall abridge the privileges or immunities of citizens of the United States; nor shall any state deprive any person of life, liberty, or property, without due process of law; nor deny to any person within its jurisdiction the equal protection of the laws.
(FOURTEENTH AMENDMENT TO THE CONSTITUTION)

OBJECTIVES

After reading this chapter, you should be able to:

- Explain how ECSE has its roots in the U.S. Constitution.
- Describe how ECSE has evolved over the past 40 years to what it is today.
- Describe what the Individuals with Disabilities Education Act (IDEA) requires of early intervention programs serving infants and toddlers.
- Describe what the IDEA requires of preschool programs serving three- to five-year-olds.
- Describe what the IDEA requires of public schools serving children six, seven, and eight years of age.

CHAPTER OUTLINE

- **OVERVIEW**
- **HISTORICAL FOUNDATIONS**
  - **Constitutional Foundations**
- **LAWS AND REGULATIONS**
  - **Beginnings**
  - **HCEEP: Planting the Seeds**
- **EDUCATION OF THE HANDICAPPED ACT**
- **EDUCATION FOR ALL HANDICAPPED CHILDREN ACT**
  - **The 1983 Amendments**
  - **The 1986 Amendments**
- **INDIVIDUALS WITH DISABILITIES EDUCATION ACT**
  - **PL 102–52**
  - **1991 IDEA Amendments**
  - **The IDEA Amendments of 1997**
  - **No Child Left Behind**
  - **IDEA 2004**
  - **The IDEA Today and Tomorrow**

OVERVIEW

To understand ECSE, you must know something about the federal legislation that supports early intervention and special education programs. You also must comprehend where these laws came from, the ways of thinking they embody, and the kinds of language they use to authorize state and local services for young children with disabilities.

The entire system of services for these young children has its foundations in these laws. In each state, the District of Columbia, Puerto Rico, and other jurisdictions subject to federal law, state law or jurisdictional statutes build on federal legislation. These state and other jurisdictional laws mirror federal laws to a remarkable extent, so much so that if we know the federal requirements, we know the gist of virtually all of the state or jurisdictional dictates as well. For example, the kinds of children who are served, the sources of payment used to finance the services, the roles parents and professionals play in deciding what services shall be provided, when, and where—all of these decisions are based on federal laws. And, although states and other jurisdictions interpret them somewhat differently, add to them, and in some cases rely as well on their own supplementary legislation, the fact remains that states and jurisdictions build on the federal statutes.

The federal legislation, in turn, has its roots in amendments to the U.S. Constitution. In particular, the Fifth Amendment and the Fourteenth Amendment are the sine qua non of Part B of the IDEA. Until those amendments were interpreted to apply to children with disabilities, in two federal court decisions in 1971 and 1972, such children and their families enjoyed virtually no rights to elementary and secondary education. Some children did receive some services, in some states and localities. However, the key word in the preceding sentence is *some.* As late as 1975, the U.S. Congress determined that millions of children and youth with disabilities of all ages either were not being served at all or were receiving inadequate services.

In 1986, Congress mandated that all 50 states, the District of Columbia, Puerto Rico, and a few other special jurisdictions must provide "appropriate" services for all under-six children with disabilities by late 1991 in order to qualify for federal financial assistance. The deadline for serving infants and toddlers was later extended to 1993.

What the state and local governments must do is spelled out in considerable detail in the IDEA, the nation's premier law in early intervention and special education. The IDEA outlines a *way of thinking*. Its approach details how children with health needs are to be identified, evaluated, and determined eligible for services. It explains how professionals and parents are to work together to plan services for those children who are eligible. It carves out major roles for families, including parental participation in decision making, and establishes for families that due process rights are exceptionally large by the standard of other U.S social service programs.

This very specific way of thinking has evolved over more than 40 years, especially over the past 30 years. The IDEA features terminology that is equally specific. It uses *language* in a particular—at times, even peculiar—way. Take the term *disabilities.* Part B lists certain disabilities as included in special education—and by doing that, excludes other disabilities. To make this use of language even more confusing, when Part C deals with early intervention services for children with disabilities under the age of three, it talks not about any disabilities as such but rather about diagnosed conditions, developmental delays, and even at-risk status.

Similarly, when the law speaks of *appropriate* early intervention services or special education services, the term *appropriate* has a particular meaning quite different from the usual definition of that word. When it describes preschool services, the IDEA uses the terms *special education* and *related services* in very precise ways to detail just what kinds of services will be provided—and what kinds are not included. Similarly, when the law speaks of family assessment in early intervention being *family-directed,* it has something quite specific in mind. In all these cases, it is necessary to know what meaning the terms carry. That understanding is best acquired by reading the statutory terms (the law itself), reviewing the federal rules interpreting the law (the regulations), and studying the history behind those terms and rules.

HISTORICAL FOUNDATIONS

The historical roots of ECSE trace back several centuries to work in Europe in the 1700s. This history may help elucidate a central concept in ECSE. That idea is that the environment matters—and matters very much—in determining whether disabilities (conditions) are handicapping (limiting) for children, youth, and adults. A physical disability, for example—combined with the massive geographic, architectural, and transportation barriers of most of 20th-century America—could overwhelm an individual, while today getting around is no more than an inconvenience for an American with the same exact condition. This background is important, particularly because recent federal legislation requires the removal of environmental barriers, one after the other. That means today's infants, toddlers, and young children with disabilities can enjoy a largely barrier-free America.

However, it was not until after the civil rights movement of the late 1950s and early 1960s that the idea arose that people with disabilities are minority group members to whom society has some obligations beyond physical restoration of "normalcy." Parents went to court in the early 1970s, demanding that their children with disabilities have access to an education in the local public schools. That led to the **Education for All Handicapped Children Act of 1975 (EAHCA) PL 94–142).** People with disabilities

Education for All Handicapped Children Act of 1975 (EAHCA) (PL 94–142)
is the landmark 1975 federal law that first established the mandate that all school-age children with disabilities must receive a free appropriate public education.

themselves testified before Congress in 1972, for the first time, arguing that they deserved some of the same rights Congress had recently granted to women and members of racial and ethnic minority groups. This movement led to Title V of the Rehabilitation Act of 1973, PL 93–112, including Section 504.

Suddenly, in the mid-1970s, Congress was deciding that the nation had an obligation to do something to the environment, to society itself, in order to accommodate people with disabilities. Now experts believe that disability by itself explains little. There is an interaction between a disability and the environment that produces a handicap. Society now is saying that it has an affirmative duty to remove that handicap by changing the environment. For example, an individual who is blind is handicapped while watching a silent film, perhaps one of the many Charlie Chaplin made, but not while listening to a symphony.

It is no accident that this new recognition was accompanied by a sharp change in language habits. Individuals who once were called *mental defects* and *morons* are now referred to as *developmentally disabled.* Institutions have come to be known as *developmental centers.* Today, people-first language is preferred; we say *individuals with disabilities* and *children with cerebral palsy.* The term *handicapped* is out of favor; its use now is restricted to instances describing how the environment *handicaps* people with disabilities.

CONSTITUTIONAL FOUNDATIONS

Under the U.S. Constitution, the states have jurisdiction over education and related services for individuals. The Tenth Amendment to the Constitution states, "The powers not delegated to the U.S. by the Constitution, nor prohibited by it to the states, are reserved to the states respectively, or to the people." The Constitution does authorize the federal government to pass any laws "necessary and proper" to carry out the responsibilities given to it by the Constitution, including the duty to "provide . . . for the general welfare of the United States." However, the Constitution contains no specific authority for the federal government in education or other fields such as early intervention. To act in those areas, the federal government must find a basis in "the general welfare" justifying such action.

Education, in particular, is a function of state and local governments. It is the states that require school attendance, usually between the ages of 6 and 16. For the federal government to become involved, some constitutional issue relating to "the general welfare of the U.S." must be invoked. In the early 1970s, that is exactly what happened. Two federal court cases, one in Philadelphia and the other in the District of Columbia, connected education for children with disabilities to two constitutional amendments. These court cases suggested that the general welfare of the United States was, and remained, at risk unless the federal government were to intervene. These cases galvanized Congress into acting to guarantee school-age children with disabilities an education (Duncan, 1993).

However, no state at the time required school attendance by children under the age of six. Thus, for the subject matter of this book, the constitutional foundations for congressional action on elementary and secondary education at times did not hold. While the Fourteenth Amendment to the Constitution guarantees equal treatment for all citizens under any state statute, if the state has no law regulating services for children under school age, there is no statute to be equally applied to all people in the state. As recently as 2005,

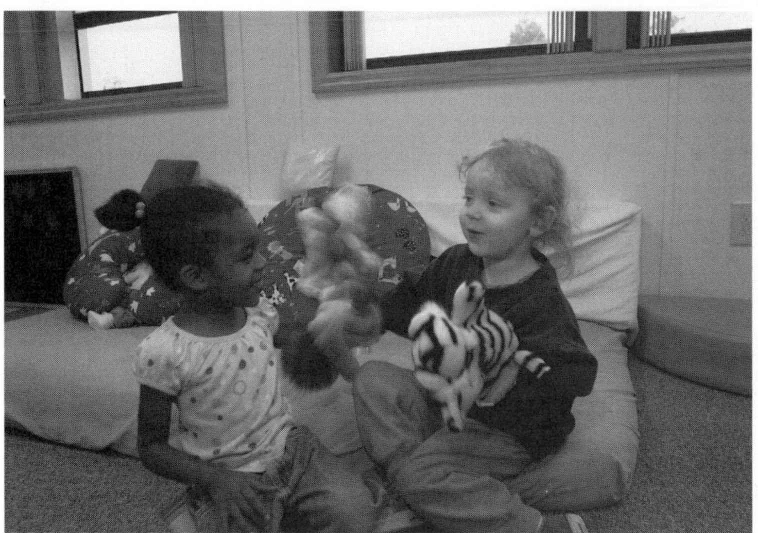

The IDEA promotes integration but only if appropriate early intervention services are provided in such integrated settings.

only about half of all three- to five-year-old children attend public school programs; far fewer birth-to-two infants and toddlers participate in local programs or activities. How, then, could Congress justify mandates for education and other services for children under school age with disabilities?

The answer, as it turns out, is that the federal government *encourages* states to serve birth-to-five children with disabilities by providing financial incentives. To qualify for federal funds under the IDEA, states must enact legislation ensuring all eligible infants, toddlers, and young children certain services. By accepting these federal funds, states obligate themselves to comply with the IDEA's requirements to make services available to all infants, toddlers, and preschool-age children with disabilities.

How this came about is our next subject. First, though, a brief detour is needed to explain a few things about federal laws and regulations.

LAWS AND REGULATIONS

In the United States, laws are given numbers indicating when they were enacted. Each number begins with the letters *PL,* for Public Law. Because each Congress lasts two years (a representative's term of office), laws are numbered according to the Congress that enacts them. The 1995–1996 Congress, for example, was the 104th Congress. Its members of Congress were elected in the November 1994 election cycle and took office in January 1995. They served until the winners of the November 1996 election took office in January 1997. Thus, the period January 1995 to January 1997 was one Congress. Usually, however, a Congress adjourns prior to a congressional election, meaning that congressional terms most often run between January of an odd-numbered year and November of the following even-numbered year. All laws enacted between January 1995 and November 1996 were given PL numbers beginning with 104. Within each Congress, laws enacted are numbered consecutively, whether they are signed by the president, or passed over a presidential veto. The first to be enacted was PL 104–1, the second PL 104–2, and so forth. To illustrate with a famous special education law, what is now known as Part B of the IDEA was first enacted in PL 94–142. It was the 142nd law passed by the 94th Congress, which served between January 1975 and November 1976.

Once enacted, laws must be interpreted by the executive branch agency with jurisdiction. For legislation related to education, the U.S. Department of Education writes *regulations,* or rules, that explain and interpret the laws. These regulations have the force of law. They are codified into a set of regulations, the *Code of Federal Regulations* (CFR). With respect to special education, the rules are embodied in Title 34 of the CFR. The IDEA, for example, is found in 34 CFR 300, 301, and 303; elementary and secondary

Year	Federal Law	Highlights
1965	PL 89–10	First federal grants for elementary and secondary education
1965	PL 89–313	Federal funds for children with disabilities
1968	PL 90–538	Created HCEEP demonstration projects
1970	PL 91–230	Education of the Handicapped Act (EHA)
1974	PL 93–380	EHA amendments requiring states to serve children with disabilities
1975	PL 94–142	Education for All Handicapped Children Act
1983	PL 98–199	State planning grants for early childhood special education
1986	PL 99–457	Required early intervention and preschool special education
1990	PL 101–476	The IDEA
1991	PL 102–52	Extends early childhood deadlines
1991	PL 102–119	Seamless services in Part B and Part H
1997	PL 105–17	Part H becomes Part C
2002	PL 107–110	No Child Left Behind (NCLB)
2004	PL 108–446	Aligns the IDEA with NCLB

FIGURE 4–1 Laws

special education in 34 CFR 300; the Section 619 Preschool Grants Program in 34 CFR 301; and the Part C early intervention program in 34 CFR 303. Copies may be found in many public libraries.

To help the reader through the sections that follow, Figure 4–1 presents a brief summary of the history of what is now the IDEA.

BEGINNINGS

Early intervention and special education, as authorized by the IDEA, trace their beginnings back some 50 years. During the early years, three laws in particular stand out as benchmarks in the development of what eventually became the mandate for services from birth to five. PL 89–313 is one; this 1965 amendment to the Elementary and Secondary Education Act (ESEA) offered federal funds the states could use on behalf of children with disabilities in the birth-to-five age range (as well as older children and youth). In 1994, it was merged into the IDEA, and it no longer exists as a separate law. In 1968, PL 90–538 launched what was then called the Handicapped Children's Early Education Program (HCEEP). HCEEP funded a network of demonstration projects serving young children with disabilities. The ESEA amendments of 1970, PL 91–230, featured the Education of the Handicapped Act (EHA), which offered federal funds to the states for serving children with disabilities.

The 1965 ESEA, PL 89–10, broke new ground by offering federal funds to assist states to improve elementary and secondary education. Prior to that time, the entire burden of financing public education had been borne by state and local governments.

Once PL 89–10 established the precedent for federal involvement in education, Congress wasted little time expanding the federal role. Throughout the balance of the decade, it amended the ESEA each year except 1969. Such rapid-fire amendments are highly unusual. In fact, just eight months after passing PL 89–10, Congress passed the ESEA amendments of 1965, PL 89–313, which provided federal grants designed to supplement state efforts on behalf of disadvantaged children in low-income areas. That law contained a program to help states pay for state-operated or state-supported programs for children and youth with disabilities. Also known as Chapter 1 of the Education Consolidation and Improvement Act (ECIA), this program supplemented state efforts on behalf of students with disabilities from birth to age 21 inclusive, often in institutions (e.g., state schools for children who are blind). The federal funds could be used to supplement a child's special education program, including instruction, physical education, mobility training, prevocational and vocational training, and purchase of equipment (PL 101–501, 20 USC 2791 et seq.).

It is difficult to overstate the role PL 89–313 played in the history of special education, despite the fact that this law did not require states to serve children and youth with disabilities. Although strictly a discretionary program that offered supplemental funding in support of whatever states wanted to do, the importance of PL 89–313 was manifold. First, it provided federal funds to expand and improve state-run programs serving children and youth with disabilities. Second, it authorized services for children in the birth-to-five age range; even the IDEA did not do that until many years later. Third, it offered funds for special education that were more generous, on a per capita basis, than those later appropriated pursuant to the IDEA. Congress justified the funding difference by pointing out that PL 89–313 monies were used at state residential and other separate schools, which have higher costs per student than do most local public schools. By the 1992–1993 school year, however, PL 89–313 provided just $9 more per child served than did the IDEA (McGivern, 1993).

PL 89–313 became increasingly controversial in the early 1990s. The program provided funds that states could use in state-operated or state-supported schools and other facilities, usually separate residential or day schools. Advocates of inclusion complained that PL 89–313 was in effect encouraging states to place children with disabilities into separate or segregated programs. Partly in response to these concerns, Congress in the 1980s and early 1990s permitted the states to use PL 89–313 monies to facilitate movement of children and youth with disabilities from state-operated or state-supported programs to local public school programs.

HCEEP: PLANTING THE SEEDS

In 1968, the HCEEP, PL 90–538, funded experimental programs in preschool education and early intervention for children with disabilities. The act created the HCEEP, the first federal special education program designed *exclusively* for young children with disabilities. (PL 89–313 authorized services for children and youth with disabilities from birth to age 21.) During 1969 and 1970, the federal government funded 24 HCEEP demonstration projects. Taken together with additional HCEEP projects funded over the next 15 years, these "model" projects showcased innovative ways of serving birth to five-year-old infants, toddlers, and young children with disabilities. Later known as **Early Education Program for Children with Disabilities (EEPCD)** projects, these efforts proved to be instrumental in leading to the eventual federal mandates to serve preschool-age children with disabilities.

Early Education Program for Children with Disabilities (EEPCD)

is the federal grant program providing discretionary support for "model" ECSE programs. EEPCD was formerly called the Handicapped Children's Early Education Program (HCEEP).

Congress's intent with HCEEP may be illustrated by citing remarks made by members of Congress in 1968 to explain why they launched the program. Commented Congressman William Dent of Pennsylvania, "[T]he legislation will lay the foundation for any future programs meeting the needs of [preschool-aged] children [with disabilities] by providing demonstrations of successful approaches to the problem." Added Representative William Ayers of Ohio, "Our task now is to find how the knowledge gained from research can be put into practice" (cited in Weintraub, 1989, p. 19). Clearly, the congressional intent was to plant seeds—to support a variety of experimental, demonstration projects that would find ways to help young children with disabilities, disseminate the knowledge they gain in those projects, and train professionals in techniques that help young children.

Between 1968 and 1975, exciting work was done in several dozen HCEEP projects. The initial demonstration projects not only provided innovative services for very young children with disabilities but did so well enough to secure state, county, and local funding to continue their work after the federal funds ran out. In time, the HCEEP projects came to be known as the *First Chance network.* In 1973, state planning efforts were begun to supplement the local demonstration projects. More than 25 states participated in these early state planning efforts (Trohanis, 1989, pp. 54 and 59). By 1975, when Congress was considering what became PL 94–142, an impressive array of evidence had accumulated showing that large numbers of very young children with disabilities needed and benefited from early intervention and preschool special education services. The evidence was sufficient to convince the U.S. House of Representatives to include services for three- to five-year-olds as part of HR 7217 in 1975, before yielding to the Senate's preference to limit such services to those states that provided services for preschoolers without disabilities (Weintraub, 1986, p. 91). Thus, mandates for preschool services were left out of what became PL 94–142.

From 1976 to 1984, the HCEEP program continued to develop model projects serving very young children with disabilities. The projects also offered technical assistance to state and local education agencies interested in inaugurating preschool programs, as well as to local and private early intervention programs. State implementation grants (SIGs) were funded beginning in 1976 to build public awareness of, and support for, preschool services. By 1984, 46 states and other jurisdictions (e.g., the District of Columbia) had used SIGs. In 1983, building on this record of activity, PL 98–199 authorized early childhood state plan programs in HCEEP. The program began in 1984. Just two years later, PL 99–457 created the Part H early intervention program and expanded the Section 619 preschool program into what were effectively national mandates to serve birth-to-five children with disabilities. The mandates emerged from the record—at that time 18 years long—that HCEEP had created in discretionary grant programs (Trohanis, 1989, pp. 59–60; see also Hebbeler, Smith, & Black, 1991, for an excellent summary of the legislative and administrative history of the HCEEP). PL 105–17 changed Part H to Part C in 1997.

EDUCATION OF THE HANDICAPPED ACT

In 1970, the ESEA amendments of 1970, PL 91–230, included the EHA and HCEEP. Both focused on the special needs of children and youth with disabilities. They were discretionary, not mandatory—encouraging but not requiring services for children with disabilities.

The EHA authorized grants to assist states "in the initiation, expansion, and improvement of programs and projects for the education of handicapped children at the preschool, elementary school, and secondary school level." Section 611 of the EHA was discretionary, as were all other programs in the law, but the authority to provide financial assistance for preschool education was noteworthy. The word *preschool* was interpreted broadly, allowing states to use Section 611 funds to identify and serve infants and toddlers under age three with disabilities as well as children in the three-to-five age range.

The Education Act amendments of 1974, PL 93–380, included as Title VI the EHA amendments of 1974. These EHA amendments for the first time *required* the states to pass state laws setting timetables during which they would move to a full services approach, under which all school-age children with disabilities would receive a public education. The states had to comply with these requirements in return for receiving greatly expanded federal grants in support of preschool, elementary, and secondary education for students with disabilities. State plans and timetables for eventually serving all children with disabilities were to be submitted to the federal government no later than August 21, 1974.

PL 93–380 is notable as well for the Family Education Rights and Privacy Act (FERPA). Another title within the act, FERPA gave parents of school-age students the right to examine records kept in students' personal files. Parents and eligible students are entitled to review and copy educational records—and to have those records explained to them by school officials. Where records contain information parents and/or eligible students believe to be erroneous or misleading, the law grants parents and students the right to request that records be changed.

The lasting importance of PL 93–380 is that it signaled what was soon to come: the landmark PL 94–142.

EDUCATION FOR ALL HANDICAPPED CHILDREN ACT

On November 29, 1975, President Gerald Ford signed into law the Education for All Handicapped Children Act (EAHCA), PL 94–142. Only seven senators and seven representatives voted against the bill after a House-Senate conference committee presented it to them. PL 94–142 was recognized from the beginning as landmark legislation (see, e.g., Abeson & Zettel, 1977; Ballard & Zettel, 1977). It represented, in Abeson and Zettel's words, "the end of the quiet revolution" in special education because it marked the shift from isolated and scattered local advocacy efforts to a nationwide commitment to full equality under the law for all school-age children and youth with disabilities. PL 94–142 contained, in Part B, a mandate to serve *all* school-age children and youth with disabilities, as of September 1, 1978. That mandate is now permanent (Harkin, 1989).

With respect to children with disabilities under age six, however, PL 94–142 holds a more modest place in history. Only states that provided public education for children aged three to five were required (as of September 1, 1980) to offer a free, appropriate public education to children with disabilities in that age range. The extension of PL 94–142's mandate to all children under school age in all states did not occur until 11 years later. So-called birth-mandate states (states that had state laws requiring the delivery of services to children with disabilities from birth) could and did use Part B funds to serve infants and toddlers. The U.S. Department of Education allowed such uses, but it forbade states from counting the infants and toddlers for purposes of the Part B child count (Bellamy, 1987).

From 1975 to 1986, states focused on complying with PL 94–142's mandate that all *school-age* children and youth with disabilities receive a free, appropriate public education. For the states, this was a massive undertaking. One unfortunate side effect was to relegate to lesser importance efforts to help infants, toddlers, and preschool-age children with disabilities. However, PL 94–142 did establish the principle of federal mandates in services for children with disabilities, a precedent that weighed heavily with Congress as it conducted oversight on and amended PL 94–142 in the years to come; it was only a matter of time before the mandate would be extended down to three and even to birth.

The 1975 act expanded Part B into a multibillion-dollar federal program assisting state and local education agencies to guarantee a free, appropriate public education for all school-age children and youth, no matter how severely disabled. Part B made it illegal for any public education agency to deny a free public education to any 6- to 18-year-old child or youth with a disability as of September 1, 1978.

Children aged 3 to 5 (and youth aged 18 to 21) were not included under Part B unless states already provided public services for nondisabled children and youth in those age ranges, in which case they were to begin serving children aged 3 to 5 and youth aged 18 to 21 with disabilities as of September 1, 1980. However, PL 94–142 did require states to *identify and evaluate* the needs of children with disabilities in the birth-to-5 age range. In addition, Part C, one of the "discretionary" components of PL 94–142, created a Preschool Incentive Grant Program. This program offered states supplementary funding (in addition to the formula grants they received under Part B) to help reimburse them for serving three- to five-year-old children with disabilities. States had to be serving children in that age range in order to receive incentive grant awards. Congress authorized up to $300 per child served; actual appropriations, however, were as little as $100 per child (Hebbeler et al., 1991). According to the U.S. Department of Education, states used these incentive grant funds to pay for development of interagency agreements, parent and professional training, and technical assistance to local providers, as well as for direct services to young children with disabilities (U.S. Department of Education, 1984; Hebbeler et al., 1991).

Because PL 94–142 demanded such revolutionary changes by state and local education agencies, Congress focused its energies over the next several years on oversight and monitoring rather than new lawmaking. By 1983, however, Congress was ready to amend the law.

THE 1983 AMENDMENTS

Evidence had been accumulating since 1977 that states and communities throughout the nation were beginning to serve infants and toddlers with disabilities. As early as 1979, almost half of the nation's 16,000 school districts reported at least some services for at least some preschoolers with disabilities. Three years later, in 1982, studies suggested that virtually all school districts had begun serving some young children with disabilities. It was a situation strikingly similar to that prevailing in the early 1970s with respect to school-age children: Some programs were serving some children—but not all children, and not always appropriately. The stage seemed set for Congress to take another step forward. On December 2, 1983, it did.

The 1983 amendments, PL 98–199, were a breakthrough for services to young children with disabilities. For the first time, Congress moved beyond supporting isolated, local programs and toward helping states coordinate services on a statewide basis. The law offered grants to states for the purpose of planning services for children under six years of age with disabilities. These state plan grants were noncompetitive awards. That also was new; prior grants had been competitive, with only some of those states applying receiving awards. PL 98–199 used a broad brush in describing the purpose of the state plan grants. The program was for "planning, developing, and implementing a comprehensive service delivery system for the provision of special education and related services to handicapped children birth through five years of age" (IDEA, Section 623[b]; Hebbeler et al., 1991). These amendments also provided significantly more funds than had been authorized in prior years for the Preschool Incentive Grant Program. For the first time, the law allowed federal funds for state grants to be used not only for three- to five-year-olds but also for children from birth to age three. (The 1986 amendments repealed this program, including the extension of services down to birth, and replaced it with a new Preschool Grants Program for children from three to five.) The message to states from PL 98–199's grants to develop service delivery systems for children under six was unmistakable: Congress was moving toward a mandate for the preschool-age population, and states should begin preparing to accept that coming mandate.

The HCEEP, now known as EEPCD, begun in 1968, continued under PL 98–199. This Part C program remained discretionary, but it was playing an increasingly important role. These model programs were demonstrating *how* preschool-age children with disabilities could be helped. The programs were providing an impressive body of evidence that early intervention and preschool special education could be effective—both for the children and their families. A rich variety of approaches was being demonstrated. Of 21 model programs examined by White, Mastropieri, and Casto (1984), for example, 7 were home-based programs, in which staff visited families in their homes; 8 were center-based programs, in which families came to centers specially equipped for young children with disabilities; and 6 used various combinations of home- and center-based approaches. Most involved parents in at least some decision making, and a few demonstrated a family-centered approach featuring strong parental decision making. Some provided services for 1 or 2 hours weekly, others for as many as 15 hours weekly, for each child served. Despite these differences, the model programs themselves—and outside evaluators—insisted that the services were both effective and cost-effective (for an excellent review, see Hebbeler et al., 1991).

THE 1986 AMENDMENTS

On October 8, 1986, Congress took the next step: *mandates* for both preschool special education and early intervention. One triggering event was the publication of the 1985 U.S. Department of Education's *Seventh Annual Report to Congress on the Implementation of the Education of the Handicapped Act.* Section 618 of the IDEA, in Part B, requires the department to issue this report each year. The *Seventh Annual Report* summarized work done by the HCEEP (now EEPCD) model projects and evaluations of their progress, as well as other research and demonstration projects in the area of services for preschool-age children. Robert Silverstein, who at the time was staff counsel for the House authorizing subcommittee, remembers one paragraph in particular that struck him and others on Capitol Hill as significant, because it suggested that the time had come to take yet more steps in early childhood services:

> Studies of the effectiveness of preschool education for the handicapped have demonstrated beyond doubt the economic and educational benefits of programs for young handicapped children. In addition, the studies have shown that the earlier intervention is started, the greater is the ultimate dollar savings and the higher is the rate of educational attainment by these handicapped children. (U.S. Department of Education, 1985; quoted in Silverstein, 1989, p. A2)

Silverstein remembers being surprised by the fact that this statement was made in an official report transmitted to Congress by the Reagan administration. He privately doubted that Reagan's team would overstate the benefits of federal social programming, since the Reagan administration was well known to oppose, on principle and with vigor, virtually any expansion of social service programs. In fact, the *Seventh Annual Report* exaggerated what had been learned but only because the initial researchers did too. Studies conducted since 1986 have helped us understand that the early intervention and preschool special education work that had been done by 1986 had not in fact "demonstrated beyond doubt" that these programs produced both educational and economic benefits (see, e.g., Innocenti & White, 1993). But much truth remains, even today, in what the *Seventh Annual Report* observed, that is, that early intervention and preschool special education can in fact help many young children with disabilities and their families.

In 1986, Congress was also concerned that the Preschool Incentive Grants and the state plan grants had not yet produced a real change in services for children with disabilities in the birth-to-five age range. The number of children under six with disabilities being served seemed to have plateaued at about 100,000 below the estimated number of children who needed services (Silverstein, 1989, p. A3). In addition, Congress responded, as it often does, to its own internal imperatives. The Gramm-Rudman-Hollings deficit reduction package was just beginning to take effect in 1986, and members of both the Senate and the House were conscious that they had a better chance to do something in ECSE for young children with disabilities if they acted in that year rather than a later year. In 1986, Senator Lowell Weicker (R-Conn.), a powerful, vocal advocate for people with disabilities, was chairman of both the authorizing and the appropriations subcommittees with jurisdiction over special education. Weicker was thus in a position to move legislation, and he very much wanted to authorize greatly expanded early intervention and preschool special education services (Silverstein, 1989, p. A2).

By 1986, evidence was mounting that the HCEEP demonstration programs and the 1983 state grant awards were raising awareness throughout the nation about early intervention and preschool special education services for young children with disabilities. States were beginning to recognize the value of these services. To illustrate, Alicia Smith, representing the National Governors Association, testified before the House in 1986: "[I]f you do a quick check of the state-of-the-state addresses around the country this past year, you will find that there are only four governors who didn't mention the word 'prevention' and/or 'early intervention'" (Smith, 1986, p. 123).

Responding to these diverse developments, Congress created an entirely new early intervention program and greatly expanded the Part B (Section 619) Preschool Grants Program. PL 99–457, the 1986 EHA amendments, gave the states a phase-in period, during which they could receive federal funds for planning services to infants and toddlers from birth to two and children from three to five with disabilities. (States could not use Section 619 funds to *serve* infants and toddlers under age three, but they could use those monies to *plan* statewide systems for the under-six population, including infants and toddlers from birth to two.) By the end of the planning period, states were required, as a condition of receiving further federal financial support, to be providing universally available services for *all* children in those age ranges.

PL 99–457 was landmark legislation, second only to PL 94–142 in its impact on services for children with disabilities. It gave states five years to begin zero-reject early intervention and preschool special education programs. Funding for the Section 619 preschool program for three- to five-year-old children with disabilities was vastly increased. From a 1986 level of $28 million, appropriations (actual dollars provided to states, not just authorization ceilings) leaped to $180 million (a sixfold increase) in 1987, to $201 million in 1988, and $247 million in 1989. In just three years, funding had grown by a factor of nine—an astonishing pace for those deficit-plagued years (Silverstein, 1989, p. A3).

Funding for the new Part H program on early intervention was much more modest. That was deliberate on the part of Congress. The intent in Part H was not to fully fund services but rather to provide "glue money" enabling states to pull together resources from many different sources. Explained Silverstein (1989), "These are funds that will facilitate cooperation and coordination. Federal money was never intended to be the primary funding source for direct services to infants and toddlers" (p. A4). What was then Part H is now Part C.

The actual structure of PL 99–457 technically did not mandate services for preschool-age children with disabilities. Rather, Congress authorized (and appropriated) funds that states could elect to accept. If a state accepted those monies, the state would be obligated to comply with the legislative "strings" accompanying the funds. Those strings required zero-reject, appropriate services for all infants, toddlers, and preschool-age children with disabilities no later than a state's fifth year of participation in the programs. Because all states were already committed to obeying the requirements of Part B, their participation in the Section 619 program was all but guaranteed (because that section is in Part B).

In Section 619, the legislation stated that the secretary of education "shall make a grant to any State which" has a state policy guaranteeing a free, appropriate public education to all eligible children aged 3 to 18, has a state plan approved by the secretary, and provides special education and related services for preschool-age children with disabilities. Nothing in Section 619 required zero-reject, full-service programs until 1991. The federal fiscal year (FY) begins on October 1 and ends on September 30. Thus, FY 1991 concluded on September 30, 1991. In education, federal programs are **forward funded;** that is, they give states and local school districts advance notice of exactly the amount they will have on hand when school begins in September. PL 99–457 authorized the secretary to make state grants in FY 1991 and in subsequent fiscal years *only* to a state that

Forward funded

refers to the fact that education programs authorized by federal laws are funded during any given federal fiscal year for the following fiscal year. The intent is to give states and schools notice of funds availability well in advance of the start of a school year.

> *has a state plan approved under section 613 which includes policies and procedures that assure the availability under the state law and practice of such state of a free appropriate public education for all children with disabilities aged three to five, inclusive.* (Section 619)

To qualify for the funds made available July 1, 1991, states had to have enacted zero-reject, free, appropriate preschool education laws. This structure—offering funds for four years without mandating zero-reject services but requiring such universal service as a condition for receiving monies in the fifth and subsequent years—is the vehicle through which Congress mandated full services for preschool-age children with disabilities. The structure was necessary because the Fourteenth Amendment equal protection clause did not apply in preschool education, which was not state-mandated for young children, whether disabled or nondisabled.

INDIVIDUALS WITH DISABILITIES EDUCATION ACT

In 1990, PL 101–476 renamed the foundation legislation, from the *Education of the Handicapped Act (EHA)* to the *Individuals with Disabilities Education Act (IDEA)*. Throughout the act, signed into law on October 30, 1990, the term *handicapped children* was replaced by *children with disabilities.* (The term *disability* had been adopted in the Technology-Related Assistance for Individuals with Disabilities Act [TRAIDA], PL 100–407, in 1988; all subsequent federal laws on disability have used the term *disability* rather than *handicapped.*) The IDEA also features people-first language (*children with* . . . , *youth having* . . . , etc.), in another effort to demonstrate greater sensitivity.

PL 101–476 added two new categories to the statutory definition of children with disabilities: children with autism and children with traumatic brain injuries. The two new labels are now recognized as disabilities for the purposes of Part B, including preschool Section 619 services. The law also expanded the scope of related services to encompass rehabilitation counseling and social work services.

PL 102–52

Congress became concerned early in 1991 that many states were not on target to meet the fall 1991 deadline for providing full services to preschool-age children. The concern was magnified by Congress's realization that many state fiscal years begin in July; thus, action had to be taken prior to that. PL 102–52 was signed into law in June 1991. To help states that otherwise might have been forced to drop out of the Part H program, the law gave them one or, in some cases, two additional years to meet all "year 5" requirements. The funding formula was designed to assist those states that were late without penalizing states that were on target. In no event, however, could the full-service mandate be postponed beyond the end of 1993. (Federal education programs are forward funded, so states could use that money until late 1994.) The law clearly stated that after a maximum of two years of extended participation, states were eligible for Part H funds only if they had in effect a statewide system of early intervention services for all eligible infants and toddlers.

1991 IDEA AMENDMENTS

In PL 102–119, Congress acted to provide a seamless transition between Part H and Part B. For the first time, states were expressly permitted to use Part H funds for toddlers past the age of three, if doing so would facilitate their transition either to preschool Part B programs or to other community service programs. In addition, states were—again for the first time—allowed to use Part B monies to serve toddlers under the age of three, whether or not those toddlers were in Part H (now Part C) programs. These statutory changes responded to state concerns about what to do when a child turned three. The U.S. Department of Education had told them (Schrag, 1990) that children with disabilities become eligible for Section 619 preschool Part B services on their third birthday but that states enjoyed broad discretion in deciding how to handle service provision, as long as no three-year-olds were denied services.

The legislation obligates states to plan the transitions occurring at or about age three, so as to effect a smooth transition, that is, a seamless one. Among other things, appropriate information may be sent by Part C service providers, with parental permission, to the local education agency and/or other community-based service providers, who will begin helping the child and the family. The law requires that both the sending and the receiving agency participate in the transition planning with the parents (Rosenkoetter, 1992).

The 1991 amendments further strengthened the roles of parents and families under Part C. The law now clearly states that parents may decline any Part C–related service without jeopardizing their rights to other services. Parents have the right to accede to or decline the transmission of personally identifiable information about their infant or toddler from one agency to another. The assessment of family resources, priorities, and concerns—which is part of the IFSP process—is to be family-directed. That is, families have the right to control what assessments are done, how the assessment data are used, and even whether a family assessment is done at all. The 1991 amendments added a preference that infants and toddlers be served in natural environments. Because parents know their infants or toddlers much better than do program personnel, this provision gives parents additional ammunition to ensure that their children are served in environments, including the home and community facilities, that the family finds comfortable and convenient.

PL 102–119 also gave states the right, at their discretion, to serve three- to five-year-old children who are developmentally delayed in preschool Part B programs. If states elect to do so, they may use the same five categories of development (cognitive, physical, communication, adaptive, and social or emotional) as are used under Part C. The House report makes clear that Congress did not intend to expand the number of children eligible for Section 619 services, or to broaden eligibility criteria, but rather to grant states greater flexibility. Among other things, Congress recognized the potential danger of labeling very young children with stigmatizing names; adoption of the kinds of broad categories used in Part C might alleviate some of that stigma (U.S. Congress, 1991, p. 4).

The 1991 amendments also focused on the special needs of traditionally underserved populations. Section 671(a) of the IDEA added a new finding for what is now Part C:

> *[T]o enhance the capacity of state and local agencies and service providers to identify, evaluate, and meet the needs of historically underrepresented populations, particularly minority, low-income, inner-city, and rural populations.*

In Section 678(b)(7), the 1991 amendments further required states to provide, beginning in FY 1992, satisfactory assurance that minority, rural, and low-income families have

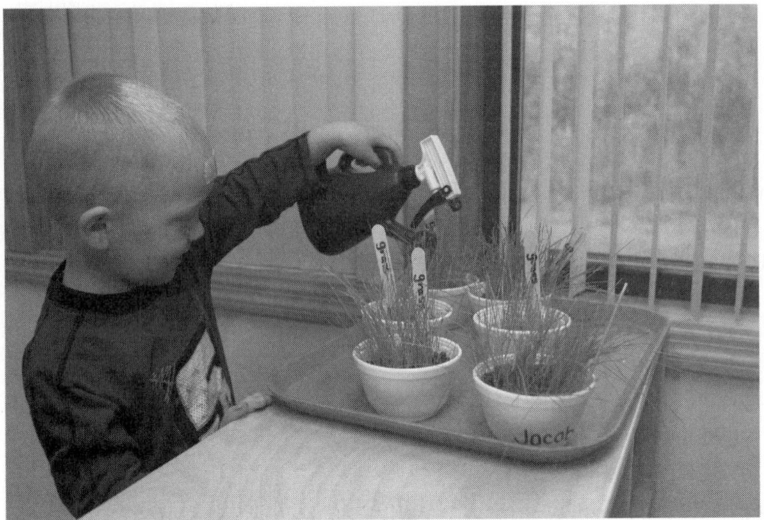

IDEA 2004 and the No Child Left Behind Act emphasize academics, including basic science.

access to "culturally competent services within their local areas" and that such families will have "meaningful involvement" in the state's implementation of Part H. The House report added, "When implementing Part H of IDEA, particular attention must be given to the inclusion and participation of minority and low-income individuals in urban as well as rural areas across the country" (U.S. Congress, 1991, p. 11). Finally, PL 102–119 amended Section 623, which authorizes the EEPCD to stimulate such demonstration programs to serve more low-income, minority, rural, and other underserved populations and to serve at-risk children.

THE IDEA AMENDMENTS OF 1997

In PL 105–17, the IDEA Amendments of 1997, Congress rearranged some of the titles in the law. Parts A and B were unaffected. Part H, on early intervention, became Part C. The discretionary titles of the act—Parts C, D, E, F, and G—were combined into one discretionary title, which was named Part D.

The 1997 amendments allowed the states to continue using the term *developmentally delayed* in lieu of disability labels until a child turned 10 years of age. Previously, a diagnostic label such as *mentally retarded* or *learning disabled* was required when a child turned six years of age. Also new in 1997 was the option of parents to use mediation services rather than litigation to resolve disputes with public agencies.

PL 105–17 also changed the funding formula for Part B, including Section 619 (preschool services). Previously, states received federal funds based strictly upon state population of children aged three-to-five inclusive. The new law continued to use that basis for funding but only up to the amount allocated during FY 1997 (October 1, 1996, to September 30, 1997). Any additional funds are to be awarded based on state population (85 percent) and childhood poverty (15 percent). The intent of the change is to provide relatively more funding to states having large numbers of poor children, in recognition of the fact that childhood disability and poverty are closely linked.

NO CHILD LEFT BEHIND

No Child Left Behind Act of 2001.

Signed into law in early 2002, this federal law requires annual assessment of children's performance and adequate yearly progress by public schools. The intent is a popular one (raise academic standards), but the intrusive federal presence in what had been local and state control has proven to be controversial.

In January 2002, President George W. Bush signed the **No Child Left Behind Act of 2001** (PL 107–110). This law is another amendment of ESEA. Its key features are several. First, NCLB requires testing of children in grades 3 through 8, and once during the high school years, in math, language arts, and science. Second, the act calls for schools and states to report each year on the scores achieved in those tests by children who are at risk of being "left behind," notably those with disabilities, children from low-income families, English Language Learners, and children of ethnic and/or racial minority groups. Those scores are to be made public. Schools may be sanctioned, and, in extreme cases, funding may be withdrawn from them, if they fail to show adequate yearly progress (AYP) in improving the academic performance of *each* of these groups of children. NCLB also sets a standard of "highly qualified" for teachers, including special educators. Briefly, a highly qualified teacher is state-certified in his or her specialty and holds at least a bachelor's degree.

For special educators, NCLB has led to major changes. First, because virtually all children with disabilities must take high-stakes tests, NCLB has focused educator attention on academic instruction, especially in language arts, math, and science. This is a seismic shift. Prior to NCLB, special educators had considered their jobs to be to respond to each of a child's unique needs in the five domains of development (adaptive, cognitive, communication, physical, and social or emotional). Suddenly, because of NCLB, much greater emphasis had to be accorded to academic instruction (i.e., to the cognitive domain of development). Second, because preparation for taking the high-stakes tests typically is given in general, but not in special, education classrooms, the act's emphasis on assessment has spurred ever-greater inclusion of students with disabilities into general classrooms.

IDEA 2004

The most recent amendment to the Individuals with Disabilities Education Act was completed in December 2004. The amendments in PL 108–446 echo the NCLB insistence that virtually all students with disabilities take, and perform well on, high-stakes tests. IDEA 2004 also repeats NCLB's requirement that special educators become highly qualified. In a third step to bring the IDEA and NCLB closer together, IDEA 2004 authorizes what it calls "early intervening services." These are support services that the IDEA pays for which are offered to students *without* disabilities, with the intent of giving them the additional assistance they need to remain in general education. In other words, early intervening services aim to prevent referrals to special education.

Other changes made in IDEA 2004 further some of the goals of earlier amendments to the IDEA. Thus, the new law permits states to use IDEA Part C funds to support the education of young children until they enter kindergarten or even first grade. This language furthers the longtime goal of the IDEA to support seamless services—that is, services with no breaks. IDEA 2004 explicitly grants to families of children with disabilities the right to decline any and all services. Previously, the IDEA had clearly reserved that "no thanks" privilege for families of infants or toddlers (i.e., under Part C but not Part B of the act). See Figure 4–2 for a summary of changes made by PL 108–446.

THE IDEA TODAY AND TOMORROW

The IDEA guides all of us who work with young children with disabilities or delays in development. It provides very specific instructions that affect virtually everything early intervention, preschool, and primary-grade programs serving children with disabilities do and how they do those things. For these reasons, a familiarity with the law is important for interventionists and special educators. Copies of the latest IDEA amendments are available in most public libraries. Readers may also get copies by writing to their U.S. senators (Washington, DC 20510) or to their U.S. representative (Washington, DC 20515). Following is a road map to reading the IDEA.

IEPs. IDEA 2004 changes the first item in IEPs to refer to "academic and functional" performance. Prior to PL 108–446, it called for IEP teams to describe "educational" performance. The change helps align the IDEA with NCLB.

In addition, IEPs no longer need to include short-term objectives or benchmarks, *except* for children with severe disabilities who are educated using alternative curricula. How an adolescent or adult functions is important for eligibility under the Americans with Disabilities Act and Section 504.

Homeless Children. School districts may not refuse to serve children with disabilities just because these children do not have a permanent domicile within the district.

Early Intervening Services. PL 108–446 encourages what formerly were called "prereferral services" for students *not* identified as children with disabilities. IDEA funds may be used to help these children, especially in K–3. The goal is to assist them in general (regular) education so that referral to special education is not necessary.

Note that this is to be distinguished from the similarly worded "early intervention services," which are those services provided to infants and toddlers with disabilities under Part C of the IDEA.

Related Services. School nurse services and sign language and other interpreting services for deaf and hard of hearing students were added as "related services."

Learning Disabilities. IDEA 2004 allows school districts to no longer use a "discrepancy" in establishing eligibility for the IDEA in the specific learning disabilities (SLD) category. Prior to 2005–2006, federal rules had required that educators document the existence of a discrepancy between ability and achievement before they could give the SLD label to a child.

In addition, PL 108–446 encourages schools to use "response to intervention" (RTI) in identifying children with SLD. One-on-one instruction is offered to children. If they respond quickly and significantly to this intervention, it is likely that their previous difficulties may be attributed to lack of appropriate instruction and not to SLD. This further aligns IDEA with NCLB.

Both are permissions, not mandates. Schools may continue to use discrepancies and may decline to use RTI in classifying children as having SLDs.

Scientifically Based Methods. IDEA 2004 adopts the NCLB emphasis on "scientifically based" interventions. Educators are to use approaches that have research behind them, particularly peer-reviewed quantitative studies of high quality.

Reducing Overidentification and Overreferral. School districts with a history of falsely identifying children from ethnic/racial minority groups as "children with disabilities" are required to take corrective action.

Medications. Educators may not require children to be on medication (e.g., Ritalin).

No Means No. Under PL 108–446, if a family refuses special education, the school district may not contest the family's decision.

Due Process. Families of children with disabilities who invoke procedural safeguards in mounting frivolous challenges to schools may disqualify themselves from court-awarded attorneys' fees. IDEA 2004 also makes explicit the disallowance of any court-awarded attorneys' fees for routine IEP team meetings and other non-due-process proceedings.

FIGURE 4–2 IDEA 2004 changes.

The IDEA, opens with *Part A—General Provisions.* Contained here is a statement of findings, which offers a "general welfare" justification for federal action in education and child care. Generally, this statement indicts the states for not meeting the needs of these children. Also in Part A are the IDEA's four main purposes:

1. To guarantee a free, appropriate public education for children with disabilities; to provide funds to states so as to assist them in offering such an education; and to provide due-process rights for children with disabilities and their parents
2. To offer funds to states to implement Part C early intervention services

3. To support research, demonstration, and training programs to improve results in special education and early intervention

4. To monitor the states as they carry out their Part B (preschool) and Part C (early intervention) responsibilities under the law

Part A continues by offering definitions of key terms. Notable here are very specific definitions for *children with disabilities* (who is eligible for Part B services) and for *special education* and *related services* (what kind of help is authorized to be provided under Part B). The only disability that is defined here is *specific learning disability;* all other disabilities included in the definition of *children with disabilities* are defined in the regulations issued to carry out the IDEA by the U.S. Department of Education.

Part B—Assistance for Education of Children with Disabilities begins by outlining the formulas to be used in calculating how much financial assistance each state will get each year from the federal government. As noted earlier, this is a combination of state population and poverty. In Section 612, Part B explains what the states must promise to receive these funds. Notable among those are (1) that the state will guarantee a free, appropriate public education to all eligible children with disabilities, "including children with disabilities who have been suspended or expelled from school"; (2) that the state will ensure that each child with a disability receives an IEP; (3) that state and local education agencies will place children with disabilities in settings that also serve children without disabilities, to the extent that such placements do not compromise the right of children with disabilities to receive an appropriate education that meets their unique needs; (4) that the state will act to protect the due-process rights of children with disabilities and their parents; (5) that the state will take whatever steps are necessary to ensure an adequate supply of special educators and related services personnel; and (6) that the state will set "performance goals and indicators" for improving special education, particularly in the areas of districtwide assessments of academic performance, and for reducing dropout rates.

Part B continues, in Section 614, to explain how the federal government expects assessments of children with disabilities to be performed. Notable here is that if parents resist or even refuse to permit an evaluation, the local education agency must contest this parental preference (through mediation or litigation) because the agency is obligated by the IDEA to provide special education and related services to all eligible children with disabilities. This section also describes, in great detail, what is to go into each IEP.

In the next section, Section 615, the IDEA outlines the rights of children with disabilities and their parents and explains how parents may assert those rights, either through mediation or through litigation. Section 619 concludes Part B. It contains very little of substance, focusing almost exclusively upon funding formulas. However, because Section 619 is in Part B, the other sections of Part B (state assurances, assessments, due process, etc.) apply to preschool programs.

Part C—Infants and Toddlers with Disabilities opens with its own statement of findings and policy in Section 631. Notable here is the intent of the federal government to support state initiatives rather than dictate terms to the states. Definitions of key terms follow, including *infants and toddlers with disabilities* and *early intervention services.* Section 636 outlines the contents of IFSPs and explains who writes them. The rights of infants and toddlers and their parents are explained in Section 639.

Part D—National Activities to Improve Education of Children with Disabilities contains many of the discretionary programs previously authorized by Parts C, D, E, and F of the IDEA as it existed prior to PL 105–17. Notable here are grant programs to assist states in enhancing services to children with disabilities, training programs for professionals and parents, research and demonstration programs, and information and referral programs. Part D differs from Part B and Part C in that nothing in Part D is mandatory; all programs authorized in Part D are discretionary—states, not-for-profit organizations, and individuals may elect to participate or not to participate.

SUMMARY

This chapter has outlined the history and major provisions of the IDEA. It has been a long journey, spanning almost 50 years of legislation. Beginning with a network of local demonstration projects, the federal government demonstrated that early intervention and preschool special education for children with disabilities could make a difference in these young children's lives. By 1986, the evidence was strong enough for Congress to take the next step: creating mandates for universal service to under-six children with disabilities. The mandate for preschool special education took effect in 1991, on target with the original timetable, but some states needed one or two additional years to complete planning for services for infants and toddlers.

The IDEA provides vital rights to families and children. So do some other federal laws. We turn now to examining those rights.

KEY TERMS

Early Education Program for Children with Disabilities (EEPCD)

Education for All Handicapped Children Act

forward funded

No Child Left Behind Act of 2001

QUESTIONS FOR REFLECTION

1. What provisions of the U.S. Constitution forced Congress to *encourage* more than *require* ECSE services for children under six who have disabilities?
2. What was the significance of PL 89–313 during its *lifetime* (1965–1994)?
3. How did the Handicapped Children's Early Education Program (HCEEP), later known as the Early Education Program for Children with Disabilities (EEPCD), build a foundation for the eventual enactment of Part C?
4. What of significance was in the 1985 *Seventh Annual Report to Congress*?
5. Why was PL 99–457 "landmark legislation, second only to PL 94–142 in its impact"?
6. What two disabilities were added to the definition of *children with disabilities* in 1990?
7. What change was made in the 1991 amendments about services for children just turning three years of age?
8. The requirements imposed by No Child Left Behind, notably that children with disabilities take high-stakes tests, are controversial. After reading this chapter and using the Web to further your study of NCLB, what is your opinion about the benefits, versus the harm, of those requirements?

9. What advantages might accompany the decision to continue using *developmental delay* (instead of a disability label) as late as a child's ninth birthday? Can you think of any disadvantages?
10. Based on what you know now, why does the IDEA guarantee a free, appropriate public education even for children with disabilities who have been suspended or expelled from school?

PRACTICAL EXERCISES

1. Spend some time examining the text of IDEA 2004. You may find it at www.nectac.org. This site also offers some documents that help explain and interpret the law. Then visit the Web site of your state education department, to review your state's "me, too" law on special education. Do you notice any differences? States are required to enact "me, too" laws that mirror IDEA, but they are permitted to go beyond IDEA 2004. Does your state add important benefits or services for children with disabilities?
2. Go to the federal site for No Child Left Behind at www.nochildleftbehind.gov. This 2001 law is set to be reauthorized in 2007. It is widely described as the single-most controversial piece of federal education legislation. After reviewing postings at this site, enter the law's name into your favorite search engine. What are educators, parents, students, and others saying about NCLB? Why do you think it is so very controversial?

WEB SITES OF INTEREST

www.nochildleftbehind.gov Federal government site offering official information about the No Child Left Behind Act of 2001.

www.dec-sped.org Division for Early Childhood, Council for Exceptional Children—offers DEC's views on services for young children

www.ed.gov Office of Special Education Programs, U.S. Department of Education, Washington, D.C.—official site of the federal agency administering the IDEA

PRACTICAL EXERCISES

WEB SITES OF INTEREST

CHAPTER

Family Rights and Services

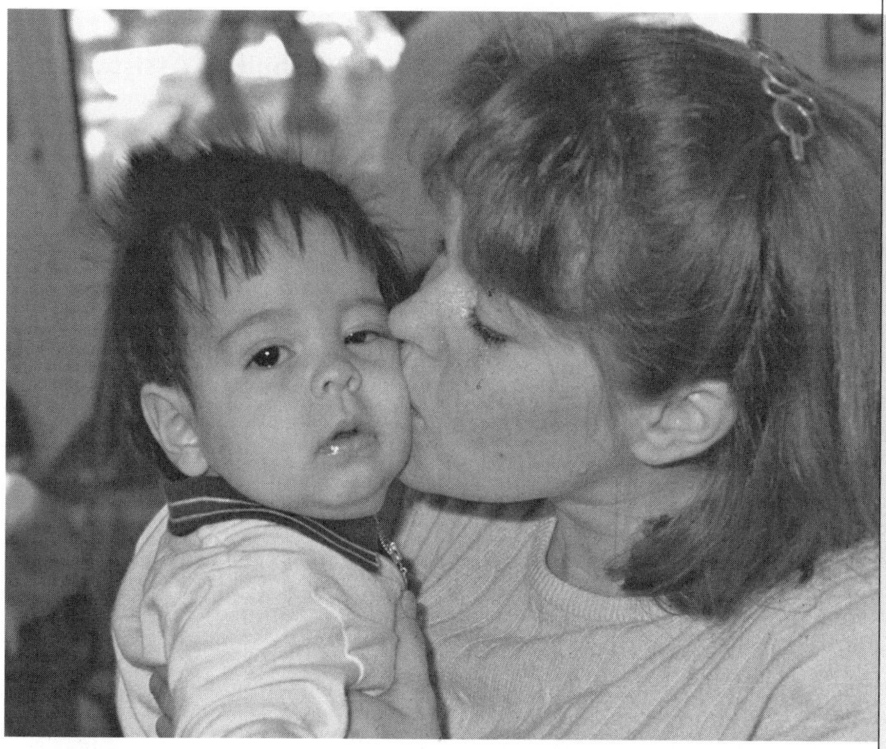

I sure wouldn't just sit there and let them tell me what they've done. I'd find out why did you do this, why is that, why do you want to do that? . . . Back then I let them tell me what they were going to do because I didn't even know I had rights. You know? Parents need to know they have rights! Speak up! . . . [Y]ou have a right to say what goes on in that child's life. Not them. They like to think they're the major authorities. They ain't. They can only tell you what they think would be best. (QUOTED IN MINKE & SCOTT, 1993, PP. 96–97; EMPHASIS IN ORIGINAL)

A child who clearly qualified for early intervention moved into a county in Minnesota. The parents were interested in providing their child some time in a typical setting with other children his age (twenty months) as he had no siblings. The county defined this setting as educational, the school district defined it as respite, and both agencies refused to provide the service. (BEHR, 1991, P. 33)

OBJECTIVES

After reading this chapter, you should be able to:

- Explain how Section 504 affects families and young children with disabilities.
- Describe how the Americans with Disabilities Act (ADA) also helps families.
- List what rights families enjoy under the IDEA.
- Describe what the one major difference is between IDEA Part C and IDEA Part B procedural safeguards.
- Describe what the Family Opportunity Act of 2005 says that may help families.

CHAPTER OUTLINE

- **OVERVIEW**
- **RIGHTS**
  - **Section 504**
  - **Americans with Disabilities Act**
  - **Procedural Safeguards**
    - *IDEA Part B*
    - *IDEA Part C*
    - *Discussion*
  - **In Brief**
    - *Fair Housing Amendments Act (FHAA)*
    - *Air Carriers Access Act*
    - *Television Decoder Circuitry Act*
    - *Telecommunications Act*
- **SERVICES**
  - **Supplemental Security Income**
    - *Significance of SSI*
    - *Definition*
  - **Medicaid**
    - *Significance of Medicaid*
    - *Covered Services*
    - *Family Opportunity Act*
    - *Early and Periodic Screening Diagnosis and Treatment (EPSDT)*
    - *State Children's Health Insurance Program (SCHIP)*
  - **Maternal and Child Health**
    - *Significance of MCH Block Grants*
  - **Respite Care**
    - *Significance of Respite Care*
  - **Developmental Disabilities Assistance and Bill of Rights Act**
    - *Definition*
    - *Significance of the DD Act*
  - **Head Start**
    - *Early Head Start*
    - *Significance of Head Start*
  - **Assistive Technology Act**

OVERVIEW

Children with disabilities and their parents enjoy extraordinary rights under the IDEA. Among them are the procedural safeguards in Part C and Part B. They enjoy other important rights, however, beyond the IDEA. This chapter examines the Americans with Disabilities Act (ADA) of 1990, one of the most significant civil rights measures ever enacted by the U.S. Congress. The ADA contains some far-reaching provisions that help young children and their families enjoy the full benefits of all a community has to offer them. The act also offers some surprising benefits for parents, who may be subjected to discrimination on the job or in other activities of daily life because of their association with a child who is disabled. The chapter also explores Section 504 of the 1973 Rehabilitation Act, a precursor to and supplement to the ADA.

As the chapter's opening quotation from Minke and Scott (1993) shows, many parents have grasped their new rights, understood them, and used them to their benefit and to the benefit of their children. Many have not, however. Accordingly, it is important that ECSE workers acquaint parents with the full range of rights—and support them in securing those rights. The material in this chapter may assist in that vital endeavor.

ECSE workers also need to familiarize themselves with—and tell parents about—services other than those authorized under the IDEA. Many families may qualify for these non-IDEA services. The need is particularly urgent for service coordinators. That is because the very nature of the service coordinator's job is to cut through red tape between agencies and secure services for the families of infants and toddlers with disabilities. This chapter concludes with thumbnail sketches of the most important of these other services.

RIGHTS

Families of infants, toddlers, preschoolers, and early-primary-age children with disabilities enjoy important civil rights. Some of these are granted by the IDEA itself. Other federal rights are accorded to families and/or to children by Section 504 of the Rehabilitation Act of 1973, by the Americans with Disabilities Act of 1990, and by a variety of less well-known federal laws.

SECTION 504

The IDEA provides rights, notably to early intervention, special education, and related services, for infants, toddlers, and young children with disabilities who are eligible under that law. Establishing eligibility for services under the IDEA is a two-step process. First, children must qualify as disabled. Under Part C, that process may be done by reference to an established condition or documentation of a developmental delay. If a state opts to serve at-risk infants and toddlers, eligibility is determined by state rules defining who is considered to be at risk. Under Part B, eligibility is by reference to one of the conditions listed in Section 602. States may, at their option, decide that preschool-age children who have developmental delays (as defined by the state) are also eligible for Section 619 preschool special education and related services. However, not all infants, toddlers, preschoolers, and school-age children qualifying under these initial steps are eligible for services. The second step is to establish that children from birth to five with disabilities *need* early intervention services (Part C) or special education and related services (Part B).

This raises some questions. What about infants, toddlers, and young children with disabilities who do not require such services? And what about infants, toddlers, and young children with disabilities who seek services not related to their disabilities? Recall that the IDEA authorizes special education and early intervention services involving instruction or therapy focusing on the disability. For many children, therefore, early intervention or preschool special education and related services will constitute only *some,* rather than all, of the services they need and desire (Ballard & Zettel, 1977).

Section 504

is a civil rights provision in the federal Rehabilitation Act. It prohibits any program receiving or benefiting from federal financial assistance from discriminating on the basis of disability. Section 504 predated but remains in effect concurrent with the Americans with Disabilities Act.

Section 504 of the Rehabilitation Act of 1973 (PL 93–112, as amended by PL 102–456; 29 USC 701) protects children who have disabilities but who may not qualify as children with disabilities under the IDEA. To illustrate, a court determined that a child with attention-deficit/hyperactivity disorder (ADHD) was in fact a person with a disability under Section 504, even though the condition was not recognized at the time under the IDEA (*Brittan [CA] Elementary School District,* 16 EHLR 1226, 1990; see also "New OCR Rulings," 17 IDELR 104–106, 1991). Section 504 is a civil rights statute comparable to Title VI of the Civil Rights Act of 1964 (minority groups) and to Title IX of the Education Amendments of 1972 (women). The basic statutory language is brief:

> *No otherwise qualified individual with a disability in the United States shall, solely by reason of the disability, be excluded from the participation in, be denied*

the benefits of, or be subjected to discrimination under any program or activity receiving federal financial assistance. (29 USC 794)

Section 504 applies to individuals with disabilities regardless of age; it protects young children, school-age children, youths, and adults. Because Section 504 is a civil rights statute, it adopts a three-part definition of *disability.* The first prong of this definition protects people who have a physical or mental impairment that substantially limits one or more of their major life activities. The second protects people who once had such a condition and have recovered; they are protected against unjust discrimination on the basis of any records of the previous condition. The final prong protects people regarded as having such an impairment, usually falsely.

The statute applies to schools, libraries, hospitals, social service agencies, nonprofit organizations, and government agencies (including federal agencies such as the U.S. Department of Education) that receive federal financial assistance. Receipt of such grants obligates these organizations and agencies to practice nondiscrimination in all of their programs and activities. The statute requires provision of auxiliary aids such as interpreters for people who are deaf and appropriate media for people who are blind, as well as other assistance necessary so that people may benefit from programs and activities. These requirements remain in effect. Although the ADA later imposed similar requirements, that act does not repeal Section 504.

With respect to public education that is supported, directly or indirectly, through federal grants, including child care and other programs for infants or toddlers and preschool programs, Section 504 says that the services offered to children with disabilities must meet their needs "as adequately as the needs of non-disabled persons are met." In other words, the federal requirement is for access to services. Section 504 says that an IEP is one means by which such access may be provided. For children who do not have an IEP (because they do not require modified instruction) or IFSP (because they do not require early intervention services), the standard that Section 504 sets is one of nondiscrimination: the services are to be as effective as are those provided by the public agency for people with no disabilities.

Regulations implementing Section 504 preceded those for what is now the IDEA's mandate to serve children with disabilities. The Section 504 rules appeared in April 1977, the PL 94–142 regulations in August of that year. The two sets of rules contained similar requirements with respect to elementary and secondary education, thus reinforcing each other. Section 504 differs from the IDEA in that it provides no funding, being, rather, a civil rights statute; the IDEA, on the other hand, is a federal funding program that sets rules for participation and for receipt of federal funds. In the late 1970s, Section 504 played an important role: it protected children in any state that declined to participate in PL 94–142—that is, rejected federal special education funds. No state now does this, though in the past, some did. To the extent that any state declines to participate in Part C, Section 504 could again play such a role.

Section 504 interprets nondiscrimination to mean equal access to admissions, fair eligibility requirements, and program accessibility that provides equal benefit from programs and activities. Program accessibility was a new concept when the initial Section 504 regulation was signed on April 28, 1977 (Bowe, 1978). It is best understood in contrast to barrier-free buildings: all rooms in a building need not be accessible if classes may be relocated to an accessible room. To take another example, were a public library to have some books shelved on the second floor of a two-story building with no elevator, the library staff would need to provide some mechanism, including personal assistance from a librarian or staff assistant, so that an individual who could not personally retrieve the book could nonetheless get it. The program is accessible, even if the building is not.

Section 504 states that it is not discrimination for a program to declare ineligible for services an individual who has unique needs that the program is not staffed or equipped to meet. A school for children who are blind, for example, may decline to admit a child who is deaf and blind on the grounds that neither the staff nor the educational programs, including the materials used, are prepared to meet the special needs of a child who is both deaf and blind. Programs may set eligibility criteria that reflect their service offerings without fear of discrimination charges from people who have different service needs.

Under Section 504, an individual with a disability may file charges alleging discrimination with the federal agency that directly or indirectly funds the offending agency's program. With respect to social service programs, that is usually the U.S. Department of Health and Human Services. With respect to schools (elementary, secondary, vocational, trade, two-year and four-year college, graduate), it is usually the U.S. Department of Education. Relief is generally limited to admission, reinstatement as a participant in a program, or provision of needed **reasonable accommodations** such as sign language interpreting for people who are deaf. In addition, Section 504 recognizes the due process procedural safeguards in Part B (see the "Procedural Safeguards" section of this chapter) as "one means" under which individuals with disabilities may enforce their rights in public education.

Reasonable accommodation

in the ADA and Section 504 refers to an adjustment enabling a qualified individual with a disability to perform a task.

AMERICANS WITH DISABILITIES ACT

The 1990 **Americans with Disabilities Act (ADA;** PL 101–336; 42 USC 12101 et seq.) protects individuals with disabilities, regardless of age, from discrimination. The act is enormously important for young children with disabilities and their families. Title I of the act proscribes discrimination on the basis of disability in employment at virtually all of the nation's private companies with 15 or more workers. Title II bans discrimination on the basis of disability at any state, county, or local government agency; it specifically proscribes less-than-equal access to public transportation. Title III of the ADA prohibits discrimination in community stores and other **places of public accommodation.** Title IV ensures users of telecommunications devices for the deaf (TDDs) equal access to local, long-distance, and international telephone networks.

The act adopts, as does Section 504, a three-part definition of *individuals with a disability.* Under the first prong of the definition, a person (of any age) who has a permanent medical condition that significantly limits one or more major life activities (going to school is a major life activity) is considered to be an individual with a disability. The other two prongs are also the same as those in Section 504 outlined previously.

The ADA has a significant feature that may surprise many parents. It protects *associates* of persons with disabilities. These include family members, who are protected against discrimination on the basis of their association with individuals with disabilities. Thus, a parent may not be denied access to services because a child has a disability. This protection is particularly important for parents with respect to their own employment and employer-provided insurance coverage. It is illegal, for example, for a company to refuse

Americans with Disability Act (ADA)

PL 101–336, is the landmark 1990 federal civil rights law for individuals with disabilities. The law bans discrimination in employment, local government services, transportation, places of public accommodation, and telecommunications.

Places of public accommodation

are restaurants, hotels, motion picture and other theaters, sporting facilities, stores and shopping malls, and doctors' and lawyers' offices. Under the ADA, Title III, these must be accessible to people with disabilities and offer these people equal enjoyment to that accorded to people with no disabilities.

to hire someone just because that person's child has a disability. It is similarly illegal for the employer to offer that person an insurance package that is less comprehensive than that provided to other workers, again because the individual is associated with (related to) a child with a disability.

While not directly affecting infants, toddlers, and preschool-age children with disabilities for a number of years to come—until they enter the labor market—Title I is nonetheless hugely important because it assures families that if their children with disabilities secure an education, they will have an equal opportunity to work—and support themselves—upon reaching adulthood. This guarantee of nondiscrimination in employment applies to more than one million American companies—virtually all employers having 15 or more workers. The knowledge that a fair chance at self-support awaits them at the conclusion of their schooling is a very significant motivating factor for children with disabilities and their parents, teachers, therapists, and counselors.

Title II of the ADA requires that state, county, and local government agencies provide nondiscriminatory treatment for people with disabilities in all programs and activities that serve members of the general public. Section 504 of the Rehabilitation Act requires such actions by recipients of federal financial assistance; all states, and most county and local governments as well, are beneficiaries of federal funds and thus covered by Section 504. Title II erases whatever doubts might have existed about that. It also moves a major step beyond Section 504 with respect to transportation. At the time the ADA was enacted (July 26, 1990), the Section 504 standard on public transportation was a vague special efforts mandate. Title II establishes specific, hard-hitting obligations on county and local public transit agencies. For example, beginning August 1990, all new mass transit buses were required to be lift-equipped. Similarly, all new rail cars on commuter rail, rapid rail, and other local train service trains had to be equipped to accept wheelchairs.

These Title II requirements are important to families with young children who have disabilities. Title II requires state, county, and local government agencies to provide services to people with disabilities as effective as those offered to individuals without disabilities. Title II forbids discrimination on the basis of disability by any state, county, or local government agency. The title became effective January 26, 1992. Title II defines a qualified individual with a disability as follows:

> *[A]n individual with a disability who, with or without reasonable modifications to rules, policies, practices, the removal of architectural, communications, or transportation barriers, or the provision of auxiliary aids and services, meets the essential eligibility requirements for the receipt of services or the participation in programs or activities provided by a public entity.* (Section 201[2])

Title III explicitly recognizes that infants, toddlers, and young children are not only people with disabilities but also citizens of their local communities. They and their families lead lives not related to their disabilities. They patronize restaurants; entertainment centers; and other public and private sources of human, medical, and other services. In the past, families of children with disabilities frequently met with discrimination from community service providers, both public and private. On May 23, 1988, Lisa Carl, who uses a wheelchair because of cerebral palsy, was denied admission to a movie theater in Tacoma, Washington. The theater manager told an advocate who called the theater to protest, "I don't want her here, and I don't have to let her in." In Denver, Colorado, on June 16, 1989, six young people using wheelchairs were told by the manager of a restaurant that they "[took] up too much space." Unless they could get out of and fold up their wheelchairs, he said, they would not be served. When they declined to do so, the manager called the local police, who took the six to jail (Bowe, 1992a; *From ADA to Empowerment,* 1991).

Such actions—denial of service at a movie theater or at a restaurant—are now outlawed by Title III, which bans discriminatory treatment by places of public accommodation. The law includes a list of such places; among them are preschool, elementary, secondary, and private schools; child care centers; social service agencies; stores; shopping malls; restaurants; hotels; movie theaters and other theaters; sports complexes and other entertainment centers; and private offices of doctors, dentists, lawyers, and other professionals serving members of the general public. Such places of public accommodation must make their facilities physically accessible to people with disabilities, unless doing so is not readily achievable. They must provide equal enjoyment for customers with disabilities unless doing so would impose an undue hardship on the business. The law defines such terms as *readily achievable* and *undue hardship*; implementing regulations issued by the U.S. Department of Justice (*Federal Register,* July 26, 1991) explain further what is meant by these and other key terms in Title III.

Among other things, if a service program or establishment such as a hotel sponsors its own client or participant transportation program (as a child care center or school might), the vehicles used and other aspects of the transportation program must be available equally to people with and without disabilities alike. Services that are less than equal to those offered to persons without disabilities are outlawed, as are opportunities that are less effective than those accorded to persons without disabilities. Any eligibility criteria that have the effect of screening out individuals with disabilities are banned. Reasonable accommodations and other assistance are required to be provided (i.e., interpreters for parents who are deaf) unless doing so would fundamentally alter the nature of the goods, services, or facilities being provided by the place of public accommodation. Title III took effect on January 26, 1992.

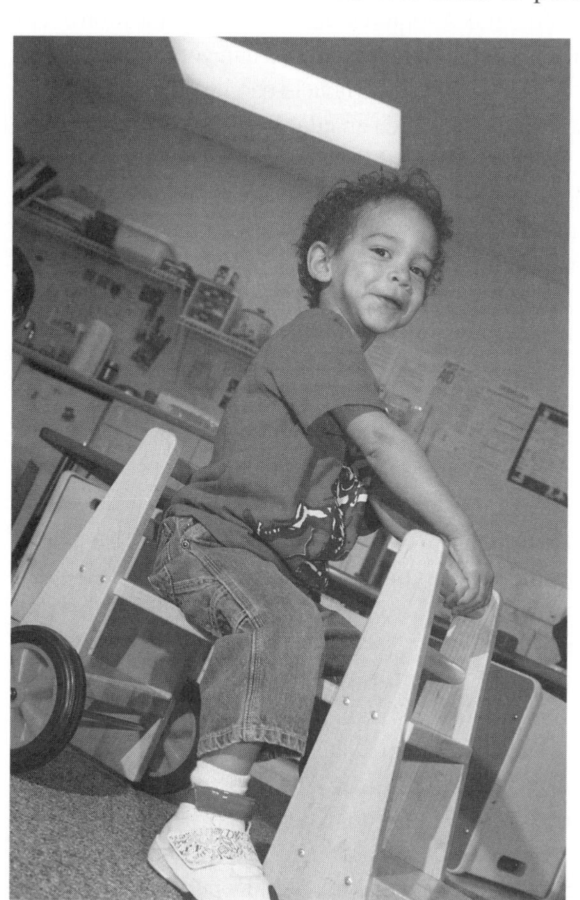

Involving fathers—who can make play objects, among many other contributions—has challenged ECSE from the beginning.

Under Title IV, all users of teletypewriters (TTYs) are entitled to free use of relay services to make and receive local and long-distance telephone calls. Since July 26, 1993, all 1,600 local and long-distance telephone companies in the United States have provided round-the-clock access to relay services, which allow individuals who are deaf, hard of hearing, and/or speech impaired to call and be called by some 100 million residential and business telephone numbers. For those who need relay services, Title IV makes a very big difference. Whether they need access to telephone service for personal or business reasons, TTY users are no longer limited in the amount or kind of calls they may make or receive.

Individuals with disabilities who win complaints under the ADA are entitled to remedies that vary from title to title. They may be awarded reinstatement of employment under Title I and reinstitution of services under Titles II, III, or IV. They may also be eligible for monetary rewards, including compensatory damages in the event of intentional discrimination, as in employment under Title I (Bowe, 1992a).

PROCEDURAL SAFEGUARDS

Procedural safeguards

(due process rights) are granted to families in both Part C and Part B. An example is the right to see all relevant records pertaining to the child.

Procedural safeguards for families were enacted as the Family Educational Rights and Privacy Act (PL 93–380; 34 CFR Part 99), were expanded in the Education for All Handicapped Children Act (EAHA) (PL 94–142), and were applied to families with infants or toddlers in PL 99–457 and PL 102–119. These statutes are powerful, and the Part B case law (collected cases and decisions) is extensive. The court decisions led to many regulatory or even statutory changes, as courts interpreted the IDEA and its meaning. Equally significant, the very existence of these due process rights may spur program-parent negotiations, as programs seek to make it unnecessary for parents to assert these rights. This may help explain why only a small minority (about 10 percent) of parents filed even one due process complaint against a local education agency during Part B's first 10 years (Harris & Associates, 1989).

IDEA Part B

Section 615 (Procedural Safeguards) of the IDEA requires state and local education agencies to provide complaint mechanisms for families and for children and youth with disabilities. Parents (the term *parents* in this context refers throughout to parents or guardians) are to have the opportunity to examine all relevant records an education agency holds about their child. These may be extensive: information on the child's health, intelligence, and academic achievement; copies of IEPs and supporting documentation; teacher assessments; and many other checklists, charts, and so on. While necessary for instructional purposes, the collection and maintenance of such comprehensive records conflicts with a family's desire for privacy. That is why the IDEA ensures the parents the right to inspect such records at any time. Parents may also secure, often at public expense, a second, independent evaluation of their child if they disagree with the school district's evaluation. Regardless of who pays for the independent evaluation, the school district is required to take into consideration the findings and recommendations of the outside evaluator.

If a child's parents are unknown or cannot be found, the education agency must appoint a surrogate to represent the child. Parents or (where appropriate) surrogates are to be given written prior notice of any school plans to evaluate, assess, place, or change services for a child with a disability. Such notices are to be given in the parents' native language unless it is clearly infeasible to do so. Prior notice allows the parents to forestall actions they believe are detrimental to the child.

If parents disagree with the IEP team about any aspect of their child's education, the IDEA urges the parents to turn first to mediation. In binding mediation, both sides agree to accept the mediator's decision. Disputes that are mediated usually are resolved much faster, and at much lower costs, than are litigated disputes. However, parents still retain the right to go to court instead of to a mediator. If they do, parents may begin by presenting complaints against an education agency to an impartial due process hearing officer, who must make a decision within 45 days. The law and the U.S. Department of Education's implementing regulations govern how the hearings are to be held. Both sides must be permitted to introduce evidence. The parents may bring an attorney or other advocate to assist them. School districts are required to inform parents about free or low-cost legal assistance that may be available (Charmatz, 1993; Turnbull & Turnbull, 1991). The losing party (the parents or the school district) may appeal an adverse decision to a state review officer. Following exhaustion of these administrative remedies, either party may proceed to state or federal district court for relief. If the case reaches the U.S. Supreme Court, its decision is final.

Section 615 requires that while a dispute is pending, the child with a disability is to continue receiving a free, appropriate public education and is to remain in the current placement. This requirement is very important, because prior to the enactment of what is now the IDEA, schools sometimes suspended or expelled students with disabilities and refused to readmit them until forced to do so by a higher authority. Such actions are no longer permissible.

Parents are explicitly permitted under Section 615 to use the protections offered by Section 504 as well. However, the IDEA administrative remedies must first be exhausted before actions under Section 504 may begin.

The relevant provisions of the Part B procedural safeguards appear in Figure 5–1. Notice especially the requirements for written prior notice, the rights at hearings, the right to go to court, and the stay-put provisions governing the pendency of any dispute. The 1997 amendments offered parents the right to use mediation, as provided for in Section 615. Attorneys fees generally are not reimbursable for IEP meetings.

IDEA Part C

Section 639 of IDEA Part C requires states to create a system ensuring timely resolution of complaints. The U.S. Department of Education's implementing regulations give states two options: First, they may adopt IDEA Part B procedures (see earlier), applying them to Part C complaints. Second, states may set up separate procedures to comply with the requirements of Section 639. The use of the Part B procedures is simplified by the fact that the Part C requirements mirror those of Part B. For example, the term *parent* is defined in the same way in Parts B and C, and in the department's 34 CFR 300 and 34 CFR 303 rules. Sections 615 and 639 both call for prior written notice in the parents' native language, and both adopt the PL 93–380 Family Educational Rights and Privacy Act (FERPA) requirements.

There are, however, differences between the procedural safeguards under Parts B and C. First, attorney's fee awards are not available under Part C. As a result, attorneys may be less willing to represent families in Section 639 procedures. Second, Part C has no explicit provision for independent evaluations (Turnbull & Turnbull, 1991). Third, complaints must be resolved within 30 days under Part C (vs. 45 days under Part B). Despite these differences, the similarities dominate, especially because states may reduce or even eliminate these differences. Nothing in the law prevents a state from providing for attorney's fee awards to the prevailing party. Similarly, a state may allow parents to introduce private, outside evaluations by physicians or other specialists during due process hearings. And states may adopt the Part B procedural safeguards, in which the 30-day time limit is eliminated in favor of the 45-day timetable.

However, another difference between Part B and Part C procedures may not be able to be resolved by state action. Unlike Part B, Part C does not specify that parents may use Section 504 as an alternative legal basis for action. Part C's apparently exclusive reliance on the IDEA safeguard routes may preclude states, and even courts, from providing alternative routes for complaint resolution (Turnbull & Turnbull, 1991).

Section 615.(a) Any State educational agency, State agency, or local educational agency that receives assistance under this part shall establish and maintain procedures in accordance with this section to ensure that children with disabilities and their parents are guaranteed procedural safeguards with respect to the provision of free appropriate public education by such agencies.

(b) The procedures required by this section shall include—
   (1) an opportunity for the parents of a child with a disability to examine all records relating to such child and to participate in meetings with respect to the identification, evaluation, and educational placement of the child, and the provision of a free appropriate public education to such child, and to obtain an independent educational evaluation of the child;
   (2) procedures to protect the rights of the child whenever the parents of the child are not known . . . ;
   (3) written prior notice to the parents of the child whenever such agency—(A) proposes to initiate or change; or (B) refuses to initiate or change the identification, evaluation, or educational placement of the child . . . or the provision of a free appropriate public education to such child; (4) procedures designed to ensure that the notice required by paragraph (3) is in the native language of the parents, unless it clearly is not feasible to do so; (5) an opportunity for mediation in accordance with subsection (e); (6) an opportunity to present a complaint . . . ;

(e) Mediation.—(1) In general.—Any State educational agency or local educational agency that receives assistance under this part shall ensure that procedures are established and implemented to allow parties to disputes involving any matter described in subsection (b)(6) to resolve such disputes through a mediation process which, at a minimum, shall be available whenever a hearing is requested under subsection (f) or (k).
   (2) Requirements.—Such procedures shall meet the following requirements: (A) The procedures shall ensure that the mediation process—(i) is voluntary on the part of the parties; (ii) is not used to delay a parent's right to a due process hearing under subsection (f), or to deny any other rights afforded under this part; and (iii) is conducted by a qualified and impartial mediator who is trained in effective mediation techniques. . . .

(f) Impartial Due Process Hearing.—(A) In general.—Whenever a complaint has been received under subsection (b)(6) or (k) of this section, the parents involved in such complaint shall have an opportunity for an impartial due process hearing. . . . [Either party may appeal the decision to the state education agency and then to federal courts. If parents are the prevailing party at court, the court may award them attorney's fees.]. . . .

(j) Maintenance of current educational placement.—Except as provided in subsection (k)(4), during the pendency of any proceedings conducted pursuant to this section, unless the State or local educational agency and the parents otherwise agree, the child shall remain in the then-current educational placement of such child, or, if applying for initial admission to a public school, shall, with the consent of the parents, be placed in the public school program until all such proceedings have been completed.

(k) Placement in alternative educational setting.—
   (1) Authority of school personnel.—(A) School personnel under this section may order a change in placement of a child with a disability—(i) to an appropriate interim alternative educational setting, another setting, or suspension, for not more than 10 school days. . . . and (ii) to an appropriate interim alternative educational setting for the same amount of time that a child without a disability would be subject to discipline, but for not more than 45 school days if—(I) the child carries a weapon to school . . . or (II) the child knowingly possesses or uses illegal drugs or solicits the sale of a controlled substance while at school.

FIGURE 5–1 Procedural safeguards: Part B (excerpts).

Relevant components of the Part C procedural safeguards are shown in Figure 5–2. Added in 1991 were the requirement for prior written consent by the family to any interagency transfer of personally identifiable information and the right of a family to decline service.

Discussion

Part C offers powerful due process safeguards for families, which mirror those provided under Part B. Section 639 of Part C requires states to create procedures to protect the

Section 639. The procedural safeguards required to be included in a statewide system under section 635(a)(13) shall provide, at a minimum, the following:

(1) The timely administrative resolution of complaints by parents. Any party aggrieved by the findings and decision regarding an administrative complaint shall have the right to bring a civil action with respect to the complaint, which action may be brought in any State court of competent jurisdiction or in a district court of the United States without regard to the amount of controversy. In any action brought under this paragraph, the court shall receive the records of the administrative proceedings, shall hear additional evidence at the request of a party, and, basing its decision on the preponderance of the evidence, shall grant such relief as the court determines is appropriate.

(2) The right to confidentiality of personally identifiable information, including the right of parents to written notice of and written consent to the exchange of such information among agencies consistent with Federal and State law.

(3) The right of the parents to determine whether they, their infant or toddler, or other family members will accept or decline any early intervention service under this part in accordance with State law without jeopardizing other early intervention services under this part.

(4) The opportunity for parents to examine records relating to assessment, screening, eligibility determinations, and the development and implementation of the individualized family service plan.

(5) Procedures to protect the rights of the infant or toddler with a disability whenever the parents of the child are not known or unavailable or the child is a ward of the State, including the assignment of an individual (who shall not be an employee of the State lead agency or other state agency, and who shall not be any person, or any employee of a person, providing early intervention services to the infant or toddler or any family member of the infant or toddler) to act as a surrogate for the parents.

(6) Written prior notice to the parents of the infant or toddler with a disability whenever the state agency or service provider proposes to initiate or change or refuses to initiate or change the identification, evaluation, placement, or the provision of appropriate early intervention services to the infant or toddler.

(7) Procedures designed to assure that the notice required by paragraph (6) fully informs the parents, in the parents' native language, unless it clearly is not feasible to do so, of all procedures available pursuant to this section.

(8) The right of any parents to use mediation in accordance with section 615(e); except that. . . .

(b) During the pendency of any proceeding or action involving a complaint, unless the State agency and the parents otherwise agree, the child shall continue to receive the appropriate early intervention services currently being provided or, if applying for initial services, shall receive the services not in dispute.

FIGURE 5–2 Procedural safeguards Part C.

rights of parents, guardians, infants, and toddlers. The state's lead agency must investigate any complaints, whether about an individual child and family or about systemic violations of law. The lead agency must correct any individual or systemic violations it identifies.

Recall that states may adopt the Part B Section 615 due process safeguards in lieu of creating new procedures under Part C's Section 639. The Part B safeguards, found in Section 615 of the IDEA, have been in place in all states for many years. They may not be familiar to officials at state health, social services, or other agencies, however. The procedures ensure that families and children with disabilities are not at the mercy of program officials. Families may challenge virtually any agency decision, from initial labeling through placement and service delivery. Parents may even challenge the qualifications of special education and related services personnel as not meeting state standards. These procedural safeguards may be invoked by parents at any time. In most states, the Part B impartial hearing officer is a school official from a neighboring school district,

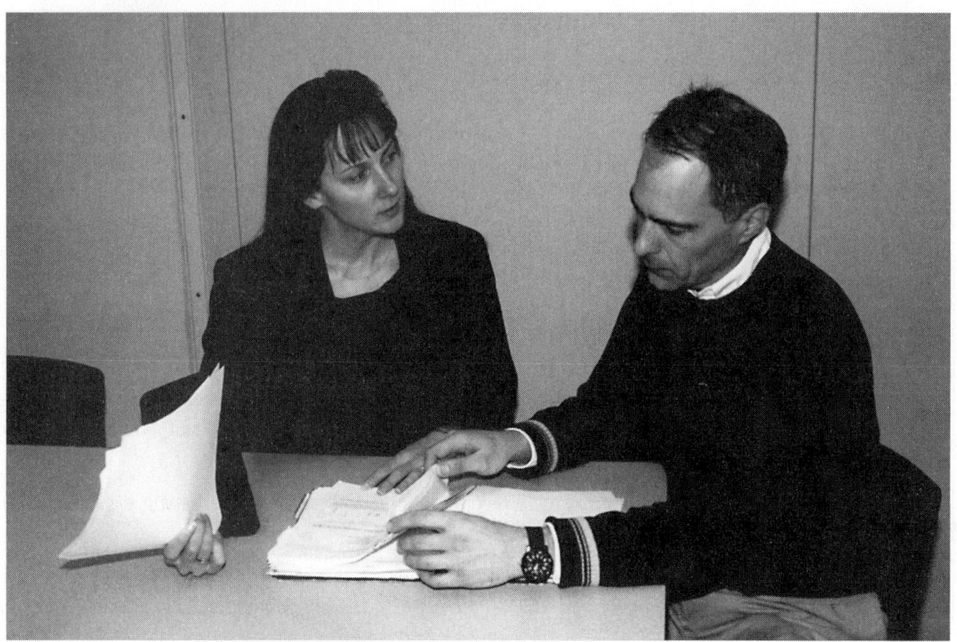

Virtually all records about a child must be open to and available for family members to inspect. They may, if they wish, append comments to such records.

a private expert, or an attorney. The IDEA provides extensive rules governing the way in which impartial hearing officers reach decisions. Either party (parents or school district) may appeal an unfavorable decision, usually to a state review officer. Either then may proceed further, to state or federal district court. Part C contains very similar rules. Accordingly, courts probably will draw on the case law concerning Part B procedural safeguards in deciding Part C cases.

The federal regulations implementing Part C (34 CFR 303) added, "It is important that the administrative procedures developed by a state be designed to result in speedy resolution of complaints. An infant's or toddler's development is so rapid that undue delay could be potentially harmful." For that reason, Section 303 insists that complaints be resolved and a written decision issued within 30 days of the date of complaint. The only exception permitted is where a state adopts Part B procedures, in which case resolution is required within 45 days.

States must also allow parents to take their complaints to state or federal courts. Part C is silent on whether parents of infants or toddlers must first exhaust administrative remedies—that is, file a complaint first with the lead agency and await its decision before proceeding to court. The statutory language of Section 639 implies that administrative complaints will usually be heard first. However, in states where the 30-day (or 45-day) timetable is routinely flouted, parents may win the right to proceed directly to court.

States also must maintain strict confidentiality of all personally identifiable information—that is, any record containing or implying the name or identity of an infant, toddler, or parent. Protection of personally identifiable information is a widespread practice in human services agencies today. The 1991 amendments to the IDEA added a requirement that parents be given written notice of, and an opportunity to provide written consent to, any reporting of personally identifiable information from one agency to another.

As specified in Part B, parents have the right to written prior notice of any significant proposal for change or other decision by an authorized Part C agency. This notice is to be provided in the parents' native language, if at all feasible. Native language may include American Sign Language (ASL) in the case of parents who are deaf. For parents who are blind, the notice may be provided in Braille or may be read aloud. Again, as in Part B, Part C contains a stay-put provision ensuring that the child and family will continue receiving services throughout the duration of any complaint or other dispute.

IN BRIEF

Other laws provide additional rights for infants, toddlers, and preschoolers with disabilities and their families. Among the more important are the following pieces of legislation.

Fair Housing Amendments Act (FHAA)

PL 100–430 protects children with disabilities and their families from unjust discrimination if they are or wish to be tenants in private housing. The bill was signed on September 13, 1988, and took full effect on March 13, 1991. In condominiums and apartment buildings having four or more units, families with members who have disabilities may not be denied the chance to rent or buy units. They are also allowed to make renovations or other alterations, at their own expense.

Private one- and two-family homes continue to be exempt from federal (and, usually, state) regulation on accessibility for people with disabilities. Until the FHAA took effect, accessibility features in apartment buildings and condominiums, as well as multiunit townhouses, were required in only a few states. As a result, finding accessible housing was a major problem for families with members who had physical disabilities; it was also a concern, though a lesser one, for families with children who had other kinds of disabilities. Even with the FHAA, most estimates suggest that less than 5 percent of all homes and other units of housing today are accessible to people with physical disabilities (e.g., U.S. Conference of Mayors, 2005). In time, new construction will result in ever more accessible housing.

Adaptability

refers to the requirement in the Fair Housing Amendments Act of 1988, PL 100–430, that new, four-unit or larger multifamily housing structures be adaptable or readily changeable to meet the special needs of individuals with severe disabilities. An example is cabinets or light switches that may be easily lowered.

The law establishes standards of accessibility and **adaptability** for new multifamily housing; apartment and condominium buildings built for first occupancy after March 13, 1991, are much more accessible and much easier to adapt than are older units. In addition, real estate agencies are now prohibited from discriminating against people with disabilities who are seeking private homes or apartments. Real estate agents who steered families with members who have disabilities away from some housing complexes were an important problem.

The law also strengthens the rights of individuals with disabilities to live in group homes. Until the FHAA was passed, only New York, Michigan, and a handful of other states that had strong laws in favor of group homes were effective in overcoming local opposition to group homes. Group homes are an important housing option for older adolescents and adults with severe disabilities. Waiting lists remain long in many states; parents are well advised to request placement eight or more years prior to the time the child is expected to need a place to live (42 USC 3601 et seq.).

Air Carriers Access Act

Although Section 504 has required since 1978 that airports be accessible, individual air carriers considered themselves not to be recipients of federal financial assistance and, therefore, believed that they were exempt from the Section 504 nondiscrimination mandates. PL 99–435 made it clear that commercial airlines must comply with Section 504, on the grounds that they "benefit from" publicly supported airports and traffic control centers. The 1986 law requires carriers using U.S. airports to provide nondiscriminatory treatment for passengers with disabilities (49 USC 1301).

Television Decoder Circuitry Act

Enacted on October 16, 1990, PL 101–431 requires all new television sets measuring 13 inches or more diagonally that are made or sold in the United States after July 1, 1993, to have built-in caption decoder chips. Such chips enable the set to receive and display captions (subtitles). In effect, PL 101–431 grants people who are deaf and people who are hard of hearing, as well as others needing captions (Americans who are illiterate, immigrants trying to learn English, etc.), the right to understand television programming. The law does not require that programs be captioned. However, the fact that tens of millions of television sets have been sold since the law took effect means that the number of households with caption-equipped sets is now very substantial, a fact that encourages program producers to caption their offerings (47 USC 609, 47 USC 303).

Telecommunications Act

The Telecommunications Act of 1996 (PL 104–104) requires that all new telecommunications equipment and services be accessible to and usable by people with disabilities, unless it is not feasible to do so. Included are customer premises equipment (including telephones, caller ID units, etc.) and services that are provided by local and long-distance telephone companies. The act also requires that virtually all new video programming be captioned. (Recall that the Television Decoder Circuitry Act, discussed previously, does not require that programs be captioned.) Captioning of broadcast and cable television offerings was phased in under the Telecommunications Act, with most entertainment programs, movies, and news programs being captioned no later than January 1, 2006.

SERVICES

Families of infants, toddlers, preschoolers, and early-primary-age children with disabilities may qualify for services under laws other than the IDEA. This is particularly true of families of infants and toddlers, because IDEA Part C is a coordinated, cross-agency program. It is also true of families of preschoolers and, to a lesser extent, those of other young children.

The interrelated nature of these various services is most clear under Part C. Figure 5–3 graphically depicts how the service coordinator—sitting at the nexus of all of these various programs—pulls together services for which a family is or may be eligible. Many of the services, however, are available to families with older children.

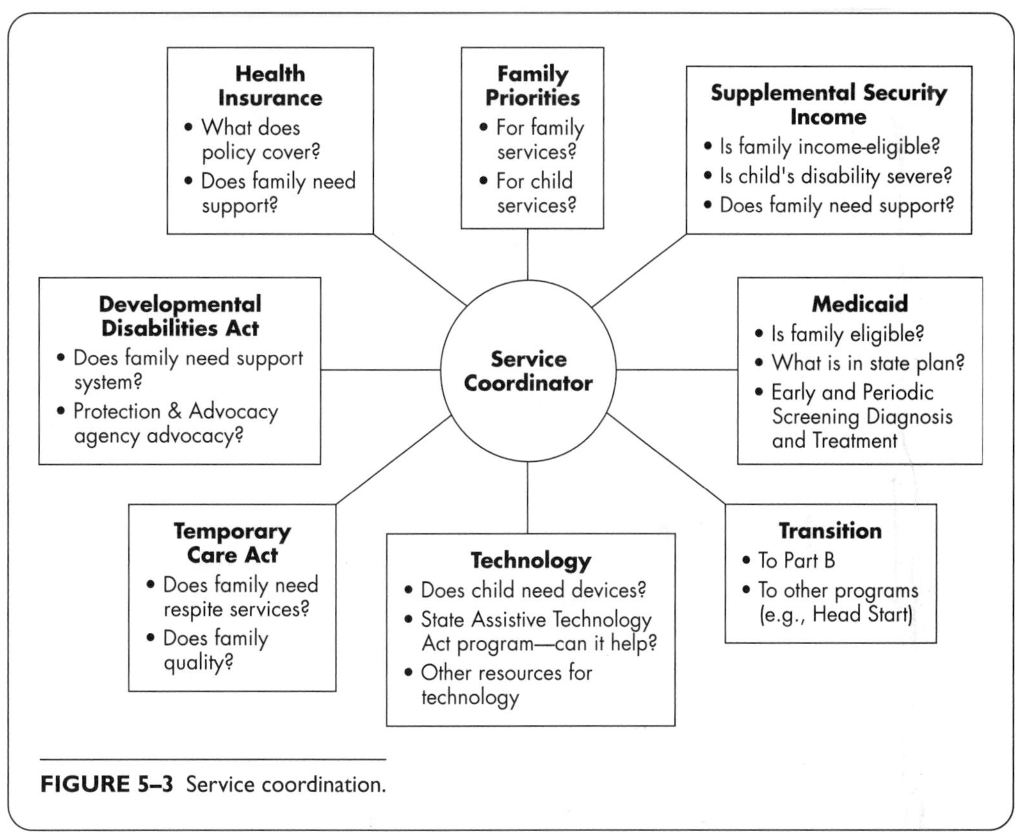

FIGURE 5–3 Service coordination.

When the children are very young, families are entitled to a service coordinator. Once children turn three years of age, they and their families lose the help of this person. From that point on, family members may direct their questions to special educators and related services personnel. Regardless of the child's age, the critical first issue in answering family questions is whether the family potentially qualifies for a particular service. If so, the service coordinator (or other professional) can work with the family to establish eligibility for any services the family desires. Eligibility requirements and the services for which these qualify families vary from state to state. That is why readers should secure up-to-date information about services in *their own states.* The resources given in this chapter—notably, the uniform resource locators (URLs)—will help readers acquire the necessary data.

There are strings attached to each source of services. Great progress has been made over the past several years to coordinate the various programs so that definitions, eligibility criteria, and other "strings" are consistent from state to state. The need for this coordination was illustrated by the chapter-opening story about the family that moved to Minnesota. When agencies define key terms differently, families may be cut off from much-needed assistance. When programs work together, by contrast, fewer families fall between the cracks.

Supplemental Security Income (SSI)

is a federal-state guaranteed minimum income program for individuals who are poor and have disabilities. Most SSI beneficiaries also receive Medicaid.

SUPPLEMENTAL SECURITY INCOME

Probably the most important of the non-IDEA programs is **Supplemental Security Income (SSI).** As the name implies, this program offers financial assistance to supplement personal or family income. It is a cash benefits program. Families become eligible by having low income and low levels of wealth. (*Income* means earned and unearned funds coming in to the family during a given year; *wealth* refers to such family assets as real estate, investments, savings accounts, etc. To qualify for SSI, *both* income and wealth must be below levels set by the Social Security Administration [SSA].) In addition, at least one family member must have a disability or be over 65 years of age. In most instances, participation in the SSI program carries with it eligibility for Medicaid, the federal-state medical insurance program (discussed later in this chapter).

Significance of SSI

SSI provides monthly checks to eligible individuals. In the case of children, family members may become designated recipients for those checks. There are few restrictions on how the checks may be used. Families may spend the money on food, housing, health care, transportation, clothing, or virtually anything else. The intent of the checks is to assure that the eligible individual (the child) has available a minimum standard of living. Thus, SSI is a *guaranteed minimum income* program in that it brings family income up to the federal poverty level. This level varies from year to year and from geographic region to geographic region. For the latest numbers, visit www.census.gov and search for "poverty level." The national federal poverty level for a family of four in 2006 was about $19,000.

Because of these benefits, families sometimes try to qualify children for eligibility under the IDEA. They do this in the mistaken belief that *disability* under the IDEA is equivalent to *disability* under SSI. Therefore, they think, if early intervention programs or schools accept a child as having a disability, the family would qualify for SSI benefits. That is not true. Service coordinators, educators, and related-services personnel need to explain to families that the IDEA and SSI are separate programs, run by different agencies, and with different eligibility criteria. Qualifying for IDEA services does nothing to help a family qualify for SSI.

Definition

Children are considered to have disabilities for purposes of SSI if they have a permanent medical condition that appears on a "listing" of impairments developed by the SSA. This listing is periodically updated. For the current version, see www.socialsecurity.gov, select "Supplemental Security Income," and search for "Listing of Impairments." (Note: This "listing" runs more than 100 printed pages.) Included are such conditions as deafness, blindness, autism, traumatic brain injury, paraplegia, and other severe impairments.

Children who do not have a "listed condition" may qualify for SSI if they have an impairment or impairments that produce a "marked" limitation in functioning in two or more broad areas of functioning or an "extreme" limitation in one such area of functioning. These areas include motor, social, and communication functioning, among others. SSA's regulations for SSI, at 20 CFR 416.902, and the Social Security Act as amended by the Personal Responsibility and Work Opportunity Reconciliation Act of 1996 (PL 104–193), in Section 1614(a)(3)(C)(i), explain that "marked and severe functional limitations" is a phrase meaning a level of severity that is comparable to that of listed conditions. It should be evident that a much higher standard applies to the term *disability* with respect to SSI than is the case under the IDEA.

Children and youth who qualify for special education and related services under the IDEA may not qualify for SSI for another reason as well. No matter how severe the child's disability may be, SSI is provided only if family income and family wealth are below certain levels. SSI is available only to very poor families. To understand how low a family's socioeconomic status (SES) needs to be for the family to be eligible, recall that SSI checks are intended to supplement family income so as to *bring the family up to the federal poverty level.*

Families may apply for SSI benefits by contacting nearby SSA district offices, which can be located using phone books. People may also visit www.socialsecurity.gov and search for the address/phone number. Because the rules are complex, professionals and families may wish to get support from an organization that is experienced in helping families with the SSA. Local independent living centers are examples. These not-for-profit organizations are located in every state and in most metropolitan areas. All centers are run by adults with disabilities. These centers specialize in helping people with disabilities deal with government at all levels (national, state, county, local) and in advocating for community change. You can identify a local center at www.ilru.org. Another good source of help is a local United Cerebral Palsy Association (UCPA), which is a parent-based group. Many of these groups provide direct services, including early intervention and special education. UCPAs may be identified at www.ucpa.org. A third possibility is state or local associations for citizens with mental retardation. Information is available at www.thearc.org. The key for professionals and family members is that eligibility and program characteristics differ so much from state to state that state or local sources of information are needed (PL 104–193; Title XVI of the Social Security Act).

MEDICAID

Medicaid
is the federal-state medical insurance program for poor individuals. Many SSI recipients receive Medicaid.

As mentioned earlier, families may qualify for **Medicaid** by establishing the child's eligibility for SSI. Medicaid is the federal-state insurance program for low-SES individuals and families. It is funded through income tax revenues (federal and state). At the federal level, Medicare is administered by the U.S. Department of Health and Human Services (HHS), through its Centers for Medicare and Medicaid Services (CMS), located at 7500 Security Blvd., Baltimore, MD 21244-1850. This unit replaced the HHS Health Care Financing Administration (HCFA). The URL is www.cms.hhs.gov. State Medicaid offices are identified on this site as well.

Many people believe that Medicaid is provided to all Americans who are of low-SES status. That is not true. It is primarily available to individuals who are on SSI, and, as noted earlier, there are strict eligibility requirements to be met for SSI.

Significance of Medicaid

For families having young children with disabilities, many of which face daunting medical bills due to the child's condition, medical insurance is absolutely essential. Thus, Medicaid is a very important program for families that can qualify. The state-based organizations identified earlier (see "Supplemental Security Income") can help families with Medicaid as well. The Balanced Budget Act of 1997 (PL 105–33) provided that Medicaid coverage may continue for families whose children had been eligible for SSI and who benefited from Medicaid for that reason but who later were dropped when SSI childhood eligibility requirements were tightened in 1996. Others eligible for Medicaid include low-SES families with children, pregnant women with incomes lower than 133 percent of the federal poverty level, and children under age six who live in families with incomes that low. These children, adults, and families may receive Medicaid but not SSI.

Covered Services

What Medicaid covers varies from state to state. A minimum set of services includes inpatient hospitalization, outpatient hospitalization, emergency room services, laboratory and X-ray services, physician services, medical and surgical dental services, pediatric and family nurse practitioner services, and the like. In addition, states may opt to provide other services. These may include optometrist services and eyeglasses, prescription drugs, prosthetic devices and other assistive technology devices and services, and regular dental services.

Medicaid Ruling 77–102 (see www.cms.hhs.gov) states that children may be eligible for Medicaid coverage *based on their own resources* following 30 days of hospitalization. This has the effect of qualifying a child who previously had not been Medicaid-eligible because of family income. The ruling is important because a child's long-term hospitalization can bankrupt mid-SES and even some high-SES families. What happens after the child is released from the hospital? In most instances, the regular eligibility rules resume; that is, mid- and high-SES families lose eligibility once the child is released. However, if Medicaid coverage for care at home is approved, this reversion to the usual rules does not occur—the child continues to be eligible for Medicaid coverage for the duration of such approved services.

Family members need to recognize that services that are offered in one state may not be available in another state. States also vary tremendously in the amount of such services provided, the frequency with which they are offered, where they are made available, and many other details. For example, states may limit the number of physician visits for which reimbursement may be claimed each year. Indeed, states may require all Medicaid recipients to go to hospital emergency rooms rather than to personal or family physicians. Another fact that is important for families to understand is that Medicaid regulations require physicians, hospitals, and other medical services providers to accept the Medicaid reimbursement as full payment. This requirement has the effect of causing some providers to decline to serve Medicaid-covered patients.

Some Medicaid services are identical to some services that appear in IFSPs and IEPs. In the event that a given service is available under both Medicaid and the IDEA, who pays for the service? The answer is, the Medicaid agency should pay on behalf of Medicaid-covered infants, toddlers, and children. Section 1903 of PL 100–360, the Medicare Catastrophic Coverage Act of 1988, remains in effect despite the fact that other components of that act later were repealed. Says Section 1903:

> *(c) Nothing in this title shall be construed as prohibiting or restricting, or authorizing the Secretary to prohibit or restrict, payment under subsection (a) for medical assistance for covered services furnished to a handicapped child because such services are included in the child's individualized education program established pursuant to part B of the Education of the Handicapped Act or furnished to a handicapped infant or toddler because such services are included in the child's individualized family service plan adopted pursuant to part H of such Act.* (42 USC 1369b)

This requirement has proven to be very helpful to states that are struggling to finance IDEA Part C and Part B services, because it provides an alternative source of financing for some services—including speech-language pathology, audiology, psychology services, physical and occupational therapy, medical counseling, and medical services for diagnosis and evaluation—for children who are covered by Medicaid (U.S. Congress, 1988, pp. 268–269).

Family Opportunity Act

The 2005 Deficit Reduction Act includes, in Section 6062, the Family Opportunity Act. This ended a seven-year effort by many disability advocates. It allows families with incomes of less than three times the federal poverty level (about $60,000 for a family of four) to *buy Medicaid coverage*. States may require cost sharing (premiums and co-pays), but those are capped. The program is optional for states. It begins, with the youngest children, in 2007.

Early and Periodic Screening Diagnosis and Treatment (EPSDT)

The EPSDT program, which is a required component of all state Medicaid plans, *must provide and pay for medical services needed due to conditions that are identified and/or diagnosed through EPSDT* even if *these services are* not *contained in the state Medicaid plan.* This makes EPSDT of great importance in early childhood special education. EPSDT assures prompt and effective treatment for conditions that are discovered during screening—at no cost to IDEA Part C early intervention programs and Part B special education programs.

States must conduct outreach activities to inform medical practitioners and families alike about EPSDT services. In addition, states must connect families seeking services to approved providers. The state Medicaid office is a good source for information about EPSDT services in a particular state (see www.acf.hhs.gov).

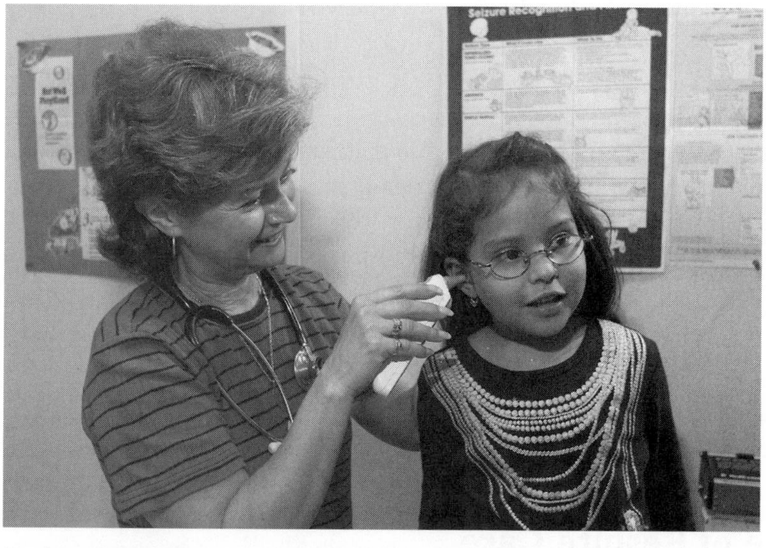

Early and periodic screening, diagnosis, and treatment (EPSDT) programs are required by law to offer treatment for conditions discovered during EPSDT screenings.

State Children's Health Insurance Program (SCHIP)

Enacted in 1997 as part of the Balanced Budget Act (PL 105–33), the State Children's Health Insurance Program is in Title XXI of the Social Security Act. SCHIP expands health coverage for children whose family members do not have health coverage from employment yet do have income and/or wealth above those required for Medicaid eligibility. States offer health insurance for children of families having incomes as high as 200 percent above the federal poverty level—for example, about $38,000 in 2004 for a family of four. All 50 states, the District of Columbia, and five U.S. territories have SCHIP programs. The fact that the annual cost of Medicaid services for covered children, as recently as 1998, was just $1,150 (much lower than the yearly cost for covered adults) contributed to this expansion of coverage (www.cms.hhs.gov). Consumer-oriented information about SCHIP is offered at www.insurekidsnow.gov. This last URL is a good one to give to families (PL 105–33; Title XIX of the Social Security Act).

MATERNAL AND CHILD HEALTH

The Maternal and Child Health Services block grant program, administered by the Maternal and Child Health Bureau in HHS, supports community-based and family-focused care for children. Thirty percent of MCH block grant funds must be used for children with disabilities. The bureau is located at 5600 Fishers Lane, Room 18-A, Parklawn Building, Rockville, MD 20857.

Significance of MCH Block Grants

The program offers relatively unrestricted funds to states for activities related to reducing infant mortality and morbidity (serious illness). Every year, hundreds of thousands of pregnant women receive prenatal care from MCHB-funded programs. Those programs also offer services directly to young children, including health assessments and follow-up diagnostic and treatment services. These family and child services include home health care and respite services (see the next section.) Following enactment of what is now Part C of the IDEA, MCH legislation was revised to require state and local MCH-funded programs to provide case management services and other services that are family-focused so as to facilitate integration with early intervention programs. Most services are offered free of charge to low-SES families. Families with more substantial resources may be charged fees on a sliding scale (PL 101–239; 42 USC 701).

RESPITE CARE

Respite services are child care services provided so that family members may receive a "respite" or brief release from what is, for many family members, a continuous responsibility. The ARCH National Resource Center for Respite and Crisis Care Services (www.archrespite.org) outlines the justification for respite services in this way:

> The stresses that challenge family stability when one member is a child with disabilities include a higher incidence of divorce or separation, inadequate health care coverage, increased financial stress, feelings of isolation, depression, loneliness, and fatigue due to the constant caregiving tasks required for the child's health and well-being. (ARCH Factsheet Number 31)

Significance of Respite Care

Respite services are not explicitly included among the "early intervention services" that Part C programs may offer to families (see IDEA Part C, Section 632[4]), nor are they specifically identified among the "special education" and "related services" that Part B programs may offer (see IDEA Part B, Sections 602[22] and 602[25]). Although Part C early intervention programs and Part B education programs may seek state agency approval for provision of respite services, a more likely source of financing is the Child Abuse Prevention and Treatment Act Amendments of 1996 (PL 104–235). Title II of this act (42 USC 5116 et seq.) authorizes respite care to "support the additional needs of families with children with disabilities through respite care and other services" (Sec. 201[b][1][F]).

The program is administered by HHS's Administration for Children and Families (ACF), contact information for which was given earlier. The ACF Children's Bureau provides formula grants to state lead agencies. This program replaces the respite care programs that had been authorized by the Temporary Child Care for Children with Disabilities and Crisis Nurseries Act of 1986 and its 1992 reauthorization (PL 104–235; 42 USC 5116 et seq.).

DEVELOPMENTAL DISABILITIES ASSISTANCE AND BILL OF RIGHTS ACT

The Developmental Disabilities Assistance and Bill of Rights Act of 2000 (PL 106–402) offers funds to states to create direct service and advocacy programs on behalf of children and adults with severe disabilities. This is not an education law. Rather, it serves to supplement the IDEA by providing family support and by funding advocacy activities within states to help to protect children with severe disabilities. The act is administered by the HHS's ACF (details are at www.acf.hhs.gov).

Definition

The act (popularly called "the DD act") defines *developmental disability* in Section 102(8):

> *The term "developmental disability" means a severe, chronic disability of an individual that—(i) is attributable to a mental or physical impairment or combination of mental and physical impairments; (ii) is manifested before the individual attains age 22; (iii) is likely to continue indefinitely; (iv) results in substantial functional limitations in 3 or more of the following areas of major life activity:*
>
> *(I) self-care*
> *(II) receptive and expressive language*
> *(III) learning*
> *(IV) mobility*
> *(V) self-direction*
> *(VI) capacity for independent living*
> *(VII) economic self-sufficiency; and*
> *(v) reflects the individual's need for a combination and sequence of specialized, interdisciplinary, or generic services, individualized supports, or other forms of assistance that are of lifelong or extended duration and are individually planned and coordinated.*

The definition clearly refers to individuals who have severe and multiple needs for services from a variety of agencies.

This act is alone among federal laws in offering a definition of "young children" with disabilities:

> *Infants and Young Children.—An individual from birth to age 9, inclusive, who has a substantial developmental delay or specific congenital or acquired condition, may be considered to have a developmental disability without meeting 3 or more of the criteria described in clauses (i) through (v) of subparagraph (A) if the individual, without services or supports, has a high probability of meeting those criteria later in life.*

These words mean that children under age 10 may be considered to have a "developmental disability" even if they do not satisfy all requirements for that classification. The intent appears to be to make reference to the IDEA's language on "developmental delay"—which, as you may recall (see the Part I opener) has an age range, "three through nine," during which children with disabilities may be given a "delay" label rather than a condition label. The age range in the DD act is the same. It is different, however, from the "birth to age eight" inclusive definition used in the EC field for "early childhood."

Significance of the DD Act

This act aims to empower family members to take part in state and local policymaking on behalf of their children. It authorizes state "DD councils" on which family members may serve. These councils engage in "advocacy, capacity building, and systemic change" (Section 121), meaning that they work to change state laws, regulations, and programs so that these are more effective for individuals with severe disabilities. No less than 60 percent of the members of a council must be parents, guardians, or other immediate family members of individuals with developmental disabilities or must be persons with such disabilities. The act also provides states with funds to finance "protection and advocacy agencies" (P&A agencies). Those state government entities are unusual in that they are expressly authorized to litigate against other state agencies, county agencies, local agencies, and not-for-profit organizations. These P&A agencies go into state institutions, local group homes, schools, and other facilities serving individuals with developmental disabilities. If agency staff find violations of law, they may (and often do) sue the service provider as well as the governmental units that fund it.

The DD act also grants certain rights to individuals with developmental disabilities. Section 109 of the act calls for services to meet certain minimum standards, for visiting privileges to be accorded to family members, and for aversive treatment techniques (chemical, physical and other restraints, isolation) to be avoided. The P&A agencies are to protect those rights (PL 106–402, 42 USC 15001 et seq.).

HEAD START

Head Start

is the federally supported program of services for preschool children that was begun in 1965. Most children served are from disadvantaged families; at least 10 percent of the children served must be children with disabilities.

The ACF at HHS also administers the **Head Start** program, through its Head Start Bureau located at 330 C Street SW, Washington, DC 20447. Its site at www.acf.hhs.gov offers information for families, professionals, and others. It includes a link to the "Head Start Performance Standards," which describe the criteria Head Start programs must satisfy in order to continue to receive federal funds.

The Head Start Act, most recently reauthorized in the Coats Human Services Amendments of 1998 (PL 105–285), defines "child with a disability" and "infant or toddler with a disability" by referencing those terms as defined in the IDEA. No less than 10 percent of children served in Head Start programs must be children with disabilities or infants/toddlers with disabilities. The proportion applies to each state. A relatively new "Early Head Start" program serves children under age three. The traditional Head Start program is for children between the ages of three and six.

The Head Start Performance Standards refer to staff qualifications, physical environments, and coordination with state and local IDEA implementation programs. A summary follows:

- **Teachers.** Head Start requires that half of the classroom teachers in any program possess an associate degree (AA), baccalaureate degree (BA), or an advanced degree such as a master's degree (MA); the other half must have a child development associate (CDA) credential. People qualify for a CDA by taking courses in child development, often at community colleges. These staff requirements are notably lower than the IDEA's "highest standards of the state" rules. Thus, Part C early intervention and Part B special education programs typically are staffed by classroom teachers possessing at least a BA and usually an MA in education, special education, or a related area. If these programs employ CDA-credentialed individuals, it is more often as paraprofessionals, teacher aides, and the like than as classroom teachers.
- **Physical environment.** Advocates have expressed concern for many years that the facilities rented or leased by Head Start programs frequently are inaccessible to persons using wheelchairs or other mobility devices. The Head Start Performance Standards address this concern by requiring programs to ensure "that the physical environments of Head Start programs are conducive to providing effective program services to children and families and are accessible to children with disabilities and their parents" (Section 640 of the Head Start Act, PL 105–285).
- **Coordination with IDEA.** Head Start programs are required to work closely with Part C and Part D programs. This includes a formal transition for participants in Early Head Start or in regular Head Start programs to pre-K–12 public school programs for special education.

Early Head Start

The Early Head Start program, which serves a population of the same age as does IDEA Part C, was begun in 1994. Thus, it is almost 30 years younger than is the traditional Head Start program (which began in 1965). Early Head Start serves children birth to age two inclusive (0–36 months) from low-SES families. The program continues to be much smaller in size than the traditional Head Start program. As of 2004, to illustrate, just 55,000 infants and toddlers participated in Early Head Start. They represented only 6 percent of the 905,000 young children enrolled in Head Start programs that year (www.acf.hhs.gov).

Significance of Head Start

Head Start programs provide options that families may consider. Both Early Head Start and regular Head Start programs offer obvious opportunities for inclusion. In communities where public services for infants, toddlers, and preschoolers are lacking or few in number, Head Start may provide some of the only such opportunities. On the other hand, families should recognize that the professional standards and (often) the physical environments of Head Start programs are lower in quality than are those of IDEA programs. Thus, for children with severe physical, mental, and sensory disabilities, Head Start may not offer appropriate services (PL 105–285; 42 USC 9801 et seq.).

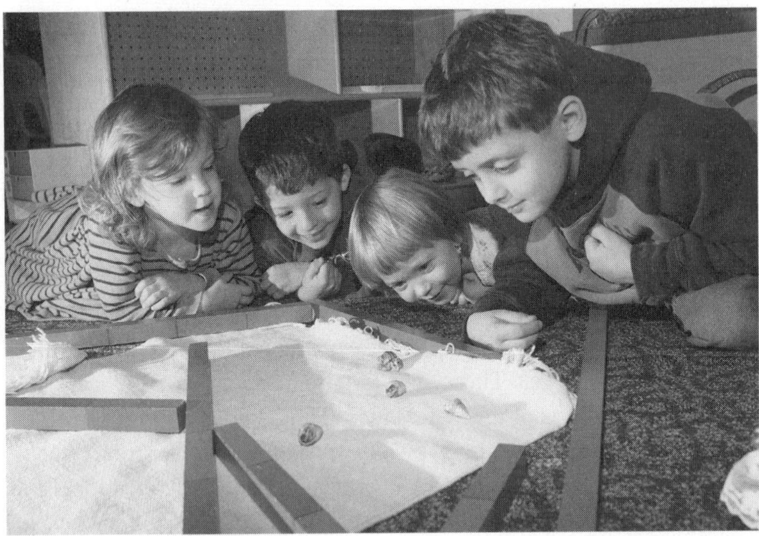

ECSE workers can help adults learn how to create inexpensive learning tools and activities for use at home.

ASSISTIVE TECHNOLOGY ACT

The Assistive Technology Act (PL 105–394) authorizes state programs designed to increase awareness among families about assistive technology devices and assistive technology services, both of which are authorized "early intervention services" under IDEA Part C and "related services" under IDEA Part B. The Assistive Technology Act adopts the IDEA definitions of "assistive technology devices" and "assistive technology services." The act also authorizes a national Web site devoted to assistive technology. This is assistivetech.net^{sm}, which sponsors the site at www.assistivetech.net. That site lets visitors search for hardware, software, and other products. Along with www.abledata.com, it is a major tool for increasing awareness about assistive technologies. Finally, the act authorizes funds that states may use to finance low-interest loan programs and revolving loan funds under which individuals with disabilities may acquire assistive technology devices (PL 108-364; 29 USC 3001 et seq.).

SUMMARY

This chapter opened by describing rights that families of young children enjoy. The IDEA itself provides procedural safeguards (due process rights). The Americans with Disabilities Act (ADA) and Section 504 are civil rights statutes that assure individuals with disabilities of nondiscriminatory treatment in much of the United States. The 1990 ADA extends to the private sector the rights that Section 504 introduced in 1977 but only with respect to organizations and agencies that received federal financial assistance. The ADA also protects family members who might be subjected to discrimination on the job or elsewhere because of their relationships with the child with a disability.

The full effect of these rights will be felt only when family members become aware of them. ECSE personnel and other advocates need to learn about these rights—and to tell family members about them.

This chapter also offered the reader information about federal programs and services that authorize supplementary funding for important services that many infants, toddlers, and preschoolers with disabilities need. States vary considerably in how they carry out these programs and in what services they provide. These variations are so numerous that it is not possible to detail all of them here. Information on provisions specific to a given state is available from organizations in the list that follows and in the Resources section of this book.

For early intervention programs in particular, but often for preschool special education programs as well, coordinating all of these varied funding sources and meeting all of their variegated requirements are both challenging and time-consuming. Since 1986, however, many of the more glaring inconsistencies and more obvious gaps have been eliminated. Continued interagency coordination efforts at the federal, state, and local levels are required for additional streamlining to occur.

The state education agency, the state Part C lead agency, the DD Planning Council, and the state Medicaid agency are all sources of information about services available in a given state. The Social Security Administration may be contacted at the following address for information about disability programs:

Social Security Administration
Office of Disability
545 Altmeyer Building
6401 Security Boulevard
Baltimore, MD 21235
www.socialsecurity.gov

In addition, the following organizations are excellent sources of up-to-date summaries of the current status of these programs. While many of the federal and private organizations discussed in the Resources section may be helpful, the groups listed here have shown interest in, and expertise about, the programs outlined in this chapter. Tracking developments at the SSA, for example, and making those understandable for parents and ECSE workers are daunting tasks.

Children's Defense Fund
25 E Street NW
Washington, DC 2001
www.childrensdefense.org

National Early Childhood Technical Assistance Center
Campus Box 8040, UNC-CH
Chapel Hill, NC 27599-8040
www.nectac.org

National Dissemination Center for Children with Disabilities
PO Box 1492
Washington, DC 20013
www.nichcy.org

United Cerebral Palsy Associations
1660 L Street NW, #700
Washington, DC 20036
www.ucpa.org

Zero to Three
2000 M Street NW #200
Washington, DC 20036
www.zerotothree.org

KEY TERMS

adaptability
Americans with Disabilities Act (ADA)
Head Start
Medicaid
places of public accommodation
procedural safeguards
reasonable accommodations
Section 504
Supplemental Security Income (SSI)

QUESTIONS FOR REFLECTION

1. Why is Section 504 of the Rehabilitation Act important for children who have attention deficit hyperactivity disorder?
2. Suppose a parent who has a child with high-cost medical needs were to seek employment. What help does the ADA offer? Why could such help be important to this parent?

3. On an everyday basis in the community, how does Title III of the ADA help families who have children with disabilities?
4. Why is "stay put" ("maintenance of current educational placement") an important right for families?
5. Why is the Fair Housing Amendments Act's prohibition against discrimination on the basis of disability by landlords and real estate brokers important for many families?
6. What do service coordinators do for families that participate in Part C programs? Does the answer help you understand the importance of these laws to service coordinators as well as to parents?
7. Supplemental Security Income (SSI) has tightened its eligibility criteria. How do these changes affect families and young children?
8. What effects do you think the SSI changes are having on families that want to benefit from Medicaid?
9. Why are early and periodic screening, diagnosis, and treatment (EPSDT) services so important for many young children with health needs?
10. How are Medicaid services financed? Of what relevance is this for a family contemplating a move from one state to another?

PRACTICAL EXERCISES

1. Imagine that you are a parent of a young child who uses a wheelchair. In your hometown, would it be possible for you and your child to

   - eat at a local restaurant (examine main entrance, space for a wheelchair to maneuver in the restaurant, and rest rooms)?
   - mail a letter at the local post office?
   - get a hair cut?
   - bank?
   - shop for clothing?

   In each instance, you should look for ramps from ground level to the first-floor entrance; doors at least 36 inches wide; a 60-inch *turnaround space* (so someone using a wheelchair can turn around); tables high enough to allow the wheelchair to slide under the table top but not so high that the individual using the wheelchair could not use the table top; and an accessible stall in the restroom.

2. Explore the two sites at the American Foundation for the Blind listed here. Then summarize, in your own words, how hotels may become accessible to people who are blind. What about health care facilities? What steps should they take to become accessible?

WEB SITES OF INTEREST

www.access-board.gov U.S. Access Board—standards for building accessibility

www.usdoj.gov U.S. Department of Justice (click on/search for "Office of the Americans with Disabilities Act—Rules for ADA and Section 504")

www.afb.org American Foundation for the Blind, Access to Hotels and Motels (search for "ADA Checklist for Hotels and Motels")

www.afb.org American Foundation for the Blind, Access to Health Care Facilities (search for "ADA Checklist: Heath Care Facilities and Service Providers")

ECSE Practices

PART 3

6 Methods

7 Evaluation and Assessment

8 Individual Planning

9 Technology

Part III centers on practices in early intervention and in preschool and primary special education. The focus in this part is *what professionals do* with families and with young children.

Chapter 6, the *methods* chapter of this text, includes information about the techniques and materials that early interventionists and special educators follow and use. We talk about *embedding* early intervention services, special education, and related services into the general curriculum. We also outline developmentally appropriate practice (DAP) and Direct Instruction (DI), two broad ways of approaching instruction. The chapter continues with suggestions on teaching language, math, and other content material to young children. It then looks at "the place of place"—where we provide these services. Chapter 6 concludes with a discussion of philosophy and values that drive ECSE.

We turn our attention in Chapter 7 to evaluation and assessment. Early interventionists and special educators tend to use observations and parent reports about young children with disabilities much more than formal tests. This is because the validity and reliability of assessment instruments with this population often are questionable. Fortunately, we can learn a great deal about infants, toddlers, preschoolers, and primary-grade students with disabilities by watching them closely and by listening carefully to the adults in their families.

Chapter 8 brings us to the next step: translating what we learn in evaluation and assessment to individual plans. We explore, in depth, IFSPs and IEPs. In study after study, early interventionists and special educators ask for specifics about how to prepare and carry out these plans. This chapter responds to those needs by explaining exactly what laws and regulations say about these plans.

Part III concludes by looking at technology. Increasingly, both *high technology* (electronics) and *low technology* (simple, one-function items) are being used in ECSE. They have proven their value both in enhancing program-parent communications and in improving the quality of services for young children with disabilities. Although high technology changes rapidly, sometimes breathtakingly fast, it is so important that all early interventionists and special educators need to master at least the basics. Chapter 9 includes links, which are uniform resource identifiers (URIs) or uniform resource locators (URLs) that allow you to visit Web sites containing the very latest information. Those URIs and URLs help "bring the book alive" by providing constantly updated information that will help you in your work.

CHAPTER

6

Methods

> [W]hat is most important is not a consensus about whether DAP [developmentally appropriate practice] or ECSE offers more appropriate frameworks for the education of young children with disabilities but, rather, a consensus about the specific aspects of implementing high-quality programs that are appropriate for all children, regardless of developmental level or individual needs. These include programmatic issues such as how to arrange environments, how teachers should interact, how programs should be monitored, and how data describing programs must be used to inform parents about their effectiveness in meeting children's needs. (Carta, Atwater, Schwartz, & McConnell, 1993, p. 243)

OBJECTIVES

After reading this chapter, you should be able to:

- Explain what a curriculum is and what it must contain.
- Describe how to use embedding in ECSE.
- Identify strategies for teaching academics in ECSE.
- Explain how to use behavior modification with young children.
- Describe what *naturalistic teaching strategies* are recommended in ECSE.
- Explain how to decide what the *natural environment* is for infants or toddlers.

- Explain how to decide what the *least restrictive environment* is for children with disabilities.
- Describe what values are important in ECSE.
- Describe how to make ECSE facilities accessible to persons with disabilities.

CHAPTER OUTLINE

- **OVERVIEW**
- **CURRICULUM**
  - **Curriculum and Individualization**
  - **EC versus ECSE Curricula**
  - **Curriculum and Structure**
  - **Curriculum Choices**
  - **Methods in Early Intervention**
    - *Embedding*
    - *Special Sessions*
    - *Family Services*
  - **Methods in Preschool**
    - *Embedding*
    - *Phonemic Awareness and Phonics*
    - *Shared Reading*
    - *Number Sense*
    - *Behavior Modification*
  - **Sign Language**
    - *Special Sessions*
  - **Methods in the Primary Grades**
    - *Response to Intervention*
    - *Embedding*
    - *Grouping*
    - *Teaching Strategies*
    - *Creating Advance Organizers*
    - *Providing Community-Based Instruction*
    - *Literacy*
    - *Mathematics and Science*
    - *Related Services*
- **THE "PLACE" OF PLACE**
  - **Natural Environments**
  - **Least Restrictive Environments**
  - **Inclusion**
- **INDOOR AND OUTDOOR ENVIRONMENTS: ACCESSIBILITY**
  - **Indoor Environments**
  - **Outdoor Environments**
- **PRACTICAL ISSUES**

OVERVIEW

Early childhood special education is far more challenging today than anyone could have envisioned just a few years ago. The goals ECSE strives to reach are many, the needs of families and children diverse, and the resources limited. ECSE programs seek to empower families, to individualize services for both families and young children, to coordinate delivery of a broad range of services across many agencies, and, while doing all these things, to practice deeply held beliefs about what is right and good. Now, on top of all of that, there is a new emphasis on academics. Two federal laws—the No Child Left Behind Act of 2001 and IDEA 2004—bring language arts, math, and science to the forefront. High-stakes tests in those areas begin as early as third grade. This means that preschool teachers as well as kindergarten and primary-grade teachers need to prepare young children to pass standardized tests in those content areas.

This chapter is the *methods* chapter of the text. We open with a brief discussion of *curriculum*—what it is and how early interventionists and other ECSE personnel use it. We then explore methods for early intervention, preschool, and the primary grades. We emphasize new research on *embedding* instruction in activities that families participate in during the course of the day and week. We also explore the more traditional methods of *direct instruction* that have characterized ECSE for many years.

Much of what we discuss was hinted at in the chapter-opening quote from Carta et al. (1993). They refer to *developmentally appropriate practice (DAP),* which you will recall is the set of recommendations developed by NAEYC for use in early childhood programs serving children. The vast majority of those children do not have disabilities. DAP, you remember, has the teacher *facilitating* learning and the children engaging in self-directed activities. Carta et al. contrast DAP to ECSE, their shorthand for direct instruction. Programs serving young children with disabilities tend to have teachers leading instruction and children engaging in teacher-directed activities.

Carta and her colleagues correctly insist that the issue facing ECSE programs is not one of choosing either of these alternatives but rather one of designing instruction that responds to the needs of the children being served. This is, in large part, a matter of curriculum. In fact, a national survey found that ECSE professionals were committed to and practiced strategies and tactics recommended by both camps (Kilgo, Johnson, LaMontagne, Stayton, Cook, & Cooper, 1999).

Early intervening services are IDEA-funded interventions that are offered to students who are *not* IDEA-eligible (not identified as having disabilities or delays in development). The intent is to provide support services that prevent unnecessary referral into special education.

Many of the methods outlined in this chapter may be used also in providing what IDEA 2004 calls **early intervening services.** Known under previous reauthorizations of the law as "prereferral interventions," these are steps that may be taken on behalf of children who are not yet identified as eligible for IDEA services (i.e., they are not classified, nor do they have individual written plans). More than a change of wording occurred in 2004. Section 612(f) of Part B now permits schools to use up to 15 percent of IDEA funds to support students with no disabilities. The law includes "*a particular emphasis on students in kindergarten through grade 3 who have not been identified as needing special education or related services but who need additional academic and behavioral support to succeed in a general education environment.*" The intent is to prevent unnecessary referrals into special education. If supports are provided on a timely basis to young children, these students may be assisted within the general education environment.

Following our discussion of curriculum is "the place of place"—a look at the emotional issues of what is meant by the terms *natural environment* and *least restrictive environment.* Those terms help us understand *where* services are to be delivered. Embedding, for example, is a practice that fits readily into inclusive settings. Direct instruction, by contrast, tends to be used more often in special settings. However, as we shall see, embedding can be used in special settings and direct instruction may be applied in inclusive settings. To anticipate a point we make throughout this chapter, what really matters in ECSE is *what* we do with young children and their families, not so much *where* we do those things. Similarly, there are instances in which the needs of particular children at particular times are better met in special settings, notwithstanding the appeal of inclusion as a philosophy. We conclude our examination of placement issues by looking at ways in which ECSE programs may make their facilities and services accessible.

CURRICULUM

Curriculum

is a planned sequence of activities, including both content and process, through which educators change children's behavior. Curriculum is a vehicle for reaching goals and objectives as identified in IFSPs and IEPs—an ordered arrangement of individually selected learning experiences that respond to children's particular needs.

The word **curriculum,** understood broadly, refers to the following:

- *Whom* to teach (the child? the family? both?)
- *What* to teach (content—facts and sequence)
- *How* to teach it (philosophy, methods)
- *Accommodations* to make for children's disabilities (devices, procedures, etc., allowing children to "hear" despite deafness, "see" despite blindness, "move" despite physical disability, and more)
- *Materials* to use (tangibles, paper, etc.)
- *Room layout* (activity centers, etc.)

Understood in this way, a curriculum represents decisions about what is important for young children to learn: should early childhood learning be about preacademics, or should it be about play and social interaction? A curriculum also reflects decisions about how early childhood special educators should act in the classroom or play center: should teachers and interventionists be active in instructing children, or should they remain in the background as children teach themselves?

Thus, curriculum is a very big subject. It is the subject of entire texts. Rather than attempt to treat curriculum comprehensively here, an impossible task, this chapter focuses on key issues facing ECSE. The reader is referred to book-length treatments for additional

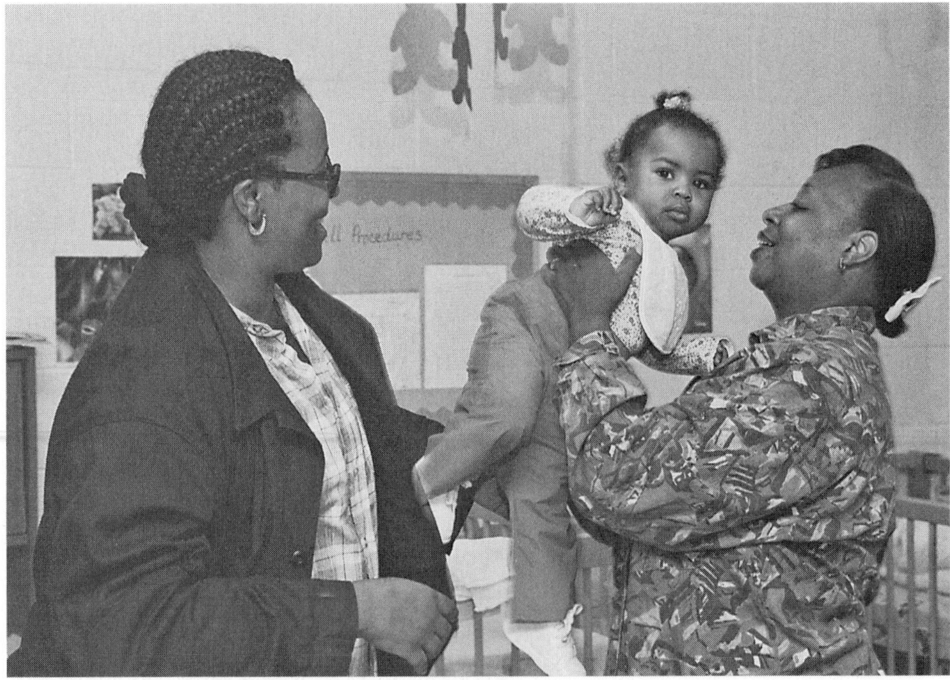

"Methods" include what professionals do and say with family members and young children.

information. Among those recommended as resources for ECSE personnel are the following titles:

Bigge, J. (1988). *Curriculum-based instruction for special education students.* Mountain View, CA: Mayfield. This text is especially strong on direct instructional techniques for use with children who have severe disabilities or delays.

Borich, G. (2007). *Effective teaching methods: Research-based practice* (6th ed.). Upper Saddle River, NJ: Merrill/Prentice Hall. This 440-page book is especially helpful in articulating what "research-based practice" means for educators.

Charlesworth, R., & Lind, K. (2007). *Math and science for young children* (5th ed.). Clifton Park, NY: Thomson Delmar Learning. This book focuses on problem solving, observation, and other approaches for teaching math and science to children in the birth-to-eight age range.

Goodman, J. (1992). *When slow is fast enough.* New York: Guilford Press. While not a curriculum textbook as such, this book is very enlightening as to actual practice in preschool special education programs serving children with moderate retardation and other disabilities. Goodman offers a memorable portrayal of what special educators do on a day-in and day-out basis with three- to five-year-olds who have special needs.

Machado, J. (2007). *Early childhood experiences in language arts: Early literacy* (8th ed.) Clifton Park, NY: Thomson Delmar Learning. This text helps teachers integrate activities in listening, speaking, reading, writing, and viewing information. It includes curricula and instructional ideas for poetry, finger play and puppetry.

McGinnis, E., & Goldstein, A. P. (2000). *Skillstreaming in early childhood: Teaching prosocial skills to the preschool and kindergarten child.* Champaign, IL: Research Press. This publication offers 40 lessons in resolving conflicts and other interpersonal issues.

Odom, S. L., McConnell, S. R., Ostrosky, M., Peterson, C., Skellenger, A., Spicuzza, R., et al. (2000). *Play time, social time: Organizing your classroom to build interaction skills.* Minneapolis: University of Minnesota Institute on Community Integration. This curriculum features sharing and other interpersonal activities. It includes a 100-day sample intervention schedule.

Ostrosky, M., & Sandall, S. (Eds.). (2001). *Teaching strategies: What to do to support young children's development.* (Monograph Series No. 3). Longmont, CO: Sopris West. This monograph includes articles on time delay, embedding, and other practices.

Paasche, C., Gorrill, L., & Strom, B. (2003). *Children with special needs in early childhood settings.* Clifton Park, NY: Thomson Delmar Learning. This text focuses on techniques for helping students with disabilities who are integrated into regular EC programs.

Schiller, P. (2003). *The complete resource book for toddlers and twos.* Beltsville, MD: Gryphon House. One of a series of "complete resource books" by the author, this one focuses on children one and two years of age.

In very general terms, the basic choice facing early childhood special educators is between *Direct Instruction* and *developmentally appropriate practice (DAP).* Directive strategies feature a strong role for the educator or interventionist; the teacher decides what the content will be, individualizes both content and process to respond to the unique needs of each child, and delivers much of the instruction personally in an active manner. DAP, by contrast, has the educator in a facilitative role; the teacher decides on content (e.g., by selecting the materials, placing them strategically throughout the room, etc.) but from that point forward allows the children to individualize the ways in which they experience that content in self-directed learning activities. These alternatives are not necessarily mutually exclusive (Bailey, 1997). EC educators and ECSE personnel alike are finding ways to fashion a third, integrated approach that features the best aspects of each philosophy.

The state of the art in the early years of the 21st century is one of ECSE personnel remaining dissatisfied by the commercial alternatives available to them (Bruder, 1997). Early interventionists and special educators alike find that they must pick and choose among competing packages. The balance of this chapter's section on curriculum considers the issues around which early childhood special educators are basing their choices.

Curriculum is a planned sequence of activities, including both content and process, through which educators aim to change children's behavior. Wolery and Sainato (1993), in their curriculum section of the DEC recommended practices document, suggest that curriculum includes content (behaviors and skills, whether academic, adaptive, or other), methods of delivering this content, and ways of individualizing it for particular children. Cole, Dale, and Mills (1991) emphasize the importance of matching different methods of instruction to children's individual characteristics. Examining learning by language-delayed children, they found no direct effect for type of instruction (direct vs. interactive), but they did note an important interaction: children with relatively lesser language delays seemed to learn more from direct instruction, whereas those with comparatively greater language delays appeared to learn more with interactive approaches. Those findings were opposite from what previous studies had suggested. The work of Wolery, Sainato, Cole, Dale, and Mills cautions us to individualize content according to what actually helps children learn.

Curriculum is a vehicle for reaching goals and objectives as identified in IFSPs and IEPs: it is an ordered arrangement of individually selected learning experiences that responds to children's particular needs. Both NAEYC, in its DAP guidelines, and DEC, in its recommended practices, urge that curriculum decisions reflect the principles of individualization, family involvement, cultural competency and sensitivity, and fulfillment of the children's needs.

The urgency of reforming ECSE curricula so as to enhance young children's mastery of academics can hardly be overstated. New studies demonstrate that children with disabilities are, overall, failing to meet the new, higher learning standards imposed by NCLB and IDEA 2004. To illustrate, the SEELS study (see "Is ECSE Effective?" in Chapter 3) found that disturbingly high proportions of young children are held back (retained), even in the primary grades. They seem to begin acceptably well, with 88 percent of six-year-olds in first grade, as would be expected. However, while eight-year-olds typically are in third grade, among those with disabilities just 4 percent are there. A remarkable 60 percent are in second grade, and a dismaying 31 percent are in first grade (U.S. Department of Education, 2003, p. 53, Table 1–12). Other SEELS data help explain why. On tests of letter-word identification skills, a rather basic assessment (students need not know the meaning of words), more than half of students with disabilities in the 6- to 12-year-old age range scored as low as the worst-performing 20 percent of their general education peers (U.S. Department of Education, 2003, p. 56, Figure 1–42). Similarly, in math, young children with disabilities were twice as likely to be in the lowest-performing quintile than were others (p. 59, Figure 1–45). Standardized assessments in science were not given nationwide until 2006–2007.

The challenge for ECSE is to figure out how to bring the academic skills and knowledge of young children with disabilities up to acceptable levels while at the same time continuing to meet their (often many) unique needs. From all indications, it will not be easy.

CURRICULUM AND INDIVIDUALIZATION

Perhaps the opening question for ECSE staff is whether NCLB and IDEA 2004 should be understood as calling for the wholesale dismantling of existing curricula and their replacement by curricula that focus squarely on preacademics and academics. This question can be answered, quickly and easily, by examining IDEA 2004. The law does not alter *any* of the long-standing requirements that instruction be individualized or that it be appropriate to the unique needs of each child. Clearly, ECSE is expected to continue to custom-design instruction so that the needs identified in IFSPs and IEPs are met.

That being the case, we should also agree that retention in grade is not the answer. The SEELS study shows that IEP teams and primary-grade teachers seem to have decided that they will respond to the increased demands for academic instruction by holding young children back. In other words, "if we can't do all of this at once, we'll do it twice." The research evidence on the issue of retention in grade is humongous, and it is unambiguous: holding children back for a year is unquestionably associated with later failure and with dropping out of school (see, e.g., *Analysis of the Five-Year PACT Longitudinal Data*, 2005; a brief summary of evidence on this point appears in Lange, 2004). If, as SEELS shows, many young children with disabilities are being retained in grade for two or more grades, those effects may be even more deleterious.

A better approach is to integrate instruction in preacademics and academics into the existing fabric of individualized and appropriate instruction for young children with disabilities. That is easier said than done. However, there are obvious places to begin. As anyone who has spent much time in primary-grade inclusive classrooms knows, related services often involve pulling children out of the classroom. **Pullout** for speech, for example, is done so frequently that first- and second-grade teachers routinely complain that at least one and often two or more students miss any lesson they give. Is it any wonder, then, that the academic performance of young children with specific learning disabilities, speech and language impairments, mental retardation, or deafness suffers? A better alternative to pullout is **push-in:** the therapist enters the classroom and provides the support services there, supplementing the teacher's academic instruction (see, e.g., Bowe, 2005).

Pullout

describes an arrangement in which the child leaves the classroom. The related-services professional works with the child in another setting, typically a therapy room.

Push-in

is the arrangement in which the child remains in the classroom. The therapist enters the classroom and performs work with the child there. This may be seat by seat, or it may be in a corner of the room.

Another way to enrich instruction is to weave academics into everyday activities. Such *embedding*, as was shown in Chapter 3, has much research evidence behind it. It requires early interventionists, special educators, and related-services personnel to think on their feet. In the coming pages, we will discuss one method that works: *parallel talk*. As young children engage in play, professionals give them words to go with what they are doing. Similarly, as children participate in a music activity, teachers work with them on *phonemic awareness*. Song lyrics are well suited for phonemic awareness exercises because words are sung more slowly than they are spoken (Gabreli et al., 2005).

If teachers find that young children are not learning as much, as fast, as needed, the solution is not to "do it again" by holding the child back. Rather, educators should change what they are doing. There is no shortage of information on effective strategies.

Guralnick (2005) recommends adopting a developmental approach in early intervention; ideas for preschool and kindergarten are offered by Deiner (2005), Allen and Cowdery (2005), and Gargiulo and Kilgo (2005).

In the area of reading instruction, there is much support for a three-tier approach (O'Connor, Harty, & Fulmer, 2005): early intervening services in kindergarten, small-group reading instruction three times a week, and one-on-one individualized help daily.

Experts also concur that educators cannot hope to be more effective if they do not gain and keep control of behavior in the classroom. A great deal of evidence has accumulated behind positive behavioral supports (Conroy, Dunlap, Clarke, & Alter, 2005; see also Chapter 14 of this book).

Translating this body of research into everyday classroom activities is essential if ECSE is to reach what clearly is its most pressing current challenge: helping young children with disabilities meet today's higher learning standards.

EC VERSUS ECSE CURRICULA

As suggested earlier, differences are apparent between EC and ECSE programs. ECSE programs tend to develop IFSPs and IEPs based on identified needs of children and their families. There is an orientation toward those needs and the services that meet them. EC programs generally look less to children's individual needs and more to the developmental needs of all children in a given age range. McLean and Odom (1993) suggest that ECSE curricula in general place more emphasis on performance of behaviors and skills, while EC curricula attend more to children's thinking processes. Graham and Bryant (1993) observe, "While similar themes are common to both orientations (e.g., independence, adaptation, contingent responsiveness, social competence, individualization), developmental and behavioral ideologies have often been translated into distinctly diverse approaches toward teaching and learning for the child with special needs" (p. 31). This diversity of approach has often been described as a contrast between informal, child-oriented, and permissive EC programs and formal, professional-oriented, and behavioral ECSE programs. Graham and Bryant state:

> Practices used in early childhood education often vary from those used in early childhood special education. Theoretically, early childhood practices tend to reflect the developmental principles of Piaget, Erikson, and Montessori; early childhood special education is grounded in the behavioral constructs of Skinner, Pavlov, and Watson. (p. 31)

This is, of course, an overly generalized statement. Many EC programs use behavioral approaches, and many ECSE programs model themselves after Piaget. To illustrate the point, incidental teaching, or child-initiated approaches during which the teacher takes advantage of opportunities a child presents to help the child learn new things, is an approach more associated with EC than with ECSE. Yet, as Carta et al. (1993) point out, it was developed by two behaviorists working in ECSE-type settings (Hart & Risley, 1968). Nonetheless, there is much truth in Graham and Bryant's (1993) observations. Service delivery strategies and tactics that are effective in helping many young children with disabilities do tend to have a strong behavioral orientation. To take just one example among many, Lovaas (1987) showed that young children with autism can achieve far more in a highly structured environment than previously had been believed. This finding raises the question of structure in the curriculum.

CURRICULUM AND STRUCTURE

Graham and Bryant (1993) state that research "repeatedly [has] shown the effectiveness of programs that are more structured and directive for children with severe disabilities" (p. 33). Cole et al. (1993), however, raise questions about popular assumptions of how program structure interacts with severity of children's disabilities. Educators have assumed that children with more severe disabilities and those who function at a lower level benefit most from a structured Direct Instruction (DI) approach, while less severely disabled children and those who function at a higher level learn better from less structured, more interactive learning opportunities (Snow, 1989). But Jenkins, Cole, Dale, and Mills (1989) found the opposite effects in a preschool population. And further research with a more typical ECSE population by the same authors (Cole et al., 1993) produced the same results: relatively higher-functioning children with disabilities did better in structured DI programs, whereas relatively lower-functioning children learned more in an interactive approach. "The conventional wisdom that slower children should receive DI and relatively higher functioning children should be placed in more interactive, cognitively based programs should be reconsidered" (p. 26). Cole et al. also suggest that more structured, DI approaches require children to understand and follow specific instructions, while interactive approaches allow children who cannot participate effectively in such structured curricula nonetheless to benefit from spontaneously occurring incidents. In a follow-up report, the researchers found that similar effects persisted as late as ages 12 and 16 (Dale, Jenkins, Mills, & Cole, 2005). It may be, they suggest, that DI and other highly structured methods impose heavy cognitive burdens on young children who have cognitive limitations. Those children, including many with mental retardation and severe learning disabilities, may learn more, and remember it better, if taught using discovery learning approaches.

Perhaps the best guidance for ECSE programs is not to assume that any given approach is the best practice for all children and not to select curricula according to assumptions about their effectiveness with children functioning at different levels of disability. Rather, curricula designed and selected to respond to individual needs of children are likely to prove more successful. Such an approach may require more planning, but the evidence is that no single curriculum or type of curriculum has yet been shown to be more effective with ECSE populations than others.

CURRICULUM CHOICES

ECSE curricula include instruction in language, cognitive, social, and both fine motor and gross motor development. Some are targeted toward specific populations. These include the Early Partners curriculum for preterm, low-birthweight infants (Sparling, Lewis, & Neuwirth, 1993); the Learning through Play curriculum for children with motor impairments (Fewell & Vadasy, 1983); and the SKI*HI curriculum for children with hearing impairments (Clark & Watkins, 1985).

Other curricula suitable for more general ECSE populations include the Carolina Curriculum (Johnson-Martin, Jens, & Attermeier, 1986); the Portage Guide to Early Education (Bluma, Shearer, Frohman, & Hillard, 1976); the Hawaii Early Learning Profile (HELP) (Furuno, O'Reilly, Hosaka, Inatsuka, Allman, & Ziesloft, 1985); and the cognitive-linguistic infant intervention of Dunst (1981).

Specific curricula may, of course, be adapted from general EC curricula, such as the "partners for learning" and "learning games" publications by Sparling and Lewis

(1979, 1985), the "active learning" program by Cryer, Harms, and Bourland (1987a, 1987b), and Badger's (1981) "joy of learning" plan for infants and toddlers. Fewell has stressed play-based curricula (Fewell, 1991; Fewell & Glick, 1993).

DEC's recommended practices suggest that ECSE professionals select or design curricula that, in the words of curriculum section authors Wolery and Sainato (1993), "cause rapid learning and use of important skills" (p. 53). They add, "[O]nly strategies should be used that result in rapid learning. Such learning often provides feelings of success and mastery, and it saves time for other goals" (pp. 53–54). They suggest that a variety of behaviorist and naturalistic approaches have attracted research support and that such approaches—including response prompting, differential reinforcement, and response shaping, as well as adult responsiveness to child behavior and milieu or naturalistic teaching—may be recommended practices.

The concern Wolery and Sainato (1993) demonstrate for rapid learning reflects a decision commonly made in ECSE programs across the nation: the unique needs of young children with disabilities are such that educator control, including use of the principles of applied behavior analysis, is appropriate because it "saves time," to quote Wolery and Sainato. Carta et al. (1993), in the chapter's opening quotation, express a similar philosophy, saying that curriculum decisions come first. ECSE programs frequently determine that preacademics are critical for young children with disabilities. Following from that decision are others about how the day is structured, how the teacher behaves, and how materials are used. Stating it differently, ECSE programs do not reach abstract conclusions about the relative merits of child-initiated versus educator-initiated instruction. Rather, the pressing need for time to teach preacademics dictates the approach to be adopted.

Coming from a background in EC, Joan Goodman (1992) was struck by the ways in which this played out in the 20 ECSE programs she visited in 10 states. These programs worked with preschool-age children with moderate mental retardation. Summarizing her observations, Goodman writes:

> Teachers are rarely sidetracked from their serious and earnest pursuit of the curriculum [selected largely from developmental checklists]. Despite their difficult charge and charges, they maintain a remarkably unflappable poise, mild-mannered but always in control of their children. . . . Teachers operate all day within this narrow, sedate, "professional" behavioral range and expect children to do likewise: sit, listen, respond when spoken to ("use your words"), stay "on tasks." . . .
>
> The problem is that moderately retarded children have difficulty meeting these expectations—both academic and behavioral. They do not catch on to preacademics, forget the right answers they may have given the day before, and are restless with the work demands. . . . Teachers, therefore, must work very hard to accomplish their goals. They cannot, Summerhill style, just put out the materials and let the children loose. (pp. 89–90)

Notwithstanding the legitimate concerns raised by Goodman, the fact is that ECSE professionals are even more challenged today to save time, to teach preacademics and academics, and to demand that young children attend to instruction. Moreover, their choices for curricula are increasingly being curtailed. NCLB uses the term "scientifically based" (or variations thereof, such as "research-based") no fewer than 100 times to refer to the kinds of interventions that are approved for use under that Act. IDEA 2004, too, calls for "scientific, research-based interventions." The U.S. Department of Education maintains a Web site that lists instructional methods shown to, and those not shown to, be effective, at the What Works Clearinghouse (www.whatworks.ed.gov). That site details numerous approaches for beginning reading. To date, though, it has fewer approved interventions for primary-grade math or science.

What are "scientifically based" or "research-based" approaches to instruction? Briefly, according to the Department's Institute of Education Sciences, scientifically based research

- employs systematic, empirical methods that draw on observation or experiment; involves data analyses that are adequate to support the general findings; relies on measurements or observational methods that provide reliable data; makes claims of causal relationships only in random-assignment experiments or other designs (to the extent such designs substantially eliminate plausible competing explanations for the obtained results);
- ensures that studies and methods are presented in sufficient detail and clarity to allow for replication or, at a minimum, to offer the opportunity to build systematically on the findings of the research;
- obtains acceptance by a peer-reviewed journal or approval by a panel of independent experts through a comparably rigorous, objective, and scientific review; and
- uses research designs and methods appropriate to the research question posed.

Thus, for reading and language arts, the federal government asserts that research-based interventions focus on phonemic awareness, phonics, reading fluency, vocabulary development, and reading comprehension. For examples in other disciplines, see Borich (2007).

METHODS IN EARLY INTERVENTION

Infants and toddlers who have developmental delays or established conditions need a wide variety of services. Their family may as well. The IDEA calls for services for very young children and their families to be provided in what it calls the *natural environment (NE).* This is most often the home. It may be any other setting that the family considers to be *natural* not only for the infant or toddler with a disability but also for its other children. The term *NE,* then, may refer to any of many possible settings.

You will recall that infants and toddlers tend to be more comfortable with family members, especially the mother, than with people outside the family. They also tend to learn most by doing things. Physical activity leads to cognitive development. Very young children enjoy imitating adult actions. By the time they are two to three years of age, they typically enjoy pretend play. Knowing these things helps you select interventions.

Embedding

A key for early intervention personnel is to practice what experts refer to as *embedding.* This important term means inserting specialized instruction into activities in which the family engages during the normal course of its day. Bricker and colleagues (1998) define it as follows: "a procedure in which children are given opportunities to practice individual goals and objectives that are included within an activity or event in a manner that expands, modifies, or adapts the activity/event while remaining meaningful and interesting to children" (p. 13).

This definition explains that embedding is a method through which early intervention personnel may help very young children to reach IFSP goals in a nondisruptive way. The key to embedding is to examine carefully what the family does during any given day or week. Those family activities potentially offer opportunities for learning. Seizing those opportunities to deliver the extra help infant and toddlers with disabilities need is what makes embedding so helpful.

Self-talk

is a form of *elaboration.* The ECSE professional articulates what he is doing and thinking. This offers a model for the young child. It also gives the young child labels for objects, feelings, and actions.

Parallel talk

is a kind of *elaboration.* The ECSE professional speaks about what the young child is doing, seeing, hearing, and so on. See *self-talk.*

Elaboration

is expanding on an answer, a decision, or a question so the child understands more fully and learns words associated with an occasion, event, or object.

To take one example from many, consider a toddler who has a delay in language development. The early interventionist engages in **self-talk** (articulating what he is doing and thinking) and in **parallel talk** (talking about what the toddler is doing). Self-talk and parallel talk are both examples of **elaboration.** The key is to put into words what the toddler is seeing, hearing, touching, and doing, as well as what the early interventionist is doing and thinking. This use of words offers the toddler a rich language environment. It labels objects, colors, activities, and emotions. It gives the toddler words he may adopt to express his desires, feelings, and behaviors. At the same time, self-talk, parallel talk, and other forms of elaboration by ECSE workers show adult members of the family how to improve the quality of their everyday activities for the benefit of the infant or toddler.

All of this may become more clear when we look at natural environments. Dunst and his colleagues have identified an impressive variety of family activities into which specialized instruction may be embedded (Dunst, Bruder, Trivette, Hamby, Raab, & McLean, 2001; Dunst, Bruder, Trivette, Raab, et al., 2001; Dunst, Herter, et al., 2001). Table 6–1 illustrates this broad range of activities and settings. The reader should take some time to study the table. Consider how such outdoor activities as biking, bird-watching, gardening, hiking, and others, for example, may provide natural opportunities for learning. These are things that families do: they are natural environments. Yet each can be so much more. Take bird-watching, for example. Were the adults in the family and the early intervention professionals accompanying them to talk about all the sights, sounds, and experiences involved, articulating what they do and giving the toddler words to describe his own experiences and feelings, the activity would become so much more than just bird-watching. It would be transformed into a science lesson, a language lesson, and even a physical education lesson.

To continue, consider "magic shows" in Table 6–1. Families often take young children to local libraries, schools, and other community centers for magic shows. Many birthday parties, whether in private homes or in local fast-food restaurants, too, feature magic shows. These activities are natural environments for families that want to take part in them. Yet each may be enriched by embedding. Early interventionists may take advantage of magic shows to expand on the experience. As the family prepares to depart for the event, for example, professionals may ask young children what they expect. Adult and child may talk about what is and is not *magic:* Is it typical, for example, for rabbits to suddenly appear in hats? Do we each check our hats before putting them on to make sure that no rabbit is inside? If it were to happen that a rabbit popped out of a hat that we had just seen was empty, where could that rabbit have come from? Early interventionists could also talk with the toddler about where the family was planning to go. Where is Jimmy's house? How far away is it? In what direction? About how long should it take the family to get there? As this example illustrates, embedding offers opportunities for language, science, and geography lessons.

TABLE 6–1

Examples of Sources of Community-Based Natural Learning Opportunities.

CATEGORY/EXAMPLES
Amusements and Attractions
Amusement parks
Aquariums
Arcades
Aviaries, bird sanctuaries
Displays and attractions
Duck ponds
Farms: seasonal/holiday activities
Fish ponds
Planetarium
Playlands
Science centers
Train rides
Zoos and wildlife preserves
Arts and Culture Activities
Children's museums
Historic sites
Museums
Musicals/plays/ballet
Outdoor concerts
Performing arts for children
Regional attractions
Clubs and Organizations
4-H
Big Brothers/Big Sisters
Community centers
Ethnic heritage clubs
Family centers
Hobby/activity clubs
MOMS clubs
Play groups
Scouting/Camp Fire/Indian Guides
Service clubs
Toy lending libraries
YMCA/YWCA
Youth groups
Community Celebrations
Block parties
Children's festivals
Church festivals
Community Day
Community garden
Farm shows
Folk festivals
Hayrides
Heritage festivals
Historic reenactments/celebrations
Holiday festivals (light shows)
Local/county/regional fairs
Parades
Picnics
Family Outings
Car/bus/subway rides
Church/synagogue
Circus, Ice Capades, etc.
Family reunions
Holiday gatherings
Movies
Picnics
Pumpkin patches, tree farms
Shopping, eating out
Special family celebrations
Visiting friends/relatives
Learning and Education Activities
After-school programs
Art
Bookstore story hours
Bookmobile
Ceramics
Children's museum activities
Creative movement
Dance
Daycare/preschools
Drama classes
Enrichment classes
Gymnastics/tumbling
Library story times, movies, and activities
"Lunch Bunch" for toddlers
Magic shows
Music
Nature center activities
Parent education classes
Petting zoos
Puppet shows
Religious education
Science center activities
Storytellers
Outdoor Activities
Biking
Bird-watching
Boating/canoeing
Camping
Fishing
Gardening
Hiking
Horseback riding
Kite flying
Skating/sledding/skiing
Walks/races
Parks and Recreation
Nature trails
Open/family gym time
Organized activities
Parks
Playgrounds
Swimming pools
Summer camps

(*continued*)

Table 6.1 (Continued)

CATEGORY/EXAMPLES	CATEGORY/EXAMPLES	CATEGORY/EXAMPLES
Parent and Child Activities	Time for Mommy & Me	Ice skating/sledding
Baby/toddler gym (e.g., Gymboree)	Water Babies	Karate
Neighborhood games (dodgeball, kickball, etc.)	**Sports Activities**	Roller skating/blading
Pajama Story Time, Read to Me (public library)	Baseball/T-Ball	Soccer
Playful parenting	Basketball	Softball
Play groups	Bowling	Swimming
	Football	Tennis
	Golf/miniature golf	Track and field

Reprinted with permission from C. J. Dunst, S. Herter, H. Shields, & L. Bennis (2001). Mapping community-based natural learning opportunities. *Young Exceptional Children, 4*(4), 16–25.

We *embed* instruction into activities that families take part in for several reasons (Horn et al., 2000). First, embedding allows early interventionists to supplement the everyday activities of the family. This means that the instruction is less intrusive. Second, embedding permits early intervention services to be more natural than would be the case were those services to be separate and different from activities that others in the family were pursuing. Third, embedding works in a very wide variety of activities. As illustrated in Table 6–1, the possibilities are almost limitless. Finally, embedding requires little additional staff and thus is economical. Early intervention personnel may accompany the family on a few family-selected activities and during those occasions teach adults and older siblings how to embed instruction. Thereafter, as the family continues to engage in these kinds of activities, the continued presence of early interventionists may not be necessary.

How to Embed Instruction

Embedding instruction requires that the ECSE professional conduct an advance examination of the activity. It must be thoroughly understood who will be doing what when and where (Horn et al., 2000). This should be evident from the examples given earlier. To continue with the magic show example, early intervention personnel need to know where the show will be held, how that location relates geographically to the family's place of residence, what the show entails (e.g., what kinds of tricks will the magician perform?), and much else. The professional then should consult the child's IFSP to identify goals and objectives that could relate to the magic show. Choosing appropriate goals and objectives is the next step. Following that, the early interventionist needs to select methods to use.

As suggested earlier, verbal guidance, including elaboration, is one approach. Words that are age- and developmental-level-appropriate for the young child need to be

Filling a basket for a picnic involves manipulatives and allows for embedding of instruction in vocabulary.

selected. The early interventionist needs to identify natural occasions during the activity to introduce those words, how to define them, and what responses to expect from the child. The key is for the professional to use appropriate words liberally, explaining and defining each with the use of manipulatives, examples, and other techniques, and giving the child opportunities to demonstrate understanding.

Another technique involves use of **performance cues.** These are prompts of various kinds. They *cue* the child to produce behavior. Examples of performance cues are **verbal prompts** ("What do we call this?" Pause. "Yes, we call it a hat!"); **modeling** (the early interventionist does the desired behavior while the child observes, then gives the child an opportunity to do it); and **visual prompts** (the professional points to a "wand" as a cue for the child to wave it).

Performance cues

are prompts alerting children that certain behaviors are expected. These cues may be physical, verbal, or visual.

Verbal prompts

are spoken cues signaling to the child what behavior is desired.

Modeling

is showing the child what behavior is desired.

Visual prompts

are visible cues signaling to the child what behavior is desired.

Adaptations

are adjustments to processes and materials so they may be used by children with disabilities.

For some very young children, **adaptations** of materials are necessary for embedding to be successful. Horn and her colleagues (2000) use the example of adding a spout to a paint can so that children with limited mobility skills could pour paint. There are, of course, many other examples of adaptation. For a child who is blind, a community map with raised features may be used to illustrate the family's planned trip to the magic show. An interpreter may sign the words spoken by the magician so a deaf child can follow the show.

Special Sessions

As useful as embedding can be, ECSE personnel need to recognize its limitations. Not all early intervention services can be embedded, nor should early interventionists *try* to embed all such services. Some are appropriately provided as separate activities. A good example is the specialized instruction some children with physical disabilities require. Another is a speech-language pathology session to give a very young child practice in articulating sounds with which he has difficulty.

Direct Instruction

Direct Instruction

is structured, teacher-led instruction. It often is contrasted to less didactic, more interactive approaches to learning, such as *developmentally appropriate practice.*

Some young children require specialized teaching to master the prerequisites of reading, counting, and other skills. While this instruction may be embedded into family activities, more often it is offered in a special session. This is because it is time-consuming, because it requires the professional to have appropriate materials on hand, and because it is most successful when the activity has the child's full attention. Frequently used by ECSE professionals is a set of techniques, briefly described earlier, collectively known as **Direct Instruction.** By Direct Instruction, we mean the explicit teaching of material, careful review by teachers of the kinds of mistakes children make, reteaching of information as needed to help students correct those mistakes, sustained practice of newly learned skills, and regular review to be sure that students retain learned information. These steps have a strong research basis (see, e.g., Gersten, Carnine, & Woodward, 1987).

The *explicit teaching* part emphasizes clear presentation of exactly the knowledge and skills that students need. The *careful review* element comprises item analysis and other probes that teachers use to discover what kinds of thinking mistakes and knowledge gaps are lowering scores. The *reteaching* component features the teacher presenting, again, the information that the child has not yet mastered. The *sustained practice* aspect is self-explanatory: The child is given lots of opportunities to practice the skills. The final portion of Direct Instruction is *periodic review and retesting* over long periods of time to maintain learning.

One example of Direct Instruction is DISTAR (Englemann & Bruner, 1984; Kuder, 1990). This is *programmed instruction* that is highly structured. DISTAR uses a *say, show, do* approach. The teacher directs all activities. He may say, for example, "This is a _____." He repeats that sentence, then asks the child to do so. He may show something, and he may ask the children to do something, such as choosing among three objects. DISTAR is so regimented that it generally is used in special, rather than in regular, sessions.

Physical Therapy

The U.S. Department of Education's (1993a) rules for the IDEA define "physical therapy services" as

> *services to address the promotion of sensorimotor function through enhancement of musculoskeletal status, neurobehavioral organization, perceptual and motor development, cardiopulmonary status, and effective environmental adaptation. These services include . . . [p]roviding individual and group services or treatment to prevent, alleviate, or compensate for movement dysfunction and related functional problems.*

It should be evident from this definition that much physical therapy needs to be conducted on its own. Physical therapists aim to maintain the child's physical capabilities (i.e., to prevent muscle atrophy or wasting away from nonuse). With many children, especially those who have cerebral palsy, positioning is a vital service. Supports need to be designed, made, and installed to help the very young child sit, stand, and eat/drink. Physical therapists also help very young children balance themselves when seated or standing, as well as teaching them how to move despite physical limitations. Toddlers may "ride" oversized balls to develop the ability to balance. As these examples suggest, much physical therapy requires special sessions and even special facilities. Those are not often available in the environments that families frequent on their own.

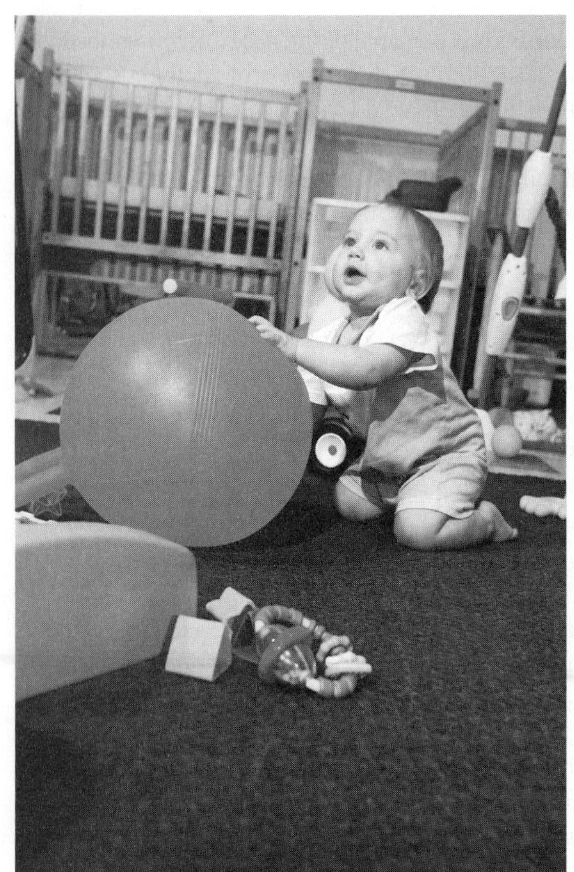

"Riding" an oversized ball can help a young child to learn balance.

Tying a shoelace can challenge a young child.

Occupational Therapy

The department's regulations define "occupational therapy" in these words:

> *(i) services provided by a qualified occupational therapist; and (ii) includes—(A) improving, developing, or restoring functions impaired or lost through illness, injury, or deprivation; (B) improving ability to perform tasks for independent functioning if functions are impaired or lost; and (C) preventing, through early intervention, initial or further impairment or loss of function.* (U.S. Department of Education, 1999)

As this definition makes clear, occupational therapy focuses more on practical, everyday skills than does physical therapy. Although occupational therapists can do many of the things that physical therapists do, occupational therapists tend to concentrate more on functional abilities. An example is dressing. Some young children have great difficulty buttoning shirts. Occupational therapists know what adaptive devices are available to make this task easier (e.g., hooks) and what bypass methods may be used (e.g., shirts with no buttons). Similarly, occupational therapists can help young children turn the pages of a book, either independently or with the help of an adaptive device. By contrast, physical therapists tend to focus on helping young children maintain the physical abilities they possess and perform gross motor activities such as walking or running.

Speech-Language Pathology

What used to be called *speech pathology* is now known as *speech-language pathology* to reflect greater emphasis on language development. The federal rules define "speech-language pathology services" in these words:

> *(i) Identification of children with speech or language impairments; (ii) diagnosis and appraisal of specific speech or language impairments; (iii) referral for medical or other professional attention necessary for the habilitation of speech or language impairments; (iv) provision of speech and language services for the habilitation or prevention of communicative impairments; and (v) counseling and guidance of parents, children, and teachers regarding speech and language impairments.* (U.S. Department of Education, 1999)

Speech-language pathologists work on (1) speech, (2) language, and (3) feeding. In the latter efforts, they take steps much like those performed by occupational therapists. Some young children, including many with cerebral palsy, need professional help with eating and swallowing. Much of this work must be done separately, because it is so time-consuming that it would disrupt typical family routines.

Family Services

Early intervention services include services provided directly to family members and not just to infants and toddlers with disabilities. This is why the written plans are called Individualized *Family Services* Plans.

A vital component of early intervention is the work of the service coordinator. This person is named in the IFSP (often with his phone number and e-mail address). Service coordination includes, as the name implies, coordinating on behalf of the family services from a variety of local, county, and state agencies.

Counseling

is the broad term referring to support, guidance, help in decision making, and information and referral.

Respite services

are early intervention services offering breaks for family members from child care.

Counseling services may be provided for adults in the family and for siblings. Some early intervention and preschool programs offer **respite services** in which adult caregivers are offered an afternoon or even a weekend "off" as ECSE professionals care for the child. Such services can be invaluable, particularly when young children have behavioral disorders. A variety of social work services may also be offered to families.

METHODS IN PRESCHOOL

When ECSE personnel work with children in the three- to six-year age range, they typically do so in classrooms. While early intervention services commonly are delivered in the home and in community settings that families frequent, preschool services generally are provided in schools. These may be public preschools, Head Start programs, or private preschools. They may be preschools that serve a general population, or they may be specialized preschool classes or schools.

The new stress on readiness to learn is placing increasing emphasis on academics in preschool and kindergarten. No Child Left Behind envisions all children being ready to learn by first grade and able to read by third grade.

Recall that preschoolers typically engage in parallel play. They are just beginning to master turn taking and other aspects of joint play. Possessions can become prized objects at this stage. For that reason, disputes over who can play with an object may lead to altercations. They tend to like puzzles and simple card games. They also enjoy construction with LEGO™ blocks and other plastic or wooden pieces. Artwork with crayons, paint, chalk, and collage materials can engage their attention for sustained periods of time (and they will want to keep what they produce!). This information helps you design effective interventions for this age group.

Embedding

Embedding is particularly appropriate in inclusive preschools. The practice is minimally disruptive of ongoing classroom activities, because it usually may be performed by regular educators and because the activities occurring in typical preschool classrooms tend to lend themselves well to embedding (Horn et al., 2000). Wolery and Gast (2000) have shown that embedding may be done during art instruction, dramatic play, snack periods, and in-class transitions from one activity to another. The keys, they found, are for teachers to alter what children do during regularly scheduled activities. Educators should look for opportunities to embed instruction into many different activities and to embed different kinds of instruction within each of those activities. The same instruction (e.g., vocabulary development) may be embedded across activities so that repetition occurs naturally in a variety of settings. This promotes **generalization** of learning; that is, children who learn how to do something in one environment with one adult demonstrate the ability to perform that activity in at least one other setting with at least one other adult.

Generalization

occurs when a child who has learned a new behavior in one environment with one adult performs that behavior in a different environment and/or with a different adult.

Principle of partial participation
is the concept of creating a meaningful role for a child who cannot fully participate in a given activity.

Time delay
is a procedure through which prompts are offered and then gradually phased out.

Some suggestions on embedding instruction in a preschool classroom are offered by Horn and her colleagues (2000). These include seating children with disabilities up front, using assistive technology devices as appropriate, and providing performance cues and physical assistance to children who need it. A related idea is the **principle of partial participation** (Anderson, 1992). If a child who is mentally retarded or one who has a physical disability cannot fully participate in an activity, the educator should provide whatever support is needed so that the child can do a meaningful part of it. Anderson emphasizes that the role be a valuable one.

Wolery (2001) adds that **time delay** may also be embedded into classroom activities. In time delay, ECSE workers provide prompts to young children to signal what the children are expected to do. Prompts include modeling, physical prompts, and other assistance. Gradually, prompts are delayed and then removed altogether. The techniques have been used to help children learn to answer questions, to put on their coats, to use spoons and other implements, and to label pictures. The guiding principle is to demonstrate the desired behavior, make sure the child can perform it, prompt for it when it is desired, and gradually phase out the prompts so that the child performs the activity when appropriate.

A wide variety of strategies and tactics lend themselves well to embedding. Table 6–2 describes some that have been used in preschool classes.

TABLE 6–2

Description of Naturalistic Teaching Strategies.

STRATEGY	DESCRIPTION
Use novel materials.	Incorporate materials that are novel and/or unique into the activity. These may be items in which the child has shown a previous interest, such as Pooh characters, balloons, bubbles, and so forth.
Join the activity.	The teacher joins the activity and engages in play-related actions and themes with the children.
Invite child to make choices.	The teacher invites the child to make choices about desired actions and/or materials. This can be done through questions or nonverbal overtures (e.g., holding out a container of markers so the child can select one).
Use incidental strategies.	Place items out of reach, block the child's access to desired items, sabotage the materials, and act in ways that violate the child's expectations (use materials incorrectly or respond to child's overtures in the wrong way).
Use comments and questions.	The teacher uses comments and questions to facilitate the child's interest and/or play-related talk (e.g., "I think that I'll put my baby right next to yours" or "Why are you coloring your turtle purple?").
Require expansion of talk.	Respond to the child's talk in a manner that generates elaboration. If the child requests a ball, the teacher might ask, "What color is the ball?" and "What are you going to do with it?" before giving the child the ball.
Invite interaction with peers.	The teacher encourages interaction with other children by drawing the child's attention to peers or prompting peers to direct overtures to the focal child (e.g., "Maybe you could ask Sam if he will play with you").

From "Teaching social interaction skills in the integrated preschool: An examination of naturalistic tactics," by Kohler et al., 2001, *Topics in Early Childhood Special Education, 21,* 93–103, 113. Copyright (2001) by Pro-Ed, Inc. Reprinted with permission.

Phonemic Awareness and Phonics

Embedding is a useful tool for enhancing learning by young children with disabilities in the "early reading" programs that are part of the December 2001 federal law, No Child Left Behind. This law provides federal funds for prekindergarten programs, especially language development efforts, that are designed to help all children begin school "ready to learn" (to quote that law and also the earlier "Goals 2000" legislation). Young children with disabilities may benefit from these early reading and other programs if additional help is provided during those sessions. Embedding is probably the most efficient means of offering that extra assistance. This is because it fits supplementary instruction naturally into ongoing activities.

Phonemic awareness

is a set of abilities to combine and separate phonemes. It is a fundamental skill, probably one we are born with and one we perform with little cognitive effort. Sometimes called *phonological awareness,* this ability allows us to decode many hundreds of phonemes per minute to comprehend speech that we hear.

To illustrate, consider instruction in phonemic awareness. **Phonemic awareness** is the ability to manipulate phonemes in spoken syllables and words—both to *decode* syllables and words that are heard and to *encode* words by combining syllables. Most young children acquire skills of phonemic awareness during the pre-kindergarten years by playing with language. They take delight in their developing abilities, which is one reason many enjoy the Dr. Seuss books such as *The Cat in the Hat.* Some children, however, need explicit instruction to master these competencies. Techniques for teaching phonemic awareness include the following (National Reading Panel, 2000, www.nichd.nih.gov). If you think about each for a few moments, ways of teaching will occur to you.

- *Phoneme isolation.* Instruction in recognizing sounds within words ("What is the first sound in 'Mommy'?")
- *Phoneme identity.* Teaching children to recognize phonemes that occur in different words ("What sound is the same: kite, calendar, kid, kitchen?")
- *Phoneme categorization.* Categorizing phonemes as "same" or "different" ("Which word does not belong: man, map, mat, orange?")
- *Phoneme blending.* Instruction in combining phonemes into words ("What word is made up of these sounds: /s/, /uh/, and /n/?")
- *Phoneme segmentation.* Teaching children to count phonemes ("How many sounds are in 'mouse'?")
- *Phoneme deletion.* Instruction in isolating phonemes ("What word do I get if I take the /k/ out of 'couch'?")

Phonics instruction

is a method of reading instruction which emphasizes the sounding-out of words on the page. The assumption is that children have heard these words, many times, and simply need to connect the printed/written version of the word (which is new to them) to the sound(s) of the word (which is/are known to them).

Consider, too, **phonics instruction**—teaching children the connections between sounds (phonemes) and letters (graphemes). Phonics instruction helps young children to decode words on a page and also to encode them (spell them). If we see that a child consistently has difficulty distinguishing between *b* and *d* on a page (to choose one example), we may embed instruction on that differentiation within our ongoing instruction. The teaching of phonics includes the following (National Reading Panel, 2000):

- *Analogy phonics*—teaching new words by analogy to known words and word parts (*pear* includes sounds also in the known word *tear*)
- *Analytic phonics*—teaching children to analyze known words to determine their sounds (*cake* includes two /k/ sounds as well as a long "a" sound)
- *Embedded phonics*—teaching sound-letter relations in materials children are reading (words used in circle time, such as children's names)

- *Phonics through spelling*—teaching children to spell phonetically
- *Synthetic phonics*—teaching children to sound out letters and then to blend those sounds to produce words

Shared Reading

Shared reading

has adults and children reading predictable stories together in short time periods.

Shared reading of predictable stories is a good way to develop literacy skills. A "predictable" story is one that has a structure that is transparent to the children. Their guesses about "what happens next" are more often right than wrong. In shared reading, adults and children read the same predictable stories again and again. They talk about the stories, act them out, and write about them. Initially, the adult reads and the child listens. Gradually, in what Lonigan and his colleagues call "dialogic reading," the child assumes increasing responsibility for storytelling. The adult offers prompts, asks questions, and provides information. The adult might ask, for example, "What is the dog doing?" By this time, the child should know the story well enough to answer that question. Even modest investments of time (20 sessions of 15 minutes each) can produce marked improvements in literacy among preschoolers with special needs (Lonigan, Anthony, Bloomfield, Dyer, & Samwel, 1999).

Number Sense

Number sense

is the facility with numbers that allows young children to count, categorize, and perform other mental operations with numbers.

Number sense refers to a child's comfort level and flexibility with numbers, what they mean, and how to play with them. Number sense is a general facility with numbers that develops in most children before they start kindergarten. It includes the core ideas that discrete items are other countable, that some collections of items are higher in number than are collections, and that one counts within categories (e.g., four apples, four oranges, but eight pieces of fruit). It also incorporates the idea that numbers are symbols, shorthand representations of things and people. The construct of number sense is as important in the teaching of mathematics to students with learning disabilities as is the idea of phonemic awareness in the teaching of reading.

Manipulatives

are concrete objects children may touch, name, and count.

As with the prereading abilities of phonemic awareness, number sense must be developed in young children by the adults around them. ECSE professionals and parents may talk about numbers as these appear in every day activities (embedding). They may also play number games with preschoolers. **Manipulatives,** or concrete objects that children may count, are invaluable in developing number sense. Wooden blocks are a good example. Have the child count a small number of blocks, disregarding color. Then comment that some blocks are red and others yellow. Ask the child to count the yellow ones.

Behavior Modification

Young children who have behavior problems (including those identified as having social or emotional delays as well as those with emotional/behavioral disorders and many with ADHD) often require the structure that behavior modification provides. Educators may use behavior modification in inclusive preschools and also in special preschools.

Here, *behavior modification* refers to the specialized set of tools that research in psychology and education has given us over several decades. Behavior modification features the provision of reinforcers for behavior that we want to see more of—called *presentation reinforcement* or, less usefully, positive reinforcement. If José speaks words we are teaching him, we may offer him praise ("Good work, José!"). We may also give him tokens, such as chips, that he may later trade in for a favorite toy. We may even give him small candies, such as M&Ms.

The method frowns on *punishment,* which is the presentation of consequences that children dislike. Research has demonstrated that although punishment can and often does reduce the incidence of undesired behaviors, it frequently leads to *other* "bad behaviors"—particularly if the child believes that he has been unfairly punished. Rather, behavior modification teaches educators to ignore behavior they want to see less of—called *extinction,* because with no rewards following the behavior, it should eventually cease to occur.

Less used but helpful is *removal reinforcement.* This set of tools, sometimes called by the confusing term *negative reinforcement,* features action by adults to remove consequences that children dislike. We see removal reinforcement more often in K–12 education. A good example is when the teacher tells Ana, "Because you've done so well in class today, I am excusing you from tonight's homework. You're free to enjoy the evening, while your classmates have to do the assignment." This removes from Ana something she does not want. That, in turn, reinforces (or rewards) the good behavior she displayed in class that day.

Time delay (discussed earlier) is a technique of behavior modification. When used one on one with a child, it is also an example of applied behavior analysis.

Applied Behavior Analysis

Applied behavior analysis (ABA)

is a form of *behavior modification.* The term refers to techniques employing trials, usually one-on-one. It does not emphasize, as does cognitive behavior modification, teaching children why some actions are reinforced and some are not.

A subset of behavior modification is known as **applied behavior analysis (ABA).** This is "the process of applying sometimes tentative principles of behavior to the improvement of specific behaviors and simultaneously evaluating whether or not any changes noted are indeed attributable to the process of application" (Baer, Wolf, & Risley, 1968, p. 91). More generally, we use ABA in one-on-one sessions with young children, whether we conduct those in an inclusive classroom or not. As the definition indicates, ABA features continuous monitoring. We count the number of responses children make and plot those over time, usually on a chart. The term is also used to describe the intervention strategy promoted by Lovaas (1987) for use with young children having autism (see Chapter 15).

SIGN LANGUAGE

Signed English

is literally "English on the hands" because it presents signs in English word order.

Signing, whether in Signed English or American Sign Language (ASL), is a very helpful tool with many preschoolers. In **Signed English,** signs follow English word order. This approach lets ECSE providers speak while they sign. In ASL, signs are ordered according to the rules of that language (Klima & Bellugi, 1979), for which reason professionals should not simultaneously speak. Basic competency in Signed English, sufficient for simple communication needs, may be acquired in a few courses. Such courses are offered in most U.S. communities, often in continuing/adult education programs at local high schools and community colleges.

Young children who do not have intelligible speech (whether because of mental retardation, severe apraxia, cerebral palsy, or deafness) often can express themselves effectively by using signs. Studies reaching back more than 20 years have shown that young signers with unimpaired hearing can make themselves understood even when their speech cannot be comprehended (e.g., Kiernan, Reid, Jones, & Bowler, 1983; Grove & Dockrell, 2000). Children with limited ability to understand what is said to them (whether because of mental retardation, auditory processing difficulties, or deafness) may comprehend much more if it is offered to them in signs as well as in speech. This is particularly true when the visuospatial and temporal features of sign language are tapped to express meaning (e.g., Goldin-Meadow, McNeil, & Singleton, 1996; McNeil, 1992). A signer may use space to explicate an event that a young child will not understand via speech. To illustrate, the right index finger (representing another person) may be brought close to the signer to indicate, "She came up to me," while the index finger moving from the signer out into space represents "I went to her."

For some young children, signs are their primary means of expressive communication (e.g., Grove & Dockrell, 2000). The point is that it offers them a means they can use, even if their speech is unintelligible. For other young children, signs are their preferred ways to receive communication. The signs for *small, large, stop,* and *milk,* to illustrate, are so strongly associated with their referents that even children with moderate mental retardation usually can comprehend what is meant. This is true of many of the "survival words and phrases" that all young children need to learn (Polloway & Polloway, 1981).

American Sign Language (ASL)

is a language of its own, as is English. Because the first users of what is now ASL were speakers of French, ASL has grammatical and syntactical similarities to French. Words that do not have known signs may be finger spelled. Finger spelling is literally "spelling in the air" as one letter after another is produced using the fingers.

Personnel skilled in **American Sign Language (ASL)** can be valuable in ECSE programs. Trained ASL instructors, sign language interpreters, and others fluent in the language may teach children, family members, and other staff in ways of finger spelling and signing ideas and words. For young children who do not have intelligible speech, signing and finger spelling offer quickly learned and easily implemented modes of expressive communication. The reader needs to bear in mind that teaching the child alone, without also instructing staff and family members, helps little. The adults need to understand what the child is trying to say.

Special Sessions

Some activities are better offered separately. A good example is learning to use an assistive technology device for the first time. Some direct instruction, as well, is more suitable for special sessions. However, both may also be embedded.

Assistive Technologies

Young children who need assistive technology devices to learn need, first, to learn to use those devices. This point is, of course, self-evident, but it has implications for service delivery. Take, for example, a child who is blind or has low vision. Such children typically can do well in integrated K–12 settings if they have and use appropriate assistive technology devices. Some of these devices let children take notes in the classroom. Other products read printed materials, including textbooks, out loud. Still other products enlarge print and images. These devices can make a very substantial difference for children who need them. Learning to use them takes time. Instruction may be provided by assistive technology specialists or orientation and mobility specialists.

The preschool years are good ones for introducing these devices to young children, training the children in their use, and giving the children ample opportunities for practice with the devices. Training in assistive technologies is often better done in special sessions than in regular ones. After mastering the use of assistive technologies in special

Animals offer high-interest activity for instruction.

settings, children who are blind or have low vision are better equipped for inclusion in K–12 classrooms.

Direct Instruction

Direct Instruction continues to be important during the preschool years. Although it may be done in inclusive settings, separate sessions are sometimes appropriate. As is shown later in this book, intensive language instruction for children who are deaf or hard of hearing may be a good example of an activity that is better done separately from the regular preschool program. This is because the language needs of these children often are greater by orders of magnitude (i.e., *much, much* greater) than those of other preschoolers. The instruction may be provided by teachers of the deaf or by speech-language pathologists.

METHODS IN THE PRIMARY GRADES

Early childhood services continue through the age of eight (until the child turns nine), meaning, in most cases, through second or third grade.

Recall that children in primary grades are much more aware than are preschoolers that there is a world beyond their neighborhoods. They typically express interest in field trips to local places. That interest can be tapped to teach the basics about geography, political science, and much else. Primary-grade children can learn through independent reading, and they can write simple stories. They rapidly learn such skills as turn taking, following classroom and school rules, and solving concrete problems. By the time they are about eight years of age, they begin to be able to engage in symbolic thought. That is, they can comprehend such ideals as democracy by relating it to their experiences in shared decision making in the classroom. Understanding these basics about this age group helps you to decide on methods of instruction. Table 6–3 offers a quick summary.

Response to Intervention (RTI)

Response to intervention (RTI)

has educators trying out one technique, then another, with a child, and tracking the student's progress, to discover what works with that child. It is one of the tactics IDEA calls "early intervening services" and is also a new element in the federal definition of specific learning disabilities.

New in IDEA 2004 is the approach known as **response to intervention (RTI).** The reauthorized IDEA introduces the concept as one of the ways in which educators may reach a decision about whether or not a child has a specific learning disability (SLD).

Previously, teachers and related-services personnel such as psychologists were using a "discrepancy" model. In that diagnostic method, tests were used. An IQ test was given along with an achievement test. If there were sharp discrepancies between ability (the IQ test results) and performance (the achievement test), this was taken as evidence of SLD. The discrepancy approach became controversial in the 1990s and early in the 21st century as some experts, notable among them G. Reid Lyon (2002), observed that schools typically did not even administer achievement tests until children were in third grade

TABLE 6–3

Instructional Methods in Primary Grades.

WHAT WORKS: PRIMARY GRADES

Small Groups	One-on-one support in a variety of strategies and tactics	*In Situ Instruction*
Peer tutoring	Progress assessment	Community-based instruction
Cooperative learning	*Direct Instruction*	Field trips
Advance Organizers	*Embedding*	*Discovery Learning*
Kidspiration® charts	Parallel talk	Directed discovery learning
Inspiration® charts	Self-talk	Guided discovery learning
Response to Intervention		*Manipulatives*
Strategy instruction		*Task Analysis*

(i.e., were about nine years of age). The inevitable result, Lyon told the U.S. Congress, was that diagnosis of SLD was delayed. The discrepancy model was, he said, "a wait to fail" model (p. 3).

He proposed RTI as an alternative. In this technique, teachers give lessons. The key is to try this teaching strategy, then that one, in an effort to discover what works with a particular child. Thus, the teacher might give a lesson on word attack, suggesting "try another way" and then "break the word into its parts and pronounce each one" and so on. Or the student might listen silently as a fluent reader reads a passage, then read it herself. Or the teacher might provide the student with a checklist of strategies to use while reading.

RTI requires educators to assess individual student progress on a continuous basis (at least twice weekly). Over time, as teachers try this strategy and that one, a record is produced that assists members of the IEP team to reach a decision about SLD. Importantly, RTI may begin at any time, even in the preschool years. It could lead to a diagnosis of SLD as early as age six. That, in turn, might result in delivery of special education and related services designed to meet the child's unique needs in first rather than third grade.

Another advantage of RTI is that it helps distinguish between two groups that in the past may have been lumped together in the SLD category: children who genuinely have learning disabilities and those who simply had not been given appropriate instruction. RTI is a number of what IDEA 2004 calls early intervening services. Previous reauthorizations of the law had used the term *prereferral interventions,* which had the unfortunate connotation of being a step toward referral to special education. The point, of course, always was to *avoid* unnecessary referrals. IDEA 2004 authorizes schools to use a portion of funds appropriated under that law for early intervening services. This means that some IDEA monies may be targeted to help students *without* disabilities, particularly in the primary grades (K–3).

In addition, RTI may help educators detect overlooked learning disabilities. Children with Down syndrome, for example, may be classified as mentally retarded. That some also have reading disabilities may never be detected. With RTI, it is more likely that the secondary condition of SLD will be discovered, and the child given the needed assistance.

In volumes 38 and 39 of 2005 and 2006, the *Journal of Learning Disabilities* published a special series of issues about RTI. In these volumes, seven guest editors (including Lynn and Douglas Fuchs of the University of Tennessee, Donald Deshler of the University of Kansas, and others) and a wide range of authors examined different aspects of RTI. The papers are recommended for readers seeking additional information about the method.

Embedding

Embedding continues to be an important method in the primary grades, particularly in inclusive classrooms. Instruction in reading, writing, mathematics, social studies, art, music, physical education, and many other subjects can be augmented by selective use of embedding techniques. Educators may, to illustrate, embed behavior modification techniques into ongoing instruction by gently and quietly cuing behavior for students with disabilities who are included in a classroom. Similarly, adaptations permitting students with physical disabilities to paint or play a percussion instrument may be offered during art and music lessons.

Grouping

Peer tutoring occurs when one good reader works to help an emerging reader, when a child who is good in mathematics helps one who is not, and so on.

Cooperative learning is teamwork, usually in pairs or small groups, where children work together under rules and procedures established by an adult.

Group-based techniques, including **peer tutoring** and **cooperative learning,** can be effective at this level. In peer tutoring, ECSE personnel pair dissimilar students (e.g., one good at mathematics one not; one accomplished reader, one emergent reader). Douglas and Lynn Fuchs and their colleagues have demonstrated the effectiveness of such pairings for students with disabilities. In cooperative learning, ECSE professionals set the rules for small groups, then let them work cooperatively on a project. An important advantage of cooperative learning for students with disabilities is that it teaches these children how to work as members of a team (Fuchs et al., 2001). Both approaches work well in the primary grades because they are quickly mastered by educators, because they are minimally disruptive of standard classroom routines, and because they help individualize instruction.

Teaching academics to students with disabilities, so that they master content well enough to perform well on high-stakes tests in third and later grades, can be a real challenge for ECSE professionals. Fortunately, well-established interventions are available for educators. We know, for example, that peer tutoring and other variations on cooperative learning are highly effective. Pairing a student who is weak in a subject area with another student who is strong in that area can help both children. The latter receives individualized instruction and answers to his questions, while the former gains deeper understanding of the content by explaining it in ways that make the material understandable to another child. Similarly, assessing where children are as part of the teacher's preparation for instruction is widely recognized as effective (see Chapter 7). Such formative assessment tells the educator precisely what to teach. In these as in other areas, the whole thrust of IDEA 2004 is to urge educators to improve instruction. It is much preferable to retention in grade, which may simply expose children to more of the same ineffective instruction.

Teaching Strategies

Students with disabilities often benefit greatly from explicit instruction about and practice in strategies they may use to learn. A good use of time is to help primary-grade students identify which strategies are most applicable to a given problem or assignment, employ that strategy, and monitor their own learning with it. ECSE professionals should model their own decision-making and problem-solving strategies. Self-talk (i.e., talking out loud so the child learns how you think as you work) helps children learn how to attack problems. A few hours each week over the first few weeks of school will pay dividends, because the student will need much less help for the rest of the school year.

Creating Advance Organizers

Advance organizer

is an outline, list of key terms with definitions, or other support that helps a student to prepare to learn new information.

Primary-grade students who have disabilities frequently need help in structuring and organizing what they read and write. An **advance organizer** gives them this support. Think of it as scaffolding. An outline, a list of key words with definitions, a concept map, a picture—advance organizers can have all or any of these elements. You can create good concept maps using such software as Inspiration or Kidspiration (www.inspiration.com). These are useful for *all* students, but those with special needs tend to need them more.

Providing Community-Based Instruction

Another way to "make learning come alive" is to deliver instruction in the community. The "community" may be the school cafeteria, the school playground, or an area adjacent to the school property. It may also be a local firehouse, museum, or store. The key is to show young children *real-life* applications for what they are learning. A big advantage: because the children learn at the site where they are expected to display competencies, it is much less of a problem, later, to teach them to generalize that behavior.

Literacy

Literacy

is the use of reading and writing skills in activities children find to be meaningful. The term emphasizes the practical utility of these skills, in contrast to traditional drill-and-practice routines that are devoid of real-world meaning for most young children.

Literacy is a child's ability to use reading and writing in everyday life—that is, in activities that the child finds important. Because children bring meaning to what they read and write, educators need to create opportunities that the children themselves find to be meaningful. This may mean that students select stories and books that interest them. It may also mean that teachers encourage groups of children to react to what they read by drawing parallels between literature and their own everyday lives.

As such, literacy builds on the foundation skills of phonemic awareness and knowledge of phonics. As is shown later in this book, some students with specific learning disabilities will need continued instruction and practice in phonemic awareness and phonics even beyond the primary grades. That is why best practice in ECSE is to combine literacy's emphasis on meaningful reading and writing activities with explicit instruction in the "nuts and bolts" of using the sounds of the language.

Evolution has hardwired our brains to put phonemes together rapidly, in speech, and to segment them quickly, in listening. The act of reading print, however, is too new to be "in the genes." The difference is an important one. When we speak and listen, we attend to the meaning of words, rather than to the sounds that make them up. We are able to do this because evolution equips us to handle the phonemes that comprise words in the background, so to speak. In other words, we need not pay much attention to the putting together of phonemes to create words and of their dismantling to understand words. That is not the case, however, with many children having specific learning disabilities. They must be taught these skills. The term we use for this is *phonemic awareness*.

When we learn to read, we need to attend to the sounds of words. That is why phonics instructs us to "sound it out." Doing so helps us understand how speech is represented on the page by print. Young children with reading disabilities, the most common learning disabilities, need help in doing this. Again, the term we employ to refer to the instruction they require is *phonemic awareness.*

Shared reading of predictable stories continues to be helpful in the primary grades. Children should be expected to assume greater responsibility than was the case in preschool. In addition, they should be encouraged to write about the stories and to produce artwork illustrating them.

Words with practical meaning that are vital for ECSE professionals to teach to young children with disabilities are *survival words.* These include such words as *stop, danger, poison,* and the like. Even if drill-and-practice routines that develop rote memory are required, these words *must* be learned by all young children.

Miscue analysis

is the coding of behaviors children exhibit, including errors they make while reading as well as their spontaneous corrections of those errors.

A means of assessing reading skills is **miscue analysis.** Developed by Ken and Yetta Goodman (Goodman, Goodman, & Hood, 1989), miscue analysis is used with oral reading. As students read out loud, teachers note what mistakes they make and also what spontaneous corrections they make of those errors. The Goodmans use copy editors' marks to code these errors. The approach differentiates between three categories of miscues. First are miscues involving letter/sound connections. These grapheme-related miscues are functions of the child's level of phonemic awareness. Second are miscues related to prefixes, suffixes, phrases, and clauses. These syntax-related miscues have to do with how those elements convey meaning. Third are miscues involving knowledge about the world. These pragmatics-related miscues illustrate what the child knows about how language is used by members of the society.

Mathematics and Science

Teaching from the concrete to the abstract, or from specific to general, can really make a difference for many young children with disabilities. This is especially true in mathematics and science. Manipulatives are of obvious utility. Objects they can touch, count, and move help children translate conceptual information into practical knowledge. Teachers have found, too, that peer tutoring and cooperative learning help as well (e.g., Fuchs et al., 2001). Direct instruction, emphasizing those specific mathematics skills with which students have difficulty, is also of demonstrated effectiveness with primary-grade students with disabilities (e.g., Gersten et al., 1987). A variation on miscue analysis may be used. By analyzing the errors young children make in mathematics or science, ECSE professionals may identify precisely where the children are having difficulty—which tells them specifically what to teach.

The greatly increased emphasis on math and science in today's schools raises the question of how ECSE can raise the achievement levels of young children with disabilities in those fields. Science particularly is taught using discovery learning. Can ECSE personnel adapt that approach so as to make it more appropriate for children with disabilities? The answer is yes.

Guided discovery learning

is a variation on discovery learning in which teachers offer suggestions to students in their inquiries. It is more structured than traditional discovery learning but less so than directed discovery learning.

One modification is called **guided discovery learning.** We use this most with students having specific learning disabilities or ADHD. In guided discovery learning, professionals and paraprofessionals offer a road map for the student. This may be a checklist of steps to follow, in order. They may also stop by the student's desk from time to time, redirecting his attention and offering encouragement. Another variation is known as

Directed discovery learning

is a variation on discovery learning in which teachers direct a student's inquiry. It is more structured than guided discovery learning and much more so than traditional discovery learning.

directed discovery learning. This is a much more hands-on method. ECSE personnel sit with the child, prompting each step in turn.

Related Services

Such related services as speech pathology and occupational or physical therapy may be pushed in or pulled out during the primary grades. Arguments in favor of pushing them in include improved teacher-therapist communication and less "dead time" for the student. Pullout, on the other hand, may be more economical for schools, because one therapist can work simultaneously with several students drawn from a number of classrooms.

THE "PLACE" OF PLACE

The question of *where* services should be delivered is an emotional one in the field of ECSE. This long-running controversy began in elementary and secondary education, where it generated a heated debate that has yet to still. In a review of the issues in K–12 special education, James Kauffman (1993) uses words like *clangorous* and *rancorous* to describe journal articles and convention speeches on the question of where. He suggests that the field has forgotten the "place" of place, its relative importance in service delivery:

> Place has varied literal and metaphorical meanings, including location, perspective, status, and power. The issue of where students are taught has been at the center of efforts to restructure special education. Physical place has been the hub of controversy because it defines proximity to age peers with certain characteristics. A student's being in the same location as others has been assumed to be a necessary if not sufficient condition for receiving educational opportunity. Physical place can be measured easily, can be reduced to simple images, and has immediate and deep emotional overtones; thus it is fertile ground for fanaticism. (p. 7)

Kauffman deplores that "fanaticism." He points out that the very core of IDEA is that services be individualized for children. After all, the statute's statement of purpose ensures children with disabilities "a free appropriate public education which emphasizes special education and related services designed to meet their unique needs" (IDEA, Section 601[c]). He adds that while special education has many problems and needs improvement in many different areas, the location in which services occur is hardly the fulcrum for improvements. Although many K–12 children with disabilities do feel stigmatized, this is not, Kauffman suggests, principally because of where they are served.

The same comments could be made about ECSE. It is equally important in ECSE that each child be looked at as a unique individual and that services be specially designed to meet that child's needs. We can, and do, alleviate stigmatism in ECSE programs by reducing or even eliminating the use of labels, by looking to and talking about children's characteristics other than their disabilities, and by writing into IFSPs and IEPs the resources and strengths of children and families, as well as their needs. Location is not the only way in which we can be sensitive to these issues. Place is important, but it has its place.

NATURAL ENVIRONMENTS

The words *natural environment* (NE) were added to Part C in 1991. The term appears in three places. First, the statute now defines the term *early intervention services* as including services that

> *to the maximum extent appropriate, are provided in natural environments, including the home, and community settings in which children without disabilities participate.* (Section 632[4][G])

The second mention of "natural environment" occurs in Section 635(a)(16), where states are told to ensure services are provided in nonnatural environments *only* when appropriate services may not be delivered in a natural environment. Finally, Section 636(d)(5) states that IFSPs include "a statement of the natural environments in which early intervention services shall appropriately be provided." Notice that Congress took care in all three instances to subordinate the NE preference to the requirement that early intervention services be appropriate. The 1991 House Report explained:

> *The term "natural environments" refers to settings that are natural or normal for age peers who have no apparent disability. The descriptor "to the maximum extent appropriate" is not meant to qualify the appropriateness of the natural environment as the primary setting for the child. Rather, it is intended to allow flexibility and individualized programming for the infant or toddler with a disability.*
>
> *For example, the primary natural environment for an infant or toddler is the home. Where group settings are utilized, the infant or toddler with a disability should be placed in groups with age peers without disabilities, such as play groups, day care centers, or whatever typical group setting exists for infants and toddlers without disabilities.* (*House Report 102–198,* 1991)

Nothing in Part C precludes the family from deciding what is the natural environment for the infant or toddler; parental discretion would make sense, given that parents know their children far better than intervention personnel do. Parental determination of what is the natural environment also fits in well with the ECSE field's emphasis on family-focused programming (DEC Task Force, 1993).

What we do with very young children and their families is more important than where we do those things. As early intervention pioneer Diane Bricker (2001) puts it, "The activity in most cases is more important than the setting" (p. 23). She objects to an interpretation of "natural environment" as being "a code word for inclusion" (p. 23), adding, "The field's definition of the natural environment as including only settings that are designed and operated primarily for nondisabled children . . . has resulted in making the child's placement paramount to all other considerations in many programs" (p. 26). Bricker insists that appropriateness and individualization of services are much more important. In fact, she writes, "I recommend that the definition of the natural environment be separated from the concept of inclusion," and "For me, natural environments are those authentic physical and social surrounds in which children generally find themselves. . . . I believe that the word authentic better captures the important concept that underlies placement" (p. 28). These sentiments conform with the central theme of this book: ECSE workers should strive to provide the services that children and their families need, in settings that those families frequent, and to give priority to the individualization and appropriateness of those services over where they are delivered.

LEAST RESTRICTIVE ENVIRONMENTS

The term *least restrictive environment* (LRE) appears in Section 612(a)(5), where state education agencies are told what assurances to provide in their triennial state plans so as to qualify for Part B funding. The state must assure the U.S. Department of Education that

> *to the maximum extent appropriate, children with disabilities . . . are educated with children who are not disabled, and that special classes, separate schooling, or other removal of children with disabilities from the regular educational environment occurs only when the nature or severity of the disability is such that education in regular classes with the use of supplementary aids and services cannot be achieved satisfactorily.* (Section 612[a][5])

This language is somewhat ambiguous. First, the preference for placement in the LRE is declared subordinate to the requirement for appropriate services. Thus, the LRE language is not an unqualified mandate. On the other hand, the subsequent language on removal does appear to suggest that children should be placed in regular settings, with necessary support services, unless appropriate education cannot be provided in such settings. This suggestion appears to be the principal basis for the "inclusion" movement, which is discussed in the next section.

The potential of integration in preschool settings has excited the attention of many researchers in ECSE. Among those examining LRE in preschools are McEvoy and Odom (1987), Odom and McEvoy (1990), and Strain (1990). McGinnis and Goldstein (2000) discuss "skillstreaming" with preschool children, to prepare them for mainstreaming in kindergarten and elementary school. Despite all the attention preschool LRE has attracted, misconceptions about it and about what the law requires remain widespread.

A key statement by the U.S. Department of Education makes clear that the intent is to ensure appropriate services. The October 30, 1992, "Notice of Policy Guidance" on the primacy of appropriateness over LRE is worth repeating here. The statement dealt with the meaning of "free appropriate public education" (FAPE) for children who are deaf, but the implications are far broader:

> *The provision of FAPE is paramount, and the individual placement determination about LRE is to be considered within the context of FAPE. . . . Any setting, including a regular classroom, that prevents a child who is deaf from receiving an appropriate education that meets his or her needs, including communication needs, is not the LRE for that individual child.* (U.S. Department of Education, 1992d, p. 49275)

With respect to removal of children from regular classes, which the statute restricts to instances in which services cannot be provided satisfactorily, the department adds:

> *Just as placement in the regular educational setting is required when it is appropriate for the unique needs of a child who is deaf, so is removal from the regular classroom setting required when the child's needs cannot be met in that setting with the use of supplementary aids and services.* (U.S. Department of Education, 1992d, p. 49275)

What all of this means is that LRE is a *principle,* not a *place.* It is an idea that teaches ECSE workers to look first at a continuum of service or placement options and then to identify those that offer the services needed by a particular child and family. From among these "appropriate" placements, ECSE workers select the one that is most integrated. The principal test, then, is that of appropriate services; the IDEA ensures that children receive an appropriate education, individually designed to meet their unique needs.

Bricker (2000) agrees, saying that the least restrictive environment must be, above all, a setting in which young children learn. "Although many more mainstream options exist for young children with disabilities [today, as compared with the 1970s], the quality of the instruction and the social interactions that occur in these settings is often contrary to best practice" (p. 16). Particularly for preschoolers who need specialized equipment and/or services, integrated preschool programs may not be suitable because the staff lacks training, the facility lacks resources, and the classroom lacks the supports that these children require to receive an appropriate education. Expressing concern about the attitudes, skills, and knowledge of general educators in mainstream preschool programs, Bricker emphasizes that young children with disabilities often require exactly the supportive attitudes, competencies, and routines of instruction that special educators bring to their work. She deplores what she perceives as misguided advocacy on the part of some so-called experts: "Many of the outspoken advocates for inclusion are not in the classroom or community delivering services" (p. 18). As is shown subsequently, Bricker's concerns are shared by this author.

INCLUSION

The principle of full inclusion is, in some respects, a logical extension of the ideals implicit in "natural environment" and "least restrictive environment." It arose in the late 1980s and early 1990s in response to the fact that children with severe disabilities were far less likely to be placed in integrated settings than were children with less severe disabilities (Biklen, 1985; Salisbury, 1991; Salisbury & Vincent, 1990). Its advocates insisted that children with severe disabilities have just as much right to integrated services as do children with mild or moderate disabilities (Manegold, 1994).

Inclusion is an ideal, a principle that builds on the earlier "mainstreaming" (Guralnick, 1990; Klein, 1975) and "regular education initiative" (Will, 1986) movements. It differs from those approaches, however. Mainstreaming, particularly in the mid- to late 1970s and early 1980s, featured placement of children with disabilities in separate classrooms but integrated them in nonacademic activities such as recreation, lunch, gym, and so on. The regular education initiative advocated placing children with mild disabilities in regular classrooms and assigning responsibility for their instruction to regular classroom teachers; it did not, however, insist on such steps on behalf of children with severe disabilities. Inclusion, by contrast, recognizes no distinctions of severity and insists on placing all children in regular classrooms in neighborhood schools.

This research was reviewed in Chapter 3. Inclusion advocates are correct in stating that regardless of how severely disabled a child may be, he is entitled to services that do not compromise his liberty and that do not unduly stigmatize him. They are incorrect, however, in insisting that one placement or type of placement is appropriate for all children with disabilities. That view violates the IDEA's core principle of individualization of services. Inclusion advocates are also wrong in stating that children must be served in a particular place, regardless of unique need. That approach runs counter to the IDEA's cardinal principle of appropriateness.

However emotionally appealing, inclusion must be understood as a philosophy that goes beyond the IDEA. It is not something the law requires or even promotes. Rather, the IDEA in its very essence is a law that looks at each child with a disability as being unique, with particular needs and strengths. It guarantees each eligible child the services that are appropriate. While movement of children with disabilities into regular settings is an admirable goal, it must be subsumed—as are all other values cherished by professionals and parents alike—to the IDEA's mandates of individualization and appropriateness. Children with disabilities should be served in integrated settings *only* when such placements benefit them.

Inclusion must also be understood as a misrepresentation of the ideals of the IDEA. Both NE and LRE support the act's overarching emphasis on individualization and appropriateness because both preferences are superseded by these higher-order mandates of individualization and appropriateness. Congress was at pains in PL 102–119, the 1991 amendments to the IDEA, to say that the NE preference is not intended to qualify appropriateness of services (*House Report 102–198,* 1991). Rather, NE guides services only to the extent that appropriateness is not compromised. LRE, similarly, is a principle, not a place, and it is subordinate to appropriateness (U.S. Department of Education, 1992d).

Inclusion, however, places the location of services above their appropriateness. Rather than suggesting, as does the IDEA, that ECSE professionals evaluate children, identify needed services, and review a continuum of placement options to select the most integrated setting that is appropriate, the concept of inclusion suggests that children be placed in integrated settings irrespective of individual differences. It implies that children must first fail in such settings before other placement options will be considered.

Educators of children who are deaf have been particularly disturbed about inclusion. Donald F. Moores (1993), editor of *American Annals of the Deaf*, wrote an editorial for that journal in which he points out:

> For many deaf children, the concept of total inclusion, as currently promulgated, could in reality be *exclusionary* in practice. Placing a deaf child in a classroom in physical contiguity to hearing children does not automatically provide equal access to education. In fact, it can be isolating, both academically and socially. (p. 251; emphasis in original)

Chapman (1992) makes much the same point with respect to another group of children: "For children with learning disabilities, whose needs have barely been met, inclusion in the mainstream seems like exclusion from remedial assistance" (p. 369).

Having said all of this, the concept of inclusion still has much merit. Provided that services in an integrated setting do meet all of the child's unique needs, inclusion of children with disabilities in regular classrooms offers social and other benefits. The keys, as always, are individualization and appropriateness. Also arguing for inclusion, at least in kindergarten and the primary grades, is a practical reality. Young children with disabilities must take the high-stakes tests required by NCLB. As much as educators and parents may express disgust over "teaching to the test," the fact is that test preparation routinely is offered for months prior to a given test date. This "test prep" most frequently is provided in general (inclusive) classrooms.

That reality does not hold in early intervention, nor does it have much cogency in preschool. Another reality also argues against inclusion at those levels. Teachers and other staff members working in child care and preschool settings typically are not trained about the special needs of young children with disabilities. Early Head Start (which serves infants and toddlers) and Head Start (which helps preschoolers), for example, rarely have special educators on staff. These and other EC programs serving general populations commonly require that staff members hold CDA certificates, which may be earned with just a handful of college-level courses. Special programs, by contrast, are required by the IDEA to meet "the highest standards of the state," for which reason they often feature professionals with master's degrees. These practical realities suggest that professionals and families planning services for young children with disabilities, particularly severe ones, may value the quality of special early childhood settings over the integration of inclusive ones.

INDOOR AND OUTDOOR ENVIRONMENTS: ACCESSIBILITY

Graham and Bryant (1993) suggest that the way in which ECSE programs use space, materials, and activities to create environments suitable for learning by young children with disabilities is important. They note that the Infant Toddler Environment Rating Scale (ITERS) (Harms, Cryer, & Clifford, 1989) and the Early Childhood Environment Rating Scale (ECERS) (Harms, Clifford, & Cryer, 1980) offer reliable and valid measures of children's settings. The ITERS and the ECERS assess environments from the point of view of young children with no disabilities. Harms, Clifford, and Bailey (1986), however, suggest additional ECERS items that look specifically at use of space and materials for children who have disabilities.

Remarkably little attention has been given in ECSE professional literature to the architectural design of program space. Young children with physical and sensory disabilities need accommodations that allow them to move about freely. Among the few efforts to provide ECSE programs with guidance on designing or retrofitting space are recommendations developed by a small federal agency, the U.S. **Architectural and Transportation Barriers Compliance Board (ATBCB),** sometimes called the *Access Board.*

Architectural and Transportation Barriers Compliance Board (ATBCB)
is a small independent federal agency charged with monitoring accessibility at many federal buildings. The agency sometimes is referred to as the *Access Board.*

INDOOR ENVIRONMENTS

In 1986, the ATBCB and the U.S. Department of Education (ATBCB/ED) worked together to prepare the board's *Recommendations for Accessibility to Serve Physically Handicapped Children in Elementary Schools.* This brief document was limited, as the title suggests, to design issues involved in helping elementary school students with physical disabilities. Six years later, North Carolina State University developed a set of *Recommendations for Accessibility Standards for Children's Environments* (Center for Accessible Housing, 1992). The ATBCB used these suggestions to prepare its own official guidelines for 1995. The 1992 Center for Accessible Housing and 1995 ATBCB specifications extended the 1986 ATBCB/ED recommendations to incorporate early childhood settings, that is, child care centers, facilities serving young children, ECSE programs, and EC programs such as Head Start. The 1992 and 1995 guidelines also incorporated specifications for meeting the needs of children whose disabilities are not issues of physical mobility (i.e., children who are blind or deaf). These publications can help ECSE programs nationwide in selecting, designing, and retrofitting space. The board may be contacted at ATBCB, 1331 F Street NW, Suite 1000, Washington, DC 20004-1111.

The 1992 Center for Accessible Housing report (available from ATBCB) included a review of literature on architectural design for young children. One important finding from that review was that as of 1992, very few states had building, fire, or safety codes that included specifications for programs that include young children with disabilities among their target populations. Florida, with its *Building Standards for Educational Facilities for Handicapped Children* (Florida Department of Education, 1988), and North Carolina were the only states identified by the center as having such guidelines. The center noted that the voluntary national accessibility standards of the American National Standards Institute (ANSI), ANSI A117.1, did not contain standards for children's facilities. Neither did the three most important model codes—the Standard Building Code, the Building Officials and Code Administrators International Code, and the Uniform Building Code. Accordingly, most states do not require facilities that serve young children with disabilities to meet architectural standards ensuring their accessibility. The 1992 recommendations also discussed children's needs for access to technology, including augmentative communication devices and wheelchairs.

More recently, the ATBCB (1997a, 1997b) has issued guidelines for "children's elements" and for "play facilities." These are very important documents for ECSE programs to obtain and to use.

Among the most important design issues for ECSE program administrators to consider are the following:

- *Doors.* The 1992 Center for Accessible Housing report found that doors are often very difficult for young children, especially children with physical disabilities, to open, close, and hold open. Although door specifications are often set to comply with fire codes, the center's research team recommends consideration of doors that are easier for young children to use. Automatic doors are one option. Although costly, such doors help young children move about in a facility much more independently; they also make it easier for them to get out fast in an emergency.

- *Ramps.* The center found that while ramps 36 inches wide (the width needed to accommodate a wheelchair) are acceptable, much wider ramps are better. Ramps 80 inches wide or more allow two wheelchairs to pass each other going in opposite directions, helping avoid congestion and accidents in programs serving more than a few children with severe physical disabilities. The slope (steepness) of ramps was also a concern. The common 1:12 slope specification, while suitable for facilities serving adults, is too steep for young children to negotiate alone. A 1:12 slope rises 1 inch every 12 inches of distance. The center reports that many facilities serving young children with disabilities required teachers, volunteers, or parents to push children up or down 1:12 ramps, thus unnecessarily limiting the children's mobility and independence; 1:20 ramps are better.

- *Stairs.* The center's report notes that detectable warnings such as changes in flooring patterns are necessary to help children with visual impairments avoid accidents at the tops of stairs.

- *Elevators.* The center's evaluation of facilities serving young children identified the height of elevator control buttons as an important issue. These buttons (including call buttons located in lobbies and control buttons in cars) should be positioned no more than 34 to 36 inches above the floor. In addition, the report found that buttons three-quarters of an inch wide, or even an inch wide were too small for many young children with physical disabilities to use with accuracy.

- *Desk height.* The center recommends that work surfaces, such as desks and tables, be provided in adjustable heights. Most of the facilities that center staff visited had work surfaces 25 inches or less from the floor. Although these are suitable for many young children, the report suggests that some children, in some situations, will need higher or lower work surfaces. Fortunately, a wide variety of desks and tables with adjustable surface heights is available.
- *Storage areas.* The report found that shelves and other storage surfaces 36 inches high suffice to meet the needs of young children (including children using wheelchairs) but that surfaces 43 inches high are too high. Adjustable shelving is strongly recommended, because desirable shelf height is a function not only of body stature but also of body position and the child's forward-reach and side-reach capacities.
- *Toilets.* Toilet seats, the report suggests, should be about 11 or 12 inches high, and certainly lower than the 15- to 17-inch heights recommended for adult toilet seats. Toilet stalls should be more than 36 inches wide to facilitate child transfers from wheelchairs to toilets.

These suggestions are most helpful when viewed from the perspective of their capacity to enhance children's independence. Especially in ECSE programs with severe staff limitations, architectural design features that alleviate pressure on staff to assist children physically throughout the building and throughout the day are highly desirable. An important consideration in serving children with physical and sensory limitations is giving them opportunities to develop and display suitable adaptive behaviors. When children are not only permitted but expected to do things for themselves, they are more likely to develop the skills necessary for functioning well in subsequent environments. By contrast, when poorly considered design specifications impede children's mobility, ECSE staff unnecessarily restrict the ability of young children with physical or sensory disabilities from learning the behaviors they will need for success in later schooling.

The design and accessibility of outdoor environments are as important in ECSE programs as those of indoor facilities.

These considerations are related to other, broader concerns. A 1994 report by the HHS Office of the Inspector General, based on inspections of 149 licensed child care centers and Head Start programs in six states, found that the majority of such facilities had health or safety hazards that put children at risk ("Audit Finds Day-Care Safety Flaws," 1994). The report states that Head Start centers, which are subject to federal safety standards and receive federal funds, often fail to protect young children from chemicals placed under sinks, improperly filled fire extinguishers, sewage, and debris. Other child care facilities are state-licensed and subject to state safety standards.

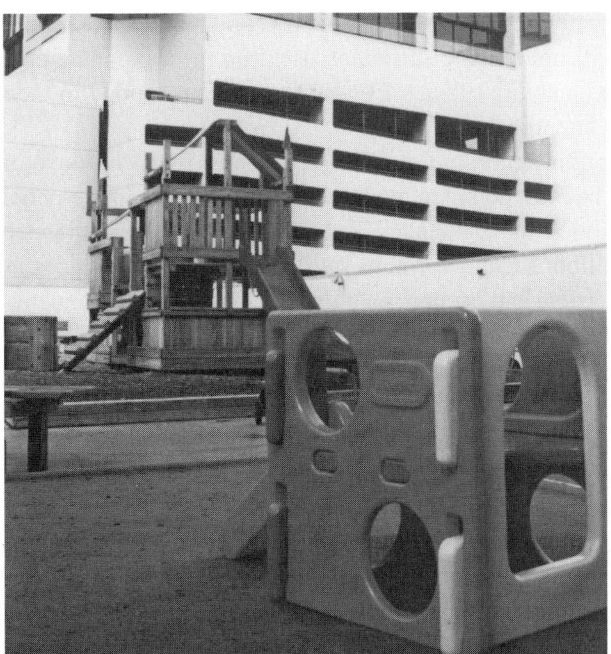

Early childhood personnel need to identify access features not only of program play areas but also of the community beyond the program grounds. Family members appreciate suggestions on how to locate accessible shopping, banking, and other sites.

The HHS report found that budget cutbacks in many states had limited auditors' ability to ensure that programs met such standards. Safety standards need to be upgraded in all programs.

OUTDOOR ENVIRONMENTS

The ATBCB guidelines for children's environments address outdoor settings in such places as child care centers, nurseries, preschool programs, and kindergartens. In addition, the Access Board recently offered recommendations for accessibility to recreation facilities. Work done by the National Park Service, the National Forest Service, and the National Accessibility Center at Bradford Woods, operated by Indiana University, paved the way for ATBCB recommendations on how to make playgrounds and other outdoor recreation areas more accessible for young children with disabilities. This issue was largely overlooked in the 1980s, but the ATBCB-led Recreation Task Force, formed in mid-1993, recommended specifications for access to swimming pools, amusement parks, winter recreation areas, and outdoor sports facilities.

The 1997 ATBCB report on play facilities offers two sets of specifications: one for young children aged 2 to 5 and another for children aged 5 to 12. The ATBCB believes there is not yet enough information available with respect to children under the age of two. Regarding routes to and from play facilities, the ATBCB recommends that these be 60 inches wide and clear of protrusions at or below 80 inches above the surface. The slope of the routes should be 1:16 or less (i.e., rising 1 inch per 16 inches of length). Any ramp in the play area should rise no more than 12 inches. No handrail should be more than 28 inches above the ramp surface. These very specific suggestions should prove helpful to ECSE programs throughout the nation. For more information, contact the Access Board at www.access-board.gov or ATBCB, 1331 F Street NW, Washington, DC 20004.

PRACTICAL ISSUES

Individualization of services is an ideal. At times, practical realities prevent it from being realized. Examples of conflicts between ideal and real situations abound in ECSE. Most ECSE programs offer only a limited range of services. They may, for example, provide group activities for young children with disabilities but lack the facilities to offer integration into similar programs for nondisabled children. This problem is particularly evident in preschool services for three- to five-year-olds. There may be no such programs for nondisabled children in the community; where such services do exist, they may be targeted toward disadvantaged children, who have pressing needs of their own. Alternatively, an ECSE program may offer integrated group programming but lack the capability to provide separate, specialized activities for children with severe disabilities. Families concerned that their children will not receive sufficient attention in large, integrated settings may be frustrated by the inability of such ECSE programs to respond to their requests for more individualized attention.

In the area of early intervention, according to NEILS, the most frequent mode of service delivery is home visits. The most common model of service delivery in preschool programs—as in special education at the elementary and secondary levels—features a large-group activity area and pullout (resource room) settings where such services as speech and language therapy, physical and occupational therapy, and the like, are delivered. Additional funding may be needed to add other capabilities-based services for infants and toddlers to supplement or even supplant home visits; or integrated settings in preschools, where specialized services are provided in the same room as other activities. Unfortunately, the reality of human service programming in many areas is one of severe and increasing budgetary pressures. For these reasons, individualization may be possible only within a range of affordable options.

Another very common practical constraint on individualization of services is perhaps the most basic: time. Service coordinators, early childhood special educators, physical and occupational therapists, and the many other professionals working in ECSE programs may have large caseloads. Often they experience conflicts between their professional obligations to provide more time and attention to each child, on the one hand, and severe time constraints, on the other. Burnout is a frequent result of such conflicts. One survey of ECSE professionals found that they experienced so much conflict as a result of having too many cases and too little time that they would respond positively to job offers promising them more time for each child and family (Kontos & File, 1992).

A variation on the time theme is the availability of services at times that are convenient for the family. The principle of individualization requires ECSE programs to make child and family services available when the family can take advantage of them. This may conflict, however, with the hours at which key professionals are available. Speech-language pathologists, physical and occupational therapists, and other such professionals are frequently freelance operators who split their time among several programs scattered over a wide geographic area. It may not be possible for them to schedule therapy sessions at a time or place that meets family needs.

In-service training is a "must" so that educators keep up with new developments in the field.

These examples raise another basic issue: cost. Often, it is possible to arrange therapy at a time and place convenient for the family but only at extra cost to the program. For example, professionals may be hired as salaried workers and assigned to the hours at which freelance therapists are not available. Overtime pay arrangements are another possibility, both with salaried and freelance professionals. Extra time and attention to individual children and their families may similarly be provided at additional cost to the program. Although these steps theoretically are possible, human services agencies, including EC programs, are under increasing budgetary constraints in many states and localities. The practical ability of programs to individualize services in these ways may be seriously limited by such economic pressures.

SUMMARY

This chapter opened with a quotation from Carta et al. (1993) stating that meeting children's needs is more important than the means by which this is done—whether with steps recommended by NAEYC in its "developmentally appropriate practice," by DEC in its "recommended practices," or, alternatively, with more traditional practices. The chapter went on to examine the "place" of place and the importance of individually designed, appropriately delivered services versus the comparatively lower importance of the location where they take place.

ECSE is challenged now to raise academic performance of young children with disabilities, while at the same time continuing to provide services that are both appropriate to the children and individualized to their unique needs. It is a tall order. To meet the new mandates, ECSE personnel need to find ways of being more efficient. Each hour—indeed, each half hour—needs to be used more productively. That is why embedding of academics into nonacademic activities is potentially so valuable. Teaching in situ (on site) alleviates the need, later, to engage in instruction to help young children to generalize. Similarly, in preschool and in the primary grades, imbuing Direct Instruction into discovery learning activities, via guided or directed discovery learning, layers each activity with more opportunities for instruction.

What takes place in ECSE is, at bottom, more important than where it occurs. Many people allow themselves to be seduced by the prospect of integration of children with and without disabilities. Although such proximity does confer many advantages, it is also true that many young children with disabilities simply need additional time to learn "how to swim" before they sign up for a race in the pool. Children who are blind, for example, need to master the assistive technologies that are so valuable for them in school. Young children who are deaf need to learn how to sign and (this takes longer) how to read the signs of other people. Children with behavioral disorders need to learn how to monitor their own behavior and how to stifle impulsiveness. In all of these instances, inclusion at the elementary and secondary levels may actually be advanced—more likely and more successful—if young children are provided with "special" ECSE services, in special education settings if necessary.

KEY TERMS

adaptations
advance organizer
American Sign Language (ASL)
applied behavior analysis (ABA)
Architectural and Transportation Barriers Compliance Board (ATBCB)
cooperative learning
counseling
curriculum
Direct Instruction
directed discovery learning
early intervening services
elaboration
generalization
guided discovery learning
literacy
manipulatives
miscue analysis
modeling
number sense
parallel talk
peer tutoring
performance cues
phonemic awareness
phonics instruction
principle of partial participation
respite services
self-talk
shared reading
Signed English
time delay
verbal prompts
visual prompts

QUESTIONS FOR REFLECTION

1. What questions does a curriculum answer?
2. What are some ways you could use embedding in ECSE?
3. Why do you think direct instruction is so widely used in ECSE programs?
4. How could miscue analysis help you teach a young child to read?
5. How does phonemic awareness differ from phonics?
6. How do you feel about applied behavior analysis (ABA)?
7. With what kinds of young children might you use sign language?
8. Why do you think ECSE professionals often become emotionally involved in the debate about inclusion?
9. Which values important to ECSE professionals might conflict with practical realities?
10. Where can you find guidance on making a facility accessible to children and adults who use wheelchairs?

PRACTICAL EXERCISES

1. Visit a local EC program (e.g., a Head Start program) or an ECSE program (e.g., a special preschool or an early intervention program serving infants and toddlers). Observe for a morning or an afternoon. Talk with program staff members. Then describe, as best you can, the program's teaching methods.

   Does it appear to emphasize DI, ABA, and/or other teacher-led activities? Or does it seem to be more of a Montessori-type discovery learning program? Or is it both?

   Do the teaching strategies you saw in action conflict in any way(s) from what staff members told you? (That is, do program staff seem to "say one thing and do another"?) If so, why do you think that happened?

2. Spend a morning or an afternoon in a third- or fourth-grade classroom. Thinking back to your own experiences at that level, does the amount of emphasis on math and science, as well as language arts, seem to be greater today? What are the methods used in each content area? Do you see more discovery learning in science, for example, than you do in math?

   Recalling the performance levels of young children with disabilities whom you have observed, do you think they are at the academic levels in these fields that you see among typically developing children in this classroom? If not, do you think the gap is one that could be bridged? How?

WEB SITES OF INTEREST

www.aota.org American Occupational Therapy Association—information on OT services and professional standards

www.apta.org American Physical Therapy Association—information on PT services and professional standards

www.handspeak.com Hand Speak is a subscription-based on-line service. It has a free Demo that features full-motion video (click on "ASL Sign Dictionary").

www.access-board.gov U.S. Architectural and Transportation Barriers Compliance Board—information on making facilities accessible

www.nochildleftbehind.gov U.S. Department of Education—information on scientifically based interventions

CHAPTER

7

Evaluation and Assessment

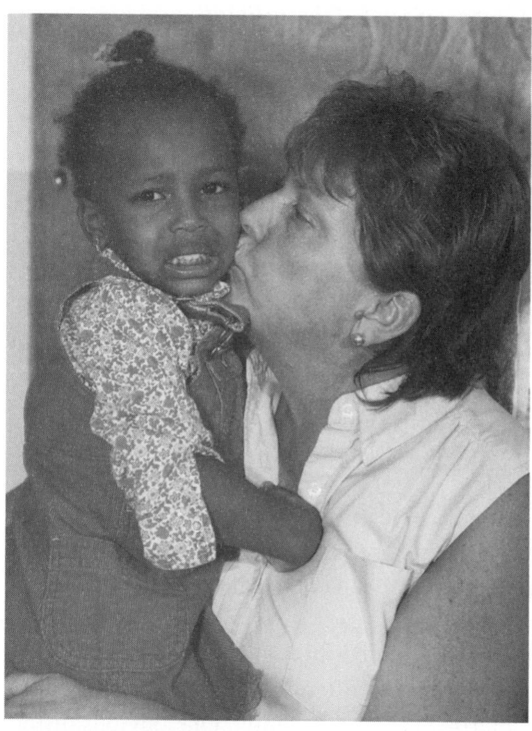

The psychologist experienced in testing school-aged children may expect a young child to exhibit appropriate "testing behavior"—sitting quietly at a desk, attending to the task at hand, and being motivated to complete the tasks presented. Such characteristic testing behavior is not present in this age group or, if present, is limited to a few brief moments.
(CULBERTSON & WILLIS, 1993, P. 4)

OBJECTIVES

After reading this chapter, you should be able to:

- Explain why informed clinical opinion is an important part of assessment.
- Explain what the federal law known as No Child Left Behind requires in the way of testing young children with disabilities.
- Describe why and how we screen young children and how screening is limited.
- List what factors complicate testing of young children with disabilities.
- Explain how evaluation differs from assessment.

- Explain what transdisciplinary play-based assessment is and how you may use it.
- Describe how ECSE professionals communicate with families about test results.
- Explain how and why ECSE programs should evaluate their activities.

CHAPTER OUTLINE

- **OVERVIEW**
- **CHILD FIND**
  - **Screening**
- **TESTING**
  - **Legal Issues**
  - **Variables in Children**
  - **Variables in Examiners**
  - **Variables in Instruments**
  - **Test Interpretation**
- **CULTURAL DIVERSITY ISSUES**
- **EVALUATION**
  - **The Federal Requirements**
    - *Infants and Toddlers*
    - *Children with Disabilities*
  - **Evaluation Instruments**
- **ASSESSMENT**
  - **Infants and Toddlers**
  - **Families**
  - **Children with Disabilities**
- **COMMUNICATING WITH FAMILIES**
- **PROGRAM EVALUATION**

OVERVIEW

Evaluation

is a formal process through which a child's initial and continuing eligibility for services under the IDEA is established. It is periodic, occurring at specific intervals. Evaluation may establish, for example, that a child qualifies for Part C services under the act as an at-risk toddler; similarly, it may establish that a child meets a state's developmental delay criteria.

Assessment

is the process of collecting data to use in determining how an individual child's development is proceeding in each of the five domains of development (cognitive, adaptive, physical, communication, social or emotional) or in academic areas. In family assessment, a family's resources, priorities, and concerns are identified.

This chapter explores the often difficult processes of evaluation and assessment of young children, discussing the critical issues of screening, testing, and interpreting test data, as well as communicating with parents. The chapter concludes with observations on program evaluation.

The terms ***evaluation*** and ***assessment*** are often confused. To the layperson, they are synonyms; and, indeed, specialists in assessment often use them interchangeably. Part C of the IDEA, however, gives each term a specific meaning. One obvious difference between the two is that while evaluation is usually carried out only by qualified licensed and/or certified specialists who administer standardized tests, assessment is an ongoing process in which workers from many ECSE disciplines participate—early childhood special educators, speech-language pathologists, physical and occupational therapists, nurses, classroom aides, and others who work with children and families on a daily basis.

Evaluation, then, is a formal process through which a child's initial and continuing eligibility for services under the IDEA is established. It is periodic, occurring at specific intervals. Under Part C, evaluation documents the child's current performance or status in all five developmental domains. With respect to preschoolers and primary-grade children, evaluation describes the child's current educational performance and need for special education and related services. In evaluation, federal and state criteria for eligibility are applied, setting against them the individual child's characteristics as determined through testing, observation, parent report, and other measures.

their recommendations to parents and to state agencies, and defending these recommendations without the benefit of incontrovertible proof.

Under the No Child Left Behind Act of 2001, states are to test young children annually in the areas of reading, writing, and mathematics. These assessments begin in third grade. Children with disabilities or delays in development are to be tested, with few exceptions. The major issue for ECSE professionals is whether these children require test accommodations. The answers are to appear in the children's IEPs. If an IEP calls for accommodations in assessments, these must be offered. If not, they may not be provided. A good source for information about test accommodations, including options that you may consider, is the National Center on Educational Outcomes (NCEO) at the University of Minnesota (www.education.umn.edu).

A few children are exempted from such tests. Usually, this is because they have cognitive or other limitations that are so severe that they cannot successfully take part in such assessments. An alternate assessment is provided. These may be observations of the child as she performs activities that are highlighted in the IEP. Sometimes, parent and/or teacher reports are used. The NCEO is a good source for information about alternate assessments.

CHILD FIND

Under both Part C and Part B, states are responsible for identifying, locating, and evaluating children who have disabilities or are suspected of having disabilities or delays. The requirement to evaluate young children as part of a child find program has been in place since 1980, although the mandate to serve all such young children who have disabilities or delay is, of course, much more recent. States are required to identify children from birth to age eight inclusive and to evaluate their disabilities and needs.

The Part B regulation (U.S. Department of Education, 2006b) mandates that states ensure that all children with disabilities are identified, located, and evaluated. Early

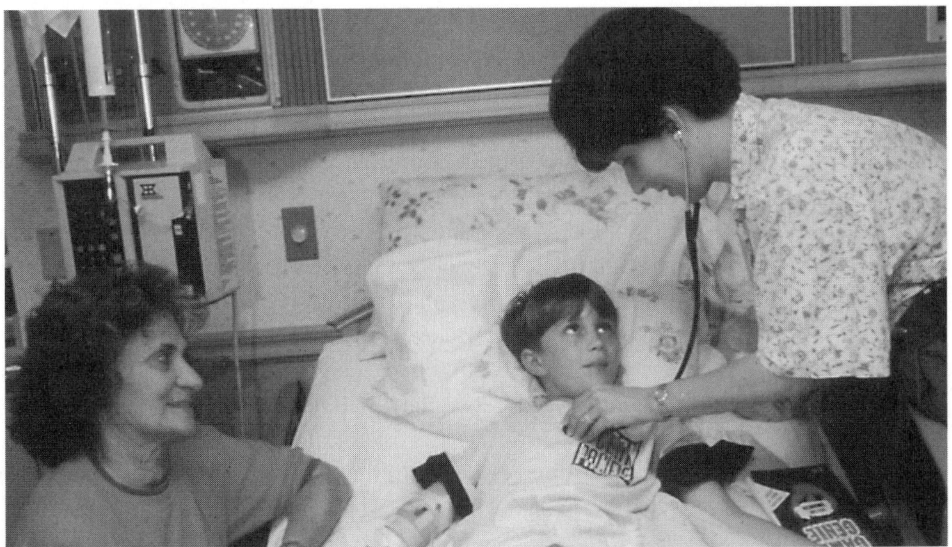

Routine screening may be performed at any time, including occasions when accidents bring children to medical facilities.

identification and assessment is a related service under Part B. States must report to the department on those children being served. The child find program is intended to locate not only children receiving no developmental services but also children in public and private service agencies and in institutions.

Although states must report to the department on children identified through child find efforts, strict confidentiality rules govern how personally identifiable information may be released. Under Part C, not even the referral for early intervention services may be made without prior written parental permission.

SCREENING

Child find often uses screening instruments to identify children as potentially eligible for IDEA services. By their very nature, screening instruments are broad-brush measures. They should never be used for diagnostic purposes, nor should they be used to establish unique needs or to select interventions. Rather, screening procedures are used to identify children who should be evaluated further. Screening sometimes produces "false positives"—instances in which a child is screened in for further testing although in fact there is no disability or delay. Screening also produces some "false negatives"—cases in which children who do have disabilities or delays are wrongly screened out. The reality is that such errors are inevitable. Unlike evaluation and assessment, which by law are multidisciplinary, screening may be conducted by a single individual. Physicians and other primary care providers are excellent choices to perform screening, because families routinely take children to doctors, well-child pediatric clinics, and hospitals. Because of their early contact with and comprehensive coverage of the birth-to-eight population, pediatricians and other physicians are logical persons to conduct screening and to make referrals for more in-depth evaluation.

Why do we screen? First, screening is much faster and much less costly than a full-scale evaluation. For example, excellent screening of infant hearing is now available for as little as $25; a follow-up test on infants "screened in" as possibly having a hearing loss costs at least four times that much. A formal evaluation of hearing impairment runs six to eight times as much as the initial screening cost, or $175 to $200.

Time is also relevant. To continue with the example on hearing, the initial screening takes only a few minutes; the follow-up test takes quite a bit longer. The second reason for screening is to establish demographic parameters (Kenny & Culbertson, 1993). No one knows the true prevalence of different disabilities in young children. To illustrate, the usual estimate is that some 2.5 percent of birth-to-eight children are mentally retarded, but that is for statistical reasons. By definition, *mental retardation* is intelligence that falls at least two standard deviations below the mean. Statistical theory tells us that 2.27 percent of children are two or more standard deviations below the mean on intelligence. No one has actually counted the number of children under nine who are mentally retarded. Until comprehensive screening and the necessary follow-up evaluations are performed, researchers will not discover how prevalent mental retardation is in this population. The same is true of other disabilities.

A number of instruments are available for use in screening. A notable example is the new neonatal hearing test mentioned earlier; an infant's vision, too, may now be screened at a very young age. The choice of which screening test to use involves many factors: what one is screening for (some tests tap all five developmental domains recognized by the IDEA, while others explore specific domain areas such as behavior or emotional development); who is administering the test (e.g., physicians use different measures than do speech-language pathologists); how old the child is (some tests are suitable for use with infants, whereas others are used with preschool-age children); and other factors. Several frequently used general-purpose screening instruments are described briefly in the following paragraphs. For a much more comprehensive discussion of screening instruments, see Kenny and Culbertson (1993).

The Denver II (Frankenburg et al., 1990) screens for language skills, gross motor and fine motor control, and personal-social concerns, through 125 items. It may be used from birth to about six years of age. The norms are quite current, and data are available to indicate at what ages 25, 50, 75, and 100 percent of the norming sample succeeded on any given test item. Delays may be noted, and the screening test may be given repeatedly over a period of time—a very important consideration with ECSE populations. The instrument requires about 20 minutes to administer.

The Battelle Developmental Inventory (Newborg, Stock, Wnek, Guidubaldi, & Svinicki, 1984) has a screening version, suitable for use from birth to about eight years of age. This screening test taps into all five areas of development recognized by the IDEA: personal-social, adaptive, motor, cognitive, and communication. Both standard and age-equivalent scores may be obtained. The Battelle focuses on school-readiness skills more than on specific disabilities or conditions. The screening version takes about 10 to 20 minutes to administer; the full version requires about an hour.

Ireton and Thwing have proposed four screening versions of the Minnesota Child Development Inventory (MCDI), a parent report instrument. Suitable for use in the birth-to-six age range, the MCDI (Ireton & Thwing, 1974b) has 320 questions organized into areas such as self-help, gross motor and fine motor development, and situation comprehension. The four screening versions are briefer and are targeted to more restricted age ranges. The Minnesota Infant Development Inventory (Ireton & Thwing, 1974c) is intended for use from birth to about 15 months. For children aged one to three years, the Minnesota Early Child Development Inventory (Ireton & Thwing, 1974a) offers 60 parent report items plus a problem report list. The Minnesota Preschool Inventory—Form 34 (Ireton & Thwing, 1974e) is intended for use with three- to six-year-olds; overlapping it is the Minnesota Pre-kindergarten Inventory (Ireton & Thwing, 1974d), which focuses on 4.5- to 5.5-year-olds. Both assess school readiness.

Bricker and Squires (1989) suggested that parents are excellent sources of information about children who require testing; that is, parent reports may be used in place of or in addition to screening tests. According to Bricker, Squires, Kaminski, and Mounts (1988), mailing parents report forms every four months during an at-risk child's first two years of life is inexpensive (averaging about $2.50 per child) yet very accurate, yielding only moderate over- and underscreening rates (false positives or false negatives).

Screening instruments and parent reports should not be used for diagnostic purposes or for planning either interventions or preschool special education services. Rather, screening tests and parental symptom or problem reports should function as indicators pointing to the need for more thorough diagnostic and medical examinations.

TESTING

Testing infants, toddlers, and preschoolers is not an easy task even under the best of conditions. Difficulties arise because of legal requirements and because of variables in the children themselves, the examiners, and the tests and other procedures used.

LEGAL ISSUES

Testing young children who have or are believed to have disabilities, delays, or deviations in development requires prior parental consent. The IDEA, Part B, Section 615(b)(3)(B) requires that parents or guardians receive prior written notice of any proposal to test a child; Section 639(a)(6) in Part C requires the same steps. In addition, communication of test results is limited by the IDEA's procedural safeguards. The law insists that no one test be used to make intervention, education, or placement decisions. The IDEA also requires a multidisciplinary approach that draws on the particular expertise of specialists in different areas as well as that of caregivers and teachers who know the child well. Again, this is an approach that is widely recommended (Bredekamp, 1987; DEC Task Force, 1993). Part C proscribes communication of personally identifiable information about a child, including test results, from one agency to another without prior written parental permission. Both Part B and Part C expressly grant parents or guardians permission to examine relevant records, including test results. A child may not be denied services even if the parents withhold permission for testing.

Assessment with young children is a subject of entire texts (e.g., Bondurant-Utz 2002, *Practical Guide to Assessing Infants and Toddlers with Special Needs*) and instruments used are thoroughly addressed elsewhere as well (e.g., Pierangelo & Giuliani, 2006a, *Assessment in Special Education*). Standardized, norm-referenced instruments may be limited in utility with young children. Much better is observation. Recent research with authentic, activity-based approaches is very promising (e.g., Macy, Bricker, & Squires, 2005).

Particularly important in the early childhood years are rating scales for use by family members and professionals. That is why we are so fortunate to have available a number

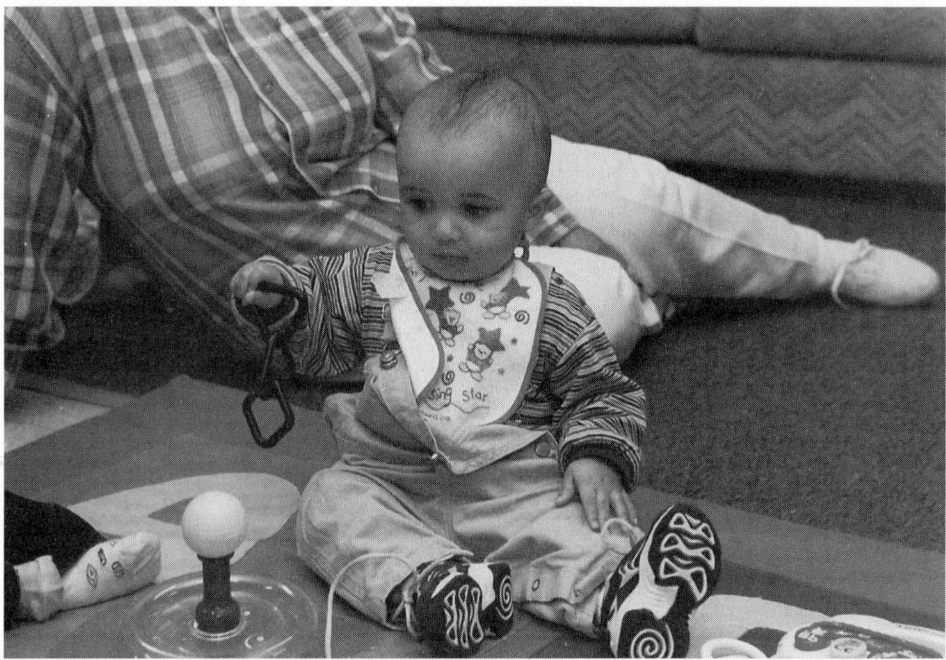

Evaluation and assessment of infants are very different from the same activities with older children. Not surprisingly, prediction from infant tests to elementary tests is not good.

of easy-to-use scales that have good validity and reliability (Mooney, Epstein, Ryser, & Pierce, 2005). The Social Skills Rating System (SSRS; Gresham & Elliott, 1990a) is an example. It has 55 items on the elementary level (grades 1–6), 38 of which relate to behavior and 17 to problem-solving skills. The Behavioral and Emotional Rating Scale—Second Edition (BERS-2): Parent Rating Scale (PRS), which was renormed in 2002, correlates well with the SSRS. Both help educators screen and identify young children who may have, or be at risk for, social and behavioral problems. They explore cooperation (sharing, helping others), empathy (showing interest in and concern about others' feelings), and self-control (handling teasing well). The AAMR Adaptive Behavior Scales—School (Lambert, Nihira, & Leland, 1993) is especially useful when examining the self-help and other coping skills of children with mental retardation.

VARIABLES IN CHILDREN

Infants in particular, but also toddlers and even preschoolers, require special treatment for testing to be effective. Infants have only a few hours each day in "alert status" when they are rested, fed, and attentive. The examiner must therefore work closely with the family and be ready to conduct testing at virtually any time during the day. Infants spend a great deal of the day sleeping. At other times, they may be irritable or drowsy. They cry a lot. They must virtually always be tested with the primary caregiver, usually the mother, present. From the age of eight months to one year in particular, the infant may be strongly attached to the primary caregiver, although stranger anxiety also occurs at later stages in early childhood.

Psychologists accustomed to testing school-age children need to modify their approaches when testing younger children. Such children usually do not have a good understanding of the testing process. They do not arrive for testing primed to perform at their optimal level. Even after they have been told, "Do your best—this is a test," most young children do not comprehend the importance of doing well in these situations. Children with severe disabilities may lack the background that test writers assume children bring with them. Many children who are physically disabled, blind, deaf, or mentally retarded have been sheltered by their parents. Such experiential deprivation hurts the children in many ways. In this context, it limits their performance on tests, simply because they have not had the opportunities to learn about and practice certain skills. In addition, children's performance in test situations may be affected by medication related to their disabilities. Children with physical disabilities may not have the endurance to persist with lengthy tasks.

Examiners must also contend with the more obvious child-related factors. Children with physical disabilities such as cerebral palsy may not be able to grasp and manipulate an object, as a test may require. Children who are deaf do not hear test instructions. The deafness interferes not only with speech comprehension but also with language development, meaning that even if the instructions are presented visually, these children may lack the linguistic competency to understand them. Children with other disabilities may not have the linguistic or even the cognitive capabilities to reflect on their own thinking, as is required in many psychoeducational assessments that are used with school-age children and youth.

For all of these reasons, examiners should look not only at the child but also to the family. Tests should be supplemented with liberal amounts of parent and professional interviews as well as firsthand observation of the child in different settings.

Testing children who are deaf challenges examiners in both administration of tests and interpretation of results.

Especially in infants and toddlers, development is very closely linked to family factors. For example, the degree of permissiveness parents show in allowing the child to explore play areas powerfully affects physical development. Parental insistence that children perform appropriately in different situations greatly influences adaptive development. Conversely, parents who excuse children with disabilities from self-help and other kinds of adaptive behavior contribute mightily to delays or deviations in that domain.

VARIABLES IN EXAMINERS

For these reasons, examiners must modify their own behavior when testing very young children. Frequently, they must also modify test instructions. The examiner may physically have to guide the hand of a child with mental retardation through a drawing task, rather than just verbally describe what is desired. In the event that stranger anxiety unnerves a young child, it may be necessary for the examiner to instruct a caregiver how to administer a test and observe the procedure from a distance. These kinds of divergences from established procedure are so often necessary that they have become common practice in ECSE. However, all such changes in procedure should be fully described in the test report and to the multidisciplinary team, because these modifications might alter, even if subtly, the meaning of test results.

The IDEA requires extensive testing of young children with disabilities. The statute assumes that psychologists and others administering tests are experienced in working with this population. The fact is, however, that most school psychologists are not trained for work in early childhood. They are familiar with tests administered in elementary and secondary schools but not with instruments used with preschool-age children. Their test-giving patterns assume that most children being tested will exhibit good test-taking

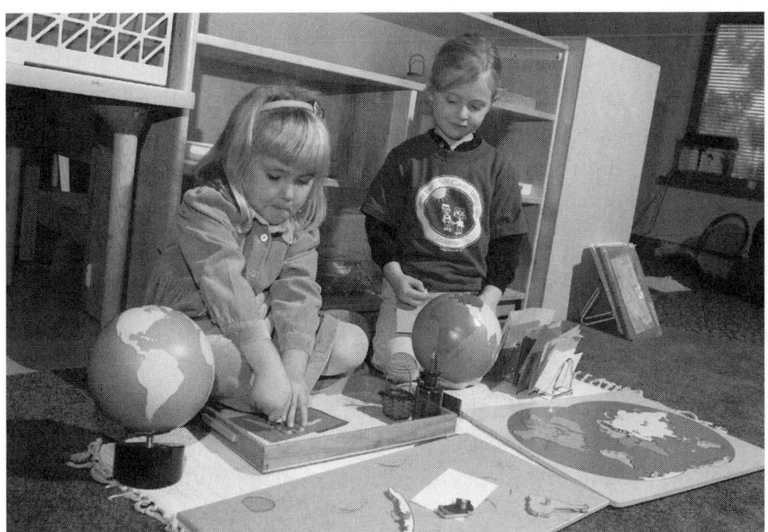

Selection of appropriate test instruments is very important in the birth-to-eight age period because many instruments are not designed for use with young children having severe disabilities. Geography is a good example.

habits. The fact that relatively few psychometricians have experience with ECSE populations is a severe constraint. This is particularly true because testing young children with disabilities demands a thorough knowledge of the instrument being administered and a great deal of flexibility in deciding which subtests to give, in what order, and with what modifications. The same kinds of personnel shortages that plague ECSE in other areas permeate testing as well.

VARIABLES IN INSTRUMENTS

Evaluation and assessment of young children are made even more difficult by the fact that few tests are available for use. Test authors typically report a range of validity and reliability data on their tests to help examiners understand how to use the instrument. Usually, these figures are relevant to examiners only when used with the same kinds of children as were tested to generate those validity and reliability measures. But because children with disabilities often were not included in those original studies, the validity and reliability data have very limited meaning to examiners working with ECSE populations.

In fact, some test authors specifically caution against using the instrument at all with children who have severe disabilities. For example, some tests require children to listen to instructions and then respond. But using such a test with a child who is deaf measures not the construct ostensibly being assessed but rather the child's hearing and linguistic competencies. Other tests require rapid manipulation of objects; cerebral palsy, by its very nature, slows and limits such activities.

A related problem has to do with what the scores mean. How does one interpret a score of 7 on a motor skills scale, for example? Norm-referenced tests handle this problem by reporting norms data on the scores that children of different ages achieved on those scales. Again, however, in most cases these data are based on samples that excluded young children with disabilities. In addition, the norms hold only when tests are administered in the same way as they were to the norming sample. Instruments are often administered differently to children with disabilities than to children without disabilities.

The federal legislation requires, rather optimistically, that tests used with young children who have or are suspected to have delays, deviations, or disabilities meet a number of standards. The tests are to be valid and reliable for the purposes for which they are used. Few tests used in early childhood meet these psychometric criteria. Tests are to be administered in the child's native language or mode of communication, yet not all tests are available in Spanish, German, Japanese, or French. Few come in Braille, in large print, or on audiocassettes for use with children who are blind. Meanwhile, few examiners are fluent in American Sign Language. The IDEA stipulates that tests are to be administered as test manuals say they should, but examiners often have to modify testing protocols. Strict adherence to the instructions in manuals may be worse than modifying them.

Finally, the IDEA requires that tests measure what they are intended to measure, and not the child's disability (unless that is what is being tested). Yet again, inadvertently measuring the child's disability sometimes is unavoidable; adjustments in interpretation of test results may be both necessary and preferable to discarding the test altogether.

Fortunately, the IDEA generated considerable excitement in fields related to psychometrics with young children who have disabilities. Each year, hundreds of thousands of young children with disabilities, developmental delays, or deviations must be tested. There is a large market now, and test developers are responding to it. While state-of-the-art techniques for testing these children still leave a great deal to be desired, the good news is that many more—and better—tests are on the way. The 1993 release of the Bayley II is a good example. It appears to be more useful in ECSE than was the original Bayley (1969), although that instrument certainly was a good one.

More generally, intelligence in infants, toddlers, and preschoolers is not the same as intelligence among school-age children. Especially in the domain of cognitive development, tests used in early childhood are different from tests for school-age children of what ostensibly are the same constructs. To adopt for the moment the terminology Piaget gave us, with infants and toddlers, intelligence tests tap sensorimotor skills, particularly physical and mobility capabilities; with school-age children, they tap operations. Not surprisingly, the power of intelligence tests administered to infants or toddlers to predict the results of intelligence tests administered to school-age children is modest at best; that is, a child's IQ at two is a poor predictor of the same child's IQ at eight. Early IQ test scores may account for only 16 to 26 percent of the variance in later IQ test scores—even for young children who have no disabilities. Correlation between IQ tests given to children with disabilities at 7 months and tests given at 18 months may be as low as .20 (McCall, 1976). The argument is sometimes made that higher predictive validity holds with children who have severe disabilities. Fagan and Singer (1983), reviewing research on that question, conclude that predictive validity coefficients may be as low as .18 between tests given at one year of age and those administered to the same children aged four to six.

TEST INTERPRETATION

Professionals working with ECSE populations often need to use considerable judgment to interpret test results properly. Test interpretation in this field is rarely routine. One cannot simply turn to a norm table and use those figures to explain how a child compares with other children, because very few EC tests included children with disabilities in their norming samples. Even scoring subtasks requires judgment. In particular, the examiner should allow evidence of correct responses if the response is not completed for disability-related reasons. A child with cerebral palsy, for example, might look in the direction of a hidden object during an object permanence test, because she has been conditioned at home and in early intervention programs to expect others to read the glance and retrieve the object. It should not be a surprise if such habits appear in testing situations as well. The key to test interpretation in this case is to recognize that by looking steadily at where the object was last placed before being hidden, the child is in fact demonstrating awareness of object permanence. The glance is as convincing a demonstration as actual physical movement to fetch the object would have been.

With children who are deaf, examiners need to recognize that a child's cognitive processing of information may be slowed by the child's need to focus attention on information acquisition. Serial information, in this case spoken test instructions, can be processed by normally hearing children "in background," so to speak, allowing them to think about information even as they are listening to it. However, when serial information is received visually, all of it must be acquired and understood before it may be processed. Children who are deaf may demonstrate a somewhat slower response than do children who can hear because they must wait until they capture and understand all the information before they can process it.

The predictive power of most tests used with young children who have disabilities is very limited. Examiners are best advised to use test results as a snapshot of a child's current performance—and not attempt to predict from a test how a child will do in later years. The suggestion made several times in this text that examiners use serial testing (periodic tests over several months) is relevant here. So many factors influence the test performance of a young child with a disability that no one test should be used for programmatic purposes, and certainly not for affixing a permanent label on a child.

The DEC-recommended practices document includes assessment as well as other aspects of ECSE (DEC Task Force, 1993). The recommendations are particularly helpful when it comes to test interpretation. Whether one is interpreting evaluation or assessment results, findings should be expressed in specific developmental and behavioral terms that lend themselves directly to interventions; global labels that do not suggest treatments or other activities should be avoided. The guidelines also recommended that a broad base of information supplement a test. In particular, strengths as well as weaknesses should be tapped. DEC recognizes the legislative mandate to conduct assessment and evaluation in all five domains of development as an appropriate way to obtain a more complete picture of the child and the family (see Figure 7–2).

- Assessment should be used to identify children's strengths, not just their weaknesses.
- Family assessments should be conducted only if the family requests them—and then family members should participate actively in all aspects.
- Assessment should have clear, concrete outcomes for the benefit of the child and the family. It should not be done only to satisfy funding or licensing agencies.
- Evaluating programs and interventions is a good use of assessment. Outcomes should be "fed back" to create program changes.
- Assessment and evaluation emphasize strengths as well as weaknesses, resources as much as needs.
- ECSE personnel should communicate evaluation and assessment findings to parents in ways that are understandable and useful to parents, avoiding both jargon and stigma.
- Assessment and evaluation procedures and tests should be culturally sensitive. Whenever feasible, ECSE program staff should use nonbiased instruments.
- Multiple "takes" are essential in assessing young children and their families. A wide variety of measures should be taken, notably including the views of family members. "Serial" testing, that is, sampling behavior on numerous occasions, is critical to obtaining accurate measures.

Adapted from Neisworth, in DEC Task Force (1993).

FIGURE 7–2 DEC-recommended practices on assessment.

Clearly, considerable expertise is required to test ECSE populations. Examiners should be trained in working with young children and in how disability affects development. They also should be able to draw on extensive experience in administering each test they use so that they may respond rapidly with test modifications when necessary. Experience may be one of the only ways in which examiners can learn the answers to some questions. Suppose, for example, that test instructions are signed to a child who is deaf, rather than spoken as dictated by a test manual. This variation from standard testing protocol will clearly affect the interpretation of the test results, but how and to what extent are things examiners usually learn only after testing large numbers of children who are deaf.

CULTURAL DIVERSITY ISSUES

The IDEA places increased emphasis on early childhood services for traditionally underserved children with disabilities. The law calls for ECSE workers, including test examiners, to have greater cultural awareness. Asian American children, for example, may avoid eye contact with the examiner. In almost all cases, this is indicative not of any psychopathology, certainly not of autism, but rather of cultural norms. Native American children are often taught that to look directly into an adult's eyes is a sign of disrespect. A white, middle-class examiner may think such children shy. African American and Native American mothers may use language less expansively at home, for which reason their children may also appear less verbal than white, middle-class children from homes where parents make liberal use of elaboration strategies to explain and reason with their children while disciplining them. Cultural competence in testing includes knowledge of these and related variables. Good practice requires that such aspects be incorporated not only into how tests are administered but also into how they are interpreted.

That point brings up a long-standing issue in special education. DEC's recommended practices on assessment include the following injunction: "Assessment approaches and instruments are culturally appropriate and nonbiased" (DEC Task Force, 1993, p. 17). As unobjectionable as this statement seems to be, it may also be unrealistic, given the state of the art in bias-free testing. For many years, IQ tests in particular have been used in such a way as to result in overreferral of ethnic and racial minority children, especially African Americans, into special education programs. The problem is widely recognized. Despite more than three decades of concerted effort, however, psychometrics experts continue to differ on what is a "culturally fair" test and how to design one.

ECSE personnel need to be aware that almost any test or other instrument they use may be culturally biased in favor of white, middle-class, suburban children and against African American or Hispanic American, poor, rural, or inner-city children. The answer is not to use only culturally fair tests—few, if any, exist—but rather to select, administer, and interpret tests and other instruments with awareness of and sensitivity to cultural variables. African American and Hispanic American children, in particular, and other ethnic and racial minority children as far as possible, should be tested by examiners who are members of the same minority group. When African American children are tested by white examiners (Epps, 1974) and when children from a linguistic minority are tested by English-speaking examiners not familiar with cultural and linguistic variables

(Figueroa, 1990), the children's performances suffer. In addition, young children do worse on tests when the examiner is a stranger to them than when someone with whom they have had at least some informal contact performs the examination.

EVALUATION

Evaluation is a process of establishing an individual child's initial and continuing eligibility for services under the IDEA. It compares an individual child's characteristics, as determined by testing, observation, parent reports, and other measures (notably medical records and medical history), against federal and state criteria. Children must meet those criteria to qualify for services. Evaluation establishes eligibility. It is periodic, recurring at specific intervals.

Infants and toddlers are evaluated in all five developmental domains recognized under Part C; in each, established conditions or developmental delays, as defined by states, may be identified. Preschoolers and primary-grade children are evaluated for one or more of the recognized disabilities and as needing special education and related services as a result. If a state elects to use delays with the three- to nine-year-old population, evaluation establishes developmental delays in one or more of the same five domains.

Under Part C, evaluation is to be comprehensive. That is, it must incorporate all the measures discussed here (tests, observations, parent reports, medical evidence) and be applied in all five developmental domains. Part B, too, requires a comprehensive evaluation, in this case to determine the child's needs for special education and related services. Both parts of the IDEA also require that evaluation be multidisciplinary, conducted by a team whose members may also plan intervention, preschool special education, and related services (Campbell, 1991). Although ECSE personnel, including psychologists, do not perform medical tests, a medical history is an essential component of any evaluation. In particular, evidence of any pre-, peri-, or postnatal incidents; any early childhood illnesses or accidents; and any assessments of hearing, vision, and general motor coordination are critical to evaluation. The discussion turns now to an examination of those mandates.

THE FEDERAL REQUIREMENTS

The statutory language, together with the U.S. Department of Education's implementing regulations, provides very specific guidance on what is to be done, how it must be done, and when it must be done. Both Part C and Part B recognize that informed judgments by expert personnel are necessary. Both parts proscribe the use of any single test or procedure. The Part B regulation, for example, requires that "[t]he evaluation is made by a multidisciplinary team or group of persons, including at least one teacher or other specialist with knowledge in the area of suspected disability" (Section 300.532[e]).

Infants and Toddlers

The U.S. Department of Education's regulations on evaluation of infants and toddlers are extracted in Figure 7–3. Note that very young children's functioning is to be evaluated in all five domains.

The Department of Education's Part C regulation explains that evaluation is to

(1) Be conducted by personnel trained to utilize appropriate methods and procedures

(2) Be based on informed clinical opinion; and

(3) Include the following:
- *(i) A review of pertinent records related to the child's current health status and medical history*
- *(ii) An evaluation of the child's level of functioning in each of the following developmental areas:*
  - *(A) Cognitive development*
  - *(B) Physical development, including vision and hearing*
  - *(C) Communication development*
  - *(D) Social or emotional development*
  - *(E) Adaptive development*

U.S. Department of Education (1993; 2006a, Section 303.322[c]).

FIGURE 7–3 Evaluation of infants and toddlers.

Part C requires the evaluation to be timely, that is, it must occur as soon as possible after the child has been identified, whether through a state child find effort; an EPSDT screening; referral from a primary care provider such as a family physician; or some other means. The department's regulation for Part C defines timely as "within 45 days after . . . referral" (34 CFR 303.321[e], 303.322[e]). The words *comprehensive* and *multidisciplinary* mean that the infant or toddler is to be evaluated on a broad range of questions by a team including specialists on those various issues. Those questions are established by the statutory definition of "infants and toddlers with disabilities" as relating to all five areas of development: cognitive, physical, communication, social or emotional, and adaptive. If applicable, development is to be measured against state criteria for "delay" in each of those five areas.

Children with Disabilities

The U.S. Department of Education (1992b, 2006b) has offered detailed instructions about evaluation of children with or suspected of having disabilities. Figure 7–4 offers selected extracts from that guidance. Note that some provisions are not included in the figure (e.g., [a] and [b] from Section 300.532, [a] from Section 300.534, etc.).

EVALUATION INSTRUMENTS

The Bayley II Scales of Infant Development (Bayley, 1993) is a standardized, norm-referenced instrument suitable for use with infants and young children aged one month to 3.6 years. The second edition of this widely used instrument offers updated norms on mental, motor, and behavior domains of development in infants, toddlers, and young preschoolers. The mental scale assesses, among other things, sensory and perceptual skills, object permanence, language, and mathematical concept formation. The motor scale assesses gross body and motor coordination, fine motor skills, and movement. The behavior rating scale has 30 items on attention, orientation, and emotional regulation.

The Part B regulation defines *evaluation* as follows:

procedures to determine whether a child has a disability and the nature and extent of special education and related services that the child needs. The term means procedures used selectively with an individual child and does not include basic tests administered to or procedures used with all children in a school, grade, or class (U.S. Department of Education, 1992b and 2006b, Section 300.500[b]). . . .

Tests and other evaluation materials:

(1) Are provided and administered in the child's native language or other mode of communication, unless it is clearly not feasible to do so;

(2) Have been validated for the specific purpose for which they are used; and

(3) Are administered by trained personnel in conformance with the instructions provided by their producer. . . .
(c) Tests are selected and administered so as best to ensure that when a test is administered to a child with impaired sensory, manual, or speaking skills, the test results accurately reflect the child's aptitude or achievement level or whatever other factors the test purports to measure, rather than reflecting the child's impaired sensory, manual, or speaking skills (except where those skills are the factors that the test purports to measure).
(d) No single procedure is used as the sole criterion for determining an appropriate educational program for a child.
(e) The evaluation is made by a multidisciplinary team or group of persons, including at least one teacher or other specialist with knowledge in the area of suspected disability.
(f) The child is assessed in all areas related to the suspected disability, including, if appropriate, health, vision, hearing, social and emotional status, general intelligence, academic performance, communicative status, and motor abilities . . . (Section 300.532).
(b) That an evaluation of the child . . . is conducted every three years, or more frequently if conditions warrant, or if the child's parent or teacher requests an evaluation (Section 300.534).

FIGURE 7–4 Evaluation of children with disabilities (excerpts).

Although the Bayley II appears to retain the features that made the original Bayley one of the most widely used and respected instruments in ECSE, very little independent evaluation of the scales' validity and reliability was available when this book was written.

Another widely used scale is the Battelle Developmental Inventory, which was mentioned earlier. The Battelle, which may be used from birth to eight years of age, assesses development in all five domains recognized by the IDEA. McLean and McCormick (1993) identify several limitations of the Battelle. It can take almost an hour longer to administer than does the original Bayley. Because each item must be administered in the order specified, it is a more difficult test to use than the original Bayley, which gave examiners flexibility in this respect. Such flexibility is often necessary with very young children.

The Kaufman Assessment Battery for Children—Second Edition (K-ABC; Kaufman & Kaufman, 2004) is a norm-referenced, standardized instrument for use with children between the ages of 2.5 and 12.5 years. It requires about one hour and 15 minutes to administer. The K-ABC yields scores of cognitive, fine motor, verbal, and quantitative development. An advantage of the K-ABC is that it does not require a lot of verbal interaction between examiner and child; it is therefore useful with children who have language or hearing limitations.

The McCarthy Scales of Children's Abilities (McCarthy, 1972) is a similar instrument, requiring about the same amount of time to administer. Designed for use with children aged 2.5 to 8.5, the McCarthy has a gross motor component that the Kaufman lacks.

Transdisciplinary play-based assessment (TPBA)

(Linder, 1993) is a qualitative approach to testing in which young children interact with play materials, professionals, and other children.

Toni Linder (1993) has promoted **transdisciplinary play-based assessment (TPBA)** as an approach that taps the natural desire of young children to play. In this technique, one professional (often aided by a parent) interacts with the child in a setting that features a variety of play materials. Linder suggests that the session begin with a free-play period, followed by a time during which the professional guides further play. These periods may be followed by child-child and child-parent interactive sessions and later by a snack session. The sessions are all videotaped. Afterward, the interdisciplinary team reviews the tapes, looking for evidence of developmental delays as well as capabilities.

Many other options are available. The interested reader is referred to Culbertson and Willis (1993), an excellent reference on testing with ECSE populations for descriptions and comparisons of many different instruments. Rosetti (1986, 1990) discusses assessment of infants and toddlers specifically; McLean and McCormick (1993) offer a shorter discussion, also helpful, on many of the same issues.

ASSESSMENT

To write IFSPs or IEPs, one must know far more than simply that a child is eligible for ECSE services. Among children evaluated as being eligible, initial assessment is needed to determine what specific limitations the child has, so as to plan intervention, special education, and related services. Assessment thus probes more deeply than does evaluation; it looks to unique needs and how those change over time as services are provided. It is a continuing, rather than a periodic, procedure.

Part C calls for a family assessment, if the family concurs. Discussion on that topic follows. Part B requires assessment only of the child and her unique needs, although special educators are encouraged to consider family factors in assessing children with disabilities.

INFANTS AND TODDLERS

The Part C regulation (U.S. Department of Education, 1993, 2006a) calls for assessment in all five areas of development and outlines the process to be used. Figure 7–5 offers the regulatory wording.

An assessment of the unique needs of the child [shall be conducted] in terms of each of the developmental areas [cognitive, physical, communication, social or emotional, adaptive], including the identification of services appropriate to meet those needs (34 CFR 303.322[c][iii]).

Assessment means the ongoing procedures used by appropriate qualified personnel throughout the period of a child's eligibility under this part to identify

(i) The child's unique strengths and needs and the services appropriate to meet those needs; and

(ii) The resources, priorities, and concerns of the family and the supports and services necessary to enhance the family's capacity to meet the developmental needs of their infant or toddler with a disability. (Section 303.322[b][2])

FIGURE 7–5 Assessment of infants and toddlers.

Communication (each is rated as able to do well; the number is the age in months 90 percent of typical children do it)
- Babbles (3)
- Says "mama" or "dada" (12)
- Responds to simple gestures (e.g., "bye bye") (17)
- Repeats or imitates a word (18)
- Follows a two-step verbal direction (24)
- Says two or three words in a sentence (25)

Cognition
- Laughs in response to peek-a-boo (8)
- Explores objects by shaking and banging (11)
- Puts things into and takes them out of things (12)
- Does simple pretending in play like feeding a doll (18)
- Recognizes two body parts (28)
- Refers to things as "mine" (30)
- Gives his or her first name (35)

Physical
- Grasps object and lets go (10)
- Crawls, scoots, or creeps (11)
- Sits up (11)
- Picks up small objects with finger and thumb (12)
- Holds a crayon or pencil (16)
- Walks without holding on (17)
- Walks quickly or runs (25)
- Unwraps paper from candy (25)

Adaptive
- Eats bite-size pieces with fingers (11)
- Lifts cup and drinks from it (18)
- Takes off socks independently (23)
- Washes and dries hands thoroughly (28)

Social or Emotional (no age level given)
- Does things on own even if hard
- Pays attention/stays focused
- Jumpy and easily startled
- Very active and excitable
- Trouble playing with other children
- Aggressive toward other children

Source: Hebbeler et al. (2003), Tables IV–6, IV–7, and IV–8.

FIGURE 7–6 Assessment areas, infants and toddlers.

Figure 7–6 outlines areas of assessment for infants and toddlers with disabilities. It draws from the NEILS research (Hebbeler et al., 2003). The figure identifies the age (in months) at which the vast majority of infants and toddlers display a given behavior.

To establish eligibility under Part C is only the first step. The second is to answer the question "Eligibility for what?" There is no requirement in the federal law that all eligible infants, toddlers, and families receive the full range of possible services under Part C. Rather, the decision about services is made on a case-by-case basis. For some infants or toddlers, periodic observation, occasional testing, and parent information and referral services will suffice. For others, a comprehensive, multidisciplinary, multiagency effort requiring a great deal of coordination and costing considerable sums will be required. The point is that establishing eligibility under Part C does not qualify a child for any particular service or group of services.

Assessment involves, to take an example, plotting a baseline of social or emotional behavior, using behavior modification techniques, and tracking how the child's activities change under different reinforcement schedules. The ECSE worker tries something and sees how it works. When a teacher inaugurates a new language development curriculum for a child who is deaf, she monitors progress, always asking, "Is this working?" and "Should we try something else instead?" That, too, is assessment.

FAMILIES

One special kind of assessment is the "family-directed assessment of the resources, priorities, and concerns of the family and the identification of the supports and services

[Part C] recognizes the central role played by families in designing and implementing effective early intervention services for their infants and toddlers with disabilities. Second, it states that the assessment must be family-directed and may, with the concurrence of the family, include an assessment of the family's resources, priorities, and concerns and identification of family preferences, supports, and services necessary to enhance the parents' and siblings' capacity to meet the developmental needs of their infant or toddler with a disability. (House Report 102–198, 1991, p. 18)

(1) Family assessments under this Part must be family-directed and designed to determine the resources, priorities, and concerns of the family related to enhancing the development of the child. (2) Any assessment that is conducted must be voluntary on the part of the family. (3) If an assessment of the family is carried out, the assessment must—

(i) Be conducted by personnel trained to utilize appropriate methods and procedures;
(ii) Be based on information provided by the family through a personal interview; and
(iii) Incorporate the family's description of its resources, priorities, and concerns related to enhancing the child's development.

U.S. Department of Education (1993, 34 CFR 303.322[d]); see also U.S. Department of Education (2006a).

FIGURE 7–7 Family-directed assessment.

necessary to enhance the family's capacity to meet the developmental needs of the infant or toddler" (IDEA Section 636[a][2]). This assessment is important for several reasons. First, Part C, unlike Part B, specifically includes services for families. The plan that is developed following assessment is, after all, called an Individualized *Family* Service Plan. Before services for the family can be identified and planned, ECSE professionals need to identify family needs. Second, infants and toddlers cannot be understood apart from their families. Tests and other evaluation and assessment processes are not as helpful with very young children as they are with older children. Bailey (1991) offers a definition of family assessment that helps frame the issue: "the ongoing and interactive process by which professionals gather information in order to determine family priorities for goals and services" (p. 27).

The statute and the regulations are clear that family assessments are voluntary on the part of the family. The law specifically states that they are to be "family-directed," which means that the family decides whether and to what extent to participate. To make the meaning of "family-directed" clearer, Figure 7–7 shows the explanatory language from the House Report accompanying what became the 1991 amendments (PL 102–119) and the department's additional explanations from its Part C regulation (1993a).

Bailey (1991) reports that, in family assessments, families themselves tend to prefer informal rather than formal approaches and open-ended rather than forced-choice conversations. Interviews are a good example of both preferences. In an appendix to his article, Bailey offers a family needs survey as a means of determining family priorities in advance of such interviews. Such a written instrument may be used only as an option, that is, as a means through which parents may voluntarily indicate priorities and interests. It cannot be presented to parents as a requirement for program participation. The form includes questions about the family's need for information, family and social support, financial support, child care, community services, professional support, and communication with others about their child.

CHILDREN WITH DISABILITIES

The department's Part B regulation does not define assessment with respect to preschool-age children with disabilities. It does note that psychological services, which are related

Reading

Comprehensive Test of Phonological Processing (CTOPP; Wagner, Torgeson, & Rashotte, 1999)—rapid letter naming and segmenting
Standard Reading Passages (Marston & Deno, 1986)—oral reading fluency
Woodcock Johnson III (Woodcock, McGrew & Mather, 2001)—
Letter-word identification; passage comprehension

Math

Woodcock Johnson III—math calculation, math problem solving

Social or Emotional

Student self-concept scale (Gresham & Elliott, 1990b)
Student attitude measure (Wick, 1990)
Loneliness scale (Asher, Hymel, & Renshaw, 1984)

Source: Blackorby et al. (2005), SEELS Report, A-5.

FIGURE 7–8 Assessment scales, children with disabilities.

services, include assessment. The Part B rule also uses the term *identification and assessment* to refer to initial screening, as noted earlier (see "Child Find"). Such activities are also considered related services.

Neither the statute nor the department's Part B regulation provides for family-directed assessments of family priorities, resources, and concerns. However, programs striving to offer seamless services may provide such family assessments, at the family's request. "Social work services in schools," a related service under Part B, incorporates such assessment-related steps as "preparing a social or developmental history on a child with a disability," "group and individual counseling with the child and family," and "working with those problems in a child's living situation (home, school, and community) that affect the child's adjustment in school" (U.S. Department of Education, 1992b, Section 300.16[12]).

Figure 7–8 identifies some often-used assessment scales, which are cited in the References. The information comes from the SEELS research (Blackorby et al., 2005).

COMMUNICATING WITH FAMILIES

Services to a child may not be withheld just because the family declines to participate or cooperate in a family assessment, which many families do. While evaluation and assessment of the child may strike them as both necessary and desirable, many parents resist the notion that they themselves be assessed by ECSE professionals. Such concerns are understandable. Assessment is by its very nature invasive, and some families feel that family assessments may result in their being blamed for whatever problems a child has. ECSE personnel, who are sensitive to the potential privacy violations that worry many families, can usually overcome such resistance.

ECSE personnel should open discussion of family assessment by acknowledging the central role of the family in early childhood. At no other stage in development is the family as crucial as it is during the birth-to-eight period. For this reason, it is essential that early intervention and preschool special education personnel understand family dynamics and know how the child functions as a member of the family unit.

A second point ECSE personnel may stress with the family is that the law, particularly Part C, expressly authorizes services for the family, not only the child. A family assessment assists in identifying such needs. If the family assessment is presented as an option, to be conducted at any time, families may be more receptive to the idea.

Finally, ECSE personnel may address privacy concerns overtly by acknowledging that all data collected will be shared with the family and will not be released by the ECSE program staff to any other public or private agency without prior written parental consent. Indeed, the law requires family assessments to be family-directed, optional, and strictly confidential. Many families will respond positively to truthful and open communication from ECSE personnel.

Communication with families about other kinds of evaluation and assessment activities also requires honesty. Most parents do not have training in psychometrics; they may have unrealistic expectations of tests as somehow magically revealing hidden truths. It is essential for ECSE personnel to explain forthrightly that standardized and other tests and instruments used in this field are limited in what they can do. They should acknowledge the weaknesses of tests in validity, reliability, and norming. Such acknowledgment should, however, be paired with an assurance that the program will draw on the varied skills of many professionals in a multidisciplinary evaluation and will combine test results with observations, interviews, and other sources so as to provide families with information and recommendations that are useful and helpful. Another suggestion is to speak with families of samples and of sampling behavior. Given the reality of testing with very young children, it is more accurate to state that what is being done is sampling behavior more than actually testing the child.

Child and family assessments should begin with consultation with the family. Without going into details about the relative merits of various approaches, ECSE personnel should explain to the family the evaluation or assessment procedure they recommend, what it involves, what kinds of results might be expected, and why it is important. They should note family questions and promise to answer them as far as possible following the activity. Parents and other family members should be assured that all findings will be kept strictly confidential, as required by law.

The NEILS longitudinal study found high levels of family satisfaction with early intervention services. The questions they asked are posted at the project Web site: www.sri.com/neils. Other sources of good questions include the *Beach Center Family Quality of Life Scale* (www.beachcenter.org) and the Family-Professional Partnership Scale (Dillman, 2000; Summers et al., 2005). Researchers at the University of Kansas reported good validity and reliability for both the 18-item FPPS and its two nine-item subscales (Summers et al., 2005). Family members are asked, for example, whether the child's service providers "help you gain skills or information to get what your child needs" and "provide services that meet the individual needs of the child."

Accardo and Capute (1979) provide another framework for communicating with families about results of evaluation and assessment procedures. They suggest that cognitive information—the nature of the activity, the findings, and what those mean—must be communicated clearly yet comprehensively, using as little jargon as possible. Key findings should also be presented on an operative level. That is, families should be given specific suggestions on how they may use the test results. Findings should be paired with recommendations, documented weaknesses matched with programs and curricula for intervention and treatment. Finally, affective aspects of communication with families are crucial. Whether the results being presented are of child or family assessments or of psychological or other evaluations, parents and other family members will have feelings about this information. These feelings should be acknowledged, particularly where evaluation indicates the need for long-term treatment.

Accardo and Capute (1979) add that, if at all possible, both parents, as well as other adults identified by the family as responsible for a child's care, be invited to meetings at which test or other assessment results are presented. If only one parent attends and returns home to explain results to other family members, that parent shoulders an unfair burden. She may not be able to answer questions from other family members, for example, or may not be able to articulate findings and their implications. Families should be permitted to designate whoever they consider to be family. Each person should be offered an opportunity to question the evaluation team, and all such questions should be accepted and answered courteously. At the meeting's end, a statement should be made along the lines of "We know you may have more questions, so feel free to call or visit at any time."

The most important part of communicating with families about evaluation and assessment is explaining what the findings mean for the child and for the family and recommending specific programs to the family. While evaluation and assessment activities are important, what is done with the information they generate is far more important. ECSE personnel should advise families that they have a legal right to a second opinion. They should also assure families that evaluation will be periodic and that assessment is ongoing. Finally, ECSE workers should remind families that family services are an integral component of ECSE services and that they should not hesitate to request support or other assistance they feel they need.

PROGRAM EVALUATION

Program evaluation

attempts to answer the following questions: Did a program do what it promised? Did it do these things efficiently and effectively?

ECSE administrators may schedule evaluations of the program itself. **Program evaluation** is the review, analysis, and reporting of what actually happened over a period of time, as distinct from program goals and other standards of performance. Program evaluation attempts to answer the following questions: Did we do what we said we would do? Did we do it as efficiently as we could have, making good use of available resources? Were our approaches effective in meeting the needs of the children and families we serve?

Formative evaluation

looks to process issues such as how many families apply for services, how many are served, and how many of what kinds of services are provided. Formative evaluation may take place during an activity or program, whereas summative evaluation tends to occur afterward.

In **formative evaluation,** the focus is on process issues. Planning and implementation in ECSE programs are reviewed with the aid of such methods as needs assessments (which inquire about the potential demand in the program's service area and the extent to which the program offers the kinds of services that are needed) and program data analysis (which looks to determine how many children and families were served in a given period of time, with what kinds of services, and at what cost to the program). Such information may be used to assure funding agencies that the program is in compliance with federal, state, and other licensing or other requirements and is carrying out the plan of services that had been proposed. For example, formative evaluation may show that an ECSE program that promised to make at least two home visits monthly to each family being served actually averaged just 1.5 visits per month. These kinds of process evaluations examine the program's performance, as compared to its goals. Formative evaluation seldom compares two or more programs against one another.

Summative evaluation

looks to outcomes, or results, to assess programs and activities, usually in comparison with other activities or programs. It is in contrast to formative evaluation, which focuses more on process than product.

In **summative evaluation,** the emphasis shifts to outcomes. It may be, for example, that family reports, child assessments, and other measures indicate that as much progress was made in those home visits as had been projected to occur under the full number of visits. Program evaluators may also find that center-based services are as effective as, but much more expensive than, home visits. These kinds of outcome data usually involve comparisons—in such cases, between outcomes as a function of more or fewer home visits and outcomes as a function of home versus center delivery (Escobar, Barnett, & Goetze, 1994).

Annual program evaluations can be very helpful in planning; they are also useful in communicating with funding and licensing agencies, because they provide independent evidence that the program does what it says it does. Murray (1992) suggests using program evaluation to answer critical questions about the program's impact on the people it serves. For example, are family-friendly approaches more effective in program-family relations than more traditional child-focused or professional-centered relations? Are more intensive services of greater assistance to children than less intensive services? Program evaluation may also help ECSE programs monitor costs and justify reimbursement claims. Murray notes, however, that few early intervention programs use computer database management. Cost allocation is far more easily managed with the assistance of computers than with calculators and paper records.

Program evaluation is most successful when an outside evaluator is contracted to perform the review. This evaluator should visit with the program staff early in a fiscal or academic year, propose and gain administrator acceptance of instruments and other measures to be used, and establish a means of maintaining ongoing communication throughout the year. At year end, when all programmatic and fiscal data have been collected, the evaluator reviews these data and prepares a draft report. After the program staff consider the draft, and perhaps submit explanations for or elaborations on the evaluator's findings, a final report is issued.

Large and midsize accounting firms often perform pro bono audits and program evaluations. They can also recommend staff financial officers and independent evaluators. Pro bono accounting and program evaluation work by established accounting firms can be very helpful to program administrators who lack training and background in business and finance.

The involvement of ECSE personnel, including senior administrators, in program evaluation should not be minimized, even if an outside evaluator is retained. Critical decisions must be made before the evaluation can be conducted. Consider, for example, cost allocations. What kinds of costs will be included on the expenses side of the register? This question is particularly urgent when it comes to placing a value on presumed costs or intangibles. To take an obvious example, family membership on planning and policy committees involves expenses, as does family member participation in support group sessions. Often, parents do not charge the program for their time. Should some dollar figure be assigned to that time to reflect more fully all actual and opportunity costs involved in running the program? If so, what dollar amount is fair and reasonable? Other examples involve results (outcomes). What kinds of measures should be sought? Parent evaluations? Student test scores? Placements of graduates in public school programs? Administrators and other workers in ECSE programs need to provide input to the outside evaluator on these and many other questions.

There is an unfortunate tendency in some human services fields to resist truly independent program evaluations. White (1988) points out that cost analysis is subject to bias. Where programs exist to meet human needs and must be justified to policymakers on an annual basis in order to retain funding, some program "administrators cannot allow data to be collected that show that the program is not completely successful" (p. 441). This bias may show up in subtle ways. Administrators may not allow certain costs (notably opportunity costs) to be included, for example, thus making expenses appear lower than they otherwise would. Alternatively (or even additionally), administrators may use very liberal definitions of benefits or other outcomes as a way of inflating program results.

However costs and outcomes are defined, results may not be as clear-cut as one might wish. Program evaluation is difficult to carry out, for many reasons. Suppose it costs $10,000 per year to provide ECSE services to Jane Doe. How can one measure whether those costs are justified? In almost all cases, programs could do things in less expensive ways. Some cost-cutting measures make sense (and should be included in the outside evaluator's report). Others, however, would compromise program quality and might even subject the program to loss of its license for failing to meet state standards. And what about outcomes? It is possible to look at where Jane attends kindergarten and elementary school in subsequent years; if she is mainstreamed into a regular classroom, with few support services, one could say that the ECSE services succeeded with her—that the local community saved the extra dollars that separate classes, resource room services, and so on, might have cost. Yet the matter is not so simple. How can anyone be sure that Jane would have needed such services absent ECSE? Perhaps, had no intervention and preschool special education been offered, she could have functioned well enough in a regular classroom to make it there. Even if one can establish that Jane could not have done these things without help, how does anyone know that it was the ECSE services that rendered separate instruction unnecessary? Perhaps it was parental assistance at home; perhaps it was a supportive, encouraging kindergarten teacher.

Murray (1992) points out that traditional program evaluation models are heavily quantitative in nature, that is, they look at numbers. In ECSE, such numbers unfortunately are often "soft." In particular, securing comparison data may be difficult or even impossible. There may be no other program serving the same kinds of children and families against which an ECSE program may be compared. Alternatively, a program may offer only center-based services or home-based services but not both, meaning that no comparisons across service placement may be made. In addition, using traditional pretest-posttest designs may not be feasible, because changes in children or families may be confounded with changes in the program itself, making it impossible to separate out what events contributed to what outcomes. Finally, as indicated throughout this chapter, instruments measuring child and family functioning that are both valid and reliable continue to be few and far between.

Whether the programs are effective, cost-effective, or cost-beneficial is often difficult to establish; it may not be possible to state definitively for even a single program or a particular child whether a program works and whether the expenditures were worth it. However, given continued budgetary pressures from all levels of government (federal, state, county, and local), ECSE programs will likely need to perform independent, outside evaluations so that program administrators, county officials, and state policymakers may obtain, as far as possible, objective evidence on what the program does and how well it does those things.

SUMMARY

Early screening and identification of children potentially eligible for ECSE services have been required in all states since 1980, yet the process remains inconsistent. Pediatricians and other physicians are the logical professionals to conduct such screenings, but to date few test more than a handful of their patients. As awareness of the importance of early identification grows, screening should become more systematic.

Evaluation establishes initial and continuing eligibility for services. ECSE workers use assessment to identify specific interventions and to track progress of children as services are provided. Tests and other instruments for use in evaluation and assessment tend to have significant limitations. The state of the art in evaluation and assessment of young children who have disabilities, delays, or deviations in development, however, is evolving. The IDEA is stimulating vigorous growth in the field of ECSE instrumentation and procedures, and we can look forward to much-improved tests and other assessment activities in the years to come. Family assessments, which are more informal activities based on interviews and observation, may be used to supplement child assessments if the family concurs. Program evaluation in ECSE is often problematic, both because many programs do not have the computer technology necessary to track data and because information is frequently ambiguous, making it difficult to pinpoint what activities had what outcomes.

As important as evaluation and assessment activities are—and they are important—these procedures are but steps toward individualization of service delivery. Programs evaluate children and assess their progress because of a recognition that they differ between and within themselves. We know that children in this age range change rapidly. They also respond differently to intervention. What works with one child may not succeed with another. For all of these reasons, evaluation and assessment lead to individualized planning, the topic of the next chapter.

KEY TERMS

assessment
evaluation
formative evaluation
informed clinical opinion
program evaluation
summative evaluation
transdisciplinary play-based assessment (TPBA)

QUESTIONS FOR REFLECTION

1. Identify at least two differences between evaluation and assessment.
2. Why are evaluation and assessment particularly challenging for professionals working with young children?
3. What is informed clinical opinion, and why does it matter so much in ECSE?
4. Explain false negatives and false positives that may occur in screening.
5. How should psychologists who are experienced in testing K–12 children adjust their approaches when working with children under six years of age?
6. If a test is not normed on young children with delays in development or disabilities, how does that fact affect how test results are interpreted and used?
7. Identify an important difference between the meanings of the construct intelligence with respect to preschool-age children versus K–12 children.
8. How does parental elaboration help young children in cognitive and language development?

9. Why does the IDEA insist that assessments of family resources, priorities, and concerns be voluntary on the part of the family?
10. Explain Goodman's concept of the best interest of the client as it applies to program-family communication.

PRACTICAL EXERCISES

1. Ask your professor to let you examine a widely used instrument, such as the Bayley, the Batelle, the Kaufman, or the McCarthy (see text for details). After reviewing one or more of these, contact a local early intervention, preschool, or elementary program to request permission to observe the instrument in use. (You will most likely need signed permission from your professor, and you will also need to sign a confidentiality agreement with the program, agreeing not to reveal any personally identifiable information about the child.) After observing the test session, reread this chapter. What insights have you gained about testing young children with disabilities?
2. Visit a local elementary school to talk with teachers and parents about the high-stakes tests now being given to virtually all children beginning in third grade. Ask about participation in these tests by young children with disabilities. Are all such children tested? Are test accommodations offered? Are student score summaries published and/or otherwise made public? Overall, how are children with disabilities performing on these tests?

WEB SITES OF INTEREST

www.education.umn.edu National Center on Educational Outcomes—information on testing children with disabilities

www.nochildleftbehind.gov U.S. Department of Education—information on testing requirements of the federal law No Child Left Behind

www.naeyc.org National Association for the Education of Young Children—position paper on testing young children on their progress toward meeting state learning standards

CHAPTER

8

Individual Planning

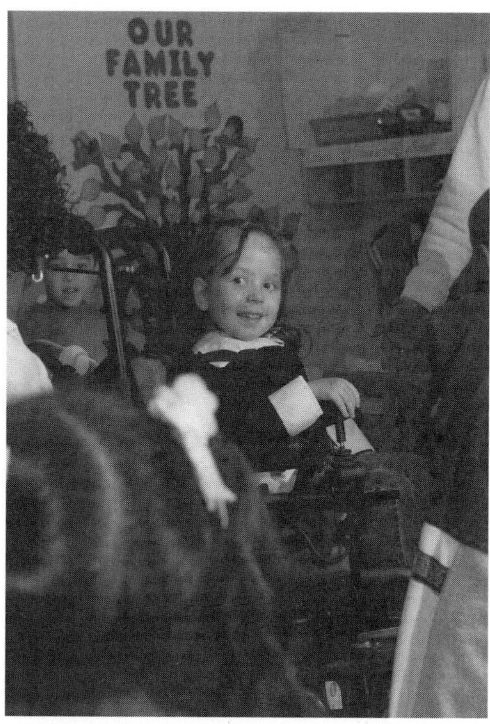

Stated simply, the target population for early intervention must be thought of in terms of eligibility for assessment and ongoing formulation of an appropriate service plan—not in terms of eligibility for a fixed set of comprehensive services.
(SHONKOFF & MEISELS, 1991, P. 24)

OBJECTIVES

After reading this chapter, you should be able to:

- Describe what goes into an Individualized Family Service Plan (IFSP).
- Explain what the law and the federal regulations require of each part of the IFSP.
- Describe what goes into an Individualized Education Program (IEP).
- Explain what is meant by the important term *appropriate*.
- Explain why IFSP and IEP teams emphasize communication with families.

- Describe how to plan transition from early intervention to preschool.
- Describe what other kinds of transition are important in ECSE.

CHAPTER OUTLINE

- OVERVIEW
- USING ASSESSMENT AND EVALUATION FINDINGS
- INDIVIDUALIZED FAMILY SERVICE PLANS
  - Assessment of Infants or Toddlers
  - Family Assessment
  - IFSP Team
  - IFSP Review
  - Timing of the IFSP
  - IFSP Contents
  - Natural Environment
  - Start Date and Duration
  - Service Coordinator
  - Transition
  - Informed Consent
- INDIVIDUALIZED EDUCATION PROGRAMS
  - IEP Meeting
  - Educational Performance
  - Goals and Objectives
  - Services
  - Districtwide Assessments
  - Transition
  - Date and Duration
  - Progress Reports
- "APPROPRIATE"
- WRITING THE PLANS
- TRANSITION
  - Within Part C
  - From Part C to Part B
  - From Part C to Other Service Programs
  - Parents and Transition from Part C
  - From Preschool to Elementary School

OVERVIEW

As a profession, ECSE values individualization of services. In fact, individualizing services for children and their families can fairly be said to be one cardinal principle of ECSE. The other is providing appropriate services. These twin values explain ECSE's overarching goal: to provide each child and family with what they need. The IDEA subsumes other values, however cherished, to those of individualization and appropriateness.

Early intervention services are "designed to meet the developmental needs of an infant or toddler with a disability" (Section 632[4]). They are to be individually designed and delivered. They are also to be "appropriate"—that is, to meet those needs. Similarly, special education is "specially designed instruction" to "meet the unique needs of a child with a disability" (Section 602[3]). Here, too, the IDEA stresses that appropriate services are to be selected and delivered in a custom-designed manner. ECSE programs are told to evaluate and assess the needs of children and, using such information, to develop unique plans of service. Individualization and appropriateness are the core concepts that separate this field from other kinds of human services programs.

Individualizing instruction is challenging for the early childhood educator, who must cope with widely varying needs.

At the same time, individualization and appropriateness are concepts that link ECSE with the broader field of early childhood. NAEYC anchored its "developmentally appropriate practice" (DAP) recommendations to two core ideas: age appropriateness and individual appropriateness.

The values of individualization and appropriateness are implemented in ECSE programs through Individualized Family Service Plans (IFSPs) and Individualized Education Programs (IEPs). These plans first identify the unique needs, priorities, concerns, and resources of particular children and their families and then outline how services will be delivered to meet these. Chapter 2 briefly described the contents of IFSPs and IEPs; this chapter elaborates in much more detail how such plans are to be prepared and what information they are to contain. The discussion meshes federal statutory and regulatory requirements to make clear how individualization is expressed in the plans.

In the opening quotation of this chapter, Shonkoff and Meisels (1991) suggest that individualization has another facet. Early intervention programs offer as many as 19 different kinds of services, in addition to service coordination services. Special education authorizes 13 kinds of related services, in addition to specially designed instruction. Not all children need, nor should they be offered, all the services. Not all families need or want all, or even most, of the kinds of family services the law identifies either as early intervention services under Part C or as related services under Part B. The services individual children and their families are to receive must be determined through customized, individualized process that identifies which services are appropriate—that is, which services children and families need in order to benefit from the program.

One very important set of services under both Part C and Part B may be grouped together under the rubric of transition services. Infants and toddlers and their families, being served under Part C, must be assisted in the transition from early intervention to programs that serve children aged three and above. In many cases, these will be Part B preschool services; in others, however, they may be community health, respite care, or other kinds of noneducational services. In addition, five-year-old children with disabilities and their families often need help to make the transition from preschool or other service programs to elementary school.

USING ASSESSMENT AND EVALUATION FINDINGS

Shonkoff and Meisels (1991) recommend tailoring services to the unique needs of individual children and their families. Early intervention and preschool special education both begin with assessments to identify those needs, followed by individualized planning of

Collaboration, or co-teaching, can often help individualize instruction.

services to meet them. Neither adopts a mass-produced, all-for-all approach. Shonkoff and Meisels continue, "[The] definition of early intervention [emphasizes] a continuum of individualized services ranging from periodic assessment to the intensive mobilization of highly specialized therapeutic and educational resources" (p. 22). They recommend that a wide range of services be considered: "varying combinations of phone monitoring, information and referral, periodic reassessment, brief home visits, participation in activity centers, parent support groups, intensive home or center-based intervention, individual parent counseling, or specialized therapeutic interventions" (p. 23).

The approach Shonkoff and Meisels recommend draws on a considerable body of research over the past several years that suggests that what researchers call aptitude treatment interactions are very important in ECSE programming, because young children with disabilities, delays, or deviations in development differ so much from one another in how they respond to different kinds of interventions and other offerings, including education. Four researchers in particular have doggedly pursued this notion. Beginning in 1991 (Cole et al.) and continuing through 2005 (Dale et al.), University of Missouri professor Philip Dale and his colleagues Kevin Cole, Paulette Mills, and Joseph Jenkins have shown us that "What works?" is a question that can only be answered with "For whom?" Their work challenges the notions that Direct Instruction seems to be most helpful for young children with cognitive impairments and that constructivist or discovery approaches appear to be more suited for use with children with few such limitations. They found, counterintuitively, that Direct Instruction may in fact impose heavy cognitive burdens on young children with severe learning needs. The bottom line, according to Dale et al., is that children's aptitudes (i.e., their skills) and teachers' interventions (i.e., our treatments) interact in such ways that we must individualize instruction.

Infants and toddlers are to be evaluated in all five areas of development: cognitive, physical, communication, social or emotional, and adaptive. If desired by the family, a measure of "the supports and services necessary to enhance the family's capacity to meet the developmental needs of the infant or toddler" (Section 636[2]) may also be conducted by trained professionals. Part B requires an assessment that looks more narrowly at the child's needs for special education and related services. However, one related service is "parent counseling and training," another is "counseling services," and a third is "social work services in schools" (34 CFR 300.16). These potential offerings suggest that children's needs be described broadly rather than narrowly.

The sections that follow outline the provisions of IFSPs and of IEPs and offer suggestions for making these documents useful in providing services for birth-to-eight children with special needs. Figure 8–1 highlights the statutory requirements for developing and using IFSPs. (Figure 8–5 does the same for IEPs later in the chapter.) The key provisions, including interpretations from committee reports and the U.S. Department of Education's regulations, are described.

(a) For each infant or toddler with a disability—

(1) a multidisciplinary assessment of the unique strengths and needs of the infant or toddler and the identification of services appropriate to meet such needs;

(2) a family-directed assessment of the resources, priorities, and concerns of the family and the identification of the supports and services necessary to enhance the family's capacity to meet the developmental needs of the infant or toddler; and

(3) a written individualized family service plan developed by a multidisciplinary team, including the parents, as required by subsection (e).

(b) The individualized family service plan shall be evaluated once a year and the family shall be provided a review of the plan at 6-month intervals (or more often where appropriate based on infant or toddler and family needs.)

(c) The individualized family service plan shall be developed within a reasonable time after the assessment required by subsection (a)(1) is completed. With the parents' consent, early intervention services may commence prior to the completion of such assessment.

(d) The individualized family service plan shall be in writing and contain—

(1) a statement of the infant's or toddler's present levels of physical development, cognitive development, communication development, social or emotional development, and adaptive development, based on objective criteria;

(2) a statement of the family's resources, priorities, and concerns relating to enhancing the development of the family's infant or toddler with a disability;

(3) a statement of the measurable results or outcomes expected to be achieved for the infant or toddler and the family, including pre-literacy and language skills, developmentally appropriate for the child, and the criteria, procedures, and timelines used to determine the degree to which progress toward achieving the results or outcomes is being made and whether modifications or revisions of the outcomes or services are necessary;

(4) a statement of specific early intervention services based on peer-reviewed research, to the extent practicable, necessary to meet the unique needs of the infant or toddler and the family, including the frequency, intensity, and the method of delivering services;

(5) a statement of the natural environments in which early intervention services shall appropriately be provided, including justification of the extent if any, to which the services will not be provided in a natural environment;

(6) the projected dates for initiation of services and the anticipated length, frequency, and duration of the services;

(7) the identification of the service coordinator from the profession most immediately relevant to the infant's or toddler's or family's needs (or who is otherwise qualified to carry out all applicable responsibilities under this part) who will be responsible for the implementation of the plan and coordination with other agencies and persons; and

(8) the steps to be taken supporting the transition of the toddler with a disability to preschool or other appropriate services.

(e) The contents of the individualized family service plan shall be fully explained to the parents and informed written consent from the parents shall be obtained prior to the provision of early intervention services described in such plan. If such parents do not provide consent with respect to a particular early intervention service, then the early intervention services to which such consent is obtained shall be provided. (Section 636)

FIGURE 8–1 Developing IFSPs.

INDIVIDUALIZED FAMILY SERVICE PLANS

The statutory language in Section 636 is explicit in insisting that every infant or toddler receive an IFSP describing the child's strengths and needs in all five developmental areas and outlining proposed services. IDEA 2004 (PL 108–446) made a few changes in IFSP contents. Notable in particular is the addition, in Section 636(d)(3), of "*measurable results*" and of "*pre-literacy and language skills, as developmentally appropriate for the child.*" These changes reflect the growing importance in the IDEA, as well as the thrust of NCLB, of academics. Also new in IDEA 2004 is the addition, in Section 636(d)(4), of

Developing IFSPs and IEPs can be time-consuming, but the plans may be short, tight-worded documents.

"*based on peer-reviewed research, to the extent practicable*," in the discussion of early intervention services. As we saw in Chapter 3, IDEA 2004 and NCLB have stressed the need to base services on scientific evidence of effectiveness.

ASSESSMENT OF INFANTS OR TODDLERS

Part C opens its discussion of IFSPs by explaining that all eligible infants and toddlers and their families are to receive certain minimum services under Part C, including "*(1) a multi-disciplinary assessment of the unique strengths and needs of the infant or toddler and the identification of services appropriate to meet such needs*" (Section 636). The term *assessment* is used here because the evaluation should already have been conducted and used to establish eligibility. The questions now are, What are the child's immediate needs, and what services would meet those needs?

FAMILY ASSESSMENT

Part C continues by calling for

> *(2) a family-directed assessment of the resources, priorities, and concerns of the family and the identification of the supports and services necessary to enhance the family's capacity to meet the developmental needs of the infant or toddler.* (Section 636[a][2])

The use of the term *family-directed* indicates that families have discretion about this family needs assessment. The literature suggests that many families that have no problems with an assessment of the infant's or toddler's needs are often uncomfortable being assessed themselves (Bailey, 1991; Garshelis & McConnell, 1993; Minke & Scott, 1993). Family members may decline such an assessment; if they agree to one, they determine what is assessed, how it is assessed, and what is done with the findings.

IFSP TEAM

Following child assessment and (if requested by the family) a family assessment, Part C requires "*(3) a written individualized family service plan developed by a multidisciplinary team, including the parents, are required by subsection (e).*" The parent clearly is a key member of the IFSP-writing team. Part C calls for the IFSP to be "developed" by a multidisciplinary team but not necessarily in a meeting. The U.S. Department of Education's regulations, however, speak of meetings to develop IFSPs (34 CFR 303.321 [e][2][ii] and 303.342).

IFSP REVIEW

Part C continues: "*(b) The individualized family services plan shall be evaluated once a year and the family shall be provided a review of the plan at 6-month intervals (or more often where appropriate based on infant or toddler and family needs)*" (Section 636[b]). The IFSP needs to be reviewed every six months because infants and toddlers change so rapidly.

TIMING OF THE IFSP

The law requires prompt action: "*(c) The individualized family service plan shall be developed within a reasonable time after the assessment required by subsection (a)(1) is completed. With the parents' consent, early intervention services may commerce prior to the completion of such assessment.*" The reasonable time requirement has been interpreted by the U.S. Department of Education to be 45 days after referral (34 CFR 303.421[e][2]). In some instances, even that is an unacceptable delay, so the statute permits services to begin immediately after eligibility is established, without waiting for the IFSP.

IFSP CONTENTS

Part C continues:

> *(d) The individualized family service plan shall be in writing and contain—*
> *(1) a statement of the infant's or toddler's present levels of physical development, cognitive development, communication development, social or emotional development, and adaptive development, based on objective criteria;*
> *(2) a statement of the family's resources, priorities, and concerns relating to enhancing the development of the family's infant or toddler with a disability;*
> *(3) a statement of the measurable results or outcomes expected to be achieved for the infant or toddler and the family, including pre-literacy and language skills, as developmentally appropriate for the child, and the criteria, procedures, and timelines used to determine the degree to which progress toward achieving the results or outcomes is being made and whether modifications or revisions of the outcomes or services are necessary.*
> *(4) a statement of specific early intervention services based on peer-reviewed research, to the extent practicable, necessary to meet the unique needs of the infant or toddler and the family, including the frequency, intensity, and the method of delivering services.* (Section 636)

(1) To the extent appropriate, the IFSP must include
(i) Medical and other services that the child needs, but that are not required under this part; and
(ii) The funding sources to be used in paying for those services.

(2) The requirement in paragraph (e)(1) of this section does not apply to routine medical services (e.g., immunizations and "well-baby" care), unless a child needs those services and the services are not otherwise available or being provided (34 CFR 303.344). . . .

The "other services" in paragraph (e) of this section are services that a child or family needs, but that are neither required nor covered under this part. While listing the nonrequired services in the IFSP does not mean that those services must be provided, their identification can be helpful to both the child's family and the service coordinator, for the following reasons. First, the IFSP would provide a comprehensive picture of the child's total service needs (including the need for medical and health services, as well as early intervention services). Second, it is appropriate for the service coordinator to assist the family in securing the nonrequired services (e.g., by (1) determining if there is a public agency that could provide financial assistance, if needed, (2) assisting in the preparation of eligibility claims or insurance claims, if needed, and (3) assisting the family in seeking out and arranging for the child to receive the needed medical-health services). (34 CFR 303.344, Note 3)

FIGURE 8–2 Other services in IFSPs.

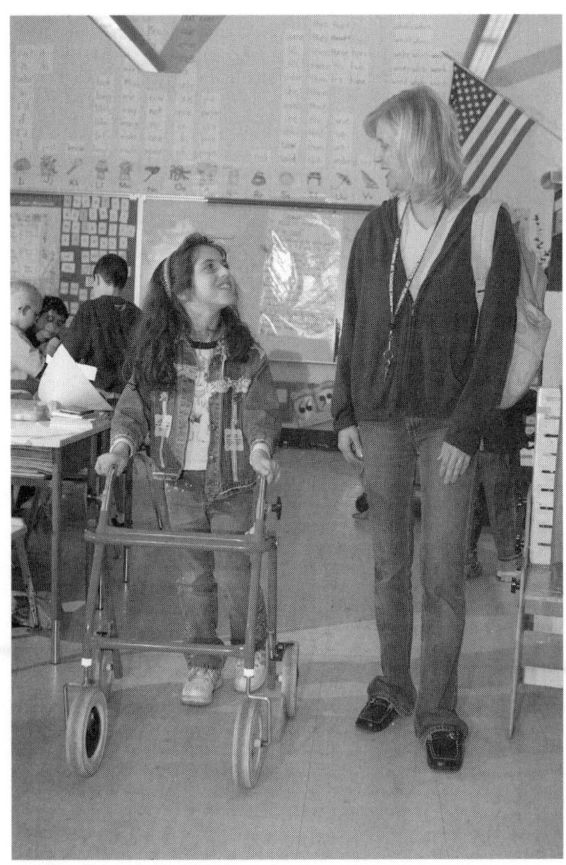

Social and emotional development is an important element in all IFSPs and IEPs, even when children have no special needs in that developmental domain.

The statutory language at Section 636(d)(4) refers to "specific" early intervention services. The U.S. Department of Education's regulations add that other services a family may need—but that are not early intervention services and therefore not reimbursable under Part C—may also be listed in the IFSP if doing so may assist the family in planning to meet its needs and those of the infant or toddler. This provision on "other services" is important, but it is widely misunderstood. For that reason, Figure 8–2 quotes the department's guidance on this issue.

The 1991 House Report provided congressional concurrence to the department's regulations:

> *The definition in this section distinguishes between the health services that are required under this part, and the medical-health services that are not required. The IFSP requirements in subpart D provide that, to the extent appropriate, these other medical-health services are to be included in the IFSP, along with the funding sources to be used in paying for the services. Identifying these services in the IFSP does not impose an obligation to provide the services if they are otherwise not required to be provided under this part.* (U.S. Congress, 1991, p. 14)

To summarize, the IFSP may include non–Part C services if by adding such "other services" the plan becomes more practical and more useful to the family.

NATURAL ENVIRONMENT

The statute continues, in Section 636(d)(5), as follows: "*a statement of the natural environments in which early intervention services shall appropriately be provided, including justification of the extent, if any, to which the services will not be provided in a natural environment*." Section 635(a)(16) adds, "*[T]o the maximum extent appropriate, [services] are provided in natural environments*." The natural environment preference does not limit the obligation to provided appropriate services. Part C does not further explain what are considered to be appropriate services.

START DATE AND DURATION

The law continues, in Section 636(d)(6), as follows: "*the projected dates for initiation of services and the anticipated length, frequency, and duration of such services*." Many ECSE programs provide year-round services, as opposed to public schools' nine-month academic year. Because the IFSP covers a one-year period, the anticipated duration never exceeds 12 months.

SERVICE COORDINATOR

Part C requires "*(7) the identification of the service coordinator from the profession most immediately relevant to the infant's or toddler's or family's needs (or who is otherwise qualified to carry out all applicable responsibilities under this part) who will be responsible for the implementation of the plan and coordination with other agencies and persons*" (Section 636).

TRANSITION

Part C requires that IFSPs include "*(8) the steps to be taken supporting the transition of the toddler with a disability to preschool or other appropriate services*." Note that the statute again uses the term appropriate to describe the services required under Part C. The U.S. Department of Education (1993) provided additional details about **transition,** as indicated in Figure 8–3.

Transition

is movement from one stage or program to another. An important transition in early childhood special education is that from early intervention programs to preschool programs.

INFORMED CONSENT

Section 636 concludes, "*(e) The contents of the individualized family service plan shall be fully explained to the parents and informed written consent from the parents shall be obtained prior to the provision of early intervention services described in such plan. If such parents do not provide consent with respect to a particular early intervention service, then the early intervention services to which such consent is obtained shall be provided*." Section (e) was added in 1991.

The U.S. Department of Education (1993) emphasizes that IFSPs need not be lengthy. An outline containing the required eight items would suffice, so long as the necessary documentation is appended. The department explains:

> *Although the IFSP must include information about each of the items in paragraphs (b) through (h) of this section, this does not mean that the IFSP must be a detailed, lengthy document. It might be a brief outline, with appropriate attachments that*

Transition at age three.

(1) The IFSP must include the steps to be taken to support the transition of the child upon reaching age three, to
   (i) Preschool services under Part B of the Act, in accordance with section 303.148, to the extent that those services are considered appropriate; or
   (ii) Other services that may be available, if appropriate.

(2) The steps required in paragraph (h)(1) of this section include
   (i) Discussion with, and training of, parents regarding future placements and other matters related to the child's transition;
   (ii) Procedures to prepare the child for changes in service delivery, including steps to help the child adjust to, and function in, a new setting; and
   (iii) With parental consent, the transmission of information about the child to the local educational agency, to ensure continuity of services, including evaluation and assessment information required in section 303.322, and copies of IFSPs that have been developed and implemented in accordance with sections 303.340 through 303.346. (34 CFR 303.344[h])

FIGURE 8–3 Transition for three-year-olds.

> *address each of the points in the paragraphs under this section. It is important for the IFSP itself to be clear about (a) what services are to be provided, (b) the actions that are to be taken by the service coordinator in initiating those services, and (c) what actions will be taken by the parents.* (34 CFR 303.344, Note 4)

INDIVIDUALIZED EDUCATION PROGRAMS

IEPs may be used for two-year-old children who will turn three during an academic year, as well as for three- to eight-year-olds. Alternatively, ECSE programs may continue to use IFSPs as long as they include in those plans all of the elements that must be incorporated into IEPs—all the way through kindergarten.

The statutory language in Section 614(d) on preparing IEPs appears in Figure 8–4. Following, the process of preparing IEPs is reviewed, provision by provision.

IEP MEETING

The department's rule states that parents are to be full and equal participants in IEP meetings. Video conferences, conference calls, and other means are allowed precisely for this reason—to encourage family participation. The appendix interpreting the purposes of IEPs added:

> *The IEP meeting serves as a communication vehicle between parents and school personnel, and enables them, as equal participants, to jointly decide what the child's need are, what services will be provided to meet those needs, and what the anticipated outcomes may be.* (U.S. Department of Education, 1992b, p. 44833)

One concern many parents have expressed is that they often feel overwhelmed by large numbers of school personnel at IEP meetings. This section requires that three, and sometimes four, people attend the IEP meeting: (1) parent(s) or guardian, (2) teacher(s) of the child, (3) a representative of the local education agency who is qualified to provide

(i) a written statement for each child with a disability that is developed, reviewed, and revised in accordance with this section and that includes—

(I) a statement of the child's present levels of academic achievement and functional performance, including—
(aa) how the child's disability affects the child's involvement and progress in the general education curriculum;
(bb) for preschool children, as appropriate, how the disability affects the child's participation in appropriate activities; and
(cc) for children with disabilities who take alternate assessments aligned to alternate achievement standards, a description of benchmarks or short-term objectives;

(II) a statement of measurable annual goals, including academic and functional goals, designed to—
(aa) meet the child's needs that result from the child's disability to enable the child to be involved in and make progress in the general education curriculum; and
(bb) meet each of the child's other educational needs that result from the child's disability;

(III) a description of how the child's progress toward meeting the annual goals described in subclause (II) will be measured and when periodic reports on the progress the child is making toward meeting the annual goals (such as through the use of quarterly or other periodic reports, concurrent with the issuance of report cards) will be provided;

(IV) a statement of the special education and related services and supplementary aids and services, based on peer-reviewed research to the extent practicable, to be provided to the child, or on behalf of the child, and a statement of the program modifications or supports for school personnel that will be provided for the child—
(aa) to advance appropriately toward attaining the annual goals;
(bb) to be involved in and make progress in the general education curriculum in accordance with subclause (I) and to participate in extracurricular and other nonacademic activities; and
(cc) to be educated and participate with other children with disabilities and nondisabled children in the activities described in this subparagraph;

(V) an explanation of the extent, if any, to which the child will not participate with nondisabled children in the regular class and in the activities described in subclause (IV)(cc);

(VI) (aa) a statement of any individual appropriate accommodations that are necessary to measure the academic achievement and functional performance of the child on State and districtwide assessments consistent with section 612(a)(16)(A); and
(bb) if the IEP Team determines that the child shall take an alternate assessment on a particular State or districtwide assessment of student achievement, a statement of why—
(AA) the child cannot participate in the regular assessment; and
(BB) the particular alternate assessment selected is appropriate for the child;

(VII) the projected date for the beginning of the services and modifications described in subclause (IV), and the anticipated frequency, location, and duration of those services and modifications; and

(VIII) beginning not later than the first IEP to be in effect when the child is 16, and updated annually thereafter—
(aa) appropriate measurable postsecondary goals based upon age appropriate transition assessments related to training, education, employment, and, where appropriate, independent living skills;
(bb) the transition services (including courses of study) needed to assist the child in reaching those goals; and
(cc) beginning not later than 1 year before the child reaches the age of majority under State law, a statement that the child has been informed of the child's rights under this title, if any, that will transfer to the child on reaching the age of majority under section 615(m).

FIGURE 8–4 Preparing IEPs.

or supervise the provision of special education, and (4) the child, if appropriate. In instances in which related services are to be provided, it makes sense for a professional from that related service (e.g., an occupational therapist) to attend. In addition, parents may wish to bring with them someone knowledgeable about the law and their child's unique needs (Ballard & Zettel, 1977).

The parents of a child with a disability are expected to be equal participants along with school personnel, in developing, reviewing, and revising the child's IEP. This is an active role in which the parents

(1) participate in the discussion about the child's need for special education and related services, and

(2) join with the other participants in deciding what services the agency will provide to the child. (U.S. Department of Education, 1992b, p. 44836).

(a) Each public agency shall take steps to assure that one or both of the parents of the child with a disability are present at each meeting or are afforded the opportunity to participate, including

(1) Notifying parents of the meeting early enough to ensure that they will have an opportunity to attend; and

(2) Scheduling the meeting at a mutually agreed upon time and place. . . .

(e) The public agency shall take whatever action is necessary to ensure that the parent understands the proceedings at a meeting, including arranging for an interpreter for parents with deafness or whose native language is other than English.

(f) The public agency shall give the parent, on request, a copy of the IEP. (U.S. Department of Education, 1992b, p. 44815)

FIGURE 8–5 Family participation in IEPs.

The department was at pains to urge that IEP meetings be "small." The interpretation section of the September 1992 final rule states:

> *Generally, the number of participants at IEP meeting should be small. Small meetings have several advantages over large ones. For example, they (1) allow for more open, active parent involvement, (2) are less costly, (3) are easier to arrange and conduct, and (4) are usually more productive.* (U.S. Department of Education, 1992b, p. 44835)

The same document adds, "*The legislative history of the Act makes it clear that attendance at IEP meetings should be limited to those who have an intense interest in the child*" (p. 44836). The department's other guidance on family participation is summarized in Figure 8–5.

EDUCATIONAL PERFORMANCE

An IEP contains "*a written statement of the child's present levels of academic achievement and functional performance*" (Section 614[d]). Notable here is the requirement that children's abilities and needs as these relate to special education and related services are to be outlined. The IFSP, by contrast, calls for statements of children's needs in all five developmental areas recognized under Part C. If the state adopts the developmental delay criteria for preschoolers, as it is permitted to do, it clearly would be appropriate here to describe the child's current performance and needs in those five areas of development and not to restrict the statement.

This language clearly implies that the needs of preschool- and primary-grade children in the domains of physical, communication, adaptive, social or emotional, and cognitive development may be described as part of the statement on educational performance.

GOALS AND OBJECTIVES

The law says the IEPs should include "*(b) a statement of measurable annual goals, including academic and functional goals.*" Academic goals are to include one-year targets in language arts, math, and other content subjects. Functional goals are appropriate for young children whose disabilities are so severe that measurable annual progress in formal academics is not appropriate, but whose gains in adaptive behavior, self-care, and other areas may be tracked.

Note that IDEA 2004, PL 108–446, removes from most IEPs the language on "benchmarks or short-term objectives" that was in IDEA for more than 20 years. That wording was controversial, because it was widely misunderstood. Some educators were actually writing daily lesson plan–type objectives in IEPs. IDEA 2004 kept that wording only for the IEPs of children with very severe disabilities. Their plans may describe functional and behavioral progress in steps (i.e., for each month or for each marking period) so as to assist educators in tracking their performance.

SERVICES

Part B continues by calling for "*(c) a statement of the special education and related services and supplementary aids and services . . . to be provided to the child.*" This section also is to describe support services needed for integration in the general curriculum. This section of the IEP also is widely misunderstood. The program should specify the services that are to be provided in response to each of the child's unique needs. This may, for example, be "occupational therapy for 30 minutes three times weekly" for the purpose of meeting a child's need to acquire the upper-body strength to use a Braille writer. The regulations make clear that this section of the IEP should outline the services a child needs, regardless of whether or not the local education agency will provide them:

> *[T]he services must be listed in the IEP even if they are not directly available from the local agency, and must be provided by the agency through contract or other arrangements.* (U.S. Department of Education, 1992b, p. 44838)

The IEP must note not only the kinds of services but also their intensity:

> *The amount of services to be provided must be stated in the IEP, so that the level of the agency's commitment of resources will be clear to parents and other IEP team members* (p. 44839)

Note that the statement is not required to identify the placement here. The federal regulations clearly indicate that the placement decision is to be made following development of the IEP, not beforehand or as it is being written:

> *An IEP must be in effect before special education and related services are provided to a child. The appropriate placement for a given child with a disability cannot be determined until after decisions have been made about what the child's needs are and what will be provided. Therefore, the IEP must be developed before placement.* (U.S. Department of Education, 1992b, p. 44834)

DISTRICTWIDE ASSESSMENTS

IEPs for preschool-age children need not contain these elements because such testing is not usually done with this population. It is also seldom performed with primary-grade children under nine. However, they do begin in third grade with math and language arts assessments. Tests in science begin in 2007. States may develop and use their own tests. Many do. The federal Department of Education runs the National Assessment of Education

Progress (NAEP), known as "the Nation's Report Card" (www.nationsreportcard.gov). These fourth- and eighth-grade assessments are intended as a "check" on state tests.

In many elementary schools, preparation for the "big tests" begins in second grade. For this reason, the IEPs of children as young as seven or eight may include statements about state- and districtwide assessments.

Some young children with mental retardation, full-scale autism, deaf-blindness, and other disabilities may be excused from those tests. Instead, they are given alternate assessments. The IEPs of these children need to contain a justification for this and identification of the methods to be used to track progress.

TRANSITION

For all children about to turn three, the IFSP must contain a statement of the transition services needed as children move from early intervention to preschool or other programs. If the IEP is used instead of an IFSP for such children, the IEP may contain the necessary information about transition services. The IEP may also be used to describe transition services for five-year-olds moving from preschool programs to kindergarten or elementary schools.

DATE AND DURATION

IEPs must also contain "*the projected date for the beginning of the services and modifications . . . and the anticipated frequency, location, and duration of those services and modifications.*" The IEP is an annual statement, so the duration here will be under 12 months. Academic year schedules usually apply (9 months), but some children require extended school year services to prevent regression or to maintain skills. If year-round services are necessary to meet a particular child's unique needs, that should be specified here.

PROGRESS REPORTS

Section 614(d) requires that IEPs contain a statement of how parents will be apprised of progress. The IEP is a planning and tracking document. The progress reports are to be measures allowing school officials and parents both to agree that goals are or are not being met. This keeps everyone posted on the child's performance and facilitates preparation of the following year's IEP.

"APPROPRIATE"

The term *appropriate* is used repeatedly throughout the IDEA. It is used several times in describing IEPs and IFSPs. However, the word itself is never defined in the IDEA. That it is an important term is abundantly clear. It surfaces, for example, at the very beginning of the IDEA, in Section 601(c), where Congress explains why Part B was created:

> *to ensure that all children with disabilities have available to them a free appropriate public education that emphasizes special education and related services designed to meet their unique needs.*

According to the definitions contained in the Act, a "free appropriate public education" consists of educational instruction specially designed to meet the unique needs of the handicapped child, supported by such services as are necessary to permit the child "to benefit" from the instruction. Almost as a checklist for adequacy under the Act, the definition also requires that such instruction and services be provided at public expense and under public supervision, meet the State's educational standards, approximate the grade levels used in the State's regular education, and comport with the child's IEP. Thus, if personalized instruction is being provided with sufficient supportive services to permit the child to benefit from the instruction, and the other items on the definitional checklist are satisfied, the child is receiving a "free appropriate public education" as defined by the Act. (*Board of Education, Hendrick Hudson School District v. Rowley,* 1982, 102 S.Ct. 3034 [EHLR 553:656], pp. 188–189)

FIGURE 8–6 "Appropriate" in *Rowley.*

The word *appropriate* also appears in Section 602(8), where "free appropriate public education" is defined as "*meet[ing] the standards of the State education agency*" and "*provided in conformity with*" an IEP. Nowhere else does the IDEA explain what *appropriate* means.

That, as it turns out, was a very significant oversight. The law guarantees young children with disabilities appropriate early intervention services and appropriate education services—but what does this mean?

In 1982, the U.S. Supreme Court decided its first-ever case on what is now the IDEA. At issue was whether Amy Rowley, an elementary school student who was deaf and whose parents also were deaf, was entitled to a sign language interpreter in class. The decision, in *Board of Education, Hendrick Hudson School District v. Rowley*, turned on the Court's interpretation of the meaning of the word *appropriate*. The Court's decision is excerpted in Figure 8–6. An "appropriate" education, the Court decided, is one that meets the child's unique needs through specially designed instruction and any necessary related services.

The word *appropriate* sets a floor, but it also creates a ceiling. Services must "meet" individual children's needs; services that do not enable children to benefit are not sufficient. On the other hand, the word *meet* limits the amount or kind of services necessary. There is no requirement to provide more services, or more expensive ones, than are needed to "meet" the child's unique needs. Thus, if two hours a week of speech and language therapy meet the needs of a child, there is no requirement to provide four hours. Similarly, if therapy offered in small groups suffices to meet the need, there is no obligation in the IDEA to provide one-on-one services instead.

The requirement in Part C that early intervention services be appropriate and in Part B that education be appropriate is, accordingly, that these services benefit the child. This requirement outweighs the placement preferences in the statute (natural environment, least restrictive environment). That is, whatever placement is made, the services provided there must meet unique needs so that the child benefits from them. It is noteworthy that both the IEP and the IFSP specifications qualify their environmental preferences by insisting that placements and services be "appropriate." The IFSP, to illustrate, calls for a "statement of the natural environments in which early intervention services shall appropriately be provided" (Section 636[d][5]; emphasis added). Similar language applies to IEPs in Part B.

The U.S. Department of Education has issued a statement on "appropriate" that reaffirms the primacy of appropriateness over placement. Suitably enough, since the

Court ruled about the education of a deaf child, this statement discusses services for deaf children:

> *The Secretary is concerned that the least restrictive environment provisions of the IDEA and section 504 are being interpreted, incorrectly, to require the placement of some children who are deaf in programs that may not meet the individual student's educational needs. Meeting the unique communication and related needs of a student who is deaf is a fundamental part of providing a free appropriate public education to the child.* (U.S. Department of Education, 1992d, p. 49275)

To reinforce the point that the requirement to provide "free, appropriate public education" (FAPE) services is primary and the least restrictive environment (LRE) preference secondary, the department's statement continues:

> *The provision of FAPE is paramount, and the individual placement determination about LRE is to be considered within the context of FAPE. . . . Any setting, including a regular classroom, that prevents a child who is deaf from receiving an appropriate education that meets his or her needs, including communication needs, is not the LRE for that individual child.* (U.S. Department of Education, 1992d, p. 49275)

Finally, family services may be provided, as appropriate, both under Part C and under Part B. Appropriate family services are those kinds of assistance a family needs to enhance the development of the child. Part C calls these "early intervention services" and specifies that they be recorded in IFSPs to the extent that the family approves, while Part B calls them "related services" and says they may be incorporated into IEPs. In fact, ECSE programs may continue to use IFSPs through a child's fifth year of life (Schrag, 1990; U.S. Department of Education, 1992b). The important point is that services that a family needs so that the child will benefit are appropriate services and may be provided under Part C and Part B.

WRITING THE PLANS

The IFSP and the IEP are written documents prepared after several preliminary steps are completed. First, eligibility must be established. Second, a multidisciplinary assessment of the infant, toddler, or child must be performed. The assessment should suggest services needed to meet the child's unique needs. The document must describe those services, together with ways in which progress will be monitored and evaluated. The IFSP includes a family-directed assessment of family resources, priorities, and concerns, to the extent that the family desires such a statement. Because Part B allows family counseling and other family assistance as "related services," an IEP may also contain such a review of family priorities and needs. In both cases, unfortunately, the actual preparation of these documents does not always comport with the ideals expressed in the IDEA.

The most important concern is that the process of creating the plan must feature mutual respect and information sharing between parents and professionals. So important is this sharing that it is fair to say that the process of developing the plan is more important than the plan itself. That is because parents and ECSE professionals may bring to the IFSP/IEP planning process different priorities, values, and goals. If the process features mutual respect and information sharing, both parties move toward a consensus position—to the child's benefit.

If, however, the process is characterized by mutual distrust, hidden agendas, and lack of respect, the plan likely will ill serve the child, the family, and the program itself.

To illustrate, as far back as 1992, Minke and Scott (1993) studied three early intervention programs to see how actively parents actually participated in writing the IFSP. They found that parents usually made "basic decisions" (p. 92), for example, about interagency transfers of personally identifiable information, about applying for other services such as Medicaid, and about how active a role they wished to play in the ECSE program. Finally, parents usually decided overall goals for physical, cognitive, adaptive, communication, and social or emotional development for their children.

Minke and Scott found that service selection—which services would be provided in order to help reach each goal—was most often made jointly by parents and early intervention program staff. Programs varied in which services they had available. Typically, early intervention program staff would recommend certain of these services and would tell the parents about additional services available elsewhere. Parents were usually asked to decide which services they wanted delivered and which they did not; and generally they did so. However, Minke and Scott found that early intervention program staff at times steered the parents toward or away from certain services. They also found that program staff, directly or obliquely, determined the frequency with which such services would be provided more than parents did. As one program staff member put it: "[The parent] was expected to listen to our suggestions. If she disagreed with anything, she could tell her reasoning behind why she didn't want certain things done. And we've had that happen on occasion. It's very rare" (p. 94).

Parental decision making was weakest, Minke and Scott found, in the later, detailed decisions, such as what strategies would be used to reach goals, which tactics would be adopted to pursue each strategy, and how progress would be measured. Said Minke and Scott: "Parents were not asked for input on strategies to achieve the selected goals in any of the nine [IFSP] meetings taped. Most ($n = 10$) of the staff members interviewed indicated that they see this process as their own prerogative and that it is carried out without parent input" (p. 99). They added, "Staff members reported keeping a set of goals separate from the parents' goals and noted having 'unwritten' goals that guide their interventions" (p. 100).

IEP development, too, sometimes departs from the ideal. Parents told one congressional commission, for example, that they were presented with a completely written IEP document and asked to sign it (Commission on Education of the Deaf, 1988). The U.S. Department of Education's (1992b) final regulations expressly forbid such practices:

> *It is not permissible for an agency to present a completed IEP to parents for their approval before there has been a full discussion with the parents of (1) the child's need for special education and related services, and (2) what services the agency will provide to the child. . . . [T]he agency should make it clear to the parents at the outset of the meeting that the services proposed by the agency are only recommendations for review and discussion with the parents.* (p. 44839)

The IDEA clearly and explicitly forbids ECSE programs from preparing complete plans in advance and just presenting them to parents for signature. Section 636(e), Part C, for example, says:

> *The contents of the individualized family service plan shall be fully explained to the parents and informed written consent from the parents shall be obtained prior to the provision of early intervention services described in such plan.*

TRANSITION

Transition must be addressed both in IFSPs and in IEPs. The principal concern in each case is with interagency coordination—that is, when a child and family are preparing to move from one agency and its services to another. The IFSP contains a statement of how the child's transition from Part C services to subsequent programs, whether preschool special education under Part B or some other service system, will proceed. The IEP, similarly, may outline the transition from preschool to kindergarten or elementary school and, for older children, from school to work, postsecondary education, or other postschool activities.

Intensive care unit (ICU)

is a hospital ward for premature, low-birthweight, and other infants needing comprehensive care. When used with infants under one month old, ICUs are called *neonatal intensive care units* (NICUs).

There are, however, other kinds of transitions. These, too, are important. Infants may move from hospital settings such as **intensive care units (ICUs)** to home- and/or center-based early intervention programs. Children of relocating families may move into new programs. And children may move from one preschool class to another. Each of these changes requires careful planning. They often cause stress for families and for young children as well. In many instances, changes involve transfer of personally identifiable information from one agency or program to another. Such transfers are subject to due process safeguards in the IDEA.

The legislation and the U.S. Department of Education's regulations address interagency transitions. The key requirements are discussed in the following sections for the most common of these interagency transitions.

WITHIN PART C

The families of infants moving from hospital-based services, such as ICUs, to home- and center-based services need assistance in negotiating important shifts in priorities and services. While ICUs and other hospital-based programs focus on survival and health promotion, early intervention programs in the community—whether home- or center-based—tend to place priority on family-child interactions, developmental milestones, and family empowerment to facilitate parents' efforts to enhance the child's growth. Wolery (1989) suggests that despite the dramatic shift in focus from ICUs to community-based programs, "it is imperative that the needs and services that were given priority in the sending program not be ignored in the receiving program" (p. 3). In this instance, the infant's health should be monitored by the intervention program, even as parents are helped to move beyond immediate concerns about health to longer-term issues of their child's development.

FROM PART C TO PART B

When what is now the IDEA was amended in 1986, resulting in the creation of Part H (now Part C) and expansion of Part B's preschool services, the need for smooth transition between the two programs was a key concern of Congress. The 1990 and 1991 IDEA legislation continued to stress transition from Part H to Part B. The law now requires that a meeting between the sending agency, the receiving agency, and the parents take place to plan transition. The receiving agency, in this case a local education agency (LEA) or intermediate education unit, or other program offering services, must actually meet with the sending agency and with the family. The statute places the responsibility for initiating these transition meetings with the Part C agency, requiring the Part C state plan to include a

> *description of the policies and procedures to be used to ensure a smooth transition for toddlers receiving early intervention services under this part to preschool or other appropriate services, including a description of how the families will be included in the transition plans and how the lead agency will notify the appropriate local educational agency for the area in which the child resides that the child will shortly reach the age of eligibility for preschool services under Part B, as determined in accordance with State law; in the case of a child who may be eligible for such preschool services, with the approval of the family of the child, convene a conference among the lead agency, the family, and at least 90 days (and at the discretion of all such parties, up to 6 months) before the child is eligible for the preschool services, to discuss any such services that the child may receive; and . . . to review the child's program options for the period from the child's third birthday through the remainder of the school year; and to establish a transition plan.* (Section 637)

The receiving agency, usually a state education agency (SEA), and its LEAs must cooperate. The law requires the Part B state plan to include procedures for transitions from Part C to Part B at about the time of the child's third birthday.

The references in Sections 637 and 612 to the child's third birthday should not be interpreted literally. Schrag (1990) makes clear that plans and placements may occur at more convenient times, before or after the third birthday. Parents must give prior written permission for the sending agency to discuss or otherwise release with or to the receiving agency and personally identifiable information about the family and/or the child (IDEA Section 639; U.S. Department of Education, 1993, Section 303.460). Families may reject or defer any early intervention services, presumably including referral to preschool programs (IDEA Section 680; U.S. Department of Education, 1993, Section 303.405). The parental prerogative to decline or postpone any early intervention services, without jeopardizing any other such services, is absolute. It is not subject to service agency appeal through the Part C Section 639 due process procedures or any other such mechanism. Because state law generally does not require program attendance by under-six children, the state has no compelling interest in overriding parental desires.

FROM PART C TO OTHER SERVICE PROGRAMS

Similar requirements hold in other kinds of interagency transition planning. The IDEA places the major obligation for initiating such steps with the Part C lead agency and its service providers. Transition to community service, public health, or other services involves transmission of personally identifiable information—including assessment and evaluation data, copies of IFSPs, and similar material—from the sending agency to the receiving agency. The law is explicit in stating that such information may not be transmitted from the current service agency to any other agency without prior written parental permission. Referral of a child from an early intervention program to some other program constitutes a change in services. Section 639 in Part C requires written prior notice to parents whenever a service provider proposes to change placement of services.

These state plan requirements address the need for state, county, and local agency officials to prepare whatever interagency agreements or other procedures are necessary to ensure the transition of any individual toddler from a Part C program to a Part B preschool program or other program is smooth.

On a more individual level, each child's IFSP contains a statement of "*the steps to be taken supporting the transition of the toddler with a disability to preschool or other appropriate services*" (Section 636[d][8]). If an IEP is used for a two-year-old about to turn three, the IEP must contain a similar statement. That is because IEPs may be used in place of IFSP, and vice versa, only if all required elements appear in the document.

PARENTS AND TRANSITION FROM PART C

Guidance for parents in transition planning is offered by Fowler, Chandler, Johnson, and Stella (1988) and by Hanline and Knowlton (1988). The Fowler et al. process uses two interviews, one during the fall and one during the spring preceding the transition to preschool. In the fall interview, parents identify priorities and concerns, which early intervention staff then use to plan transition. The spring interview is more specific (with exit to preschool just a few months away) and focuses on selecting one preschool program and making transition arrangements to it. The Hanline and Knowlton checklist helps parents assess their family's readiness for transition and provides a basis for family-professional discussions. The 12-item checklist identifies those specific areas in which parents need additional information. Many preschools publish their own guides for use with parents during the preplacement transition period. Whatever materials are used, the critical element is providing families with information that not only allows them to choose a specific program but also to receive both factual and emotional reassurance that their child's needs will be met.

FROM PRESCHOOL TO ELEMENTARY SCHOOL

Aside from the requirement that IEPs be in effect prior to the beginning of a school year, there is no statutory requirement covering movement from preschool Part B programs to K–12 programs under Part B. (The same is true for transitions from nonpreschool community programs to K–12 schools.) However, this transition is no less important than those addressed in the IDEA. In fact, it may be more important, because while not all states require programming for under-six children, virtually all require that children at or about six years of age be placed in formal public or private educational programs. Moving from one program to another produces stress for the family and for the child, as new relationships must be formed and new rules of behavior learned. Wolery (1989) explains that such transitions are stressful because so many changes are involved:

> [T]he sending and receiving programs may differ in terms of location of services, schedule, transportation systems, staff members involved, manner and frequency with which communication with families occurs, contact with social support such as other families, cost of services, expectations for family participation, and many others. Further, the receiving program may hold many unknowns for the family. (p. 3)

Fowler et al. (1991) notes that information about the receiving program and the behaviors necessary for success there can help to inform preschool curricula. "The logic of future environmental surveys," they say, "is straightforward: Look to the next environment to identify required skills, and use these skills to set goals and objectives for the

1. Parents and program staff jointly decide what criteria will be used upon exit from preschool.
2. Program staff discuss with family members the family's role in transition, including consent for release of information.
3. Program staff alert the receiving agency (local education agency, kindergarten, or elementary school) about the need for planning meeting(s).
4. A multidisciplinary team does an assessment of the child to document the current level of educational and related performance.
5. The receiving program staff establishes eligibility.
6. The IEP team develops the IEP in consultation with the family (it must be "in effect" prior to start of school year).
7. The team selects a placement from a continuum of appropriate placement options. This includes a visit to each by the family.
8. The sending program transfers records, with prior written parental permission, to the receiving program.
9. Child and family visit receiving program.
10. Sending program and family follow up with the receiving program to ensure "goodness of fit."

Adapted from Fowler et al. (1991).

FIGURE 8–7 Planning transition from preschool.

current program" (p. 137). They caution, however, that although teaching such skills smoothes the transition, acquisition of these skills "must be viewed as optimal goals, not as behavioral prerequisites for placement in that setting" (p. 137). Figure 8–7 summarizes the key steps Fowler et al. recommend.

Particularly helpful to young children making the transition to kindergarten or first grade, Fowler et al. (1991) note, are the ability to work independently and as a member of a small group, the ability to follow directions, and the ability to pay attention in class over sustained periods of time. Also helpful is action by preschool program staff to involve parents in planning the timing of exit from the preschool and in writing the next year's IEP if the child is eligible for continuing special education services. Ideally, both parents and sending program staff will visit the alternative placement options. Once a placement is decided, the receiving program staff should visit the current placement as well. These and other recommended practices are outlined in Repetto and Correa (1996).

SUMMARY

Individualizing services for young children and their families is perhaps the greatest challenge facing ECSE programs. The IDEA prescribes that the process begin with evaluation and assessment, to identify the child's unique needs and strengths, after which a formal written document is prepared outlining the needs, services to be provided, and means of monitoring progress. Parents and ECSE staff should work as a team to develop these plans. The law offers sufficient flexibility so that families desiring to receive services from the program may do so throughout the birth-to-eight period. It also provides that services be appropriate—that is, meet the individual needs of the child and, when suitable, the family's needs to enhance the child's development. These steps are statutorily required so that ECSE services are both individualized and appropriate, these being the two most important characteristics of ECSE services.

In most instances, the early childhood years feature several critical transitions. Some young children move from hospital-based program to home- and/or center-based early intervention programs; some move from early intervention to preschool programs; others move from early intervention to respite, community health, or other noneducational programs. At the age of five or six, all young children with disabilities move into kindergarten or first grade. These transitions must be planned well in advance and should feature strong family participation. Although such transitions may be made more smooth and effective by teaching skills and behaviors needed in the next environment, mastery of such skills should not be made a prerequisite for placement into the next setting.

Parents may reject or postpone any transition except the last. State laws in all 50 states require that children begin formal education at or about six years of age. Because similar laws do not always apply to children under six, the parental option of declining or delaying services for such children must be respected.

Although the field places great importance on the principle of individualization, ECSE as a profession—and individual programs from coast to coast—struggle to translate the ideal into an everyday reality, much as other EC programs do (Bredekamp, 1987). These and related program design issues are the topic of the next chapter.

KEY TERMS

intensive care unit (ICU) **transition**

QUESTIONS FOR REFLECTION

1. How does individualization of services draw from what we know about "aptitude treatment interactions"?
2. What questions does the multidisciplinary assessment of infants and toddlers seek to answer?
3. Why are IFSPs to be reviewed twice yearly, while IEPs are to be reviewed annually?
4. Why could it help to include in an IFSP services that the IDEA will not cover?
5. Why is the early intervention program responsible for planning transition for children about to turn three years of age?
6. What are the IDEA requirements if a program elects to continue to use an IFSP after a child turns three years of age?
7. Who must be at an IEP meeting?
8. IDEA 2004 added wording to IFSPs about "pre-literacy and language" and to IEPs about "academic achievement." However, it left intact all of the preexisting requirements of both plans. The net effect is to increase the responsibilities of early interventionists, special educators, and related-services personnel beyond what already were extensive duties. What do you think about all this? (See also Practical Exercise 2.)
9. In your own words, what does *appropriate* mean?
10. Which kinds of transition are described in IEPs and IFSPs—and which kinds are not?

PRACTICAL EXERCISES

1. Ask a family member of an infant, toddler, preschooler, or early elementary student with a disability if you may look over his or her IFSP and/or IEP. If you do not know any such parents or other relatives, ask a local early intervention, preschool, or elementary program if you may read an IFSP and/or IEP. The program staff likely will photocopy the plan and white out the child's name and other personally identifiable information.

   Read the plan over, comparing it with what this chapter says should be in it. Are the required elements present? Does the plan include specific goals and objectives—or are those worded in general terms? Does the plan explicitly say what services will be provided, how often, and so on—or, again, is that information nonspecific?

   Is there anything in the plan that surprises you (i.e., that this chapter did not alert you to expect)? If so, discuss that with your professor.

2. Interview special educators as well as general educators who teach inclusive classes in local elementary schools. How have the new "high-stakes" tests changed their jobs? How well (or badly) are the young children with disabilities responding to the pressure?

WEB SITES OF INTEREST

www.cec.sped.org Council for Exceptional Children

www.nectac.org National Early Childhood Technical Assistance Center—helpful page about IFSPs and IEPs for family members

www.birth23.org Connecticut Birth to Three System—how one state interprets the rules about IFSPs

CHAPTER

Technology

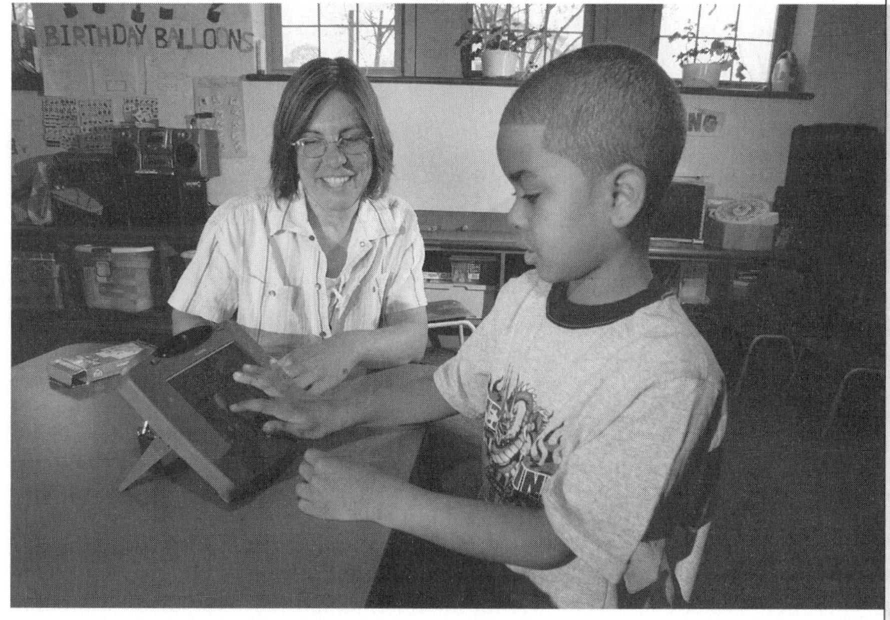

Technology is a lot like freedom. . . . Once it's uncorked, there's no putting it back. Its fruits are there for everyone's enjoyment and benefit. It is often said that assistive technology is liberating, and that is certainly the case. But it is time to be clear that assistive technology is liberating not just for the individual with a disability but indeed for America as a whole.
(WILLIAMS, 1991)

OBJECTIVES

After reading this chapter, you should be able to:

- Explain what *low-tech* is and why it is so important in ECSE.
- Describe how the IDEA defines *assistive technology devices* and *assistive technology services.*
- Explain why speech recognition is so helpful for young children.
- Explain how you can make good use of touch screens.
- Describe how a group of e-mail addresses can help you keep in touch with families.

- List some financing options for assistive technology products.
- Describe where more information is available.

CHAPTER OUTLINE

- OVERVIEW
- "LOW-TECH"
- ASSISTIVE TECHNOLOGY DEVICES
  - In the Classroom
  - Reaching the Potential?
  - Broadband—An Exciting Technology
- ASSISTIVE TECHNOLOGY SERVICES
- FINANCING OPTIONS
- ECSE PROFESSIONALS AND TECHNOLOGY
  - Getting Started
- TELEVISION
- MULTIMEDIA
- INFORMATION SOURCES
  - Not for Profit
  - For Profit

OVERVIEW

Technology holds great promise for young children with disabilities or developmental delays, for families, and for professionals in ECSE. This chapter explores all these potential uses of technology.

Nothing in ECSE changes as rapidly as does technology. For this reason, Chapter 9 and its electronic resource, Online Companion, for the fourth edition (www.earlychilded.delmar.com) include many Web site addresses. These let the reader keep up-to-date. They quite literally update these pages.

Probably most useful for young children and their families are low-tech rather than high-tech products. Velcro fasteners, dycem table pads, and the like, have no moving parts and are nonelectronic. Those two features make them low-tech. A wide variety of toys and other products feature just one or a few moving parts and few electronics. Low-tech in a different way are new cell phones specifically designed for use by young children. These products let them call family, friends, and teachers at will and be called by them as needed. These wireless phones feature high technology, yet their simple human interfaces make them seem to be low-tech.

Some products are intermediate in complexity. These include touch-screen-enabled laptop and desktop PCs. The personal computer has become so ubiquitous in American society that even preschoolers are using it. With a touch screen, very young children can make choices and operate programs. Similarly, text to speech (speech synthesis) and speech to text (speech recognition) programs allow young children to use sophisticated computer hardware and software by listening (rather than, or in addition to, reading) and speaking (rather than, or in addition to, typing). Instant messaging (IM) services now offer voice, music, and video, making IM user-friendly even for young children.

Broadband

is high-speed, always-on, digital communications. One broadband connection can provide several high-speed "lines" plus a voice line and a fax line. People can talk to and see each other and exchange faxes and e-mails, all without hanging up.

At the other end of the spectrum are cutting-edge high-tech products and services. Among these are the high-speed, always-on, voice/video/data communications technologies collectively known as **broadband.** Professionals may "attend" advanced training anywhere in the world, seeing and hearing professors and other experts as if in the same room. Similarly, family members may "attend" team meetings to prepare IFSPs or IEPs without leaving the home. Young children may "visit" far-off locations such as the Grand Canyon, the Great Barrier Reefs, or the frozen tundras of Antarctica. Broadband also brings to the home or classroom Google maps showing neighborhood buildings as seen from the sky, digital videos of hurricanes as seen from the storms' eyes, and much, much more.

Finally, technology can connect ECSE professionals to a vast array of information and support resources throughout the nation and, indeed, the world. When an early interventionist first meets a young child who has a rare syndrome, for example, she can acquire much-needed information about that syndrome in minutes—by surfing the Web—and can exchange views about intervention strategies with other professionals all over the world.

Technology is not without its challenges. This chapter discusses those concerns. It concludes with sources readers may contact for more information, as well as with Questions for Reflection.

"LOW-TECH"

Inexpensive, "low-tech" products can make life much easier for children with physical disabilities and for their caregivers. A good example is Velcro. It is a great fastener and can be used in jackets, slacks, pants, skirts, shoes, and a wide range of other items. Velcro-equipped products are widely available in clothing and home furnishing stores. Another useful product is dycem. This is a no-slip surface. Placed on a table or on a wheelchair lapboard, it helps prevent spilling of liquids and accidental dropping of objects. You can find dycem products at hardware or home furnishing stores (e.g., Home Depot, Lowe's, etc.). As should be clear from these examples, low-technology products have no or few moving parts; they also tend not to be electronic.

Kitchen utensils, pencils and pens, and other items often found in ECSE settings now come equipped with wide, easily held grips. A good example is the Good Grip family of knives and other items. You can also find rocker knives, weighted cups, two-sided cup holders, and pizza cutters at Williams-Sonoma stores, as well as at Home Depot. Harder to find are plate guards, which are rims that fit around a plate; people with mobility limitations can use those in place of a second utensil to scoop up peas, applesauce, and so on. A good source for hard-to-locate items is the Maxi Aids catalog, (800) 522-6294; www.maxiaids.com. Another is Island School & Art Supply, at www.educationalmaterialcatalog.com.

Low-tech products that young children with disabilities in ECSE programs can use are both many and diverse. For children with vision impairments, there are talking clocks and calculators (and hundreds of other talking products), beeping balls, magnifiers of all descriptions, and raised-relief maps. Children with limited fine motor control may use extralarge cards and other play products, wheelchairs of every imaginable size and function (including special "sport" chairs for recreation), extralarge utensils and double-handled cups for mealtimes, automatic seat lifters, sock and stocking dressing aids, and thousands of others (see, e.g., www.theraproducts.com). For PCs alone, there are key guards (plastic covers for keyboards that allow the user to rest a hand while the holes guide fingers or

AdaptAbility
Department 2292
Colchester, CT 06415

Attainment Company
504 Commerce Parkway
Verona, WI 53593

Flaghouse Inc.
150 N. MacQuesten Parkway
Mount Vernon, NY 10550

Hygeia Medical
555 Westbury Avenue
Carle Place, NY 11514

Madenta Communications
9411 A-20 Avenue
Edmonton, AB Canada

Maxi Aids
PO Box 3209
Farmingdale, NY 11735

Maddak Inc.
6 Industrial Road
Pequannock, NJ 07440

Sammons/Preston
PO Box 5071
Bolingbrook, IL 60440

Source: Kornreich Technology Center, National Center for Disability Services, Albertson, NY.

FIGURE 9–1 Assistive technology catalogs.

sticks to the correct keys), light pens, mouth sticks, and extralarge keyboards. Children who are deaf or severely hard of hearing may benefit from flashing lights to signal rings or other sounds, telephone amplifiers, and telecommunications devices for the deaf (TDDs). See Figure 9–1 for sources of low-tech products.

ASSISTIVE TECHNOLOGY DEVICES

This chapter opened with a quotation from testimony presented to the U.S. House of Representatives by an individual with a physical disability, who commented on the revolutionary impact assistive technology could have. In an important report, the privately funded National Task Force on Technology and Disability said that assistive technology now has become indispensable for Americans with disabilities (www.ntftd.org). The need is not new, however. The National Council on Disability (NCD), a small federal agency, a decade ago reported on a survey of adults with disabilities. Asked to assess assistive technology's impact on their lives using a scale of 1 to 10, with 10 being the highest, assistive technology users reported that such devices make a tremendous difference. Without such products, they said, they would rate the quality of their lives at 3, whereas with assistive technology, the ratings zoomed to 8.4 on average (NCD, 1993, p. 2). Clearly, assistive technology is enormously important to individuals with disabilities who need it.

The council also surveyed 136 families with members who have disabilities, including some with infants and toddlers. These families reported that a majority of the infants and toddlers benefited from assistive technology. In addition to fewer health problems, families reported less need for child care services and fewer hours of parental child care.

Overall, as many as 10 to 15 hours weekly were freed for recreation and other family needs (NCD, 1993, p.51).

Assistive technology devices

are any products that may be used by individuals with disabilities to do things they otherwise would have difficulty doing.

The IDEA defines the term ***assistive technology devices*** as follows:

> *[A]ssistive technology devices means any item, piece of equipment, or product system, whether acquired commercially off the shelf, modified, or customized, that is used to increase, maintain, or improve functional capabilities of individuals with disabilities.* (Section 602)

This definition is an expansive one, including commercial, general-purpose products that have potential uses for people with disabilities as well as specially designed or customized items. The operative aspect of the definition is that assistive technology devices are "used to increase, maintain, or improve functional capabilities of individuals with disabilities." The same definition is used in other federal laws, including the Assistive Technology Act (ATA), the Americans with Disabilities Act (ADA), and the Rehabilitation Act.

Many adaptive products fit into or work with PCs. The first PCs, in the late 1970s and early 1980s, were similar to the first cars in that they were one-for-all models. The Ford Model T, for example, came in any color you wanted, as long as it was black. Similarly, the first PCs let you enter and retrieve information in any way you wanted as long as it was visual. The most important trend in PCs today for children with disabilities is the increasing ability of users to select the modalities through which they will interact with the machine. Today, one need not even touch a key to operate a PC. Children may speak commands to the machine using speech recognition. They may use joysticks, head wands, and other alternative or supplementary communication add-ons. Similarly, while most PC information is still presented visually, some software programs use music or even synthesized speech.

Speech to text (speech recognition)

is computer comprehension of spoken words or sounds. Speaker-dependent speech recognition systems can understand one person's voice, while speaker-independent systems can comprehend the speech of many different individuals.

Speech to text (speech recognition) is an important alternative means of communication with PCs. Many of today's PCs feature "speaker-independent" speech recognition. Such systems can understand any speaker's voice. Earlier systems were "speaker dependent"; that is, they had to be trained on one user's voice and could respond only to that individual's speech. Earlier PCs also required speakers to pause between words, speaking . . . like . . . this. Today's machines can often handle continuous speech at or near conversational speed. IBM and Dragon Systems offer inexpensive (about $100) software programs that recognize continuous speech. Just a few years ago, such programs cost in the thousands of dollars.

Touch screens

are technologies that sense the user's finger on the screen, activating software commands.

Touch screens are also widely used in early childhood programs. These are familiar to teachers from automated teller machines (ATMs). Young children find touch screens to be easier to use than is the case with most other input mechanisms. That is because they are used to pointing to what they want. Touch screens work by means of software that "maps" the computer screen, much as latitude and longitude map a globe. The software can triangulate your touch to determine where on the screen your finger is. You can find touch screens in most good-sized computer stores, including those that have on-line capabilities (e.g., www.compusa.com). You may also get them from specialty retailers such as Tom Caine and Associates (www.caineassociates.com), which sells a variety for $180 to $270, and from Don Johnston, Inc. (www.donjohnston.com).

Many ECSE programs use such screens with computer games and instructional programs that take advantage of touch screens. An example is Away We Ride, a program that teaches matching skills, word awareness, and object/sound association to young children. The program uses six songs about transportation to instruct children in these concepts. Made by SoftTouch (www.funsoftware.com), it is intended for children below kindergarten age. As useful as touch screens are, they are more limited than are speech recognition programs. That is because speech recognition is not limited to a finite set of choices displayed on a screen.

To illustrate the potential of speech recognition, consider the case of a speech and language pathologist who is trying to diagnose a four-year-old's problems with the English language. Ideally, the pathologist would like to see written samples of the child's language to analyze them for grammar, syntax, vocabulary, and other aspects of language use. Four-year-olds, however, seldom write long essays. A PC-based speech recognition system would allow the pathologist to tell the child to talk about favorite toys, life at home, or anything else. The PC automatically would produce a transcribed, printed version of the child's output. After the session, the speech pathologist could read the printout at leisure, searching for the linguistic rules that must have been used to create that language.

Electronic mail (e-mail) involves digital transfer of written messages.

Speech recognition also gives young children who do not yet know how to write access to **electronic mail (e-mail).** Mueller (1992) describes the use of e-mail in a pediatric psychiatric unit classroom by children as young as eight. She reports that while the children began hesitantly with such sentences as "I am fine. How are you?" they gradually opened up in their communications, producing messages that conveyed real emotional content and provided emotional support to the children with whom they were communicating. During the same period, the e-mail messages gradually became longer and grammar and spelling improved. The children became excited about e-mail, in part, Mueller says, because of the rapid turnaround; messages sent to other cities, states, or even countries could be answered within hours or days versus weeks to months via air or surface mail. In addition, she notes, the medium caused the children's disabilities to "disappear" because all messages, whether from children with or without disabilities, appeared identical on the screen. This "anonymous" feature of e-mail is vital in that it gives these young children some of their only chances to have others focus exclusively on the content of their messages, not on their disabilities or even their personalities.

One commercial product that young children may use to speak to the PC is Nuance's Naturally Speaking, a speech-to-text program (www.nuance.com). Naturally Speaking requires little user training; it can be used with a fairly high degree of accuracy within minutes of unpacking. With training, the program works well even for very young children who have never before used a computer. The child simply speaks into a microphone and sees his words appear instantly on the screen, free of misspellings and typographical errors. Very young children who know words but do not know how to spell them accurately can produce high-quality communications. An obvious application for Naturally Speaking is as an addition to a communications program to produce e-mail. Another exciting possibility is its use by children who have physical disabilities that make typing difficult or impossible.

Many Americans with disabilities and members of their families do not know what assistive technology devices are "out there" that could help (Carlson, Ehrlich, Berland, & Bailey, 2001). This is a long-standing problem.

IN THE CLASSROOM

ECSE professionals may be aware of some controversy about the use of technology with young children. For example, NAEYC has expressed skepticism about such uses (see www.naeyc.org). In that statement about technology, revised in 2005, NAEYC focused primarily on computers. It noted that much so-called educational software does not follow sound educational practice. Some of the first programs marketed for use by young children were in fact drill-and-practice oriented. Newer programs, however, let young children explore on their own. NAEYC urges professionals to screen software, picking programs that comply with the organization's DAP recommendations. Thus, computer programs should be age-appropriate, individually appropriate, and culturally appropriate. Young children should use computers in pairs or small groups, rather than alone. Perhaps most important, according to NAEYC, is that technology be *integrated* into the curriculum. That is, there should not be a separate "technology time" in the schedule. Similarly, computers should not be located in a "computer room" but rather in the early childhood classroom itself. These should be used in regularly scheduled activities, just as are crayons, paper, and other materials.

Technology, both low- and high-tech, is *more* important for young children with disabilities than it is for those without disabilities. This is because disabilities often limit what young children learn on their own and because disabilities can restrict children's ability to communicate. For these reasons, ECSE professionals need to become aware of what is available, learn how to use it, and make intelligent choices from among the many products on the market.

Young children with specific learning disabilities, mental retardation, and several other disabilities will find it much easier to use touch screens than to use keyboards or other input devices. This is particularly an issue in assessment. The federal law No Child Left Behind, for example, requires annual testing in mathematics and English for all third graders in the United States. Children with learning disabilities and mental retardation in particular may have difficulty with the answer sheets used in such tests. It is cognitively more demanding to make a choice in one place (on the test booklet) and then enter that choice elsewhere (on the answer sheet) than it is simply to point to the chosen answer on a screen.

Communication products, known as *augmentative and alternative communication technologies,* are also important. These range from low-tech, in the case of Picture Exchange Communication System (PECS) to high-tech, in the case of DynaVox® machines. In PECS, teachers assemble pictures on a board to represent what a young child might want to say. Thus, there usually is a "Yes" image at one upper end of the board and a "No" image at the opposite end. Key images in the middle include symbols for "I," "want," and other often-used words and ideas. Boards may be swapped between activities. There may be one board for snack and lunch periods, one for morning start activities, one for recess, one for music, and so on. The child points to one picture after another to compose a message. A teacher or other person (e.g., a mature peer) needs to stand near the board to read the message as it is composed.

Midway between PECS and the high-tech DynaVox® devices are such products as Frame Technologies' (www.frame-tech.com) Voice-in-a-Box® communicators. These are battery-operated machines. The basic preschool edition, priced at about $200, features pictures in a 4×4 matrix. The child touches a picture to activate the voice (which the child recorded, in advance, as part of setting up the program). A newer edition, the VB 6-16/PrS, costing about $450, offers six levels of messages. At 16 messages per level, this means the device can store and produce 96 messages.

At the high level, the DynaVox and DynaMyte® devices (www.dynavoxsys.com) are "dynamic" in that they offer even more flexibility than does Voice-in-a-Box. However, these machines cost about $7,000 each. They must be programmed so that they will say what the child desires to say. This means that someone needs to follow the child throughout the day to see what the child does on a typical day and what kinds of messages the child may wish to create.

Software programs are available in a wide variety of subject matter. Teachers may visit www.teachersfirst.com for some suggestions. Two other sites—www.assistivetech.net and www.abledata.com—are also helpful. Be sure to specify that you are looking for products suitable for use with young children. Many companies offer a no-cost 30-day trial option. This can be invaluable in ECSE, because sometimes it is not evident what features of the program pose barriers for children with vision, hearing, mobility, cognitive, or other limitations until the software is actually used.

Text to speech (speech synthesis) is computer-generated speech.

Large numbers of young children are using Kidspiration, a graphic organizer from Inspiration (www.inspiration.com). This program gives children a wide variety of pictures to insert on the computer screen, connecting them with arrows, and with these graphics tell a story. Kidspiration uses **text to speech (speech synthesis)** to speak out loud whatever is on the screen, including the function icons that control the program. All of this makes Kidspiration user-friendly. Another nice feature, particularly for the primary grades, is an automatic outlining program. With one click of the mouse, the child sees a written outline she can follow in writing an essay.

Also increasingly popular among young children is PowerPoint, a program in the Microsoft Office suite. Even first and second graders are producing slide shows that feature sophisticated capabilities, including eye-catching graphics, impressive sound effects, and cascading words in a wide variety of typefaces.

REACHING THE POTENTIAL?

ECSE as a field needs to examine the extent to which it is fully tapping the potential of today's technologies. Lending urgency to the task is the looming pressures of the "big tests" that begin in third grade—in math, in English and language arts, and, in 2007, in science as well. The evidence suggests that young children with disabilities are not well prepared to succeed in these high-stakes assessments (see Chapter 3).

Today's young children tend to enjoy, and learn from, computer games.

Tremendous resources are available on the Web to help these young children catch up. Computer games that foster number sense and that call for use of important math skills are many in number and easily found via search engines such as Yahoo! or Google. Lesson plans that teach math through sports, through art, and through other interests that children may have also are available on the Internet. The Web-based resources in science are even greater in number and often richer in content. And the simple acts of exchanging e-mails and IMs develop children's reading and writing abilities. Are we as interventionists and educators doing enough to bring these resources into our programs and services?

As another example of potential that to date seems to be untapped, consider two new cell phones. Both were designed for use by preschoolers, kindergartners, and other young children. They have very simple interfaces, with just a handful of large and colorful buttons. Phone numbers are preprogrammed by adults, so the child need only touch a button to reach the family home, the school, or police. Each costs about $100. The TicTalk Mobile Phone (www.mytictalk.com) is one; the FireFly is another (www.fireflymobile.com). These cell phones could grant children with disabilities, even those with such severe conditions as mental retardation or autism, a level of freedom and independence unknown in years past. Are ECSE professionals and families taking advantage?

BROADBAND—AN EXCITING TECHNOLOGY

Traditional telecommunications networks offer what is now being called *narrowband* communication, meaning that it transmits voice well, data pretty well (think: slow-loading Web pages), and video badly (think: jerky images). Another word to describe this is *analog*. Traditional voice telephony is analog. So is dial-up Internet service. Now becoming widely available is *broadband,* which conveys voice, data, and video on one line, at one time, very fast. Homes, schools, and businesses get broadband services via cable modems, DSL modems, or other high-speed connections.

Broadband offers revolutionary possibilities for ECSE programs, because it allows ECSE workers to see and hear family members and family members to see and hear ECSE workers over phone lines. An early intervention specialist could consult with the family without having to travel to the home. IFSP and IEP meetings may be held that way, too. In fact, with broadband, the ECSE team could even fax the agreed-on plan to the family, without hanging up on the voice/video call. This is because one broadband line not only provides a high-speed voice/video/data connection but also allows people to send and receive faxes.

Coming soon is a rather amazing feature of broadband. Called "telepresence" in a report issued by the Committee on Broadband Last Mile Technology (2002), it is a "window" that "opens" to another space. Imagine that an ECSE professional is in the program playroom. Telepresence opens a window to a child's home. The professional sees the infant or toddler and the parent on a large screen. At the home, the parent and the young child can see the professional on a screen. The window may remain open as long as desired. This technology permits the delivery of early intervention services without necessitating home visits. The cost savings, even after accounting for the monthly fee for the phone line, are very considerable. Needed are very high-speed connections both at the ECSE program's offices and at the home. It may be a few years before a majority of families with young children have such high-speed broadband services. However, the trend is a strong one (Bowe, 2002).

At the preschool and primary levels, other features of broadband offer intriguing possibilities as well. One is speech synthesis or computer talk. Because everything transmitted over broadband connections is digital—that is, in bits or 1s and 0s—young children can dictate e-mail, surf the Web, and even write brief stories simply by talking. The telephone network can translate what is spoken into text. Another feature of broadband is remote interpreting. If their services are needed only for short periods of time (say, an hour or less), sign language interpreters do not need to travel to the school. Rather, they can use the "window" of telepresence to interpret from a remote location. A third is **telemedicine.** Physicians who specialize in such uncommon disorders as apraxia may be

Telemedicine

links medical specialists in one location with a patient in another, usually via fiber optic cable, which can transmit high-quality video as well as voice and data.

consulted at a distance. Not only can the specialist see the child and listen to the family, but she can also view a high-quality CAT scan or other document.

Some of these possibilities stagger the imagination. To get the latest about broadband, enter the word *broadband* in your favorite search engine's "search" box. You may also contact local and long-distance phone companies for more information.

ASSISTIVE TECHNOLOGY SERVICES

Assistive technology services include assessment, selection of devices, instruction in their use, and related services to support individuals with disabilities in the use of technology.

Parts C and B of the IDEA recognize **assistive technology services** as allowable early intervention and related services, respectively. These are services provided by professionals to assist ECSE programs, families, and children to identify what technologies are needed; to select suitable devices; to install or configure the machines so that they do what is needed; and to train children, family members, and ECSE workers how to use them. The term is defined in Part A:

> *[A]ssistive technology services means any service that directly assists an individual with a disability in the selection, acquisition, or use of an assistive technology device. Such term includes*
>
> *(A) the evaluation of the needs of an individual with a disability, including a functional evaluation of the individual in the individual's customary environment;*
>
> *(B) purchasing, leasing, or otherwise providing for the acquisition of assistive technology devices by individuals with disabilities;*
>
> *(C) selecting, designing, fitting, customizing, adapting, applying, maintaining, repairing, or replacing of assistive technology devices;*
>
> *(D) coordinating and using other therapies, interventions, or services with assistive technology devices, such as those associated with existing education and rehabilitation plans and programs;*
>
> *(E) training or technical assistance for an individual with disabilities, or, where appropriate, the family of an individual with disabilities; and training or technical assistance for professionals (including individuals providing education and rehabilitation services), employers, or other individuals who provide services to, employ, or are otherwise substantially involved in the major life activities of individuals with disabilities.* (Section 602)

Assistive technology services clearly are important for ECSE programs, ECSE workers, families, and children. Many thousands of technology devices are out there, and choosing among them is difficult. Fortunately, several sources can assist ECSE programs to identify experts who can help. Two are on-line. The advantage this offers is major. Technology, including assistive technology, changes with great speed. Web-based resources can update their information in minutes. You can get the latest data at any time. One that is very helpful is AbleData (www.abledata.com). This site has information on tens of thousands of assistive technology devices. Another, also very useful, is assistivetech.net (www.assistivetech.net). Both are supported by federal grants. They specialize in describing assistive technology devices. Each site gives you a "search" button and offer "channels" that you can use to find data in categories of interest.

AbleData and the Job Accommodation Network (JAN), another Web-based resource (www.jan.wvu.edu), differ from assistivetech.net in that they also give you information about products that are not commercially available. These may be one-of-a-kind devices

Multimedia programs give young children multiple modes of input and output, facilitating learning.

that were designed by a rehabilitation engineer. Your need for such products likely is limited. However, some young children have very unusual needs, so it is good to be aware that you can learn about rare products at AbleData, JAN, and also the Rehabilitation Engineering Society of North America (RESNA).

Rehabilitation engineering is a relatively new professional specialty. Emerging out of vocational rehabilitation in the late 1970s and early 1980s, it attracted people who combine knowledge about individuals with disabilities and expertise in engineering and technology. RESNA is the major professional organization representing rehabilitation engineers. The work of these professionals has changed over the years. In the early 1980s, they specialized in custom-designed solutions because few off-the-shelf devices were commercially available to meet the special needs of people with disabilities. Today, with many thousands of such products available, rehabilitation engineers spend less time creating new solutions and more time screening, selecting, installing, and configuring off-the-shelf products to meet individual needs.

Environmental control system (ECS)

enables people to operate electric equipment via remote control, usually with the assistance of a small personal computer.

One exciting kind of assistive technology service is the creation of an **environmental control system (ECS).** Linking an inexpensive PC to lights, alarm systems, and other electric appliances in the home allows a child with a physical disability to control many aspects of the environment from a remote location. Such systems can increase greatly the child's freedom and sense of personal responsibility. They may even prove lifesaving, because the child is able to set or release alarms, make 911 calls, and take other steps to protect herself in the home. Some products, such as NanoPac's CINTEX2, allow voice control of as many as 256 devices through as many as one hundred commands (channel up/down, volume up/down, rewind/fast forward, play, record, on/off, etc.). In each of these instances, technology promotes adaptive development by enabling young children with disabilities to do important everyday tasks by themselves, reducing pressure on parents and other caregivers, while encouraging the children to become self-reliant.

In all of these areas—extending the classroom by using Web-based instructional resources, tapping the educational benefits of some computer games, using preprogrammed cell phones to give young children unprecedented freedom from constant adult supervision, using the graphics capabilities of Kidspiration and PowerPoint to let young children express themselves in writing, mining computer games for incidental lessons in math and science, equipping the homes of young children with environmental control systems that increase their independence—the story in ECSE continues to be one of catching up to potential. This may be because families of young children with disabilities are not familiar with the technologies. It may be because many professionals in ECSE are more comfortable with older rather than newer technologies. It may also be for reasons related to money, a topic to which we now turn.

FINANCING OPTIONS

Third-party funding for assistive technology devices and assistive technology services is available from a large number of sources (Figure 9–2). However, persistence is necessary in many instances because financing is not automatic. A convincing case must be made that an individual's needs do in fact meet the criteria of a particular funding source.

The first source to which ECSE professionals should look is the IDEA itself. Part D offers discretionary funds for which school programs may apply in order to create advanced technology capabilities. The U.S. Department of Education's Office of Special Education Programs (OSEP) annually announces grant competitions under Part D. For more information, contact OSEP at the U.S. Department of Education, 400 Maryland Avenue SW, Washington, DC 20202.

Part C states that assistive technology devices and services may constitute early intervention services that may be financed with Part C monies. Similarly, Part B allows such devices and services to be paid for as related services. In both cases, reimbursement is available if the IFSP or IEP provides for devices and services that children require so as to benefit from the early intervention or preschool special education program.

Devices and services that have purely personal uses—wheelchairs, braces, and the like—are not included. The test to apply is fairly simple: If a device and/or service is

IDEA, Part C (if in IFSP)

IDEA, Part B (if in IEP)

Medicaid (Mandated and Optional Services)

Medicaid EPSDT (Early and Periodic Screening, Diagnosis, and Treatment)

Supplemental Security Income

Developmental Disabilities Programs

Maternal and Child Health Block Grants—Title V

Assistive Technology Act

FIGURE 9–2 Selected financing options.

required for program participation and is used only at the program or school, it is eligible for Part C or Part B funding. If, however, the child uses it all day, seven days a week, in program and out of program, then it is a personal device or service and is not reimbursable under Part C or Part B.

In some cases, this test is misleading. Parents may argue successfully that devices and/or services that are primarily program-related are also needed at home and during vacations for intervention or educational purposes. In such instances, their cost may be reimbursed under Part C or Part B. As another illustration of exceptions to this test, OSEP issued a groundbreaking policy letter stating that, contrary to previous policy, hearing aids were to be acquired by schools and made available without cost to children with hearing impairments if the children's IEPs contained such devices (Hehir, 1993). The precedent appears to be such that other low-tech products may also be considered *assistive technology devices* and thus eligible for provision in IFSPs and IEPs.

Medicaid is a second, very important source of funding for assistive technology devices and services. Officially, Medicaid will reimburse costs for medically necessary equipment and services. However, the federal regulations governing Medicaid (42 CFR 440.10) state that physical therapy, occupational therapy, and speech and language pathology—all of which are allowable services—*include* "any necessary supplies and equipment." This phrase opens a wide door for all kinds of technologies. As Medicaid expert Allan Bergman, of the Brain Injury Association, put it in an interview, "For example, when an OT [occupational therapist] recommends assistive eating devices, Medicaid must pay for them. In the speech/language area, hearing aids, alternative and augmentative communication devices, computers, and voice synthesizers are Medicaid reimbursable" (quoted in Kyes, 1994, p. 28). Bergman added that the same regulation allows reimbursement for vision aids.

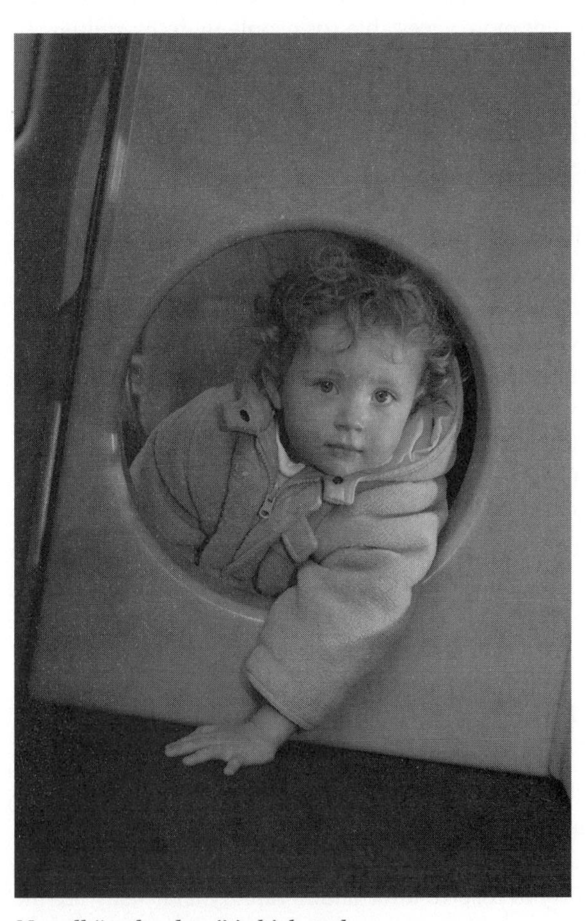

Not all "technology" is high-tech.

In addition, state Medicaid programs are authorized by law to acquire "rehabilitation and other services to help . . . families and individuals attain or retain capability for independence or self-care." This opens what may be an even wider door. The quoted passage was written into the Medicaid statute in 1965, yet a surprising number of federal and state Medicaid officials are unaware of it. Bergman commented that a request for reimbursement for these kinds of devices and services "is not welcomed by Medicaid, but it does happen when people push" (quoted in Kyes, 1994, p. 28).

Products and services identified during early and periodic screening, diagnosis, and treatment (EPSDT) developmental screenings may be reimbursable even if not medically necessary. Again, families may need to persist in the face of stonewalling by Medicaid and EPSDT staff who are not familiar with these rules. When products and services are in fact medically necessary, securing reimbursement should be much easier (Brown, Perry, & Kurland, 1994). Review Chapter 6 for much more information about Medicaid and EPSDT.

Supplemental security income (SSI) is a possible source of financing for assistive technology for children of families

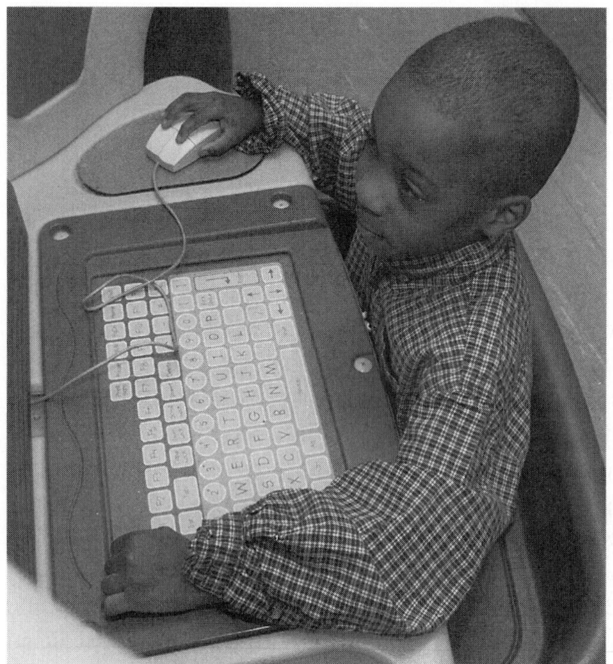

Today's speech recognition and other alternative input devices can help young children use e-mail and bulletin boards even before they learn to write or type.

that qualify for this federal-state program. The most important role SSI plays with respect to technology is that becoming eligible for SSI automatically qualifies the family for Medicaid and EPSDT in all but a handful of states. In addition, the monthly SSI checks are largely unrestricted; they may be used, if needed, to rent, lease, or purchase devices. Developmental Disabilities and Bill of Rights Act (DD act) funds also may be used for acquiring technology, as may Maternal and Child Health (MCH) block grants. Each of these programs is described in much more detail in Chapter 6. Also useful in learning about these programs are the Brown et al. (1994) article and Kyes's (1994) interview with Allan Bergman.

Other possibilities include state-run revolving fund and equipment distribution programs. Some states—California, Massachusetts, and Minnesota—offer free or low-cost telecommunications equipment, including TTDs for deaf individuals and Tele-Brailler machines for people who are both deaf and blind. The programs frequently feature flashing-light ring signalers, large-button dials, and other products useful in making telephones and related equipment more accessible for people with disabilities. In California, this equipment is available on request at no charge; families must simply certify that a family member has a disability. In Minnesota and Massachusetts, the equipment is free only to low-SES families; others pay part or all of the cost.

The National Cristina Foundation (591 West Putnam Avenue, Greenwich, CT 06830; www.cristina.org) distributes free PCs and adaptive devices. The foundation receives these as donations from companies and individuals. Additional sources include private, nonprofit organizations specializing in services for individuals with disabilities. Local chapters of the National Easter Seals Society (230 W. Monroe Street, Chicago, IL 60606-4802; www.easterseals.com) and United Cerebral Palsy Associations, Inc. (1660 L Street NW, Washington, DC 20036; www.ucpa.org), for example, often provide financial assistance for purchase, rental, or lease of assistive technology devices and services. Other assistance may be available from local Lions, Kiwanis, or other civic organizations. One interesting resource is the Used Equipment Referral Service, an on-line information source for matching individuals who need equipment with those who have used products to sell.

ECSE PROFESSIONALS AND TECHNOLOGY

ECSE professionals report that telecommunications helps them combat professional isolation, a big problem for many educators. Forums and bulletin boards let them post queries and exchange information rapidly and efficiently. The opportunity to communicate with far-flung peers and the ability to receive information rapidly and easily are the two most motivating aspects of telecommunications use.

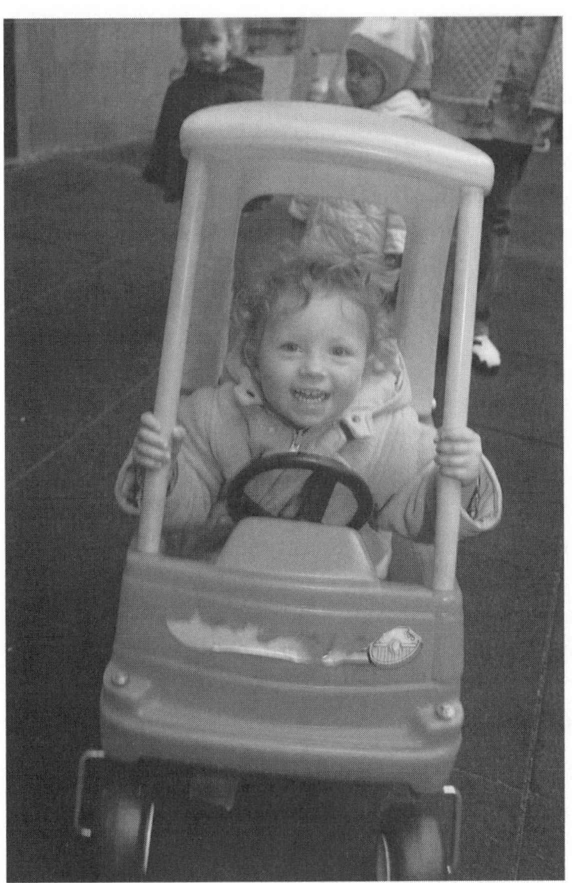

Low-tech products can facilitate exploration and imagination.

The Division for Early Childhood (DEC), of the Council for Exceptional Children (CEC), sponsors discussion groups, forums, and e-mail groups for members. In addition, DEC posts the names and e-mail addresses of state leaders and subdivision (state) presidents so as to encourage interaction. A good place to start is the DEC home page: www.dec-sped.org. DEC's parent CEC sponsors Webcasts. Here is a link to current ones: www.cec.sped.org.

The National Center for Learning Disabilities (NCLD) has monthly forums and on-line chat sessions. These allow individuals around the country to post questions in advance. Previous sessions are archived. LDTalk, the on-line chat site, is at www.ldtalk.org.

The Independent Living Resource Utilization (ILRU) center, in Houston, sponsors both teleconferences and Webcasts, at www.ilru.org.

In addition, some college and university programs in EC and in ECSE offer **distance learning.** Typically, these courses use Blackboard or other text-based interaction tools to connect professor with far-flung students. Some augment those text sessions with live two-way video conferences.

In all of these ways, today's technologies, particularly broadband, are promising to end the isolation of ECSE professionals and families having young children with disabilities. Once again, the promise of the technology leads practice. We need to take advantage of what these technologies offer if we are to benefit fully from them.

Distance learning

links an instructor in one geographic location with students at other sites. Students see and hear the instructor, who in turn sees and hears them. The connections may be via satellite broadcast or, increasingly, via fiber optic cable.

GETTING STARTED

Creating a telecommunications capacity for an ECSE program is not difficult. Local and long-distance telephone companies have specialists working with educational and social service agencies and programs who can help. The first step is to assess the program's current telecommunications capabilities. These probably are insufficient for more than routine office functions. Telephone lines should be added to activity rooms, classrooms, and media centers. Telephone companies can provide information about cost containment, including blocking of unauthorized calls.

A second step is to acquire the necessary "customer premises equipment" to use on these telephone lines. If the program's objective is to provide for e-mail and bulletin board system (BBS) access, all that is needed is an inexpensive PC, a modem, and communications software. An excellent way to choose these items is to ask a telecommunications enthusiast who may be a staff member, a volunteer, or a parent. In selecting this person, the critical skill to look for is an ability to communicate to laypeople in real English as well as an understanding of what the program wants to accomplish.

The PC need not be a powerful one; an older IBM-compatible or Macintosh is sufficient for most purposes. If the ECSE program wants to create a BBS of its own, into which parents and staff alike may call, it is important to bear in mind that the machine must be dedicated to this function. If the PC is turned off or being used for other things, users will be unable to connect to the BBS (unless, as mentioned, the lines are broadband).

The next step is to pick out communications and other software. Most word-processing software programs, such as WordPerfect, allow text to be saved as American Standard Code for Information Interchange (ASCII). This is a no-frills way to store data; there are no codes for bold, italic, underlining, and so on. ASCII often is used for e-mail and BBS communications. Communications programs often may be acquired free or at low cost from BBS services, as "shareware." More sophisticated software is needed if the ECSE program wants to create its own BBS or if it wants to use broadcast fax as a means of communicating with parents.

Training for staff, volunteers, and parents is important. Probably most helpful will be two levels of training—one for newcomers who have little or no prior experience with telecommunications and a second, much briefer, training for experienced users. Some schools and universities provide communications software to their staff members for use from the home; ECSE programs may wish to consider such off-site access for staff and volunteers as a means of enhancing ongoing communications.

These steps may appear to be complicated, but they really are not. Electronic communication today is a relatively simple process in most cases. Most communications software is designed for easy use by beginners, as are most BBS services. ECSE programs should encourage staff, volunteers, and parents to learn to use these capabilities because they do so much to facilitate communication.

TELEVISION

Television sets are among the most widely used low-tech products in the United States today, with virtually all households having at least one. Many ECSE programs have television sets as well, and many also have videocassette recorders (VCRs) and/or digital video disk (DVD) players. The ubiquity of television technology is potentially of tremendous importance in ECSE. That is especially true because television recently has become far more accessible to and usable by young children with disabilities.

Perhaps the most exciting television-related advance in recent years is the remarkable distribution of caption-ready television sets. All sets measuring 13 inches or more diagonally manufactured in and/or sold in the United States after mid-1993 contain built-in "caption chips," which, when activated, display closed **captions,** or subtitles. Because 15 to 20 million television sets are sold in the United States annually, some 100 million American households had caption-ready sets as of 2002, and the number will grow with each passing year. The caption capability is offered at no additional cost; previously, caption users had to acquire and attach decoder boxes costing about $200 (Bowe, 1991). Industry analysts estimate that virtually every home in the United States has caption-ready television sets today.

Captions

are subtitles for video programming. Captions may be *open,* in which case all viewers see them, or *closed,* in which case caption decoders are required to make the subtitles visible.

Federal law calls for virtually everything on TV to be captioned as of January 1, 2006. The only exceptions are commercials of less than five minutes and programs (including local news) produced by small stations. Captions have obvious benefits for young children who are deaf. Indeed, without captions, most children who are deaf cannot follow television programming at all. However, to consider captioning as a technology only for people who are deaf would be a serious mistake. Potential uses with other populations were so widely recognized when Congress considered what became the Television Decoder Circuitry Act of 1990 (PL 101–431) that more than 100 organizations serving people with mental retardation, learning disabilities, and other special needs endorsed the legislation (Bowe, 1991). Young children with mental retardation or learning disabilities benefit when the audio signal is supplemented by subtitles because they receive information in a multisensory mode, something we know helps them learn more and better (Adler & Drew, 1988; Bos & Vaughn, 1988; Clements, Nastasi, & Swaminathan, 1993). Many ECSE programs may also find that captioning helps parents and other primary caregivers learn English. Literacy organizations strongly endorsed the Decoder Circuitry Act because captions may dramatically increase literacy in the American population.

The technology will reach its potential only if it is used. ECSE staff should advise parents of young children with cognitive or communication limitations or delays to activate the captions whenever captioned programming is being watched. Similarly, early childhood special educators should consider activating the caption capability as a routine matter whenever educational programming is shown during program hours. Of course, where educational videotapes are available in captioned or uncaptioned versions, ECSE staff should order the captioned tape.

Activating captions is a simple matter. To display captions, the viewer touches a button on the remote control unit or on the television itself or activates an on-screen menu via the remote control unit. Captions appear if they have been prepared and transmitted by the broadcaster or video producer.

Descriptive video service (DVS)

transmits spoken descriptions of on-screen television action so that individuals who are blind may learn about actions they do not see.

Descriptive video service (DVS) is another recent development. In DVS, spoken descriptions of on-screen action are inserted during natural pauses in program dialog. This narration articulates the visual image for the benefit of viewers who are blind. As of 2006, few programs feature DVS. Advocates continue to press Congress, however, and families with young children who are blind may look forward to greatly increased video description in the coming years.

MULTIMEDIA

Multimedia

personal computers can display video as well as words, sound, data, and still images.

CD-ROM

stands for compact disk—read-only memory. CD-ROMs store information that computer users may read, scan, and search at high speed. The user may read the disk but not write to it.

Perhaps the newest buzzword in computers these days is ***multimedia,*** a shorthand term for PCs that can display video as well as words, data, and still images. Once much more costly than ordinary PCs, today's multimedia PCs are no more costly than their unadorned counterparts. For $600—even less with education discounts—ECSE programs get not only a Pentium-class PC but also a **CD-ROM** player, a video-graphics-array color monitor, a sound card, speakers, and a microphone. (The term *CD-ROM* stands for compact disk—read-only memory. As the term implies, the user may read the disk but not write to it.)

A major advantage of multimedia PCs for ECSE is the ability of these machines to provide information to children in a variety of media. Children who are deaf can see the information, children who are blind can listen to it, and children with mental retardation or dyslexia can use sound to reinforce video. The evidence is that such multiple-mode input helps, often considerably (Adler & Drew, 1988; Clements et al., 1993). Multimedia is one means of making computers "appropriate" for very young children, to adopt the NAEYC term. That is because multimedia PCs offer young children individualized, customizable, and interactive opportunities for learning.

INFORMATION SOURCES

A wealth of information about technology and people with disabilities is readily available to ECSE programs. *Exceptional Parent* magazine publishes an "Annual Guide to Products and Services," which lists state-by-state agencies and organizations providing technical assistance on assistive technology and also provides toll-free numbers for products and services. *Closing the Gap* (PO Box 68, Henderson, MN 56044) is a tabloid-style newspaper published bimonthly that describes new assistive technology devices and products in an easy-to-read format. Special education uses are well covered in this publication. Somewhat more difficult to read is the professional *Journal of Special Education Technology.* Edited by Herbert Rieth of the Peabody College at Vanderbilt University (Box 328, Nashville, TN 37203), it is a publication of the Technology and Media Division of the Council for Exceptional Children.

An excellent way to keep abreast of low-tech devices is to write to mail-order catalog publishers requesting a copy of their latest catalog; doing so gets you on their mailing list, and they will send you catalogs at least annually. A number of companies serve as distributors of low-tech products for people with disabilities. Independent Living Aids (ILA, 27 East Mall, Plainview, NY 11803) offers hundreds of products in a 64-page catalog. The Lighthouse, Inc. (111 E. 59th Street, New York, NY 10022), annually describes more than 300 classroom, play, and household products for people who are blind or have low vision in its *Product Catalog.* TeleConsumer Hotline (T-C Hotline, 1910 K Street NW, #610, Washington, DC 20006) annually publishes guides to products that people with hearing, vision, mobility, and other limitations can use with the telephone. Figure 9–1 gives additional sources of catalogs, and the following sections offer some other sources of information.

NOT FOR PROFIT

AbleData
8455 Colesville Road, #935
Silver Spring, MD 20910-3319
www.abledata.com
Offers a database describing 17,000 products for people with disabilities, from more than 2,000 companies.

Alliance for Technology Access
2175 East Francisco Blvd., #L
San Rafael, CA 94901
www.ataccess.org
Through 45 community-based centers in 38 states, provides information on devices.

American Association for the Advancement of Science Project on Science, Technology, and Disability
1333 H Street NW
Washington, DC 20005
www.aaas.org
Has an outstanding directory of scientists and engineers who are individuals with disabilities. Also has a wealth of technology-related publications, as well as a respected guide to accessible meetings and conferences.

assistivetech.net
Georgia Institute of Technology
Center for Assistive Technology
490 Tenth Street, NW
Atlanta, GA 30332-0156
www.assistivetech.net
A good on-line resource for hardware and software products.

Closing the Gap
PO Box 68
Henderson, MN 56044
www.closingthegap.org
A tabloid bimonthly newspaper, *Closing the Gap* includes many articles on special education uses of PCs.

ERIC Clearinghouse on Information & Technology
Center for Science/Technology
Syracuse University
Syracuse, NY 13244-4100
www.ericit.org
A good source of brief summaries on technology as applied to special education.

Job Accommodation Network (JAN)
918 Chestnut Ridge Road
PO Box 6080
University of West Virginia
Morgantown, WV 26506
www.jan.wvu.edu
An outstanding source of information on products and people with disabilities.

RESNA
1700 N. Moore Street
Suite 1540
Arlington, VA 22209
www.resna.org
An organization of engineers and scientists who specialize in meeting the needs of children and adults with disabilities.

Trace R&D Center
S-151 Waisman Center
1500 Highland Avenue
University of Wisconsin
Madison, WI 53705
www.trace.wisc.edu
Sponsors research on "cutting-edge" devices and services for people with disabilities.

World Institute on Disability
510 16th Street, #100
Oakland, CA 94612
www.wid.org
Sponsors WIDNet, a bulletin board, as well as reports on such issues as access to telecommunications.

FOR PROFIT

Apple Computer, Worldwide
Disability Solutions
20525 Mariani Avenue
Cupertino, CA 95014
www.apple.com
Offers information and referral for products that work with the Apple Macintosh.

HITEC Group International
8160 Madison
Burr Ridge, IL 60521
www.hitec.com
Distributes a wide range of fairly low-tech devices, some for young children.

IBM Accessibility Center
PO Box 2150
Atlanta, GA 30055
www.ibm.com
Provides information on IBM products and IBM-compatible products and services.

Nuance (formerly ScanSoft, Inc.)
9 Centennial Drive
Peabody, MA 01960
www.nuance.com
Offers Dragon Dictate and other speech recognition systems.

SUMMARY

The United States is a generation into the knowledge age, an era in which the collection, analysis, and reporting of information is our nation's principal economic activity. The technologies driving this period of our history affect ECSE as they do other sectors of the economy. Perhaps most urgent is the need for ECSE workers and parents to learn how today's technologies can help young children with disabilities do things they might not be able to do otherwise. In particular, the fact that PCs may be modified to meet unique needs of children with disabilities is tremendously important. With PCs and adaptive technology devices and services, children who are blind can "see," children who are deaf can "hear," children with mental limitations can "remember," and children who have mobility disabilities can "move" virtually without boundaries.

Also important, though, is the potential of today's technologies to alleviate isolation among ECSE workers. In many towns and cities, only one ECSE program is available. Experts who work with very young children with disabilities need to maintain close contact with others specializing in similar work, regardless of where those others are located geographically. Modern technology makes it possible for ECSE workers even in the most remote locations to maintain daily, even hourly, contact with experts from coast to coast.

The ability of today's telecommunications to enhance family-program communications promises to make a reality of one of the most cherished values in all of ECSE: family-focused programming. In the years to come, technology will provide real-time machine translation of languages, allowing ECSE programs to communicate instantly in whatever languages the families they serve speak at home.

KEY TERMS

assistive technology devices

assistive technology services

broadband

captions

CD-ROM

descriptive video service (DVS)

distance learning

electronic mail (e-mail)

environmental control systems (ECS)

multimedia

speech to text (speech recognition)

text to speech (speech synthesis)

telemedicine

touch screens

QUESTIONS FOR REFLECTION

1. Explain in your own words the differences between *low* and *high* technologies.
2. Children with what kinds of special needs might benefit from speech-to-text (speech recognition) programs such as Naturally Speaking?
3. What is the difference between *assistive technology devices* and *assistive technology services?*
4. Explain why old, slow, and outdated PCs might find new uses in environmental control systems.
5. Under what circumstances will Medicaid pay for assistive technology devices?
6. What about the IDEA—under which circumstances does it authorize reimbursement of assistive technology costs incurred on children's behalf by ECSE programs?
7. What is broadband, and why does it matter to ECSE programs?
8. How can telemedicine bring children to faraway specialists?
9. How could an ECSE program use closed captioning to enhance cognitive and language development of *hearing* children?
10. How can the Alliance for Technology Access help ECSE programs and families to get helpful devices?

PRACTICAL EXERCISES

1. Visit a local early childhood program (e.g., a Head Start program) or an ECSE program (e.g., a special preschool or an early intervention program serving infants and toddlers). Observe for a morning or an afternoon. Talk with program staff members. Then describe how the program uses technology.
   a. Are one-switch toys or other special toys in use?
   b. Are other low-tech products in use (e.g., Velcro, crayon or pencil holders, etc.)?
   c. Are PCs in use? If so, do they have touch screens?
   d. How do program staff use technology to keep up with the field?
   e. How do program staff communicate with families (e.g., by phone, e-mail, use of a program Web page, etc.)?

2. Visit the Web sites for the TicTalk (www.mytictalk.com) and the FireFly (www.fireflymobile.com). Study the features of these cell phones, which are designed for use by young children. Consider how these might be used by (a) a family of such a child and (b) a program serving such children.

WEB SITES OF INTEREST

www.assistivetech.net assistivetech.net—easy-to-use "search engine" on assistive technology

www.abledata.com AbleData—another search engine, even larger than assistivetech.net

www.enablingdevices.com Enabling Devices/Toys for Special Children—one source for low-tech products, such as switches

www.naeyc.org National Association for the Education of Young Children—has NAEYC's position statement, revised in 2005, on technology and early childhood education

Domains of Development

PART

10 Practical and Ethical Issues

11 Communication Development

12 Physical Development

13 Cognitive Development

14 Social or Emotional Development

15 Adaptive Development

Early Childhood Special Education: Birth to Eight now turns to an in-depth examination of the primary population served by ECSE programs: the children and their families. We open with Chapter 10, where we begin with demographics. What do we know about young children with disabilities and their families? Much new information has surfaced since the third edition of this text. We also look, in Chapter 10, at program-family relations, including how to form effective teams. The chapter concludes with an exploration of issues. We define the word *issues* to mean questions about which equally well-informed persons may have very different opinions. ECSE professionals need to be prepared to grapple with these issues, notably when family members seek advice and information.

Chapters 11–15 explore the five domains of development. The order of these chapters is one of descending prevalence. Thus, Chapter 11 looks at communication development, because disabilities and delays are most often seen among young children in this domain, notably delays and conditions in speech and language. Chapter 12 explores physical development, which is much more frequently a focus in ECSE than in the middle or high school years. Chapter 13 examines cognitive development, which is now assuming a place of prominence it did not enjoy in years past. That is because of the increasing stress on preacademics and academics that are placed on ECSE programs by recent federal laws. Chapter 14 looks at social or emotional development. The domain-specific material concludes with Chapter 15, on adaptive development.

As we open this final part of the book, we need to sharpen our focus on some new realities. ECSE has always taken pride in its ability to individualize instruction according to the strengths and needs of each child. The stress was on helping young children improve functioning in areas in which they were behind age peers, while also building on their strengths. Now, however, new mandates are raising questions about this traditional mission. Table IV–1 offers some data. The numbers themselves are striking. What they mean is an issue: we may disagree as to what the figures are telling us. In reading the

TABLE IV–1

Ages of Young Children in Various Grades.

	AGES			
GRADE	**6**	**7**	**8**	**9**
Ungraded	12	3	3	2
1st	88	86	32	2
2nd		10	60	31
3rd			4	61
4th				4

Data source: SEELS School Survey. Adapted from U.S. Department of Education (2003, p. 53, Table 1–12).

table, bear in mind that the typical nine-year-old is in fourth grade, the typical eight-year-old in third grade, and so forth.

In 2001, the SEELS longitudinal study found that just 4 percent of nine-year-olds with disabilities were, as would be anticipated, in fourth grade. Instead, 61 percent were in third grade. Three in 10 (31 percent) were in second grade. The story is very similar among students with disabilities who were eight years of age: just 4 percent were in third grade, as would be anticipated for students without disabilities, whereas 60 percent were in second grade, and 32 percent were in first grade. These figures may be showing us that young children with disabilities, especially boys, may be starting primary grades a year or so later than is typical. Perhaps family members, or educators, or both, suggested that entry into kindergarten or first grade be put off a year. Another possibility is that we are seeing a lot of retention in grade here. Young children may be held back for another year of first, second, and/or third grade.

We need to ask, Were educators and family members acting in the best interests of these young children with disabilities? Are these children really not developmentally prepared for the grades in which their age peers attend? Or are we seeing here retention in grade of children because the instruction the young children had received was not appropriate for their needs? If the latter, ECSE professionals need to look at what is being taught—and how. Are educators giving young children just another year of the same ineffective instruction? If so, reforming the curriculum is a far better response than is holding children back.

Readers should bear in mind that these data were collected in 2001. While it is true that students with disabilities were, at that time, taking the tests administered by the U.S. Department of Education as part of the NAEP (www.nationsreportcard.gov), it is also true that the No Child Left Behind Act of 2001 was signed into law in early 2002. These data, accordingly, were gathered *before* children with disabilities were required to take the NCLB "big tests" of the third and fourth grades. Now that young children with disabilities are taking not only the NAEP assessments but also state tests called for under NCLB, pressures may be building for even more "holding back."

These data also raise troubling questions about the mission of ECSE. Traditionally, ECSE has focused on children's strengths and needs in all five domains of development. Given the distressing figures in Table IV–1, the question must be asked: At the primary-grade level, and even at the preschool level, should that mission be altered? Should the cognitive domain, including as it does preacademics and academics, become the primary focus of attention, even if this means that many young children will not receive the amount of assistance they require in order to achieve their potential in other domains of development?

Practical and Ethical Issues

CHAPTER

10

As Mary drives away from her home visit with Alex, she can not get Mrs. Clanton's words out of her mind. Normally, Mrs. Clanton is so attentive to what Mary is doing with her two-year-old son, Alex, but the family is having a stressful week. And, in addition to seeing Mary, a special instructor, Alex sees a speech therapist, physical therapist, occupational therapist, neurologist, gastroenterologist, and an ophthalmologist. By the end of the week, Alex and his mother have been seen by seven different professionals, each with a different focus. Ms. Clanton is overwhelmed by all of the appointments and information. During the home visit she began to cry and remarked, "I feel like a secretary and a taxi. My life is consumed with Alex's appointments." (Jung, 2005, p. 19)

OBJECTIVES

After reading this chapter, you should be able to:

- Describe where information about young children with disabilities is available.
- Describe where most infants and toddlers with disabilities are served.
- Explain what likely causes some infants and toddlers to be served later than others.
- Tell which disability first becomes prominent in the primary grades (grades 1–3)

- Explain how a program becomes *family-friendly.*
- Describe how ECSE workers can empower families.
- Identify ethical issues of concern in ECSE
- Discuss your views about inclusion

CHAPTER OUTLINE

- OVERVIEW
- INTRODUCTION: STATISTICS AND THE IDEA
- THE FAMILIES
- CHILDREN BEING SERVED
  - Infants and Toddlers
  - Preschoolers
  - Primary-Grade Children
- LABELS
- FAMILY INVOLVEMENT
  - Traditional Approaches
  - A "Reconceptualization"
  - Family-Focused Programs
  - Family-Centered Programs
- EMPOWERING FAMILIES
- INVOLVING FATHERS
- SIBLINGS
- TEAMING
- ETHICAL ISSUES
  - Prenatal Services?
  - Gene Therapy
  - Surgical Interventions
- PROGRAM ISSUES
  - Mission
  - Inclusion
  - Diversity
  - Deafness Is Different

OVERVIEW

Professionals in ECSE need information about the more than two million young children who receive early intervention services and preschool and primary special education and related services. ECSE personnel also need to know something about the families of these children. This chapter summarizes current information about children with disabilities or delays in the birth-to-eight-inclusive age group and about their families.

We have quite a bit of knowledge about these young children and their families. This is new. As recently as 15 years ago, few data were available to help ECSE workers understand the needs of these children and their families. Statistical information was largely limited to children in primary grades; little was available that described the population of young children who were eligible for services under Part C and preschool Part B of the IDEA. Today, not only do we have a good picture of young children who are being served and of their families; we also have information about those who are potentially eligible but who, for one reason or another, are not currently receiving services under the IDEA. This chapter describes this corpus of data.

The pictures we are now able to draw of the population tell us much about what ECSE professionals need to do. In particular, we now know that the most common needs of young children with disabilities are in the domains of communication and physical development. We know that families of these young children tend to be of lower-than-average **socioeconomic status (SES)**; that is, they have household assets and incomes that are below the means for all families in America. We recognize that a team approach that involves family members as well as a variety of professionals is required. Contributions from many disciplines are needed to meet the many needs of young children in all five domains of development and also to respond to the resources, priorities, and concerns of the families. This chapter ends with a discussion of ethical and program issues in working with young children and their families.

Socioeconomic status (SES)

refers to family income and other demographic characteristics. Disability is disproportionately common among low-SES families.

INTRODUCTION: STATISTICS AND THE IDEA

More than 2,200,000 children in the birth-to-eight-inclusive early childhood age range receive services under the IDEA's Part C (early intervention for infants and toddlers), Section 619 (preschool special education), and Part B as it applies to primary-grade children. These numbers raise some questions. First, who are these children? What are their needs? What kinds of families do they come from? Another important question, a different one, is, Are these all, nearly all, most, or only some of the potentially eligible young children?

In the sections that follow, we offer a lot of numbers in answer to those questions. A few words about statistics may help the reader wade through the numbers. It is important, first, to understand that terms need to be defined before data may be gathered. Different agencies use different definitions. Thus, the U.S. Bureau of the Census (www.census.gov) has definitions for such words as *disability* and *delay* that are not the same as the definitions used by the U.S. Department of Education. The department, in turn, reports data it receives yearly from state agencies. The state agencies, for their part, collect information from local and county agencies. While the department continually strives to get other units of government to use its definitions properly, the historical fact is that some do and some do not. There are, to use statistical terms, *errors of measurement* in the studies reviewed in this chapter. Such errors of measurement occur, too, in special studies such as that of the National Early Intervention Longitudinal Study (NEILS; www.sri.com/neils) and the Pre-Elementary Education Longitudinal Study (PEELS).

This chapter offers numbers from three sources. The first is the U.S. Department of Education's annual reports on children served under the IDEA. The most recent of these, as this book was written, was the *Twenty-eighth Annual Report to Congress on Implementation of the Individuals with Disabilities Education Act* (U.S. Department of Education, 2006c). These yearly reports compile data from the states on implementation of Part C and Part B. The *Annual Report* is a direct-count source; the numbers it contains are of young children who receive early intervention services and special education and related services. There is some overcounting in these figures. State and local agencies may overreport the numbers of young children being served. In some cases, this occurs simply because two agencies serve the same child, and both report serving that child. Although the department tries to correct duplications, it acknowledges in its *Annual Reports* that interagency coordination at the state level to discover and remove duplicated counts is a work in progress.

The second source we use is NEILS. This is a long-term follow-along study that looks at a sample of families with infants or toddlers, and at the early intervention programs that serve those families and children. NEILS is a sample study. It does not attempt to count the number of children being served. Rather, it looks at a relative handful of such children and at their families in more depth and over a longer period of time than is the case with the *Annual Reports.*

PEELS had not generated much information at the time this book was written; the interested reader is referred to www.peels.org. It is our third source.

The most important implication of the data presented in this chapter is that ECSE has reached a critical turning point. About 20 years after beginning its effort to reach and serve *all* eligible young children and families, the field seems to have succeeded in at least reaching out to the vast bulk of the potential population. In other words, the focus may now shift. In earlier years, as documented in the first three editions of this text, ECSE was struggling to identify and extend services to families and their young children. Today, the emphasis no longer is on what the IDEA calls child find—outreach to bring families and children into the service delivery system. Rather, our priority now is to provide the high-quality services these families and young children need.

THE FAMILIES

The U.S. Bureau of the Census (2005), in its *Disability and American Families* report, found that, on average, the family incomes of families having members with disabilities, as compared with families having no such members, were lower. Those families were more likely to reside in rural areas, in the South, and in rental rather than owned housing. Adults in these families were less likely to be employed and more likely to depend on public assistance (i.e., Supplemental Security Income). One in every three families with a female householder with no husband present reported members with a disability. More information is available from www.census.gov.

The NEILS study found that many families of infants or toddlers being served under Part C of IDEA were of low SES. Four in 10 (42 percent) were receiving public assistance such as Aid to Families with Dependent Children or food stamps. Finally, the NEILS report indicated that most infants or toddlers receiving Part C services were from racial or ethnic minority families: 21 percent were African American, 15 percent were of Hispanic origin, 4.8 percent were Asian/Pacific Islanders, and 0.5 percent were Native American/Alaskan.

Helping us place these findings into context is the Early Childhood Longitudinal Study (ECLS) conducted by the National Center for Education Statistics (NCES) at the U.S. Department of Education. This massive study follows more than four million young children and their families (Flanagan & West, 2004). When the cohort born in 2001 turned nine months of age, the ECLS team interviewed the family. They found that 23 percent of those families lived in poverty, 27 percent had mothers who lacked a high school diploma, and 36 percent were not living with married biological parents. With respect to race and ethnicity, ECLS found that 54 percent were non-Hispanic white, 26 percent were Hispanic, 3 percent were Asian American, and 14 percent were Black non-Hispanic.

What does all of this tell us about working with families? It suggests, first, that we respect the fact that many young families have limited resources. While it has always been true that people just beginning their work careers tend to earn much less than do employees in their peak earning years (45–54), the fact that so many young children now live in single-adult households magnifies the effect. We also see in these statistics that ECSE workers cannot expect that adults have a lot of discretionary time. Whether because there is only one adult in the household or because both parents work, the reality today is that families of young children tend to be starved for free time. All of this helps explain—and justify—the trend toward ever-more service delivery in the home. By providing services where young children live, ECSE programs relieve single-parent families of transportation costs as well as the expenses they would incur were they to pay for child care at home while visiting the ECSE program.

These figures also suggest that the term *family* should be *family-defined*. It should be up to the family itself to identify who will represent it and the child. This may be a grandparent or even an aunt or uncle. For the same reasons, ECSE personnel should refer to "the family" and not "the parents." We want to respect the family's right to decide who are the persons it regards as "family" and who it authorizes to speak on its behalf.

Furthermore, ECSE programs need to be sensitive to the fact that family members may need flexibility in scheduling meetings. Whether we are talking about writing IFSPs or providing training for family members, we as professionals need to open our minds to nontraditional times for meetings. This may be during evening hours or on weekends. If so, the program should offer professionals and paraprofessionals alike sufficient flex-time that they can respond to family needs (Overton, 2005).

It also means that many families of young children with disabilities depend on SSI and Medicaid (see Chapter 5). For ECSE professionals, the fact that so many families are recipients of benefits from these programs has several implications. First, SSI checks come with few, if any, strings attached. Families may use the monthly income for food, clothing, utilities, and even toys. Second, Medicaid will pay for some services, such as speech pathology sessions, and for some assistive technology products, such as a personal communicator (see Chapter 9). If Medicaid pays for these, that frees up ECSE program resources for meeting other needs.

There are also family planning implications. ECSE professionals, especially the service coordinator, should review with the family some of the rules of SSI and Medicaid. For example, the family should meet with an attorney specializing in these programs. The family should have a will that assures that the child will not be impoverished were a parent or guardian to die. The problem arises because under SSI rules, assets above $2,000 may disqualify the child for continued benefits. A study by MetLife found that 88 percent of parents having children with disabilities had not set up a trust to preserve the child's eligibility, and 72 percent had not named a trustee to administer the child's finances. More than half (53 percent) had not identified a guardian to care for the child in the event of their death (see www.metlife.com). Although these subjects are sensitive, of course, the urgency of protecting the child compels ECSE professionals to at least raise the issues with the family and to encourage adults to take appropriate steps.

To illustrate, adults may not realize that the child automatically becomes independent at age 18. Unless the family has taken legal steps to appoint a guardian, the parents and other adults may not have the legal right to make decisions about the child's life after age 18. A parent may name him- or herself as guardian. Applying for guardianship is a simple process that's usually just a matter of filling out paperwork properly and going to either a state supreme court or a surrogate court. Guardianship may be of the person, the person's property, or both, depending on the child's capabilities. While many young children with disabilities will become teens who are capable of living independently, some may not. The family may always revoke guardianship arrangements in the event that they prove not to be necessary.

Insurance is a key part of the answer for many families. Life insurance policies typically name the child as primary beneficiary. But if the child depends on SSI and Medicaid, doing so may disqualify the child from those benefits. In addition to guardianship, a parent's financial plan should include a special-needs trust—a legal document established to hold title to assets that will be used to provide for a child with a disability. This trust does not adversely affect eligibility for government benefits, and parents have a legal right to establish it. Most special-needs trusts are funded with some type of insurance. Assets such as the house and investments can all be put into the trust. Legal fees to set up the trust may range from $1,000 to $5,000. MetLife offers a disability insurance calculator that can help the family work through these matters.

CHILDREN BEING SERVED

According to the *Twenty-eighth Annual Report* (www.ideadata.org), a total of 2,219,158 infants, toddlers, preschoolers, and primary-grade students in the birth-to-eight-inclusive age range received services under the IDEA as of December 2000. Part C (Infants and Toddlers) served 279,154 young children in the birth-to-two-inclusive age range that year. Part B, Section 619 (preschool), served 701,949 young children in the three-to-five-inclusive age range. Part B also served 1,237,209 young children aged six to eight inclusive. Thus, of the total, 12.8 percent were infants and toddlers, 31.6 percent were preschoolers, and 55.6 percent were primary-grade children.

The numbers steadily increase. This is so for several reasons. First, it takes time for delays in development to become evident. Second, it requires time for disabilities to be diagnosed. Third, illnesses and accidents occur during the early childhood period, adding new young children to the total as the years go by. We can see the progression if we examine the numbers by age (Table 10–1).

INFANTS AND TODDLERS

The 279,154 infants and toddlers represent 2 percent of all Americans in the birth-to-two-inclusive age range. However, great variation exists within states. To illustrate, consider that the proportion of all infants and toddlers identified as having disabilities or delays in Massachusetts (5.75 percent) is almost five times as large as the proportion identified in Georgia (1.33 percent), according to the *Twenty-eighth Annual Report* (Table 6–1). Possibly, Massachusetts overcounted while Georgia may have undercounted.

The most common location where early intervention services were provided continues to be the home (80 percent). Much smaller proportions were served in early intervention centers (8 percent) or programs for developmental delays (7 percent). The balance (5 percent) of infants and toddlers were scattered among a variety of other settings, including hospitals and residential facilities (U.S. Department of Education, 2005). This continues a strong trend toward ever-more home-based services. In 2000, 72 percent of infants and toddlers were served at home. In 1996, 56 percent were. NEILS, drawing on its sample of 3,338 families with very young children having disabilities or delays in

TABLE 10–1

Disability and Delay by Age: Early Childhood Years.

AGE	NUMBER OF CHILDREN	PERCENT OF ALL ECSE CHILDREN
<1	40,236	1.8
1–2	89,205	4.0
2–3	149,713	6.7
3–4	156,988	7.1
4–5	246,592	11.1
5–6	298,369	13.4
6–7	365,263	16.4
7–8	409,742	18.5
8–9	462,204	21.0

Source: www.ideadata.org in Tables 6–1 and 1–7, as of December 1, 2004.

development, agreed that the home was the most frequent location for delivery of early intervention services.

The *Twenty-eighth Annual Report* added more details about infants and toddlers who are served under Part C. With respect to race and ethnicity, 60 percent were white, 15 percent were African American, and 21 percent were of Hispanic origin; the balance consisted of small percentages who were American Indian/Alaskan or Asian/Pacific Islander.

Offering further information about infants and toddlers is the first data report from NEILS (Hebbeler et al., 2001). A study of a sample of families residing in 93 counties located in 20 states, NEILS made important contributions to reinforce the point made by the Census Bureau data that Part C is reaching its goal of serving all eligible infants and toddlers. The major insight offered by the NEILS report is that the ages at which young children are first served seem to be appropriate. There had been concern, as reflected in the first two editions of this book, that early intervention programs may have been identifying and beginning to serve infants and toddlers later than one might desire. In fact, NEILS found that the average age of the child at referral for early intervention services was 15.5 months, and the average age when the IFSP was completed was 17.1 months. The NEILS researchers convincingly showed that these averages obscure the nature of the data. The numbers formed a bimodal distribution, with two peaks—one at 3 months of age (primarily children with disabilities that are visible) and the other at 28 months of age (principally children with delays in development). Figure 1 in their report, reprinted here as Figure 10–1, is eye-opening. It clearly shows that the average of 17.1 months is not the key to understanding age at IFSP. Rather, the critical element is whether the young child has a disability or a delay. This is because children with diagnosed

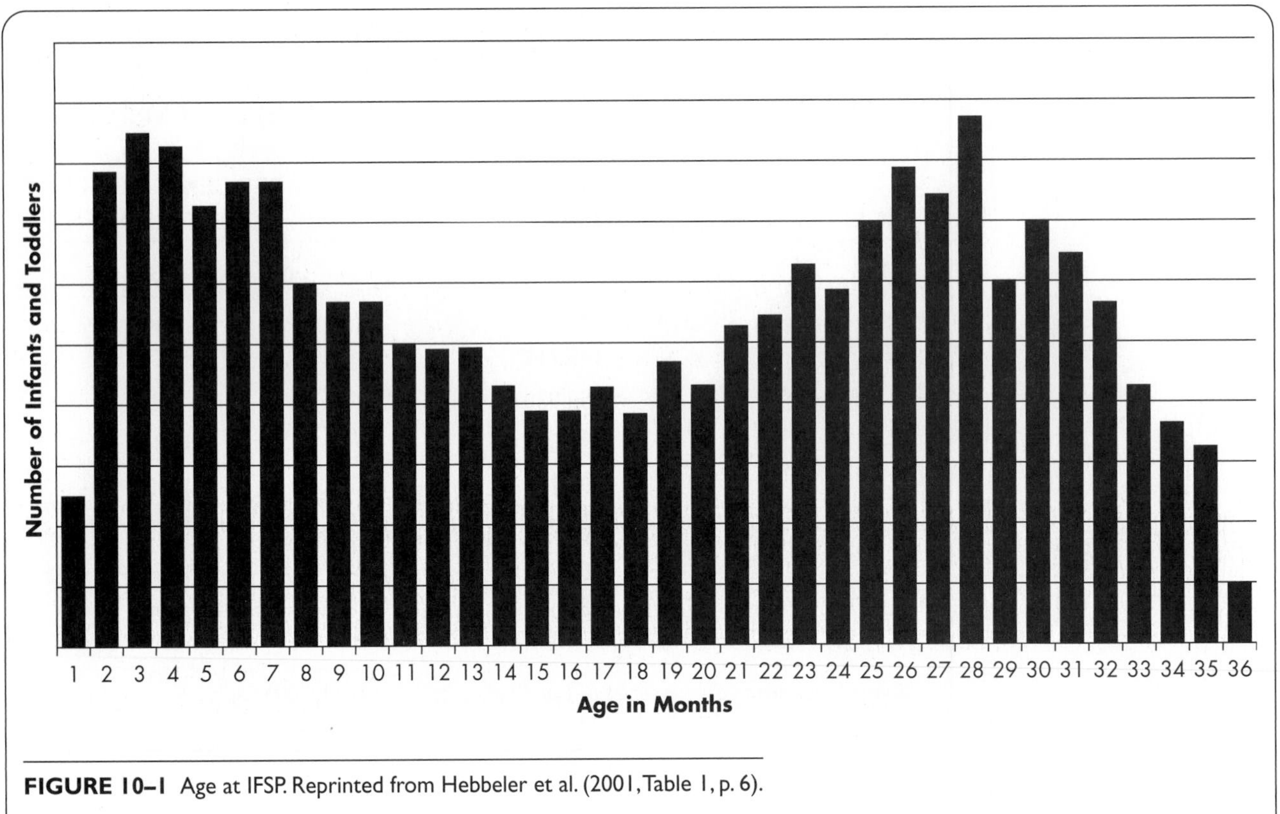

FIGURE 10–1 Age at IFSP. Reprinted from Hebbeler et al. (2001, Table 1, p. 6).

conditions tend to be identified early in life, and those with delays in development tend to be identified much later.

The NEILS report was also helpful in pointing out that the most common kinds of delays or conditions were in the area of communication development and of physical development. Table 5 in the NEILS report (Hebbeler et al., 2001, p. 12) shows that 41 percent of infants and toddlers had speech-language impairments or delays. For example, only 58 percent of those who began early intervention between 12 and 24 months of age could say "mama" or another simple word—something virtually all infants can do by 12 months of age. Another 30 percent had disabilities or delays in the domain of physical development (17.5 percent motor impairment or delay, 6.5 percent in central nervous system disorders such as cerebral palsy, 2.2 percent in physiological or neurological system impairment, 2.0 percent in musculoskeletal disorders, and 1.6 percent in physical growth abnormalities).

Where do toddlers go once they "age out" of early intervention? Not all go on to special education preschool programs. Most (55 percent) do. Although two out of every three (63 percent) are eligible for Part B Section 619 preschool services, some exit with no referrals reported, while others enroll in general preschool programs such as Head Start (U.S. Department of Education, 2005). NEILS also found that most, but not all, toddlers continued to receive special education services after reaching their third birthday (Hebbeler et al., 2004). One helpful point made in that report is that 62 percent of the infants and toddlers served in early intervention were there because of developmental delays, 22 percent because of a diagnosed condition (disability), and 17 percent because of at-risk status. It may be that by the time these children turned three, some of the 79 percent who did not have disabilities were no longer in need of special education services.

PRESCHOOLERS

The *Twenty-fourth Annual Report* indicated that 598,922 young children in the three-to-five-inclusive age range received special education and related services under Section 619 of Part B of the IDEA in 2000–2001. This number represents 5 percent of all preschool-age Americans. In some states, as many as 8 percent of three-to-five-inclusive young children were being served.

Over the past 15 years (1991–2006), the number of preschool-age children with disabilities served under the IDEA's Part B Section 619 has increased from 422,217 to 701,949. That is a 66 percent increase. The most rapid growth occurred in the early 1990s. The first years of the 21st century have seen relatively modest continued increases.

The most frequent classification for these three-to-five-inclusive children is speech or language impaired (SLI) (49 percent), followed by developmentally delayed (35 percent). Few have disability labels such as specific learning disabilities. These facts reflect the difficulty professionals have in reaching definitive diagnoses of children this young.

Preschool-age children with disabilities tend to be served in general preschool programs (about one-third) or special preschool programs (another one-third). About one in every six is served part of the time in a general preschool and part in a special preschool. One in every 10 receives itinerant (visiting) services. A few (3 percent) are served at home or in a reverse mainstream program (a special preschool class into which a number of nondisabled children are placed) (www.ideadata.org).

PRIMARY-GRADE CHILDREN

The *Twenty-eighth Annual Report* (www.ideadata.org) shows that the number served increases with age throughout the primary-grade period:

Age 6: 350,670
Age 7: 402,009
Age 8: 458,835

These children represented, respectively, 16, 18, and 21 percent of all young children in the ECSE birth-to-eight-inclusive age range. Stated differently, 58 percent, or a clear majority, of all ECSE-aged young children are in the primary-grade years.

The *Twenty-seventh Annual Report* (U.S. Department of Education, 2005) provides some additional information about primary-grade children with disabilities, those who are six through eight years of age. Half (52 percent) have the SLI label. One in five (20 percent) is classified as SLD. Other disabilities were far less common. The figures from Table AA7 in the report appear in Table 10–2. The number and proportion with the SLI label and those identified as delayed in development decline after peaking at ages seven and six, respectively. By contrast, the number and proportion with most other labels increase yearly during this age period.

TABLE 10–2

Number and Percentage of Children Aged 6–8, by Disability Classification (2003–2004 School Year).

DISABILITY CLASSIFICATION	NUMBER	PERCENT
All Disabilities	1,211,514	100.0
Speech or language impairments	627,247	52.0
Specific learning disabilities	242,225	20.0
Mental retardation	67,825	5.5
Other health impairments	66,610	5.5
Developmental delay	43,456	3.6
Autism	42,839	3.5
Emotional disturbance	33,135	2.7
Multiple disabilities	22,771	1.9
Orthopedic impairments	15,828	1.2
Hearing impairments	14,340	1.1
Visual impairments	4,353	0.4
Traumatic brain injury	2,825	0.2
Deaf-blindness	1,227	0.02

Source: U.S. Department of Education (2005, Table AA7).

Notice in Table 10–2 that SLIs continue to dominate in the six-to-eight-inclusive age range. Beginning when children are nine years of age, the category "specific learning disabilities (SLD)" assumes top rank. This reflects the requirement over the past several decades that the SLD label may not be used unless schools demonstrate a "discrepancy" between ability and achievement. Importantly, IDEA 2004 removes this requirement. Schools may continue to use a discrepancy-based definition, but they may instead adopt a different one. The discrepancy approach was highly controversial. One reason: we rarely test achievement in young children until third grade. This has the effect of delaying the SLD diagnosis until the child is at least nine years of age. Now that schools need no longer follow the discrepancy formula approach, we may expect to see in coming years more children under age nine with the SLD diagnosis. We discuss these issues further in Chapter 13.

Notice, too, that the number of children in the primary grades with the autism spectrum disorder diagnosis continues to increase. As recently as 2000, there were 25,000 children in the six-to-eight-inclusive age range with this label. They were 2.0 percent of all such children. The latest numbers show that 42,839 children in this age range have the autism label and that they comprise 3.5 percent of all children in that age group. Chapter 15 discusses autism.

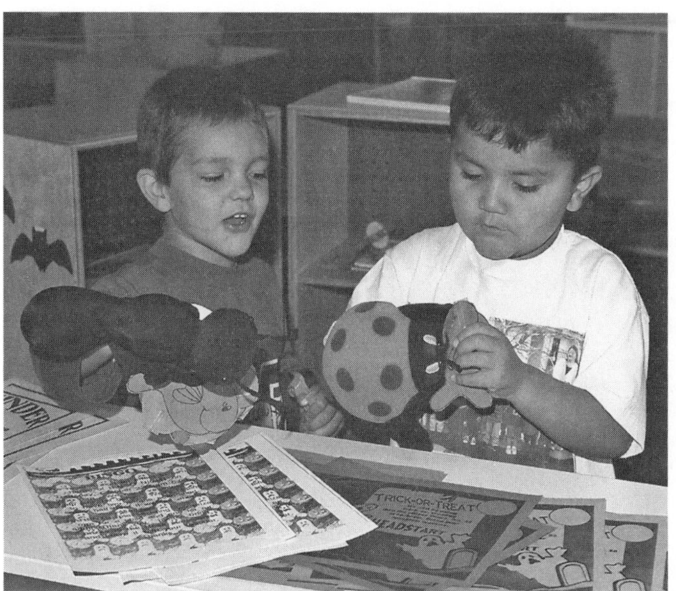

Disability appears to be least common among children from white or Hispanic American families.

As for where young children are educated, the *Twenty-seventh Annual Report* shows that virtually all (97 percent) are educated in neighborhood public school buildings. Six in every 10 spend virtually all of their time in inclusive (general) classrooms. However, the proportions taught in inclusive versus separate (self-contained) classrooms vary sharply by disability. Nine in every 10 (91 percent) of those with the SLI label are placed in inclusive classrooms. A lower but still impressive 51 percent of young children with SLD are in such placements. On the other hand, just 15 percent of young students identified as mentally retarded are in inclusive classrooms, versus 51 percent in separate ones. Those with emotional or behavioral disorders are also more likely to be in self-contained environments (36 percent) than in inclusive ones (32 percent). These placement patterns are becoming ever more important. Because virtually all third graders with disabilities are expected to take high-stakes tests in math and reading, and because test preparation for those assessments is most often provided in general (inclusive classrooms), we may see pressure build for more inclusion of students with disabilities, if for no other reason than to enhance their performance on statewide and district tests.

LABELS

For convenience, researchers, including census takers, use labels in communicating with parents. It is easier to ask a parent to report a single word (e.g., "blind") than it is to ask the parent to explain the child's special needs. However convenient labels may be for this purpose, they sometimes lead to problems. As the five domains are discussed in Chapters 11 to 15, labels are used; the text names and describes some of the more common physical, cognitive, emotional, and other conditions or disabilities that affect children's development. This means using labels. Hence, a few words about labeling are appropriate here.

For many years, professionals in education and related fields have been concerned about negative effects of labeling on children. Nicholas Hobbs (1975) and his colleagues explored the labeling issue at length in their landmark *Issues in the Classification of Children.* They examined sociological implications of labels, including how labels function as a means of social control. That same year, Congress enacted PL 94–142, now Part B of the IDEA. In the 1975 law, Congress explicitly required states to report the conditions (labels) of children being served. The confluence of cautions against labeling in Hobbs et al. and the congressional mandate to report conditions caused professional conflicts that have yet to subside.

Some parents and educators have suggested that a compromise is to "label the service, not the child." That is, rather than refer to a child as having cerebral palsy, one

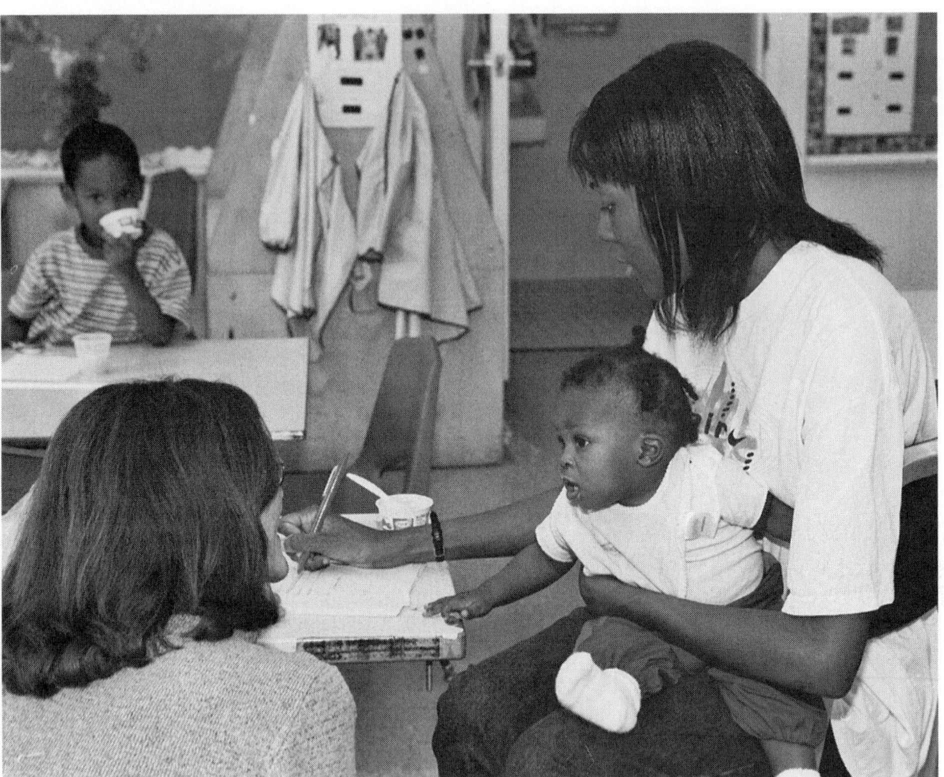

Record keeping—recording the outcomes and results of services and observations—is a key component of ECSE.

would report that the child needs—and is receiving—physical, occupational, and speech pathology services. Writing in the *Harvard Educational Review,* kindergarten teacher Anne Martin (1988) objects strongly to early labeling of young children:

> Our entering children tended to be labeled and pigeonholed through screening and testing procedures. . . . I have been repeatedly dismayed and angered by their effects on the lives of children. . . . One of my brightest students was said to be possibly learning disabled, and my most skilled artist deficient in fine motor ability. My most cooperative learner was "oppositional" and displayed "negative attitudes." . . . The more I remonstrated and gave counterevidence (I was already starting to know these children, after all), the more I was met by grave, implacable insistence on the validity of the judgments. (pp. 488–489; emphasis in original)

By 1986, when the mandate to serve children from birth to five was enacted, Congress was very sensitive to issues related to labeling. Part C explicitly proscribes labeling in favor of broader, less stigmatizing developmental domains such as physical development. The definition of "children with disabilities" in Section 602 of the IDEA was changed in 1990 to allow states to serve three- to five-year-olds with developmental delays and, thus, to avoid labeling children until they reached six years of age. The 1997 IDEA Amendments (PL 105–17) extended that until children reach 10 years of

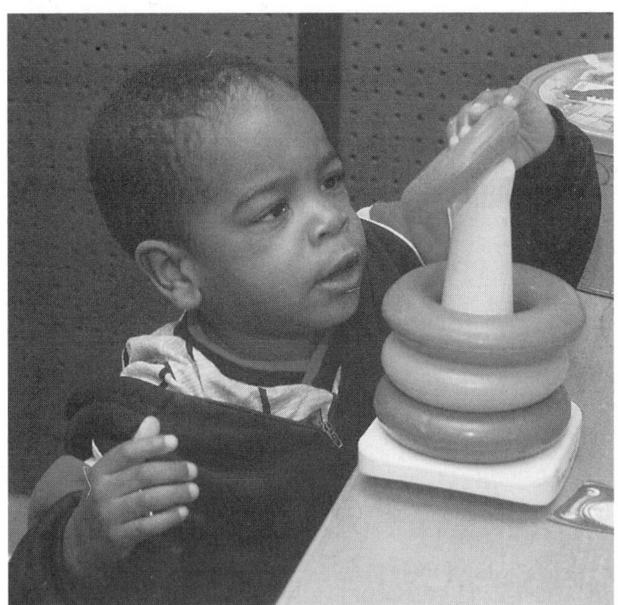

Disability is most frequently reported, according to the Census Bureau, in African American families.

age. One of the guiding philosophies of ECSE as a field is avoidance of labeling. This philosophy preceded the legislation; it followed it in even stronger form. The ECSE preference is clearly to eschew labels whenever possible.

Despite all of this, parents consulting physicians are often told of a diagnostic condition, or disability. They may ask ECSE professionals about these labels. Referrals to Part C and to preschool Part B programs, similarly, are often accompanied by labels. Whether they like it or not, ECSE professionals must deal with labels. That is why this book discusses them.

The issue is not whether to use labels but rather *how* to use them. Certainly, labels must not be used where they are not needed. Children should not be labeled in conversation they, or other children, hear. Labels should be used in reporting only when required by funding, licensing, and other agencies and authorities. Labels may also be used in professional literature—for example, when intervention strategies are described as having been administered with experimental groups and withheld from control groups. In both requisite reporting and professional literature, the intent of using labels is clarity and specificity. To write in a journal article, for example, that young children "have delays in communication development" is to obscure much important information; readers of the article deserve to be told in very concrete terms precisely what kinds of children participated in the experiment (Goodman, 1992). For exactly these reasons, readers of this text have the right to expect specific information, not just generalized observations.

Diversity among ECSE staff optimally should be similar to that in the surrounding communities.

Similarly, when parents mention a label and request clarification on what it means, they have a right to be told by ECSE professionals in specific terms what a given condition usually means and what kinds of interventions have been reported in the literature as effective with children having that condition (see Table 10–3).

Aside from those rather restricted exceptions, ECSE professionals are well advised to eschew use of stigmatizing labels. Their gratuitous use in casual conversation, especially when they are the only characteristics used to describe a child, can be damaging in many ways. Professionals may find themselves unable to get past the label. In spite of their best efforts, they may not be able to escape using the lens the label provides—and may see what they expect to see, based on the label, rather than what the child is actually doing. Parents may lower expectations based on labels. Children themselves may internalize these labels and define themselves by them. For all of these reasons, labels should be used judiciously, cautiously, and rarely.

TABLE 10–3

Labels and Their Meanings.

Label	Meaning
Speech/language impairment (SLI)	There is a speech impediment such as stuttering and/or a language impairment such as a word-finding problem.
Developmental delay	No disability has been diagnosed, but the child is measurably behind age peers in some area(s) of development.
Specific learning disabilities	The child has a reading disability, a writing one, a math one, or an auditory processing disorder, or some combination of these, perhaps with organizational issues as well.
Mental retardation	Measured IQ is below 70 or 75, behavior is not age-appropriate, and the cognitive limitations began prior to age 18.
Emotional disturbance	The child's behavior is very atypical of age peers and/or of typical behavior in a given situation; the child is extremely withdrawn or extraordinarily aggressive toward others and/or toward property.
Autism spectrum disorders	Interpersonal interaction is nonexistent or very atypical, the child does not play well with others and does not engage in pretend play, and verbal behavior is nearly absent.
Orthopedic impairments	The child has cerebral palsy, muscular dystrophy, or other physical disability(ies).
Other health impairments	The child has ADHD, asthma, AIDS, a cardiac condition, epilepsy, or some other health-related condition.
Hearing impairments	The child is deaf or hard of hearing.
Vision impairments	The child is blind or has low vision.
Traumatic brain injury	The child was seriously injured in the head and as a result has short-term memory or sensory or other limitations.
Multiple disabilities	The child has more than one "primary" (educationally important) disability.
Deaf-blind	The child is both deaf/hard of hearing and also blind/has low vision.

FAMILY INVOLVEMENT

Family-friendly programs involve parents and other family members (as defined by the family) and value their input.

A **family-friendly** philosophy took hold in early intervention with infants and toddlers when Congress created Part H (now Part C) in 1986. It has since infused preschool special education as well. This new family-friendly emphasis is revolutionary in human service delivery. Today, family friendliness takes on even more importance. This chapter explores what is meant by two variations on family-friendly philosophies: **family-focused** and **family-centered.** It also discusses **teaming,** an approach in which individuals from

Family-focused

programs see families as partners with professionals, while **family-centered** programs tend to be planned by and conducted with parents, guardians, and other family members in a dominant role.

Teaming

is an approach in which individuals from different professions come together on multidisciplinary teams. Family members are integral parts of such teams.

different professions come together on multidisciplinary teams. Family members are integral parts of such teams.

An important point made by the recommended practices group of the Division for Early Childhood (DEC) is that families be self-defined (DEC Task Force, 1993). That is, the family itself decides who is considered to be "family." Many families of young children with disabilities consist of single mothers, adoptive parents, grandmothers, or other members of an extended family. The NEILS study reviewed earlier in the chapter suggested that large numbers of families with children under six who have disabilities are lower-SES units, with many other pressing needs. This part of the chapter includes some ideas on helping families secure needed literacy training, forge community and interest group linkages, and become empowered to solve their own problems.

Another important issue relating to families is how ECSE programs can increase participation by fathers. Traditionally, the words *parent* and *family* referred, in practice, to mothers. However, some programs are demonstrating innovative thinking on how to get fathers more involved.

EC programs, including ECSE programs, have long valued family involvement. The family-friendly beliefs espoused by ECSE practitioners, beginning in the late 1960s and early 1970s, consistently have included respect for family members, recognition that the family is the major constant in a child's life, and understanding that children's needs cannot fully be met unless the family joins with the program in meeting those needs. Family-friendly approaches involve a way of thinking in which professionals recognize their own natural tendencies to be directive and even to turn parents into lay professionals by instructing them in the tools of their trades. A family-friendly philosophy teaches ECSE program staff to look to the family for identification of resources, needs, and especially priorities while writing IFSPs and IEPs. It also responds to the IDEA provisions granting parents the right to decline both early intervention services and family assessments. The philosophy now is permeating preschool and, to a lesser degree, primary-grade special education as well, despite the fact that Part B is not as explicit on such parental prerogatives.

That families should be involved is a cardinal value defining ECSE as a field. To say that family involvement is important is not to say, however, that this philosophy translates in any uniform way to day-to-day practices in ECSE programs nationwide. Rather, the core value of family involvement is one on which many professionals in the field have strong differences of opinion. They agree that traditional approaches, in which professionals make most decisions unilaterally, are wrong for this field. They disagree, however, on the extent to which ECSE programs should be family-focused or family-centered. Implementing family-friendly values in day-to-day program operations has been—and continues to be—a real problem in many ECSE programs.

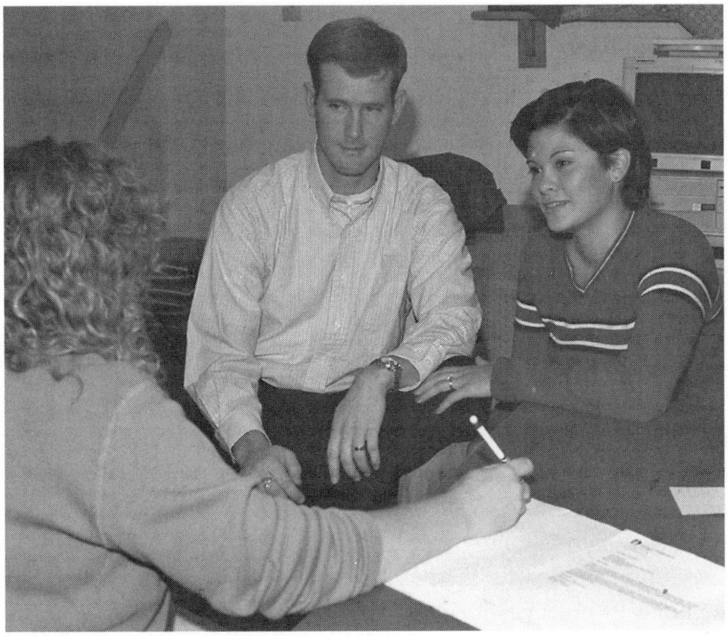

Program-family interactions should be informal, small-group sessions that do not intimidate or overwhelm family members.

TRADITIONAL APPROACHES

The traditional approach, in ECSE as in EC, features the professional in the central role, with support staff and family members revolving around that professional. Mahoney and O'Sullivan (1990) have shown that the most common way in which family members actually have been involved in ECSE programs is very limited; they have been trained by ECSE practitioners to serve as at-home instructors for their children. Casto and Mastropieri (1986a) and White, Taylor, and Moss (1992), reviewing large numbers of studies on family involvement in ECSE, concur with Mahoney and O'Sullivan that home visits and other family-program interactions in ECSE have tended to be limited to training parents to offer therapy and other interventions in the home. Guralnick (1991) adds that "family involvement typically meant parent participation in a series of informational and support meetings" (p. 178).

Donald Bailey of the University of North Carolina has done considerable work on family involvement in ECSE. In one article arising from that work, Bailey et al. (1992) suggest that traditional approaches continued to be standard practice as recently as 1992; that is probably still the case in many programs. They comment that "most programs currently are offering services that are primarily child focused" (p. 73). That should not be a surprise, because most ECSE personnel were trained in "child-focused" or "professional-focused" methods (Bailey, Simeonsson, Yoder, & Huntington, 1990; Bailey et al., 1991). Another reason for the persistence of professional-focused approaches is the continuing existence of traditional state licensing and other requirements governing who may deliver services. A third is professional accountability; professionals may feel that they cannot protect themselves against liability or other accountability claims unless they are permitted to make decisions with which they are comfortable.

Whatever the reasons, the evidence is that ECSE personnel do know they need training in family-friendly thinking. A survey of program administrators and service providers in six states (Johnson, Kilgo, et al., 1992), for example, found that professionals recognized their needs for training in family-friendly approaches. Asked to rank-order a variety of training topics, administrators, supervisors, and service providers in programs for infants and toddlers all ranked highest the following training need: "the ability to communicate effectively in response to family concerns and needs" (p. 143). Staff in preschool programs ranked this item high but not as high as did early intervention personnel, perhaps because Part C places far more emphasis on family interactions than does Part B.

What exactly does a "family-friendly approach" mean? How is it different from more traditional approaches? Figure 10–2 offers contrasts between family-friendly and more traditional service delivery approaches. The most striking difference may be that a family-friendly program brings the family into decision making, whereas traditional programs reserve most decision making for professionals.

Note that the family-friendly practices in Figure 10–2 remain ideal more than real in many ECSE programs. The extent to which local programs practice what they preach is a matter of some controversy in the ECSE field today. Among other things, economics plays a role. Providing services during family-friendly hours at locations preferred by the family can be expensive, for example. But there is no disputing the fact that the field is moving away from the kinds of practices identified as "traditional" in Figure 10–2 and toward those called "family-friendly." This widespread recognition of the urgency of learning new and better ways of working with families is part of a "reconceptualization" (Guralnick, 1991) of ECSE practices.

Family-Friendly Approach

- ECSE programs see empowering families and offering supports as their highest goals.
- Family priorities are respected. If family desires, "urgent" services are postponed.
- Family members are key players on IFSP/IEP development teams.
- Services are offered at family-friendly hours (i.e., at the family's convenience), whenever feasible.
- Services are delivered where convenient to the family.
- Family members approve assessments in advance and receive full reports.
- Child care is offered during parent meetings or child therapy/class sessions.
- Family communication is a key part of every staff member's job.

Traditional Approach

- Diagnosis and treatment of the child are the top goals.
- Professionals decide on priorities and inform families.
- Professionals write the plan and give it to parents to sign.
- Professionals and programs have set office hours, at their own convenience, with few exceptions.
- Services are delivered at the professional's office or clinic.
- Professionals decide on, select, administer, and interpret tests and other assessment instruments.
- Parents are on their own with respect to child care arrangements.
- Family communication is delegated to a low-ranking staff member.

FIGURE 10–2 Family-friendly versus traditional.

A "RECONCEPTUALIZATION"

During the late 1980s, what Guralnick (1991) called "a major reconceptualization" of the family's role in ECSE service delivery took place. Spurring this change was PL 99–457, the 1986 federal law that created the Part H program and greatly expanded the preschool Part B program. In hearings held in Washington, D.C., as well as in committee reports accompanying the law, a new view of family involvement began taking shape. Variously called "family-focused" or "family-centered," this approach emphasized family involvement not so much in assisting with service delivery as in determining priorities and in deciding what services would be delivered and how they would be provided. Families moved, in this reconceptualization, from positions of subservience to professionals into positions of decision makers and full partners in planning.

Today, there is broad consensus that parents should not be limited to surrogate provider roles. Similarly, there is wide agreement that families should participate in decision making on behalf of their children. The question today is how best to support families in these new roles. At issue is the relative centrality of the family in program design, planning, and operation. That is, disagreement remains as to the extent to which family members participate in (as equal partners) or actually control (as final decision makers) what is done in ECSE programs on behalf of the child and the family (Goodman, 1994). The words *family-focused* and *family-centered* are used to describe these two variations on current practice.

FAMILY-FOCUSED PROGRAMS

Family-focused programs seek to empower families, helping them reach their own goals and to function more effectively (Dunst & Trivette, 1988). Traditional programs,

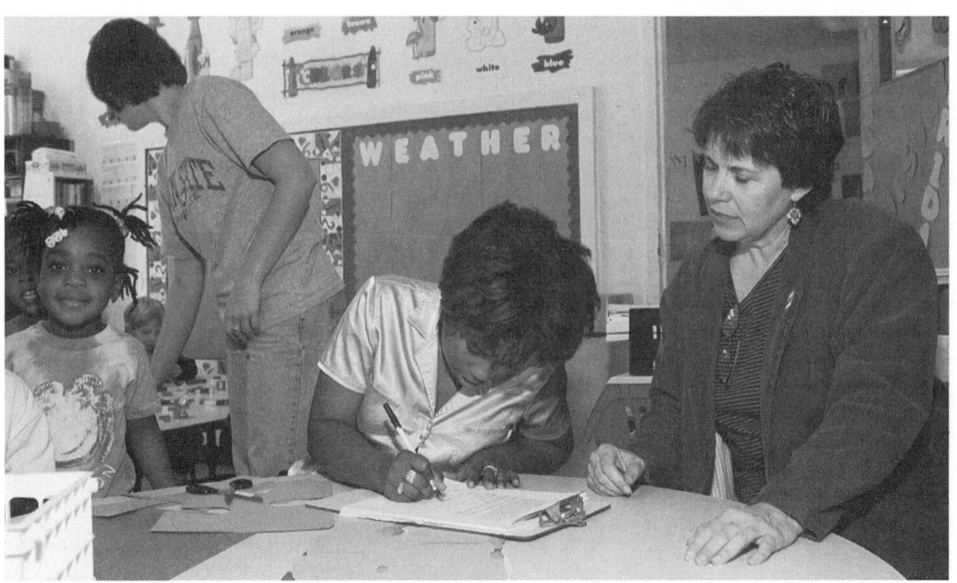

Interdisciplinary planning in advance of and subsequent to IFSP or IEP development is essential so that families receive the support and services they need.

by contrast, see their major role as diagnosing and treating a particular child's problem, regarding family issues as of secondary importance. Similarly, family-focused programs involve parents as peers in assessment and treatment, welcoming parental perspectives and concerns. More traditional programs, by contrast, regard assessment as a strictly professional responsibility, relegating family members' roles to those of passive recipients of professional summaries of outcomes and other results. Family-program communication is regarded as so important in family-focused programs that it is a critical job function for all staff members; in traditional programs, by contrast, a staff aide or even receptionist might be given the principal responsibility of communicating with parents.

Because families with very young children seldom know how to negotiate the maze of social services, family-focused programs appoint a service coordinator whose job is to cut through red tape and get services delivered. On the federal and state levels, such moves were supported as program after program—Medicaid, SSI, Developmental Disabilities, and others—changed their rules, altered their eligibility criteria, and rewrote definitions so as to comply with the needs of families for coordinated, seamless ECSE services. (Those changes were reviewed in Chapter 5.) At the county and local levels, service coordinators empower parents by making them aware of community resources. In some states, this function is performed by a direction center, which is the family's first stop after referral by a family physician or other primary care provider. Such centers tell parents not only about local ECSE programs but also about other social service programs for which the family may be eligible. In yet other cases, where there are no county- or city-wide direction centers, each ECSE program and each service coordinator must perform these vitally important roles.

Today, such practices are widely accepted in ECSE. The issue now is whether and to what extent programs should move even further away from traditional practices and embrace what is called the *family-centered* approach.

FAMILY-CENTERED PROGRAMS

Much of the professional literature in the 1990s used the term *family-centered approach* to describe what some experts believe ECSE programs should do. The titles of professional articles are revealing: "Family-Oriented Early Intervention Policies and Practices: Family-Centered or Not?" (Dunst, Johanson, Trivette, & Hamby, 1991); "Building Family-Centered Practices in Early Intervention: A Team-Based Model for Change" (Bailey et al., 1992); and "Creating Family-Centered Services in Early Intervention: Perceptions of Professionals in Four States" (Bailey, Buysse, Edmondson, & Smith, 1992).

Figure 10–3 highlights some differences between a family-focused approach and a family-centered approach. These differences are best explained by noting what is *not* statutorily required by the IDEA. A family-centered program, at least in theory, grants the family the decision-making authority on virtually every aspect of ECSE services. The process of assessment offers a good example of how the law does not place parents in quite that position. The IDEA, however, explicitly states that assessments are to be "multidisciplinary"—that is, conducted by professionals who are trained in different aspects of assessment and evaluation. It provides that family members are to be integral members of such teams. That is not to say that the IDEA envisions families directing child assessments. Family assessments, however, by law must be family-directed. The parental role in child assessment principally is one of granting advance written permission to a program's request that child assessment occur. The IDEA, in sum, does not go quite as far as a family-centered approach might suggest.

Another way of describing the difference is to say that under a family-centered approach, parents and professionals are not coequal partners. Rather, the parents exercise ultimate authority over what is done, how it is done, and who does it. Under a family-focused approach, however, professionals share power with parents on an equal basis and consensus governs decision making. What family-focused programs do not do but the

Family-Focused Approach

- Family and ECSE program jointly decide on priorities and services outlined in IFSP/IEP.
- Families make global decisions on goals; program staff make technical decisions.
- ECSE programs teach families how to help children at home.
- Family members serve as equal partners in child assessments, but the multidisciplinary team conducts them.
- Family members set annual goals, but ECSE staff select curricula and materials.
- Family members and ECSE staff work as a team to select placements and levels of integration.

Family-Centered Approach

- Families decide on IFSP/IEP contents, including priorities and services. They may veto staff ideas.
- Families make both global and specific decisions, which ECSE program staff then implement.
- ECSE programs teach home care skills only if the family requests that help.
- Family members may, if they wish, decide all aspects of child assessments, even technical details.
- Family members may, if they wish, choose not only goals but also curricula and materials.
- Family members may, if they wish, choose placements and/or levels of integration.

FIGURE 10–3 Family-focused versus family-centered approaches.

family-centered approach implies should be done is to give parents the ultimate decision-making authority, even over selection of curricula, materials, and methods. Note that law authorizes family-focused approaches; it does not require family-centered techniques. ECSE programs that continue to be family-focused are not out of compliance with the law. The IDEA envisions partnerships in which parents make the broad decisions—whether their child needs help, what the goals should be—and professionals, in consultation with family members, make subsequent decisions and recommendations that draw on their special knowledge. Such an approach is what this book calls *family-focused.*

EMPOWERING FAMILIES

Empowerment
is the process of helping people feel as if they are in control. It involves feelings as well as facts.

Respite services
are early intervention services offering breaks for family members from child care.

Empowerment involves feelings as well as facts. Empowered families feel as if they are in control; stated differently, empowerment is a shift from professional to parent of control over what happens in ECSE programs. Guralnick (1991) argues that early intervention (and, by extension, preschool special education as well) is most effective when it focuses on empowering families. Affleck, McGrade, McQueeney, and Allen (1992) concur; supporting and enhancing "natural parent-child relationships" is far more important than training parents to be surrogate service providers. White et al. (1992) and Guralnick (1991) review research showing that little long-term benefit for children or for families is associated with the traditional approach of parents-as-trainers, alone. The aim, Guralnick (1991) proposes, should not be only to train parents as caretakers capable of providing direct services to children but rather to empower families more broadly to function effectively.

The Variety Children's Learning Center (VCLC) in Long Island, New York (see Figure 10–4), has learned from over 30 years of working with families that empowerment

The Variety Children's Learning Center (VCLC) in Syosset, New York, has demonstrated innovative ways of empowering families. The program, founded in the mid-1960s by Judith Bloch, involves family members in all aspects of service delivery. The Variety center specializes in work with young children having behavior and/or emotional disorders. The program uses what it calls "The Five Ps" (Parent/Professional Preschool Performance Profile) to obtain parent input on goals, needs, and objectives (Bloch & Seitz, 1989). The Variety social worker trains family members how to complete the instrument. Parents and program staff then independently rate the child's performance both at home and in the classroom. These ratings lead directly to intervention goals and objectives.

Bloch and Seitz (1989) report that parents take part in four separate assessments over the two-year period in which children typically are enrolled at the program. These assessments look at self-help, motor skills, language, social and emotional development, cognitive activities, and classroom adjustment. Where parents indicate priority needs, the program staff accepts those: "the behavior items become the goals" (p. 227). Staff-parent divergences in ratings are rare; Bloch and Seitz report that teacher-parent correlations were strong, suggesting that parental ability to judge behaviors was good (p. 240).

In addition, VCLC offers **respite services,** social and recreational activities, child care, and educational support to family members. Supports are emphasized, both by ECSE program staff and by other families. As Bloch and Seitz (1985) put it: "Parents become confidants, form mutual-aid networks, and often assume the role of a caring extended family" (p. 7). Two afternoons each week, and every Sunday, the building is open to families for respite care as well as social and recreational activities.

This comprehensive approach emerged over a period of years. Initially, Bloch and Seitz (1985) report, families came to the center seeking help for the child but did not see themselves as potential program clients. In fact, some family members found it demeaning that program staff even brought up the possibility of family services. "Therefore, we chose to remain sensitive both to their needs and to their rights, to decide whether or not their family or they were clients" (p. 11)

FIGURE 10–4 How one program does it.

The role of the father in early childhood programs is just now being recognized after a long period of neglect. Some ECSE programs have found that fathers are excellent volunteers and recruiters of other fathers.

activities are not only desirable but indeed necessary for programs to succeed in helping both family members and young children with disabilities. Many ECSE programs find that **family support groups** are a helpful mechanism for empowering families. VCLC offers a number of such groups.

Family support groups are loosely organized bodies of parents and other family members who come together, often at an ECSE center, to share information and offer each other assistance.

INVOLVING FATHERS

Since their beginnings, EC and ECSE programs alike have tended to accept without much questioning but also without much effort to change things that "parent" and "family" translated, in almost all instances, to "mother" (Pearl, 1993). The family member most often accompanying the child to service appointments was the mother; she also was typically the only family member attending parent-program meetings. It was not until the late 1980s that child care literature began to focus on the fact that fathers, too, had much to contribute in EC services and began to recommend that EC and ECSE programs actively bring fathers into programs serving their children.

Pearl (1993) comments that fathers may not participate as actively in the day-to-day care of young children as do mothers, but their acceptance of a child's disability or delay is essential to the entire family's response to the child's special needs. Few studies have looked at fathers' perceptions of ECSE programs and service needs

According to the Association for the Fathers Network (www.fathersnetwork.org), fathers are more likely to attend meetings if goals, times, and procedures are clearly specified in advance. Program staff should conduct needs assessments among fathers prior to a meeting, using priorities expressed in the survey to demonstrate to fathers, both in the invitation letter and follow-up phone calls, that the support group sessions will be specific and concrete, responding to issues they themselves have raised. Each session should begin—and end—with roundtable comments from all participating fathers. The session leader should target discussion toward feelings, avoiding abstract or intellectual discussions that are not on target. Program staff should follow up after group sessions by providing fathers with specific information on community resources and other solutions to problems identified during the group discussion.

Further work on involving fathers has been done at the Beach Center on Families and Disabilities at the University of Kansas. This center offers a video, *Including Fathers: Strategies for Service Providers* (1997), as well as article reprints on the topic. For more information, visit the center's Web site at www.beachcenter.org, or write to 3111 Haworth Hall, University of Kansas, Lawrence, KS 66045.

SIBLINGS

The VCLC (see Figure 10–4) has shown that an important part of making a program family-friendly is providing support to families with respect to siblings who do not have disabilities or delays. Siblings are often overlooked, just as fathers are. However, both have important contributions to make. Brothers and sisters of children with disabilities may resent the seemingly excessive attention given to the child with special needs. Such anger may, in turn, produce acting-out behavior as the sibling seeks attention. These problems may be overcome in a number of ways. ECSE staff may suggest to parents that they set aside time for each sibling, perhaps a Saturday morning breakfast out each week. Other ideas include bringing the child with a disability to events such as plays, athletic contests, and concerts in which the sibling is performing, to counterbalance those occasions on which he must go places and do things with his brother or sister who has a disability.

Other sibling-related problems include instances in which children and adolescents are—or feel they are—forced prematurely into adult roles. They may be surrogate caregivers, especially when parents or other primary caregivers need respite. When a child is deaf, hearing children sometimes become "interpreters," hearing what is spoken and translating that into ASL. While some children adjust well to such roles, others report feeling rushed into adulthood and denied their right to enjoy childhood and adolescence. ECSE workers may suggest to parents that they watch siblings closely for such reactions. Most parents know that siblings who have no disabilities do have needs and that those needs are as important to these children as are the disability-related needs of other children. Parents may, however, benefit from occasional gentle reminders to give all of their children quality time and not allow a crisislike atmosphere in the home to overwhelm the day-to-day functioning of the family.

A good resource is the Siblings Support Project, a unit of the Children's Health Care System, in Seattle. It offers a well-received book by Meyer and Vadasy (1996), *Living with a Brother or Sister with Special Needs: A Book for Sibs*; sponsors a "SibKids" e-mail group for young brothers and sisters; and issues a newsletter, *Sib to Sib*. A *e-mail group* is an electronic service linking many e-mail users who share an interest in a specific subject. For information, visit www.thearc.org or write to the Siblings Support Project, Children's Hospital and Medical Center, PO Box 5371, CL-09, Seattle, WA 98105-0371. See also "The Impact of ADHD on Siblings" (www.helpforadd.com).

Especially useful may be efforts by parents to arrange for a child with a disability to have more opportunities to function as a "big sister" or "big brother" to younger siblings. Such chances are too often overlooked, yet they have tremendous potential for the entire family. A child with a disability takes as much pride in guiding younger sisters and brothers as do children without disabilities. He enjoys being assigned by parents as temporary surrogate caregiver. ("You're responsible for Susie while we're away this afternoon. And, Susie, John's in charge. Do what he says.") Such assignments also help siblings see their sister or brother as a whole person, not just someone with a disability.

TEAMING

The IDEA calls for family members to join professionals on teams to plan individualized services. The plans for infants and toddlers (IFSPs) are to be reviewed twice a year and, if necessary, revised. For preschoolers and primary-grade children with disabilities, the plans (IEPs) must be reviewed and/or revised at least once annually.

IFSP and IEP team meetings are intended to be forums for discussion. They are not voting sessions (if they were, of course, family members would be outnumbered and thus outvoted by staff members). Earlier editions of this text demonstrated that at times there has been confusion about roles and responsibilities. The general rule, as the process is envisioned in the IDEA, is for family members and professionals to seek consensus. Minke and Scott (1993) observed teams in action during the early 1990s. They found that professionals typically respected family members' views about annual goals and priorities. However, professionals commonly reserved for themselves the prerogative to determine which instructional and assessment methods to adopt. Those can be, and often are, appropriate divisions of labor, because professionals have much more knowledge about educational techniques and assessment tools.

At the early-intervention level, especially, resource constraints increasingly are affecting team functioning. In many states, reimbursement of expenses is available only for "face time"—the periods of time when professionals work directly with children. This means that programs may not be compensated for the time that professionals and paraprofessionals spend in family-program team meetings. In addition, funding limits may also reduce the number of staff available to serve on teams and to limit program ability to pay staff members for evening and weekend team meetings.

There are rising constraints on the family side, as well. With both parents of many young children employed full-time, there may be no family member available to attend daytime team meetings. Understandably, mothers and fathers may prefer evening or weekend team meetings.

How might ECSE programs respond to these pressures? Jung (2005) looked at how early intervention programs are grappling with these issues. Noting that what she calls the "problem-centered focus" (p. 21), as illustrated in the chapter-opening quote, could result in family members relying on professionals rather than assuming responsibilities themselves, Jung suggests that a "primary service provider model" (p. 21) be adopted. In this approach, the professional who is trained in the domain most of concern to the family serves as the team leader. This person makes the home visits, at a time convenient to the family. Other ECSE staff members play supportive roles. They do not make home visits unless the family and the lead professional agree that their in-person services are necessary. This model emphasizes empowering the family. It also has the advantage of reducing the number of professional visits to the home, and in that way helps to control costs.

Minke and Scott (1993), observing teams in action, were disturbed by failures they witnessed in collaboration and joint decision making. Specifically, they found instances of program staff withholding information from parents and other cases in which goals and objectives were entered into written plans without parental knowledge. They suggest some possible steps to avoid such problems, including the following:

1. Goals should be family-set, reflecting family priorities and concerns. They should not be staff-selected goals presented to parents for approval.
2. The final set of goals in the plan should be presented to the family prior to implementation. Program staff should regularly check back with families to ensure that their goals for the child and for themselves have not changed.
3. Family assessments, if conducted, should be fully and openly discussed in advance with family members. They should understand how the assessment would be conducted and how information would be used. Their statutorily defined right to direct this assessment must be made clear to them.

Professionals may also differ in their opportunities to contribute to the process. Teaming ideally involves all team members and gives each a chance to offer information and to participate in decision making. When the process works as envisioned in the IDEA, it can be surprisingly effective; research by Garshelis and McConnell (1993) found that teams were more successful in identifying and understanding family concerns than was even the single most knowledgeable and experienced team member acting alone. Team members may, however, bring sharply contrasting views of the child's needs, service priorities, and desirable interventions. Understandably, professionals tend to see problems and identify solutions to which their training and experience make them sensitive. It takes time, in many instances, before people begin to understand the need for and appreciate the value of the potential contributions of other disciplines.

Other considerations are more practical. One may be archaic state reimbursement rules. Some states reimburse programs and personnel for direct service hours (time spent treating a child) but not for planning or meeting hours (time spent in teams). Such pay arrangements may discourage participation by some team members. Perhaps the most central concern about teaming in many ECSE programs is that of the amount of time required for teams to work. It is not just that effective teams do not come together overnight but require many months or even years to develop, as already pointed out; more practically, it is that each member of the team likely has a very large caseload and many other pressing obligations. Just getting the whole team together in one place at one time may be quite an accomplishment.

In focus groups, DeGangi, Royeen, and Wietlisbach (1992) found that despite such pressures, teams can be effective. They identify the ability to listen as perhaps the most important characteristic of effective team members. Also critical are cultural competency and sensitivity, as when white team members react appropriately to behavior different from that they themselves would have exhibited. Highly valued are professional knowledge and competence when staff members communicate their unique information in a warm and caring way. DeGangi and her colleagues identify problem solving and empowerment as areas of training from which professionals may emerge as better team members. Minke and Scott (1993) add that professional offering of information so that parents can make informed decisions is another critical element in successful teams.

ETHICAL ISSUES

Issues are questions on which well-informed individuals have differences of opinion. In ECSE, there are many such questions. Particularly important are issues about what services ECSE should and should not provide. Professionals and paraprofessionals working in ECSE programs need to know when to accede to family desires and when to contest family preferences. Also important for ECSE workers are ethical issues about which family members often seek consultation and advice.

PRENATAL SERVICES?

The first issues we review here relate to the ever-greater capacity of medical science to intervene prior to birth. It has long been recognized that good prenatal care for expectant mothers is in the best interests both of the woman and of the child. We have known for about a decade that it is possible to identify likely conditions, including disabilities, prior to birth. That capacity continues to pose ethical dilemmas for many people. What is even more recent is the potential of surgery to ameliorate or even prevent disabilities prior to birth. If an unborn child is known to have a condition, and if surgical intervention could alter that condition, how should family members make decisions about such prenatal surgeries?

The first observation we need to make here is that the IDEA authorizes services from birth to the year in which children turn 22 years of age. For our purposes here, the operative term is *from birth*. Prenatal services are explicitly excluded. Accordingly, whatever decisions families make, they cannot look to ECSE programs to finance those interventions.

That being said, family members may consult with ECSE professionals for information and advice. Accordingly, ECSE workers should become knowledgeable about the issues involved and should remain current with the professional literature. A good source on prenatal tests is www.baylorhealth.com.

Prenatal tests are available, if requested by families, to screen for some conditions. The most prominent among these is Down syndrome, which includes mental retardation as well as cardiac conditions and characteristic facial features. At about 11 weeks, the first screen may be performed. It measures the mother's levels of two pregnancy-related proteins, PAPP-A and free beta hCG, and also the thickness of the skin of the fetus. Down syndrome causes thicker skin. One month later, women are offered a "quadruple screen" blood test during the second trimester (three-month period) of pregnancy. The test looks for four proteins: alpha-fetoprotein, total hCG, estriol, and inhibitin A. Results of these tests are entered into a computer program together with the woman's age. The program produces an estimated risk that the baby has Down syndrome. According to studies reported in professional journals, including the prestigious *New England Journal of Medicine,* these procedures, taken together, can detect up to 95 percent of instances of Down syndrome (Malone et al., 2005).

Not all prospective mothers want the tests done. If the family will not do anything differently based on test results, whether for religious or other reasons, there is no point in doing the tests. The tests cost between $200 and $800, and typically they are not covered by health insurance.

Many families will benefit in assessing the risk from consultation with ECSE professionals who can tell them about the quality of life that people with Down syndrome may achieve. About 80 percent of women told that there is a risk of Down syndrome elect to abort the fetus. This choice is a difficult one and should be made only after weighing the pros and cons. Among the considerations that should be weighed so that families reach informed decisions is that the computer programs produce a risk estimate. What is a "high" risk is a judgment call. Some women will consider a 1-in-300 (0.3 percent) risk to be high. Others will not. A woman who is in her late 30s and has tried for many years to become pregnant will assess the issues differently than will one who is in her late teens and feels she will easily become pregnant again. People need to be reminded that false positives are many, particularly when the prospective mother is older; for this reason, there is a risk of aborting a fetus that does not have Down syndrome. Especially helpful to families may be referral to a parent group where the prospective parents may meet adults with children who have Down syndrome and also talk with adults who themselves have Down syndrome.

Adults with disabilities and others who have thought deeply about these issues have strong views on these matters. ECSE professionals may benefit from reading a very thoughtful article, "The Problem with an Almost-Perfect World" (Harmon, 2005). This unusually sensitive mass media piece opens by quoting an adult who has Down syndrome, as well as mothers and fathers of children with disabilities. The issues they raise are important. Among other things, they express concern that if most pregnant women order prenatal tests, and most of those opt for abortion based on risk estimates, the result over time will be a smaller number of Americans with disabilities. As a consequence, society will feel less of a need to accommodate for persons with disabilities. That, in turn, will diminish the quality of life enjoyed by Americans who do have disabilities. It may even lead to **genetic discrimination**—people may be denied jobs, training, and/or insurance on the grounds that they carry genetic predispositions for certain diseases or disabilities. For a thoughtful review of these issues, see Parens and Asch's book *Prenatal Testing and Disability Rights* (2000). Parens is a senior research scholar at The Hastings Center, a think tank on ethical issues located north of New York City. Asch is the Edward and Robin Milstein Professor of Bioethics at Yeshiva University in New York City. A longtime member of the National Federation of the Blind (NFB), she was recently recognized by NFB as "Blind Educator of the Year." Readers of previous editions of this text will recall Asch's previous affiliation with Wellesley College in Massachusetts.

Genetic discrimination is decision making on the basis of an individual's real or perceived genetic characteristics.

Also weighing in with thoughtful opinions about prenatal tests is Little People of America (www.lpaonline.org). This self-advocacy group of dwarfs notes that little people are quite normal in virtually all respects except for height. They worry about a future in which dwarfs are aborted prior to birth without regard for all of the positive characteristics and talents they may have if the pregnancy were carried to term.

ECSE professionals and family members might also consider the "slippery slope" aspect of prenatal diagnosis and intervention. We have known for some time, for example, that ADHD are genetic in origin, at least in part. There is an inborn predisposition toward hyperactivity, impulsivity, and inattentiveness that is translated into a disorder by environmental factors that we are just beginning to understand. Should prenatal tests that screen for ADHD-related factors become widely available, should prospective mothers abort as a response to a report of "high risk" of giving birth to a child with ADHD? Today, that question likely strikes most readers as absurd. It may not be seen that way in years to come. The temptation to "permit birth" only for "perfect" fetuses may become irresistible. Even if we reject this thesis, we must still recognize that it causes us to ask, Where do we draw the line? With which fetuses having what severities of which disabilities do we as a society consider abortion to be appropriate? Further down the road are prenatal surgical interventions. Again, should we attempt those when a fetus has ADHD? If not, where is the line dividing acceptable from unacceptable interventions?

Genetic engineering, also called *gene therapy,* is a process in which interventions are effected to eliminate or at least alleviate a condition. Prior to gene therapy, a pregnant woman had only two choices in responding to fetal test results: proceed to term, or abort the fetus. Genetic engineering gives her a third option: to "fix" the fetus.

GENE THERAPY

A related field, one that is further afield than is surgical intervention, involves the use of defanged viruses as vectors (delivery mechanisms) to insert into the body genes that are missing or, if present, are damaged. The promise of **genetic engineering** or gene therapy, as it is more popularly known, has excited researchers for many years. Results to date have been few and far between. Now, however, the field seems to be maturing to the point where researchers believe that they can solve the many complex problems that prevented success in past years. In particular, new techniques permit genes to be transported only to specific parts of the body, so as to minimize harmful side effects. They are also delivering very small amounts of genetic material, at least until they are satisfied that extensive experience demonstrates the safety of the procedures. The current state-of-the-art features new ways of turning on the new genes (and, if needed, turning them back off), new and safer transporters (e.g., the common adeno-associated virus [AAV], which does not cause disease in humans), and more effective mechanisms for sending genes to precisely the locations where they are most needed (and not where they might cause havoc by interacting with other metabolic processes).

If, indeed, the technologies are becoming more feasible, we may need to ask questions about whether and when genetic engineering is appropriate. The temptation to use the techniques for "designer babies"—that is, to design the DNA of a fetus for the athletic talent, intelligence, and good looks desired by the parents—may well prove irresistible (Cowley, 1990). The fact that genetic engineering will first be available to people who can afford the high costs raises another issue: should we as a society make gene therapy available to poor persons as well? These are challenging questions. It is probably fortunate, then, that we may have a very long wait before we need to confront such issues. First, despite the tendency of mass media to say that a particular gene "causes" a given disability, the fact is that it is proteins that are more typically the active agents. When genes are expressed, as scientists say, it is through the proteins whose construction they guide that they are expressed. For these reasons, gene therapy may well require medicine to learn how proteins act. We are a long way from comprehending how the folds of proteins affect their work (see, e.g., Socolich et al., 2005).

In addition, the cautionary words of Hubbard and Ward (1993) still apply: most characteristics of humans, including disabilities, result not from one, or even a few, but rather many genes interacting in ways that we still do not understand. More recently, scientists have come to realize that chemical and environmental factors are at least as important as genes in affecting the behavior of proteins. This is why genetic tests result in risk assessments rather than definitive diagnoses. We have long known that one person with a gene gets a disability, whereas another with the same gene does not. These other causative agents may well be why.

Finally, the 98 percent of our genetic makeup that once was called "junk DNA"—the snippets of our DNA that do not seem to code for proteins—may not be junk after all. They seem to play a role in creating the messenger molecules known as RNA and, in that way, control important cell functions. All in all, contrary to the excited chatter of researchers, genetic engineering may be a generation removed from reality.

SURGICAL INTERVENTIONS

Just as many people who have not given much thought to the matter might summarily conclude that "of course" a fetus suspected of having a disability should be aborted, so too will many say that "of course" surgical interventions that might improve the bodies and perhaps the lives of children with disabilities should be performed. Every year thousands of infants, toddlers, preschoolers, and primary-grade children who are deaf are implanted with devices designed to enhance their hearing. Surgical intervention is also widely available to make little people (dwarfs) taller. Several hundred little people have surgeries that add a few inches to their height.

But is surgical intervention always a "good"? As with prenatal medical procedures, many questions need to be asked. One is often overlooked. A child is, unlike a fetus, a human being with opinions, hopes, and desires. Should the child's views on surgery be a consideration? Even if they take the decision as being properly theirs to make, parents may nonetheless benefit from consultation and advice that helps them to think through the often-complex issues involved.

Thoughtful examination of these issues is offered by The Hastings Center, in Garrison, New York (www.thehastingscenter.org). One of its recent publications is *Surgically Shaping Children* (Parens, 2006). Erik Parens's introductory chapter is a model of balanced thinking about the ethical quagmires involved in making decisions about surgery for children and adults with disabilities. One of the contributors is Paul Steven Miller (2006), whose "Toward Truly Informed Decisions about Appearance-Normalizing Surgeries" explores legal issues that help shape ethical thinking about limb-lengthening in little people. He argues that family decisions must be truly informed ones and that such decisions may only be made after family members seek out, and have thoughtful discussions with, adults with disabilities.

In 1995 the American Academy of Pediatrics (AAP) issued its influential policy statement "Informed Consent, Parental Permission, and Assent in Pediatric Practice" (www.aap.org). The statement says, "Patients should participate in decision-making commensurate with their development; they should provide assent to care whenever reasonable." The academy does not venture to hazard a guess as to the age by which children could be presumed to offer informed consent, but it does emphasize that even young children can contribute to their parents' decisions. In *Surgically Shaping Children*, Miller and Asch relate that even as young children they recall having strong opinions about their bodies and their futures. Asch (2006) particularly cautions that children may perceive parental desires for surgery as indicating rejection ("You are not good enough as you are, so we will fix you").

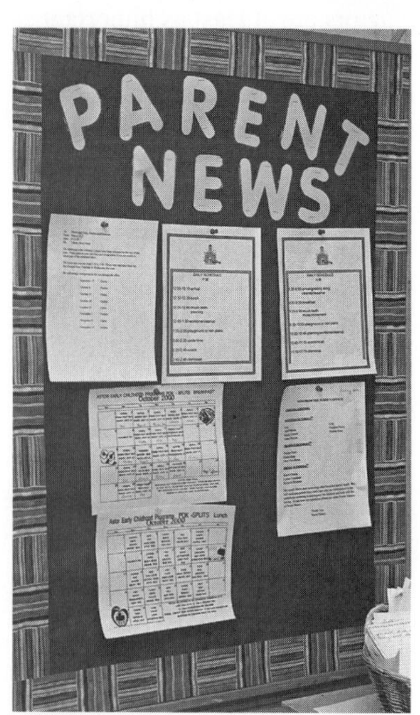

Bulletin boards, whether physical ones or cyberspace-based computer ones, are effective means of disseminating information.

Other considerations are more technical. ECSE professionals might advise families that the cochlear implant decision is an irrevocable one. A child who can hear to some extent with the assistance of a hearing aid no longer will have that ability once the surgery is done. The surgery effectively destroys residual hearing in the implanted ear. Another consideration is that while today's 22-channel implants are very good at helping many children hear environmental sounds, their contributions to speech comprehension are more mixed. Some children become able to talk on the phone and to understand conversational speech with implants, but others do not. A review of these technical issues is offered online by the National Association of the Deaf (NAD), at www.nad.org. The site includes an official NAD position paper about cochlear implants as well as a frequently asked questions (FAQ) page.

With respect to limb lengthening, too, there are both ethical and technical considerations. The procedures involve the breaking of bones. The bone fragments then are separated. A surgical sleeve is inserted between the fragments. The child wears a brace for several months while the bone grows through the sleeve. The procedures are repeated several times over a period of years. The result of these surgeries is alteration of the child's *appearance*. Limb-lengthening surgeries, then, are qualitatively different from surgeries performed to enhance the child's *functioning*—so that the child may breathe, sit, and walk normally. For more about these matters, ECSE professionals will find much help at the Web site of Little People of America (www.lpaonline.org), particularly the FAQ page.

PROGRAM ISSUES

ECSE has a number of issues relating to program matters that are exciting debate. One of these has to do with the overall mission of ECSE as a field. The traditional mission has been called into question by new mandates. Also stirring discussion is inclusion. While it is popular among many families and educators, inclusion may not always be an appropriate choice for young children. A continuing issue relates to diversity, particularly the roles played by adults with disabilities. Finally, another long-standing concern has to do with the field's ability to respond adequately to the special needs of young children who are deaf.

MISSION

As recently as 2002, the mission of ECSE remained as it always was: to offer individualized and appropriate services in response to the unique needs and strengths of young children in all five domains of development (adaptive, cognitive, communication, physical, and social or emotional). The signing of the No Child Left Behind Act of 2001 in early 2002 and the 2004 reauthorization of the IDEA, however, have changed things considerably. Neither NCLB nor IDEA 2004 released ECSE from its traditional responsibilities. Both, however, added new ones.

High-stakes tests in math, language arts, and science now are administered in third grade. The evidence to date, notably from the SEELS longitudinal study (see Chapter 3), is that very large numbers of young children are being retained in grade (held back) in first, second, and third grade. The figures are startling. To illustrate, by third grade, only a small minority of children with disabilities are still with their age peers. The overwhelming majority are in second or even in first grade. Although it may be argued that retention is appropriate because it gives these children more time to master the material that will be assessed in the third- and fourth-grade tests, this massive amount of holding back may also signal something else. It may be that ECSE has not yet adjusted to the new demands for much higher levels of academic achievement in the post-NCLB and IDEA 2004 eras. And it may be that these new requirements, on top of the many mandates dating from earlier years, are proving too much to handle.

Reports from the field indicate that kindergarten increasingly is a full-day program and that in many localities not even a midday nap is allowed, all in the interest of providing more instructional time. Anecdotal accounts from teachers about parents bringing five-year-olds in for extra help, something we used to associate with middle and high school grades, add to the concern. Teachers report that third graders cry out of frustration and that parents are adding to their angst by pressuring these young children ("You have to do well on these tests, or you won't get into a good college").

ECSE as a field needs to engage its different audiences (professionals, family members, etc.) in a dialog about all of this. NCLB comes up for reauthorization in 2007. Congress will hold hearings in the months preceding the actual rewrite of the law. While the IDEA itself will not be rewritten until 2009 or 2010, special educators and families of children with disabilities have much at stake in how Congress revises the NCLB rules. In particular, given the fact that many young children need extensive and very time-consuming support as a result of their disabilities, it is vital that ECSE's traditional "job" of responding to those needs not be compromised. At the same time, we need to ask questions about whether it is appropriate to administer high-stakes tests to children who are so young that they are not cognitively prepared to handle abstract ideas—and high-stakes assessment is, by any definition, an abstract notion. Can we really expect eight- and nine-year-old children to understand and respond appropriately to high-pressure standardized tests? If we can, should we?

INCLUSION

Inclusion is an idea of obvious appeal to many families (Bowe, 2005). It offers their children opportunities for social and emotional development, through interaction with age peers who do not have disabilities. With respect to academics, too, there are benefits: in a period in which high-stakes assessments begin as early as third grade, and "test prep" for those examinations is most intensive in general (inclusive) classrooms, young children with disabilities may do better academically in such settings. In spite of all of this, there are some considerations that may dampen the enthusiasm of professionals and parents alike for inclusion as a placement option in early childhood.

A key concern is that specialized programs that are authorized by and funded under the IDEA are required to employ educators who meet "the highest standards of the state" (to quote the IDEA). Typically, professionals in ECSE programs are state-certified in special education. Many possess master's degrees in the field. They are, then, highly trained in diagnosing and responding to the unique needs of young children with disabilities. Other early childhood programs, by contrast, have no such personnel rules. It is not uncommon to find early childhood teachers and Head Start educators only to qualify for CDA certifications—that is, to have taken a handful of courses on child development. Figure 10–5 summarizes skills that these CDA-certified persons may not have, yet are essential to help children with disabilities.

Another concern has to do with individualization. ECSE programs are well known to customize instruction according to the specifications of an individual child's IFSP or IEP. By contrast, many early childhood and Head Start programs design and carry out instruction for *groups*. Indeed, it is the individualization of ECSE early childhood

1. Ability to observe objectively child and family behaviors relevant to ECSE programming
2. Flexibility to function well in inter-, multi-, and transdisciplinary settings and on teams
3. Good listening skills, including ability to reflect on experience
4. Knowledge of and demonstration of skill in problem-solving behavior
5. Negotiation skills
6. Knowledge of and ability to communicate to families about community supports for families
7. Ability to act as consultant (facilitator) for family members, encouraging family members to be advocates and decision makers for their own child
8. Knowledge and skill in direct service delivery including therapy and other interventions

Adapted from Bennett and Watson (1993).

FIGURE 10–5 Skills essential for ECSE workers.

programs that is most attractive to many families having children with no disabilities. Reverse mainstreaming, in which a handful of children having no disabilities join in at specialized programs, is so popular in some communities that there is a lively lottery to gain coveted seats (see, e.g., Brenna, 2003). PreKNow, the advocacy organization, provides a checklist families may use to identify quality general early childhood programs that individualize services, at least to some extent (see www.preknow.org).

A third has to do with funding. ECSE programs tend to be well funded, spending as much as $15,000 per year per child or even more (Levin et al., 2004). General early childhood programs, by contrast, struggle to find even a fraction of that amount. To illustrate, when New Mexico planned, in late 2005, to expand prekindergarten offerings, lawmakers budgeted just $2,278 per child per year. Even at that level, the state projected that only 1,500 young children could be served, versus 25,000 who could benefit from such services. Nationwide, the picture is similar. For more on this topic, see the National Institute for Early Education Research's annual yearbooks, at www.nieer.org. Another helpful resource is Kauerz (2005), a report on full-day kindergarten published by the Education Commission of the States.

Finally, there is the matter of capacity. ECSE is a zero-reject program. No child with a disability or qualifying delay in development may be denied services. General early childhood programs, by contrast, are available only in certain states and, often, even there, only within specific communities. There is no nationwide zero-reject policy. The resulting scarcity of general (inclusive) early childhood "seats" is another reason why many families scramble to find reverse-mainstreaming "seats" in ECSE programs (Brenna, 2003).

DIVERSITY

Strong majorities of young children in ECSE are boys. There are advantages for boys when their teachers are male. Yet among those working with boys in the one-to-five-year age range, only 1 percent are men, according to the most recent data (2002) from the Study of Personnel Needs in Special Education (SPeNSE) (www.spense.org; Table 6.2). Among those teaching students aged 6–12, just 10 percent are male. Similarly, while large numbers of young children are African American, just 6 percent of the teachers of children aged 1–5 are African American; among teachers of children aged 6–12, the proportion rises to 10 percent (Table 6.4).

All of the young children served by ECSE programs are, of course, persons with disabilities. Many would benefit greatly from being exposed to role models. We also noted, earlier in this chapter, that family members need to talk with adults having disabilities in order to reach informed decisions about medical interventions. Despite all of this, just 7 percent of teachers of children aged 1 to 5 years, and 10 percent of teachers of children aged 6 to 12, consider themselves to have disabilities; only 4.8 percent and 4.0 percent, respectively, are seen by others to have disabilities (Table 6.1).

DEAFNESS IS DIFFERENT

Young children who are deaf have needs that are qualitatively different from those of children with most other disabilities. The whole concept of integration—whether one calls it mainstreaming, least restrictive environment, inclusion, or something else—assumes a fundamentally different meaning when applied to children who are deaf

(Dolnick, 1993). The first and most obvious reason for this is that because such children cannot hear and understand conversational speech through the ear alone, simply placing them in a room alongside children who can hear does nothing to advance interaction. Antia, Kreimeyer, and Eldredge (1994) note that a deaf child placed in a regular nursery or preschool program will likely be ill served unless teachers, aides, and classmates practice special communication methods throughout the day. These researchers found that integration benefits faded once social support intervention ended.

The second, less obvious reason is that the primary challenge in early intervention and preschool special education for young children who are deaf is to help them acquire language. If they learn English, especially if they master reading, they will be well positioned for success in K–12 schools. That is particularly true as technology improves in its ability to convert speech to text. In fact, speech recognition technologies promise to revolutionize the lives of people who are deaf, but *only* if they can read—and read well. Similarly, closed captions have opened up television for enjoyment by people who are deaf and soon will do so even for theatrical movies; again, however, their use requires very well-developed reading skills. For these reasons, the emphasis in programming for birth-to-eight children who are deaf must be on acquisition of the English language.

These considerations bother some ECSE workers, because they appear to call for separate programming for young children who are deaf. But the IDEA's statutory requirements for an appropriate education and for individualized programming mean little unless ECSE staff are flexible enough to recognize that the children's unique needs, not program philosophy, should dictate how services are delivered.

SUMMARY

More than two million young children and their families participate in ECSE. Most (56 percent) are in kindergarten or in the primary grades, another 32 percent are preschool age, and 12 percent are infants or toddlers in early intervention. In this chapter, we saw that delays and disabilities in speech and language are most common among these birth-to-eight-inclusive young children, with delays and disabilities in physical development second in prevalence. Much less common are delays and disabilities in the other three domains: cognitive, social or emotional, and adaptive development. We also saw in this chapter that large numbers of families having ECSE-eligible children are of low-SES. Many, too, are members of ethnic and/or racial minority groups. These families typically face pressures above and beyond those connected to their child who has a disability or delay in development.

This information helps ECSE workers in several ways. First, programs and staff with the competence to run them will be needed in the areas of speech and language development among young children. Chapter 11 takes up that domain. Second, disabilities and delays in the domain of physical development are quite common in the birth-to-eight-inclusive population, particularly among infants, toddlers, and preschoolers. For this reason, physical accessibility of program buildings and classrooms is important. We look at those issues in Chapter 12. Third, the limited incomes and resources of many ECSE families create strain for adults in those families. ECSE workers need to recognize the importance of accepting as "family" whoever family members designate to represent their interests, the need to be flexible in scheduling meetings with family members, and the fact that some families may be embarrassed by home visits from ECSE personnel.

These are examples of how ECSE programs may adopt *family-friendly* approaches. Whether the program elects to follow a *family-focused* structure, in which family members and ECSE professionals are partners with equal standing, or a *family-centered* philosophy, where family members take the lead, the important point is to respect and involve family members. The traditional *child-centered* approach, which had professionals making most decisions, has been discredited. Even in the primary grades, educators should welcome involvement of families and find ways to help families support their young children with special needs.

Family members may consult ECSE professionals about troubling ethical issues, including prenatal tests, genetic interventions, and surgery for young children having disabilities. The appropriate roles for ECSE personnel is to assist family members by providing information as requested and referring the family to helpful community and national resources.

Another set of issues relates to ECSE programs themselves. While NCLB and IDEA 2004 have increased the emphasis on preacademics and academics, neither law relieved ECSE programs from their preexisting obligations to provide appropriate services to help young children in all five domains of development. Indeed, in the view of the author, those responsibilities remain paramount. IDEA stresses appropriateness so much that providing individualized services that respond to the unique needs of young children with disabilities is the choice to make if ECSE professionals cannot at one and the same time fulfill those obligations and also teach academics. If it comes to that, future reauthorizations of NCLB and of IDEA will need to clarify that early intervention and special education are primarily about individually appropriate services, and only secondarily about academics.

Inclusion is often a good idea, but in some instances the approach may not offer appropriate services. Two long-standing program issues continue to call for attention: (1) the need for ECSE staffs to reflect community demographics and to include among their members adults with disabilities and (2) the special, often-misunderstood needs of young children who are deaf.

KEY TERMS

empowerment
family support groups
family-centered
family-focused
family-friendly
genetic discrimination
genetic engineering
respite services
socioeconomic status (SES)
teaming

QUESTIONS FOR REFLECTION

1. Why should ECSE professionals and researchers have information on sex, race, ethnic group membership, disability, delay, and so on, among under-nine children?
2. Why do you suspect many parents reported speech-related conditions among under-six children? What kinds of disabilities feature speech impairments or delays?
3. Why might indiscriminate use of labels harm children?
4. Why might use of labels be acceptable in journal articles that report on large numbers of children, yet not be acceptable in ECSE programs when used to describe particular children?
5. Reflecting on the chapter as a whole, what kinds of needs, other than disabilities, could you expect to find among children served in ECSE programs?
6. In your own words, what is a *family-friendly* approach? How does it differ from *traditional* approaches?
7. Differentiate in as many ways as you can *family-focused* from *family-centered* approaches.
8. What are some practical realities that might make it difficult for ECSE programs to become more family-friendly?

9. In your own words, respond to this question from a prospective parent: "We are undecided about ordering prenatal tests. Can you direct us to some resources that will help us reach an informed decision?"
10. What are some pros and cons of inclusion for young children with disabilities?

PRACTICAL EXERCISES

1. Visit a local EC program (e.g., a Head Start program) or an ECSE program (e.g., a special preschool or an early intervention program serving infants and toddlers). Observe for a morning or an afternoon. Talk with program staff members. Then answer the following questions:
   A. Are the children served demographically similar to those served nationally, as reported in this chapter?
   B. If not, what local factors may account for the differences?
   C. If the program serves infants and toddlers, about how old are those young children when they first receive services?
   D. Do you think this program is finding eligible children early enough?
   E. Are program staff demographically similar to, or different from, families served? Do you think any differences matter to families?
   F. How does the program make itself family-friendly?
   G. Are efforts made to involve fathers? If so, what are those efforts?
2. Talk with ECSE professionals at a local special education preschool program. Does the program enroll any preschoolers who do not have disabilities? If so, how is the reverse mainstreaming being handled? How does the program decide on the number of young children with no disabilities to accept? In the opinion of ECSE professionals at the program, is reverse mainstreaming helping children with disabilities? If so, in what ways? Is it beneficial for the children who have no disabilities? If so, how and why?

WEB SITES OF INTEREST

www.ideadata.org IDEA Data—latest statistics on ECSE

www.sri.com/neils SRI's NEILS Project—the site for this important longitudinal study

www.beachcenter.org Beach Center on Families and Disabilities, at the University of Kansas—good information on including families and fathers in ECSE programs

Communication Development

CHAPTER

Parents were asked to report their children's ability to carry out the several skills of communication—speaking clearly, communicating effectively despite difficulty speaking, carrying on a conversation with others, and understanding what others say—compared with their perceptions of the abilities of other children of the same age.... Substantial numbers of students (from 35% to 45%) experienced at least some difficulty speaking, conversing, or understanding others, and almost three-fourths of those who had difficulty speaking still had some trouble communicating through other means in addition to or instead of speech.... Seventy percent or more of students with a hearing loss whose primary disability classification was learning disability, speech impairment, mental retardation, orthopedic impairment, or traumatic brain injury were reported to have mild hearing losses. (Blackorby et al., 2003, pp. 3-22–3-23)

OBJECTIVES

After reading this chapter, you should be able to:

- Explain why the domain of communication development is so large in ECSE.
- Describe what kinds of impairments are included in this domain.
- Explain how blindness and other vision impairments affect communication.
- Describe what you can do for a young child who stutters.
- Explain how to help a deaf child who has a cochlear implant.
- Explain why a noninclusive preschool program might be the appropriate placement for a young child who is blind.

- Describe what orientation and mobility specialists do.
- Describe how you can help family members enhance communication by young children.

CHAPTER OUTLINE

- OVERVIEW
- PREVALENCE
- DEVELOPMENTAL DELAYS
- ESTABLISHED CONDITIONS
  - Speech and Language Impairments
  - Deafness and Hearing Impairments
  - Blindness and Low Vision
- ASSESSMENT
  - Hearing
  - Speech and language
  - Vision
- INTERVENTION
  - Speech and Language Impairments
  - Deafness and Hearing Impairments
  - Blindness and Low Vision
  - Technology
- WORKING WITH FAMILIES

OVERVIEW

Communication is the number one area of development in which young children have disabilities or delays. NEILS found that most families of infants and toddlers reported concerns in these areas. The most frequent disability classification in preschool special education (IDEA Part B, Section 619) is speech and language impairment (SLI), with 333,000 of the 701,000 preschoolers (47 percent) identified. In addition, many of the 258,000 three- to five-year-olds identified as delayed in development had communication delays; those young children accounted for another 37 percent of all preschoolers served (U.S. Department of Education, 2006c; www.ideadata.org). Disabilities or delays in communication also were found by SEELS to be very common among six- to nine-year-olds. A major reason, which is apparent in the chapter-opening quote from a recent SEELS report, is that communication limitations are frequent not only in children whose primary disabilities are SLI or hearing impairments but also in those with other primary classifications.

Communication is the expression and reception of meaning. It may occur through speech/hearing, reading/writing, signing/seeing, gestures, or other means.

Congress defined **communication** development broadly. In the U.S. House of Representatives committee report on the 1991 IDEA amendments, the Subcommittee on Select Education and Civil Rights, state:

> *[T]he term "communication development" is intended to include language, speech, and hearing. Communication development includes acquisition of communication skills, during pre-verbal and verbal phases of development, receptive and expressive language, including spoken, non-spoken, and sign language means of expression, the use of augmentative communication devices, and speech production and perception. Communication development also includes oral-motor development, specifically those neuromuscular and structural conditions affecting pre-speech oral-motor development, speech sound production, and feeding and swallowing processes. Related to hearing,*

communication development includes development of auditory awareness, auditory, visual, tactile and kinesthetic skills, and auditory processing for speech or language development. (p. 12)

The definition focuses attention on language, speech, hearing, vision, and nonvocal means of communication such as ASL. This chapter addresses normal and abnormal communication development. The disabilities of deafness and blindness, as well as stuttering, are considered, as are interventions to help young children.

PREVALENCE

Prevalence

is the number of cases in a population, as contrasted to incidence, the number of new cases.

Incidence

is the number of new cases annually, as contrasted with prevalence, which is the total number of such cases.

In demographics, the term ***prevalence*** refers to the number of instances of a given condition or characteristic in a population at any one time; the word ***incidence*** refers to the number of new instances or cases per year. This section presents prevalence data. The parallel sections in Chapters 12–15 do the same with respect to other domains of development.

The *Twenty-eighth Annual Report* (U.S. Department of Education, 2006c, www.ideadata.org) shows that SLI continues to be the number one classification through age eight, at which point specific learning disabilities assume the top spot. Among three-year-olds, 58,000 have the SLI label; the number rises annually to a peak of 192,000 at age eight. Hearing impairments, by contrast, are relatively uncommon in the ECSE age range, with just 2,000 three-year-olds to 5,600 eight-year-olds identified. Young children who are blind or visually impaired are even less common in this age group, with about 1,000 identified at age three, rising to some 2,000 by age eight.

For many children who are deaf, American Sign Language (ASL) is their first (native) language.

DEVELOPMENTAL DELAYS

State definitions of *delays* in communication tend to stress late-developing speech. This delay may be expressed in terms of first words occurring at 12 months following expected appearance—that is, at or after two years of age. Delays are also frequently expressed in terms of standard deviations (SDs) from the mean; the most frequent usage is two SDs below the mean. Many states accept 1.5 SDs below the mean in two or more domains as well. That combination is common with communication delays, because physical and cognitive delays in particular often accompany delays in communication development—a good example is cerebral palsy. Finally, delays may be expressed in percentage terms, such as a 25 percent delay in communication development. To illustrate, infants who are visually impaired are often delayed in head righting in the prone position (which usually occurs by three to four months of age); a 25 percent delay would mean this occurred at six months or later.

Deviations

are behaviors that are not normal at any age. Delays in development, by contrast, feature behavior that is normal but for children of younger ages.

Developmental **deviations** are as much a matter of concern as delays, if not more so. Some children do not develop functional language; children born deaf, for example, will not master the native language without intensive and extensive intervention. They are not just delayed; the expected behavior is not late but absent or nearly so.

Professional judgment, or informed clinical opinion, is very important in communication assessment. That is because speech and language delays or deviations may signal some other problem, as in the case of deafness. It is also because measures of communication development in young children are not so much tests as they are documentation of behavior. Psychologists and other ECSE personnel should bear in mind that delays in speech and language may indicate other problems, notably mental retardation.

Neonate (Birth to 28 Days)
- Does not show a startle response to a loud noise
- Does not look eye-to-eye when being held

1 to 4 Months
- Does not exhibit the social smile
- Does not follow a moving object with eyes
- Does not turn head in direction of sound

4 to 8 Months
- Does not babble
- Does not laugh
- Does not search for hidden objects (or shows no awareness that an object has been hidden)
- Does not demonstrate interest in new, different sounds
- Does not calm to primary caregiver's voice

8 to 12 Months
- Does not obey no or other simple commands
- Does not blink eyes in defensive movement when objects rapidly approach head
- Does not play with sounds or make first word

12 to 18 Months
- Does not speak in variety of one-word utterances
- Does not answer questions with yes or no or other appropriate responses
- Does not appear to recognize self in mirror
- Is not delighted by new, different objects or pictures

18 Months to Two Years
- Does not speak variety of two-word utterances in speech that is intelligible to people familiar with the toddler's speech
- Does not obey simple spoken commands unless the request is also made in gestures or other visual mode
- Does not stop to explore objects on path while walking

Three Years
- Does not speak in variety of three- or four-word utterances
- Does not have speech that is at least occasionally intelligible to strangers
- Does not tell own name upon request

Adapted from Prizant and Wetherby (1993).

FIGURE 11–1 Indicators of possible delay: communication.

Young children with delays in speech development should also be screened for possible hearing loss (see "Assessment" later in this chapter).

Possible delays or deviations in communication development are listed in Figure 11–1. Generally, indicators are conservative (if any one of the indicators holds true for a child, it is cause not for alarm but for a checkup with a specialist or clinic). Some suggest a hearing loss, some a vision impairment, yet others a delay or disability in speech. Problems in communication should be identified prior to three years of age.

ESTABLISHED CONDITIONS

Most states recognize speech impairments, deafness or severe hearing loss, and blindness or serious visual impairment as established conditions known to result in developmental delays. Deafness, for example, is widely accepted by states as being an established condition; it usually results in severe speech and language delays if intervention is not accomplished quickly and effectively. Most states accept as established other conditions that result in communication delays as a secondary problem; such conditions include cerebral palsy, muscular dystrophy, and others. This section discusses the more common established conditions and outlines what ECSE professionals can expect with each.

SPEECH AND LANGUAGE IMPAIRMENTS

Speech

is the oral expression of meaning, usually—but not always—with symbols (words).

Because the infant's first word and subsequent utterances attract so much family attention, delays or deviations in **speech** are among the first noticed and most reported of problems by parents. Impairments of speech are among the leading indicators of a wide range of disabilities. Language impairments, such as aphasia, are less common, but delays in langue development are quite frequent. Hearing losses are first noticed by parents when infants and toddlers do not speak at expected ages; similarly, parents first bring children with autism to community clinics due to concerns about the child's speech. Only later do parents notice other indicators of these disabilities. Similarly, young children with cerebral palsy, Down syndrome, and learning disabilities, to name just three conditions, may display delays in speech development or speech impediments.

Stuttering

is dysfluent speech or disrupted oral communication.

Stuttering is a common concern in many young children. LaBlance, Steckol, and Smith (1994) suggest that stuttering is more common among boys than girls by a ratio of five to one, with most children who stutter beginning to do so in early childhood, between two and six years of age. They report that stuttering is often preceded by delays in development of both speech and language. Van Riper (1993) explores the contributions of disturbed communication, disrupted feedback, and organicity in stuttering and attempts to synthesize the many diverse theories advanced to explain why children stutter. The consensus? So far, no one theory successfully explains stuttering (Guntupalli & Kalinowski, 2006).

DEAFNESS AND HEARING IMPAIRMENTS

Hearing loss is relatively uncommon in young children. More than half of those with hearing losses have congenital (present at birth) or early (first year) adventitious impairments.

When hearing loss occurs, one cause may be congenital cytomegalovirus infection (CMV). Such infections are very common, but in most instances there are no lasting health effects. Of those who do develop symptoms, about half have a hearing loss. Another cause is birth defects. An infant's hearing can be damaged even before birth. For example, if a woman contracts rubella (German measles) during pregnancy, her baby may be born deaf. Abuse of certain drugs by a pregnant woman could also damage or destroy her baby's hearing. Hearing loss occurring after birth often are a result of noise or injury. Exposure to excessive noise (including loud music) can damage hearing structures. This is called "noise-induced" hearing loss. It is usually gradual and painless, but it is often permanent.

A severe blow to the head, as may occur in an auto accident, also could cause hearing loss. Some childhood diseases, such as measles, mumps, and chicken pox, can cause hearing loss. In some instances, heredity is involved. Several patterns of inheritance may lead to **deafness.** The most common is *autosomal recessive inheritance*. In this pattern, a child acquires two recessive genes for deafness, one from each parent. Usually neither parent is deaf. Instead, each is a carrier. Less common is the pattern of *autosomal dominant inheritance*. In this pattern, a child acquires a dominant gene, and it may come from just one parent. That parent's family usually has a history of deafness, with half or more of the members of the family showing some degree of hearing loss. Because the recessive pattern is by far the most common cause of inherited deafness, it happens that most (90 percent) deaf children are born to hearing parents. Also, most deaf adults (also about 90 percent) have hearing children.

Deafness

is the inability to hear and understand conversational speech through the ear alone.

The effects of deafness or other severe hearing impairment on young children are a function, in large part, of the *age at onset.* That is, a congenital loss of hearing has a much greater and much more broad-ranging effect than does the same degree of loss occurring at age five. This is because children's development of language, speech, and much incidental knowledge occurs principally through the ears during early childhood. The trend in recent years has been for the average age at onset to decline; that is, today's children who are deaf are much more likely to have been born deaf or to become deaf during the first year of life. Prior to the 1970s, age at onset of nine or even later was much more common.

About one out of every three children who are deaf has a secondary disability as well. Most common is cerebral palsy, although learning disabilities also are frequent. In many cases, the medical condition that caused the deafness also produced the other condition. Thus, oxygen deprivation prior to, during, or just after birth may lead to both cerebral palsy and deafness.

SEELS (Blackorby et al., 2003) reports that young children identified as having hearing impairments use a wide variety of modalities for receptive and expressive communication. Virtually all (98 percent) use sounds (nonwords), and almost as many (97 percent) use gestures/pointing. Two-thirds (66 percent) use lipreading, and almost half (45 percent) use signs (p. 3-33). According to their parents, a plurality (45 percent) speak with "a little trouble," while about one-third (35 percent) speak "as well as others" and one in five (20 percent) speak "with a lot of trouble or not at all" (p. 3-30).

Blindness

is 20/200 vision or tunnel vision where central vision subtends at an angle of 20 percent or less as measured with corrective lenses.

BLINDNESS AND LOW VISION

Blindness and **low vision** are also relatively rare in young children, occurring in about 1 per 1,000 young children. Visual impairments occur as secondary conditions with cerebral palsy and, less frequently, with Down syndrome. The two most frequently used classifications for children with significant visual impairments are blindness and low

Low vision

is 20/70 vision or worse to 20/200 vision, which is blindness.

vision. In each case, vision is measured with use of appropriate corrective lenses and is compared with that of unimpaired individuals. Blindness is 20/200 vision or tunnel vision where central vision subtends at an angle of 20 percent or less as measured with corrective lenses. Low vision is between 20/70 to 20/200 vision. Normal vision is expressed as 20/20, meaning that an individual standing 20 feet from an eye chart correctly identifies the letters/symbols it displays. In 20/200 vision, a child with normal (average) vision standing 20 feet from a chart could see the same letters or symbols that a child who is blind could see only if standing 2 feet from the same chart. A child with low vision can see a symbol at 20 feet that normally sighted children could see from 70 feet.

The distinction between blindness and low vision is drawn for intervention and education purposes. Children who are blind usually do have residual vision (less than 20 percent are totally blind), but their vision is so poor that they learn best through other senses, chiefly hearing and touch. Children who have low vision, by contrast, have enough residual vision to be able to use it as a primary sense for learning and daily living purposes. Thus, with children who are blind, the emphasis is on auditory and tactile means of communication; with children who have low vision, it is on visual means.

The cause of a child's blindness or other vision impairment frequently cannot be identified. The best-known and most common cause of blindness in infants continues to be **retinopathy of prematurity (ROP),** once known as *retrolental fibroplasia*. It is associated with prematurity, affecting about 4 percent of very low-birthweight (less than 1,000-gram) infants. The condition once occurred when premature infants were placed into incubators and given excessive amounts of oxygen. With careful monitoring of oxygen levels, ROP all but disappeared in the late 1960s and 1970s. Other important known causes of blindness are inheritance (as with retinoblastoma, a malignant tumor in the retina—or the "screen" in the rear of the eye—and congenital cataracts) and pre-, peri-, and postnatal illnesses and accidents that also may cause cerebral palsy, retardation, and other disabilities. Such illnesses and accidents tend to occur prior to age one, if they happen at all. Diabetes may also cause blindness but rarely in early childhood.

Retinopathy of prematurity (ROP)

once known as *retrolental fibroplasia,* is a limitation of vision occurring during the neonatal period.

Children who are blind or have low vision are affected by the condition to different degrees depending in large part on the age at onset. A congenital condition is likely to cause much greater developmental delays than a later-occurring loss. Young children who once had good vision have formed mental images of themselves, their environments, and nonverbal communication techniques, including body posture. Children who were born blind, by contrast, lack these firsthand mental images and must acquire substitute versions by other means.

As with deafness, blindness is congenital much more often today than in years past; that is, a child who is blind today is far more likely to have been born blind than were children in the 1950s and 1960s. And today's child who is blind is more likely than were such children in the past to have other disabilities. Cerebral palsy is a common accompanying condition. That is not surprising, since illnesses producing high fevers may damage the optic nerve and also damage motor control areas in the brain.

Young children who are blind but who have no other major limitations will usually acquire communication competence by the time they enter school. During early childhood, however, many are delayed in communication development. Selma Fraiberg has contributed greatly to our understanding of blindness in young children. Her longitudinal studies of infants blind from birth (Fraiberg, 1968, 1970, 1975, 1977; Fraiberg & Freedman, 1964; Fraiberg, Smith, & Adelson, 1969) suggest that when early intervention and preschool instruction are not undertaken, children who are blind may demonstrate autistic-like behavior, have difficulty establishing and maintaining ties with other people, have echolalic speech, have poor definition of body boundaries, display motor stereotypes of the head and hands, and be delayed in achieving independent mobility. Examining the importance of sight in early childhood development, Fraiberg et al. (1969) comment:

> The response smile to the configuration of the human face, the selective smile for the face of the mother, the father and siblings, the discrimination of mother and stranger, the entire sequence of recognition experience which leads to mental representation and evocative memory, are organized through visual experience. To a large extent, eye to eye contact is the matrix of a signal system which evolves between mother and child. (p. 122)

Similarly, Fraiberg (1970) found that children with blindness tend to be delayed in use of the pronoun *I,* in part because they are restricted by parents in exploration and mobility. With appropriate parental and early intervention assistance, such delays often are temporary. The delays occur because children who are blind or have low vision do not see objects to which words refer, thus learning their names later; do not see nonverbal communication cues that indicate expected behavior, including communication; and may not be invited to join in social activities with sighted peers.

Parents also may restrain the child who is blind from exploratory and independent play, fearing for the child's safety. Such *experiential deprivation* is a major factor in developmental delays among children who are blind. In an excellent overview of blindness and low vision, Warren (1984) urges parents and educators to provide young blind children with enriched linguistic stimulation, as well as extended opportunities to learn auditorially and tactually about their environments.

ASSESSMENT

Assessment in the domain of communication development is improving rapidly. The early 1990s witnessed dramatic advances in early detection of hearing and vision impairment, for example. Such progress is much-needed. Children with delays or disabilities in any of the five domains should be assessed in the area of communication. Young children with Down syndrome, for example, frequently have losses of hearing and sometimes of vision as well. Expressive communication is a well-recognized concern among children with cerebral palsy. Children with autism may not use situation-appropriate language; they may be delayed in **pragmatics.** The examples are legion, and the point is basic. The IDEA requires that children be looked on holistically, that assessment be multidisciplinary, and that ECSE workers focus not only on children's deficits or delays but also on their strengths and resources.

Pragmatics
is the social use of language or the knowledge of what expressions to use in which contexts.

HEARING

Recent research has given us very early identification of hearing loss. Procedures developed in the early 1990s permit screening of virtually all newborns even before they leave the hospital. These new tests have revolutionary implications. As recently as 1988, the U.S. Congress Commission on Education of the Deaf reported that the average age at which hearing loss was first identified in the United States was as late as three years of age.

For a cost of just $25 per newborn, *otoacoustic emission testing* can screen infants for hearing loss even before they leave the hospital. Low-level, inaudible emissions are produced as the inner ear functions; otoacoustic emission testing measures those sounds. The full name of the procedure is *transient evoked otoacoustic emissions* (TEOAE). Otoacoustic emissions were first reported by David Kemp (1978) of the Middlesex School of Medicine in London in 1978. No physical response by the infant is required by the process, which was validated by the Rhode Island Hearing Assessment Project (RIHAP). For infants who test positive, follow-up auditory brainstem response (ABR) audiometry, which costs about $100, can be done. Again, no physical response by the infant is required. Electrodes attached to the head record electrical activity in the auditory nerve as the infant sleeps or rests quietly. Neither test is invasive, neither is time-consuming, and neither requires the infant's cooperation. For a very helpful review of the state of the art, see Smith, Bale, and White (2005).

The U.S. Department of Education's (1993) regulations on early intervention services describe the assessment function of "audiology" in Section 303.12(2) as follows:

> *(i) Identification of children with auditory impairment, using at risk criteria and appropriate audiologic screening techniques;*
> *(ii) Determination of the range, nature, and degree of hearing loss and communication functions, by use of audiological evaluation procedures; [and]*
> *(iii) Referral for medical and other services necessary for the habilitation or rehabilitation of children with auditory impairment.*

Audiograms

are graphic displays of hearing loss along two dimensions: pitch (frequency) and intensity (volume).

The degree of hearing loss may be equated with the sound intensity (measured in decibels, or dB) needed for a person to hear. Sound intensities are measured in hearing tests. The faintest whisper that most people can hear is 0 dB. An ordinary conversation between people several feet apart is about 65 dB. A person is considered deaf if he or she cannot hear sounds below 90 dB. An **audiogram** displays results of audiological assessments. At each frequency or Hertz (Hz) (250, 500, 1,000, 2,000, 4,000, and 8,000), the level of sound pressure at which young American adults report hearing tones half the time or more is set at zero. The most important frequencies are those in "the speech range" (500, 1,000, and 2,000 Hz). Thus, a 0-dB hearing level across the speech range represents "average" or "typical" and not "perfect" hearing. Hearing in the better ear generally is most of interest. Persons with audiograms showing responses between 0 and 20 dB across the speech range, in the better ear, are considered to have typical hearing (i.e., 0–20 dB). When audiograms show 21- to 40-dB hearing levels in the speech range for the better ear, the person is said to have a "mild" level of hearing loss. A moderate loss is 41–55 dB, and a moderately severe one is 56–70 dB. While there is not uniform agreement on this, usually a severe loss is 71–90 dB and a profound one 91+ dB. The line between "hard of hearing" and "deaf" is typically set at 90+ dB, although many experts use 80+ dB.

The most used approach to test hearing is pure-tone audiometry. This technique requires the active participation of the subject. It establishes air, bone, or both air and bone conduction thresholds by identifying the sound pressure level at which the subject reports hearing tones at specific frequencies at least half the time. For air conduction, earphones are used. For bone conduction, vibrators are used. (The reason your voice as recorded on a tape recorder sounds "different" to you is that you receive it solely through air conduction, whereas you hear yourself speaking in real time through both air and bone conduction.)

Newer approaches do not require active participation by the subject. These include auditory brainstem response testing, in which electrodes on the skin record reactions, and otoacoustic emission testing, in which sounds originating in the cochlea are measured in the external auditory canal (the sounds themselves may be evoked by acoustic stimuli, in which the response is known as evoked otoacoustic emissions).

A hearing loss of 40+ dB (i.e., one that is "mild" or "moderate") may affect education. The Acoustical Society of America (asa.aip.org) reports that ambient sound in the typical classroom can adversely affect learning. Given that conversational speech typically is in the 60-dB range, and the *maximum* recommended ambient sound level is 35 dB, one can appreciate the problem. The ASA and the federal Access Board jointly developed those standards (ANSI S12.60-2002). They may be downloaded, free of charge, at asastore.aip.org.

Particularly significant for speech comprehension are consonants. These tend to be higher-frequency sounds. Differentiating between *feet* and *feel*, for example, requires hearing attuned to the high-frequency "t" and "l" sounds. Understanding conversational speech effectively requires the ability to perceive and use high-frequency sounds.

The third step in the federal regulation on audiology is referral for services. These services may include medication (as with otitis media and other ear-related illnesses), surgery (as with outer- and middle-ear problems), hearing aid and other amplification selection, and speech and language services if appropriate. For more information, see www.asha.org and www.infanthearing.org.

SPEECH AND LANGUAGE

The U.S. Department of Education (1993) defines "speech-language pathology" in Section 303.12(14) as including this assessment role:

> *(i) Identification of children with communicative or oropharyngeal disorders and delays in development of communication skills, including the diagnosis and appraisal of specific disorders and delays in those skills;*
>
> *(ii) Referral for medical or other professional services necessary for the habilitation or rehabilitation of children with communicative or oropharyngeal disorders and delays in development of communication skills.*

What is a "delay" in communication development? The answer to that question is not as obvious as it may seem. Children vary greatly in the ages at which they speak their first words and in the ways in which they develop both receptive and expressive language. The speech and language pathologist needs to use observation with infants, toddlers, and preschoolers—preferably in natural environments. While a strict assessment protocol of stimulus and response can be very helpful, children this young do not perform all of the linguistic functions of which they are capable in such structured settings. It is essential to look for prespeech modes of communication, particularly gestures, as well as vocalizations. A variety of observations should be used, in different settings; indeed, communication assessment must be an ongoing process, not a onetime phenomenon. One instrument that may be used is the Communication and Symbolic Behavior Scales (CSBS), which is helpful in assessing both preverbal and verbal communication abilities in young children. Standardized on 8- to 24-month-old infants and toddlers, the instrument analyzes and rates children on 22 scales. Composite scores may be obtained on gestures, speech, social-affective signaling, and other aspects of communication development. The Psychological Corporation's catalog, *Assessment and Intervention Products for Speech, Language, and Hearing,* features more than a hundred pages describing tests and other instruments. Virtually all available instruments are limited, particularly in evaluating the full range of communication options young children use.

All assessments of language and communication should include efforts to identify any other condition, delay, or deviation that may be present. Communication impairments frequently do not appear alone. Communication behavior tends to be obvious, attracting parental and professional attention. Other, perhaps more subtle, problems should be explored whenever communication development is evaluated or assessed.

With infants and toddlers, ECSE professionals should look for a variety of indicators. A "Clinical Practice Guideline" from the New York State Department of Health (1999b) suggests these possible signals: not using gestures for communication, not imitating heard words, not spontaneously producing single words to convey meaning, not persisting in efforts to communicate, understanding fewer than 50 words or phrases without gesture/context clues, speaking fewer than 10 words, and demonstrating a lack of growth in expressive and receptive vocabulary over a six-month period. The American Academy of Pediatrics (2002), in its *Developmental Milestones* at its Web site (www.aap.org), and similar material at the Web site of the American Speech-Language-Hearing Association (www.asha.org) extend the guidelines through the EC age range.

The most common SLI disorders are dysfluencies of speech (notably stuttering), childhood apraxia of speech (a planning but not a production problem in speech), and aphasia (a word-finding problem). A good source on stuttering is Judith Kuster's, www.mnsu.edu. ASHA offers brief tutorials on assessment and intervention in apraxia of speech and aphasia (www.asha.org).

Well-regarded is the Rossetti Infant-Toddler Language Scale (LinguiSystems, 1990). This scale examines children's gestures, language comprehension and expression, play, interaction attachment, and pragmatics (social use of language). Used together with the Rosetti Interview Guide (which asks questions of parents), it can identify delays in development and help diagnose disabilities

VISION

The U.S. Department of Education's (1993) regulations for early intervention services describe the assessment component of "vision services" in Section 303.12(16) as follows:

> *(i) Evaluation and assessment of visual functioning, including the diagnosis and appraisal of specific visual disorders, delays, and abilities;*
> *(ii) Referral for medical or other professional services necessary for the habilitation or rehabilitation of visual functioning disorders, or both.*

Infants may be checked for redness in the eyes, excessive tearing, oversensitivity to light, and a cornea that is larger than normal. Newborns' eyes may be examined to make sure they move. The next screening examination should be between 6 and 12 months; thereafter, vision should be assessed at three and five years, with the first formal examination occurring during that time. Parents should be especially alert to eye rubbing, squinting, and closing one eye. Less obvious signals of possible vision impairment include frequent daydreaming, avoidance of close work, and short attention span. Frequent headaches, nausea, and clumsiness are additional possible indicators (Teplin, 1995).

Diagnosis of a visual impairment should immediately trigger measurement of visual acuity by an eye specialist. Vision may be measured with young children by means of a Snellen Illiterate E chart; in this variation on the Snellen chart, all symbols are the letter E, and the child's response is to point in the direction of the letter's "legs." Of course, the Snellen Illiterate E chart (or the Snellen chart, for older children) measures vision at a distance—in this case, some 20 feet. Most schoolwork occurs at much closer range. For these reasons, X/20 measurements of visual acuity in young children are of limited utility. Fortunately, several tests of vision impairment with respect to the kinds of work children do in preschool and later are available. Tests of preferential viewing, for example, are fairly simple and may be done by an observer trained to watch the child's gaze shift (Teller, McDonald, Preston, Sebris, & Dobson, 1987).

Deitz and Ferrell (1993) summarize evidence on developmental delays in children who are blind or have low vision that may assist ECSE professionals in the assessment process:

> Although they exhibit rolling, independent sitting, independent standing, and stepping movements at the same general time as sighted infants, motor milestones that require projection of their bodies into space, such as elevating the upper torso by their own support, raising self to sitting, pulling to stand, crawling, or walking, have shown delays. Also, reaching for objects, searching for a lost object, and joining hands at midline seem to appear later in children with visual impairments than in their sighted peers. Delays in speaking two-word utterances and two-word sentences and in using self-referent pronouns have been reported. The clearest cognitive delay reported by Fraiberg [1977] was development of object concept and object permanence. (pp. 72–73)

Even more important than measurements of visual acuity are assessments of *functional* vision. Young children with blindness or low vision communicate with the world around them in three fundamental ways; each child will have her preference, and this should be respected. The first is use of residual vision; in this instance, the child taps whatever vision is left as her primary means of receptive communication. The second is auditions; she prefers to listen to spoken instructions, taped materials, and computer speech synthesis. Finally, there is touch; she uses Braille and other raised symbols (Teplin, 1995). How the child functions is an urgently important question in any assessment. While the child's preferred mode should be given considerable weight, ECSE workers may decide to focus on developing her abilities in other areas, as when she is helped to make better use of her vision. Such decisions should be reached in consultation with experts on adaptive technology. Such experts can recommend technology that will convert material from one mode to another; to illustrate, printed material such as this book may rapidly be converted to computer speech synthesis or to Braille. These and other steps are now discussed further.

INTERVENTION

Communication interventions should be planned by multidisciplinary teams with extensive parental involvement. Whether implemented at the early intervention or at the preschool/primary programming level, services in all five domains of development should be included to the extent appropriate—first, because communication delays, deviations, and disabilities often have wide-ranging effects; and, second, because communication-related problems frequently coexist with physical, mental, and emotional or behavior conditions or delays. For a child who is deaf, a certified teacher of the deaf should be on the multidisciplinary team; for a child who is blind, a certified teacher of the blind is appropriate.

The issue of environmental stimulation is urgently important in poorer, less well-educated families. Such families at times tend to use language more for purposes of controlling the child ("No!") than for purposes of developing communication competency in the child. ECSE workers suspecting communication impoverishment in the home may want to assist parents and other family members to learn how to expand on and explain their communication with their children. When commands are not merely given but also explained, the child learns much more, much faster. Language development is most rapid when the child is surrounded daily with elaborations that offer new and different ways of expressing things. A parent who expands on a command can at the same time teach the child synonyms, antonyms, and alternative sentence structures. Such expansion appears to be very important in adaptive development as well.

SPEECH AND LANGUAGE IMPAIRMENTS

One of the most common impairments of speech in young children, stuttering, is not easily eliminated (Figure 11–2). Telling a child to "slow down and take your time" seldom works. Rather, LaBlance et al. (1994) suggest that child care workers and teachers should slow down their speech, because children who stutter tend to have more problems when conversing with fast speakers than with slow speakers. They urge teachers to ignore much stuttering, attending to fluent speech instead. In this way, fluent speech is reinforced (rewarded), while stuttering is not. LaBlance et al. also suggest that child care workers ask the child to cease another activity while speaking, because some young children find it difficult to do several things at once. They caution teachers not to expect miracles from these interventions; stuttering remains a much-misunderstood phenomenon despite several decades of research. In a text on stuttering, Van Riper (1993) concurs that although theories abound, interventions that cure stuttering or even alleviate

- **Model fluent speech—and dysfluencies.** Giving the child examples of good speech, at a moderated rate of speed, helps; by displaying some nonfluencies yourself (e.g., "uh," "that is," "you know," etc.), you set a relaxed tone that comforts the child.
- **Ignore dysfluencies.** Children who stutter fear adverse reactions; this creates more tension, which in turn leads to more stuttering. By ignoring dysfluencies, you reduce pressure on the child. By attending to fluent moments, you reinforce (reward) such behavior.
- **One thing at a time.** Suggest that the child stop doing something else when talking. On your part, model such behavior. Often it is difficult for young children to speak clearly while also running, playing, or doing something else.

Adapted from LaBlance et al. (1994) and Van Riper (1993).

FIGURE 11–2 What works: stuttering.

it significantly in a wide variety of children remain to be found. Stuttering is and likely will continue to be an enigma.

The issue of "How much is enough?" arises in speech and language pathology. The field has not given us clear answers. Although IEPs and IFSPs differ greatly in describing children's needs, they vary much less when it comes to intervention, typically calling for two or three sessions per week. Hanft and Feinberg (1997) urge that interventions vary according to need and that they specify the outcomes desired (something they report is usually missing in IEPs and IFSPs).

Embedding speech and language in child-initiated activities was recommended in Chapter 6. It is a well-regarded technique. The approach builds on the fact that the child has demonstrated interest in, and attention to, an object or activity. ECSE staff should take advantage by offering the child words that go along with these objects and activities (parallel talk). *Elaboration* is another tactic discussed in Chapter 6. This draws on evidence that low-SES families tend to expose their children to far fewer words and ideas than do professional families (indeed, Hart & Risley [2003] report that the difference could reach three million words by the time the child turns three).

Also popular as interventions are *phonemic awareness* activities. ECSE professionals may help young children in phoneme segmentation (identifying the individual phonemes in heard words and phrases) and phoneme blending (putting phonemes together). Although phonemic awareness is undoubtedly important, there is some controversy as to the extent to which phonemic awareness interventions in the EC years lead to literacy gains (e.g., Nancollis, Lawrie, & Dodd, 2005).

These techniques, together with the interventions delivered by speech-language pathologists, seem to help many young children. The NEILS longitudinal study, for example, shows that, according to family members, infants and toddlers improve in their communication abilities. PEELS results about preschoolers were not available at the time this book went to press (for an update, see www.peels.org). At the primary-grade level, according to the SEELS longitudinal study, parents say that children's expressive and receptive communication skills improve. It must be noted, however, that developmental factors may contribute to these improvements. Young children become better communicators over time, even without intervention. Because ECSE is an entitlement program, we cannot design studies comparing two groups of young children with communication delays or disabilities, one group receiving treatment and the other not. We can compare two different kinds of interventions or two different intensities of treatment, but that is not the same thing. We do know that the number of young children with the SLI classification declines in the primary grades, beginning at about age eight, and this may be evidence of effectiveness of services. It may also be, however, that some young children given the SLI label are later reclassified as having specific learning disabilities. We will revisit that issue in Chapter 13.

DEAFNESS AND HEARING IMPAIRMENTS

If a young child who is deaf is referred to you for early intervention and/or preschool special education, I urge you to consider very seriously recommending placement in a special program specifically designed for children who are deaf. That is because deafness is a severe disability when it comes to education. If you think about it a moment, you will recognize that the overwhelming majority of teacher-child and child-child communication in early childhood special education is oral (speaking and listening) and the underlying vehicle used is language (words, syntax, grammar). Without hearing, language—the coin of the realm—does not develop, absent extraordinary measures. Thus, even if the interventionists or teachers sign or if an interpreter is present, the child's ability to understand what goes on is severely compromised. Very intensive programming—mostly on language development—is required. That programming is so qualitatively and quantitatively different from what usually occurs in early childhood special education that a separate placement may well be needed if the child is to have any chance of succeeding in an integrated placement in elementary school.

Language is learned by children during early childhood—if hearing is intact. This suggests immediately that the single-most important task of ECSE professionals and of parents in working with a child who is deaf or severely hearing-impaired is to facilitate language development. Without immediate and effective early intervention and preschool special education instruction in language, children who are deaf or severely hearing-impaired will enter first grade knowing just a few words—and virtually no grammar, syntax, or other aspects of language. This is not an exaggeration; every year in every state, five- and six-year-olds who are deaf begin schooling knowing their names, a few object names, and virtually nothing else about the English language.

The urgency of the child's task—to learn *language,* any language—during early childhood cannot be overemphasized. The developing brain creates connections for the purpose of using language. After the age of two, synapses specializing in language that have not been tapped to perform those functions apparently begin to be suppressed or even eliminated in the brain, a process that continues into adolescence. Thus, after the age of two, the brain's language-learning ability gradually dissipates. It is a slow process. Enough plasticity remains, fortunately, throughout the early childhood period and into the early elementary years for language to be acquired later. The evidence from work with young children who are deaf is that the longer first-language acquisition is delayed, the harder it becomes for the child to demonstrate fluency. Children with deafness who learn some language, notably ASL, early in life are known to learn English much better and much more easily than do children who do not master any language before they begin their schooling (Commission on Education of the Deaf, 1988; Moores, 1982).

This is not to say that speech development is the top priority. Speech is not language. Speech is one mode, certainly the most frequently used mode, of expressing language; but language is a system of rules and symbols quite independent of speech. One can have language without speech. You are reading this text and understanding the language in it without either of us talking. Speech, by contrast, is largely a motor function, involving fine coordination of many hundreds of muscles. It is extremely hard to learn for many children born deaf and enormously frustrating for virtually all of them. To appreciate this point, consider how even an accent or a minor speech impediment is immediately noticed by most people. Hope should not be held out to parents or to the children themselves that children born deaf will ever speak even that well.

Parents of young children who are deaf may not see it quite this way; to them, often, the most obvious need of the child is to speak. Whereas *speech* delays are immediately noticed by parents of children who are deaf, *language* delays are less obvious, though in the long run much more important. That is because language is necessary, while speech really is not, for children to learn academic subjects in school and to perform gainful work as adults. Today's assistive technology devices can "talk" for children and adults, but no machine can yet generate grammatical English—what computer experts refer to as *natural language processing.* ECSE personnel must firmly explain to parents how speech and language differ and must try to educate the parents on why language acquisition is more urgent a task for the early childhood years than is speech. As important as speech is—and it undeniably is important—it pales in significance in comparison with language. Language—whether read and written, signed, or spoken—is the vehicle through which most learning—and virtually all academic learning—takes place in modern American society. Only if the child acquires a working knowledge of language will she later be able to learn mathematics, history, and biology.

The role of hearing in language acquisition is inescapable. The brain appears to be wired in such a way that it will generate the rules of language if and only if it is presented with the raw materials of spoken language and allowed to create, *de novo,* patterns and rules. To force the point, the brain is not wired to accept input about structure ("Nouns are the names we give things and ideas," "Verbs are action words," etc.), together with lists of many examples of such parts of speech. Given such input, the brain will record the information and store it as rote memory. The individual will attempt to apply these rules when requested to generate language but will usually fail.

This is exactly what has been done to generations of children who were deaf or severely hearing-impaired. They were *taught* language—not helped to learn it. The evidence on teaching language is in, and it is incontrovertible: the approach does not work. As the U.S. Congress Commission on Education of the Deaf reported in 1988, "The educational system has not been successful in assisting the majority of students who are deaf to achieve reading skills commensurate with those of their hearing peers" (p. 17). To illustrate, reading comprehension scores of students who are deaf or severely hearing-impaired, the commission reports, plateau at just third-grade levels, even after 15 to 18 years of schooling. Not surprisingly, "The present status of education for persons who are deaf in the United States is unsatisfactory" (p. viii) (see also Moores, 1982, 1991).

That is why ECSE professionals need to set as their top goal giving young children who are deaf or severely hearing-impaired linguistic input—of the same kinds, varieties, and amounts as hearing children get—visually as well as auditorially. Most young children who are deaf or severely hearing-impaired do have residual hearing, but it is not sufficient to serve as a primary vehicle for language acquisition. At most, the hearing of these children is a supplement to visual input. Whether the words and structures of English are presented in signs, finger spelling, and/or reading and writing is much less important than that the input be as comprehensive and variegated as possible and that it track the auditory input hearing children receive. That is, the input should consist of the same kinds of sentences, in all their tremendous range and scope, as hearing children hear. This task may appear daunting, but with today's technology, it is possible. Both television captioning and computer speech recognition can present these exact sentences in visual form to children who are deaf or severely hearing-impaired—allowing them to use vision to get the raw materials at the same ages, in the same sequences, and to something approximating the same extent as do hearing children through the auditory channel.

The IFSP or IEP should include an explicit statement of the child's communication needs, including personal and parental preferences. A range of communication modes is available. The choice of mode is a highly individualized one and, often, an emotion-laden one as well. Hearing aids amplify but also distort speech; while very helpful for children with mild to moderate losses of hearing, careful fitting and daily checking of batteries are necessary for them to work as intended. In addition, children using hearing aids may need visual input to understand conversational speech. ECSE workers need to be sensitive to those needs, because EC programs rarely involve stationary seatwork; with teachers, aides, and children constantly moving about in the room, a child's ability to keep up may be seriously compromised unless all concerned are cognizant of the need to make communication visual. One helpful approach is for ECSE workers from time to time to ask questions that cannot be answered with a yes. This permits checking on the child's comprehension yet avoids the ambiguity of yes responses (the child may nod, agree, or say yes to avoid embarrassment or confrontation; this is particularly a problem with children who have severe hearing impairments, including deafness).

Additional suggestions may be gleaned from the U.S. Department of Education's regulations on early intervention services, which define the early intervention services component of audiology in Section 303.12(2) as follows:

> *(iv) Provision of auditory training, aural rehabilitation, speech reading and listening device orientation and training, and other services;*
> *(v) Provision of services for prevention of hearing loss; and*
> *(vi) Determination of the child's need for individual amplification, including selecting, fitting, and dispensing appropriate listening and vibrotactile devices, and evaluating the effectiveness of those devices.*

The department further describes "speech-language pathology" services in Section 303.12(14) to include the following:

> *(iii) Provision of services for the habilitation, rehabilitation, or prevention of communicative or oropharyngeal disorders and delays in development of communication skills.*

Cochlear implants are electronic devices that simulate "hearing" for children who are deaf.

Cochlear implants for children who are deaf have been widely publicized in recent years. Today's implants have as many as 22 channels for electronic transmission of sound, making them much better than the early, one-channel versions. However, even 22-channel cochlear implants are limited in what they can do. They are most useful as an early warning safety system, helping children hear environmental sounds, including approaching cars. They are less helpful in the area of speech comprehension; while some children with implants can understand some speech through the ear alone, many continue to need lipreading and other visual cues. Children must undergo regular training sessions for six months to a year following the surgery to learn how to interpret the sounds the implant sends to their auditory cortex. Accordingly, cochlear implants are not "magic bullets" to cure deafness, nor are they appropriate for all children who are deaf.

Options for communicating with children who are deaf include *total communication,* in which children use speech reading, residual hearing, finger spelling, and sign language—together with gestures and facial expressions—to communicate. Total communication generally adopts Signed English, because when speech and signs are used simultaneously it is necessary for the signs to track English word order. American Sign Language, a rich, expressive language, usually cannot be used in a total communication environment because it has its own grammar and syntax (Figure 11–3) very different from Signed English. ASL is highly valued by many deaf parents and a treasured part of deaf culture (Dolnick, 1993).

Most audiology, auditory training, speech reading, speech and language pathology, and related services are available in local hearing and speech clinics or other community centers. Such clinics and centers are used by children with no disabilities, thus allowing early intervention programs to observe Part C natural environment (NE) and Part B least restrictive environment (LRE) preferences.

In recent years, deaf culture advocates have sought to advance ASL as the first (native) language for use with young children who are deaf. This approach repositions English as a second language; it is taught using second-language techniques and only after ASL has been mastered.

The approach responds to criticism of total communication, an approach in which teachers and other caregivers spoke while also signing and using finger spelling. ASL advocates objected that the children were seeing neither English nor ASL but, rather, some muddled amalgam vaguely resembling English. Was it any surprise, they asked, that children's expressive language was similarly muddled "deaf English"?

To understand how radical the change would be, consider that under this approach, teachers and other caregivers would neither speak nor move their lips. That is because ASL uses a different order than does English; one cannot simultaneously sign in ASL and speak in English. Similarly, because ASL has no written form, reading and writing in English would be postponed until perhaps third or fourth grade, after the children had mastered ASL.

The approach is probably best suited to the 10 percent of young children who are deaf whose parents also are deaf; in most such homes, ASL is in fact the native language.

For children who are deaf but whose parents are hearing, however, parental preferences should be carefully considered before this approach is adopted. For a discussion of the many controversies concerning the use of ASL as the primary language of instruction for children who are deaf, see Bowe (1992b) and Stuckless (1992).

FIGURE 11–3 Controversy in deafness.

The Part B LRE preference is very controversial in deafness education. Research with children who are deaf suggests that the LRE mandate, as currently implemented, may actually be harming some children who are deaf (Moores, 1991). The Commission on Education of the Deaf (1988) expressed reservations about how LRE was being implemented by the U.S. Department of Education. In response to the commission's concerns, the department published a guidance in the October 30, 1992, *Federal Register* explaining that any placement (including a center-based program) that meets a child's unique needs may be the LRE for that child (Bowe, 1993). The Part C NE preference is much less controversial in deafness. Very few studies have examined NE, despite the fact that it is now as new as LRE was in 1980. Research by Antia, Kreimeyer, and Eldredge (1994) suggests that social interaction can be stimulated between young children with hearing impairments and same-age children with no hearing losses, but that those beneficial effects that do occur fade rapidly after intervention to enhance such interactions is withdrawn. Consistent and persistent support both to children with no hearing impairment and to children with hearing losses is essential if interaction is to move beyond mere physical proximity to genuine interpersonal communication and joint play.

All of this requires that early intervention and preschool special education staff trained in techniques of working with children who are deaf or hard-of-hearing be made available to ECSE programs. Unfortunately, a national survey by Roush, Harrison, Palsha, and Davidson (1992) found that "fewer than half the programs currently preparing teachers of deaf students in the United States offer specializations in early intervention. Moreover, very few students are electing to specialize in early intervention even when such a specialization is available" (p. 428). That continues to be the case.

BLINDNESS AND LOW VISION

Separate placements for young children who are blind or have low vision merit serious consideration by early interventionists and preschool special educators, as they do when young children are deaf. The reasons for recommending separate placements are different from

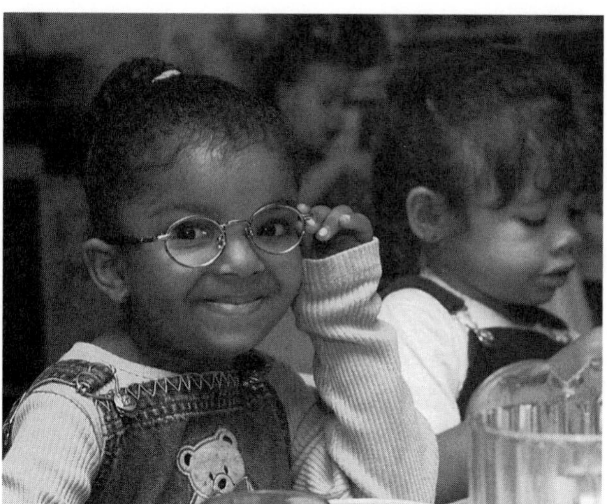

Vision is measured with appropriate corrective lenses, in contrast to hearing, which is assessed without the use of any assistive devices.

those with deaf children but almost as compelling. Children who are blind have very good prospects of succeeding in elementary school if and only if they have mastered use of the technology that makes such integration feasible. They have a lot to learn. They need to acquire good orientation and mobility skills, using canes and other navigation devices. They need to become accustomed to note-taking devices, such as Braille 'n Speak or Versabraille—to say nothing about learning Braille itself! They need to learn how to operate scanners, special tape recorders, and other products. While it is true that all of these capabilities could be acquired during the elementary school years, it is also true that the child is likely to do far better if she enters first grade already possessing these vital skills.

Glass (1993) expresses concern about the high-intensity, continuous lighting found in most NICUs. Ambient light as intensive as 30 to 150 footcandles, or well in excess of adult office light, is common. In addition, preterm infants are often exposed to other lights, including heat lamps and the Mini Bili-Lite (which can produce 10,000 footcandles). All of this light may produce phototoxicity. Conceding that "the optimal level of NICU lighting has not been determined," she adds nonetheless that "no study supports the safety of the bright light levels still common in many NICUs" (p. 17).

Glass also recommends the human face as the best stimulus for infant visual development. Her reasons are obvious ones: "The face is three dimensional. It contains some contrast at the edge of the hair or at the features; provides slow, contingent movement around the eyes and mouth; and it is situated at a variable distance from the infant" (p. 18).

For children diagnosed as blind or having low vision, perhaps the most urgent tasks of ECSE professionals and of parents are to facilitate the development of independent mobility and tactual exploration skills and to introduce the use of modern assistive technology. Children who are blind or have low vision have the same jobs as other children during the early childhood years. In addition, however, they must learn orientation and mobility skills so as to get around independently. Independent mobility is a sine qua non (literally, "without which not") of early childhood development. It is essential for the infant's, toddler's, and preschooler's learning. Getting around in the environment, including new and strange as well as familiar settings, is an added responsibility of early childhood for children who are blind or have low vision. It cannot be neglected; it should not be postponed.

The federal regulations on early intervention describe "vision services" in Section 303.12(16) as the following:

> *(iii) Communication skills training, orientation and mobility training for all environments, visual training, independent living skills training, and additional training necessary to activate visual motor abilities.*

Orientation and mobility specialists

help young children who are blind or have low vision learn to navigate around the home; the early intervention program; the neighborhood; and, later, the community as a whole.

These are to be provided by "qualified personnel" including **orientation and mobility specialists** (U.S. Department of Education, 1993). The work of these specialists is outlined in Figure 11–4.

Another important task of early childhood for children who are blind or have low vision—and for ECSE workers and parents—is training in use of today's assistive technology devices and services. These are discussed in more detail later in the chapter and

Orientation and mobility specialists are trained professionals who are experts in helping children who are blind or have low vision learn how to make maximum use of residual vision, hearing, and touch so as to navigate safely. They are also specialists in teaching children how to use public transportation in the community so as to get around independently. In addition to the prosaic skills of traveling, using the long cane, and so on, they develop in children who are blind or have low vision the confidence and feeling of independence so necessary for these children's development.

In most cases, orientation and mobility specialists work with families in the home, the immediate neighborhood, and the local child care center or nursery or preschool. This enables ECSE programs to observe the NE preference in Part C and the LRE preference in Part B. However, if orientation and mobility training are only available in a center program, or if specialists in working with very young children are employed only there, such settings are natural or least restrictive because the necessary services are available nowhere else.

Young children who are blind or have low vision need to master independent orientation and mobility skills in addition to all the other capabilities children learn during the preschool years. That is why orientation and mobility training is a recognized related service under Part B and an authorized early intervention service under Part C.

FIGURE 11–4 Orientation and mobility.

in Chapter 9. The point to be made here is that, thanks to this new technology, the lives of these children—now and throughout public education and into adulthood—are vastly richer and immeasurably easier today than they were even 20 years ago. As illustrated in Figure 11–5, the contributions these products and services can make are so substantial that they merit careful consideration by ECSE personnel.

Finally, it is very important that ECSE programming not be limited only to the needs and resources of the child with respect to vision. Children who are blind or have low vision are, despite their pressing vision-related needs, the same jumble of impossible contradictions that all children this age are. That needs to be borne in mind—and reflected in ECSE programming. Research reminds us that children who are blind or have low

One child's story illustrates how early intervention, preschool special education, and today's assistive technology can help a child who is blind succeed in elementary school. Olivia, who was born prematurely, is blind from retinopathy of prematurity (ROP). The ophthalmologist told her family that Olivia was eligible for early intervention services.

These began when Olivia was 3.5 months of age. A social worker and parent-infant specialist visited her home, teaching her parents to touch and massage her, to tie bells to her wrists and ankles so she would learn where her hands and feet were, and to put things in her crib so that when she moved she would touch something.

Olivia entered a center-based preschool program specializing in services for children who are blind or have low vision when she was three. There she learned to become "tactually observant" and to interpret verbal descriptions of ideas. Meanwhile, her parents learned Braille.

Three years later, she entered first grade, the only student who was blind out of the 450 in her local elementary school. A vision teacher came to the school weekly to teach Olivia Braille, to translate her school books and materials into Braille, and to teach her how to use an abacus for math, to type, to use a computer, and to develop her auditory skills so that she could listen to texts on tape. In addition, a mobility specialist came to the school weekly to teach her to use a cane. Beginning in second grade, an occupational therapist also helped Olivia increase her upper-body strength enough to use a Braillewriter.

In the classroom, Olivia's teachers spelled out loud whatever they wrote on the chalkboard and described any other visual materials. They touched Olivia frequently—and let her touch them—throughout the day, to "keep in touch."

Adapted from "Side by Side," by Debra Viadero, in Teacher Magazine Reader, *undated.*

FIGURE 11–5 Olivia: one child's story.

vision may be at greater risk for non-vision-related problems than are other children. Developmental delays may occur, absent early intervention and preschool programming, in adaptive (self-help), motor, social, cognitive, and language development (Scholl, 1986). Early intervention research with children who are blind or have low vision has been summarized by Olson (1987) and White et al. (1987). These studies suggested that such children benefit from early intervention services. However, as Behl, White, and Escobar (1993) point out, these studies had small subject populations, lacked comparison groups, and performed only short-term follow-up measures.

Ten infants blind from birth made up Fraiberg's longitudinal intervention study (Fraiberg et al. 1969). Of these 10, 5 would have been considered at risk even if they had not been blind, due to factors such as extreme poverty, unemployment, and mental illness in their families. These 10 infants received home intervention that began before one year of age. All reached the normal human-object relations expected at 18 months of age. Their performance placed them in the upper half of children who are blind. All were found to have normal or near-normal intelligence.

TECHNOLOGY

Technology is tremendously important for many young children with communication-related limitations, but particularly for children who are deaf or blind. The potential of technology for children with developmental delays or established conditions that limit their receptive or expressive communication is impressive with respect to two particular capabilities. One is *computer speech recognition,* or the ability of computer systems to "hear." The other is *computer speech synthesis,* the ability of computers to "talk."

The principal concern of young children with hearing loss is understanding what other people say. Speech comprehension is the basis for language development in early childhood; children learn the language they hear. If they hear little or no language, they do not learn it. Today's personal computers may help children with severe or profound hearing loss dramatically, because they can hear—and print out as they are hearing it—what teachers, caregivers, and other children say.

Some of the newer personal computers feature *speaker-independent, continuous speech recognition.* This capability represents an enormous breakthrough in technology for young children with communication-related limitations. Earlier computer speech recognition capabilities were limited in two important ways. First, they could not understand most voices but, rather, were limited to the voice that trained them. One person "trained" the system by speaking many words and phrases over and over again so that the system could learn to match that person's voice with English words stored in its memory. This process is called *speaker-dependent speech recognition* because the computer's ability to recognize speech is dependent on one particular speaker. Second, earlier computers required speakers to pause . . . like . . . this . . . when . . . speaking . . . to . . . the . . . machine. That is, they could not handle continuous, or conversational, speech—today's machines can. They are not perfect, however. Commonly, computer speech recognition achieves 95 percent accuracy; that is, it correctly recognizes 19 out of every 20 words it "hears." Background noise, unusual accents, and other factors can throw it off, bringing down the accuracy rate. To put the 95 percent rate into context, consider that if you achieved that rate and no better using a computer keyboard, you would toss it out and get a new one. But for children who need speech recognition, 95 percent accuracy is quite sufficient.

Offered by Nuance, IBM, and others (see Chapter 9), continuous speech recognition capabilities are now remarkably affordable (about $100 for the software). These packages also offer speech synthesis (computer talk) as well. Today's speech synthesis has a natural-sounding rhythm, at least as compared with the earlier, flat-pitched voice that pronounced everything in the same machinelike monotone. The user can select from among several voices; typical choices include a man, a woman, a child, and a Spanish accent. For children who are deaf, the synthesized speech is their voice, so it should be one that they feel sounds right and reflects well on them. As with any voice, it is a very personal thing. But the fact that technology has reached this state of the art is wondrously liberating. Children who cannot speak intelligibly can prepare messages in advance and can program a laptop computer to "speak" those as needed. Of course, the computer also can provide real-time speech in response to words as those are typed on the keyboard.

Children who are blind can use the same speech synthesis capability with a scanner, a product that "reads" books, newspapers, and so on, and sends those to the computer, which then speaks them aloud or translates them to Braille. Small, handheld Braille Speak or Versabraille machines can be used to take notes and to read them later. The fact that these technologies are all computer-based means that translation from print to voice is as readily done as is print to Braille or Braille to voice. In years past, parents, friends, and volunteers had to read textbooks or other printed materials into a tape recorder or translate them by hand into Braille. The translations now can be performed in a matter of a few minutes, not the hours or weeks required in the past.

WORKING WITH FAMILIES

Successful early intervention and preschool special education programs for young children who are deaf or severely hard-of-hearing work closely with families. The single-most important advice ECSE workers can give to families is that they must establish in the home some means of reliable communication with their young child. Work performed at the Kendall Demonstration Elementary School, located on the Gallaudet University campus, and at other programs shows that families who accept the child's deafness and learn ASL greatly reduce their own and their children's frustration levels. Other programs, such as those at the Clarke School for the Deaf in Massachusetts and the Central Institute for the Deaf in St. Louis, Missouri, as well as the correspondence program of the John Tracy Clinic in California, have shown results with oral approaches. Communication choice is a matter of family preference. More important than how communication is effected is *that* it is established—and maintained—on a daily basis between the child, her siblings, and her caregivers. As noted earlier, ECSE workers should call families' attention to the urgent need for language development. This may be effected not only through closed captioning on television but also by family caregivers reading with the child on at least a weekly, and preferably a daily, basis. Third, families need to be cautioned against overprotection. Children only develop adaptive behaviors when their caretakers give them ample opportunities to practice such behaviors. Experiential deprivation in the name of caution does not serve the best interests of the child.

It is imperative that young children who are blind establish independent mobility, not only to facilitate development of the self-concept but also for cognitive and adaptive development to proceed apace. Families of school-age children who are blind express most concern about adaptive behavior and functional independence. Knowing this, ECSE workers should help families take appropriate steps during the early childhood years to foster in the child a sense of independence and an ability to care for herself. ECSE workers should also introduce families to modern adaptive technology so they may understand how revolutionary is the impact of computer-based communications for children who are blind.

SUMMARY

This chapter included a look at children who have special needs in the area of expressive and receptive communication. Children who are blind principally face a limitation in receptive communication. Today's technology can translate inaccessible information from print into voice, Braille, or large print in a matter of minutes or even seconds. Equally important for young children who are blind are mobility skills, which allow them to achieve independence from family and professional care. Such independence is vital for cognitive and adaptive development.

Children with severe hearing impairments are often limited in expressive communication. In fact, most children who are born deaf have great difficulty speaking intelligibly. Today's technology provides a "voice" for such children. It is a voice that can be very high in quality, affordable, and easy to learn to use. For young children who are deaf, the voice is a tremendous help, because its quality exceeds what most such children will achieve on their own even after many years of speech training. However, computer speech synthesis is of secondary importance with young children who are deaf or severely hearing-impaired. That is because their primary need is to acquire language. Deafness is only secondarily a limitation on expressive communication; it is primarily a restriction on receptive communication. The real task is to make spoken English comprehensible to children who are deaf. Although computer speech recognition has advanced remarkably in recent years, to the point that it can now be used to translate from voice to text what parents, ECSE workers, and other children say, even this amazing capability does not solve the problem. Young children who are deaf must learn how to read before they can benefit from computer speech recognition. That is why parental and ECSE communication skills, as well as closed captioning on television, are so urgently important. It is through these means, especially the former—parents and professionals who sign, finger spell, gesture, and speak clearly so as to make it easy for the child to lip-read them—that young children who are deaf learn language.

With all of these kinds of communication limitations, ECSE's goal is to prepare children for success in school. Children who are blind can acquire the orientation, mobility, and adaptive equipment skills they will need to compete in integrated environments in the public schools. Achieving integration is far more challenging for children who are deaf, because the solutions are far more elusive. Deafness so disrupts the language acquisition process in early childhood that very intensive efforts are required for a period of many years before mastery of the language occurs—if it ever does.

We have much to learn about providing effective ECSE services to children with severe communication limitations. Both deafness and blindness are severe disabilities. The evidence to date is that ECSE programs tend to be much more successful with mild or moderate disabilities than with severe or profound ones. One of the field's greatest challenges in the years ahead is to help most those who need the most help.

KEY TERMS

audiograms
blindness
cochlear implants
communication
deafness
deviations
incidence
low vision
orientation and mobility specialists
pragmatics
prevalence
speech
stuttering

QUESTIONS FOR REFLECTION

1. The text says most deaf children (90 percent) have two hearing parents. What implications can you draw from this statement?
2. Why might earlier identification of hearing loss make a big difference for young children?
3. Differentiate *blindness* from *low vision.* What do the differences suggest for intervention strategies and techniques?
4. Explain the significance of age at onset with respect to vision impairment.
5. Name three senses through which young children who are visually impaired might acquire information.
6. What language use patterns often are seen in poorer families and why are those of concern to ECSE workers?
7. Differentiate *speech* from *language*. Why is the difference an important one in ECSE?
8. What is wrong with *teaching language* to children who were born deaf, according to the text?
9. What is *total communication*?
10. What do orientation and mobility specialists do?

PRACTICAL EXERCISES

1. Spend some time in an ECSE program that serves young children having communication delays, deviations in development, or disabilities. Ask the early intervention staff or teacher to tell you about the children's needs. What is known about how family members communicate with their children? Observe as teachers and speech-language pathologists work with children. Compare everything you learn with what was suggested in this chapter. Write up your observations and conclusions. Share these with your professor.
2. Check out such sign language resources as "Signing Time Videos" and "Signing Time Songs" (Two Little Hands Productions, Draper, UT; www.signingtime.com) and *Sign Language for Kids* (Heller, 2004). A wide variety of other video and book resources will do as well. At a local EC or ECSE program, use these to teach staff members and, with their permission, young children basic signs (for colors, emotions, animals, etc.). Ask staff members to report back to you in a week or so about whether the children used the signs to increase their verbal production.

WEB SITES OF INTEREST

www.asha.org American Speech-Language-Hearing Association—the professional organization of speech-language pathologists

www.infanthearing.org Utah State University Project on Infant Hearing—information on in-hospital testing for newborns

www.cochlearimplant.com and **www.cochlearimplants.com** Two commercial Web sites of companies marketing cochlear implants

CHAPTER

Physical Development

Growing up a dwarf, I was not a shy or retiring kid. Being different, I experienced a good deal of attention, both negative and positive. I recall that sometimes adults would ask me, "If there was a pill that would make you tall, would you take it?" As a ten-year-old boy, I knew that I wanted the teasing to stop. As a fifteen-year-old boy, I just wanted the girls to kiss me.

And yet, even as a child, I recognized that my entire identity was connected to being a dwarf. I did not view that fact as either good or bad, it just was. (Miller, 2006, p. 211)

OBJECTIVES

After reading this chapter, you should be able to:

- Explain why the domain of physical development is so large in ECSE.
- Describe what kinds of impairments are included in this domain.
- Explain how asthma can affect young children—and what you can do about it.
- Explain what cerebral palsy is and what causes it.
- Discuss how to assess the accessibility of an ECSE facility.

- Describe what occupational and physical therapists do.
- Discuss how you could help a young child with a traumatic brain injury.

CHAPTER OUTLINE

- **OVERVIEW**
- **PREVALENCE**
- **DEVELOPMENTAL DELAYS**
- **ESTABLISHED CONDITIONS**
  - **Asthma and Cystic Fibrosis**
  - **Back, Leg, and Side Impairments**
  - **Cerebral Palsy**
  - **Amputation**
  - **Traumatic Brain Injury/Spinal Cord Injury**
  - **Arthritis and Other Fingers/Hands Impairments**
  - **Medically Fragile, Technology-Dependent Children**
- **ASSESSMENT**
- **INTERVENTION**
  - **Traumatic Brain Injury**
  - **Spinal Cord Injury**
  - **Asthma**
  - **Muscular Dystrophy**
  - **Spina Bifida**
  - **Cerebral Palsy**
  - **Amputation**
  - **Medically Fragile, Technology-Dependent Children**
- **WORKING WITH FAMILIES**

OVERVIEW

Virtually everything a young child does is affected if physical development is delayed or limited. The "work" of young children is to develop their abilities. They do that in large part by exploring their environments, finding things, and manipulating them. Infants, toddlers, and preschoolers play with physical objects, thereby learning size, color, and other characteristics of things such as their texture or firmness. Children use these objects to construct castles, to play house, to practice counting, to develop gross and fine motor control and eye-hand coordination, and to perform many other tasks of early childhood development.

Limitations or delays in physical development, accordingly, can have substantial and far-reaching effects. Consider, for example, how physical disability may affect cognition. Young children learn by *doing* things, especially in the toddler stage (1 year to 2.5 or 3 years), when movement dominates their lives. A physical disability such as cerebral palsy interferes in two major ways. First, the condition makes movement itself difficult and slow. The infant or toddler explores less territory and manipulates objects less effectively and, for these reasons, tends to learn less than does a young child with no disabilities. Second, overprotection by parents and other caregivers further constrains mobility (Gerales & Ritter, 1991). Both phenomena lead to experiential deprivation; the infant or toddler with cerebral palsy is deprived of developmentally necessary experiences.

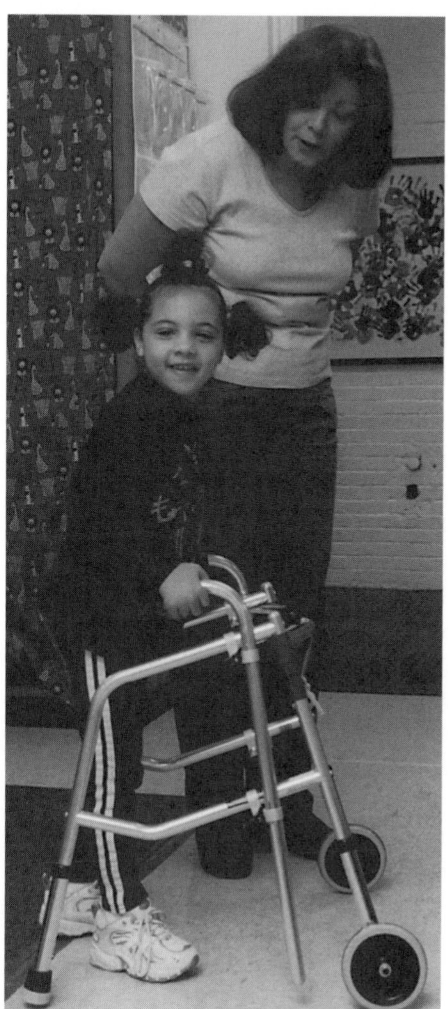

Aids for physical mobility are now widely available, making it much more feasible for young children with disabilities to engage in an active, physically demanding childhood.

Nor is that all of it. Cerebral palsy also affects performance on tests. Intelligence tests for young children typically involve the child using objects. By its very nature, cerebral palsy may sharply constrain how well and how quickly a child may manipulate objects or describe them to an examiner. This may lead to an overestimation of the prevalence of mental retardation among children with cerebral palsy. The usual estimate is that 30 percent of children with cerebral palsy are also mentally retarded (Levine, 1986; Verhaaren & Connor, 1981). Given that tests may inappropriately measure physical skills while ostensibly measuring cognitive ones, that proportion may be too high. Or consider how physical development delays may affect adaptive behavior. Not only do many physical limitations constrain self-help behavior, but caregivers often do things for the child, frequently unnecessarily, thereby delaying the child's development in self-care.

Despite these many potential pitfalls, the fact remains that America as a society and thousands of cities and towns as individual communities are more accessible to people with physical disabilities today than ever before. Children using wheelchairs can now travel safely on public mass transit buses, something that simply did not happen 15 years ago. In many communities, too, playgrounds and movie theaters alike today have ramps, elevators, and automatic doors so that families with children who have physical disabilities can enjoy close to the same variety of recreation as can other families. Even wheelchairs themselves are different today than they were 15 years ago. Sports chairs and other aids for physical mobility are now widely available, making it much more feasible for young children with physical disabilities to engage in an active, physically demanding childhood.

This chapter discusses normal physical development during the first eight years of life. The information may help ECSE workers and parents identify delays in development. Among the conditions discussed in this chapter are amputations, asthma, cerebral palsy, muscular dystrophy, spina bifida, spinal cord injury, and traumatic brain injury. Suggestions on working with medically fragile and technology-dependent children also given. The detailed discussion of different disabilities may be particularly helpful in answering parents' questions about specific labels or conditions. The chapter continues with material on assessment and intervention. Some suggestions for working with families are offered at the conclusion of the chapter.

A considerable number of rare disorders affect physical development in some young children. A condition such as dysautonomia, which limits a child's ability to self-regulate the body and to feel, can have catastrophic effects on walking, which requires biofeedback, and even on eating and speaking, which also require the ability to feel. Another rare disorder is "–18Q syndrome," which also limits mobility and speech. A full discussion of these conditions is beyond the scope of this book because the disorders are so unusual. Interested readers are referred to the National Organization for Rare Disorders (NORD), 100 Route 37, P.O. Box 8923, New Fairfield, CT 06812; www.rarediseases.org. It is an outstanding voluntary organization concerned with identification, treatment, and cure of "orphan diseases."

PREVALENCE

The domain of physical development is becoming even more prominent these days, due to two trends in American society. First, we as a nation are becoming much more obese. Three times as many 6- to 11-year-olds are overweight as compared with 30 years ago. The rate among preschoolers has doubled in the same time period (Institute of Medicine, 2005, *Progress in Preventing Childhood Obesity*, available at www.nap.edu). Second, the number of babies born premature and/or with a very low birthweight each year has passed the half-million mark; they now account for 12 percent of all births (Hack et al., 2005).

Childhood obesity is a worrisome risk factor. Diabetes, a chronic health condition, is associated with it. According to the Institute of Medicine, 30 percent or more of obese young children may develop diabetes. More—some 80 percent—will be overweight as adults. Extremely low birthweight and prematurity, which some would characterize as "physical" conditions, are also associated with a wide range of chronic health conditions, including lung diseases that develop into asthma, neurological conditions including learning disabilities, and behavior problems.

ECSE programs are not required by the U.S. Department of Education to report the conditions, or even the developmental domains most of concern, for the under-six children whom they serve. Even among primary-grade students, only broad categories are reported. Among six- to nine-year-olds, for example, the U.S. Department of Education (2006c) notes that 3 percent have physical conditions such as "orthopedic impairments" or "multiple disabilities" as their primary disabilities. The specific conditions are not listed in the *Twenty-eighth Annual Report*. We must turn to other sources for prevalence estimates on these. The Brain Injury Association (www.biausa.org) estimates that 1.5 million Americans sustain a brain injury each year. Fortunately, the vast majority have few if any long-lasting effects. The Centers for Disease Control and Prevention report that 11,000 individuals have a traumatic spinal cord injury annually (www.cdc.gov). The National Multiple Sclerosis Society (www.nmss.org) estimates that about the same number (11,000) Americans are diagnosed with MS each year. The Spina Bifida Association of America reports that some 70,000 Americans have spina bifida, virtually all of whom were born with the condition (www.sbaa.org).

DEVELOPMENTAL DELAYS

Within each domain, states define "developmental delays." These may be expressed in terms of first appearance of behavior as a function of expected date of appearance—for example, a 12-month delay in walking alone. Delays may also be expressed in terms of standard deviations (SDs) from the mean; the most common usage is two SDs below the mean in one domain. Most states accept 1.5 SDs below the mean in two or more domains as well. Many children with delays or disabilities in physical development are also limited in cognitive or adaptive behavior in particular.

Neonates who suffer respiratory problems often have delayed motor development. Neonates with low Apgar scores (well-baby ratings) are more likely to have delayed motor development than those with high scores. Low birthweight (LBW) and prematurity (which often go together) may lead to delays in motor development as well, with later ages of attaining sitting, standing, and walking. Malina (1982) has shown that environment strongly affects age at attainment of motor development milestones. While heredity is important, whether or not a child has the opportunity to explore freely has a lot to do with how fast he reaches physical development milestones. There is a direct relationship between how much and how freely the infant/toddler can explore, for family or for disability reasons (e.g., "environment"), and how fast development proceeds.

The needs of young children born prematurely and/or with low birthweight can be many. Looking at such children who were about eight years old, Boyce, Saylor, and Price (2004) at Utah State University's Early Intervention Research Institute found that most had benefited from early intervention and preschool special education services. Most had typical development and IQ scores. In communication and cognitive areas, those who were raised in homes that emphasized verbal and other interactions fared best. Beginning early matters.

We should not minimize the needs of young children with delays or disabilities in this domain, however. Barlow, Thomson, Johnson, and Minns (2005) report that shaken-infant syndrome children, when examined at age five, had delays or conditions in all five domains of development. There were cognitive limitations, visual impairments, speech and language delays, behavioral problems, and epilepsy. Adaptive functioning was compromised in many of these young children. In daily living skills, communication, socialization, and motor development, these children were measurably behind age peers.

ESTABLISHED CONDITIONS

Orthopedic impairments including spinal cord injury and cerebral palsy, are recognized disabilities under the Individuals with Disabilities Education Act (IDEA).

Cerebral palsy, muscular dystrophy, traumatic brain injury, spinal cord injury, and other physical disabilities are recognized by many states as "established"—that is, known to result in developmental delays. Under the IDEA, it is not necessary to demonstrate a delay when such conditions are present. This section discusses the more common established conditions, notably **orthopedic impairments,** including what ECSE professionals can expect with each and how treatment may help children with limitations of physical development. This material, summarized in Table 12–1, may also assist in answering questions from parents and other family members.

TABLE 12–1

Capsule Descriptions of Physical Disabilities.

PHYSICAL DISABILITIES	CHARACTERISTICS
Asthma	Difficulty breathing and frequent attacks, some resulting in hospitalization
Cerebral palsy	Volitional control of muscles is compromised, limiting fine motor as well as gross motor activities
Cystic fibrosis	Mucus inflammation in the lungs
Muscular dystrophies	Gradual weakening of muscles
Spina bifida	Loss of control and feeling below site of origin on spinal cord
Spinal cord injury	Similar to those of spina bifida, but of adventitious onset
Traumatic brain injury	Memory and sensory impairments (many temporary) and personality changes (often permanent)

ASTHMA AND CYSTIC FIBROSIS

Asthma

is a condition in which people have difficulty breathing because of obstructions in the airways of the lungs. It is a chronic respiratory disorder (sometimes called a chronic obstructive pulmonary disease). The U.S. Department of Education recognizes asthma as a disability when it affects a child's education.

Asthma is a condition in which people have difficulty breathing because of obstructions in the airways of the lungs. It is a chronic respiratory disorder (sometimes called a *chronic obstructive pulmonary disease*) that often appears within the first year of life. However, because symptoms may be mistaken as something else (i.e., congenital heart disease), diagnosis may not occur until a child is in preschool. Asthma is quite common in children; in fact, some one-third of all Americans with asthma are school age or younger. Among school-age children, asthma is one of the most frequent causes of absenteeism. According to the Centers for Disease Control and Prevention, about 10 million Americans of all ages have asthma (www.cdc.gov).

Symptoms include not only difficulty in breathing but also vomiting and a dry cough. The principal effect of asthma on children from birth to eight is frequent absence from early intervention, preschool special education, or other programs. Hospitalization is often necessary; some families report taking an asthmatic child to the hospital several times during one night. Excessive absenteeism, in turn, constrains a child's progress in the program. It may also lead to social and emotional problems, because other children in the program learn not to rely on this child's being there; children like a friend who is reliably there and may not form close attachments to children when they cannot rely on their presence.

Attacks result in most cases from allergic reactions. These may be to pollens, molds, dusts, or animal hair. Infection of the respiratory system is another cause. Generally, the body produces excess antibodies in response to pollens or other antigens. This is an allergic reaction to the antigens. In someone with asthma, the antibodies are not effective in combating the antigens but, rather, trigger production or release of histamines, deleterious chemicals that in turn cause swelling in the airways. This swelling makes breathing difficult.

Sometimes, asthma develops following a respiratory infection that is not promptly and thoroughly treated. A viral infection, in particular, is a common precursor to asthma in young children.

Psychological and genetic factors are also involved in asthma. Children with emotional difficulties are more prone to asthma; the onset of asthma may in turn exacerbate those emotional conditions. Somewhat more than half of all children who develop asthma have relatives with the condition. However, the genetic basis, if one exists, for this inheritance is not yet well understood.

An asthma attack can start suddenly, and the fear this causes may prolong the attack. Cold triggers asthma attacks, as can fatigue after exercise. What happens is that the bronchioles in the lungs become swollen and clogged with mucus, and the muscles surrounding them contract so that the air that should pass through is unable to do so. The body reacts to the lack of oxygen, and the child forces more and more air into the lungs. However, due to the blockages, the child has difficulty exhaling that air; this leads to the wheezing noise characteristic of asthma. Most asthma attacks last a few hours, although some may persist only for a few minutes. Emotional stress can also trigger an asthma attack. Asthma was in the news in 2006 with reports that film star Lindsay Lohan (*Chapter 27, Herbie: Fully Loaded, The Parent Trap,* etc.) was hospitalized after an asthma attack. The actress's mother reported that Lohan has had asthma since she was two years old. Dina Lohan was quoted as saying, "I don't think people understand how truly terrifying it is to have an asthma attack."

Cystic fibrosis

is an inherited condition that causes mucus to build up in the lungs, compromising lung capacity and usually resulting in death by the age of 30. Children with cystic fibrosis need to have physical therapy, get lots of exercise, and receive dietary supplements.

A somewhat similar condition is **cystic fibrosis.** Here, the body cannot make a protein called (after the condition) the *cystic fibrosis transmembrane regulator* (CFTR). This protein facilitates the transport of chloride (which, with sodium, makes up salt). Without CFTR, chloride cannot readily enter and leave cells. Thus, not surprisingly, one of the first indications of the condition is a salty-tasting sweat. More serious, the person's lungs become covered with a sticky mucus. This inflammation gradually destroys the lungs. Eventually, most people with the condition die from it, usually at about 30 years of age. According to the Cystic Fibrosis Foundation (www.cff.org), cystic fibrosis is the most common fatal genetic disease in America, at some 30,000 individuals (prevalence), with another 1,000 people added annually (incidence).

People with cystic fibrosis need antibiotics, enzyme supplements, and frequent hospitalization. Because of their reduced lung capacity, they typically expend more energy in any given activity than do other people. For this reason, they need frequent rest. Physical therapy, mostly "chest thumping" to loosen the mucus, is needed daily. Regular exercise, similarly, helps maintain breathing and muscle strength.

Congenital

conditions appear at or prior to birth; they are present at birth, as contrasted to *acquired* conditions.

Adventitious (acquired)

conditions appear after birth, usually as a result of illness or accident. They differ from *congenital* conditions, which are present at birth.

Muscular dystrophy (MD)

is a condition characterized by muscle weakness. There are several types of MD. Duchenne MD, the most serious form, is a progressive, usually fatal condition. Other dystrophies are less serious and rarely fatal.

BACK, LEG, AND SIDE IMPAIRMENTS

Congenital conditions occur infrequently—about one in every 20,000 live births—and include shortened (truncated) limbs and shortened limb bones. **Adventitious (acquired)** limb impairments result from surgery or from accidents; these are somewhat less frequent than are congenital ones. Some 200 neuromuscular diseases affect 500,000 Americans of all ages. Among them are *myasthenia gravis,* a hereditary condition affecting the myoneural junction; *congenital and metabolic myopathies,* also hereditary, which affect muscles; and *spinal muscular atrophy,* affecting the anterior horn cells. Two of the most common in children are muscular dystrophy and spinal bifida.

In **muscular dystrophy (MD),** tiny leaks in the muscle membranes allow calcium to enter the muscle cells, activating enzymes that proceed to destroy the muscle. In time, the muscles of the legs, chest, and arms progressively weaken as fatty tissue replaces muscle tissue. Recent research has suggested that the absence of a protein, which the scientists identifying it called *dystrophin,* causes muscles to deteriorate. This was one of the first instances in which researchers found that an absence of a protein causes disease. About 20,000 boys and young men have MD, of whom 15,000 are children, according to the Muscular Dystrophy Association.

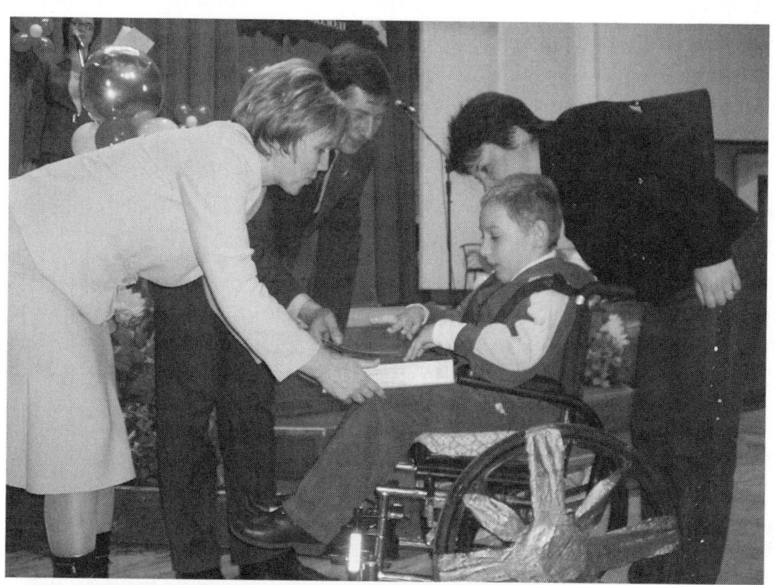

A wide variety of wheelchairs is now available for use by young children.

There are several dystrophies. The most common and severe is *Duchenne MD,* which usually leads to death by the early twenties. It affects about one in every 3,500 young boys. Duchenne MD has been linked to a gene located on the X sex chromosome; because females have two X chromosomes, the affected one is suppressed by the normal one, making the female a carrier of the disease. Males, however, have one X and one Y sex chromosome, which is much smaller. With no normal X chromosome to counter the affected one, boys develop the disease. Duchenne MD usually becomes evident in the toddler years, as the child is unable to walk or run as easily as before. The muscles that had been growing begin to atrophy between the ages of two and six. Usually, the individual needs a wheelchair by about age 13. In the late teens or early twenties, muscle atrophy has weakened the lung and heart muscles, leading to death.

In *Becker MD,* a less common and less severe version, muscles weaken but not to the point of causing premature death. Several other, also less common, versions also occur. *Congenital dystrophy* is evident at birth when muscles appear small and weak; life span usually is short. *Facio-scapulo-humeral dystrophy* may appear in infancy but is more common in adolescence and adulthood. It begins in muscles of the face, shoulder, and upper arms, hence its name. *Limb-girdle dystrophy* begins in the lower trunk and legs; it may begin in the shoulders, in which case progression is slower. Life expectancy usually is normal with limb-girdle dystrophy. *Myotonic dystrophy* starts with the fingers, hands, feet, and lower legs; however, it rarely appears in children. Females as well as males can have some of these forms of MD.

Spina bifida

is a condition in which the spinal cord does not close completely during fetal development.

Spina bifida is a condition in which the spinal cord does not completely close during the first month (28 days) of fetal development during pregnancy. In fact, the name refers to the spine being "divided into two" or "open spine." The condition may be caused by folic acid insufficiencies in the diets of pregnant women, especially if these women also have a genetic-related inability to process folate. Thanks to more use of folic acid by women who are pregnant, spina bifida is becoming less frequent. According to the Spina Bifida Association of America (www.sbaa.org), spina bifida occurs about once every 1,000 pregnancies. The SBAA notes that more children have spina bifida than have muscular dystrophy, multiple sclerosis, and cystic fibrosis combined.

Spina bifida is the most common neural tube defect. Of the three main kinds of spina bifida, the most severe is *myelomeningocele,* where nerves of the spinal cord protrude through the back. Although surgery can and usually does help, the condition leads to significant, permanent limitations. An important side effect is *hydrocephalus,* a buildup of cerebrospinal fluid in the brain. This fluid cushions and protects the brain and spinal cord. In spina bifida, the spinal lesion prevents the brain from draining normally. Thus, the fluid collects in and around the brain, enlarging the head and leading to mental retardation. Other secondary conditions often found with spina bifida include some learning disabilities and attention deficits (with or without hyperactivity). Clearly, spina bifida can have consequences well beyond the domain of physical development.

The site of the lesion has much to do with these effects. As is the case with spinal cord injuries as well, spina bifida interferes with *afferent* (to the brain) and *efferent* (from the brain) messages. Thus, the child's ability to monitor bodily functions and pain (afferent) and to control voluntary muscle and other brain-directed patterns (efferent) is limited. The higher the lesion, the more pervasive these problems are. Regardless of the site of the lesion, pressure sores (decubitus ulcers) often occur, as they do with spinal cord injuries.

Cerebral palsy (CP)

is a condition in which oxygen deprivation or damage to the brain limits voluntary control of muscles.

CEREBRAL PALSY

Cerebral palsy (CP) is a condition that in virtually all cases occurs during the pre-, peri-, or postnatal period and one that affects gross as well as fine motor control. CP is almost immediately noticeable. Common estimates are that CP occurs about three times in every 1,000 live births. This may be an underestimation, however, because much CP occurs in families with limited access to medical care, a population well known to be underrepresented in morbidity statistics. It is 25 to 30 times more common in infants weighing less than 1.5 kilograms at birth than among normal-weight infants (www.ucpa.org).

CP is a condition that is perhaps best described as limiting voluntary control of muscles. If you think of it that way, you see that the principal issue is that of the brain's ability to control the body's muscles; the muscles themselves are of secondary concern. That is, the muscles are not the source of the child's problems; the brain's motor control centers are.

This suggests several things that are important. One is that CP is a physical condition affecting both movement and expressive communication. The movement limitations are urgently important in infants and toddlers, because they rely so much on motor activity to learn other things. As the children grow, the expressive communication limitation becomes, if anything, more important. That is why use of today's computer-based technologies to facilitate expressive communication is so urgent with children who have severe cases of CP.

A second important implication of this way of viewing CP is that the muscles themselves, not being manipulated on a voluntary basis by the brain, may atrophy or weaken over time unless intervention is taken. But it goes beyond that; speech is a motor control function, one in which many hundreds of small muscles are manipulated very precisely to produce intelligible sounds. In CP, too, these muscles are not controlled as well or as easily by the individual. Speech and language services, accordingly, may be needed. Other aspects of expressive communication, including writing, are also limited. Indeed, it is not going too far to say that the principal limitation in CP is one of expressive communication.

Secondary conditions are quite common in children with CP. Hearing loss is frequent, visual impairments somewhat less so, and some degree of retardation exists in a minority of cases. Often the same cause triggered each of these problems. CP frequently occurs as a result of oxygen deprivation prior to, during, or just after birth. Other causes include maternal infections such as rubella (German measles), birth trauma, and chronic diseases, including fetal infections. The same conditions may affect hearing, vision, and intelligence as well.

For all these reasons, CP is very likely to require multidisciplinary intervention. Children with CP frequently have problems related to learning, social and emotional growth, perception, vision, hearing, and intellectual functioning. Assistance from early childhood special educators, speech and language pathologists, physical and occupational therapists, and others will be required.

Cruickshank (1976) showed that CP is not progressive; the condition does not worsen over time. This is not to say that muscles do not atrophy if not used; they do, which is why physical and occupational therapy are so important. CP also is not contagious; and it is not remittent, coming and going. The condition varies from mild to very severe. In mild cases, children need a little more time to do things and may need assistive technology devices to hold and manipulate objects (Gerales & Ritter, 1991). In severe cases, by contrast, they literally cannot express themselves through speech, handwriting, or other conventional means and must use assistive technology devices, such as "talking" personal computers. Such technologies help children with severe CP dramatically reduce their dependence on others. Before the advent of modern microprocessor-based assistive devices, such children depended on others for virtually every activity of daily life.

Words frequently used to describe the problems of children with CP include *spasticity* (stiffness, hypertonia, muscle contractions), *atonia* (lack of muscle tone; also *hypotonia,* less than normal muscle tone), *ataxia* (uncontrolled, jerky, irregular movements caused by fluctuating muscle tone, balance problems, overreaching for things), and *athetosis* (contortions, twisting motions). These words all suggest problems controlling voluntary muscles.

Hypotonia is a frequently reported condition in children who have Down syndrome (see Chapter 13). This illustrates a central theme in ECSE; children should be assessed and helped in all five domains, regardless of whether their primary needs lie in one particular domain. In this instance, children with Down syndrome may have pressing needs for intervention in cognitive development, but they also need physical and other therapy for hypotonia. The point is to think of needs and respond to them, rather than thinking only of a child's primary deficits.

Physical therapy and occupational therapy aim to slow down the atrophying of muscles. They also assist the spastic and athetoid child in the morning to loosen muscles that became tight during the night. Maintaining good posture while standing or sitting is another goal of physical and occupational therapy, as severe atrophy may result from chronic abnormal posture.

AMPUTATION

In some cases, limbs are missing at birth; in others, they are amputated for survival reasons, as when a bone is cancerous. Amputations are three or four times as likely to be *congenital* (occurring at or prior to birth) as *adventitious* (happening after birth) (Jones, 1988). Therapeutic amputations are more frequent among boys than girls, as boys tend to be more adventurous physically and have more accidents. Congenital conditions may result from drugs, as when a pregnant woman abuses controlled substances or when medicinal drugs are administered to the woman before she realizes she is pregnant. Maternal rubella in pregnancy may cause congenital conditions as well.

TRAUMATIC BRAIN INJURY/SPINAL CORD INJURY

Traumatic brain injury (TBI)

was added to the IDEA as a recognized disability in 1990. Automobile, motorcycle, sports, and gun-related accidents resulting in sharp blows to (closed head injuries) or penetration of (open head injuries) the head cause TBIs.

Traumatic brain injury (TBI) was added to the definition of "children with disabilities" under Part B in 1990. The disability is relatively rare in young children but is quite common among adolescents and young adults. According to the Brain Injury Association (www.biausa.org), every year 200,000 children sustain TBIs; one in every 30 Americans will have a significant brain injury before reaching driving age. While teenagers are the group at highest risk (due to motor vehicle and sporting accidents), preschool-age children are second. The absolute number of instances, however, is low. Boys are two to four times as likely to sustain TBI as are girls. Nine out of every 10 TBIs are caused by falls and by bicycle, motor vehicle, and sporting injuries (Allison, 1992). Others result from child abuse, gunshot wounds, and injuries from other projectiles.

Cognitive losses due to TBI frequently are temporary. A good example is short-term memory loss after damage to the temporal lobe; with therapy, good nutrition, and—perhaps most important—time, the ability to lay down new information returns. However, in some cases, longer-term effects are hidden, not surfacing for months or even years after the accident. As the child reaches a new stage of development and is expected to do new things, long-hidden damage in the brain becomes apparent. The child does not progress intellectually or behaviorally as expected, and it is this delay or impairment that reveals the extent of the injury. Reports Mark Ylvisaker, of the College of St. Rose in Albany, New York:

> A two-year-old may leave the emergency room walking and talking, and look like he's recovered. But years later, he may still be displaying the type of behavioral disregulation—inability to control impulses, inappropriate behavior in a social context, inability to plan, etc.—that is typical of a two- to four-year-old, but which is now drastically out of place in an older child. (quoted in Allison, 1992, p. 4)

Particularly evident is damage to just-emerging capabilities. Infants and toddlers who are acquiring receptive language skills may demonstrate linguistic deficits if they sustain TBIs, while preschoolers may show deficits in interactive play with other children.

TBI is also a common cause of epilepsy. Almost half of all head traumas result in some form of epilepsy.

Spinal cord injury (SCI)

occurs when the spinal cord is stretched, bruised, or even severed. It is one of many conditions categorized in the IDEA as orthopedic impairments.

Spinal cord injury (SCI) occurs when the spinal column is damaged or ruptured. Many of the accidents that cause TBI can also cause SCI; the difference is that the spine, rather than the brain itself, is traumatized. As with TBI, accidents are the most common cause of SCI in childhood—automobile, bicycle, and sports accidents in particular. The spinal cord is the principal mode through which afferent (to the brain) and efferent (from the brain) messages are transported. Accordingly, when the cord is injured, both kinds of messages may stop. Children with SCI may injure or burn a toe, for example, and not feel any pain. They also are unable to "tell" the legs what to do.

The extent of the effects of SCI depends in large part not only on how severely the cord is damaged but also on the site of the lesion. The higher (closer to the head) the cord is traumatized, the more pervasive the effects. High-level SCI produces paralysis not only in the legs but in the arms and hands as well. That is called **quadriplegia.** Lower-level SCI, by contrast, principally affects the legs in what is called **paraplegia.** Wheelchairs may be needed in both cases, although occasionally physical and occupational therapy can help a child avoid the need for a chair. Some individuals even become "walking quads," overcoming quadriplegia to walk independently, perhaps with a cane or other means of support. Secondary problems from SCI include **pressure sores** (decubitus ulcers), which develop when the child does not shift weight on a wheelchair cushion or on a bed. ECSE professionals should become acquainted with techniques, some of which are illustrated in Figure 12–1, including special seating pads as well as rotation procedures, to prevent pressure sores. Urinary tract infections also may occur; again, as with pressure sores, the lack of afferent messages to the brain means that the child does not complain about urinary pain. ECSE professionals need to be alert to signs of such infections.

Quadriplegia

occurs when all four limbs (arms and legs) are affected, usually by a spinal cord injury.

Paraplegia

occurs when the lower limbs (legs) are affected, usually by a spinal cord injury, but upper limbs (arms) are not.

Pressure sores

(decubitus ulcers) develop when the child does not shift weight on a wheelchair cushion or on a bed.

Young children often express keen interest in active recreation, for which everyday wheelchairs frequently are not suited. Fortunately, over the past 5 to 10 years, a fast-growing market in sport chairs has developed in response to this interest. Sport chairs are very different from everyday chairs; they are much lighter, more streamlined, with fewer parts. Some come with wheels that are angled outward for greater stability at high speed and for more maneuverability in wheelchair basketball, soccer, and other sports. Unfortunately, most insurance plans (including Medicaid and Medicare) reimburse costs only for one, primary wheelchair.

1. Initiate seating as soon as possible following the acute stage.
2. Use rental and manufacturer-loaned chairs for evaluation.
3. Look for solid seat, contoured cushion, and pelvic support.
4. Involve physical and occupational therapists in evaluation and ongoing assessment.
5. Monitor child's posture, head position, visual field, skin condition, alertness, comfort, and ability to function independently.
6. Use a second, "sporty" chair for recreation purposes. Sport chairs are light, easily maneuvered, and have only essential seating and positioning features.
7. Reassess both regular and sport chairs every few months, because rapid physical growth in young children dramatically affects needs.

Adapted from Kreutz (1993) and Smith (1994).

FIGURE 12–1 Wheelchair seating and positioning.

ARTHRITIS AND OTHER FINGERS/ HANDS IMPAIRMENTS

Juvenile rheumatoid arthritis
is a condition in which joints become inflamed, and usually appears between the ages of 18 months and four years; it generally has few if any lasting effects on children.

Juvenile rheumatoid arthritis usually appears between the ages of 18 months and four years, often after a respiratory infection caused by bacteria or viruses (Schumacker, Klippel, & Robinson, 1988). Its principal effects are joint pain and swelling, especially after midafternoon. As often happens with asthma, children may miss parts or all of day programs or preschool if the condition becomes severe. Most children with juvenile rheumatoid arthritis recover within a few years, experiencing few, if any, permanent effects.

Juvenile diabetes (Type I) is a disorder of metabolism in which the body is unable to retain sufficient energy from food. One important effect may be reduced finger sensation. Diabetes also can cause visual impairment, including blindness. The loss of finger sensation may make it all but impossible for the individual to read Braille or even raised letters and symbols in buildings. Type II diabetes, once rare in children, is increasing rapidly as obesity rises.

MEDICALLY FRAGILE, TECHNOLOGY-DEPENDENT CHILDREN

Medically fragile, technology-dependent children
require a range of intensive medical and other services as well as specialized equipment for ventilation and feeding.

Medically fragile, technology-dependent children require the use of one or more pieces of equipment to prevent death or to forestall further disability. Formerly, such children usually died within hours or days of birth. Now, as reported by the now-defunct U.S. Congress Office of Technology Assessment (OTA) in a 1987 report, medical and technological advances are giving thousands of such children an opportunity to live. They may need long-term hospitalization or other intensive care. More and more, however, they are being discharged to the home for care by the family (Beck, Hammond-Cordero, & Poole, 1994).

Technology-dependent children may need machines for ventilation or for feeding. Often, child care workers and family members must monitor the infant, toddler, or preschooler virtually 24 hours a day. This creates tremendous needs on the family's part for respite care. The extensive support system required for monitoring may begin to fail over time, as the demands of employment, care for other children, and other deferred or delayed needs resurface (Beck et al., 1994).

Medically fragile, technology-dependent children include children who require vigilant monitoring and extensive technological support for ventilation, children who have had tracheostomies, and children using machines ("iron lungs") for ventilation. Often, very complex support arrangements must be made between the home, the hospital, a pediatric pulmonary center, and early intervention programs. Baroni, Tuthill, Feenan, and Schroeder (1994) offer a vivid case history describing how one young boy was helped through such teamwork. It is impossible to read their account without coming to appreciate the remarkable constellation of support services required to help children with severe pulmonary needs. Baroni et al. comment, for example, "Over the subsequent three years of his life, the array of services necessary to care for this one little boy expanded to include four hospitals, eight clinics, three financial agencies, five home care components (including therapies), and countless physicians, nurses, social workers, and therapists across services and settings spanning three states" (p. 74).

ASSESSMENT

The IDEA calls for a "multidisciplinary assessment" of all potentially eligible young children. It is important that ECSE professionals consider each child's status and needs in the domain of physical development, even if the child's primary needs appear to be in some other domain. In part, this holistic approach reflects recognition in the field that development in one domain may be affected by disabilities or delays in another domain. More broadly, however, it emerges from the focus inherent in ECSE as a field on "the whole child."

The federal rules for early intervention programs outline the assessment functions of physical therapy in Section 303.12(9) as follows:

> *(i) Screening, evaluation, and assessment of infants and toddlers to identify movement dysfunction; [and]*
> *(ii) Obtaining, interpreting, and integrating information appropriate to program planning to prevent, alleviate, or compensate for movement dysfunction and related functional problems.* (U.S. Department of Education, 1993)

The Bayley Scales of Infant Development (second edition) offer a psychomotor scale; this scale in the first edition of the Bayley was widely used for assessment of physical development. Another widely used set of scales is the Peabody Developmental Motor Scales (Folio & Fewell, 1983), which offer well-standardized gross and fine motor scales. Regardless of what scales or other measures are chosen, tests should be interpreted with care when a child has a physical disability, particularly CP, but also SCI, TBI, and other conditions such as MD. Assessors must remind themselves that these kinds of disabilities affect not only the child's daily activities but testing as well. Tests designed for use with infants and toddlers rely heavily on physical activity by the child; parental reports, developmental checklists, and other measures also look to what the child does motorically. Yet CP, SCI, MD, and many other physical disabilities by their very nature slow motoric response and limit fine motor control in all of these areas. The ECSE professional should interpret test results or reports with care, recognizing that test results and assessed activities may be skewed by the disability.

INTERVENTION

Accessible

refers to a standard such that at least one entrance, at least one path through a facility, at least one restroom, and so on, is usable by individuals with disabilities. This standard, which applies to existing facilities or buildings, is lower than the *barrier-free* standard.

Barrier-free

relates to buildings or facilities. All entrances, all rooms, and all levels or floors need to be accessible to people with disabilities. This standard applies to new construction and to newly renovated parts of existing facilities. The standard contrasts with *accessible,* which is a lower standard.

The design of the built environment is a major consideration in serving children with physical disabilities. Whether services are delivered at the home, in a child care center, or in a public school, the facility should at a minimum be **accessible** and optimally be **barrier-free.** An *accessible* environment offers at least one route into the facility; at least one way to reach any given room within the building; at least one restroom that has wide stalls, grab bars, and lowered sinks and mirrors; and at least one way to do the things other children do, including removable chairs, adjustable desktops, and the like. Programs and classes may be reassigned to ground-floor rooms if the building has no elevator. The *accessible* standard applies to existing buildings. The intent is to offer access that is "reasonable" and not excessively costly.

Barrier-free, by contrast, applies to new construction and to newly renovated parts of existing facilities. The barrier-free requirement sets a much higher standard. In barrier-free buildings, each entrance is accessible, all rooms are reachable in a wheelchair or with the use of crutches, and all important switches and furnishings are usable by people with physical disabilities.

The U.S. Architectural and Transportation Barriers Compliance Board, a small independent federal agency, offered guidelines for making facilities usable by people with physical disabilities. The guidelines, developed for use under the ADA, addressed the issues raised when young children use a facility. Particularly important are lowered switches and controls (for room lights, elevator call buttons, etc.); turnaround space in halls, restrooms, and other common areas so that children using wheelchairs may reverse direction easily; and the height of workspaces such as tables and desks. Libraries should have lowered bookshelves and may have revolving book displays and revolving turntable stacks on tabletops so that children can easily reach any object on the table. Automatic doors and doors that open or close with relatively little pressure are other important aspects of design for young children with physical disabilities.

In addition, toys themselves may be adapted. Velcro, now a widely used convenience item, was originally developed for people who have fine motor control limitations. Virtually anything can be equipped with Velcro, heavy duct tape, or other fasteners. These may be used to secure toys to a surface, making it much easier for the child to play independently. Heavy cardboard may be added to the base of game pieces to give them greater stability. As Wershing (1994) reports, many such modifications are suggested by the children themselves as they play with toys. Game rules, too, may be changed. Wershing suggests that all such rule changes apply to all players, not only to the child with a physical disability.

Use of adaptive toys is but one part of what should be a broad-ranging program of ensuring that all children participating in an ECSE program have an equal opportunity to engage in active play. Every child needs to be able to play, because as Piaget said, "the child's work is play"—it is through play that cognitive and other kinds of development

Switch Kids Inc. 8507 Rupp Farm Drive West Chester, OH 45069	Flaghouse Inc. 601 Flaghouse Drive Hasbrouck Heights, NJ 07604
ChildCraft Education Corp. 2920 Old Tree Drive Lancaster, PA 17603	S & S P.O. Box 513 Colchester, CT 06415
Access to Recreation 2509 E. Thousand Oaks Boulevard Thousand Oaks, CA 91362	Constructive Playthings 1227 East 119th Street Grandview, MO 64030
Community Playthings P.O. Box 901, Route 213 Rifton, NY 12471	Abilitations Select Service & Supply One Sportime Way Atlanta, GA 30340

Source: Kornreich Technology Center, National Center for Disability Services, Albertson, NY.

FIGURE 12–2 Adapted toys catalogs.

Physical therapy helps prevent and reduce muscle atrophy and promotes musculoskeletal development.

occur in young children. Children communicate with other children most often while they are playing, so communication development, as well, depends heavily on the child's ability to play freely. Adaptive development, too, is spurred when young children have a chance to respond creatively to new situations in play. Figure 12–2 offers addresses for catalogs of adapted toys and related products.

Much learning by young children occurs as a result of physical movement.

Much intervention in this domain involves **physical therapy.** The profession of physical therapy focuses on preventing or reducing muscle atrophy. The federal regulation for early intervention programs (U.S. Department of Education, 1993) defines physical therapy in Section 303.12.(9) as follows:

> *[S]ervices to address the promotion of sensorimotor function through enhancement of musculoskeletal status, neurobehavioral organization, perceptual and motor development, cardiopulmonary status, and effective environmental adaptation. These services include . . . (iii) Providing individual and group services or treatment to prevent, alleviate, or compensate for movement dysfunction and related functional problems.* (U.S. Department of Education, 1993)

The department's earlier definition had been considered by many in Congress to be too narrow. For example, *House Report 102–198* (1991) urged a broader view of the role of physical therapy:

> *The Committee is concerned that the existing definition of "physical therapy" in the regulations implementing Part H has not kept pace with advances in the field. The current definition lacks a clear scope of practice for*

physical therapists in the pediatric setting. The definition does not currently reflect the physical therapist's role in the promotion of sensorimotor function through enhancement of musculoskeletal status, neurobehavioral organization, perceptual and motor development, cardiopulmonary status, and effective environmental adaptation. Additionally, the current regulation is unclear with respect to individual and group treatment, as well as consultation services. (p. 12)

Occupational therapy helps children learn to perform specific tasks (brush teeth, dress, maintain good posture, etc.) despite physical disabilities or other conditions such as Down syndrome.

While physical therapy focuses on prevention of atrophy in muscles, **occupational therapy** concentrates on helping children perform daily activities and self-care functions. In occupational therapy, the therapist teaches the child how to do something concrete and specific—how to dress, how to brush her teeth, and so on. The federal regulation for early intervention describes occupational therapy in Section 303.12(8) as follows:

[S]ervices to address the functional needs of a child related to adaptive development, adaptive behavior and play, and sensory motor and postural development. These services are designed to improve the child's functional ability to perform tasks in home, school, and community settings, and include—
(i) Identification, assessment, and intervention;
(ii) Adaptation of the environment, and selection, design, and fabrication of assistive and orthotic devices to facilitate development and promote the acquisition of functional skills; and
(iii) Prevention or minimization of the impact of initial or future impairment, delay in development, or loss of functional ability. (U.S. Department of Education, 1993)

Augmentative and alternative communication (AAC) devices are important assistive technology products for some young children with physical conditions. Such devices as the Dynamyte and Dynavox, from Dynavox Systems (www.dynavoxsys.com), are popular in many ECSE programs, despite high prices and maintenance costs. In a helpful review of AAC with infants, toddlers, and preschool-age children, Romski and Sevcik (2005) respond to several myths that may dissuade ECSE professionals from using such products. Communication via AAC does not slow nor stop vocalizations by young children, so AAC devices should not be perceived as "last resort" options. It is also not true that children must have a set of typing and other skills before they can make effective use of the machines.

TRAUMATIC BRAIN INJURY

Interagency coordination is particularly important for children with physical disabilities, because hospital, community health, and other agencies have important contributions to make. With TBI, the need for interagency cooperation is especially urgent due to the rapidly changing abilities of the child. TBI was added to the list of disabilities recognized under Part B in 1990. TBI challenges ECSE program staff to be unusually flexible. Psychological adjustment following TBI may be difficult because the recovery process is often prolonged (Figure 12–3). The greatest potential for improvement occurs during the first two years following discharge from the hospital; frequent reevaluations of the child during that time are essential because brain functions often return, increasing the child's ability to do things he could not perform earlier.

1. Arrange for older child, adolescent, or adult who has gone through rehabilitation to spend time with the child. Such modeling and peer counseling can be very effective.
2. Expect variations from the Kübler-Ross (1969) stages; children with SCI or TBI often cycle through emotional states rather than proceeding through each in sequence.
3. Early denial is good, as it shows hope. By the time equipment must be ordered, however, denial becomes harmful. Engage the assistance of a child mental health specialist as needed.
4. Focus on practical realities as soon as possible. By solving concrete, day-to-day problems, children gain confidence and move beyond initial worries.
5. The entire child care team should offer support and encouragement.
6. Any behaviors that are self-destructive or otherwise harmful should be ignored so as to cause them to extinguish, and more adaptive behaviors taught in their place.

Adapted from Madden (1993) and Page and Chew (1993).

FIGURE 12–3 Psychological adjustment to SCI and TBI.

A longitudinal study, completed in 2005, followed children with TBI, many of them victims of shaken-infant syndrome. At about five years of age, the children had a range of problems. Two out of every three (68 percent) had neurological, motor, visual, speech and language, and behavioral problems. Some also had cognitive and adaptive delays or limitations, including specific learning disabilities. The researchers concluded that "inflicted TBI has a very poor prognosis" requiring "extended follow-up" (p. e174) (Barlow et al., 2005).

SPINAL CORD INJURY

Orthosis

is a device that enhances the function of a body part, as a leg brace helps a child walk. It contrasts with a *prosthesis,* which replaces a body part.

Prosthesis

is an artificial replacement, such as a mechanical arm or knee, for a missing limb or body part.

Individuals with SCI learn to use new muscles to perform functions now limited by the injury. They also learn from physical and occupational therapists how to use **orthoses** and **prostheses** and how to take advantage of any and all residual muscle strength. Assistive technology experts train people with SCI (and individuals with other disabilities as well) in the use of a wide range of assistive technology devices and services, including environmental control systems (ECSs).

ASTHMA

Intervention is primarily medical. A child may use a portable air compressor, which delivers antihistamine medication, with assistance from ECSE professionals. In asthma, swelling in the lungs makes breathing difficult. Antihistamines are often used to treat asthma, because they reduce the body's supply of histamines, thereby alleviating clogging in the lungs and easing the task of breathing. Other asthma medications include cromolyn sodium and steroids, which may be taken in pill form. The child should take medication prior to activities that in the past triggered attacks, such as exercise or test taking. In some cases, a nurse or physician injects medication.

ECSE personnel can take several other steps. First, unnecessary or prolonged physical activity should be avoided, because it may trigger an attack. Second, allergens such as pollen should be removed from the program environment if at all possible or at least reduced via heating, ventilation, and air-conditioning (HVAC) systems and filters. The recent increase in the reported incidence of asthma may be related to greater environmental allergens, which may flourish in carpets, in the air of tightly sealed rooms, and in furniture as dust mites. Third, events known to be stressful to the child should be minimized; if such events are unavoidable, ECSE personnel should consider antihistamine medication in advance of the activity and should monitor the child during that activity. They should learn to recognize signs that an asthma attack is coming or is under way. The characteristic patterns of labored breathing, dry coughing, and other indications of respiratory stress should alert ECSE personnel to the need to take action. Finally, ECSE personnel should watch for possible side effects of medication and know how to respond to those. Monitoring the condition is an important function for ECSE personnel.

MUSCULAR DYSTROPHY

Some studies suggest that the steroid prednisone slows the muscle deterioration. Boys taking prednisone did not need wheelchairs until about three years after boys not taking it did. Steroids, however, have serious side effects—including high blood pressure, cataracts, diabetes, and significant weight gain, which can be a particular problem for boys with weakened muscles to carry. Researchers are now trying to identify the active ingredient in prednisone that slows MD and isolate it, in the hope that they can offer help without the side effects. They are also trying to design treatments that will replace dystrophin or compensate for its absence. (This research was funded by the Muscular Dystrophy Association, the group for whom Jerry Lewis holds his Labor Day telethons.)

Now that a gene associated with Duchenne MD has been identified, it is possible that at some time in the near future genetic interventions may alleviate or even eliminate the effects of the disease. Until that time, physical therapy to slow down muscle atrophy and occupational therapy to help the child cope with muscle weaknesses are the principal interventions. Assistive technology devices can enable the child to do things that he no longer can do alone, such as sitting in an upright position. Mobility can also be enhanced by braces, crutches, and wheelchairs; and fine motor control functions can be facilitated by pointing, switching, and similar devices.

SPINA BIFIDA

The SBAA has estimated that the incidence of spina bifida could fall by as much as 75 percent if all women of childbearing age took appropriate amounts of folic acid. This is beginning to happen.

Children with spina bifida often have allergies to latex (natural rubber), which is often found in catheters, diapers, elastic bandages, rubber bands, balloons, pacifiers, and many other products. Latex-free substitutes are readily available for most of these items. The SBAA offers an extensive list of such substitutes at its Web site (www.sbaa.org). Bladder and/or bowel problems also are common with spina bifida. A *shunt,* or straw-shaped drain, can relieve the fluid buildup in hydrocephalus (Shaer, 1997). This shunt tubing empties the fluid into the abdominal cavity. Unfortunately, shunts sometimes become infected and may fail for other reasons as well (Shaer).

Most children with spina bifida do not require specially designed instruction because their learning needs are not affected by the condition (unless, of course, the children also have learning disabilities or attention deficits). However, assistive technology devices and services can help children with spina bifida to learn to walk, after surgery, using canes, crutches, and/or leg braces; others use manual or motorized wheelchairs (Shaer, 1997).

CEREBRAL PALSY

Computer speech synthesis can help children with CP much as it does children who are blind, deaf, retarded, or learning disabled. As with other children, speech synthesis systems offering a choice of voices (male, female, child, etc.) are important psychologically, because this will be the child's "voice." Because CP is a disability limiting expressive communication, children with CP need more than just a voice. Alternative means of input are often required, ranging from the simple (a "key guard" or plastic covering for the keyboard) to the complex (still experimental systems that translate brain patterns into words). Many alternatives to the keyboard are available. Any child with voluntary control over at least one muscle (even an eyebrow) can use alternative input mechanisms. Through microprocessor-based technologies, children with CP can express themselves in precise and complete ways.

Providing these children with such assistive technology devices and services is urgently important. Both the IFSP under Part C and the IEP under Part B may provide for assistive technologies. With such aids, many young children with CP can function well in integrated settings. More controversial are such interventions as conductive education (Kozma & Balogh, 1995), for which little empirical evidence exists.

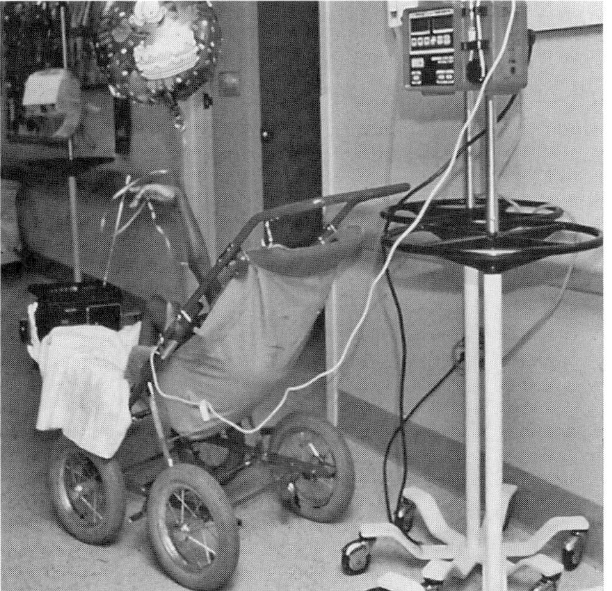

Medically fragile and technology-dependent children may have multiple, intensive needs that challenge child care professionals.

AMPUTATION

As a general rule, children who never had (or who have no memory of) the missing limb adjust more readily to the condition than do children who lose the limb later in childhood. They more quickly accept braces, artificial limbs, and assistive technology devices and services. By contrast, children who vividly remember life before amputation may resist the introduction of artificial devices and aids.

Orthoses (products that help children do things the amputation might otherwise prevent) and *prostheses* (devices that replace a missing body part) play important roles in intervention with children who have amputation. Other assistive technology devices and services are also frequently helpful. Chapter 9 offers an in-depth discussion of such technologies.

MEDICALLY FRAGILE, TECHNOLOGY-DEPENDENT CHILDREN

Nolan, Young, Hebert, and Wilding (2005) and Freund, Boone, Barlow, and Lim (2005) echo Lantos and Kohrman (1992) in suggesting that newborns who are technology-dependent require much greater degrees of hospital-home coordination than most intensive care unit (ICU) programs offer. The needs of these infants for complex life support devices—which must not only be selected, acquired, and operated but also maintained and, at times, repaired—brings technicians and computer experts into the family-hospital follow-up process. Renée Waissman (1993), of the Centre de Recherche Médecine in Paris, has commented that many parents who decide to accept responsibility to raise technology-dependent children, including children with chronic illnesses, "behave with conviction and a sense of responsibility when they decide to treat their child at home. However, they don't necessarily consider all possible consequences of their decision" (p. 29). Helping parents explore those possible outcomes is the responsibility of the professional. One aspect of that role is assisting parents to overcome what Waissman calls the "guilt of being healthy and being unable to transmit that health" (p. 30).

When medically fragile children begin early intervention or preschool programming, family relief may be short-lived. Public support for nursing or other monitoring during program hours may not be available under the IDEA, which does not authorize most medical care services. Unless the family is able to locate private health insurance or other coverage, the costs of having a nurse with the child throughout the day may soon bankrupt the family. Then, too, the fact that these children have one-on-one, constant adult monitoring limits their independence and may slow social and emotional growth. One solution to these problems is to place the child in a specialized setting, where child care workers and early childhood special educators are trained in maintaining the equipment and caring for the child.

An excellent guide to the legal aspects of related services for children with severe physical and health care needs is offered by Rapport (1996). She reviewed federal and state cases brought under the IDEA. Rapport notes that the U.S. Supreme Court's 1984 decision in *Irving Independent School District v. Tatro* (468 U.S. 883) continues to be the controlling case with respect to what are "medical services" (not covered by the IDEA) versus "educational services" (included in the IDEA). Under *Tatro,* services that can be performed by a nurse or other qualified person but that do not require a physician are the responsibility of educators if these services are necessary for the child to take part in the educational program.

WORKING WITH FAMILIES

Perhaps the most important information ECSE professionals can share with families of young children with physical disabilities is the existence of powerful federal accessibility laws. A physical disability in a child affects the family in many ways every day. The family must think about accessibility when making restaurant or movie reservations, when visiting the library, and even when calling for a doctor's or dentist's appointment. That is why the ADA and other legislation reviewed in Chapter 5 are so important. Yet surveys show that most parents have only limited understanding of what the ADA says, what it means to them, and how to file complaints. With families whose children's physical limitations are both significant and permanent (i.e., are disabilities), understanding these laws and how to make them work makes a tremendous difference in a family's ability to function every day in the community.

TBI can drain families as can few conditions other than autism. That is because the condition does not stabilize for years following the accident. The ability to remember new information, for example, may disappear for months or even a year. This may make the child unable to learn anything new. In most cases, the ability returns; however, until it does, no one knows when it will. Educational and therapeutic interventions are based on an intact ability to remember what is taught. This problem often traumatizes families, who find it not only frustrating but frightening. Meanwhile, functions that children had learned may be lost, even if only temporarily; still, it is disconcerting for a caretaker to see a toilet-trained three-year-old return to diapers. In all of these cases, ECSE programs may work in close collaboration with hospital staff and the family to plan and carry out interventions while waiting for the condition to stabilize.

Using lay language to explain needs and plans to families is essential. Keeney (1994) offers suggestions on empowering families of young children with TBI (these are summarized in Figure 12–4). Many of the suggestions also apply to children with other severe physical disabilities or conditions.

When children have delays in physical development but not disabilities, the issues are different. Usually, physical access is not a major concern (the child is not using a wheelchair, braces, a cane, etc.). ECSE personnel need to focus instead on helping the family understand how they may accelerate physical development by providing more opportunities to explore and play in safe locations. Meanwhile, developmental milestones in the domain of physical development are so well known to parents—the first step at one year comes to mind—that ECSE professionals may need to caution parents

1. Seek to empower the family to act as the child's primary caregiver and decision maker.
2. Eschew professional jargon in favor of clear, lay language.
3. Make sure the family understands that discharge does not mean the child is recovered; rather, it signals another in a long series of steps to rehabilitation.
4. Suggest that the family start a "recovery book" or journal into which family members enter changes in the child's condition and abilities. Such a record can provide encouragement when needed, by showing how far the child has come since discharge.
5. Work with the family to assess home accessibility, dietary requirements, equipment and financing for equipment, and whether the child needs an attendant.
6. Support family members (including siblings) to prepare them for major changes in their routines as they provide long-term care for the recovering child. Offer respite care if available.
7. Offer the family a "map" of every important facility or building in the child's life (home, clinic, school, church/synagogue, neighbor homes, playgrounds, etc.), together with names and telephone numbers of professionals who can provide assistance as needed at each location. Encourage the family to seek recreation and other "fun times" both for themselves and for the child.

Adapted from Keeney (1994).

FIGURE 12–4 Helping parents of young children with TBI.

that very considerable variation occurs even among "normal" infants, toddlers, and preschoolers. Flexibility is necessary so that parents do not become unduly worried when children are late in reaching developmental targets.

SUMMARY

Physical and occupational therapy are authorized under both Part C and Part B. Their importance is difficult to overstate. Young children are naturally active physically—as indeed they must be, because so much of their cognitive, social or emotional, communication, and adaptive development emerges as they act physically on their environment. That is why physical therapy (to develop muscles and to prevent atrophy) and occupational therapy (to teach children how to perform everyday tasks despite physical limitations) are so essential in ECSE. Today's wide variety of seating and mobility devices help, too; especially useful for children needing wheelchairs are sport chairs with which they may take part in recreational activities.

As important as these interventions are, much more may also be done. The built environment is far more accessible today than in past years, and this fact alone greatly increases the ability of families with young children who have physical disabilities to get around in the community. ECSE program staff should ensure that early childhood program facilities are accessible to people with physical limitations, that buildings and other facilities such as play areas at programs to which ECSE staff often refer children and their families are also accessible, and that families of children with physical disabilities themselves make their homes accessible as well. An important way in which ECSE staff may empower families is by making them aware of such laws and assisting them, where necessary, in filing complaints about violations with the appropriate authorities.

Some physical disabilities present special challenges both to families and to ECSE workers. Children who are medically fragile or technology-dependent, children recovering from TBI, and children with spina bifida often require ongoing medical, therapeutic, and other interventions over a period of years. Psychological adjustment can be challenging, because the children do not have the luxury of adjusting only once to a new level of functioning; rather, they often must readjust to what is almost a new disability as their condition alters.

KEY TERMS

accessible
adventitious
asthma
barrier-free
cerebral palsy (CP)
congenital
cystic fibrosis
juvenile rheumatoid arthritis
medically fragile, technology-dependent children
muscular dystrophy (MD)
occupational therapy
orthosis
paraplegia
physical therapy
pressure sores
prosthesis
quadriplegia
spina bifida
spinal cord injury (SCI)
traumatic brain injury (TBI)

QUESTIONS FOR REFLECTION

1. Explain in your own words what *experiential deprivation* means, and illustrate it with a child who has a physical disability such as cerebral palsy.
2. Differentiate *prevalence* from *incidence.*

3. Can you think of a good reason why physical conditions are proportionately more common among under-six children than among older children?
4. How might asthma affect a child's participation in an ECSE program? If you were an ECSE worker, how would you address those problems?
5. Which disability discussed in this chapter is closely associated with low birthweight?
6. Explain how brain damage as a result of a traumatic brain injury might not become apparent for several years after the accident.
7. What are *pressure sores,* and how can they be avoided?
8. How might a physical disability affect a child's performance on an IQ test?
9. Differentiate *accessible* from *barrier-free.* Which standard applies in which cases?
10. In your own words, what are the differences between physical therapy and occupational therapy?

PRACTICAL EXERCISES

1. Visit two ECSE programs in your town or city. Look for features of building accessibility (e.g., main doors that are level with the sidewalk or have ramps leading from the sidewalk to the main door, doors that are 36 inches wide, etc.). Could a family member (e.g. a grandfather) who uses a wheelchair visit the facility? If not, what changes would be required to make the facility *accessible,* according to information in this chapter?

   Ask facility staff whether they considered accessibility needs when they leased, rent, or bought the building. Ask, too, whether any family members or any young children being served have a need for accessibility features. If an accessibility study has been conducted, ask what the cost estimates were for making the building accessible. Write up your observations and conclusions. Share these with your professor.
2. Visit the Web sites of Dynavox Systems (www.dynavoxsys.com), and Prentke Romich (www.prentkeromich.com) to learn about augmentative and alternative communication (AAC) devices. Then contact local early intervention, preschool and primary-grade programs to find out at which, if any, ACC devices are in use. Make an appointment to observe the products in action. Do you agree with Romski and Sevcik (2005) that these devices are appropriate for use with young children?

WEB SITES OF INTEREST

www.access-board.gov U.S. Architectural and Transportation Barriers Compliance Board—the key federal agency on building accessibility

www.usdoj.gov U.S. Department of Justice—accessibility of existing facilities

www.apta.org American Physical Therapy Association—professional organization of physical therapists

www.abilityhub.com Portal about assistive technology products

CHAPTER

13

Cognitive Development

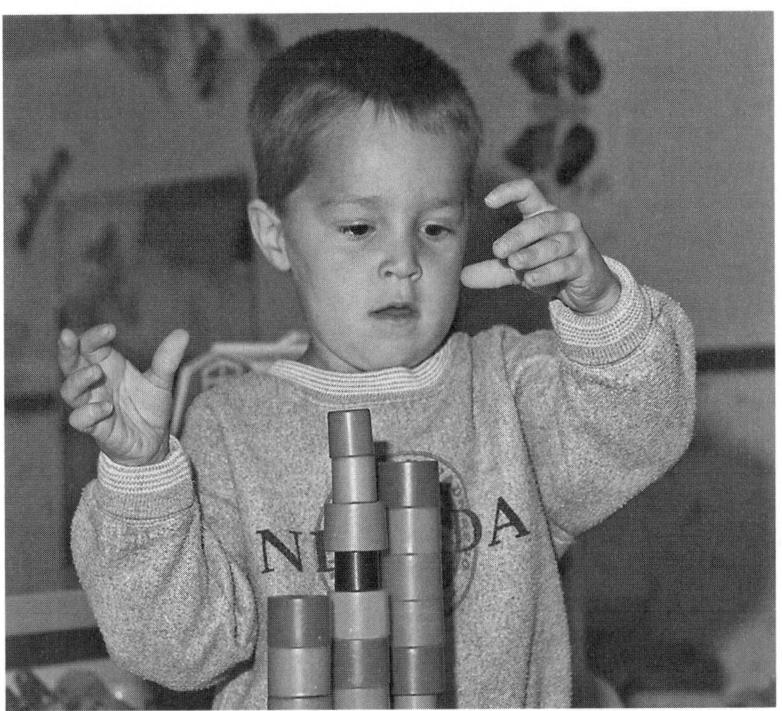

(Studying five year-olds who had shaken-infant syndrome or other inflicted traumatic brain injury as very young children): A wide range of neurologic sequelae were seen, including motor deficits (60%), visual deficits (48%), epilepsy (20%), speech and language abnormalities (64%), and behavioral problems (52%).... Adaptive functioning showed a wide range of difficulties across all domains: communication domain, daily living skills domain, and socialization domain.... Inflicted TBI has a very poor prognosis and correlates with severity of injury. Extended follow-up is necessary so as not to underestimate problems such as learning disabilities and attentional and memory problems that may become apparent only once the child is in school. (BARLOW ET AL., 2005, P. e174)

OBJECTIVES

After reading this chapter, you should be able to:

- Describe what the domain of cognitive development includes.
- Describe what learning disabilities are.
- Explain how mental retardation affects learning in young children.
- Describe what Down syndrome is.
- Explain why it is often difficult to diagnose learning disabilities in young children.

- Discuss how mental retardation can be prevented.
- Explain why direct instruction is often used in ECSE programs.

CHAPTER OUTLINE

- **OVERVIEW**
- **PREVALENCE**
- **DEVELOPMENTAL DELAYS**
- **ESTABLISHED CONDITIONS**
  - **Learning Disabilities**
  - **Mental Retardation**
  - **Down Syndrome**
  - **Fragile X Syndrome**
- **ASSESSMENT**
- **INTERVENTION**
  - **Prevention**
  - **Stimulation**
  - **Curriculum**
    - *Mental Retardation*
    - *Learning Disabilities*
    - *Fragile X Syndrome*
- **WORKING WITH FAMILIES**

OVERVIEW

The young child's "work," Piaget said, is play: to do things; explore; touch/feel/smell/taste things in the environment; and practice new skills such as walking, running, skipping, and rolling a ball. Cognition proceeds directly from such "work." Cognitive development has to do with age-appropriate functions involving perception, understanding, and knowledge.

Young children learn by doing. By walking, the child frees the hands; that, in turn, speeds up the child's exploration of the environment, leading to more cognitive growth. Chapter 12 also showed that through movement the child physically distances herself from caregivers, which naturally leads to psychological distance. The child, in large part, displays her cognitive accomplishments in physical activity. The child is also tested that way; tests and other procedures assess what she does physically. For these reasons, physical and cognitive development are closely linked. Adaptive development, as well, depends on both physical and cognitive growth.

Delays or disabilities in the cognitive domain of development are very common among young children. In this chapter, we will examine specific learning disabilities and mental retardation. The chapter-opening quote reminds us that children with primary conditions in other domains frequently have cognitive limitations.

PREVALENCE

According to the *Twenty-eighth Annual Report* (U.S. Department of Education, 2006c), relatively few young children have cognitive domain labels. Preschoolers with learning disabilities totaled 14,000 nationwide, while those with mental retardation added up to about 23,000. Among those in the six-to-eight-inclusive age range, 237,000 had learning disabilities and 65,000 had mental retardation.

These figures understate the prevalence for technical reasons. Until fall 2005, programs were not permitted to use the "specific learning disabilities" label unless they could show a "discrepancy" (difference) between intelligence and performance. Because achievement tests rarely are given earlier than third grade, this requirement had the effect of depressing the use of that classification. The requirement to show discrepancies was removed by IDEA 2004. Similarly, it is difficult to test intelligence in young children. The instruments used with preschoolers emphasize hand-eye coordination. Those used with older children are very different, looking more at factual knowledge and abstract reasoning.

DEVELOPMENTAL DELAYS

Most states define a "delay" in cognitive development as two standard deviations (SDs) below the mean, or about 70 to 75 IQ, or as 1.5 SDs below the mean if there are other kinds of developmental delays as well. Some states look to adaptive behavior, such as with a 12-month delay in expected cognitive accomplishments. In particular, infants, toddlers, and preschoolers who walk, feed themselves, and talk later than other children do may be classified as delayed in cognitive development; these, of course, are also indicators of possible delays in physical and communication development. Additionally, they may be considered to be delays in adaptive development. The boundary lines are not clear. Professional judgment (clinical opinion) is important in many state definitions of delay.

ESTABLISHED CONDITIONS

LEARNING DISABILITIES

Learning disabilities (LDs) are conditions interfering with or limiting academic kinds of activities. They are believed to have neurological bases. Dyslexia is an example of an LD.

The IDEA, from 1975 through the 1997 amendments, defined **learning disabilities (LDs)** as follows (Section 602[26]):

> *The term "specific learning disability" means a disorder in one or more of the basic psychological processes involved in understanding or in using language, spoken or written, which disorder may manifest itself in imperfect ability to listen, think, speak, read, write, spell, or do mathematical calculations. Such term includes such conditions as perceptual disabilities, brain injury, minimal brain dysfunction, dyslexia, and developmental aphasia. Such term does not include a learning problem that is primarily the result of visual, hearing, or motor disabilities, of mental retardation, of emotional disturbance, or of environmental, cultural, or economic disadvantage.*

IDEA 2004 kept that definition, now in Section 602(30), but made important changes elsewhere in the law. In Section 614 of Part B, IDEA 2004 added:

> *[W]hen determining whether a child has a specific learning disability as defined in section 602, a local educational agency shall not be required to take into consideration whether a child has a severe discrepancy between achievement and intellectual ability in oral expression, listening comprehension, written expression,*

basic reading skill, reading comprehension, mathematical calculation, or mathematical reasoning.

(B) ***ADDITIONAL AUTHORITY.****—In determining whether a child has a specific learning disability, a local educational agency may use a process that determines if the child responds to scientific, research-based intervention as a part of the evaluation procedures described in paragraphs (2) and (3).*

Dyslexia

is a learning disability that interferes with reading and writing, because letters seem to float across a page, reverse, or otherwise become difficult to read. Children with dyslexia display reading difficulties despite normal or near-normal intelligence and adequate opportunities to learn to read.

Metacognition

is awareness of one's own behavior and ways of thinking and learning.

It is quite possible that in coming years, we will see more young children identified as having learning disabilities now that the requirement to show a discrepancy has been removed. The language in (B) quoted here suggests that schools may use *response to intervention* as one of the considerations in deciding on classification. As explained earlier (see Chapter 6), response to intervention is an approach in which educators try different means of instruction to discover what works with an individual child.

The term *specific learning disabilities* begins with the word *specific* because there are several distinct kinds of learning disabilities. Dr. Mel Levine (2002), an expert in this area, explored those in his book *A Mind at a Time.* Levine showed that children may have difficulties with handwriting but not with any other intellectual functions. Alternatively, they may find it difficult to understand what is said to them but easy to understand what they read—or vice versa. Most common are *reading disabilities* (also known as **dyslexia**). Less common are auditory processing disorders, math-related learning disabilities, and LD-related organizational difficulties.

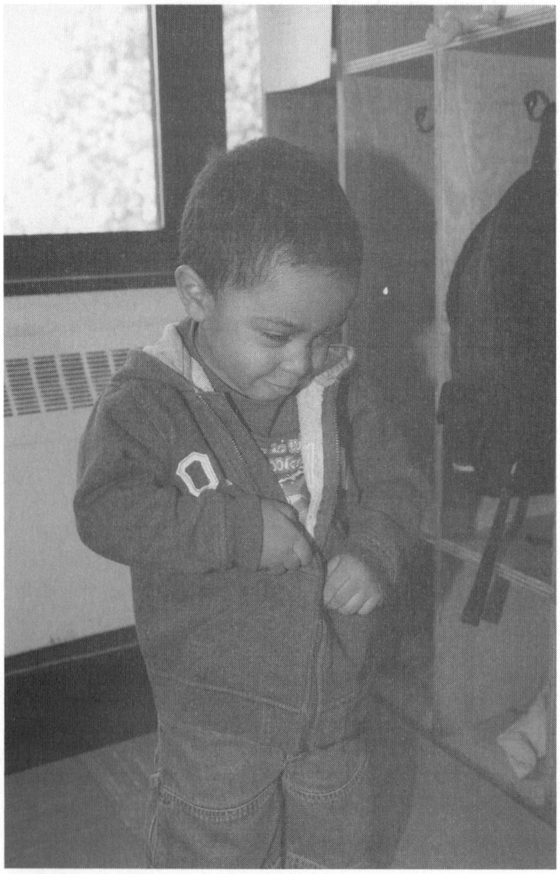

Despite the differences, children with specific learning disabilities typically are characterized as displaying limitations in **metacognition,** or understanding one's own thinking and learning patterns. They know that they are having problems learning, but do not understand why. These children also may find it hard to distinguish signal from noise (figure from ground). If reading, they may find illustrations, sidebars, and so on to be distracting. If listening, they may have trouble distinguishing a speaker's voice from ambient sounds.

Particularly interesting is work by Paula Tallal of Rutgers University. Examining young children with and without reading disabilities, Tallal discovered that those who had learning disabilities needed somewhat longer to process sensory input. Those with reading disabilities lagged well behind those with no disabilities in identifying the different sounds they heard and the different taps they felt from an examiner's fingers (Tallal, Stark, & Mellits, 1985). It is possible that delays in the brain's processing of sensory input may be an underlying characteristic of many different kinds of specific learning disabilities. It is possible that these delays may have neurological roots (e.g., Galaburda, Menard, & Rosen, 1994). Tallal's work, including material on phonemic awareness and on computer games that help stimulate the brains of young children with learning disabilities, is at www.cmbn.rutgers.edu.

Task analysis reveals that putting on a jacket may involve as many as 17 discrete steps.

Specific learning disabilities are difficult to identify in young children. Often, it is necessary to test for everything else before settling on a diagnosis of LD. This is especially true with young children. Tallal's work suggests that it may be possible, in the near future, to test for LD by looking at the brain's processing delays as it deals with input from the visual, auditory, and even tactile sensory channels.

MENTAL RETARDATION

Mental retardation

refers to a combination of adaptive behavior characteristic of younger age ranges and intellectual functioning significantly lower than normal when onset occurs prior to age 18. The current definition stresses that individuals with mental retardation need extensive systems of support.

The term ***mental retardation*** is used here because the IDEA continues to use it. The term is controversial in many quarters. The American Association on Mental Retardation (AAMR), the major professional association in the field, now downplays the words, preferring to use the initials. Many professionals have adopted such terms as *cognitive disabilities* or *intellectual disabilities*. The federal regulations for the IDEA define mental retardation along three dimensions: first, a measured intelligence test score that is two or more standard deviations below the mean (i.e., IQ of 70 or 75 or lower); second, adaptive behavior that is not age-appropriate; and third, onset during the developmental years (prior to about age 18). In addition, the definition notes that mental retardation "adversely affects a child's educational performance" (34 CFR 3000.7(b)(5). The AAMR definition is similar.

Mental retardation, from whatever cause, is defined along three variables. First, there are adaptive behavior deficits that are characteristic of much younger age ranges. Second, intellectual functioning is significantly lower than normal, with IQ test results at or below 70 to 75, or about two SDs below the mean. Third, the disability arises during the developmental period, usually understood as the first 18 years of life. The American Association on Intellectual Disabilities (AAID), formerly the AAMR (Luckason et al., 2002), puts it somewhat more formally:

> Mental retardation is a disability characterized by significant limitations both in intellectual functioning and in adaptive behavior as expressed in conceptual, social, and practical adaptive skills. This disability originates before age 18. A complete and accurate understanding of mental retardation involves realizing that mental retardation refers to a particular state of functioning that begins in childhood, has many dimensions, and is affected positively by individualized supports. As a model of functioning, it includes the contexts and environments within which the person functions and interacts and requires a multidimensional and ecological approach that reflects the interaction of the individual with the environment, and the outcomes of that interaction with regards to independence, relationships, social contributions, participation in school and community, and personal well being. (Luckason et al., 2002, p. 1)

The most important part of this definition has to do with functioning—it is the child's behavior, more than a score on a test, that signals mental retardation. Behavior that is acceptable in a one-year-old would be evidence of possible mental retardation if displayed by a three-year-old. Virtually all states recognize mental retardation as an established condition under Part C.

Down syndrome

is the most common identifiable cause of mental retardation, accounting for perhaps one-third of all cases. In addition to mental retardation, characteristic facial features, hypotonia (floppiness in muscles), and hearing loss are common in Down syndrome.

DOWN SYNDROME

First identified in 1866 by Dr. John Langdon Down, **Down syndrome** causes mild or moderate retardation. About 5,000 infants are born each year with Down syndrome; the majority are males. Down syndrome is the most common identifiable cause of mental retardation, accounting for perhaps one-third of all cases of retardation. Most other cases cannot be linked to a specific cause; they may have dietary, environmental, or other roots. Down syndrome includes characteristic facial features, hypotonia (floppiness in muscles), hearing loss, and numerous other physical problems (Msall, DiGaudio, & Malone, 1991). This condition is now known to be genetically caused in about 95 percent of cases, with unbalanced translocations of chromosome 21 accounting for most of the remainder. There are more than 1,000 genes on chromosome 21. The genetic basis for Down syndrome was first identified in 1959 by Dr. Jerome Lejeune (Cooley & Graham, 1991). In what is called *trisomy 21,* cells have three rather than two 21st chromosomes.

Down syndrome occurs about 1 in every 800 live births (Roizen, 1997). However, the condition is much more common than that proportion would indicate, not only because most fetuses with the syndrome are spontaneously aborted (through miscarriage) but also because readily available prenatal tests (including amniocentesis, chorionic villus sampling, and early amnio) can now identify the condition early in pregnancy. Many prospective parents choose to abort rather than proceed to term.

Although mental retardation is the best-known effect of Down syndrome, the condition is far more complex than that. Most children with Down syndrome have a measurable hearing loss, particularly in the high frequencies. Visual impairments are also common. Hypotonia is very common in Down syndrome. It can interfere with breast feeding (causing tongue protuberation that makes feeding a more laborious process than usual) and can also produce constipation due to hypotonic gut musculature. The syndrome includes cardiac conditions in about 44 percent of cases, including congenital heart disease (Cooley & Graham, 1991). These cardiac conditions are a major cause of premature death and remain a concern throughout the early childhood years; indeed, most cardiac-related deaths in people with Down syndrome occur during the first five years of life. Other common causes of premature death include susceptibility to infection, immature digestive tracts (including duodenal atresia), and respiratory problems. Absent these or other physical problems, people with Down syndrome typically live to 50 or 55 years of age, some longer.

During the first year of life, parents and professionals alike need to be alert to acquired loss of hearing and/or vision. In addition, tonic/clonic seizures (formerly called *grand mal seizures*) may occur in about 10 percent of cases. In the subsequent early childhood years, generalized delays will likely become evident. As should be evident by now, the syndrome affects physical, adaptive, and communication behavior, not just cognitive development. It is important for parents and ECSE professionals alike to bear in mind that Down syndrome infants, toddlers, and preschoolers have the same range and types of childhood problems as do other children; thus, they should not focus their attention exclusively on syndrome-related concerns.

FRAGILE X SYNDROME

Fragile X syndrome

is a condition resulting from damage to the X chromosome. Hyperactivity and mental retardation are common symptoms in males; females are usually only carriers.

Fragile X syndrome results from damage to the X chromosome (which is also implicated in Duchenne muscular dystrophy). Females have two X chromosomes, so if one is damaged but the other is not, symptoms usually do not appear; instead, females become carriers of the condition. In the few females who do have symptoms, these are mild, usually limited to learning difficulties; they rarely call for drugs or other treatment. Males, however, have only one X chromosome; the other sex chromosome, the Y chromosome, cannot overcome problems in the X chromosome. Fragile X syndrome is now recognized as the leading cause of mental impairment in males. Symptoms in males include mild to severe hyperactivity, mild to severe retardation, moderate LD, autism—or no symptoms at all. Fragile X syndrome is believed to occur in 1 in every 1,000 male live births and 1 in every 2,000 female live births. In only one-third of the women, however, do symptoms appear.

New tests are now available to screen family members in cases where inheritance of fragile X syndrome is a concern, costing as little as $250 (they previously were $700). Some states routinely screen public school children for the condition if family history suggests that it may occur. However, the disorder can appear with no prior family history.

ASSESSMENT

Assessment may identify delays or deviations. Delays are typical behaviors but at later-than-expected ages. Babbling at three years of age, for example, constitutes a delay. Deviations, however, are very atypical behaviors. Copying drawings backward, for example, is unusual in children at any age. The IDEA insists that all potentially eligible young children be assessed by a multidisciplinary team. That team should examine cognitive development in each child, regardless of the fact that a given child may have primary needs in some other domain of development. The interconnections between domains are so dramatic that a multidisciplinary approach is essential.

Frequently used in assessment of young children suspected of having mental retardation is the Peabody Picture Vocabulary Test (AGS Publishing). The PPVT-III (www.agsnet.com) is a test of receptive vocabulary. The examiner states a word, and the child indicates, by pointing or speaking, which picture corresponds to the word. Popular, too, are the Vineland Adaptive Behavior Scales, also from AGS Publishing. The second edition (www.agsnet.com) includes a family interview and a teacher rating scale. Because children with mental retardation typically have limitations in several areas of functioning, ECSE professionals may also use the Denver Developmental Screening Test (Frankenburg et al., 1990) and the Battelle Developmental Inventory (Newborg et al., 1984). Especially with Down syndrome, hearing and vision should also be assessed (see Chapter 11).

Diagnosing LD during the early childhood years is very difficult, because the definition refers to academic work—notably reading, writing, and calculation—that may not be developmentally appropriate for the early childhood years. Yet some children do show the perceptual problems, seeming inability to do metacognition (examining one's own behavior and adjusting it to learn better), excessive distractibility, and/or poor coordination that are indicators of possible LD. But actually diagnosing learning disabilities is problematic. Ariel (1992), for example, in a text on LD, states:

> The early identification of learning disabilities is a complex process due to the following factors: (a) learning disabilities are viewed primarily as an academic handicap, making it difficult to predict academic difficulty before kindergarten or first grade; (b) learning disabilities are more difficult to detect early than are severe handicaps; (c) differential developmental patterns make it difficult to distinguish between the existence of learning disabilities and a developmental lag; (d) the

> impreciseness of the definition of learning disabilities makes it difficult to establish widely accepted eligibility criteria; and (e) the use of labels permeates the identification of any of the "mildly handicapping conditions." (p. 205)

The findings by Tallal and other researchers on processing problems in children may be used someday soon in ECSE assessment. Her technique of touching two fingers under a table in rapid succession, described earlier in this chapter, does not require elaborate laboratory settings. Tallal's work suggests that requiring children to perform rapid speech production may help in differentiating children who have LD from children whose problems are due to other factors.

Giving children very rapid visual signals and then asking them to report what they saw may be a third method of assessment when one is testing for LD. That possible indicator draws on the work of Livingstone, Rosen, Drislane, and Galaburda (1991). In all three cases, the suggestion is that one key to diagnosing dyslexia and other learning disabilities in young children may be testing for ability to process information rapidly. Livingstone et al. suggest that auditory, tactual, and perhaps other brain processing functions may be impaired in ways similar to those they found in visual information processing among children with dyslexia.

The most practical approach in assessment of LD probably remains the one most commonly used in special education: test the child for everything else, and if the problems are not due to other conditions, it may be a learning disability. Complete physical, psychological, and sensory examinations should be given together with a comprehensive family medical history. As noted earlier, response to intervention (RTI) should also be used.

Assessing children with fragile X syndrome can be challenging. Freund (1994) suggests that assessors look for behavioral indicators (extreme hyperactivity, autistic-like activities) believed to be associated with the condition, as well as for wide, protruding ears and a long face—both thought to be physical indicators of possible fragile X syndrome. Genetic factors are critical in this syndrome, so a thorough family history should be taken. As noted, screening tests may also be used.

INTERVENTION

Interventions or—to adopt a term popularized by AAMR—supports range from intermittent (occasional, as needed) to pervasive (continuous and of high intensity). Early intervention, preschool, and primary-grade programs aim to prevent or ameliorate mental retardation by offering environments that are intellectually stimulating. Family members are encouraged to engage young children in word-rich conversations, to expose them to a variety of activities, and to protect them from exposure to lead-based paints and other toxins.

PREVENTION

Good prenatal and pediatric medical care and good nutrition, together with stimulating environments, are known, from two decades of research, to be effective in preventing or lessening mental retardation (Infant Health and Development Program, [IHDP] 1990; Martin et al., 1990). In addition, physicians now advise women to avoid alcohol during pregnancy. ECSE professionals are sensitive to any indication of child abuse, recognizing that shaken-infant syndrome includes substantial cognitive impairments. They also arrange for, and encourage parents to engage in, physically active pursuits for young children, in recognition that movement is a major way by which these children learn.

In Chapter 3, we summarized the very encouraging findings of McCormick and her colleagues (2006). Their study was a longitudinal follow-up on one of the major prevention studies of the 20th century, the IHDP. This project worked with nearly a thousand children and their families in eight cities. Focusing on low-birthweight (LBW) (<2,500 grams, or about 5.5 pounds) and premature <37 weeks' gestational age) infants and toddlers, the IHDP aimed to prevent mental retardation in these at-risk populations. The program used a center-based approach supplemented by home visits. Children began in the program at 12 months of age and continued until the age of three. A control group of similar infants received routine medical follow-up services. This experimental-control design is what allowed McCormick, 16 years later, to compare different levels of intensity in services.

The original IHDP program obtained impressive results, especially with the experimental group. Stanford-Binet test scores at age three were much higher with experimental subjects than with control subjects. While many control infants had IQs of 85 or lower at age three, most experimental subjects tested at 95 or better.

Looking again at the IHDP data, Ramey and Ramey (1992) conclude that those LBW/premature infants whose families participated most frequently in the program gained most. Participation was measured by the number of home visits completed, the number of parent group meetings attended, and the number of sessions the infant attended at the eight program centers. Infants from high-participation families did much better, with just 2 percent testing as mentally retarded (IQ ≤ 70) at age three, compared with 4 percent of medium participants, 13 percent of low participants, and 17 percent of control subjects (nonparticipants) (Ramey & Ramey, 1992). The findings held even for very LBW and very premature infants. This is important, indicating that family involvement is a key to successful prevention of mental retardation.

Children with needs in the domain of cognitive development have physical development needs as well. As is true with other children in this age range, they tend to learn most through physical activity. Such activity should be as unrestrained as possible so they may learn by doing.

STIMULATION

The issue of environmental stimulation is urgently important, especially in low-SES families where parents or other primary caregivers have attained low education levels (see Figure 13–1). It is vitally important for children with cognitive delays, deviations, or disabilities that parents and ECSE professionals alike make use of *linguistic elaboration* techniques. That is, they should talk out what they are doing, why they are doing it, and not only what the child should do but why, and in what steps. ECSE workers suspecting communication impoverishment in the home may want to assist parents and other family members to learn how to expand on and explain their communication with their children.

Particularly helpful to many children with Down syndrome is the personal computer (PC). PCs equipped with speech synthesis (computer talk) are especially valuable, because the computer's monotonous "voice" gives equal emphasis to each phoneme. The hearing impairment that is common in children with Down syndrome often causes them to miss word endings, prepositions, and other sentence elements that are spoken rapidly, in higher pitches, and merged into other words (as "howdjadue" for "How do you do?"). The computer pronounces each sound with the same speed and at much the same pitch, making it much easier for children with Down syndrome to hear, attend to, and learn these sounds and parts of speech (Adler & Drew, 1988).

Ironically, then, the preferred speech synthesis hardware and software system for use with children who have Down syndrome is one of the older, less sophisticated ones. Newer, state-of-the-art speech synthesis systems that produce high-quality speech with greater variability in pitch are less suitable, because children who have Down syndrome often display mild to moderate hearing losses. To some extent, properly fitted hearing aids may help the child understand even the newer, more variegated speech synthesis systems.

Early infant stimulation and continued high-quality communication interaction make a tremendous difference to young children who are mentally retarded. This kind of early and rich stimulation, combined with use of technology discussed in Chapter 9, is having a profound impact on children who are mentally retarded today, as compared with years past. PCs presenting information both auditorially and visually can be very helpful to young children who are mentally retarded. Multimedia presentations offer the child

1. Nutrition interventions, because much mild retardation in particular appears to result from poor diet
2. A rich variety of activities providing stimulation
3. Multisensory input, because when young children with mental retardation hear, see, and touch things, they learn more, and faster
4. Behavior modification, because it helps clarify for the child what behaviors are desired
5. Modeling, because studies by Albert Bandura (1977) and Marc Gold (1980) demonstrate that showing a child what is desired may be the clearest, most direct means of instruction available to us
6. Instructing parents and other primary caregivers on how to use language to elaborate on directions and to explain what is wanted, rather than just repeating the injunction "No!"
7. Encouraging children to explore, limiting caregiver control to essential constraints

FIGURE 13–1 What works: mental retardation.

redundancy, or the same information in different forms, and this redundancy appears to help many young children with mental retardation learn. Interactivity is another feature of many educational software programs; these programs present information, request a response, and react to that answer by branching into one of several next steps. And of course the program has no emotions; it does not become impatient with a child who is slow or angry with a child who is error-prone.

CURRICULUM

Whatever methods they adopt, ECSE professionals face a daunting task in preparing students with cognitive disabilities for the high-stakes tests that begin in third grade. According to the SEELS longitudinal study, fully 88 percent of students with mental retardation and 66 percent of those with specific learning disabilities who are in the 6- to 12-year age range performed at the lowest level (bottom one-fifth) in passage comprehension tests. In math calculation, the numbers were similar: 82 percent of those with mental retardation and 40 percent of those with learning disabilities were in the lowest one-fifth of their age cohorts. In math problem solving, the figures, respectively, were 88 percent and 42 percent. These findings help explain why so many young children with these disabilities are retained in grade (held back) in first, second, and third grades. They also challenge educators: rather than hold children back for another year of the same kinds of ineffective instruction, ECSE staff should adopt proven techniques such as Direct Instruction, peer tutoring, and the like, so as to help these children master academics (see Chapter 6).

Mental Retardation

Teaching young children with mental retardation begins with an individual assessment. What does the child know? What can he do? Often, these children can do some, but not all, of a task or assignment. That is when early interventionists and special educators do a *task analysis*. The technique is what the term implies: you analyze the assignment to see what components comprise it. Putting on a winter coat, for example, might involve as many as 17 distinct movements. The child is shown each in turn, given practice at it, and offered opportunities to demonstrate success at it before a second, and then a third, small step is added.

A related idea is called *ecological inventory*. The early interventionist or special educator closely examines the room, the school, the neighborhood, the home, and the surrounding community, looking for what is available to help the child learn. Especially helpful with young children having mental retardation are *manipulatives*—concrete objects they can hold, look at, touch, manipulate, and even smell. Also useful are opportunities for community-based instruction, or in situ teaching. Thus an animal hospital or veterinarian's office has real animals the children can see, hear, and pet.

Because we learn and remember when our emotions are involved—think back to your most vivid childhood memories—early interventionists and special educators look for ways to evoke emotion. Singing is an example, as is physical motion—because it is playful, it can trigger joy and pride and thus make lessons memorable.

Direct Instruction—teach, test, reteach, and retest—is well established as effective with this population. The approach has teachers doing explicit instruction of precisely what it is that the child needs to learn.

In these and many other ways, early interventionists and special educators try this, try that, looking for the often-elusive "hook" that leads to the child learning. Young children with mental retardation typically have much better long-term than short-term memory. Whatever method is used to get information into long-term memory—that is, whatever works—is the key. Once they store information in long-term memory, they are much less likely to forget it.

While many early childhood professionals favor *discovery learning*, in which they put out interesting materials and give young children freedom to explore ideas with them, such approaches need to be adapted when young children have mental retardation. Some will need *guided* discovery learning, a variation in which professionals and paraprofessionals offer direction and occasional redirection to keep the child on track, while others require *directed* discovery learning, in which the staff members help the child step-by-step through the process.

Particularly with children having Down syndrome, early interventionists and special educators need to remind themselves that there are five domains of development. These children need attention in, and assistance with, communication, adaptive behavior, social and emotional behavior, and physical activity, in addition to cognitive development. The fact that high-stakes tests of academics loom in third grade may, unfortunately, limit the amount of time that educators can devote to those noncognitive domains. It is urgent, nonetheless, that these not be neglected. Young children with mental retardation need support in all five domains.

Learning Disabilities

The most important aspect of teaching young children with specific learning disabilities is instructing them in *how* to learn (Bowe, 2005; Pierangelo & Giuliani, 2006b). They need to be introduced to strategies that work for them—in reading, in doing math, in social situations. That is why *strategy instruction* is a major component of early intervention and special education with this population. Indeed, strategy instruction is largely what is done in resource rooms in elementary, middle, and high schools—and it should begin in the prekindergarten years. When these children learn what works for them, they become empowered. They gain in confidence. They become better learners.

At these age levels, children do not yet know how their brains differ from those of other students. The maxim "We learn what we live" applies here: these young children only know what their own experience has taught them. But their brains are wired differently than are other children's. General education is structured around the typical child's capabilities. Educators know, but these young children are still discovering, that specific learning disabilities make certain ways of learning difficult. The author of this text has taught many hundreds of students with learning disabilities and must admit: They were all different. There is no one technique, no one modality, no one magic "hook" that works with all of them. Rather, it is a discovery process. At the preschool and primary-grade levels, that discovery is teacher led. You need to tell the child to "do it this way" and see what happens. Much later, when they are in high school or even college, they will be able to tell you "here's what works for me." That is not the case at the early childhood level.

Deshler and his colleagues at the University of Kansas have articulated this theme in their well-regarded Strategic Instruction Model (SIM; www.ku-crl.org). Children learn different ways of attacking and identifying words. They ask themselves questions about materials. They paraphrase (use their own words to describe something). They visualize what they are reading or math problems they are trying to solve. Over time, they learn what works for them. They develop confidence in those tactics.

Because many children with learning disabilities are visual learners, software that organizes information visually can be very powerful. Kidspiration, from Inspiration (www.inspiration.com), is a good example. This computer software program lets children choose pictures or icons to represent different ideas. They can place those around a page to represent a sequence of activities or a timeframe for a story. Kidspiration automatically creates a text outline that these children may use to write an essay. The program is in widespread use in kindergarten and primary grades throughout the country for children with no disabilities, because its visual nature appeals to today's young children who grew up with video games. Thus, it is nonstigmatizing for children with learning disabilities who need it to organize their thoughts. Kidspiration includes a text to speech utility: the program talks. Text to speech can be very helpful for young children with learning disabilities because it clarifies which words are being read (thus preventing them from thinking that "fab" is "tab") and keeps them on the right line as they read.

At the primary-grade level, the looming third-grade high-stakes tests call for educators to help these young children prepare for and successfully take standardized tests in math, language arts, and science. Children with learning disabilities need strategies for test taking as much as for everyday classroom use. Mnemonics in particular can help them remember information and sequence their work in high-stakes assessments. The work of Deshler and others at the University of Kansas shows that when children create labels for each step they must follow or each piece of information they must remember and create a mnemonic from the first letter of each label, they do much better on tests. *Mnemonics* are tools that many children learn on their own. Experience shows that young children with learning disabilities typically do not independently adopt such strategies. Rather, educators need to teach them how to use mnemonics.

Fragile X Syndrome

This condition was relatively recently identified, so not much is known about working with children who have fragile X syndrome. Freund (1994), for example, observes, "No unique or specific interventions for young fragile X children have been identified through research" (p. 43). She does, however, indicate that adaptive behavior interventions are urgently important with such children: "[A]daptive social development . . . is probably the single most important issue of development for the developmentally delayed fragile X child" (p. 43). Adaptive development is considered in Chapter 15.

Suggestions made elsewhere in this book on interventions with children who have similar problems, albeit due to other conditions, may help. Extreme hyperactivity is an example. Helping children with fragile X syndrome often involves the use of prescription drugs such as Ritalin and Dexedrine to control hyperactivity; the same medications are also used with children diagnosed as having ADHD. Because many young children with fragile X syndrome display autistic behaviors, some of the interventions suggested by Frith (1993) may be useful (see Chapter 15). Offering lessons visually, especially on computer, seems to help as well.

Family counseling is an important intervention when a child is diagnosed as having fragile X syndrome. That is because the inheritance pattern is such that the condition is not merely passed on from parent to child but will occasionally worsen from generation to generation. That is not always true. In some instances, the error pattern shrinks (the number of repeats becomes smaller in child than in parent). It is not yet known why that occurs. However, once the mechanisms causing this error correction to take place are discovered, it may be just a short step to genetic therapy for fragile X syndrome.

WORKING WITH FAMILIES

ECSE workers may suggest ways to provide stimulation for young children at home, particularly in families where parents are not well educated. As Craig Ramey's Project CARE showed, efforts by early intervention and preschool specialists to help members of low-SES families can have dramatic results (Ramey & Ramey, 1992). A related approach ECSE specialists may suggest to parents is that of linguistic elaboration.

Although Ramey worked with families of young children believed to be at risk for delays in cognitive development, it must be emphasized here that cognitive development during the first six years of life is of crucial significance for *all* young children. To illustrate, consider a three-year-old child who is deaf. Unless parents and other family members act aggressively to create in the home a rich environment that provides visual information and stimulation to the child, the child will not develop normally in the cognitive domain. That is why the IDEA emphasizes that all young children should be helped, as appropriate, in all five domains of development.

Also helpful, research suggests, is specific information answering parents' questions. Fragile X syndrome, for example, can be frightening for many families. In particular, women who learn that they are carriers of the genetic defect responsible for the condition need counseling to understand their options. Families who have one child with Down syndrome understandably want to know what the likelihood is that future children will also be affected. This kind of genetic counseling will likely become an increasingly important function of ECSE programs, as more and more families turn to ECSE professionals for knowledgeable guidance in dealing with these troubling questions.

SUMMARY

Cognitive development depends heavily on environmental influences. Young children grow intellectually when they are given frequent and ample opportunities to explore; when they are surrounded by visual, auditory, and tactile stimulation; and when they receive explanations rather than just orders or directions. On the other hand, when they are overprotected (perhaps by worried parents), when they are deprived of intellectual stimulation (perhaps because of deafness or because of parental neglect), and when they hear and see little linguistic interaction between adults, their cognitive development is slowed.

Regardless of these influences, ECSE staff members need to design interventions that will help young children with mental retardation or learning disabilities. A key is to individualize instruction. With children having mental retardation, Direct Instruction helps do that. The approach calls for the early interventionist or special educator to organize the material to be learned and to sequence it in a way that it can be mastered, then explicitly to teach it, test the child, reteach what the child did not learn, and retest the child. It is an intensive, teacher-led activity.

With young children who have learning disabilities, Direct Instruction is also helpful. However, more effective is strategy instruction. That is because what these children most need are learning and memory strategies that work for them.

KEY TERMS

Down syndrome
dyslexia
fragile X syndrome
learning disabilities (LDs)
mental retardation
metacognition

QUESTIONS FOR REFLECTION

1. What are some early indications of possible learning disabilities?
2. Explain in your own words what *metacognition* means.
3. Why is it significant that IDEA 2004 removed the long-standing requirement to show a "discrepancy" between ability and achievement for classification of a child as having a specific learning disability?
4. In your own words, what is *response to intervention* (RTI)?
5. Why is low socioeconomic status associated with mild mental retardation?
6. Give at least three characteristics of Down syndrome.
7. Why does fragile X manifest itself in boys rather than in girls?
8. Why is it so difficult to diagnose learning disabilities in young children?
9. What kinds of interventions appear to help in preventing mild mental retardation?
10. Describe *direct instruction,* and explain why it is often used with young children with mental retardation.

PRACTICAL EXERCISES

1. Visit the family of a child being served in an ECSE program. You can get permission from a program administrator to contact the family, and then request the family's permission. Ideally (this may not be possible), you should try to visit with two families: one middle-class family where both parents are college graduates and one lower-class family where neither parent is a college graduate.

   Compare the language used by the family members with young children. Do you see elaboration (the use of words to explain decisions and to help young children understand a caretaker's thinking)? Or do you see short, declarative sentences being used to give orders, without much explanation?

   Look for other kinds of stimulation. Do adults in the family make a conscious effort to provide visual, auditory, and other kinds of stimulation for young children?

   Write up your observations and conclusions. Share these with your professor.

2. Visit the Web site www.inspiration.com, select Kidspiration, and call up the Quick Tour. After viewing the demo, explain what features this graphic organizer offers that may appeal to young children.

WEB SITES OF INTEREST

www.ldanatl.org Learning Disabilities Association of America—organization of persons interested in learning disabilities

www.thearc.org The Arc—organization of persons interested in mental retardation

www.ku-crl.org University of Kansas Center for Research on Learning

CHAPTER

Social or Emotional Development

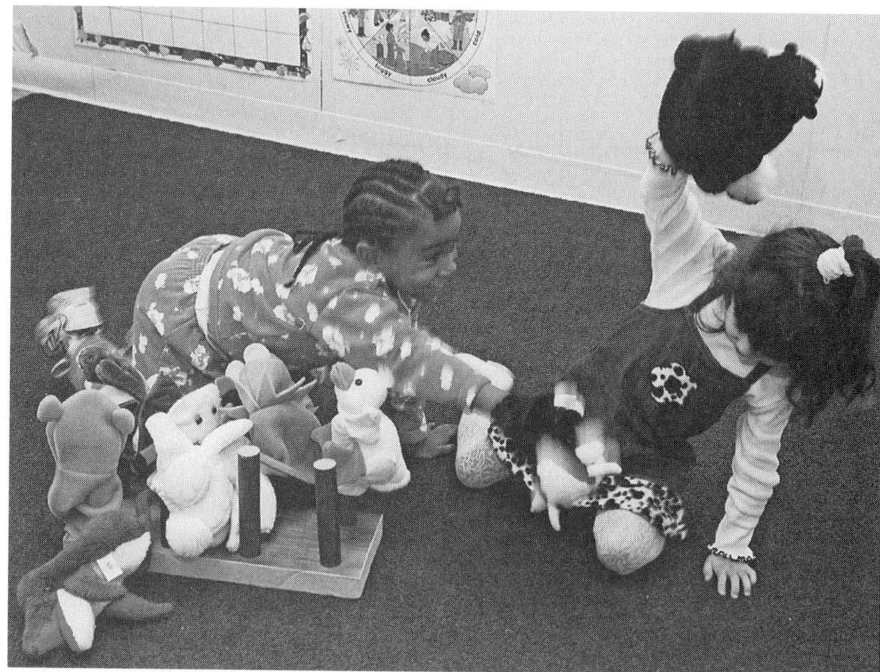

Testifying before the U.S. Senate Subcommittee on Disability Policy in 1989, Steve Forness said, on behalf of the National Mental Health Special Education Consortium:

> [W]e simply do not know enough about identifying and serving children [with emotional disturbance] in our public schools. Three of five of these children are in restrictive school settings. As a matter of fact, we are using out-of-school placements for these children half again as much as any other major category of special education. We are taking them out of their homes and even out of their communities in order to serve them, rather than developing school-based programs. Two out of five children we serve drop out of school before graduation. It is the highest dropout rate of all ten categories of special education. Something is not working. . . . There is a shortage of teachers in this category and it is the worst of all ten categories in special education. It is especially critical in recruiting minority teachers. Thirty percent of our teachers leave after three or four years, because of the stress of this job. (Forness, 1989, pp. 186–187)

OBJECTIVES

After reading this chapter, you should be able to:

- Describe what is considered to be "emotional disturbance" in the IDEA.
- List what other impairments are included in this domain.
- Explain how attention-deficit hyperactivity disorders (ADHD) are diagnosed.
- Explain how ECSE professionals decide "how much is too much" with respect to disruptive behavior.
- Describe what behavior modification teaches professionals to do—and not do.

- Explain how "shaping" can be used in ECSE programs.
- Discuss the pros and cons of medicating young children with ADHD.

CHAPTER OUTLINE

- OVERVIEW
- PREVALENCE
- DEVELOPMENTAL DELAYS
- ESTABLISHED CONDITIONS
- ASSESSMENT
- INTERVENTION
  - Behavior Modification
  - Other Interventions
  - Interagency Coordination
- WORKING WITH FAMILIES

OVERVIEW

Delays in and limitations of social or emotional development are important to ECSE personnel for two reasons. First, the domain is important in itself and has, as Dr. Forness told the Senate, received relatively less attention from special educators than have other kinds of disabilities. Speaking on behalf of the Council for Exceptional Children (CEC), Frederick Weintraub told the Senate at the same hearing, "It is generally agreed that this area (emotional development) is probably the most problematic in special education and the area that historically has gotten the least national attention and leadership" (Weintraub, 1989, p. 30). Children with social or emotional disorders need help to be successful in ECSE programs—and later in school as well. Fortunately, well-established principles of modifying inappropriate behavior are available for use in EC programs.

The domain of social or emotional development is much broader than is the Part B category "emotionally disturbed." For this reason, ECSE programs have an opportunity to serve many young children who have important needs but who may not qualify for needed services after they leave preschool. The ECSE focus on family services allows professionals to intervene in families much more readily than does the more child-centered focus of elementary and secondary education. Family services during the early childhood years can help parents understand how social and emotional development occurs, learn ways of stimulating appropriate behavior, and acquire competence in using nonpunitive methods to control behavior. By intervening early with both the child and the family, ECSE programs may prevent or at least ameliorate severe social or emotional problems.

If allowed to continue, on the other hand, these problems may become worse. The National Longitudinal Transition Study—2 shows that students with emotional/behavioral disorders have the lowest graduate rates of youth with any classification (56 percent). Released in late 2005 (www.nlts2.org), these findings are sobering. In today's society, a high school diploma is required even for entry-level jobs. While paid employment may seem far away to families with children still in the early childhood years, it really is not. As Forness (1989) told Congress, early intervention is essential if long-term consequences are to be avoided.

The domain of social or emotional development is important to ECSE professionals for another reason. Children with established conditions or delays in other domains of early childhood development may also have social or emotional problems. These may occur, for example, when a child who is blind arrives at a child care center or preschool program not having had the kinds or amount of social interaction other children take for granted. This child's experiential deprivation may surface as age-inappropriate behavior, including excessive withdrawal, self-stimulation, and other indicators that the child needs assistance in social and emotional growth. Similarly, children with severe physical disabilities may have had years of hospitalization; their experiences, the lives they have lived, are very different from those of most children. That their behavior, too, should differ is no surprise. Third, these children may have health problems or physical conditions placing them at risk for accidents or illnesses even in ordinary, everyday activities; parental worries, often internalized by the child, may lead them to avoid activity and fear social interaction. These children are not emotionally disabled, but their behavior may be similar in some ways to the behavior of children who are.

This reinforces a central theme of this book: ECSE programs should assess social or emotional development in *all* young children and should consider interventions appropriate for all of them, not merely those showing disabilities, delays, or deviations primarily in the social or emotional development domain. Indeed, the multidisciplinary approach required by the IDEA mandates that members of the multidisciplinary team perform an assessment of social or emotional development in all young children and that services be provided, as appropriate, in this domain even if the child's primary needs are in some other domain of development.

However, social or emotional development in early childhood is of most concern in one or both of two instances. One is when social or emotional problems interfere with the child's own learning; an example is a child whose thumb sucking is so excessive that he rarely participates in activities requiring the use of both hands. The second is when these problems interfere with learning by other children; an obvious example is when a child's temper tantrum disrupts a group activity. Although social or emotional disorders, delays, and deviations are challenging for ECSE professionals, the evidence is that real progress can often be made in this domain. That is fortunate for many reasons. Young children are most likely to succeed in kindergarten and beyond if they display acceptable behavior and stay on task (e.g., Kemp & Carter, 2005). They also need to know how to communicate their feelings, desires, and concerns effectively. The SEELS longitudinal study (Blackorby et al., 2005) suggests that elementary-age students with emotional disorders lag badly in communicating with others, although they can speak as clearly as can any children. When ECSE staff members are effective in helping these young children express themselves, and in understanding others' statements and emotions accurately, young children with emotional or behavioral disorders are far more likely to get along with other children well enough to be successful in school.

PREVALENCE

This chapter discusses children who most often are classified with emotional/behavioral disorders or attention-deficit hyperactivity disorders. Neither label is frequently used in the early childhood years. In large part, this relates to the subjectivity of these labels. The

IDEA category "emotionally disturbed" is one that calls for professionals to make informed judgments about behavior. ADHD, too, whether the hyperactive/impulsive variety (ADHD/HI) or the inattentive version (ADHD/I), is a judgment call. Many professionals prefer to reserve judgment ("Hopefully, he will grow out of it").

The *Twenty-eighth Annual Report* (U.S. Department of Education, 2006c), reveals that emotional/behavioral disorders were reported in 2004 for just 819 three-year-olds, 1,539 four-year-olds, and 3,455 five-year-olds—nationwide. We begin to see sizeable numbers of children with this classification after the EC period. The nationwide total exceeds 20,000 only when children are nine years of age. For purposes of comparison, speech and language impairments were identified approximately 50 times as frequently during the early childhood period. Because ADHD is not an IDEA classification, we do not have nationwide figures on this disorder. The SEELS report (Blackorby et al., 2005) includes family and teacher ratings that suggest that many young children, particularly boys, may have ADHD. The SEELS data also show that large numbers of children with ADHD are identified in the public schools with labels other than the "other health impaired" (OHI) classification that is most in use. Notably, children with specific learning disabilities frequently have ADHD as a secondary impairment.

A further finding from the SEELS study is that large numbers of children with ADHD are identified by their schools as having *other* primary disabilities. During the 2000–2001 school year, about 4 in every 10 (41 percent) had the specific learning disability classification. Another 15 percent were given the SLI label and 14 percent were classified as emotionally disturbed. One in eight (12 percent) were identified as OHI, the preferred category for placing students with ADHD as a primary disability. These data clarify an important point: ADHD is a common secondary condition. Overall, SEELS reported, 27 percent (or more than one in every four) students in special education have ADHD as a primary or secondary disability.

DEVELOPMENTAL DELAYS

States define "developmental delays" to include behavior that is not age-appropriate. For example, a one-year-old may cling to his mother when dropped off at a nursery school or child care center. Were a five-year-old to display this same fear of separation from the mother, however, it would clearly be age-inappropriate; most five-year-olds display more independence, especially in public settings. The delays may be expressed in terms of time, as in that example, in which behavior appears at least 12 months after it normally ceases. They may also be expressed in ways state rules require, as deviations from the mean on standardized tests, or in percentage terms. Despite the fact that state regulators may write such standards into state guidelines, the usefulness of these rules is questionable. Very few tests of social or emotional behavior are available for use with early childhood populations.

For this reason, informed clinical opinion is particularly important in establishing eligibility for services. Many states look to expert diagnosticians to interpret such terms as *persists* (as in inappropriate behavior) or *interferes* (with the child's own or other children's activities). Clinicians draw on what we know about normal development in making such decisions. Social or emotional delays rarely are reported by parents of infants and toddlers; parental concerns in the birth-to-two period focus much more on sleeping and feeding problems. However, during the early preschool-age period, especially from ages three to four, parental complaints about behavior rise very sharply. Parents who accepted willfulness, disobedience, and impulsivity as to be expected in the "terrible twos" become concerned when these behaviors persist.

The assessor faces a difficult task in evaluating such complaints. Major developmental changes take place, featuring (in most young children) a sharp decline in aggressive and destructive behaviors between the ages of three and four (Tynan & Nearing, 1994). On the one hand, volatility in behavior is very common between the ages of three and six, and changes are both abrupt and short-lived. What may appear at first glance to be developmental delays often are very normal variations in development. For these reasons, assessors may be reluctant to pronounce a delay, preferring to tell the parents to "wait—it will take care of itself." On the other hand, however, children whose behavior does not change spontaneously may have real problems that, left untreated, seriously impair later school performance.

ESTABLISHED CONDITIONS

A number of conditions are recognized by states as established. Differentiating them is not always as easy as is naming them. Problems of definition and of evaluation and assessment are pervasive in the domain of social or emotional development.

Children with emotional disturbance are eligible for early intervention and preschool special education services in many states. Some states recognize conduct disorders as "established," and some accept ADHD. Also recognized in some states are infants, toddlers, and preschoolers diagnosed as having other varieties of mental illness. Part B preschool eligibility in most states is recognized by means of one of the 10 conditions recognized in Section 601(a) of the IDEA; one is "emotional disturbance."

Emotional disturbance (ED)

is a category recognized under the IDEA. Sometimes referred to as "emotional and behavioral disorders," ED refers to behavior in children that is age-, culturally, and/or situation-inappropriate and interferes with their education and/or that of other children.

Emotional disturbance (ED) is recognized as a disability under Section 602 in the IDEA. A 1977 regulatory definition (there is no statutory definition), which follows, remains the official definition of "emotional disturbance" (U.S. Department of Health, Education, and Welfare, 1977, p. 42478):

> *(i) The term means a condition exhibiting one or more of the following characteristics over a long period of time and to a marked extent, which adversely affects educational performance: (A) An inability to learn which cannot be explained by intellectual, sensory, or health factors; (B) An inability to build or maintain satisfactory relationships with peers and teachers; (C) Inappropriate types of behavior or feelings under normal circumstances; (D) A general pervasive mood of unhappiness or depression; or (E) A tendency to develop physical symptoms or fears associated with personal or school problems.*
>
> *(ii) The term includes children who are schizophrenic. The term does not include children who are socially maladjusted unless it is determined that they are seriously emotionally disturbed.*

Notice the use of the word *or* in the preceding definition between statements D and E; any one of these five behaviors or characteristics may suffice to qualify a child as eligible. Childhood depression is one of the conditions included in the definition of emotional

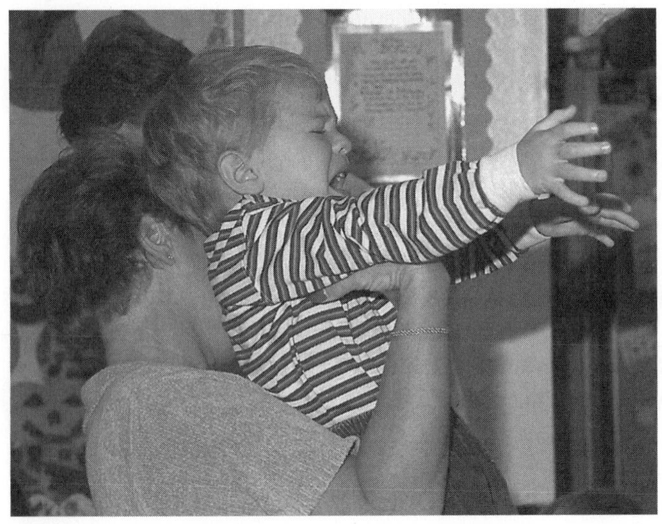

Fear of strangers is normal in very young children.

disturbance. For many years, psychiatrists insisted that depression did not occur in children. Their longstanding contention illustrates the power of an idea. Freud had said that depression occurs when the pleasure-loving id was suppressed by the superego. Because the superego did not emerge, in Freud's theory, until adolescence, it followed that depression could only occur in the teen and adult years. Today, we know that Freud was wrong about that. Depression can occur even in very young children, and does (e.g., Najman et al., 2005). The good news, researchers report, is that young children seem to be resilient: they can rebound quickly after exposure to such risk factors as dysfunctional family relationships, poor communication in the home, and other environmental influences.

Conduct disorders

include a range of emotional conditions affecting behavior. Children appear to be "undersocialized" in that they often do not exhibit socially approved behavior.

Conduct disorders include a range of emotional conditions causing limitations in social or emotional development, particularly with respect to socially approved behavior. One could say that the problem is one of undersocialization; the child has not internalized, or has not made habitual, the kinds of behaviors and attitudes that society tries to instill in all of us. Children with conduct disorders use aggression as a routine means of getting their way. Children who respond to authority figures by doing what they are told not to do and refusing to do what they are asked to do may also be socially or emotionally delayed. Serious problems may be indicated when children display emotions that are inappropriate for a situation—a child who laughs when most children would cry, for example, or one who becomes inconsolably depressed when most children would cry briefly and recover quickly. A very different kind of conduct disorder occurs when young children withdraw from social contact with both adults and other children. While occasional withdrawal is normal (and may reflect problems at home), children who persist in isolation, actually turning away from other children and from adults, may require professional help.

Attention-deficit/hyperactivity disorder (ADHD), predominantly hyperactive-impulsive type

is a diagnosis made when impulsivity and hyperactivity are present together with distractibility and short attention spans.

Attention-deficit/hyperactivity disorder (ADHD), predominantly inattentive type

is a diagnosis reached when a child is "unavailable for learning" due to distractibility and short attention spans. The diagnosis is used if hyperactivity is not present.

Attention deficits are controversial in ECSE. As with LD, diagnosis is largely a matter of testing the child for other conditions or problems, settling on attention deficit only after other labels have been rejected as inappropriate (Lerner, Lowenthal, & Lerner, 1995). *The Diagnostic and Statistical Manual of Mental Disorders, Fourth Edition* (*DSM-IV*) (American Psychiatric Association, 1994) recognizes three kinds of attention disorders (Figure 14–1). **Attention-deficit hyperactivity disorder (ADHD/HI), predominantly hyperactive-impulsive type,** is described as a condition characterized by short attention span, hyperactivity and impulsivity, and distractibility. Without hyperactivity, an attention deficit would still be characterized as **attention-deficit hyperactivity disorder (ADHD/I),** although the *DSM-IV* adds the words **predominantly inattentive type.** The *DSM-IV* also allows use of a third diagnosis of *combined type* (ADHD/C), in which criteria are met for both hyperactive-impulsive type and inattentive type. According to the *DSM-IV,* symptoms should appear prior to age six or seven. According to Goodman and Poillon (1992), the behaviors often first surface at about age three or four.

Attention deficits may occur together with other conditions. Children with ADHD may also have conduct disorders. Children who take medication (sedatives or anticonvulsants) to control epileptic seizures may develop what appears to be an attention deficit as

A. Either 1 or 2:

(1) Inattention: At least six of the following symptoms of inattention have persisted for at least six months to a degree that is maladaptive and inconsistent with developmental level:
  (a) Often fails to give close attention to details or makes careless mistakes in schoolwork, work, or other activities.
  (b) Often has difficulty sustaining attention in tasks or play activities.
  (c) Often does not seem to listen to what is being said to him or her.
  (d) Often does not follow through on instructions and fails to finish schoolwork, chores, or duties in the workplace (not due to oppositional behavior or failure to understand instructions).
  (e) Often has difficulties organizing tasks and activities.
  (f) Often avoids or strongly dislikes tasks (such as schoolwork or homework) that require sustained mental effort.
  (g) Often loses things necessary for tasks or activities (e.g., school assignments, pencils, books, tools, or toys).
  (h) Is often easily distracted by extraneous stimuli.
  (i) Often forgetful in daily activities.

(2) Hyperactivity-Impulsivity: At least six of the following symptoms of hyperactivity-impulsivity have persisted for at least six months to a degree that is maladaptive and inconsistent with developmental level:

Hyperactivity:
  (a) Often fidgets with hands or feet or squirms in seat.
  (b) Leaves seat in classroom or in other situations in which remaining seated is expected.
  (c) Often runs about or climbs excessively in situations where it is inappropriate (in adolescents or adults, may be limited to subjective feelings of restlessness).
  (d) Often has difficulty playing or engaging in leisure activities quietly.
  (e) Often talks excessively.
  (f) Often acts as if "driven by a motor" and cannot remain still.

Impulsivity:
  (g) Often blurts out answers to questions before the questions have been completed.
  (h) Often has difficulty waiting in lines or awaiting turn in games or group situations.
  (i) Often interrupts or intrudes on others.

B. Onset no later than seven years of age.

C. Symptoms must be present in two or more situations (e.g., at school, work, and at home).

D. The disturbance causes clinically significant distress or impairment in social, academic, or occupational functioning.

E. Does not occur exclusively during the course of a Pervasive Developmental Disorder, Schizophrenia, or other Psychotic Disorder, and is not better accounted for by a Mood Disorder, Anxiety Disorder, Dissociative Disorder, or a Personality Disorder.

Code based on type:
314.00 Attention-deficit/Hyperactivity Disorder, Predominantly Inattentive Type; if criterion A(1) is met but not criterion A(2) for the past six months.
314.01 Attention-deficit/Hyperactivity Disorder, Predominantly Hyperactive-Impulsive Type; if criterion A(2) is met but not criterion A(1) for the past six months.
314.01 Attention-deficit/Hyperactivity Disorder, Combined type; if both criteria A(1) and A(2) are met for the past six months.

Source: American Psychiatric Association. (1994), Diagnostic and statistical manual of mental disorders *(4th ed.). Washington, DC: Author. Reprinted with permission.*

FIGURE 14–1 ***DSM-IV*** **criteria for ADHD.**

a side effect of the drugs (Ariel, 1992). Similarly, children may have learning disabilities in addition to attention deficits. For all of these reasons, reaching a diagnosis of attention deficit challenges even experts in the field.

The distinction between LD and attention disorders is clear in theory—LD affects information processing (the information is attended to and perceived, but the third step of analyzing and interpreting information somehow goes awry) while ADHD affects attention (the information never is received, so it can neither be perceived nor processed). However, in practice, psychologists seldom can see into a young child's mind well enough to make that distinction. The outward effects that can be observed are similar in both instances; the child is not learning despite sensory integrity and adequate instruction.

The IDEA includes neither type of ADHD as a separate category under Part B. Infants and toddlers with either diagnosis may be served under Part C if the state recognizes their condition; meanwhile, preschool-age children may be provided with a free, appropriate public education under Section 504 of the Rehabilitation Act (see Chapter 6). As noted earlier, Figure 14–1 presents the *DSM-IV* criteria for ADHD.

Aggressive behavior in particular is more common among boys than among girls. Withdrawal, however, may be more common in girls. ECSE workers should not fall into the trap of thinking that children with social or emotional problems are usually boys. In fact, withdrawal can be an indicator of emotional conditions much more severe than is suggested by some aggressive behaviors.

ASSESSMENT

The U.S. Department of Education's (1993) regulations for early intervention programs define the assessment role as part of "psychological services" in Section 303.12, using this language:

> *(i) Administering psychological and developmental tests and other assessment procedures;*
> *(ii) Interpreting assessment results;*
> *(iii) Obtaining, integrating, and interpreting information about child behavior, and child and family conditions related to learning, mental health, and development.*

There are few standardized tests of social or emotional development appropriate for use with young children. Rather, ECSE workers need to rely on informed clinical opinion. Assessment focuses on the necessarily subjective process of determining whether delays exist or deviations are present. The subjectivity arises because what one professional considers normal behavior is not considered so by another; each brings his social and cultural values to the assessment process. These facts highlight the need for repeated (serial) assessments, performed over time, so that a more complete picture may be obtained.

The first step in assessment of social or emotional behavior must be to ascertain that no organic cause exists for the behavior. A frequent cause of apparent "willful disregard of authority," to illustrate, is a hearing loss; the child literally does not hear the authority figure's requests or commands. Some social or emotional problems have a physical cause and must be treated differently, perhaps with medication. A few children are hyperactive for chemical reasons; most are not, but those who are may need medical treatment.

After organic causes have been ruled out, the focus in assessment of social or emotional development is on degrees of difference. The question is one of whether and to what extent behavior is significantly different from age-appropriate norms. Cultural norms are relevant here. A Hispanic American or African American child may display more cooperative behavior than a white child because of cultural and familial emphasis on group relations. There may be a corresponding reluctance to compete on an individual basis. Similarly, children from low-SES families headed by parents with low education attainment levels may not articulate their feelings as well as may children from middle- and high-SES, well-educated families. This disparity may reflect the greater use in well-educated families of verbalized rationales and elaborated-on commands as child management techniques, in contrast to the use of much more directive language in less educated families. Variations of these kinds are well within cultural norms and expectations.

Guidelines helpful in assessing behavior include the indicators described in Figure 14–2. Notice the comparative nature of these assessment measures.

The indicators in Figure 14–2 are matters of interpretation. Looking at disruptive behavior, withdrawal, age-inappropriate parallel play, attention-getting behavior, and so on, the assessor is trying to answer the question "How much is too much?" A preschool teacher with 20 children in her class may regard some acting-out behavior as more than she can handle, given her other responsibilities. That is not the primary issue for a psychologist or other assessment professional, however. The assessor is more concerned with whether a given behavior is so different from that of other children that intervention is required. A good example is the infant's ability to attend to things and events. Serious deficits in that area will interfere with education and therapy. Modulation of behavior is another example; a young child who moves quickly from laughing to crying will unnerve other children, leading to her social isolation. More attenuated moves over a period of time, in this case from laughing to smiling to sitting quietly to shifting to frowning to crying, are more acceptable to other children.

1. *Persistence.* If an activity persists much longer with one child than it does with most children, concern is warranted. All children fight at times; fighting as a primary means of responding to conflicts with other children and fighting as a daily occurrence, however, are not normal.
2. *When displayed.* Behavior that is very normal in response to abnormal circumstances is not normal if it continues over a long period of time and is displayed under typical circumstances. Withdrawal behavior and shyness are very normal when a child returns to an ECSE program after an extended absence due to illness or hospitalization. The same withdrawal patterns appear in a very different light when displayed in more typical situations.
3. *Severity.* Aggressive behavior that is excessive in kind or duration may signal social or emotional problems. While all children will at times hit other children, violent battering of another child is not normal.
4. *Response to intervention.* When the ECSE worker or parent has used standard procedures to stop a behavior, yet it continues unabated, concern is warranted.
5. *Interference with own activities.* One of the most important indicators of social or emotional problems occurs when the child's own learning and play activities are disrupted or halted altogether because of the behavior.
6. *Interference with other's activities.* A related indicator is when other children cannot play or engage in a learning activity due to one child's behavior.

FIGURE 14–2 Assessing behavior in young children.

The next step is to watch the child over a period of time, in different settings. Is behavior triggered by some particular event? Does it occur at home, at school, or both? How frequent is the behavior? This monitoring helps the assessor create a *baseline,* or measure of existing behavior. It also helps the assessor isolate what the people around the child do immediately before the undesired behavior occurs. Bearing in mind the old saw "Children learn what they live," the assessor watches how parents and ECSE workers themselves behave both before and after instances of undesired behaviors. The emphasis is on the behavior. What is happening, when, and in response to what antecedents and what consequences?

Observing behavior is important for another reason. Such labels as ADHD may be discarded if the child displays consistent attention to a task—any task, even watching television—so the first step is very careful observation. Watching the child in different settings also helps differentiate similar conditions, something that is particularly important when the examiner suspects ADHD or a conduct disorder. Diagnosis of social or emotional conditions often involves testing for one possible disorder after another, ruling each out, and then settling on the most likely condition (Goodman & Poillion, 1992; Reid et al., 1994).

Often, the assessor will learn that the child is responding quite normally to abnormal circumstances. The problem frequently is the parents' behavior, and sometimes it is the ECSE worker's behavior. These adults may be encouraging inappropriate behavior by attending to it. Some parents, for example, unwittingly trigger acting-out behavior by withholding attention until the behavior forces them to pay attention to the child. At times, ECSE workers will also lavish attention on a misbehaving child. What is happening here is readily explained. The child is responding quite appropriately to the signals he is getting. At other times, though, the assessor will see that both parent and professional are doing what they should be doing. They are attending to good behavior and ignoring bad behavior. Still the misbehaving persists. Now there is a problem, and the focus of the problem is the child. Having ruled out organic and environmental causes for behavior, the assessor is now ready for a formal evaluation. Referral to a clinic specializing in behavior disorders may be necessary. Such referral should not be made until other causal factors have been eliminated (Wolery et al., 1988).

Very helpful diagnostic guidelines, *Diagnostic Classification of Mental Health and Developmental Disorders of Infancy and Early Childhood* (1994), together with *The DC:03 Casebook* (1997), have been issued by Zero to Three, the National Center for Infants, Toddlers and Families, in Washington, DC. The *Casebook* offers 24 case reports illustrating how the classification system may be used. This system is markedly different from earlier ones. It looks for atypical behaviors rather than just for delays in development. Especially of concern is self-regulation, including hyperactivity, underactivity, impulsivity, and other deviations from normal behavior.

Diagnosis of ADHD is typically made by a physician, a psychologist, or a social worker. The criteria in *DSM-IV* are used (see Figure 14–1). However, ECSE staff may also find that parent and teacher questionnaires and rating scales can help screen children so as to identify those who should be evaluated professionally. The Vineland Adaptive Behavior Scales may be used. The Preschool and Kindergarten Behavior Scales and the Kindergarten and Elementary Teacher Questionnaires were used by the PEELS team (www.peels.org) and may be considered by ECSE professionals. The most important indicator, experts agree, is family history. ADHD typically runs in families.

One popular tool for diagnosing ADHD is the long-form Connors Rating Scales. These are psychiatric questionnaires filled out by family members and teachers. Although a short

Turning to a trusted caregiver at times of distress is normal. Persistent clinging, however, is not—and signals a possible need for treatment.

form, with just 10 questions, is available, it may miss children who have the inattentive type of ADHD. The long version, with nine symptoms of inattention, is more sensitive to that variation on ADHD. Importantly, it asks when the child loses attention and why.

A second indicator is resistance to reinforcers that normally work to control aggressive behavior. Experience in ECSE programs that serve young children with ADHD indicates that even these powerful interventions may fail to alter behavior in children having this condition. However, before concluding that "behavior modification doesn't work," program staff should consult with an expert on behavior modification to ascertain that everything has been done correctly and that nothing else in the extensive repertoire of reinforcers remains to be tried.

INTERVENTION

The IDEA's requirement that multidisciplinary teams carry out both assessment and intervention has important implications for ECSE programs. Perhaps the most central is that *all* young children in ECSE programs be considered both for assessment and for intervention in the domain of social or emotional development. This process can become expensive. The approach dictates that children with communication-related disabilities or delays, as well as children with concerns primarily cognitive or physical in nature, be assessed on social or emotional development as well as in their primary domain of need. It also requires that early intervention or preschool special education and related services to prevent problems or to accelerate development in the social or emotional domain be reviewed for inclusion in the IFSP or IEP.

The U.S. Department of Education's (1993) regulations for early intervention programs described the service provision component of "psychological services" in Section 303.12 as follows:

> *(iv) Planning and managing a program of psychological services, including psychological counseling for children and parents, family counseling, consultation on child development, parent training, and education programs.*

Especially when a child is displaying delays, deviations, or disabilities in the domain of social or emotional development, parental resistance to psychological counseling may be strong. The adoption of an attitude of nonjudgmental, cooperative searching is central to success in this area. ECSE personnel need to focus on the behavior. Although it may be tempting to seek psychological bases for inappropriate behaviors, the initial attention should instead be on the specific behaviors that are situation-inappropriate. By attending to these rather than to the child or even the parents, ECSE personnel can avoid premature and inappropriate blaming. Even when program staff discover that a child's behavior has emerged as a direct result of inappropriate parental reinforcements, the focus must remain firmly on the behavior itself ("George took Sam's drink at lunch today") rather than on the child ("George upset all of us today") or on the parents ("Can't you teach him to leave other children's things alone?").

Children who display inappropriate behavior should not be labeled—whether "emotionally disturbed," "conduct disordered," "schizophrenic," or "ADHD"—except in rare cases, and even then with great care. Similarly, labels should never be used as excuses. Even children with severe conduct disorders can learn to behave appropriately. Making excuses for the child ("He is, after all, emotionally disturbed") solves nothing. It does not help the child, nor does it reduce future occurrences—indeed, it increases them. And it does not deal with the most frequent real reason for misbehavior—that the child does not know what to do, does not have the skills to perform a task, and finds an outlet for his frustration in acting out. Even if the child is hyperactive or aggressive, the hyperactive behaviors and the aggressive behaviors still have to be dealt with and, in time, eliminated.

With respect to ADHD, experts recommend that ECSE workers follow the principles of behavior modification that are discussed in the next section. Also frequently recommended for children with ADHD is use of stimulant medications such as Ritalin, Dexedrine, and Cylert, which have the paradoxical effect in these children of reducing rather than increasing activity levels. Some 40 years of experience in using Ritalin with hyperactive children supports its selection (Barkley, 1990; Fiore, Becker, & Nero, 1993). However, concerns were raised in 2006 about possible side effects. While we await definitive studies, parents should consult family physicians for guidance (Johns Hopkins Children's Center, 2006).

Most disabilities in this domain do not have well-established organic (physical) causes and therefore should not be treated medically. Drugs such as Ritalin and Dexedrine may also have side effects such as weight loss, insomnia, and increased blood pressure. If medication is used, then, ECSE workers should monitor the child closely and alert a physician if such effects occur. Figure 14–3 summarizes information on often-used medications.

Trade Name	Generic Name	Approved Ages	Uses
Adderall	Amphetamine	3 and older	ADHD
Concerta	Methylphenidate	6 and older	ADHD
Dexedrine	Pemoline	6 and older	ADHD
Ritalin	Methylphenidate	6 and older	ADHD
Anafranil	Clomipramine	Consult MD	Depression, OCD*
BuSpar	Buspirone	Consult MD	Anxiety
Valium	Diazepam	Consult MD	Anxiety
Xanax	Alprazolam	Consult MD	Anxiety
Prozac	Fluoxetine	Consult MD	Depression, OCD*
Zoloft	Sertraline	Consult MD	OCD*

** OCD = Obsessive compulsive disorder.*

Source: National Institutes of Health (www.nih.gov).

FIGURE 14–3 Commonly prescribed medications.

Thomas and Tidmarsh (1997) urge ECSE workers to create a safe environment for the children and to encourage parents, when appropriate, to seek marital and other counseling services. They offer three case studies to illustrate effective intervention techniques.

Perhaps the single-most important intervention ECSE workers can use is to look for positive behavior and attend to it. This is something we all know we should do, but it is also something we very rarely actually do. Parents and professionals alike are routinely astonished when they view videotapes of their own interactions with children, showing how they (unintentionally) regulate children's activities. Appropriate behavior exhibited by the child many, many times during the videotaped session almost never arouses comment by the parent or professional. Inappropriate behavior, by contrast, frequently brings immediate and total attention from the parent or professional. After watching such a videotape, many adults understand why children misbehave.

This illustrates a point made in the "Assessment" section: often the source of the problems lies not with the child but, rather, is in the child's environment. The problems may be our own behaviors. It is urgently important to broaden the focus of inquiry beyond just the child and to examine ourselves and our own behavior as well. People's attention is drawn to sudden, unexpected, and disruptive behavior; that is why many children display it—to get attention. Some researchers have even postulated that disruptive behavior is seven times more likely to get our attention as is appropriate behavior (Strain, Lambert, Kerr, Stagg, & Lenker, 1983).

BEHAVIOR MODIFICATION

Well-established procedures that work very well in helping children develop, maintain, and generalize appropriate behavior are available for use in ECSE programs (Figure 14–4). The principles of behavior modification themselves are readily learned. They are

1. *Baseline.* Document behavior in discrete time periods (1-, 5-, 10-minute intervals, etc.) in different settings, with different caregivers and different children. How frequently is unacceptable behavior exhibited? After what antecedent events? Prior to what subsequent events?
2. *Attend to desired behavior.* Give the child your attention when he does things you approve. It may be just a glance, a smile, a pat on the back. The key is to attend *immediately,* so that the child connects the behavior to the attention.
3. *Ignore undesired behavior.* As difficult as this step is, it is essential that the child *not* receive your attention after unacceptable behavior. Wait until desired behavior reappears, and then give the child your attention.
4. *Attend to incompatible behavior.* To decrease unacceptable activities, reinforce alternative actions. Let the child know that these other behaviors are more acceptable options.
5. *Shape behavior.* If the child cannot do what you want, attend to whatever she *can* do that approximates what you desire. Later, expect more before you grant the child your attention.
6. *Maintain behavior.* Intermittent, unpredictable reinforcement maintains behavior. Once desired behavior is established, attend to it only on occasion or seemingly at random.
7. *Generalize behavior.* After acceptable behavior is well established in the presence of an ECSE staff member, reinforce it when another worker is there. Later, generalize to other settings as well.

FIGURE 14–4 Altering behavior in young children.

summarized in many texts ECSE professionals have read or can easily secure (i.e., Wolery et al., 1988). Virtually any good text on educational psychology includes an introduction to behavior theory (i.e., Woolfolk, 2004). The discussion here is limited to highlights, showing how the techniques relate to work in ECSE programs.

The core concept behind behavior modification is so basic as to be banal: if you want to see more of something, attend to it. For example, when a child plays successfully with another child for five successive minutes, the adult should pay attention to the child. This may take the form of walking over to the child, touching his shoulder, and saying something like, "Glad to see you two are getting along so well," or even giving the child a hug. Once the child's behavior becomes routine or habitual, it may be reinforced by allowing him to engage in a preferred activity. Later, such privileges should be contingent on the child's playing for 10, then 20, minutes at a stretch.

This example illustrates several key principles of behavior modification. The first and most important is that behavior that is rewarded, or reinforced, increases in frequency. Neither parents nor ECSE professionals can reinforce behavior until they understand what a child considers to be rewarding. You must understand the child. Some children find personal attention from a caregiver or teacher to be rewarding, but some find it distracting or even annoying. For some children the opportunity to play with other children is reinforcing, while for others the chance to play alone is preferable. Behavior modification teaches that a *reinforcer* is anything that increases the frequency of the behavior it follows. No one knows what will reinforce a given child's behavior until he sees what the child does.

Reinforcers have several characteristics. First, they must follow behavior *immediately.* If they do not come until some time after the desired behavior is exhibited, that behavior may not be reinforced. Second, to establish a new behavior and to make it habitual, reinforcers must follow behavior *consistently.*

Shaping

is a method of successive approximations in which only ever more accurate behaviors are reinforced.

Also illustrated by the example is **shaping.** Behavior modification teaches that behaviors must be within the child's repertoire. The child must be able to do what we expect from him. If the child is unable to do that—for example, to play with another child for a 20-minute period—we must identify what *is* within the child's behavior repertoire. The first time this behavior is exhibited when we want it, it should be reinforced. Once it appears consistently and regularly, as when a child routinely plays for five minutes without acting out, it is time to shift our attention. Now, only successful play of 10 or more minutes will be reinforced. After the child manages that level of interactive play, the time period again is lengthened. This concept of shaping is an extremely powerful one for use with children who have social or emotional behavior problems. It allows us to reinforce *something,* while working steadily toward the ultimate goal.

The example also brings up something known as the *Premack principle* (Premack, 1959). Stated one way, the Premack principle tells us that a more preferred activity reinforces a less preferred activity. But how does one know which activity is more, or less, preferred? The answer is, by watching the child during unregulated times. What does the child most often do? This helps us understand the Premack principle as meaning that a more frequent activity will reinforce a less frequent one. In the example, a child was given permission to do something he liked after consistently demonstrating successful play with another child.

Giving such permission is an example of an *intrinsic* reinforcer. Play is something the child already prefers to do. Later, an *extrinsic* reinforcer may be introduced. Extrinsic reinforcers stand for, or represent, intrinsic ones. For example, the child may be told that permission has been granted to do the preferred activity but later on in the day. The promise stands in place of the activity. A token may accomplish this purpose.

Reinforcers may be positive or negative. In *positive reinforcement,* something is given or presented to the child. In the example, permission was granted to play or a token was given. In *negative reinforcement,* something the child dislikes is taken away or removed. The effect of negative reinforcement may be illustrated by lunchtime or recess time; in both cases, children are released from the regulations imposed during supervised activities. In negative reinforcement, such release is made contingent on successfully performing a desired behavior. The child is freed from supervision after, say, sitting quietly throughout story time. Because these terms are so often misunderstood, they are probably better called *presentation reinforcers* and *removal reinforcers* (as introduced in Chapter 1). The bottom line is the same in both instances; the preceding behavior increases. Both presentation and removal reinforcers, or positive and negative reinforcers, increase desired behavior.

What does an ECSE worker do if he wishes to decrease behavior (i.e., make it less frequent)? The best way may be to reinforce an *incompatible behavior.* In this approach, reinforcement is given to an activity that the child cannot do while also displaying the undesired behavior.

Meanwhile, the undesired behavior is ignored. Ignoring misbehavior is very important. It must not be reinforced in any way. Systematically ignoring behavior is called *extinction.* Extinction works; it is a useful technique. However, practicing extinction can try the patience of ECSE workers and parents. To understand why extinction often takes so long to be effective, consider the activity of gambling. People go to Atlantic City, Las Vegas, or other places that support gambling because they expect to be reinforced—that is, to win money. Even in the face of a long string of losses, most people persist in gambling behavior; after a time, they are rewarded with a win. They are thus being *intermittently* reinforced.

Establishing behavior requires that reinforcement occur both immediately and consistently. Different rules apply when one wants to *maintain* a behavior. Fortunately, it is not necessary to continue to reinforce behavior every time it occurs. In fact, better results come from making reinforcement less predictable. Reinforcement schedules may be varied in several ways. One is to reinforce after set periods of time (say, every 10 minutes); another is to reinforce after a certain number of responses (say, five correct answers). Perhaps the best method of maintaining an established behavior is to reinforce at random—that is, at unexpected intervals or rates. The child never knows, and cannot figure out, when reinforcement next will occur. This is exactly the situation the gambler experiences; she anticipates reinforcement but has no way of knowing when it will occur.

Unfortunately, the same principles that govern maintenance of behavior apply when one attempts to extinguish undesired behavior. Such actions persist in the face of well-spaced-out, even random reinforcers. The behavior does not finally extinguish until a period of time without any reinforcement, often a very long time.

Once desired behaviors have been established and maintained, the issue becomes one of *generalization.* A child may exhibit appropriate behavior with one teacher but not with another. Similarly, getting the child to behave appropriately in ECSE programs does little good if the child continues inappropriate behaviors at home. Generalization is an important concern. It should be part of any ECSE worker's plan when modifying a child's behavior. Generalization is best accomplished after a behavior is established and maintained in one setting.

Vaughn, Bos, and Lund (1986) suggest that the first step in generalizing is to vary the reinforcer. Introduce a different reinforcer—perhaps a promise in place of immediate permission to do a preferred activity—or use verbal praise in place of either. Second, vary the cue (prompt) that is expected to trigger the desired behavior. The same response may be used in another situation—for example, when the child is playing with a different child. Third, show the student another response and reinforce that. This helps the child develop alternative but equally acceptable behaviors. The response may also be changed by reducing the time allowed for completion. Fourth, vary the presenter. The child should learn that the behavior itself will be reinforced, even if the original presenter is not there. And fifth, reinforce the same behavior in a different setting, perhaps at the home during a home visit.

Interaction with other children is a major concern in ECSE. While interaction skills may be taught, at least with respect to a specific situation, getting children with severe disabilities to display those same skills in other settings is often difficult. To illustrate, using prompts and rewards, Cone and his associates taught boys with mental retardation to toss a ball to one another (Cone, Anderson, Harris, Goff, & Fox, 1988). Although the children learned at least parts of the task, they did not perform their new skills in any location other than that in which they originally had been taught. Cone et al.'s intent had been to give the boys social interaction skills valued by other children (in this case, ball-playing abilities). The researchers found, however, that the skills, once learned, did not transfer to other situations and did not appear to increase the boys' social acceptance by others. Lovaas (1987), reporting on his work with children who have autism, expresses a similar worry about generalization; each behavior had to be taught in each setting in which its display was expected. These generalization problems are especially significant in the area of social behavior, because each situation is different.

Social interaction is, by its very nature, a fluid process requiring rapid adaptation to different people, different topics of conversation, and different roles; for these reasons, it may not lend itself well to traditional behavior modification techniques. *Cognitive behavior modification,* however, because it focuses on teaching children how to assess and respond to different situations, may prove to be more successful; cognitive behavior modification is described in the next chapter.

Another principle used with children is *time-out.* In time-out, a child is removed from an area in which reinforcement is possible and placed into one in which no reinforcement is possible. The technique should be used with caution and by trained personnel. Time-out works best when an entirely separate area is used, preferably another room. The VCLC has found that such a room should be very softly lit, with approximately the amount of light that remains after sundown. It should be padded and soundproofed to remove any stimulation through sound, and there should be no interesting objects or toys. The idea is to remove any possible source of stimulation or reinforcement (www.vclc.org).

ECSE workers must bear several things in mind about time-out. First, the ground rules must be clearly understood by everyone—parent, child, and ECSE worker alike. Those rules must be objective, they must be few, and they must be explained to the point of being clearly understood in advance. First, when a rule is broken, the ECSE worker should say firmly, "I cannot allow you to do that," and escort the child out. Hard as it may be to do, the ECSE worker should give an absolute minimum of attention to the undesired behavior. Second, time-out must be used only as a last resort, after classroom or playroom management techniques have failed to control behavior. Third, it must be used for short periods of time (up to and seldom exceeding five minutes). Fourth, the child must be returned to the playroom or classroom immediately after time-out. During the trip back, ECSE workers should give the child prompts, cues, or suggestions on what activities will be approved upon reentry to the classroom or playroom. It is very important as well that ECSE workers monitor the child's actions upon return, immediately reinforcing any appropriate behaviors (Bloch, 1993).

Stay-put provision

is an important due process right under Part B of the IDEA. While a dispute is pending, the child with a disability is to continue receiving a free, appropriate public education and is to remain in the current placement.

Both Part C and Part B contain **stay-put provisions,** prohibiting changes in placement or in patterns of service delivery without prior parental permission. Excessive use of time-out rooms may constitute such a *change in placement.* The issue of what is a placement change was explored in depth in a 1988 Supreme Court decision, *Honig v. Doe.* The case concerned two emotionally disturbed boys who had been expelled from school. The Supreme Court based its decision on the Part B stay-put provision, ruling that a child may be suspended for several days (up to 10). That suspension may trigger review of the appropriateness of the placement, which may then be changed after parental notification and consent. While this review is occurring, the child stays put in the existing educational placement or in an alternative placement to which the parents concur.

OTHER INTERVENTIONS

The SEELS longitudinal study sheds sobering light on the task before ECSE workers. Students in the 6- to 12-year-old cohort who were identified as having emotional disturbance performed at low levels in passage comprehension, with 53 percent scoring in the lowest one-fifth of students with any disabilities. By contrast, just 10 percent were in the upper three-fifths of their age cohorts on these tests. In math calculation, 37 percent were in the lowest one-fifth; in math problem solving, 38 percent were. These findings appear to show that many young children with emotional disorders miss all or parts of academic instruction, either because they are not paying attention or because their behavior has resulted in their repeated removal from academic activities.

Beyond behavior modification, ECSE workers may find that *structuring the environment* to maximize learning opportunities is a good response to social or emotional needs. A structured environment has discrete areas designated for specific activities. This often helps young children with social or emotional conditions, because the setting itself provides clues as to what behavior is expected and what will be tolerated. Such a play area or classroom could also include locations in which children may be observed discreetly yet effectively; when some children may attack or otherwise harm other children, it is essential that child care workers be able to catch such behavior immediately and respond quickly. A structured environment, too, provides continuity from day to day, giving children who need predictability and structure some scaffolding on which to hang the changes each day inevitably brings.

ECSE workers may also draw on the power of *peer group interactions* to help young children with social or emotional conditions or needs. Young children, including those with behavior needs, often value other children's approval and friendship; these desires for peer acceptance may moderate even some behaviors adult caregivers find hard to control. The ECSE worker's task with small groups is twofold. First, he must give all children in the group effective tactics for responding to unacceptable behavior when it occurs; they must know how to react when threatened physically or verbally. Second, he must suggest to the child demonstrating such behavior what alternative actions may lead to the desired result. Ladd and Mize (1983) suggest that caregivers offer children specific strategies for gaining and keeping other children's support. Often, behavior that is unacceptable results because a child just does not know other ways of gaining peer acceptance. The motivating factor for the child in this case is approval from other children. That is a powerful change agent.

For the same reason, *modeling* is an effective way of teaching acceptable ways of responding to frustration. One of the major arguments given by proponents of integration of children with and without disabilities is that the former will be exposed, every day, to the kinds of behavior that children with no disabilities display. The hope is that they will then display such behavior themselves. The same holds true when children with and without behavior or emotional needs are integrated. Modeling is discussed further in the next chapter.

Giving the child a sense of security may be most important. When young children know that ECSE workers may disapprove of discrete behaviors but understand that this disappointment is specific to the behavior and not to the child, they may become more open to program staff efforts to change those behaviors. Both the DEC and the NAEYC recommended practices emphasize accepting and supporting children so that they will gain a sense of belonging.

INTERAGENCY COORDINATION

Children with social or emotional disorders and their families are particularly in need of services from a broad range of agencies, including child welfare or child protection agencies, mental health agencies, and education agencies, among others. The coordination problems are severe. Even elementary and secondary schools, which have had 30 years' experience serving children and youth with emotional disturbances, have yet to create smooth-running networks of interagency service. Knitzer (1988) reports that more than 250,000 children of all ages are in out-of-home care placements made by child welfare agencies, either at the parents' request or by court order. State custody (including foster care and adoption) commonly follows reports of child abuse or neglect, but it also comes into effect at times when overburdened families find themselves without alternative options to care for a child. Making a bad situation worse, many child welfare agencies will not assume financial responsibility for such placements unless a transfer of custody occurs.

WORKING WITH FAMILIES

Family members are often sensitive to delays, deviations, and disabilities in the area of social or emotional development. They feel that ECSE workers will blame them for anything that goes wrong; and for this reason they may deny problems, withhold cooperation, and even withdraw the child from the program. The VCLC has shown that ECSE workers can deal with these understandable family concerns by adopting a nonjudgmental posture. Particularly while the initial evaluation and assessment process is taking place, program staff should take the position that they are interested in the behavior itself, the extent to which it is manifested in different settings, and the degree to which it may be modified with standard interventions. This focus on specific behavior is in contrast to any blame placing. The attention is thus not on a "bad" child but rather on specific behaviors. ("Under what circumstances does she cry quickly, with little apparent provocation?")

In working with family members, it is also helpful to videotape sessions during which they interact with their children. As mentioned earlier in this chapter, most people (professionals as well as laypeople) truly are not aware of just how little attention they give to behavior they like. By videotaping a session and playing it back later, ECSE personnel can help family members literally see what they are doing. The aim, again, is not one of blame but, rather, one of discovery. Such taping sessions should be followed by simple instructions in the basics of behavior modification. The core principles are readily understood and in most cases easily applied. The key seems to be personal awareness. When the family members are more conscious of themselves as being able to control reinforcements and understand that behaviors that are reinforced appear more frequently, they often become quite expert at providing selective attention and dispensing other reinforcers according to a schedule. Following these principles becomes its own reward for family members as they see improvements in the child's behavior and as their family lives become more enjoyable.

SUMMARY

Delays or disabilities in the social or emotional development domain are relatively uncommon in the early childhood years. Young children may have social or emotional problems, but these may not appear to be serious until years later. Social or emotional delays or limitations may also emerge as a secondary consequence of a physical, cognitive, or other disability. This is particularly likely where parents or other primary caregivers feel sorry for the child and abandon the usual disciplinary and other child management procedures; but problems may also occur when young children with disabilities become frustrated, angry, or even depressed due to their difficulties. That is especially common when the physical or other disability is acquired rather than congenital.

EC programs work much more closely with families than do most elementary and secondary schools. The family focus of ECSE programs gives professionals important opportunities to intervene in the family to prevent, ameliorate, or eliminate inappropriate behaviors. Elementary or secondary school staff may find it much more difficult to take the same steps, because these programs do not have the same family orientation. ECSE programs have another important advantage. The enabling legislation in both Part C and preschool Part B permits ECSE programs to serve children with delays in social or emotional development. Elementary and secondary programs, by contrast, are limited to serving a much more narrowly constructed category—that of "emotional disturbance." Third, ECSE programs have a mandate to provide multidisciplinary assessment and services in all five domains of development, even when a child has a disability or delay in only one such domain. All young children are entitled to multidisciplinary assessment in each domain and to services, whether early intervention services or preschool-related services, in any domain in which assistance appears to be appropriate and to which family members agree. For these three reasons, EC programs have a unique role to play in this domain.

KEY TERMS

attention-deficit/hyperactivity disorder (ADHD), predominantly hyperactive-impulsive type

attention-deficit/hyperactivity disorder (ADHD), predominantly inattentive type

conduct disorders

emotional disturbance (ED)

shaping

stay-put provision

QUESTIONS FOR REFLECTION

1. Why might children with emotional disorders act out more in structured environments than in free-play settings?
2. Distinguish between ADHD, predominantly hyperactive-impulsive type, and ADHD, predominantly inattentive type.
3. In your own words, explain the difference between externalizing and internalizing behaviors.
4. Explain how the exclusion factor works in defining emotional disturbance.
5. Why is it important to observe behavior in different settings before making a decision about the label "emotional disturbance" or about ADHD?
6. How can ECSE workers overcome parental resistance to discussion of emotional problems in children?
7. According to the text, children most often act out because they lack what?
8. Although Ritalin often helps children who have ADHD, the text recommends using something else as well. What is that?
9. Explain *shaping*, and give an example of how you might use this technique.
10. In your own words, explain the difference between presentation and removal reinforcement.

PRACTICAL EXERCISES

1. Do you know a family in which a young child is very hyperactive? Attention deficit/hyperactivity disorders are quite common. If so, spend some time with that family. If not, ask a local early intervention or preschool program for a referral. Observe for a morning or an afternoon. Pay particular attention to what happens *after* a child breaks a house rule.

   Do family members enforce the rule? Or do they find some excuse not to? Experts suspect that one reason young children often become "uncontrollable" is that they quickly learn that the rules are without teeth. They learn to disregard those rules—and that they can get away with almost anything. If family members do not enforce the rules, document what you see happening. If, on the other hand, family members *do enforce and have been enforcing* the rules, note whether they believe misbehavior has decreased.
2. Visit www.nlm.nih.gov (the National Library of Medicine) and www.nimh.nih.gov (the National Institute of Mental Health) to learn about the drugs discussed in Figure 14–3. Which include stimulants (and so might contribute to insomnia)? Is there new information about dosages recommended for young children on any of these drugs?

WEB SITES OF INTEREST

www.aap.org/advocacy/archives/octadhd.htm American Academy of Pediatrics—guidelines for diagnosing attention-deficit disorders

www.ccbd.net Council for Exceptional Children's division on behavior disorders—has a "Resources" section with good links to other sites

cecp.air.org The Center for Effective Collaboration and Practices—on managing children with emotional disorders

CHAPTER

Adaptive Development

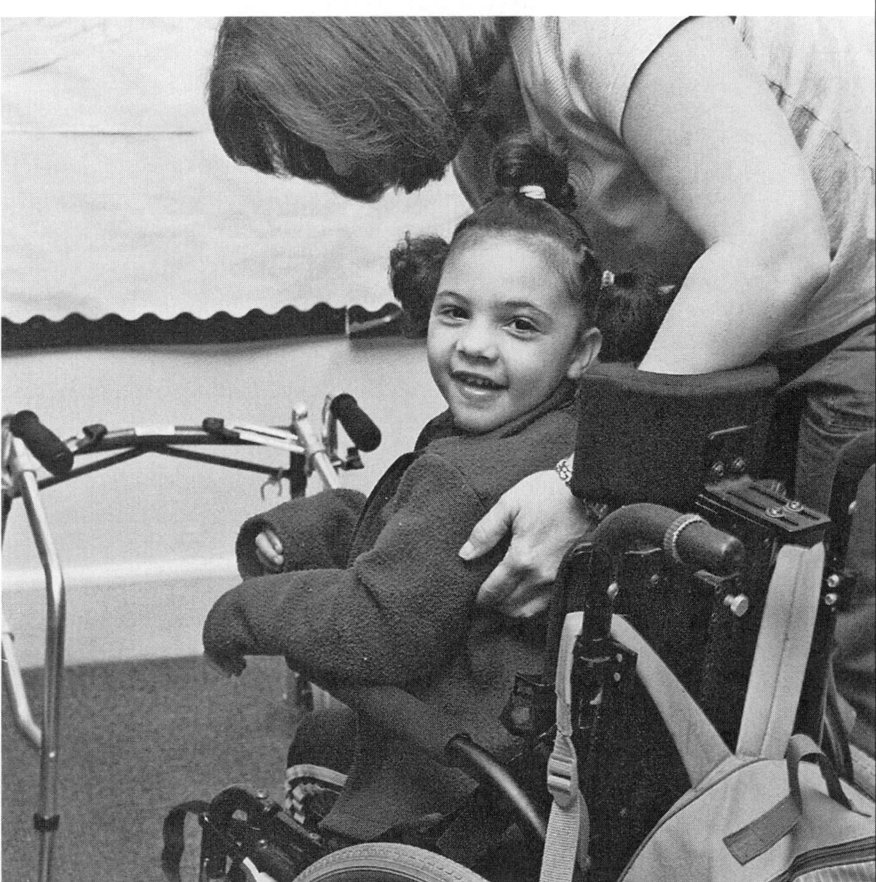

They were no more than the notes of an excited new mother, records to reflect on and share with the grandchildren when they asked about their parents' first words or how they did in school. It turns out, these hundreds of now-yellowed pages, became the basis of a medical paper published in *Neurocase,* a journal of neuropsychology, neuropsychiatry and behavioral neurology. . . . The diary starts in 1992, when the Fougeres learned Tina was pregnant. . . . Tasha and Nathan are now 12 years old. Tina still keeps the records—report cards, hair samples, first teeth, results of medical checkups—all meticulously stored in binders, photo albums, and in the tiny boxes on monthly calendars. The diaries, which also include brain scans and echocardiogram recordings, have been examined as clues to autism. The notes of a doting mother have become records of autism, presenting possible indications of the condition in a child at seven months—long before typical diagnosis. (CUKIER, 2005, P. 1)

OBJECTIVES

After reading this chapter, you should be able to:

- Explain why the domain of adaptive development is the smallest in ECSE.
- Describe what kinds of impairments might be included in this domain.
- Describe how fetal alcohol syndrome affects young children.

- Describe what effects maternal abuse of drugs may cause in children.
- Explain what autism spectrum disorders is and how to help a young child with autism.
- Describe what universal precautions help contain the spread of AIDS.

CHAPTER OUTLINE

- **OVERVIEW**
- **PREVALENCE**
- **DEVELOPMENTAL DELAYS**
- **ESTABLISHED CONDITIONS**
  - **Fetal Alcohol Syndrome**
  - **Vulnerable Child Syndrome**
  - **AIDS**
  - **Epilepsy**
  - **Autism Spectrum Disorders**
- **ASSESSMENT**
- **INTERVENTION**
  - **Autism Spectrum Disorders**
- **WORKING WITH FAMILIES**

OVERVIEW

The final domain is that of adaptive development. Sometimes referred to as *self-help,* this domain actually is much broader than that. It relates to a young child's ability to display age-appropriate self-care and other behaviors in such a way as to adapt meaningfully to different circumstances. In adaptive development, the principal concern is with behavior that is both situation-appropriate and personally appropriate.

Young children are expected, before they enter elementary school, to demonstrate a number of behaviors. These include dressing and feeding themselves, exercising safety precautions when crossing streets, playing interactively with other children, observing program regulations, obeying authority figures such as ECSE personnel, and using restroom facilities appropriately. Also important is how language is used. Dramatic divergences may occur in children with autism, for example, between language development and how it is expressed. Children with autism may have great difficulty expressing the language they learn and may for that reason be misunderstood as having no useful language. Although these areas of adaptive development are important, self-help remains a central component of adaptive behavior, one we should not lose sight of as we expand our horizons to incorporate other kinds of behavior.

This chapter considers AIDS, autism spectrum disorders, epilepsy, fetal alcohol syndrome, and vulnerable child syndrome (children with mothers who abuse controlled substances). Each affects adaptive development. Because it can be so helpful in teaching adaptive behaviors, the intervention of cognitive behavior modification is described in this chapter. All children referred for testing, not only those with disabilities or delays in adaptive behavior, should be assessed in this domain and should receive early intervention as well as preschool and primary-grade special education and related services in the area of adaptive development if appropriate and if approved by parents. The IDEA calls for multidisciplinary teams in assessment, in development of IFSPs, and in delivery of services.

PREVALENCE

No one disability is linked directly to this domain. Prevalence data are limited. The U.S. Department of Education, in its *Annual Reports*, does not break out numbers for conditions discussed in this chapter, with one exception: autism. The latest such data, in the *Twenty-eighth Annual Report* (U.S. Department of Education, 2006c), show that the number of young children with autism spectrum disorders rises with each year of age through age six. About 6,000 three-year-olds, 8,000 four-year-olds, 12,000 five-year-olds, 16,000 six-year-olds, 16,000 seven-year-olds, and 16,000 eight-year-olds are reported to have this classification as of 2004. While the absolute number of young children with autism remains fairly small by comparison with other disabilities, the rise in incidence (the number of new cases annually) and prevalence (the total number) is startling. We do not see the kinds of progressions year after year in any other category that we see in Figures 15–1 (preschoolers) and 15–2 (6- to 11-year-olds). Similarly, the Centers for Disease Control and Prevention (www.cdc.gov) reports that autism spectrum disorders occur about five times per 1,000 live births; a decade ago, the figure was once per 2,000 births.

It is common for family members to excuse adaptive behavior delays or deviations in children with developmental delays or established conditions in other areas, reasoning

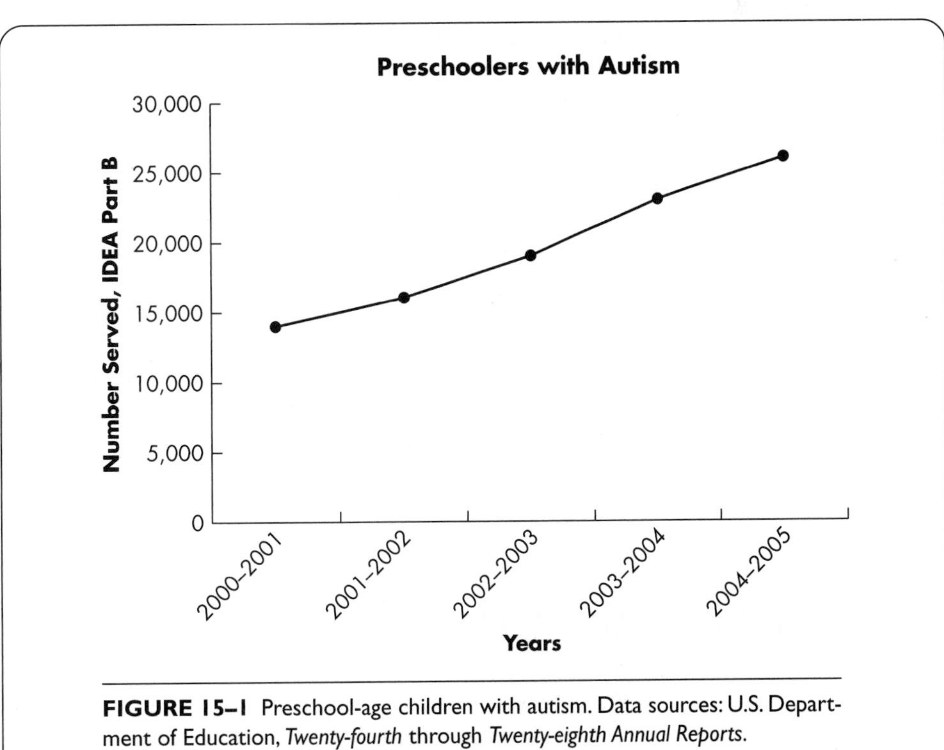

FIGURE 15–1 Preschool-age children with autism. Data sources: U.S. Department of Education, *Twenty-fourth* through *Twenty-eighth Annual Reports*.

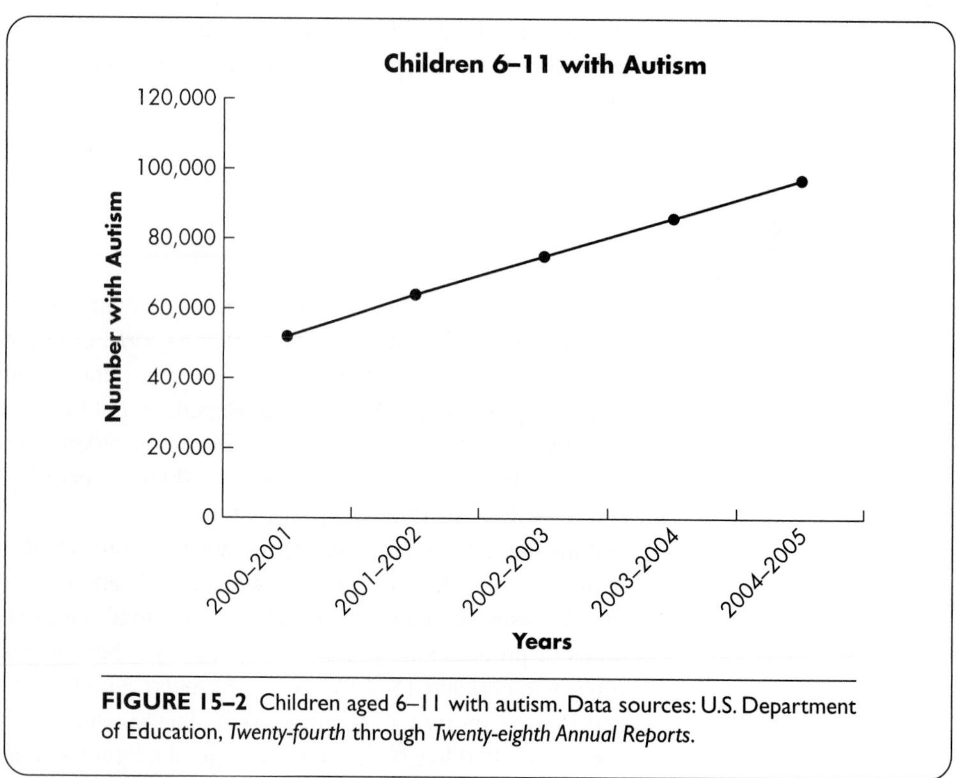

FIGURE 15–2 Children aged 6–11 with autism. Data sources: U.S. Department of Education, *Twenty-fourth* through *Twenty-eighth Annual Reports*.

that the child has other, much more important concerns. It is important that ECSE staff impress on family members the critical role adaptive behavior plays in academic success in elementary school and in social acceptance by other children, particularly children without disabilities.

DEVELOPMENTAL DELAYS

States may express developmental delays in adaptive behavior as age-inappropriate behavior, using 12-month or percentage delays for milestones like "ties own shoes" or "is toilet trained." Although some states may use measures based on standard deviations (SDs), such standards often are inappropriate in this area. The usefulness of SD is a direct function of the availability of standardized tests that provide means and SDs with which to compare individual scores. Few such measures are available in this area of development. The most appropriate indicators are those that look to behavior as it relates to specific situations.

ESTABLISHED CONDITIONS

As suggested earlier, no established condition is unique to the domain of adaptive behavior. Rather, conditions that almost invariably delay development in other domains, as cerebral palsy does in physical and communication development, also may affect

1. Physical, especially facial, features—including short eye slits that make eyes appear to be set far apart, a flat midface, and a thin upper lip
2. A growth deficiency (height, weight), placing the child in the lowest tenth of age norms
3. Evidence of central nervous system (CNS) dysfunction, including hyperactivity, seizures, attention deficits, and microcephaly

Adapted from Olson (1994).

FIGURE 15–3 Fetal alcohol syndrome indicators.

adaptive development. This chapter discusses several additional conditions that appear to relate more closely to adaptive than to the other four domains of development.

FETAL ALCOHOL SYNDROME

Fetal alcohol syndrome (FAS)

results from maternal abuse of alcohol during pregnancy and has three dimensions: facial characteristics, physical growth, and neurological aspects. In *fetal alcohol effect (FAE)*, one or two kinds of symptoms, but not all three, are present.

Fetal alcohol syndrome (FAS) is a complex of developmental effects caused by maternal use of alcohol during pregnancy. Olson (1994) suggests that the syndrome includes three kinds of symptoms: facial abnormalities, growth problems, and neurological impairments (see Figure 15–3). Many infants with FAS are premature, with low birth weight. The first set of characteristics is facial, including a small head and underdeveloped eyes that appear "too far apart." The ears may be prominent and unusually low. There often is a thin, long, or smooth upper lip. The second area is permanent growth retardation (stunted growth). The child may be limited in walking, and heart defects are common. Many children with FAS have difficulty sleeping through the night. Finally, neurological conditions may include mental retardation, hyperactivity, and speech impairments. FAS is a major cause of mental retardation in children. There are discernible differences between the brains of infants with and without FAS; infants with FAS have fissures that are notably more smooth than normal. Some children with FAS have seizures.

It is obvious from this discussion that FAS may affect cognitive and physical development. Yet the connection with adaptive development is a strong one. A particular problem of many children with FAS is learning cause and effect; they may need to learn safety rules by rote, for example, and may not understand the reasons behind rules governing social behavior. Kolata (1989) reports severe cause-and-effect deficits among Native Americans who engage in heavy drinking. The implications for teaching adaptive behavior are obvious; behavior modification or other behavior therapy approaches are necessary because just telling the child what to do often does not suffice. In *fetal alcohol effect (FAE),* children exhibit symptoms in one or two of the three categories. FAE usually has much less severe consequences for the child. See Figure 15–4 for intervention ideas for use with children having FAS or FAE.

Vulnerable child syndrome (VCS)

is an attempt to describe the condition of children exposed prenatally to cocaine, heroin, and other controlled substances; such children were formerly called *crack babies.*

VULNERABLE CHILD SYNDROME

Vulnerable child syndrome (VCS) (after Frank, 1990) includes children exposed prenatally to cocaine, heroin, and other controlled substances. Shortly after cocaine came into widespread use in the United States in 1985, neonatal intensive care unit

1. Observe the child carefully, in many different situations. She will show you what works for her.
2. Because FAS frequently results from parental substance abuse, ECSE workers should help family members obtain counseling and other assistance from community resources.
3. Identify and eliminate, where possible, excess stimulation of the child. Both at home and in the program, overstimulation may trigger hyperactivity and attention problems.
4. Use direct instruction to teach the child specific, concrete behaviors that other children may learn in less formal ways. Examples include showing her how to behave in social situations with family members and how to entertain herself when bored.
5. Adopt cognitive behavior modification strategies, including explicit explanations of what is desired and why, so that the child understands when behavior is reinforced or results in punishment.

Adapted from Olson (1994).

FIGURE 15–4 Intervention: FAS.

(NICU) intervention specialists and child care workers noticed effects in infants and toddlers born of cocaine-abusing mothers. The first reports suggested alarming numbers of such children—and a baffling variety of symptoms. (*Newsweek*'s February 12, 1990, issue, for example, focused on "The Crack Children," claiming that 11 percent of all newborns, or 375,000 infants annually, were displaying growth abnormalities, difficulty in concentrating, and a host of birth defects.) In the initial hysteria, the term *crack babies* came into widespread use. However, later research has established that the environmental quality of postnatal life for these infants may contribute much more to their problems than the mother's substance abuse during pregnancy (Frank, 1990; Williams & Howard, 1993). That is because adults addicted to illegal drugs may be so preoccupied with supporting their drug habits that they do not provide the infant with adequate nutrients and a safe, clean home environment, not to mention intellectual and sensory stimulation throughout the day (Chapman & Elliott, 1995). For a very useful summary of current data, see www.nida.nih.gov.

AIDS

AIDS
(acquired immune deficiency syndrome) is a condition in which the body's immune system fails. It is widely believed to be caused by the human immunodeficiency virus (HIV).

Human immunodeficiency virus (HIV)
is the virus associated with and widely believed to cause AIDS.

AIDS, or acquired immune deficiency syndrome, is widely accepted by states as an established condition. AIDS is believed to be caused by the **human immunodeficiency virus (HIV).** Detecting the disease in infants and very young children is problematic. Young children may be carriers of the mother's transferred antibodies and, thus, test positive for the virus until 13 or 15 months of age or perhaps as late as 18 months (Rathlev, 1994). During this period, children may passively carry maternal antibodies, but that does not mean that they themselves are infected.

In fact, only a small minority of infants, toddlers, and preschoolers born to HIV-positive mothers will develop AIDS. A strong majority (two-thirds to three-quarters) are not themselves infected (Rathlev, 1994). Caroline Johnson (1993), of Children's Hospital in Oakland, California, which has had more experience than have most programs with pediatric AIDS, estimates that about one-third of infants born to HIV-positive mothers are infected. If the mother takes the drug AZT during pregnancy, she can dramatically cut the risk of transmitting the disease to her fetus (Sack, 1994).

Initial symptoms in children include respiratory and other infections, failure to thrive, chronic diarrhea, and delays in linear growth (Johnson, 1993). In 2003, just 59 cases involving children under age 13 were reported to the CDC (www.cdc.gov).

Perhaps the first step is for ECSE program staff and volunteers to educate themselves about the disease, how it is transmitted, and how it affects not only child development but also the mother-child relationship. Although confidentiality rules prevent disclosure of any given child's HIV status, program administrators need to take steps to protect staff, volunteers, and children themselves. Program staff and volunteers may be instructed to assume that one or more children is infected and to follow such precautions as wearing gloves whenever blood may be present. Alternatively, staff and volunteers may be told that one or more children in a program have tested positive for the virus, without identifying which child(ren). The point is that standard procedures for handling cuts and other instances in which blood is spilled should be followed even if no child in the program is known to have the virus.

EPILEPSY

Epilepsy

is a physical condition producing irregular electric discharges in the brain. There are actually several types of epilepsy, many caused by head injuries.

Often caused by head injuries, as in traumatic brain injury (Chapter 12), **epilepsy** is a physical condition producing irregular electric discharges in the brain. There are actually several epilepsies, some much more serious than others. Seizures, whether *tonic-clonic* (formerly called *grand mal*) or more modest types, may cause a child to break the rules of social behavior—for example, in story time or quiet time—and may also interfere with learning. For these reasons, epilepsy is discussed in this chapter. The Epilepsy Foundation of America estimates that 7 million Americans of all ages have epilepsy (www.efa.org).

In an excellent brief discussion of pediatric epilepsy, Brunquell (1994) notes that epilepsy occurs at a rate among infants of one per thousand, much higher than the rates among older people. He explains that a single seizure does not indicate epilepsy. Rather, epilepsy is characterized by recurrent, unprovoked seizures. Each of us has a seizure threshold, Brunquell reports; epilepsy, then, may be understood as a condition in which the threshold is lower than it is with most people. His article goes into considerable detail to explain how different epilepsies are diagnosed and how medication for each is selected. Brunquell estimates that about 30 percent of individuals with epilepsy cannot achieve satisfactory control of seizures through medication. For these people, surgery may be an option. New, far more sophisticated surgical interventions, Brunquell reports, are as helpful for young children as for older individuals.

Epilepsy seizures range from the generalized tonic-clonic seizures in which electrical storms in the brain trigger loss of consciousness to the brief, transient *absence* (formerly called *petit mal*) seizures that look more like blinking or daydreaming and last for seconds. One complex, Lennox-Gastaut syndrome, affects about 20,000 children in the United States. It causes massive, repeated seizures, as many as 100 to 200 per hour and, if not treated, usually leads to mental retardation. As should be evident from this range of symptoms, epilepsy is not one condition but, rather, a variety of disorders. Common causes include blows to the head, as in automobile accidents, and heredity. Frequently, though, no cause can be located (www.efa.org).

About 85 percent of seizures can now be controlled with medication. However, many drugs have side effects, including fatigue, nausea, and weight gain.

AUTISM SPECTRUM DISORDERS

Autism spectrum disorders is a condition affecting communication, imagination, and socialization. Its most prominent characteristic is an "autistic aloneness" in which children appear to avoid and even to reject social interaction.

The CDC estimated in 2005 that 1 child in every 500 may have **autism spectrum disorders** (www.cdc.gov). That is about four times the rate (1 per 2,000) that the agency had given 15 years ago. Part of the reason is that the diagnostic criteria have changed. The disability is now recognized as existing along a continuum, hence the name "autism spectrum disorders." However, other factors doubtlessly are at work. In 2005, the NIH and three private autism organizations joined to fund a consortium to learn what is behind the surge. The five-year effort is spearheaded by Cure Autism Now (www.cureautismnow.org), the National Alliance for Autism Research (www.naar.org), and the Southwest Autism Research & Resource Center (www.autismcenter.org), as well as NIH and other federal agencies.

Many family members suspect that childhood immunizations play a role in, or even cause, autism. In particular, the measles-mumps-rubella (MMR) vaccines, and the mercury used in some vaccines, are suspected. Parents point to the fact that symptoms of autism frequently appear at about the time of vaccinations (i.e., around two or three years of age). However, as the chapter-opening story about Mrs. Fourgere's diaries suggests, medical experts are now detecting symptoms much earlier in life, which casts doubt on the theory that vaccines cause autism. What does remains unknown. The good news is that millions of dollars are being allocated to finding answers (www.cdc.gov).

Following Wing (1981), Frith (1993) describes autism as having three dimensions: impairments in communication, imagination, and socialization. Parents most often first notice delays in language and speech, and it is usually for that reason that they bring the child to a pediatrician, and later to a speech and hearing clinic, for assessment. Other speech-related problems, such as muteness and *echolalia* (meaningless repetition), are readily observed as well. Children of all kinds imitate; there is nothing unusual about a three-year-old occasionally exhibiting echolalic-like speech. Children with autism spectrum disorders, however, may be echolalic until age five or six, alarming their parents; the echolalia is not occasional but, rather, is a common occurrence. Immediate echolalia is a key symptom of autism spectrum disorders.

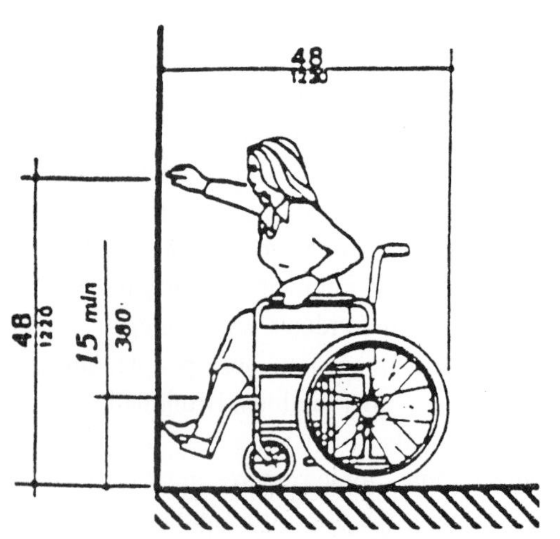

Making sure objects are reachable is a small but important step toward facilitating adaptive behavior for children who have physical disabilities.

Source: U.S. Architectural and Transportation Barriers Compliance Board (1991, July 26), Americans with Disabilities Act accessibility guidelines, *Federal Register, 56*(144), 35476.

The most prominent characteristic of autism spectrum disorders is not speech and language delay, however, but rather an "autistic aloneness" (Frith, 1989, 1993). There is an aversion of the eyes and a lack of responsiveness to others as people. The child does not seem to understand what is said to her, does not look up when called, seems to "look through" people. Children with autism spectrum disorders do not use gaze for communication; this seems not to be a matter of avoiding eye contact but rather of not using eye contact as expected. Frith (1993) notes that young children with autism do not engage in "shared attention," as when they point to something of interest so as to engage a caregiver's attention to it. When infants and toddlers point to something only when they want it, Frith (1993) comments, this may be one of the earliest indications of autism.

During the second to the fifth year of life, most children engage in pretend play virtually every day. Children with autism do not; according to Frith (1993), "Autistic children cannot understand pretense and do not pretend when they are playing" (p. 112). They may also seem to be overselective, screening out some cues, attending only to a few isolated cues. In addition, often there is self-injurious behavior. O. Ivar Lovaas (1989), an expert on childhood autism, suspects that the child is attempting to communicate something—perhaps "You haven't fulfilled my needs, you haven't taught me a more appropriate way to interact" (p. 5).

A frequent class of symptoms is an obsessive desire for sameness, a rigid repetition of certain activities. This rarely occurs in other childhood disabilities. There are very narrow, intense interests and stereotypical movements. These symptoms help us distinguish autism spectrum disorders from emotional disturbance or mental illness. In addition, autism does not feature "hearing voices" or a conviction that the environment holds personal messages; nor does it first develop in adolescence or adulthood. (Those symptoms are characteristic of schizophrenia.)

Whatever the causes, autism is a severe disability. Greenfield (1972) describes the kinds of behaviors that many parents find so disturbing:

> At the age of four, Noah is neither toilet-trained nor does he feed himself. He seldom speaks expressively, rarely employs his less-than-a-dozen-word vocabulary. His attention span in a new toy is a matter of split seconds, television engages him only for an odd moment occasionally, he is never interested in other children for very long. His main activities are lint-catching, thread pulling, blanket-sucking, spontaneous giggling, inexplicable crying, bed-bouncing, eye-squinting, wall-hugging, circle-walking, and incoherent babbling addressed to his finger-flexing right hand.
>
> But two years ago, Noah spoke in complete sentences, had a vocabulary of well over 150 words, sang the verses of his favorite songs, identified the objects and animals in his picture books, was all but toilet-trained, and practically ate by himself. (pp. 3–4)

In 1990, Congress added autism as a distinct category qualifying for assistance under Part B. The condition previously had been subsumed, in U.S. Department of Education reports, under "emotional disturbance" or "other health impaired." The 1990 addition of autism as a separate category reflected growing recognition that autism is fundamentally different from social or emotional conditions. For one thing, the symptoms do not disappear; people do not "grow out of it." For another, psychotherapy and other traditional means of dealing with emotional disturbance seldom work with children who are autistic (Lovaas, 1989).

ASSESSMENT

The domain of adaptive behavior is a broad one, encompassing many kinds of activities and situations. The interest in early childhood is evaluating the extent to which a child performs activities that are both age-appropriate and situation-appropriate. It is necessary to include in this work a recognition of cultural variables, in that behavior culturally valued in one family (i.e., individual competence, competitiveness) may not be valued in a second family, which may instead place emphasis on interpersonal relations, cooperation, and group problem solving. Given these variables, professional judgment or informed clinical opinion is particularly critical in assessing adaptive development.

Children whose disabilities or delays appear to be primarily related to another domain nonetheless should be assessed and helped in the domain of adaptive development. Freund (1994), to illustrate, calls adaptive development the single most critical area of intervention for children with fragile X syndrome, an inherited condition that often leads to mental retardation. Similarly, children with losses of hearing or vision may be overprotected by parents, who thus prevent them from learning how to behave independently in different situations. Those skills are essential for successful integration in K–12 programs. Young children with severe physical disabilities may need special help in gaining physical access to different parts of the community so that they can learn to get around independently.

Some standardized instruments are available for use in the early childhood years. One of the most commonly used measures of adaptive behavior is the Vineland Adaptive Behavior Scales (Sparrow, Balla, & Cichetti, 1984). This instrument provides a general overview of adaptive behavior, including daily living skills, communication, socialization, and motor skills. It uses a semistructured interview format and may be responded to by a teacher, caregiver, or parent. Results may be expressed as standard scores and as age-equivalent scores. Interrater reliability, internal consistency, and concurrent validity indicate that this is a good instrument for use with young children who have developmental delays or disabilities.

The Brazelton Neonatal Behavioral Assessment Scale (Brazelton, 1984) and the Index of Neurobehavioral Dysfunction (Cole, 1996) have been used with infants suspected of prenatal exposure to alcohol or drugs. The Brazelton instrument in particular is widely used during the first month of life to assess head turning, reflex action, and reaction to stimuli.

The Bayley Scales of Infant Development (second edition) include measures of adaptive development. The Carolina Record of Individual Behavior (Simeonsson, Huntington, Short, & Ware, 1982) rates a child's interaction with the environment. The clinician observes the child's behavior and rates its appropriateness. Test-retest reliabilities are reported that are well within acceptable ranges. The Battelle Developmental Inventory contains an adaptive behavior subscale as well as personal-social, gross and fine motor, and communication measures.

Both delays and deviations may be noted. Delays occur when behavior is appropriate, but for a younger age period. Parallel play, to illustrate, is appropriate for two-year-olds but not for five-year-olds. Deviations, however, are forms of behavior that are fundamentally different from those displayed by nondisabled children under six. Disinterest in self-dressing, for example, is atypical in young children; even two-year-olds want to at least help dress themselves. Self-stimulation in public is another deviation, as is aimless wandering in the halls during breaks in scheduled activities.

However demanding assessment in the domain of adaptive development may be, the IDEA looks to ECSE programs to assess each eligible child in this domain as in the others. That is crucial. Children whose primary needs lie in another domain nonetheless should also be assessed in the area of adaptive behavior. Program staff should be particularly alert to instances in which primary caregivers, whether parents or other adults, unwittingly retard a young child's development in this domain by overprotecting the child and by not expecting the child to perform self-care and other activities that are part of age-appropriate behavior.

With respect to children with autism spectrum disorders, assessment involves looking for indicators of this unusual condition. Widely used for screening purposes are well-regarded questionnaires. The autism spectrum quotient (AQ) is one (Baron-Cohen et al., 2001). It asks about the child's interest in fiction and in the personalities of people around her, among much else. The Checklist for Autism in Toddlers (CHAT) is another (Baron-Cohen et al., 1998). It requires just a few minutes to complete. A 12-question instrument developed in London has also found widespread acceptance (Skuse, Mandy, & Scourfield, 2005). The New York State Department of Health's (1999a) guidelines on autism suggest that clinical clues include lack of communicative gestures, nonattempts to imitate or produce single words to convey meaning, nonpersistence in communication, limited comprehension and production vocabularies, and lack of growth in production vocabulary over a 6-month period between 12 and 18 months of age.

INTERVENTION

Virtually all young children with disabilities, delays, or deviations in behavior can learn at least some adaptive behaviors. Children who are HIV-positive may live for years without significant symptoms; children with AIDS also may have years of productive learning. An important "staff memorandum" prepared by the U.S. Department of Education's Office for Civil Rights (OCR) confirms that children with AIDS are entitled to a free, appropriate public education, pursuant to Section 504 of the Rehabilitation Act (OCR Staff Memorandum, 16 EHLR 712, 1990; Supplement 266, June 1, 1990). That includes training and assistance in functioning independently both at home and in ECSE programs.

Other children with very severe physical disabilities or severe mental retardation can learn skills of helping others help them. Adaptive behavior skills may be taught by early childhood special educators and other ECSE professionals. The contributions an occupational therapist may make should not be overlooked. Occupational therapists teach adaptive behaviors as part of their professional responsibilities. To illustrate, the federal regulations for early intervention (U.S. Department of Education, 1993) defines occupational therapy in Section 303.12(8) as follows:

> *[S]ervices to address the functional needs of a child related to adaptive development, adaptive behavior and play, and sensory motor and postural development. These services are designed to improve the child's functional ability to perform tasks in home, school, and community settings.*

Effective intervention in the domain of affective development begins, as it does in all domains, with IFSPs and IEPs. It is imperative that these written plans identify the child's needs and specify precisely what kinds of instruction will be attempted. Goals and objectives must be written that are concrete and measurable.

Whether early childhood special educators, occupational therapists, or others do the teaching, some techniques are particularly suited to instruction in adaptive behavior. One is to take full advantage of the opportunity teaching adaptive behaviors offers to introduce and practice other concepts and behaviors. In many instances, adaptive behavior sessions are both frequent and lengthy; a considerable amount of the time children are in ECSE settings is often given over to instruction in adaptive behavior. Language is a good example. When children are learning self-care, self-dressing, and self-eating behaviors, they tend to give their full attention to the task. Such situations offer ECSE workers an ideal opportunity to introduce new words describing the activities being performed, the feelings the child has during those activities, and the implements being used. Conceptual information necessary for development may also be taught; during instruction in self-feeding, for example, children may be taught sequence, color, number, and other things, in addition to food groups.

A technique important to instruction in the adaptive development domain is behavior modification, which was discussed in the previous chapter. Those techniques certainly are applicable in the domain of adaptive behavior as well. However, since the cardinal principles of adaptive behavior are the ability to size up a situation, select appropriate behaviors to match that situation's expectations or demands, and flexibly implement that plan with modifications as the changing situation demands, a variation on behavior modification may prove especially helpful. That variation is called **cognitive behavior modification.** The major advantage of cognitive behavior modification is that it can be used to alter not only the child's behavior but also the child's thinking behind that behavior. That can be extremely helpful in the case of impulsive children, children who use aggression as their primary coping mechanism for frustration of all kinds, children with other emotional or behavior disorders, and children with adaptive behavior limitations. This approach focuses as much on faulty thinking skills as it does on behavior. It includes training for children in self-monitoring, problem solving, and relaxation. Children are offered suggestions both on analytical skills and on specific activities.

Cognitive behavior modification

stresses the importance of teaching the child ways of thinking about situations, in the belief that learning is a change in the *capacity* to behave in a certain way.

A great deal of research evidence now supports cognitive behavior modification (Woolfolk, 2004), but the evidence is more mixed on its effectiveness with children having adaptive and/or emotional or social conditions or delays (Fiore et al., 1993; Reid et al., 1994). The technique remains promising for such uses because it helps alter the way a child *thinks* about situations and responds to them. The basic principles of behavior modification outlined in the previous chapter apply as well in cognitive behavior modification. One of those is that behavior that is reinforced increases in frequency. An important assumption of behavior modification generally is that behavior must be demonstrated; one cannot study and certainly cannot modify behavior that is never shown. If a child does not display behavior, she cannot be reinforced—and therefore does not learn the desired behavior. Traditional behavior modification has great difficulty with situations in which learning occurs without behavior.

Cognitive behavior modification, however, can readily explain such occurrences. What about instances in which behavior increases—that is, learning occurs—without being reinforced? That is the question Albert Bandura (1977) forced us to consider. What Bandura did was to challenge the whole foundation of behavior modification by showing that behavior need not be demonstrated in order for learning to occur. In a series of studies, Bandura illustrated what he called *social learning.* First, he created some videotapes and films in which children did certain things and were reinforced for doing so. These "models" performed desired behavior. The subjects in Bandura's studies watched the videotape or film. After it was shown, Bandura observed their behavior. They clearly had learned that certain behaviors were desired (would be reinforced).

Over a period of years, Bandura established some rules governing social learning. One is that attention is necessary. A second is that children must have an opportunity to display the desired behavior (e.g., practice it). A third is that these children are being *vicariously* reinforced when they observe models being rewarded. In effect, Bandura said, the children were learning without performing behavior because their thinking processes were being altered. They were learning and being reinforced mentally. Vaughn, Ridley, and Bullock (1984) used puppets to model desired behavior to young children. Again, vicarious reinforcement was taking place (the children identified with the puppets, saw them do things and be rewarded for doing them, and learned from that process that certain behaviors would be reinforced).

Modeling

occurs when a child watches a high-status "model" perform positive actions and be reinforced for doing so. The child is vicariously reinforced by watching the model be rewarded.

Modeling is a major component of cognitive behavior modification. Children are asked to attend to behavior that is being modeled. As Lovaas (1989) points out, adults can start this process—they can model desired behavior—but other children need to model it as well for it to be established and maintained. In cognitive behavior modification, another step is taken. The adults—and often other children as well—talk through the steps they are taking. They articulate out loud what their thinking processes are—what they are doing, and in what order. Thus, children learn not only what to do but also how to think about it. They are encouraged to duplicate the modeled behavior. At first, particularly with young children, this may be done with *overt* talking out, but later it becomes *covert* talking out, for example talking to oneself silently, as the task is performed.

These techniques may be used to teach many adaptive behaviors. Modeling is particularly important. One benefit of integrating of children with and without disabilities is the ready availability for the former of examples of developmentally appropriate behavior by the latter; children with disabilities, delays, or deviations in behavior are exposed daily to how children with no disabilities do these things. That is why Lovaas is so concerned that young children with autism be integrated into regular preschool, kindergarten, and elementary school programs. It is only by being with, observing, and being socialized by children with no disabilities that appropriate behaviors are modeled, learned, and practiced until they become habitual.

Whether the adaptive behaviors at issue have to do with self-care, self-feeding, self-dressing, or self-regulation of desires, instruction may best be accomplished by observing the rules of cognitive behavior modification. The ECSE worker should model the desired behavior. While doing so, she should talk through that behavior—verbalizing what is being done, in what sequence, and why it is being done in that way. The conjunction of physical modeling with verbalized thinking processes helps young children see not only what behavior is acceptable but also how to think about the behavior itself.

If "developmentally appropriate adaptive behavior" means anything, it means doing what is expected in a particular situation. In play, that means assessing a situation before seeking entry into a group. In self-care, it means anticipating needs before they become uncontrollable (as in the need to go to the bathroom). In these and other situations, the child needs to be able to think through and analyze a situation. The next step is to identify alternative behaviors, or options, and to determine which are acceptable in that situation. The child then formulates and carries out a plan of action. While doing so, she notes the reactions of other children and modifies behavior accordingly. All of these are cognitive steps that children need to learn in order to demonstrate acceptable adaptive behavior.

Behavior modification and cognitive behavior modification may be especially helpful with children who have VCS. These children need structured environments and one-on-one direct instruction. Those children with VCS who exhibit extreme sensitivity to sensory input (whether being touched, hearing noises, or other stimulation) may be helped if stimulation is initially reduced. Sensory input is then gradually increased, and

1. Give children with autism love. These children do need love, even if this does not appear to be true.
2. Offer a structured environment—firm, calm, reassuring. Children with autism need structure.
3. Directly teach children how to read other people's body language, how to make people be friendly.
4. Directly teach metacognitive skills (understanding one's own and other's thought processes).
5. Teach by overteaching, by calling attention to cues the child may have overlooked. Children with autism at times are overselective and attend to only a few cues.
6. Use sign language. Signs force children to watch you.

Adapted from Frith (1989, 1993).

FIGURE 15–5 What works: autism spectrum disorders.

the child is given an opportunity to adjust (habituate) to the new level before stimulation again is increased (Williams & Howard, 1993).

AUTISM SPECTRUM DISORDERS

Interventions to help children with autism spectrum disorders remain few and far between (see Figure 15–5). The one validated approach is *applied behavior analysis* (ABA), the one-on-one repeated-trials intervention used by Lovaas (1987), discussed later. Variations include *applied verbal analysis* (AVA), which features repeated trials of words ("Say, 'Thanks!'") (www.drcarbone.net). Embedding and other incidental teaching are used in *floor time,* another popular approach (www.floortime.org). These techniques take advantage of activities the child shows interest in doing. Early interventionists and special educators give the child words to go along with those preferred activities. Although incidental learning and floor time are in use in many programs serving young children with autism, the research behind them has not yet reached the level that supports ABA. Whatever tactics are adopted, early intervention is essential. In a review of methods, Corsello (2005) notes that "children make greater gains when they enter a program at a younger age" (p. 82).

Lovaas (1987) demonstrated a home-based, one-to-one approach that restructures a child's home environment to make it functional for a child with autism. The project's aims were to demonstrate behavioral interventions useful with young children who have autism. Beginning as early as 18 months and continuing as late as five years of age, the Young Autism Project featured as many as 40 hours per week of behavior modification intervention. Staff and parents met at a clinic weekly for about two hours; virtually all other work was performed in the home. UCLA graduate students, parents, and even neighbors or relatives worked with the children.

In a 1987 article describing the outcomes of his work, Lovaas reports on 19 young children who participated in the project for two or more years. Half had entered regular elementary school and tested normal or above normal on IQ tests; most of the others entered special education classes in regular public schools and tested mildly retarded. Comparing the experimental subjects with control-group children who received just 10 hours weekly of intervention, Lovaas (1987) reports an average IQ gain of 30 points over two years. He contends that very intensive treatment is essential for progress with young children who have autism: "You're not going to do a lot with less than thirty hours of one-to-one training a week" (1989, p. 9). He adds, "But they didn't start playing with other kids; they didn't become emotionally attached to their parents; they didn't simultaneously learn to put on their pants or learn to go to the toilet" (1989, p. 4). He further points out that the children had learned only after direct instruction in each specific activity; they demonstrated very little generalization from one setting to another or from one task to a similar task. Nonetheless, he insists that the approach shows that behavior modification can help even children with severe autism. Looking to the next stage, he urges that children with autism not only be integrated into regular classes insofar as possible but be directly taught how to watch what the other children do:

> Mainstreaming is absolutely essential, because if you get the children hooked on normal peers and developing friendships, they won't regress once you stop treatment; then the development is in the hands of the child's friends. Adults can help a child get started, but it's other children that make a child normal, not adults. (1989, p. 2)

Despite his own qualifications about what his project demonstrated, Lovaas's reports elicited much skepticism from other researchers. Schopler, Short, and Mesibov (1989), for example, criticize Lovaas's choice of outcome measures, criteria for subject selection, and other aspects of his experimental design. Lovaas and his colleagues Smith and McEachin (1989) respond by defending their methods. What neither Schopler et al. nor Lovaas et al. note is another concern with the Los Angeles work: providing 40 hours weekly of intensive intervention at the homes of young children is so difficult and so costly that few ECSE programs or university programs not supported by research grants will be able to replicate it.

Recent years have seen other approaches being recommended. Barry Prizant and Amy Wetherby, two experts on speech and language impairment, have promoted the SCERTS model (*S*ocial *C*ommunication *E*motional *R*egulation *T*ransactional *S*upport) (e.g., Prizant et al., 2003). Their methods seek to promote child-to-child and child-to-adult communication, arousal and tantrum control, and transition from activity to activity. Floor time is a prominent component. Keen (2005) suggests that toddlers and preschoolers with autism spectrum disorders be taught different strategies for use in attempts to repair communication breakdowns (the children studied tended to rely heavily on simple repetition). McDonald (2004) emphasizes the importance of teaching social skills, as playing with other children is a key to success in kindergarten and the primary grades. Stahmer and Ingersoll (2004) agree, noting that whether toddlers use sign language or communication boards is much less important than what they communicate to other young children and to

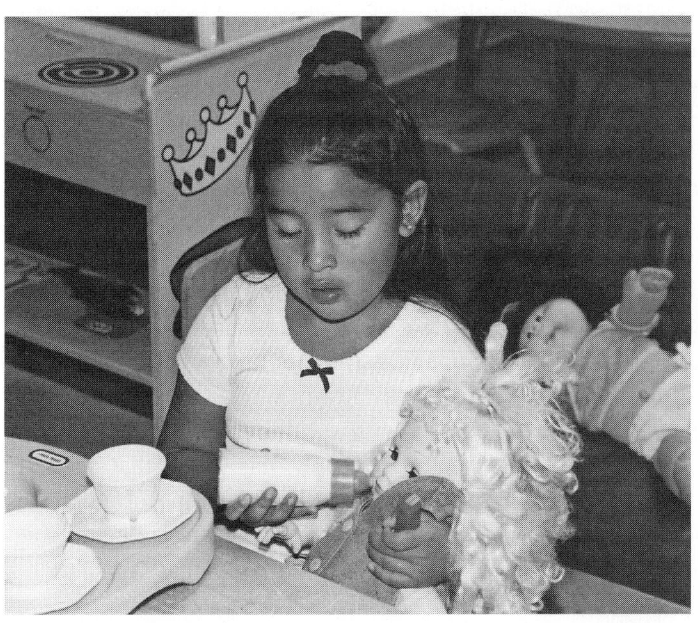

According to Uta Frith, pretend play does not occur among young children with autism.

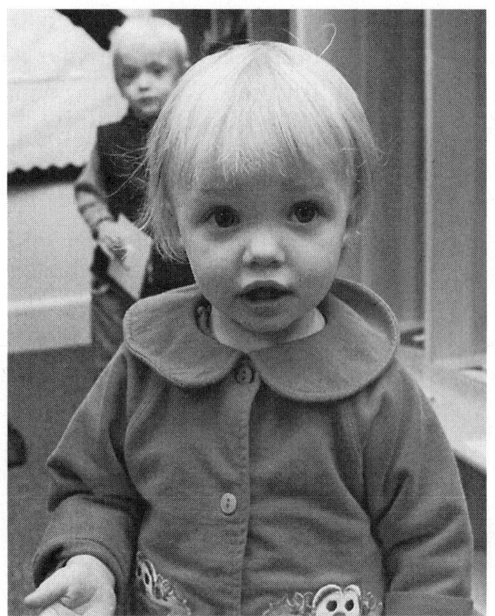

The "autistic aloneness" characteristic of autism includes nonuse of eye contact for communication purposes. There is an avoidance of direct gaze.

adults. They also find that effective communication in play and other activities reduced behavior problems in inclusive settings.

What all of these approaches have in common is a near-total command of available time. Lovaas, for example, insists that applied behavior analysis is a comprehensive intervention, to be implemented in every setting and at every moment. Here, in sharper relief than anywhere else, we confront the academic demands of NCLB and IDEA 2004: when is academic instruction to take place? The need is clear. The SEELS longitudinal study reports that 6- to 12-year-olds with autism performed at the lowest one-fifth in passage comprehension at a 66 percent rate, in math calculation at a 49 percent clip, and in math problem-solving at a 65 percent rate.

WORKING WITH FAMILIES

As noted earlier, family members sometimes excuse young children with disabilities from performing self-care activities out of a concern that the child "has so much else to worry about." Other family members may do these things for the child in the mistaken belief that they are helping. Either pattern—excusing or overdoing—harms the child. It also interferes with and delays success in ECSE program efforts to teach adaptive behavior. Adaptive behaviors are among the most likely to be the subject of adult attention both at home and in EC programs. Thus, family and ECSE worker cooperation is essential. ECSE workers should emphasize to family members that it is essential for young children with disabilities to master these self-help and other adaptive behaviors. They are critical to success in integrated settings, for example; and they are as developmentally appropriate as anything can be.

Children in the early childhood years are driven (no other word seems sufficient to describe it) to master self-control skills. From the first attempt to sit, or walk, or run, children in the early childhood years demonstrate persistence that is far beyond the capacity of many of their caregivers; children will practice a new skill for days and weeks on end, persisting in the face of almost certain frustration. To stop the child from doing that because the adult feels frustration is a disservice to the child. This point needs to be made with emphasis, not only to families but also to any ECSE worker who does things that children are trying to do by themselves.

With children who have severe disabilities, adults should limit their assistance to what is necessary and unavoidable. Let us illustrate with a child who has cerebral palsy. Before dressing, this child may need assistance in putting on braces. The adult's role should be as restricted as possible. If the braces are located in another area that the child cannot travel to, the adults may bring the braces to a point within the child's reach; however, a better solution is to establish a permanent place for keeping braces that is readily within the child's reach. If the braces require strapping, the adult may perform that task after the child has placed the braces on her legs. Again, however, there are better solutions. Braces that may be attached with Velcro straps offer a solution that even children with severe cerebral palsy can strap.

Other examples are legion. Allen (1992) illustrates appropriate assistance by noting that adults may help children who have difficulty putting on their own coats by placing the coat on a child-size chair; by sitting in the chair and reaching each arm back in sequence, the child can put on the coat. Such assistance—limiting the adult involvement to simply placing the coat on the chair back—is much more suitable than actually putting the coat on the child. Watson (1973) shows how *chaining* could be used to teach children how to take off T-shirts. The child first learns to do the final step of the process (in this case, removing the shirt from the left wrist and hand); once this is learned, the preceding step is added. Continuing backward, the child eventually demonstrates the entire process. Watson describes how the technique could be used for entire dressing patterns. At first, the adult completely dresses the child except for her shoes; she must put on her shoes to be reinforced. Later, after that is learned, the child must put on both socks and shoes; later, of course, pants, shirts, and other items of clothing are added.

Young children are powerfully driven to perform self-care and many other adaptive activities for good reasons. Being able to perform these activities is one of the child's first demonstrations of independence from caregivers. That move toward independence is itself developmentally important. Family members and professionals alike are well advised to think through how minimal their support might be, what kinds of assistive technology devices and services might be useful, and what kinds of behavior techniques might accelerate the child's learning. Those kinds of planning activities are far more helpful to a child with a disability, delay, or deviation in behavior than is direct assistance in performing adaptive behaviors.

The challenge for families of children with autism spectrum disorders is sobering by any measure. Lovaas (1987) and Kozloff, Helm, Cutler, Douglas-Steele, and Scampini (1988) caution that parenting with young children who are autistic is a demanding, full-time job. Kozloff et al. (1988), reviewing almost 20 years of their efforts to train families of children with autism, conclude that it not only can be done but that it is an essential element of an overall approach to helping children with autism. Family members report real progress in their children's behavior as a result of the behavior management techniques they used. These changes, in turn, renew family enthusiasm for the interventions. Other experts, however, echo Lovaas (1987) in pointing to significant problems in achieving generalization of training with children with autism. Progress made at home does not seem to translate to similar progress in other settings, nor do advances in school transfer to the home (Schriebman, 1988).

Stoner et al. (2005) explore reasons for the often-reported friction between families and programs. Noting that traditional approaches in ECSE have featured professionals training parents, which can have the unintended effect of making family members feel incapable, Stoner and her colleagues emphasize the importance of ECSE staff members looking at family-program relations from the perspective of the family. Professionals need to "walk a mile in our shoes," they urge, so as to learn to avoid ways in which program staff may undermine parental trust and also ways in which they may neglect family members' needs for respect and partnership.

SUMMARY

Delays in adaptive development are characteristic of children with mental retardation and emotional disturbance and indeed are central to the definitions of those terms. The availability of a fifth domain, that of adaptive development, allows ECSE programs to serve young children who are neither mentally retarded nor emotionally disturbed but who for other reasons, perhaps because of family neglect or poor child management techniques, have yet to acquire the kinds of adaptive behaviors necessary for formal schooling.

This chapter discussed a number of conditions often associated with delays in adaptive development. AIDS is one; young children who are HIV-infected or who have developed the symptoms of AIDS often display delays or even regressions in adaptive behavior. The neurological impairments common to children with FAS similarly lead to difficulties in adaptive development. To the extent that such children's primary caregivers abuse alcohol, the home environment may be one of little appropriate stimulation, leading to delays in adaptive development. Similarly, while questions persist as to what permanent effects, if any, VCS produces, there is little doubt that drug addiction in primary caregivers dramatically reduces the attention many give to adaptive development in their children. Seizures resulting from epilepsy interfere with a child's ability to attend to program activities; those seizures may also disrupt the attention of other children to program tasks.

As an intervention technique, cognitive behavior modification combines direct instruction with well-established techniques of promoting desired behaviors. The method is particularly well suited to adaptive development because of the demands of this domain; children must assess each new situation, weigh alternative behaviors, determine which is most situation-appropriate, implement that approach, and react to how it is received by others. The flexibility all of these tasks require is best taught by helping children talk through behavioral alternatives and explain or justify their behaviors as appropriate. Even though he achieved success in Los Angeles with many young children who have autism, Lovaas (1987, 1989) recognizes that replications in other programs will be limited, both because the required early childhood intervention is so extreme (more than 40 hours weekly) and because even with this intensive treatment, many children are not ready for integration when they enter school.

The domain of adaptive development is vital not only to children displaying delays or deviations in behaviors related to this domain but to all young children. Experience with applying what Salisbury and Vincent (1990) call the "criterion of the next environment" teaches ECSE workers to emphasize the acquisition during the preschool years of the kinds of adaptive behaviors necessary for success in K–12 programs. Often, the extent to which children with disabilities are able to integrate successfully in regular classrooms is a direct function of the degree to which they have mastered the demands of adaptive development. That is, their ability to care for themselves and to respond appropriately to new and challenging situations is crucial to successful integration in kindergarten and in elementary school.

KEY TERMS

AIDS
autism spectrum disorders
cognitive behavior modification
epilepsy
fetal alcohol syndrome (FAS)
human immunodeficiency virus (HIV)
modeling
vulnerable child syndrome (VCS)

QUESTIONS FOR REFLECTION

1. In your own words, what is *adaptive development?*
2. What are the three kinds of indicators of FAS?
3. How might problems in learning cause and effect manifest themselves in young children?
4. How do alcohol and illegal drugs, when used by a mother during pregnancy, differentially affect young children?

5. Explain why it would be wrong to assume that children of an AIDS-infected mother are also infected.
6. Give an example of echolalia.
7. Explain why autism spectrum disorders is not an emotional disturbance.
8. Differentiate cognitive behavior modification from behavior modification.
9. How could you use modeling to change a child's behavior?
10. What practical realities might hinder an ECSE program from adopting Lovaas's approach to autism spectrum disorders in young children?

PRACTICAL EXERCISES

1. Do you know a family having a young child with one of the disabilities discussed in this chapter, particularly autism spectrum disorders? Many families with young children having autism post requests with college teacher-training programs, seeking the part-time help of a student majoring in special education. Your professor may know of such a family. Request permission to visit the family or to observe the child in a program.

   After spending a few hours with the child, comment on the interventions being used. In particular, if you see behavior modification in action, explain the technique and illustrate with examples drawn from your observations. Why do you think behavior modification is the only intervention shown by objective research to help young children with autism? How do you think it achieves its effects?
2. What causes do you think are likely behind the recent surge in reported cases of autism spectrum disorders? This is a lively and controversial topic. Some people, including many parents, suspect that childhood vaccinations are either related to or directly causative of autism. The medical establishment is vehement in its denial of any such relationship. Much research is underway on the topic, of which some will soon appear in professional journals. Visit the URLs in this chapter and read journal articles. Then take a position on genetic, environmental, or other likely causes.

WEB SITES OF INTEREST

www.cureautismnow.org Cure Autism Now Foundation—a good site about autism in young children

www.efa.org Epilepsy Foundation of America—very helpful on epilepsy

Resources

A tremendous number of books, journals, agencies, and organizations are available to assist ECSE workers and parents. The resources listed and described here have proven useful to the author; however, no endorsement should be implied.

The World Wide Web has become an increasingly vital tool for people seeking information. The field of early childhood special education certainly is no exception. A vast wealth of material relevant to the topics discussed in this book is available on-line. Much of it is valuable; some of it is worthless. How to tell the difference? A few comments may help the reader.

A good rule of thumb is to begin your search at the Web site of a well-respected national organization that specializes in the topic of interest to you. For example, you might surf to the Web site of the National Early Childhood Technical Assistance Center (NECTAC) at www.nectac.org and then, after reaching that site, look for "hot links" or connections to other sites. Similarly, the Council for Exceptional Children (www.cec.sped.org) and CEC's Division for Early Childhood (www.dec-sped.org) are excellent starting points, as is the U.S. Department of Education (www.ed.gov). A reputable Web site generally will list only respectable resources, avoiding those that have questionable validity. You may also bring a Web site about which you have questions to the attention of a professor, teacher, or other scholar whose opinion you trust, asking her to evaluate the site and the information it offers.

Given here are the basic Web site addresses (Uniform Resource Locators, or URLs). Readers seeking specific information will need to navigate within each site, either by clicking on a link or by using a "search" button.

MEDICAL INFORMATION

Medline/Pubmed

National Library of Medicine
National Institutes of Health
www.nlm.nih.gov

Very helpful on disabilities and other medical conditions. Very authoritative source for treatment information. Some of the material is fairly technical.

4WomanGov

U.S. Department of Health and Human Services
www.4woman.gov

Easy-to-use information on women's health, including maternity issues and child rearing.

ExpressScripts

www.drugdigest.org

Invaluable for people who take more than one prescription drug. You may check on interactions between different prescriptions.

Quest Diagnostics

www.questdiagnostics.com

This is proprietary (Quest Diagnostics is in the business), but the site is still useful for information on medications and medical tests.

National Organization for Rare Disorders (NORD)

100 Route 37, PO Box 8923
New Fairfield, CT 06812-8923
www.rarediseases.org

NORD is invaluable on "orphan diseases"—rare conditions. Based in Connecticut, it offers a wealth of data on-line and even more information via U.S. mail. The author of this text has requested more information than is posted at NORD's Web site and, within a few days, received packages in the mail about very unusual conditions. There is no charge.

ADHD

American Academy of Pediatrics
www.aap.org (search for "ADHD")
Information on ADHD.

CDC

Centers for Disease Control and Prevention
www.cdc.gov

The experts on preventive medicine and demographics of chronic health conditions. At this site, search for, respectively, asthma, autism, HIV, and ADHD. CDC is the main source for epidemiological data on these conditions.

BOOKS

General

Allen, K., & Cowdery, G. (2005). *The exceptional child: Inclusion in early childhood education.* Clifton Park, NY: Delmar Learning.

This text focuses on methods for facilitating inclusion of young children with disabilities into general early childhood programs.

Deiner, P. (2005). *Resources for educating children with diverse abilities*. Clifton Park, NY: Delmar Learning.

This book offers activities for use with children having disabilities or otherwise in need of differentiated instruction.

Gargiulo, R., & Kilgo, J. (2005). *Young children with special needs*. (2nd ed.). Clifton Park, NY: Delmar Learning.

This second edition offers information about infants, toddlers, and preschoolers with disabilities or at risk.

Gould, P., & Sullivan, J. (2005). *The inclusive early childhood classroom*. Upper Saddle River, NJ: Merrill/Prentice Hall.

This 200-page book provides very brief and practical suggestions for helping young children with disabilities to learn.

Guralnick, M. (Ed.). (2005). *The developmental systems approach to early intervention*. Baltimore: Brookes.

Guralnick is also editor of the highly regarded journal *Infants & Young Children*. In this text, experts discuss how early interventionists can differentiate therapy and instruction for infants and toddlers.

McLean, M., Wolery, M., & Bailey, D. (2003). *Assessing infants and toddlers with special needs*. (3rd ed.). Upper Saddle River, NJ: Merrill/Prentice Hall.

This 640-page book offers current information about assessing young children with disabilities, including parent and professional ratings, observation in home and in center programs, and other techniques.

ADHD

Barkley, R. (2000). *Taking charge of ADHD: The complete, authoritative guide for parents* (rev. ed.). New York: Guilford Press.

From a recognized expert on ADHD, help for families.

DuPaul, G., & Stoner, G. (2004). *ADHD in the schools* (2nd ed.). New York: Guilford.

Well-regarded resource for educators and psychologists.

Autism

Exhorn, K. (2005). *The autism sourcebook: Everything you need to know about diagnosis, treatment, coping, and healing*. New York: Regan Books.

Written by a mother, this 432-page book explores the emotions as well as facts.

Heflin, L., & Alaimo, D. (2007). *Students with autism spectrum disorders: Effective instructional practices*. Upper Saddle River, NJ: Merrill/Prentice Hall.

This 354-page text outlines applied behavior analysis and other approaches, including sensory integration issues.

Zysk, V., & Notbom, E. (2004). *1001 great ideas for teaching and raising children with autism spectrum disorders*. Arlington, TX: Future Horizons.

Practical tactics for families and educators. The publisher focuses its offerings on autism.

Cerebral Palsy

Levitt, S. (2004). *Treatment of cerebral palsy and motor delay*. Ames, IA: Blackwell.

Occupational and physical therapy techniques.

Workinger, M. (2004). *Cerebral palsy resource guide for speech-language pathologists.* San Diego, CA: Singular.

As the title suggests, this brief text is intended for speech-language pathologists.

Deafness and Hearing Impairment

Legal Rights. (2005). 6th ed. Washington, DC: Gallaudet University Bookstore.

Written by attorneys at the National Association of the Deaf, this brief book summarizes civil rights and entitlements for people who are deaf or hard of hearing.

Moores, D. F., & Martin, D. S. (Eds.). (2006). *Deaf learners: developments in curriculum and instruction.* Washington, DC: Gallaudet University Press.

Marschark, M., Lang, H., & Albertini, J. (2002). *Educating deaf Students: From research to practice.* New York: Oxford University Press.

Suzuki, J., Kobayashi, T., & Koga, K. (Eds.). (2004). *Hearing impairment: An invisible disability.*

A comprehensive treatment of the subject.

Diversity

Banks, J., & Banks, C. (Eds.). (2004). *Multicultural education: Issues and perspectives.* New York: Wiley.

As the title implies, the contributed chapters in this volume offer different, and valuable, perspectives on multiculturalism in education.

Bucher, R., & Bucher, P. (2003). *Diversity consciousness: Opening our minds to people, cultures, and opportunities* (2nd ed.). Upper Saddle River, NJ: Merrill/Prentice Hall.

Brief and highly readable, with exercises on teamwork, conflicts, and more.

Family members often ask about how to use plants and other resources in and around the home to stimulate child development.

Families

Meyer, D. (Ed.). (2005). *Uncommon fathers: Reflections on raising a child with a disability.* Baltimore: Woodbine House.

Don Meyer brings together fathers of children with different disabilities to tell their own stories. Valuable as one of only a handful of such books.

Schwartzenberg, S. (2005). *Becoming citizens: Family life and the politics of disability.* Seattle: University of Washington Press.

Insightful and stimulating view of families and persons with severe disabilities.

Genetics and Ethics

Parens, E. (Ed.). (2006). *Surgically shaping children: Technology, ethics, and the pursuit of normality.* Baltimore: Johns Hopkins University Press.

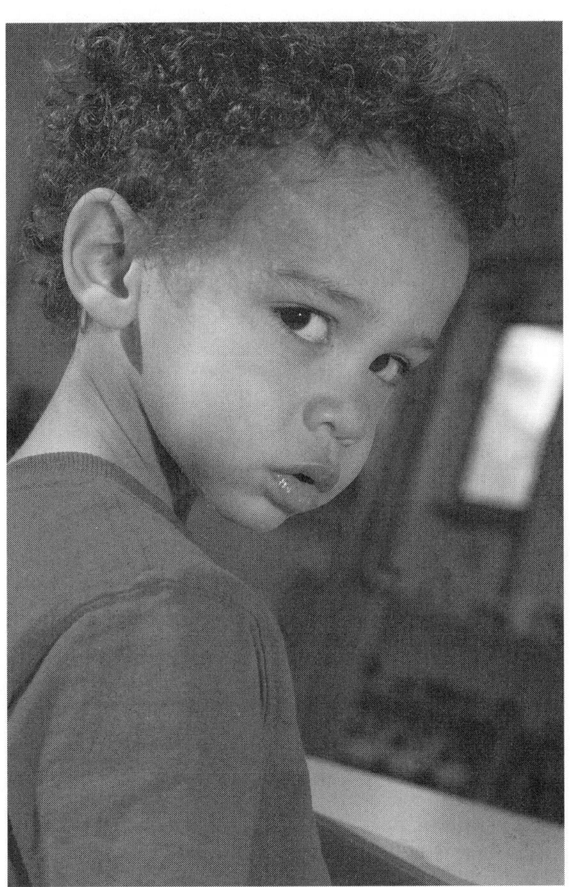
Social and emotional development is a frequent area of concern among parents.

This 266-page book offers an in-depth examination, from many viewpoints, of the ethics of cosmetic (appearance) surgery and related issues.

JOURNALS

Behavioral Disorders. Focuses on emotional and behavior-related disabilities and conditions. Division for Children with Behavior Disorders, Council for Exceptional Children, 1920 Association Drive, Reston, VA 22091.

Early Childhood Research Quarterly. Peer-reviewed journal for professionals. Sponsored by the NAEYC and published by Ablex Publishing Corporation, 355 Chestnut Street, Norwood, NJ 07648. Editorial offices are at 1267 Child Development and Family Studies Building, Purdue University, West Lafayette, IN 47907-1267.

Exceptional Children. General special education journal featuring refereed articles. Council for Exceptional Children, 1920 Association Drive, Reston, VA 22091.

Exceptional Parent. A readable journal for parents of children with disabilities. Each year, the journal issues its "Annual Guide to Products and Services," an excellent resource on technology as well as services for children and families, including toll-free numbers. Psy-Ed Corporation, P.O. Box 300, EP, Denville, NJ 07834.

Infants and Young Children. Journal on medical and other early interventions. Four times each year, this journal provides articles of practical importance for ECSE programs and personnel. Aspen Publishers, 7201 McKinne Circle, Frederick, MD 21701.

Journal of Early Intervention. Journal on working with infants and toddlers. A quarterly publication by the Division for Early Childhood, Council for Exceptional Children. Formerly called the *Journal of the Division for Early Childhood.* Council for Exceptional Children, 1920 Association Drive, Reston, VA 22091.

Journal of Special Education. General special education journal featuring refereed articles. PRO-ED, 8700 Shoal Creek Boulevard, Austin, TX 78757-6897.

Journal of Special Education Technology. Focuses on assistive and instructional devices and software. Attention: Herb Rieth, Editor, Peabody College of Vanderbilt University, Box 328, Nashville, TN 37203.

Ragged Edge. Tabloid written by adults with disabilities. *The* authoritative voice of disability advocates, the *Rag* is an outspoken, often radical voice protesting against paternalism. Indispensable for "the consumer viewpoint" on disability issues. The Disability Rag, P.O. Box 145, Louisville, KY 40201.

Teaching Exceptional Children. A readable, practice-oriented magazine for special education teachers. Council for Exceptional Children, 1920 Association Drive, Reston, VA 22091.

Topics in Early Childhood Special Education. Quarterly journal having three issues annually on selected topics and one "open." PRO-ED, 8700 Shoal Creek Boulevard, Austin, TX 78757-6897.

Young Exceptional Children. A quarterly publication by the Council for Exceptional Children, 1920 Association Drive, Reston, VA 22091.

DIRECTORIES

Directory of national information sources on disabilities. Silver Spring, MD: NARIC and ABLEDATA, 8630 Fenton Street, Suite 930, Silver Spring, MD 20910.

Resource directory of more than 500 organizations of and for people with disabilities, including what they do, who they serve, and what publications or other information they offer.

ILRU directory of independent living programs. Houston, TX: Independent Living Resource Utilization Project, 2323 S. Shepherd, #1000, Houston, TX 77019.

Excellent directory of some 500 independent living centers (ILCs), most of which are local self-help groups. By law, these centers must be governed and operated by adults with disabilities. The ILCs are excellent sources of names of local advocates who are individuals with disabilities and who may be interested in providing consumer perspectives on ECSE programs and/or on individual families.

State resource sheet. National Dissemination Center for Children with Disabilities, P.O. Box 1492, Washington, DC 20013.

A very helpful service from this federally funded center, these "State Resource Sheets" offer regularly updated information on disability-related organizations and agencies within a particular state.

White, B., & Madara, E. (Eds.). *American Self-Help Group Clearing House: Self-help group sourcebook*; on-line at www.mentalhelp.net

Electronic guide to self-help groups. The on-line resource is searchable. Highly recommended to ECSE programs because it will help so many families link up with other families having children with similar needs.

INFORMATION SOURCES

Federal

Administration for Children and Families
U.S. Department of Health and Human Services
200 Independence Avenue SW
Washington, DC 20201
www.acf.hhs.gov

The federal agency coordinating state-run programs for children with severe and multiple needs.

Architectural and Transportation Barriers Compliance Board
1331 F Street NW, #1000
Washington, DC 20004-1111
www.access-board.gov

A small, independent federal agency offering guidelines on accessibility in construction and transportation.

Department of Education
400 Maryland Avenue SW
Washington, DC 20202
www.ed.gov

The Office of Special Education Programs (OSEP) is the federal agency responsible for administering the IDEA.

Department of Housing and Urban Development
451 7th Street NW
Washington, DC 20410
www.hud.gov

The federal agency responsible for implementation of PL 100–407, the Fair Housing Amendments Act of 1990.

Department of Justice
Office of the Americans with Disabilities Act
Civil Rights Division
P.O. Box 66118
Washington, DC 20035-6118
www.usdoj.gov

The federal office responsible for implementation of ADA Title II (on state and local government) and Title III (on places of public accommodation).

Department of Transportation
400 7th Street SW
Washington, DC 20590
www.fta.dot.gov

The federal office responsible for implementation of ADA transportation requirements.

Equal Employment Opportunity Commission
1801 L Street NW
Washington, DC 20507
www.eeoc.gov

The federal agency responsible for implementation of ADA Title I (on employment).

Federal Communications Commission
445 12th Street SW
Washington, DC 20554
www.fcc.gov

The federal agency responsible for implementation of ADA Title IV (on telecommunications) and PL 101–431, the Television Decoder Circuitry Act of 1990 (on caption decoders in commercial TV sets).

National Council on Disability
1331 F Street, NW, #1050
Washington, DC 20004
www.ncd.gov

A small, independent federal agency that advocates for laws on behalf of people with disabilities.

National Institutes of Health
Bethesda, MD 20892
www.nih.gov

The NIH sponsors research on hearing (National Institute on Deafness), aging and age-related disabilities (National Institute on Aging), and so on.

Social Security Administration
6401 Security Boulevard
Baltimore, MD 21235
www.socialsecurity.gov

The federal agency responsible for administering Social Security Disability Insurance (SSDI) and Supplemental Security Income (SSI). Click on "Disability."

General

American Academy of Pediatrics: www.aap.org

Offers a number of helpful pages, including "Child Care Guidelines for Terminally Ill Children," "Newborn Screening," and "Sudden Infant Death Syndrome"—the latter noting that some 20 percent of SIDS incidents occur in child care settings.

Center for the Early Childhood Workforce
733 15th Street NW, #1037
Washington, DC 20005
www.ccw.org

Advocates for EC professionals and paraprofessionals, including political awareness and voter registration activities.

Consortium for Citizens with Disabilities
c/o The ARC
1660 L Street, NW, #700
Washington, DC 20036
www.c-c-d.org

An association of Washington-based advocacy groups, CCD has a task force on special education issues.

Division for Early Childhood
Council for Exceptional Children
1920 Association Drive
Reston, VA 22091-1589
www.dec-sped.org

DEC is the division of CEC that focuses on ECSE. An association of special educators and related services personnel, CEC is a long-standing advocate for special education and early intervention.

ERIC Clearinghouse on Elementary and Early Childhood Education (ERIC/EECE)
University of Illinois
805 West Pennsylvania Avenue
Urbana, IL 61801
npin.org

Offers on-line and off-line articles on curriculum, diversity, and other topics.

Independent Living Research Utilization Program
2323 S. Shepherd, #1000
Houston, TX 77019
www.ilru.org

A research and training project focusing on independent living centers for adults with disabilities, the ILRU Program offers an excellent *Guide to Planning Accessible Meetings,* in addition to its indispensable annual directory of ILCs.

National Association for the Education of Young Children
1313 L Street NW, #500
Washington, DC 20005
www.naeyc.org

An association promoting EC services and "developmentally appropriate practice."

National Association of State Directors of Special Education
1800 Diagonal Road, Suite 320
King Street Station 1
Alexandria, VA 22314
www.nasdse.org

An association of state special education agency directors, NASDSE coordinates information sharing among directors and represents them in Washington. Excellent source of names, titles, addresses, and telephone numbers of state agency officials.

National Early Childhood Technical Assistance Center
Suite 500, NationsBank Plaza
137 East Franklin Street
Chapel Hill, NC 27514
www.nectac.org

NECTAC is a federally funded center on ECSE. Each year, it issues numerous reports on issues important to the field. It also maintains current and comprehensive contact information about Part C and preschool Part B programs in the states, for which reason it is an excellent source of names, addresses, telephone and fax numbers, and so on, for parents and professionals alike.

National Early Intervention Longitudinal Study: www.sri.com/neils
National Pre-Elementary Education Longitudinal Study: www.peels.org

The sites for, respectively, the early intervention and the preelementary education longitudinal studies that are sponsored by the U.S. Department of Education. The NEILS study began earlier than PEELS, so more data are available.

National Easter Seals Society
230 West Monroe Street, #1800
Chicago, IL 60606-4802
www.easter-seals.org

NESS and its 200 affiliates nationwide are private, nonprofit providers of services for children and adults with physical disabilities.

Zero to Three, National Center for Clinical Infant Programs
734 15th Street NW, #1000
Washington, DC 20005
or
2000 14th Street North, Suite 380
Arlington, VA 22201
www.zerotothree.org

Specialists in serving infants and toddlers with developmental delays or at risk for delays. Zero to Three hosts important conferences on Part C–related issues, usually in Washington, DC.

Lawyers and Legal Advocacy

Disability Rights Education and Defense Fund
2212 6th Street
Berkeley, CA 94702
www.dredf.org

A private advocacy organization of and for people with disabilities, DREDF has been active in advocating for human and civil rights for Americans with disabilities. It offers legal representation and cocounsel in selected cases.

Public Interest Law Center of Philadelphia
125 S. 9th Street, #700
Philadelphia, PA 19107
www.pilcop.org

PILCOP has worked with families and children with disabilities for more than 20 years, notably in the landmark *PARC v. Commonwealth of Pennsylvania* case. It specializes in class action suits.

ADHD

Attention Deficit Disorder Association (ADDA)
1788 Second Street, Suite 200
Highland Park, IL 60035

A national organization providing information on ADHD and related disorders.

ADDult Support Network
2620 Ivy Place
Toledo, OH 43613

A national support group of individuals with ADHD and related disorders, the network is affiliated with the ADDA.

Attention Deficit Information Network, Inc.
475 Hillside Avenue
Needham, MA 02194

AD-IN is a good information and referral source for support groups, experts, and information about ADHD.

Children and Adults with Attention-Deficit/Hyperactivity Disorder
8181 Professional Place, Suite 150
Landover, MD 20785
www.chadd.org

A national support and information organization with more than 450 parent group affiliates, CHADD has grown to 21,000 members since it was formed in 1988.

AIDS

AIDS Action Council
1875 Connecticut Avenue NW, #700
Washington, DC 20009

Representing some 900 community groups, the council promotes legislation protecting people with AIDS and advocates for more research and better care.

National AIDS Clearinghouse
P.O. Box 6003
Rockville, MD 20849-6003

This information service offers materials in Spanish as well as English and operates a hot line. The clearinghouse is sponsored by the Atlanta-based Centers for Disease Control and Prevention.

Autism

Autism Society of America
7910 Woodmont Avenue, Suite 300
Bethesda, MD 20814-3067
www.autism-society.org

With 200 chapters nationwide, the ASA offers factual information about autism and urges research and treatment advances.

Cure Autism Now
5455 Wilshire Blvd., #2250
Los Angeles, CA 90036-4272
www.cureautismnow.org

A major source of funding for research into autism.

Blindness and Low Vision

American Council of the Blind
1155 15th Street NW, #720
Washington, DC 20005
www.acb.org

A consumer organization of blind and low-vision adults, ACB has 52 state or regional chapters and about two dozen affiliates. An excellent source of information about the consumer perspective.

American Foundation for the Blind
11 Penn Plaza, #300
New York, NY 10001
www.afb.org

Founded by Helen Keller, this organization advocates on behalf of people who are blind. It offers a wealth of information about blindness and low vision and sponsors a National Technology Center.

The Lighthouse, Inc.
111 East 59th Street
New York, NY 10022
www.lighthouse.org

The Lighthouse offers consumer products for persons with blindness or low vision and annually publishes a catalog describing the products. The Lighthouse purchased the American Foundation for the Blind's consumer products business in mid-1994.

National Federation of the Blind
1800 Johnson Street
Baltimore, MD 21230
www.nfb.org

A national organization competing with ACB, the federation claims to be "the voice of the organized blind." Another excellent source for consumer views.

Cerebral Palsy

United Cerebral Palsy Associations, Inc.
1660 L Street NW, #700
Washington, DC 20036
www.ucpa.org

A private organization with 183 affiliates nationwide.

Cystic Fibrosis

Cystic Fibrosis Foundation
6931 Arlington Road
Bethesda, MD 20814
www.cff.org

The authoritative source on cystic fibrosis.

Cystic Fibrosis Research, Inc.
560 San Antonio Road, #103
Palo Alto, CA 94306-4349
www.cfri.org

A major source of funding for and information about research on prevention and amelioration of cystic fibrosis.

Deafness and Hearing Impairment

Hearing Loss Association of America
7800 Wisconsin Avenue
Bethesda, MD 20814
www.hearingloss.org

A consumer association with state and local chapters throughout the nation.

National Association of the Deaf
8630 Fenton Street, #820
Silver Spring, MD 20910
www.nad.org

A national consumer advocacy organization with state associations nationwide.

Telecommunications for the Deaf, Inc.
8630 Fenton Street, #604
Silver Spring, MD 20910
www.tdi-online.org

A consumer and industry association interested in technology for communication-impaired people.

Diabetes

American Diabetes Association
505 Eighth Avenue, 21st Floor
New York, NY 10018
www.diabetes.org

Offers brochures on diabetes.

Juvenile Diabetes Foundation
432 Park Avenue South
New York, NY 10016-8013
www.jdfcure.org

Founded in 1971, it has 128 chapters in North America and funds the Diabetes Research Foundation.

Epilepsy

Epilepsy Foundation of America
National Epilepsy Library
4351 Garden City Drive
Landover, MD 20785-7223
www.epilepsyfoundation.org or www.efa.org

A private organization providing information and advocacy services for people with epilepsy.

Families

American Academy of Family Physicians
www.aafp.org

The pages on continuing education for family physicians offer useful information for families and for ECSE professionals. See, for example, the page on diabetes. A growing number of young children in America are overweight, placing some at risk of diabetes.

Association for the Care of Children's Health
19 Manuta Road
Mount Royal, NJ 08061

In addition to its regularly updated *Parent Resource Directory,* the ACCH links parents of children with disabilities or developmental delays for parent-to-parent networking and mutual support. It also offers a guidebook for developing IFSPs.

Beach Center on Families and Disability
Bureau of Child Research
University of Kansas
4138 Haworth Hall
Lawrence, KS 66045
www.beachcenter.org

A federally funded research and training center, Beach focuses on childhood disability. Its directors, H. R. and Ann Turnbull, are experts on special education law.

Children's Defense Fund
25 E Street NW
Washington, DC 20001
www.childrensdefense.org

An outstanding public interest advocacy group, CDF has a long-standing interest in lobbying for children with disabilities. It publishes low-cost (most under $6) publications on how to be an advocate, how to use the mass media, and how to lobby and raise funds for programs.

Estate Planning for People with Disabilities
3100 Arapahoe Avenue, #112
Boulder, CO 80303

A national organization focusing on assistance in financial planning to families with a child, sibling, or other family member who has a disability. Some 130 local estate-planning teams (including CPAs) in 44 states are available to help families plan.

National Dissemination Center for Children with Disabilities
P.O. Box 1492
Washington, DC 20013
www.nichcy.org

A federally funded center that offers readable information and referral services especially for families. Single copies of its many publications are free.

Parents Helping Parents
3041 Olcott Street
Santa Clara, CA 95054
www.php.com

A family-directed resource center for parents, PHP offers information and referral for parents with children who have disabilities.

Fetal Alcohol Syndrome

At CDC, search for "FAS" at www.cdc.gov.

Epidemiological data plus explanatory material.

Other sources:

www2.potsdam.edu/alcohol-info/FAS/FAS.html
www.nofas.org
www.acbr.com
www.come-over.to

Fragile X

National Fragile X Foundation
1441 York Street, #215
Denver, CO 80206
www.fragilex.org

An information resource on genetic testing, family needs, and family counseling support groups and experts, the foundation is a good source of information about this disorder.

Learning Disability

Learning Disabilities Association of America
4156 Library Road
Pittsburgh, PA 15234
www.ldanatl.org

A parent-based group offering information and advocacy for children, youth, and adults with dyslexia and other learning disabilities. Formerly called ACLD.

International Dyslexia Society
The Chester Building, #382
8600 LaSalle Road
Baltimore, MD 21286-2044
www.interdys.org

A private group specializing in dyslexia, the Orton Society has 43 affiliates or volunteer branches staffed by professionals who can offer referrals to evaluators and tutors.

LD Online
www.ldonline.org

A respected site, with a wealth of information about specific learning disabilities.

Schwab Learning
www.schwablearning.org

Another good site on learning disabilities, particularly on helping young children learn to read.

Mental Illness

American Psychological Association
750 First Street NE
Washington, DC 20002-4242
www.apa.org

A professional association for psychologists, the APA includes sections for those working in public schools and related programs.

American School Counseling Association
1101 King Street, #625
Alexandria, VA 22314
www.schoolcounselor.org

Specializing more in school-related needs than the APA does, the ASCA includes as members counselors who are not psychologists.

National Alliance for the Mentally Ill
Colonial Place Three
2107 Wilson Blvd., #300
Arlington, VA 22201-3042
www.nami.org

The alliance is a self-help, consumer organization run principally by individuals who themselves are mentally ill or mentally restored. It advocates for better treatment and greater rights. Support groups affiliated with the alliance offer help to families and to individuals alike.

Muscular Dystrophy

Muscular Dystrophy Association
3300 E. Sunrise Drive
Tucson, AZ 85718
www.mdausa.org

Sponsors the Labor Day telethon that helps support research, service, and information programs.

Other Physical Disabilities

Amputee Resource Foundation of America
2324 Wildwood Trail
Minnetonka, MN 55305
www.amputeeresource.org

The foundation provides information and referral for people with amputation and their families.

American Occupational Therapy Association
4720 Montgomery Lane
P.O. Box 31200
Bethesda, MD 20842-1220
www.aota.org

An association of occupational therapists, AOTA seeks to educate its members and to advance the profession.

American Physical Therapy Association
1111 North Fairfax Street
Alexandria, VA 22314-1488
www.apta.org

The APTA counts among its members some 57,000-odd PT professionals, as well as students. It seeks to increase public understanding of physical therapy.

Americans Disabled for Attendant Programs Today
1339 Lamar Square Drive, #101
Austin, TX 78704
www.adapt.org

An advocacy organization comprising disability activists, ADAPT urges profound change in national and state medical care policies, advocating specifically for giving control of attendant care services to consumers themselves. A good source of adults with disabilities who may be willing to serve as mentors or advisers in ECSE programs.

University of Utah Medical School
www.utah.edu (search for "MedHome")

This site is of interest because it provides information on low-incidence disabilities, including deafness and other hearing impairments, cerebral palsy, and so on. It also contains a brief, readable explanation of what is a *medical home.*

Respite Services

National Resource Center for Respite and Crisis Care Services
Chapel Hill Training-Outreach Project
800 Eastowne Drive, #105
Chapel Hill, NC 27514
www.chtop.com

The "ARCH" focuses on respite care, an allowable entry intervention service under the IDEA's Part C.

Retardation

The Arc of the United States
500 East Border Street, #300
Arlington, TX 76010
www.thearc.org

A private, nonprofit association of affiliates providing services, information, research, and advocacy on behalf of people with retardation. The ARC (formerly Association for Retarded Citizens/United States) has 1,200 chapters or affiliates.

National Down Syndrome Society
666 Broadway
New York, NY 10012
www.ndss.org

Sponsors research, information, and outreach on behalf of children and adults with Down syndrome.

Speech and Language

American Speech-Language-Hearing Association
10801 Rockville Pike
Rockville, MD 20852
www.asha.org

A professional organization for speech, language, and hearing pathologists and audiologists.

American Cleft Palate-Craniofacial Association/Cleft Palate Foundation
1504 E. Franklin Street, #102
Chapel Hill, NC 27514-2820
www.cleftline.org

A private association offering information about speech disorders due to cleft palate.

Spina Bifida

Spina Bifida Association of America
4590 MacArthur Boulevard NW, #250
Washington, DC 20007-4226
www.sbaa.org

With more than 100 chapters and affiliates, SBAA offers support for parents and other family members of individuals with spina bifida. It provides information on treatment, education, and social and medical services as well.

Technology

Parents, Let's Unite for Kids
516 N. 32nd Street
Billings, MT 59101-6003
www.pluk.org

A good starting place for family members with young children having disabilities. The page on "Publications & Information" is particularly rich.

Alliance for Technology Access
1304 Southpoint Blvd., #240
Petaluma, CA 94954
www.ataccess.org

Another excellent source for families.

Traumatic Brain Injury

Brain Injury Association
1776 Massachusetts Avenue NW, #100
Washington, DC 20036
www.biausa.org

A private organization advocating for laws benefiting people with TBI. The foundation is affiliated with more than 400 support groups nationwide.

Centers for Disease Control and Prevention
www.cdc.gov (search for "TBI")

An excellent source of information about TBI.

Glossary

A

Accessible refers to a standard such that at least one entrance, at least one path through a facility, at least one rest room, and so on, is usable by individuals with disabilities. This standard, which applies to existing facilities or buildings, is lower than the *barrier-free* standard.

Accommodation, for Piaget, is a process in which new information alters a child's understanding of reality.

Adaptability, in housing, refers to the requirement in the Fair Housing Amendments Act of 1988, PL 100–430, that new, four-unit or larger multifamily housing structures be adaptable or readily changeable to meet the special needs of individuals with severe disabilities. An example is cabinets or light switches that may be easily lowered.

Adaptations are adjustments to processes and materials so they may be used by children with disabilities.

Adaptive development (sometimes referred to as *self-help development*) refers to a child's ability to display age-appropriate self-care and other behaviors in such a way as to adapt meaningfully to different circumstances.

Advance organizer is an outline, list of key terms with definitions, or other support that helps a student prepare to learn new information.

Adventitious (acquired) conditions appear after birth, usually as a result of illness or accident. They differ from *congenital* conditions, which are present at birth.

Age appropriateness is a philosophy in which activities are designed to match children's developmental stages. It is a key concept in NAEYC's developmentally appropriate practice (DAP) guidelines. DEC's Recommended Practice Task Force suggested that programs be *chronologically* age-appropriate as well, because otherwise some young children with disabilities might wrongly be placed in settings designed for far younger children.

Age at onset is a child's age when a condition begins.

Age at start is a child's age when early intervention or other services begin.

AIDS (acquired immune deficiency syndrome) is a condition in which the body's immune system fails. It is widely believed to be caused by the human immunodeficiency virus (HIV).

American Sign Language (ASL) ASL is a language of its own, as is English. Because the first users of what is now ASL were speakers of French, ASL has grammatical and syntactical similarities to French. Words that do not have known signs may be fingerspelled. Fingerspelling is literally "spelling in the air" as one letter after another is produced using the fingers.

Americans with Disabilities Act (ADA), PL 101–336, is the landmark 1990 federal civil rights law for individuals with disabilities. The law bans discrimination in employment, local government services, transportation, places of public accommodation, and telecommunications.

Applied behavior analysis (ABA) is a form of behavior modification. The term refers to techniques employing trials, usually one on one. It does not emphasize, as does cognitive behavior modification, teaching children why some actions are reinforced and some are not.

Appropriate is a term used both in Part C and in Part B of the Individuals with Disabilities Education Act, but it is not defined precisely in the statute. It appears to mean "meets the standards of the State" and "meets the unique needs of the child."

Architectural and Transportation Barriers Compliance Board (ATBCB) is a small independent federal agency charged with monitoring accessibility at many federal buildings. The agency sometimes is referred to as the *Access Board.*

Assessment is the process of collecting data to use in determining how an individual child's development is proceeding in each of the five domains of development (cognitive, adaptive, physical, communication, and social or emotional) or in academic areas. In family assessment, a family's resources, priorities, and concerns are identified.

Assimilation, for Piaget, occurs when new information is added to existing knowledge but does not change a child's view of the world.

Assistive technology devices are any products that may be used by individuals with disabilities to do things they otherwise would have difficulty doing.

Assistive technology services include assessment, selection of devices, instruction in their use, and related services to support individuals with disabilities in use of technology.

Asthma is a condition in which people have difficulty breathing because of obstructions in the airways of the lungs. It is a chronic respiratory disorder (sometimes called a *chronic obstructive pulmonary disease*). The U.S. Department of Education recognizes asthma as a disability when it affects a child's education.

At risk is a term used to refer to infants or toddlers who do not exhibit developmental delays but who for biological and/or environmental reasons are more likely than are most infants or toddlers to develop such delays. The concept is used only in Part C of the Individuals with Disabilities Education Act.

Attention is the process through which a child acquires information through the senses. Learning cannot occur absent attention.

Attention-deficit/hyperactivity disorder (ADHD/HI), predominantly hyperactive-impulsive type, is a diagnosis made when impulsivity and hyperactivity are present together with distractibility and short attention spans.

Attention-deficit/hyperactivity disorder (ADHI/I), predominantly inattentive type, is a diagnosis reached when a child is "unavailable for learning" due to distractibility and short attention spans. The diagnosis is used if hyperactivity is not present.

Audiograms are graphic displays of hearing loss along two dimensions: pitch (frequency) and intensity (volume).

Autism spectrum disorders are conditions affecting communication, imagination, and socialization. Their most prominent characteristic is an "autistic aloneness" in which children appear to avoid and even to reject social interaction.

Autonomy versus shame and doubt is the Eriksonian stage in which toddlers learn to assume self-responsibility, including feeding and toileting activities.

B

Barrier-free, as used in relation to buildings or facilities, means that all entrances, all rooms, and all levels or floors are accessible to people with disabilities. This standard applies to new construction and to newly renovated parts of existing facilities. The standard contrasts with *accessible,* which is a lower standard.

Behavior modification is the use of presentation reinforcement, removal reinforcement, and other techniques to increase the likelihood that children will display desired behaviors and will not produce undesired behaviors.

Blindness is 20/200 vision or tunnel vision where central vision subtends at an angle of 20 percent or less as measured with corrective lenses.

Broadband is the term to describe high-speed, always-on, voice/video/data communications technologies.

C

Captions are subtitles for video programming. Captions may be *open,* in which case all viewers see them, or *closed,* in which case caption decoders are required to make the subtitles visible.

CD-ROM stands for "Compact Disc—Read Only Memory." CD-ROM discs store information that computer users may read, scan, and search at high speed. The user may read the disc but not write to it.

Cerebral palsy (CP) is a condition in which oxygen deprivation in or damage to the brain limits voluntary control of muscles.

Child development associate (CDA) paraprofessionals have a credential indicating postsecondary study in child development and child care. CDA-credentialed paraprofessionals often work in Head Start programs.

Child find is the term used in both Part C and Part B of the Individuals with Disabilities Education Act to refer to outreach and recruitment efforts by the state to identify, screen, and serve eligible children and families.

Children with disabilities refers to children who meet the criteria in IDEA Section 602(3), notably that they have a recognized disability and for that reason need special education and related services.

Cochlear implants are electronic devices that simulate "hearing" for children who are deaf.

Cognitive behavior modification stresses the importance of teaching the child ways of thinking about situations, in the belief that learning is a change in the *capacity* to behave in a certain way.

Cognitive development refers to age-appropriate mental functions, especially in perceiving, understanding, and knowing—that is, becoming capable of doing intellectual tasks.

Communication is the expression and reception of meaning. It may occur through speech/hearing, reading/writing, signing/seeing, gestures, or other means.

Communication development (sometimes referred to as *speech and language development*) refers to a young child's ability to express thoughts and feelings and to understand vocal, nonverbal, signed, or other communication by others.

Concrete operational stage, for Piaget, is the stage at which children can perform *operations* on ideas, specifically symbolic and logical thoughts. This stage begins at age 7 and concludes at age 11, according to Piaget.

Conduct disorders include a range of emotional conditions affecting behavior. Children appear to be "undersocialized" in that they often do not exhibit socially approved behavior.

Congenital conditions appear at or prior to birth; they are present at birth, as contrasted to *acquired* conditions.

Cooperative learning is teamwork, usually in pairs or small groups, where children work together under rules and procedures established by an adult.

Cost-benefit analyses look at benefits, assigning values to them, and compare those values with the costs of providing the benefits.

Cost-effective analyses look to whether one approach, or one program, provides more benefits per dollar than another.

Counseling is the broad term referring to support, guidance, help in decision making, and information and referral.

Cultural competence (cultural sensitivity) refers to the skill and knowledge of ECSE workers in relating to family members from different ethnic, racial, and cultural groups.

Curriculum is a planned sequence of activities, including both content and process, through which educators change children's behavior. Curriculum is a vehicle for reaching goals and objectives as identified in individualized family service plans and individualized education programs—an ordered arrangement of individually selected learning experiences that respond to children's particular needs.

Cystic fibrosis is an inherited condition that causes mucus to build up in the lungs, compromising lung capacity and usually resulting in death by the age of 30. Children with cystic fibrosis need to have physical therapy, get lots of exercise, and receive dietary supplements.

D

Deafness is the inability to hear and understand conversational speech through the ear alone.

Descriptive video service (DVS) transmits spoken descriptions of on-screen television action so that individuals who are blind may learn about actions they do not see.

Developmental delays are lags in child development in any one or more of the five domains (cognitive, communication, physical, adaptive, and social or emotional). How much of a lag constitutes a "delay" is to be defined by each state. The term is used in both Part C and in Part B of the Individuals with Disabilities Education Act, for Section 619.

Developmental disabilities are conditions of early onset (occurring well in advance of adulthood) that require a range of diverse services or interventions. The term formerly referred to four disabilities (autism, cerebral palsy, mental retardation, and epilepsy).

Developmental plasticity is the belief that young children in particular can develop rapidly, changing their behavior—and indeed their lives—if services are provided early in life.

Developmentally appropriate services are designed to be suitable for children at particular stages of development. Thus, very short individual activities are developmentally appropriate for infants and toddlers, while lengthy large-group activities are not.

Developmentally appropriate practice (DAP) is professional work that emphasizes activities with young children that are both age-appropriate and child-focused. In DAP approaches, children are encouraged to be active learners, while professionals guide and facilitate their activities.

Deviations are behaviors that are not normal at any age. Delays in development, by contrast, feature behavior that is normal but for children of younger ages.

Diagnosed conditions (established conditions) are disabilities or other health conditions recognized by a state as limiting or very likely to limit activities young children can do. The term is used in Part C of the Individuals with Disabilities Education Act.

Direct Instruction is structured, teacher-led instruction. It often is contrasted to less didactic, more interactive approaches to learning, such as *developmentally appropriate practice.*

Directed discovery learning is a variation on discovery learning in which teachers direct a student's inquiry. It is more structured than is guided discovery learning and more structured than discovery learning.

Discovery learning (Jerome Bruner) is an approach in which children learn things themselves as teachers structure the environment to facilitate children's discovery.

Distance education links an instructor in one geographic location with students at other sites. Students see and hear the instructor, who in turn sees and hears them. The connections may be via satellite broadcast or, increasingly, via fiber optic cable.

Domains are areas of development. Part C of the Individuals with Disabilities Education Act recognizes five such domains: adaptive, cognitive, communication, physical, and social or emotional.

Double jeopardy is a term used by some researchers to explain risks children face due to *both* biological and environmental risk factors. Children from families of low socioeconomic status tend to have more illnesses and accidents *and* to suffer more long-lasting consequences from these than do children from families of high socioeconomic status.

Down syndrome is the most common identifiable cause of mental retardation, accounting for perhaps one-third of all cases. In addition to mental retardation, characteristic facial features, hypotonia (floppiness in muscles), and hearing loss are common in Down syndrome.

Dyslexia is a learning disability that interferes with reading and writing, because letters seem to float across a page, reverse, or otherwise become difficult to read. Children with dyslexia display reading difficulties despite normal or near-normal intelligence and adequate opportunities to learn to read.

E

Early childhood (EC) education is the term referring to services for young children in the birth-to-eight inclusive period. EC is a much larger field than is ECSE.

Early childhood educators are professionals trained in work with young children.

Early Childhood Longitudinal Study is an effort by the National Center for Education Statistics, U.S. Department of Education, that follows two groups (cohorts). One tracks children from birth and the other from kindergarten.

Early childhood special education (ECSE) is the term describing early intervention, preschool, and primary-grade services for young children who have disabilities or delays in development and with their families. It is a specialized form of the broader field of early childhood education.

Early childhood special educators are professionals trained in work with young children, methods of education, and other kinds of intervention for children with disabilities or developmental delays.

Early Education Program for Children with Disabilities (EEPCD) is the federal grant program providing discretionary support for "model" Early Childhood Special Education programs. EEPCD was formerly called the Handicapped Children's Early Education Program (HCEEP).

Early intervening services are IDEA-funded interventions that are offered to students who are not IDEA-eligible (not identified as having disabilities). The intent is to provide support services that prevent unnecessary referral into special education.

Early intervention refers to services for infants and toddlers and their families to address the special needs of very young children who have disabilities, have developmental delays, or are at risk of developmental delays. The term is used in Part C of the Individuals with Disabilities Education Act.

Education for All Handicapped Children Act (EAHCA) (PL 94–142) is the landmark 1975 federal law that first established the mandate that all school-age children with disabilities must receive a free appropriate public education.

Elaboration is expanding on an answer, a decision, or a question so the child understands more fully and learns words associated with an occasion, event, or object.

Electronic mail (e-mail) involves exchange of written messages over telephone lines.

Elementary educators are professionals trained at the BA or MA level in teaching K–6 children. They usually are state-certified as meeting state-set minimum requirements.

Embedding is incorporating instruction or other support that helps young children with disabilities to reach IEP/IFSP goals into activities that these young children and/or their families are engaging in on their own.

Emotional disturbance (ED) is a category recognized under the Individuals with Disabilities Education Act. Sometimes also referred to as "emotional and behavioral disorders," it refers to behavior in children that is age-, culturally, and/or situation-inappropriate and interferes with their education and/or that of other children.

Empowerment is the process of helping people feel as if they are in control. It involves feelings as well as facts.

Entitlement means that infants and toddlers must receive early intervention services if they satisfy state criteria. Similarly, three- to five-year-old children must receive free preschool services to meet their unique needs if they satisfy federal and/or state eligibility standards. (The term *zero reject* expresses a similar idea—namely, that no child who meets eligibility criteria may be denied services.)

Environmental control system (ECS) enables people to operate electric equipment via remote control, usually with the assistance of a small personal computer.

Epilepsy is a physical condition producing irregular electric discharges in the brain. There are actually several types of epilepsy, many caused by head injuries.

Evaluation is a formal process through which a child's initial and continuing eligibility for services under the Individuals with Disabilities Education Act is established. It is periodic, occurring at specific intervals. Evaluation may establish, for example, that a child qualifies for Part C services under the act as an at-risk toddler; similarly, it may establish that a child meets a state's developmental delay criteria.

Experiential deprivation occurs when young children are not allowed to confront strange, even dangerous, situations—as when parents overprotect them. According to Erikson, overprotected children may enter school still unsure of themselves, having internalized parental fears.

Extinction occurs when reinforcement is removed altogether so that behavior decreases and then ceases.

F

Family support groups are loosely organized bodies of parents and other family members who come together, often at an ECSE center, to share information and offer each other assistance.

Family-focused programs see families as partners with professionals, whereas **family-centered** programs tend to be planned by and conducted with, parents, guardians, and other family members in a dominant role.

Family-friendly programs involve parents and other family members (as defined by the family) and value their input.

Fetal alcohol syndrome (FAS) results from maternal abuse of alcohol during pregnancy and has three dimensions: facial characteristics, physical growth, and neurological aspects. In *fetal alcohol effect (FAE),* one or two kinds of symptoms, but not all three, are present.

Formative evaluation looks to process issues such as how many families apply for services, how many are served, and how many of what kinds of services are provided. Formative evaluation may take place during an activity or program, whereas summative evaluation tends to occur afterward.

Forward funded refers to the fact that education programs authorized by federal laws are funded during any given federal fiscal year for the following fiscal year. The intent is to give states and schools notice of funds availability well in advance of the start of a school year.

Fragile X syndrome is a condition resulting from damage to the X chromosome. Hyperactivity and mental retardation are common symptoms in males; females are usually only carriers.

G

Generalization occurs when a child who has learned a new behavior in one environment with one adult performs that behavior in a different environment and/or with a different adult.

Genetic discrimination is decision making on the basis of an individual's real or perceived genetic characteristics.

Genetic engineering, also called *gene therapy,* is a process in which interventions are effected to eliminate or at least alleviate a condition. Prior to gene therapy, a pregnant woman had only two choices in responding to fetal test results: proceed to term, or abort the fetus. Genetic engineering gives her a third option: to "fix" the fetus.

Guided discovery learning is a variation on discovery learning in which teachers offer suggestions to a student in his or her discovery learning. More structured than discovery learning but less so than directed discovery learning.

H

Head Start is the federally supported program of services for preschool children that was begun in 1965. Most children served are from disadvantaged families; at least 10 percent of the children served must be children with disabilities.

Human immunodeficiency virus (HIV) is the virus associated with and widely believed to cause AIDS.

I

Incidence is the number of new cases annually, as contrasted with *prevalence,* which is the total number of such cases.

Inclusion is an approach in which children with disabilities (including those with severe disabilities) are placed in rooms with, and receive services side by side with, children who have no disabilities.

Individual appropriateness is an approach in which services are custom-designed and -delivered to respond to a child's unique needs. Often, it is a concept more honored in theory than in practice, as child care workers often find it difficult to individualize services as much as they would like.

Individualized Education Program (IEP) is a written document that identifies the unique needs of the child, the special education and related services needed to meet those unique needs, annual goals and short-term objectives, how the child's progress will be assessed, the date of initiation of services and the projected duration of those services. The IEP is used in Part B of the Individuals with Disabilities Education Act.

Individualized Family Service Plan (IFSP) is a written document outlining services for infants and toddlers and (if the families concur) their families as well. IFSPs note the infant's or toddler's development in five domains, services the child (and family) will receive, and similar information, as well as the service coordinator's name.

Individuals with Disabilities Education Act (IDEA). The IDEA is the landmark special education law in the United States. Formerly called the Education of the Handicapped Act, it includes (as Part B) PL 94–142, the Education for All Handicapped Children Act of 1975.

Industry versus inferiority is Erikson's fourth stage. Industriousness, or achievement, is the successful outcome of this stage. Failure to achieve leads to a sense of inferiority.

Infants and toddlers refers to children before they reach the age of three. Infancy begins at birth and ends with the achievement of independent walking, while toddlers are young children who have begun walking but have not yet reached the age of three. Another commonly used way to refer to this population is "birth-to-two inclusive," which more directly incorporates the first 36 months of life.

Infants and toddlers with disabilities refers to those from birth to age two inclusive who need early intervention services because they are experiencing developmental delays in adaptive, cognitive, communication, physical, and/or social or emotional development or because they have a diagnosed condition that has a high probability of resulting in developmental delay. The term may also include, at a state's discretion, at-risk children and preschool-age children.

Informed clinical opinion supplements formal testing and is especially valuable where suitable tests are not available. The word *clinical* refers to assessments in which the expertise of the clinician comprises at least 50 percent of the procedure.

Initiative versus guilt is the Eriksonian stage in which preschool-age children struggle between exploring for its own sake and feeling guilty for doing so.

Intensive care unit (ICU) is a hospital ward for premature, low-birthweight, and other infants needing comprehensive care. When used with infants under one month old, ICUs are called *neonatal intensive care units* (NICUs).

Interdisciplinary services are services provided by specialists from different disciplines working together on a team (e.g., early childhood special educators and speech pathologists). The term contrasts with services that are provided by professionals representing only one discipline (*uni*disciplinary). The term *multi*disciplinary most often refers to a team (including family members) that plans and conducts assessments or evaluations. These terms are used most often in Part C of the Individuals with Disabilities Education Act. The term *trans*disciplinary refers to an approach in which the often artificial boundaries between disciplines or professions are transcended or ignored so as to deliver "holistic" services to a child and/or a family.

J

Juvenile rheumatoid arthritis is a condition in which joints become inflamed, and usually appears between the ages of 18 months and four years; it generally has few if any lasting effects on children.

L

Language is a formal symbol system in which words are ordered according to rules to express meaning. It may be spoken, written, or signed and may be expressive or receptive.

Lead agency is the term used in Part C of the Individuals with Disabilities Education Act to refer to the state agency authorized to carry out the state Part C plan and to coordinate the work of other public and private agencies. In some states, the state education agency is the lead agency; in others, a health agency, social services agency, or child care agency serves as the lead agency. Up-to-date addresses for state lead agencies are available at www.nectac.org, the Web site of the National Early Childhood Technical Assistance Center, at the University of North Carolina. NECTAC may also be reached at 500 NationsBank Plaza, 137 E. Franklin Street, Chapel Hill, NC 27514.

Learning disabilities (LDs) are conditions interfering with or limiting academic kinds of activities. They are believed to have neurological bases. Dyslexia is an example of an LD.

Least restrictive environment is a philosophy stressing the placement of children with disabilities in appropriate settings closest (when compared with other appropriate settings) to settings used by nondisabled children. The term is used in Part B of the Individuals with Disabilities Education Act.

Literacy is the use of reading and writing skills in activities children find to be meaningful. The term emphasizes the practical utility of these skills, in contrast to traditional drill-and-practice routines that are devoid of real-world meaning for most young children.

Low vision is 20/70 vision or worse to 20/200 vision, which is blindness.

M

Manipulatives are concrete objects children may touch, name, and count.

Medicaid is the federal-state medical insurance program for poor individuals. Many Supplemental Security Income recipients receive Medicaid.

Medically fragile, technology-dependent children require a range of intensive medical and other services as well as specialized equipment for ventilation and feeding.

Memory is retrieval of information. Recent studies suggest that data actually are re-created, not merely retrieved from storage.

Mental retardation refers to a combination of adaptive behavior characteristic of younger age ranges and intellectual functioning significantly lower than normal, when onset occurs prior to age 18. The current definition stresses that mentally retarded individuals need extensive systems of support.

Metacognition is awareness of one's own behavior and ways of thinking and learning. Frith suggests that individuals with autism may be very limited in metacognition.

Miscue analysis is the coding of behaviors children exhibit, including errors they make while reading as well as their spontaneous corrections of those errors.

Modeling occurs when a child watches a high-status "model" perform positive actions and be reinforced for doing so. The child is vicariously reinforced by watching the model be rewarded. *Modeling* is also the term for showing the child what behavior is desired.

Morphemes are the smallest units of words that carry meaning.

Multimedia personal computers can display video as well as words, sound, data, and still images.

Muscular dystrophy (MD) is a condition characterized by muscle weakness. There are several types of MD. Duchenne MD, the most serious form, is a progressive, usually fatal condition. Other dystrophies are less serious and rarely fatal.

N

National Early Intervention Longitudinal Study (NEILS) is a major, long-term examination of infants and toddlers and their families. A nationally representative sample of 5,668 families residing in 20 states is being followed. The study is important because so little information is available elsewhere about very young children with disabilities and their families.

Natural environment is a philosophy emphasizing services for infants, toddlers, and their families in places that are typical or otherwise "natural." Early intervention services are to be delivered in such environments, to the extent that these are "appropriate" and meet the child's needs. The home is the usual such environment. The term is used in Part C of the Individuals with Disabilities Education Act.

No Child Left Behind Act of 2001. Signed into law in early 2002, this federal law requires annual assessment of children's performance and adequate yearly progress by public schools. The intent is a popular one (raise academic standards) but the intrusive federal presence in what had been local and state control has proven to be controversial.

Number sense is the facility with numbers that allows young children to count, categorize, and perform other mental operations with numbers.

O

Occupational therapy helps children learn to perform specific tasks (brush teeth, dress, maintain good posture, etc.) despite physical disabilities or other conditions such as Down syndrome.

Operant conditioning is a process through which behavior is altered by manipulating its consequences.

Orientation and mobility specialists help young children who are blind or have low vision learn to navigate around the home; the early intervention program; the neighborhood; and, later, the community as a whole.

Orthopedic impairments, including spinal cord injury and cerebral palsy, are recognized disabilities under the Individuals with Disabilities Education Act.

Orthosis is a device that enhances the function of a body part, as a leg brace helps a child to walk. It contrasts with a *prosthesis,* which replaces a body part.

P

Parallel talk is a kind of *elaboration.* The ECSE professional speaks about what the young child is doing, seeing, hearing, and so on. See *self-talk.*

Paraplegia occurs when the lower limbs (legs) are affected, usually by a spinal cord injury, but the upper limbs (arms) are not.

Part B is the part of the Individuals with Disabilities Education Act describing how children with disabilities aged 3 to 18 shall receive a free appropriate public education.

Part C is the state-operated program created in 1986 for infants and toddlers with disabilities and their families. It is an early intervention program for children under three years of age and (with family concurrence) their families.

PEELS (Pre-Elementary Education Longitudinal Study) is a federally funded effort tracking more than 3,000 children from preschool through the early elementary years. The project began in 2003. Initial data appeared in 2006.

Peer tutoring occurs when one good reader works to help an emerging reader, when a child who is good in mathematics helps one who is not, and so on.

Perception is a process in which information entering the sensory register takes on meaning—for example, is interpreted.

Performance cues are prompts alerting children that certain behaviors are expected. These cues may be physical, verbal, or visual.

Phonemes are units of sound that cannot be further divided. An example is "ph" in "phoneme," expressed as /f/. The study of phonemes and the role they play in speech is called *phonology.*

Phonemic awareness A set of abilities to combine and separate phonemes. It is a fundamental skill, probably one we are born with and one we perform with little cognitive effort. Sometimes called *phonological awareness,* this ability allows us to decode many hundreds of phonemes per minute to comprehend speech that we hear.

Phonics instruction is a method of reading instruction that emphasizes the sounding out of words on the page. The assumption is that children have heard these words, many times, and simply need to connect the printed/written version of the word (which is new to them) to the sound(s) of the word (which is/are known to them).

Physical development (sometimes called *motor* or *coordination development*) is the display of age-appropriate fine motor control and gross motor control abilities.

Physical therapy helps prevent and reduce muscle atrophy and promotes musculoskeletal development.

Places of public accommodation are restaurants, hotels, motion picture and other theaters, sporting facilities, stores and shopping malls, and doctors' and lawyers' offices. Under the Americans with Disabilities Act, Title III, these must be accessible to people with disabilities and offer these people equal enjoyment to that accorded to people with no disabilities.

Pragmatics is the social use of language or the knowledge of what expressions to use in which contexts.

Pre-Elementary Education Longitudinal Study (PEELS) is another large-scale study, this one following 3,000 young children through their preschool and early elementary years. Data collection began in fall 2003, was conducted in winter 2005, and will resume in winter 2007 and 2009.

Preoperational stage, for Piaget, is the stage in child development just before children acquire the ability to engage in symbolic mental actions. A preoperational child, for example, cannot grasp the concept of reversibility.

Preschool-age children are children aged three-to-five inclusive. Most early childhood programs focus on this population.

Preschool child with a disability is a three- to six-year-old child who has one of the disabilities recognized under the Individuals with Disabilities Education Act. The term is used in some states to avoid the need to label a child prior to elementary school. (Preschool age begins at three and ends when the child enters kindergarten or first grade, usually at about age six.)

Preschool special education refers to special education and related services to meet the unique needs of three- to five-year-olds with disabilities and, in some states, developmental delays.

Presentation reinforcement occurs when something the child will work to get is presented to the child following performance of desired behaviors. Also called *positive reinforcement.*

Pressure sores (decubitus ulcers) develop when the child does not shift weight on a wheelchair cushion or on a bed.

Prevalence is the number of cases in a population, as contrasted to *incidence,* the number of new cases.

Principle of partial participation is the concept of creating a meaningful role for a child who cannot fully participate in a given activity.

Procedural safeguards, also called due-process rights, are granted to families in both Part C and Part B. An example is the right to see all relevant records pertaining to the child.

Processing occurs when information that has been perceived is analyzed and used by an individual.

Program evaluation attempts to answer the following questions: Did a program do what it promised? Did it do these things efficiently and effectively?

Prosthesis is an artificial replacement, such as a mechanical arm or knee, for a missing limb or body part.

Pullout is an approach in which the child leaves the classroom. The related-services professional works with the child in another setting, typically a therapy room.

Punishment is any consequence that decreases the frequency of the behavior it follows. One possible outcome, however, is displacement, in which some other behavior increases in frequency.

Push-in is an approach in which the child remains in the classroom. The therapist enters the classroom and performs his or her work with the child there. This may be seat by seat or, it may be in a corner of the room.

Q

Quadriplegia occurs when all four limbs (arms and legs) are affected, usually by a spinal cord injury.

Qualitative research is an observational study and report in which nothing is manipulated or controlled.

Quantitative research usually manipulates one or more variables (*independent variables*), observing its or their effects on dependent variables. Such studies report findings as numbers, hence the name "quantitative."

R

Reasonable accommodation in the Americans with Disabilities Act and Section 504 refers to an adjustment enabling a qualified individual with a disability to perform a task.

Related services are noninstructional support services such as transportation, therapy, and counseling. The term is used in Part B of the Individuals with Disabilities Education Act.

Removal reinforcement occurs when something the child will work to avoid is removed following performance of desired behaviors. Also called *negative reinforcement.*

Respite services are early intervention services offering breaks for family members from child care.

Response to intervention (RTI) is an approach in which educators try out one technique, then another, with a child and track the student's progress to discover what works with that child. It is one of the tactics IDEA calls "early intervening services" and is also a new element in the federal definition of specific learning disabilities.

Retinopathy of prematurity (ROP), once known as retrolental fibroplasia, is a limitation of vision occurring during the neonatal period.

S

Seamless system is a term referring to a set of services that has no gaps or delays between Part C early intervention and Part B services.

Section 504 is a civil rights provision in the federal Rehabilitation Act. It prohibits any program receiving or benefiting from federal financial assistance from discriminating on the basis of disability. Section 504 predated but remains in effect concurrent with the Americans with Disabilities Act.

Section 619 of Part B of the Individuals with Disabilities Education Act authorizes preschool special education and related services for children from three to five inclusive.

SEELS (Special Education Elementary Longitudinal Study) is a research project funded by the U.S. Department of Education to track 11,000 young children with disabilities and their families. The children were aged 6 through 12, and were receiving special education and related services in first or higher grades on September 1, 1999. Parents were first interviewed in the summer of 2000.

Self-talk is a form of *elaboration.* The ECSE professional articulates what he or she is doing and thinking. This offers a model for the young child. It also gives the young child labels for objects, feelings, and actions.

Sensorimotor stage is the Piagetian period in which young children perform goal-directed actions and acquire the idea of object permanence.

Service coordinators facilitate service delivery to families and represent the family in negotiations with public and private service providers.

Shaping is a method of successive approximations in which only ever-more-accurate behaviors are reinforced.

Shared reading has adults and children reading predictable stories together in short time periods.

Signed English is literally "English on the hands" because it presents signs in English word order.

Social or emotional development (sometimes called *psychosocial* or *affective* development) refers to young children's age-appropriate ability to understand their own feelings and those of others and to respond to both with behavior that is socially acceptable for children of that age. It also includes behavior children exhibit in play.

Social workers are trained human services professionals who help the family qualify for and receive needed services for which the family and/or the infant or toddler is or are eligible. Social work services also are "related services" under Part B of the Individuals with Disabilities Education Act.

Socioeconomic status (SES) refers to family income and other demographic characteristics. Disability is disproportionately common among low-SES families.

Special education is specially designed instruction to meet the unique needs of the child. The term is used in Part B of the Individuals with Disabilities Education Act.

Speech is the oral expression of meaning, usually—but not always—with symbols (words).

Speech to text (speech recognition) is computer comprehension of spoken words or sounds. Speaker-dependent speech recognition systems can understand one person's voice, while speaker-independent systems can comprehend the speech of many different individuals.

Spina bifida is a condition in which the spinal cord does not close completely during fetal development.

Spinal cord injury (SCI) occurs when the spinal cord is stretched, bruised, or even severed. It is one of many conditions categorized in the Individuals with Disabilities Education Act as orthopedic impairments.

Stay-put provision is an important due process right under Part B of the Individuals with Disabilities Education Act. While a dispute is pending, the child with a disability is to continue receiving a free, appropriate public education and is to remain in the current placement.

Stuttering is dysfluent speech or disrupted oral communication.

Summative evaluation looks to outcomes, or results, to assess programs and activities, usually in comparison with other activities or programs. It is in contrast to formative evaluation, which focuses more on process than product.

Supplemental Security Income (SSI) is a federal-state guaranteed minimum income program for individuals who are poor and have disabilities. Most SSI beneficiaries also receive Medicaid.

Supports are links to neighbors, friends, and community resources on which the family may rely in times of need. Supports may empower the family so it functions more effectively on behalf of the infant or toddler.

Syntax is a rule system for language governing the order of words or parts of sentences.

T

Teaming is an approach in which individuals from different professions come together on multidisciplinary teams. Family members are integral parts of such teams.

Telemedicine links medical specialists in one location with a patient in another, usually via fiber optic cable, which can transmit high-quality video as well as voice and data.

Text to speech (speech synthesis) is computer-generated speech.

Therapists and other services personnel include speech and language pathologists, occupational therapists, and other professionals delivering related services to preschool-age children or early intervention services to infants and toddlers with disabilities.

Time delay is a procedure through which prompts are offered, then gradually phased out.

Touch screens are technologies that sense the user's finger on the screen, activating software commands.

Traditionally underserved children with disabilities come from rural or inner-city families, and/or are members of ethnic or racial minority groups. Native American tribes and tribal organizations are among "traditionally underserved" groups. The 1991 Individuals with Disabilities Education Act amendments call for greater emphasis on serving children and families from such groups.

Transdisciplinary play-based assessment (TPBA) (Linder, 1993) is a qualitative approach to testing in which young children interact with play materials, professionals, and other children.

Transition is movement from one stage or program to another. An important transition in ECSE is that from early intervention programs to preschool programs.

Traumatic brain injury (TBI) was added to the Individuals with Disabilities Education Act as a recognized disability in 1990. Automobile, motorcycle, sports, and gun-related accidents resulting in sharp blows to (closed head injuries) or penetration of (open head injuries) the head cause TBIs.

Trust versus mistrust is the Eriksonian stage in which infants learn to trust their caregivers, particularly parents.

V

Verbal prompts are spoken cues signaling to the child what behavior is desired.

Visual prompts are visible cues signaling to the child what behavior is desired.

Vulnerable child syndrome (VCS) is an attempt to describe the condition of children exposed prenatally to cocaine, heroin, and other controlled substances; formerly called *crack babies*.

Z

Zone of proximal development (Lev Vygotsky) is the edge to which children's development has brought them, that is, what they can learn if helped. Teachers should not attempt to introduce more cognitively challenging material, however, until children progress to higher levels of development.

References

Abeson, A., & Zettel, J. (1977). The end of the quiet revolution: The Education for All Handicapped Children Act of 1975. *Exceptional Children, 44,* 115–128.

Accardo, P. J., & Capute, A. J. (1979). Parent counseling. In P. J. Accardo & A. J. Capute (Eds.), *The pediatrician and the developmentally delayed child* (pp. 167–177). Baltimore: University Park Press.

Achenbach, T. M. (1992). *Manual for the Child Behavior Checklist 2/3 and 1992 profile.* Burlington: University of Vermont Department of Psychiatry.

Adler, J., & Drew, L. (1988, March 28). Waking sleeping souls. *Newsweek,* 70–71.

Affleck, G., McGrade, B., McQueeney, M., & Allen, D. (1992). Promise of relationship-focused early intervention in developmental disabilities. *Journal of Special Education, 26,* 413–430.

Affleck, G., Tennen, H., Rowe, J., Roscher, B., & Walker, L. (1989). Effects of formal support on mothers' adaptation to the hospital-to-home transition of high-risk infants: The benefits and costs of helping. *Child Development, 60,* 488–501.

Allen, K. E. (1992). *The exceptional child: Mainstreaming in early childhood education.* Clifton Park, NY: Delmar Learning.

Allen, K., & Cowdery, G. (2005). *The exceptional child: Inclusion in early childhood education.* Clifton Park, NY: Delmar Learning.

Allen, K., & Marotz, L. (2007). *Developmental profiles: Pre-birth through twelve* (5th ed.). Clifton Park, NY: Delmar Learning.

Allen, M. C., Donohue, P. K., & Dusman, A. E. (1993). The limit of viability: Neonatal outcome of infants born at 22 to 25 weeks' gestation. *New England Journal of Medicine, 329*(22), 1597–1601.

Allison, M. (1992). The effects of neurologic injury on the maturing brain. *Headlines, 3*(5), 2–6, 9–10.

Alper, J., Natowicz, M., & Ard, C. (1993). Discrimination on the basis of perceived genetic disabilities. *Disability Studies Quarterly, 13*(3), 27–30.

American Academy of Pediatrics. (1995). *Informed consent, parental permission, and assent in pediatric practice.* Retrieved from www.aap.org

American Association on Mental Retardation. (1992). *Mental retardation: Definition, classification, and systems of support.* Washington, DC: Author.

American Psychiatric Association. (1994). *Diagnostic and statistical manual of mental disorders* (4th ed.). Washington, DC: Author.

Analysis of the five-year PACT longitudinal data. (2005). Columbia: South Carolina Education Oversight Committee (P.O. Box 11867, Blatt Building, Columbia, SC 29211; www.sceoc.org).

Anderson, F. E. (1992). *Art for all the children: Approaches to art therapy for children with disabilities.* Springfield, IL: Thomas.

Anderson, S. M. (1989). Secondary neurologic disability in myeldomengingocele. *Infants and Young Children, 1*(1), 9–21.

Antia, S., Kreimeyer, K., & Eldredge, N. (1994). Promoting social interaction between young children with hearing impairments and their peers. *Exceptional Children, 60*(3), 262–275.

Aram, D. M., Morris, R., & Hall, N. E. (1992). The validity of discrepancy criteria for identifying children with developmental learning disorders. *Journal of Learning Disabilities, 25*(9), 549–554.

Ariel, A. (1992). *Education of children and adolescents with learning disabilities.* New York: Merrill/Prentice Hall.

Asch, A. (1993). The human genome and disability rights: Thoughts for researchers and advocates. *Disability Studies Quarterly, 13*(3), 3–5.

Asch, A. (2006). Appearance-altering surgery, children's sense of self, and parental love. In E. Parens (Ed.), *Surgically shaping children* (pp. 227–252). Baltimore: Johns Hopkins University Press.

Asher, S., Hymel, S., & Renshaw, P. (1984). Loneliness in children. *Child Development, 55,* 1459–1464.

Association for the Care of Children's Health. (1992). Guidelines for facilitating father support groups. *ACCH Network, 9*(4), 2.

Audette, B., & Algozzine, B. (1992). Free and appropriate education for all students: Total quality and the transformation of American public education. *Remedial and Special Education, 13*(6), 8–18.

Audit finds day-care safety flaws. (1994, January 24). *Newsday,* p.13.

Badger, E. (1981). *Infant/toddler: Introducing your child to the joy of learning.* New York: McGraw-Hill.

Baer, D. M., Wolf, M. M., & Risley, T. R. (1968). Some current dimensions of applied behavior analysis. *Journal of Applied Behavior Analysis, 1*(1), 91–97.

Bagby, J., Rudd, L., & Woods, M. (2005). The effects of socioeconomic diversity on the language, cognitive, and social-emotional development of children from low-income backgrounds. *Early Child Development & Care, 175*(5), 395–405.

Bailey, D. (1989). Issues and directions in preparing professionals to work with young handicapped children and their families. In J. J. Gallagher, P. L. Trohanis, & R. M. Clifford (Eds.), *Policy implementation and PL 99–457: Planning for young children with special needs* (pp. 97–132). Baltimore: Brookes.

Bailey, D. (1991). Issues and perspectives on family assessment. *Infants and Young Children, 4*(1), 26–34.

Bailey, D. (1997). Evaluating the effectiveness of curriculum alternatives for infants and preschoolers at high risk. In M. Guralnick (Ed.), *The effectiveness of early intervention.* Baltimore: Brookes.

Bailey, D., Buysse, V., Edmondson, R., & Smith, T. M. (1992). Creating family-centered services in early intervention: Perceptions of professionals in four states. *Exceptional Children, 58*(4), 298–309.

Bailey, D., Buysse, V., & Palsha, S. A. (1990). Self-ratings of professional knowledge and skill in early intervention. *Journal of Special Education, 23,* 423–435.

Bailey, D., McWilliam, P. J., & Winton, P. J. (1992). Building family-centered practices in early intervention: A team-based model for change. *Infants and Young Children, 5*(1), 73–82.

Bailey, D., Palsha, S. A., & Simeonsson, R. J. (1991). Professional skills, concerns, and perceived importance of work with families in early intervention. *Exceptional Children, 58*(2), 156–165.

Bailey, D., Scarborough, A., & Hebbeler, K. (2003). *Families' first experiences with early intervention*. Menlo Park, CA: SRI International. Retrieved from www.sri.com/neils

Bailey, D., Scarborough, A., Hebbeler, K., Spiker, D., & Mallik, S. (2004). *Family outcomes at the end of early intervention*. Menlo Park, CA: SRI International. Retrieved from www.sri.com/neils

Bailey, D., Simeonsson, R. J., Yoder, D., & Huntington, G. (1990). Preparing professionals to serve infants and toddlers with handicaps and their families: An integrative analysis across eight disciplines. *Exceptional Children, 57*(1), 26–35.

Ballard, J., & Zettel, J. (1977). Public Law 94–142 and Section 504: What they say about rights and protections. *Exceptional Children, 44*(3), 177–184.

Bandura, A. (1977). *Social learning theory.* Englewood Cliffs, NJ: Prentice Hall.

Barkley, R. (1990). *Attention deficit hyperactivity disorder: A handbook for diagnosis and treatment.* New York: Guilford.

Barkley, R. (2000). *Taking charge of ADHD: The complete, authoritative guide for parents* (rev. ed.). New York: Guilford.

Barlow, K., Thomson, E., Johnson, D., & Minns. R. (2005). Late neurologic and cognitive sequelae of inflicted traumatic brain injury in infancy. *Pediatrics, 116*(2), e174–e185 [on-line document].

Baron-Cohen, S., Bolton, P., Wheelwright, S., Short, L., Mead, G., Smith, A., & Scahill, V. (1998). Autism occurs more often in families of physicists, engineers, and mathematicians. *Autism, 2,* 296–301.

Baron-Cohen, S., Wheelwright, S., Skinner, R., Martin, J., & Clubley, E. (2001). The autism-spectrum quotient (AQ): Evidence from Asperger syndrome/ high-functioning autism, males and females, scientists and mathematicians. *Journal of Autism and Developmental Disabilities, 31*(1), 5–17.

Baroni, M., Tuthill, P., Feenan, L., & Schroeder, M. (1994). Technology-dependent infants and young children: A retrospective case analysis of service coordination across state lines. *Infants and Young Children, 7*(1), 69–78.

Batshaw, M., & Perrett, Y. (Eds.). (1992). *Children with disabilities: A medical primer.* Baltimore: Brookes.

Bayley, N. (1969). *Bayley Scales of Infant Development.* San Antonio, TX: Psychological Corporation.

Bayley Scales of Infant Development: Second edition. (1993). San Antonio, TX: Psychological Corporation.

Beach Center on Disability. (2005). *Beach Center Family Quality of Life Scale user's manual*. Lawrence: University of Kansas.

Beck, L. R., Hammond-Cordero, M., & Poole, J. (1994). Integrated services for children who are medically fragile and technology dependent. *Infants and Young Children, 6*(3), 75–83.

Behl, D., White, K. R., & Escobar, C. M. (1993). New Orleans early intervention study of children with visual impairments. *Early Education and Development, 4*(4), 256–274.

Behr, J. (1991). Testimony before the Subcommittee on Disability Policy, March 15. *Senate report S. Hrg. 102–133.* Washington, DC: U.S. Government Printing Office, 29–33.

Bellamy, G. T. (1987, December 8). *OSEP memorandum to state school officers.* Unpublished document. Washington, DC: U.S. Department of Education, Office of Special Education Programs.

Belson, S. I. (2003). *Technology for exceptional learners.* Upper Saddle River, NJ: Prentice Hall/Merrill.

Benson, A. M., & Lane, S. J. (1993). The developmental impact of low-level lead exposure. *Infants and Young Children, 6*(2), 41–51.

Bigge, J. (1988). *Curriculum-based instruction for special education students.* Mountain View, CA: Mayfield.

Blackorby, J., Wagner, M., Cameto, R., Davies, E., Levine, P., Newman, L., Marder, C., & Sumi, C. (2005). *SEELS: Engagement, academics, social adjustment, and independence: The achievements of elementary and middle school students with disabilities.* Menlo Park, CA: SRI International.

Blakeslee, S. (1991a, September 10). Brain yields new clues on its organization for language. *New York Times,* pp. C1, C10.

Blakeslee, S. (1991b, September 15). Study ties dyslexia to brain flaw affecting vision and other senses. *New York Times,* pp. 1, 30.

Bloch, J. S. (1993). Personal communication, August 5.

Bloch, J. S., & Seitz, M. (1985). *Empowering parents of disabled children: A family exchange center.* Syosset, NY: Variety Preschoolers Workshop.

Bloch, J. S., & Seitz, M. (1989, July). Parents as assessors of children: A collaborative approach to helping. *Social Work in Education,* 226–244.

Bluma, S., Shearer, M., Frohman, A., & Hillard, J. (1976). *Portage guide to early education.* Portage, WI: Cooperative Educational Service Agency #12.

Board of Education, Hendrick Hudson School District v. Rowley, 458 U.S. 176, 181 (1982).

Bondurant-Utz, J. (2002). *Practical guide to assessing infants and preschoolers with special needs.* Upper Saddle River, NJ: Merrill/Prentice Hall.

Borich, G. (2007). *Effective teaching methods: Research-based practice* (6th ed.). Upper Saddle River, NJ: Merrill/Prentice Hall.

Borja, R. (2005, October 19). Growing niche for tutoring chains: Prekindergarteners' academic prep. *Education Week,* 10.

Bos, C. S., & Vaughn, S. (1988). *Strategies for teaching students with learning and behavior problems* (2nd ed.). Boston: Allyn & Bacon.

Bowe, F. (1978). *Handicapping America.* New York: Harper & Row.

Bowe, F. (1985a). *Black adults with disabilities.* Washington, DC: President's Committee on Employment of People with Disabilities.

Bowe, F. (1985b). *Disabled adults of Hispanic origin.* Washington, DC: President's Committee on Employment of People with Disabilities.

Bowe, F. (1991). *Approaching equality.* Silver Spring, MD: T. J. Publishers.

Bowe, F. (1992a). *Equal rights for Americans with disabilities.* New York: Franklin Watts.

Bowe, F. (1992b). Radicalism v. reason. In D. F. Moores, M. Walworth, & T. J. O'Rourke (Eds.), *A free hand.* Silver Spring, MD: T. J. Publishers.

Bowe, F. (1993). Getting there: Update on recommendations by the Commission on Education of the Deaf. *American Annals of the Deaf, 138*(3), 304–308.

Bowe, F. (1994). Population estimates: Birth-five children with disabilities. *Journal of Special Education, 28*(4), 28–37.

Bowe, F. (2000). *Physical, sensory, and health disabilities: An introduction.* Columbus, OH: Merrill/Prentice Hall.

Bowe, F. (2002). Broadband and Americans with disabilities. Retrieved from www.newmillenniumresearch.org

Bowe, F. (2005). *Making inclusion work.* Upper Saddle River, NJ: Merrill/Prentice Hall.

Boyce, G., Saylor, C., & Price. C. (2004). School-age outcomes for early intervention participants who experienced intraventricular hemorrhage and low birth weight. *Children's Health Care, 33*(4), 257–274.

Boyce, G., Smith, T. B., Immel, N., Casto, G., & Escobar, C. (1993). Early intervention with medically fragile infants: Investigating the age-at-start question. *Journal of Early Education and Development, 4*(4), 327–345.

Boyce, G., White, K. R., & Kerr, B. (1993). The effectiveness of adding a parent involvement component to an existing center-based program for children with disabilities and their families. *Early Education and Development, 4*(4), 327–345.

Brandt, P. (1993). Negotiation and problem-solving strategies: Collaboration between families and professionals. *Infants and Young Children, 5*(4), 78–84.

Brazelton, T. (1984). *Neonatal Behavioral Assessment Scale.* Philadelphia: Lippincott.

Bredekamp, S. (Ed.). (1987). *Developmentally appropriate practice in early childhood programs serving children from birth through age 8: Expanded edition.* Washington, DC: National Association for the Education of Young Children.

Bredekamp, S. (1993a). Myths about developmentally appropriate practice: A response to Fowell and Lawton. *Early Childhood Research Quarterly, 8,* 117–119.

Bredekamp, S. (1993b). The relationship between early childhood education and early childhood special education: Healthy marriage or family feud? *Topics in Early Childhood Special Education, 13*(3), 258–273.

Bredekamp, S., & Copple, C. (Eds.). (1997). *Developmentally appropriate practice in early childhood programs: Revised edition.* Washington, DC: National Association for the Education of Young Children.

Brenna, S. (2003, November 9). Very special ed. *New York Times*, Education Life, pp. 30–32.

Bricker, D. (2000). Inclusion: How the scene has changed. *Topics in Early Childhood Special Education, 20*(1), 14–19.

Bricker, D. (2001). The natural environment: A useful construct? *Infants and Young Children, 13*(4), 21–31.

Bricker, D., Pretti-Frontczak, K., & McComas, N. R. (1998). *An activity-based approach to early intervention* (2nd ed.). Baltimore: Brookes.

Bricker, D., & Squires, J. (1989). Low-cost system using parents to monitor the development of at-risk infants. *Journal of Early Intervention, 13,* 50–60.

Bricker, D., Squires, J., Kaminski, R., & Mounts, L. (1988). The validity, reliability and cost of a parent-completed questionnaire system to evaluate at-risk infants. *Journal of Pediatric Psychology, 13*(1), 55–68.

Bricker, D., & Veltman, M. (1990). Early intervention programs: Child-focused approaches. In S. J. Meisels & J. P. Shonkoff (Eds.), *Handbook of early childhood intervention* (pp. 373–399). New York: Cambridge University Press.

Brinkworth, R. (1975). Early treatment and training for the infant with Down syndrome. *Royal Society of Health, 2,* 75–78.

Brittan (CA) Elementary School District. (1990). *Education for the Handicapped Law Report,* 16 EHLR 1226. (Now *Individuals with Disabilities Education Law Report.*)

Brockenbrough, K. (1991, August 26). Preparing personnel for pluralism. *NEC*TAS Notes.* Chapel Hill, NC: National Early Childhood Technical Assistance Center.

Brodsky, P., Brodsky, M., Lee, H., & Sever, L. (1986). Two evaluation studies of Reitan's REHABIT program for the retraining of brain dysfunctions. *Journal of Perceptual and Motor Skills, 63,* 501–502.

Bronfenbrenner, U. (1979). *The ecology of human development: Experiments by nature and design.* Cambridge, MA: Harvard University Press.

Bronfenbrenner, U. (1989). Ecological systems theory. *Annals of Child Development, 6,* 187–249.

Bronfenbrenner, U., & Morris, P. (1998). Ecological processes of development. In W. Damon (Ed.), *Handbook of child psychology: Theoretical issues* (Vol. 1, pp. 993–1028). New York: Wiley.

Bronowski, J. (1973). *The ascent of man.* Boston: Little, Brown.

Brown, C. W., Perry, D. F., & Kurland, S. (1994). Funding policies that affect children: What every early interventionist should know. *Infants and Young Children, 6*(4), 1–12.

Bruder, M. B. (1997). The effectiveness of specific educational/developmental criteria for children with established conditions. In M. Guralnick (Ed.), *The effectiveness of early intervention.* Baltimore: Brookes.

Bruder, M. B. (2000). Renewing the inclusion agenda: Attending to the right variables. *Journal of Early Intervention, 23*(4), 223–230.

Bruder, M. B., Lippman, C., & Bologna, T. M. (1994). Personnel preparation in early intervention: Building capacity for program expansion within institutions of higher education. *Journal of Early Intervention, 18*(1), 103–110.

Bruininks, R., Thurlow, M., & Ysseldyke, J. (1992). Assessing the right outcomes: Prospects for improving education for children with disabilities. *Education and Training in Mental Retardation, 27*(2), 167–175.

Bruner, J. (1966). *Toward a theory of instruction.* New York: Norton.

Bruner, J. (1981). The social context of language acquisition. *Language and Communication, 1,* 155–178.

Brunquell, P. J. (1994). Listening to epilepsy. *Infants and Young Children, 7*(1), 24–33.

Buysse, V., & Bailey, D. (1993). Behavioral and developmental outcomes in young children with disabilities in integrated and segregated settings: A review of comparative studies. *Journal of Special Education, 26*(4), 434–461.

Calem, R. E. (1992, August 30). Coming soon: The PC with ears. *New York Times,* p. 9.

Cardon, L. R., Smith, S. D., Fulker, D. W., Kimberling, W. J., Pennington, B. F., & DeFries, J. C. (1994). Quantitative trait locus for reading disability on chromosome 6. *Science, 266,* 276–279.

Carlson, D., Ehrlich, N., Berland, B. J., & Bailey, N. (2001). *Assistive technology survey results: Continued benefits and needs reported by Americans with disabilities.* Posted at www.ed.gov

Carnegie Corporation of New York. (1994). *Starting points: Meeting the needs of our youngest children.* New York: Author.

Carta, J. J., Atwater, J. B., Schwartz, I. S., & McConnell, S. R. (1993). Developmentally appropriate practices and early childhood special education: A reaction to Johnson and McChesney Johnson. *Topics in Early Childhood Special Education, 13*(3), 243–254.

Casto, G., & Mastropieri, M. A. (1986a). The efficacy of early intervention programs: A meta-analysis. *Exceptional Children, 52*(5), 417–424.

Casto, G., & Mastropieri, M. A. (1986b). Much ado about nothing: A reply to Dunst and Snyder. *Exceptional Children, 53*(3), 277–279.

Casto, G., & White, K. R. (1985). The efficacy of early intervention programs with environmentally at-risk infants. *Journal of Children in Contemporary Society, 17,* 37–48.

Center for Accessible Housing. (1992). *Recommendations for accessibility standards for children's environments.* Washington, DC: U.S. Architectural and Transportation Barriers Compliance Board.

Centers for Disease Control and Prevention. (1992, September 11). Recommendations for the use of folic acid to reduce the number of cases of spina bifida and other neural tube defects. *Morbidity and Mortality Weekly Report, 41,* Number RR-14.

Chaikind, S., Danielson, L., & Brauen, M. (1993). What do we know about the costs of special education? A selected review. *Journal of Special Education, 26*(4), 344–370.

Chapman, J. W. (1992). Learning disabilities in New Zealand: Where kiwis and kids with LD can't fly. *Journal of Learning Disabilities, 25,* 362–370.

Chapman, J., & Elliott, K. (1995). Preschoolers exposed to cocaine: Early childhood special education and Head Start preparation. *Journal of Early Intervention, 19*(2), 118–129.

Charlesworth, R. (1992). *Understanding child development* (3rd ed.). Clifton Park, NY: Delmar Learning.

Charlesworth, R., & Lind, K. (2007). *Math & science for young children* (5th ed.). Clifton Park, NY: Thomson Delmar Learning.

Chasnoff, I. J. (1989, July). *National epidemiology of perinatal drug use.* Paper presented at Drugs, Alcohol, Pregnancy and Parenting Conference, Spokane, WA.

Chomsky, N. (1957). *Syntactic structures.* The Hague: Mouton.

Chomsky, N. (1968). *Language and mind.* New York: Harcourt Brace Jovanovich.

Clark, T. C., & Watkins, S. (1985). *SKI*HI curriculum* (4th ed.). Logan, UT: SKI*HI Institute at Logan State University.

Clements, D. H., Nastasi, B. K., & Swaminathan, S. (1993, January). Young children and computers: Crossroads and directions from research. *Young Children,* 56–64.

Cole, J. (1996). Intervention strategies for infants with prenatal drug exposure. *Infants and Young Children, 8*(3), 35–39.

Cole, K. N., Dale, P. S., & Mills, P. S. (1991). Individual differences in language delayed children's responses to direct and interactive preschool instruction. *Topics in Early Childhood Special Education, 11,* 99–124.

Cole, K. N., Dale, P. S., Mills, P. S., & Jenkins, J. R. (1993). Interaction between early intervention curricula and student characteristics. *Exceptional Children, 60*(1), 17–28.

Coleman, L. (1993). A method for studying the professional practical knowledge of service providers. *Journal of Early Intervention, 17*(1), 21–29.

Commission on Education of the Deaf. (1988). *Toward equality: Education of the deaf.* Washington, DC: U.S. Government Printing Office.

Committee on Broadband Last Mile Technology. (2002). *Broadband: Bringing home the bits*. Washington, DC: National Academy Press.

Cone, J. D., Anderson, J. A., Harris, F. C., Goff, D. K., & Fox, S. R. (1988). Developing and maintaining social interaction in profoundly retarded young males. *Journal of Abnormal Child Psychology, 6,* 351–360.

Connolly, B. H., Morgan, S. B., & Russell, F. F. (1984). Evaluation of children with Down syndrome who participated in an early intervention program. *Physical Therapist, 64,* 1515–1518.

Conroy, M., Dunlap, G., Clarke, S., & Alter, P. (2005). A descriptive analysis of positive behavior intervention research with young children with challenging behavior. *Topics in Early Childhood Special Education, 25*(3), 157–166.

Constantino, J., et al. (2006). Autistic social impairment in siblings with pervasive developmental disorders. *American Journal of Psychiatry, 163,* 294–296.

Cooke, R. (1993, May 30). Fragile-X: Genetic screenings raise new hopes of treatment, and a whole new set of problems. *Newsday, 7,* pp. 58–59.

Cooley, W. C., & Graham, J. M. (1991). Down syndrome: An update and review for the primary paediatrician. *Clinical Paediatrics, 30*(4), 233–253.

Corsaro, W. A. (1985). *Friendships and peer culture in the early years.* Norwood, NJ: Ablex.

Corsello, C. (2005). Early intervention in autism. *Infants & Young Children, 18*(2), 74–85.

Cowley, G. (1990, Winter/Spring). Made to order babies. *Newsweek,* special edition, 94–95, 98, 100.

Cox, G. A., Cole, N. M., Matsumura, K., Phelps, S. F., Hauschka, S. D., Campbell, et al. (1993). Overexpression of dystrophin in transgenic *mdx* mice eliminates dystrophic symptoms without toxicity. *Nature, 364*(6439), 725–729.

Creswell, J. W. (2002). *Educational research: Planning, conducting, and evaluating quantitative and qualitative research.* Upper Saddle River, NJ: Prentice Hall.

Cruickshank, W. (Ed.). (1976). *Cerebral palsy: A developmental disability* (3rd ed.). Syracuse, NY: Syracuse University Press.

Cryer, D., Harms, T., & Bourland, B. (1987a). *Active learning for infants.* Menlo Park, CA: Addison-Wesley.

Cryer, D., Harms, T., & Bourland, B. (1987b). *Active learning for ones.* Menlo Park, CA: Addison-Wesley.

Cukier, A. (2005, August 12). Mother's journal offers early look at child with autism. *Stoney Creek News.* Retrieved from www.stoneycreeknews.com

Culbertson, J. L., & Willis, D. J. (Eds.). (1993). *Testing young children: A reference guide for developmental, psychoeducational, and psychosocial assessments.* Austin, TX: PRO-ED.

Cystic Fibrosis Foundation. (1998). *Facts about cystic fibrosis* [On-line pamphlet]. Retrieved from www.cff.org

Dale, P. S., Jenkins, J. R., Mills, P. E., & Cole, K. N. (2005). Follow-up of children from academic and cognitive preschool curricula at 12 and 16. *Exceptional Children, 71*(3), 301–317.

Damasio, H., & Damasio, A. (1989). *Lesion localization in neuropsychology.* New York: Oxford University Press.

DC:03 casebook. (1997). Washington, DC: Zero to Three.

DeGangi, G., Royeen, C. B., & Wietlisbach, S. (1992). How to examine the individualized family service plan: Preliminary findings and a procedural guide. *Infants and Young Children, 5*(2), 42–56.

Deiner, P. (2005). *Resources for educating children with diverse abilities.* Clifton Park, NY: Delmar Learning.

Diagnostic classification of mental health and developmental disorders of infancy and early childhood. (1994). Washington, DC: Zero to Three.

Diamond, K. E. (2001). Relationships among young children's ideas, emotional understanding, and social contact with classmates with disabilities. *Topics in Early Childhood Special Education, 21*(2), 104–113.

DiCarlo, C. F., Stricklin, S., & Banajee, M. (2001). Effects of manual signing on communication verbalizations by toddlers with and without disabilities in inclusive classrooms. *Journal of the Association for Persons with Severe Handicaps, 26*(2), 120–126.

Dillman, D. (2000). *Mail and Internet surveys: The tailored design method.* New York: Wiley.

Division for Early Childhood. (2004). *DEC recommended practices: A comprehensive guide.* Denver: Sopris West.

Dolnick, E. (1993). Deafness as culture. *Atlantic Monthly, 272*(3), 37–53.

Dore, J. (1974). A pragmatic description of early language development. *Journal of Psycholinguistics Research, 4,* 343–351.

Duara, R., Kushch, A., Gross-Glenn, K., Barker, W. W., Jallad, B., Pascal, S., et al. (1991). Neuroanatomic differences between dyslexic and normal readers on magnetic resonance imaging scans. *Archives of Neurology, 48,* 410–416.

Dunst, C. J. (1981). *Infant learning: A cognitive-linguistic intervention strategy.* Hingham, MA: Teaching Resources.

Dunst, C. J., Bruder, M. B., Trivette, C. M., Hamby, D., Raab, M., & McLean, M. (2001). Characteristics and consequences of everyday natural learning opportunities. *Topics in Early Childhood Special Education, 21*(2), 68–92.

Dunst, C. J., Bruder, M. B., Trivette, C. M., Raab, M., & McLean, M. (2001). Natural learning opportunities for infants, toddlers, and preschoolers. *Young Exceptional Children, 4*(3), 18–25.

Dunst, C. J., Herter, S., Shields, H., & Bennis, L. (2001). Mapping community-based natural learning opportunities. *Young Exceptional Children, 4*(4), 16–25.

Dunst, C. J., Johanson, C., Trivette, C. M., & Hamby, D. (1991). Family-oriented early intervention policies and practices: Family-centered or not? *Exceptional Children, 58*(2), 115–126.

Dunst, C. J., & Trivette, C. M. (1988). An enablement and empowerment perspective on case management. *Topics in Early Childhood, 8,* 87–102.

DuPaul, G., & Stoner, G. (2004). *ADHD in the schools* (2nd ed.). New York: Guilford.

Dyslexia may be tied to brain's last fetal stages. (1993, August 26). *Newsday,* p. 65.

Eikeseth, S., & Jahr, E. (2001). The UCLA reading and writing program: An evaluation of the beginning stages. *Research in Developmental Disabilities, 22*(4), 289–307.

Englemann, S., & Bruner, E. (1984). *DISTAR Reading.* Chicago: Science Research Associates.

Epps, E. G. (1974). Situational effects in testing. In L. P. Miller (Ed.), *The testing of black students: A symposium* (pp. 17–29). Orlando, FL: Harcourt Brace Jovanovich.

Erikson, E. (1963). *Childhood and society* (2nd ed.). New York: Norton.

Escobar, C. M., Barnett, W. S., & Goetze, L. D. (1994). Cost analysis in early intervention. *Journal of Early Intervention, 18*(1), 48–63.

Exhorn, K. (2005). *The autism sourcebook: Everything you need to know about diagnosis, treatment, coping, and healing*. New York: Regan Books.

Fagan, J., & Singer, L. (1983). Infant recognition memory as a measure of intelligence. In L. Lipsett (Ed.), *Advances in infant research* (Vol. 2, pp. 31–78). Norwood, NJ: Ablex.

Fewell, R. R. (1991). Trends in the assessment of infants and toddlers with disabilities. *Exceptional Children, 58*(2), 166–173.

Fewell, R. R., & Glick, M. P. (1993). Observing play: An appropriate process for learning and assessment. *Infants and Young Children, 5*(4), 35–43.

Fewell, R. R., & Vadasy, P. F. (1983). *Learning through play: A resource manual for teachers and parents.* Hingham, MA: Teaching Resources.

Figueroa, R. A. (1990). Assessment of linguistic minority group children. In C. R. Reynolds & R.W. Kamphaus (Eds.), *Handbook of psychological and educational assessment of children; Vol. 1. Intelligence and achievement* (pp. 671–696). New York: Guilford.

Fiore, T., Becker, E., & Nero, R. (1993). Educational interventions for students with attention deficit disorder. *Exceptional Children, 60*(2), 163–173.

Flanagan, K., & West, J. (2004). *Children born in 2001: First results from the base year of the Early Childhood Longitudinal Study, Birth Cohort* (ECLS-B) (NCES 2005-036). Washington, DC: National Center for Education Statistics, U.S. Department of Education.

Fletcher, J. M. (1992). The validity of distinguishing children with language and learning disabilities according to discrepancies with IQ: Introduction to the special series. *Journal of Learning Disabilities, 25*(9), 546–548.

Florida Department of Education. (1988). *Building standards for educational facilities for handicapped children.* Tallahassee: Author.

Folio, M. R., & Fewell, R. R. (1983). *Peabody developmental motor scales and activity cards.* Allen, TX: DLM Teaching Resources.

Ford, B. (1992). Multicultural education training for special educators working with African-American youth. *Exceptional Children, 59*(2), 107–114.

Forness, S. (1989). Testimony. *S. Hrg. report 101–287* (186–200). Washington, DC: U.S. Government Printing Office.

Fowler, S. A., Chandler, L. K., Johnson, T. E., & Stella, M. E. (1988). Individualizing family involvement in school transitions: Gathering information and choosing the next program. *Journal of the Division for Early Childhood, 12,* 208–216.

Fowler, S. A., Schwartz, I., & Atwater, J. (1991). Perspectives on the transition from preschool to kindergarten for children with disabilities and their families. *Exceptional Children, 58*(2), 136–145.

Fraiberg, S. (1968). Parallel and divergent patterns in blind and sighted infants. *The Psychological Study of the Child, 23,* 264–300.

Fraiberg, S. (1970). Interventions in infancy. *Journal of the American Academy of Child Psychiatry, 10*(3), 381–405.

Fraiberg, S. (1975). The development of human attachments in infants blind from birth. *Merrill-Palmer Quarterly, 21,* 315–334.

Fraiberg, S. (1977). *Insights from the blind: Comparative studies of blind and sighted infants.* New York: Basic Status in Books.

Fraiberg, S., & Freedman, C. A. (1964). Studies in the ego development of the congenitally blind child. *Psychoanalytic Study of the Child, 19,* 113–169.

Fraiberg, S., Smith, M., & Adelson, E. (1969). An educational program for blind infants. *Journal of Special Education, 3*(2), 121–139.

Frank, D. A. (1990, August). *Infants of substance abusing mothers: Demographics and medical profile.* Paper presented at Babies & Cocaine Conference, Washington, DC.

Frankenburg, W. K., Dodds, J. B., Archer, P., Bresnick, B., Maschka, P., Edelman, N., & Shapiro, H. (1990). *Denver II screening manual.* Denver: Denver Developmental Materials.

Franklin, M. (1992). Culturally sensitive instructional practices for African-American learners with disabilities. *Exceptional Children, 59*(2), 115–122.

Freund, L. S. (1994). Diagnosis and developmental issues for young children with Fragile-X syndrome. *Infants and Young Children, 6*(3), 34–45.

Freund, P., Boone, H., Barlow, J., & Lim, C. (2005). Healthcare and early intervention collaborative supports for families and young children. *Infants & Young Children, 18*(1), 25–36.

Frith, U. (1989). *Autism: Explaining the enigma.* Cambridge, MA: Blackwell.

Frith, U. (1993, June). Autism. *Scientific American,* 108–114.

From ADA to empowerment: The report of the Task Force on the Rights and Empowerment of Americans with Disabilities. (1991). Washington, DC: Task Force.

Fuchs, D., Featherstone, N., Garwick, D., & Fuchs, L. (1984). Effects of examiner familiarity and task characteristics on speech and language-impaired children's test performance. *Measurement and Evaluation in Guidance, 16*(4), 198–204.

Fuchs, D., Fuchs, L., Benowitz, S., & Barringer, K. (1987). Norm-referenced tests: Are they valid for use with handicapped students? *Exceptional Children, 54,* 263–272.

Fuchs, D., Fuchs, L., Garwick, D., & Featherstone, N. (1983). Test performance of language-handicapped children with familiar and unfamiliar examiners. *Journal of Psychology, 1214,* 37–46.

Fuchs, D., Fuchs, L. S., Thompson, A., Svenson, E., Yen, L., Al Otaiba, S., et al. (2001). Peer-assisted learning strategies in reading: Extensions for kindergarten, first grade, and high school. *Remedial and Special Education, 22*(1), 15–21.

Furuno, S., O'Reilly, A., Hosaka, C., Inatsuka, T., Allman, T., & Ziesloft, B. (1985). *Hawaii Early Learning Profile (HELP)* (rev. ed.). Palo Alto, CA: VORT Corp.

Gabreli, J., et al. (2005, November 16). *Music and language.* Paper presented at the Society of Neuroscience, Washington, DC.

Galaburda, A. M., Menard, M. T., & Rosen, G. D. (1994). Evidence for aberrant auditory anatomy in developmental dyslexia. *Proceedings of the National Academy of Sciences, 91,* 8010–8013.

Gandell, T., & Laufer, D. (1993). Developing a telecommunications curriculum for students with physical disabilities. *Teaching Exceptional Children, 25*(2), 26–28.

Gargiulo, R., & Kilgo, J. (2005). *Young children with special needs* (2nd ed.). Clifton Park, NY: Delmar Learning.

Garshelis, J. A., & McConnell, S. R. (1993). Comparison of family needs assessed by mothers, individual professionals, and interdisciplinary teams. *Journal of Early Intervention, 17*(1), 36–49.

General Accounting Office. (1979). *The Comptroller General's report: Early childhood and family development programs improve the quality of life for low income families.* Washington, DC: Author.

Gerales, E., & Ritter, T. (Eds.). (1991). *Children with cerebral palsy: A parent's guide.* Rockville: Woodbine House.

Gersten, R., Carnine, D., & Woodward, J. (1987). Direct instruction research: The third decade. *Remedial and Special Education, 8*(6), 48–56.

Gesell, A. (1925). *The mental growth of the preschool child: A psychological outline of normal development from birth to the sixth year.* New York: Macmillan.

Gestwicki, C. (2007). *Developmentally appropriate practice: Curriculum and development in early education* (3rd ed.). Clifton Park, NY: Delmar Learning.

Glass, G. V. (1976). Primary, secondary, and meta-analysis of research. *Educational Researcher, 5*(10), 3–8.

Glass, G. V., McGaw, B., & Smith. M. L. (1981). *Meta-analysis in social research.* Newbury Park, CA: Sage.

Glass, P. (1993). Development of visual function in preterm infants: Implications for early intervention. *Infants and Young Children, 6*(1), 11–20.

Gliedman, J., & Roth, W. (1980). *The unexpected minority.* New York: Harcourt Brace Jovanovich.

Gold, M. W. (1980). *Try Another Way training manual.* Champaign, IL: Research Press.

Goldin-Meadow, S., McNeil, D., & Singleton, J. (1996). Removing the handcuffs on grammatical expression in the manual modality. *Psychological Review, 103,* 34–55.

Goodman, G., & Poillion, M. J. (1992). ADD: Acronym for any dysfunction or difficulty. *Journal of Special Education, 26*(1), 37–56.

Goodman, J. (1992). *When slow is fast enough: Educating the delayed preschool child.* New York: Guilford.

Goodman, J. (1994). "Empowerment" versus "best interests": Client-professional relationships. *Infants and Young Children, 6*(4), vi–x.

Goodman, J., & Bond, L. (1993). The individualized education program: A retrospective critique. *Journal of Special Education, 26*(4), 408–422.

Goodman, J., Cecil, H., & Barker, W. (1984). Early intervention with the handicapped: Promising findings. *Developmental Medicine and Child Neurology, 26,* 47–55.

Goodman, K. S., Goodman, Y. M., & Hood, W. J. (1989). *The whole language evaluation book.* Portsmouth, NH: Heinemann.

Gould, P., & Sullivan, J. (2005). *The inclusive early childhood classroom.* Upper Saddle River, NJ: Merrill/Prentice Hall.

Graham, M., & Bryant, D. (1993). Developmentally appropriate environments for children with special needs. *Infants and Young Children, 5*(3), 31–42.

Gray, C. (2005). Inclusion, impact and need: Young children with a visual impairment. *Child Care in Practice, 11*(2), 179–190.

Greenfield, J. (1972). *A child called Noah.* New York: Holt, Rinehart & Winston.

Gresham, F., & Elliot, S. (1990a). *Social Skills Rating System.* Circle Pines, MN: American Guidance Service.

Gresham, F., & Elliot, S. (1990b). *Student Self Concept Scale.* Circle Pines, MN: American Guidance Service.

Grove, N., & Dockrell, J. (2000). Multisign combinations by children with intellectual impairments: An analysis of language skills. *Journal of Speech, Language, and Hearing Research, 43*(2), 309–320.

Guntupalli, V., & Kalinowski, J. (2006). The need for self-report data in the assessment of stuttering therapy efficacy: Repetitions and prolongations of speech. *International Journal of Language & Communication Disorders, 41*(1), 1–18.

Guralnick, M. (1989). Recent developments in early intervention efficacy research: Implications for family involvement in PL 99–457. *Topics in Early Childhood Special Education, 9*(3), 1–17.

Guralnick, M. (1990). Early childhood mainstreaming. *Topics in Early Childhood Special Education, 10*(2), 1–17.

Guralnick, M. (1991). The next decade of research on the effectiveness of early intervention. *Exceptional Children, 58*(2), 174–183.

Guralnick, M. (1993). Second generation research on the effectiveness of early intervention. *Early Education and Development, 4*(4), 366–378.

Guralnick, M. (Ed.). (1997). *The effectiveness of early intervention.* Baltimore: Brookes.

Guralnick, M. (2000). An agenda for change in early childhood education. *Journal of Early Intervention, 23*(4), 213–222.

Guralnick, M. (2001). *Early childhood inclusion: Focus on change.* Baltimore: Brookes.

Guralnick, M. (Ed.). (2005). *The developmental systems approach to early intervention.* Baltimore: Brookes.

Hack, M., Taylor, H., Drotar, D., Schluchter, M., Cartar, L., Andreias, L, Wilson-Costello, D., & Klein, N. (2005). Chronic conditions, functional limitations, and special health care needs of school-aged children born with extremely low birth weight in the 1990s. *Journal of the American Medical Association, 294*(3), 318–325.

Halverson, L. E. (1971). The significance of motor development. In G. Engstrom (Ed.), *The significance of the young child's motor development* (pp. 17–33). Washington, DC: National Association for the Education of Young Children.

Hanft, B., & Feinberg, E. (1997). Toward the development of a framework for determining the frequency and intensity of early intervention services. *Infants and Young Children, 10*(1), 27–37.

Hanft, B., & Royeen, C. B. (1991). Commentary. *Infants and Young Children, 4*(2), 8–11.

Hanft, B., & Striffler, N. (1995). Incorporating developmental therapy in early childhood programs: Challenges and promising practices. *Infants and Young Children, 8*(2), 37–47.

Hanft, B. E., & Pilkington, K. O. (2000). Therapy in natural environments: The means or end goal for early intervention? *Infants and Young Children, 12*(4), 1–13.

Hanline, M. F., & Knowlton, A. (1988). A collaborative model for providing support to parents during their child's transition from infant intervention to preschool special education public school programs. *Journal of the Division for Early Childhood, 12,* 116–125.

Harkin, T. (1989). Opening statement, April 2. In *S. Hrg. 101–287* (pp. 1–2). Washington, DC: U.S. Government Printing Office.

Harmon, A. (2005, November 20). The problem with an almost-perfect genetic world. *New York Times,* section 4, pp. 1, 14.

Harms, T., Clifford, R. M., & Bailey, D. B. (1986). *Special needs items for the ECERS.* Chapel Hill, NC: Frank Porter Graham Child Development Center.

Harms, T., Clifford, R. M., & Cryer, D. (1980). *Early Childhood Environment Rating Scale.* New York: Teachers College Press.

Harms, T., Cryer, D., & Clifford, R. M. (1989). *The Infant/Toddler Environment Rating Scale.* New York: Teachers College Press.

Harris & Associates. (1989). *The ICD survey III: A report card on special education.* New York: International Center for the Disabled.

Hart, B., & Risley, T. (1968). Establishing use of descriptive adjectives in the spontaneous speech of disadvantaged preschool children. *Journal of Applied Behavior Analysis, 8,* 411–420.

Hart, B., & Risley, T. (2003). The early catastrophe: The 30 million word gap by age 3. *American Educator*. Retrieved from www.aft.org

Hart, V. (1986). Testimony before the Subcommittee on Select Education, July 24. In *House report 99–120* (pp. 144–155). Washington, DC: U.S. Government Printing Office.

Hartshorne, T. S., & Boomer, L. W. (1993, Summer). Privacy of school records: What every special education teacher should know. *Teaching Exceptional Children, 25*(4), 32–35.

Hatton, D. D., Bailey, D. B., Roberts, J. P., Skinner, M., Mayhew, L., Clark, R. D., et al. (2000). Early intervention services for young boys with Fragile X syndrome. *Journal of Early Intervention, 23*(4), 235–251.

Head Start impact study: First year findings. (2005). Washington, DC: Head Start Bureau, U.S. Department of Health and Human Services. Retrieved from www.acf.dhhs.gov

Heaton, J., Noyes, J., Sloper, P., & Shah, R. (2005). Families' experiences of caring for technology-dependent children: A temporal perspective. *Health & Social Care in the Community*, *13*(5), 441–450.

Hebbeler, K., Spiker, D. Mallik, S, Scarborough, A., & Simeonsson, R. (2004). *Demographic characteristics of children and families entering early intervention.* NEILS Data Report #3. Menlo Park, CA: SRI International. Retrieved from www.sri.com/neils

Hebbeler, K., Wagner, M., Spiker, D., Scarborough, A., Simeonsson, R., & Collier, M. (2001). *A first look at the characteristics of children and families entering early intervention services.* Menlo Park, CA: SRI International.

Hebbeler, K. M., Smith, B. J., & Black, T. L. (1991). Federal early childhood special education policy: A model for the improvement of services for children with disabilities. *Exceptional Children, 58*(2), 104–112.

Hebbeler, K., Spiker, D. Mallik, S, Scarborough, A., & Simeonsson, R. (2004). *Demographic characteristics of children and families entering early intervention.* NEILS Data Report #3. Menlo Park, CA: SRI International. Retrieved from www.sri.com/neils.

Heckman, M., & Rike, C. (1994). Westwood Early Learning Center: A framework for integrating young children with disabilities. *Teaching Exceptional Children, 26*(2), 30–35.

Heflin, L., & Alaimo, D. (2007). *Students with autism spectrum disorders: Effective instructional practices*. Upper Saddle River, NJ: Merrill/Prentice Hall.

Hehir, T. (1993, November 19). *Letter to Peter J. Seiler*. Policy letter. Washington, DC: Office of Special Education Programs, U.S. Department of Education.

Hemmeter, M., Smith, B., Sandall, S., & Askew, L. (2005). *DEC recommended practices workbook*. Longmont, CO: Sopris West.

Heriza, C., & Sweeney, J. (1994). Pediatric physical therapy: Part I. Practice scope, scientific basis, and theoretical foundation. *Infants and Young Children, 7*(2), 20–32.

Heriza, C., & Sweeney, J. (1995). Pediatric physical therapy: Part II. Approaches to movement dysfunction. *Infants and Young Children, 8*(2), 1–14.

Hill, J. L., Brooks-Gunn, J., & Waldfogel, J. (2003). Sustained effects of high participation in an early intervention for low-birth-weight premature infants. *Developmental Psychology, 39*(4), 730–744.

Hobbs, N. (Ed.). (1975). *Issues in the classification of children.* San Francisco: Jossey-Bass.

Holahan, A., & Costenbader, V. (2000). A comparison of developmental gains for preschool children with disabilities in inclusive and self-contained classrooms. *Topics in Early Childhood Special Education, 20*(4), 224–235.

Horn, E., Lieber, J., Li, S., Sandall, S., & Schwartz, I. (2000). Supporting young children's IEP goals in inclusive settings through embedded learning opportunities. *Topics in Early Childhood Special Education, 20*(4), 208–223.

Howard, J., Sparkman, C., Cohen, H., Green, G., & Stanlislaw, H. (2005). A comparison of intensive behavior analytic and eclectic treatments for young children with autism. *Research in Developmental Disabilities, 26*(4), 359–383.

Hubbard, R., & Wald, E. (1993). *Exploding the gene myth.* New York: Beacon.

Humphreys, R. (1989). Patterns of pediatric brain injury. In M. Miner & K. Wagner (Eds.), *Neurotrauma 3: Treatment, rehabilitation and related issues* (pp. 115–126). Stoneham, MA: Butterworth.

Hutchins, J. (1994). A guide to purchasing a caption decoder-equipped TV set. *GA-SK, 12*(2), 1, 8. (Newsletter published by Telecommunications for the Deaf Inc., 8719 Colesville Road, Suite 300, Silver Spring, MD 20910)

Individuals with Disabilities Education Act, 20 U.S. C. 1400, as amended by PL 108–446, the IDEA Amendments of 2004.

Infant Health and Development Program (IHDP). (1990). Enhancing the outcomes of low-birth-weight, premature infants. *Journal of the American Medical Association, 263,* 3035–3042.

Innocenti, M. S., Hollinger, P. D., Escobar, C. M., & White, K. R. (1993). The cost-effectiveness of adding one type of parent involvement to an early intervention program. *Early Education and Development, 4*(4), 306–326.

Innocenti, M. S., & White, K. R. (1993). Are more intensive early intervention programs more effective? A review of the literature. *Exceptionality, 4*(1), 31–50.

Institute of Medicine. (2005). *Progress in preventing childhood obesity*. Washington, DC: National Academy Press. Retrieved from www.nap.edu/catalog/11461.html

Internet access points to ERIC. (1993, July). *The ERIC Networker, 4*(1).

Ireton, H., & Thwing, E. (1974a). *The Early Child Development Inventory.* Minneapolis: Behavior Science Systems.

Ireton, H., & Thwing, E. (1974b). *Manual for the Minnesota Child Development Inventory.* Minneapolis: Behavior Science Systems.

Ireton, H., & Thwing, E. (1974c). *Minnesota Infant Development Inventory.* Minneapolis: Behavior Science Systems.

Ireton, H., & Thwing, E. (1974d). *Minnesota Pre-Kindergarten Development Inventory.* Minneapolis: Behavior Science Systems.

Ireton, H., & Thwing, E. (1974e). *Minnesota Preschool Inventory.* Minneapolis: Behavior Science Systems.

Iversen, S., Ellertsen, B., Tylandsvik, A., & Nodland, M. (2005). Intervention for 6-year-old children with motor coordination difficulties: Parental perspectives at follow-up in middle childhood. *Advances in Physiotherapy*, *7*(2), 67–76.

Jenkins, J. R., Cole, K. N., Dale, P. D., & Mills, P. E. (1989). *A longitudinal comparison of two preschool instruction models.* Final report no. G008400646, for U.S. Department of Education. Seattle: University of Washington, Experimental Education Unit WJ-10.

Jenkins, J. R., & Sells, C. J. (1984). Physical and occupational therapy: Effects related to treatment, frequency, and motor delay. *Journal of Learning Disabilities, 17,* 89–95.

Jenkins, J. R., Sells, C. J., Brady, D., Down, J., Moore, B., Carman, P., & Holm, R. (1982). Effects of occupational and physical therapy in a school program. *Physical and Occupational Therapy in Pediatrics, 4,* 19–29.

Jenson, W. R., Sloane, H. N., & Young, K. R. (1988). *Applied behavioral analysis in education: A structured approach.* Englewood Cliffs, NJ: Prentice Hall.

Johns Hopkins Children's Center. (2006). *Press release: Popular ADHD drug safe and effective for preschoolers.* Baltimore. Retrieved from www.hopkinschildrens.org/pages/news/pressdetails.cfm?newsid=358

Johnson, L., Kilgo, J., Cook, M., Hammitte, D., Beauchamp, K., & Finn, D. (1992). The skills needed by early intervention administrators/supervisors: A study across six states. *Journal of Early Intervention, 16*(2), 136–145.

Johnson, S., Ring, W., Anderson, P., & Marlow, N. (2005). Randomised trial of parent support for families with preterm children: Outcomes at 5 years. *Archives of Disease in Childhood*, *90*(9), 909–915.

Johnson-Martin, N. M., Jens, K. G., & Attermeier, S. A. (1986). *The Carolina curriculum for handicapped infants and infants at risk.* Baltimore: Brookes.

Jones, L. E. (1988). The free limb scheme and the limb-deficient child in Australia. *Australian Paediatric Journal, 24*(5), 290–294.

Jung, L. (2005). Can we all fit? Squeezing in better support with fewer people. *Young Exceptional Children, 8*(4), 19–27.

Kantor, R., Elgas, P. M., & Fernie, D. E. (1993). Cultural knowledge and social competence within a preschool peer culture group. *Early Childhood Research Quarterly, 8,* 125–147.

Kaplan-Sanoff, M., Parker, S., & Zuckerman, B. (1991). Poverty and early childhood development: What do we know, and what should we do? *Infants and Young Children, 4*(1), 68–76.

Kauerz, K. (2005). *Full-day kindergarten: A study of state policies in the United States.* Denver: Education Commission of the States.

Kauffman, J. (1993). How we might achieve the radical reform of special education. *Exceptional Children, 60*(1), 6–16.

Kaufman, A., & Kaufman, N. (2004). *The Kaufman Assessment Battery for Children—Second Edition.* Circle Pines, MN: American Guidance Service.

Keen, D. (2005). The use of non-verbal repair strategies by children with autism. *Research in Developmental Disabilities*, *26*(3), 243–254.

Keeney, S. M. (1994). Going back to school. *REHAB Management, 7*(1), 24–28.

Keilty, B. (2001). Are natural environments worth it? Using a cost-benefit framework to evaluate early intervention policies in community programs. *Infants and Young Children, 13*(4), 32–43.

Kemp, C., & Carter, M. (2005). Identifying skills for promoting successful inclusion in kindergarten. *Journal of Intellectual & Developmental Disability, 30*(1), 31–44.

Kemp, D. T. (1978). Stimulated acoustic emissions from within the human auditory system. *Journal of the Acoustic Society of America, 64,* 1386–1391.

Kenny, T. J., & Culbertson, J. L. (1993). Developmental screening for preschoolers. In J. L. Culbertson & D. J. Willis (Eds.), *Testing young children: A reference guide for developmental, psychoeducational, and psychosocial assessment.* Austin, TX: PRO-ED.

Kerlinger, F. N. (1986). *Foundations of behavioral research* (3rd ed.). New York: Holt, Rinehart & Winston.

Kermoian, R., & Campos, J. J. (1988). Locomotor experience: A facilitator of spatial cognitive development. *Child Development, 59,* 908–917.

Kiernan, C., Reid, B., Jones, L., & Bowler, D. (1983). New sign imitation test. In C. Kiernan, M. Jones, B. Bowler, & D. Bowler (Eds.), *Other communication related assessments.* London: Thomas Coram Research Unit.

Kilgo, J. L., Johnson, L., LaMontagne, M., Stayton, V., Cook, M., & Cooper, C. (1999). Importance of practices: A national study of general and special early childhood educators. *Journal of Early Intervention, 22*(4), 294–305.

Kirp, D. L. (2005, July 31). All my children. *New York Times,* Education Life, pp. 20–22.

Klein, J. W. (1975). Mainstreaming the preschooler. *Young Children,* July, 317–327.

Klima, E., & Bellugi, U. (1979). *The signs of language.* Cambridge, MA: Harvard University Press.

Knitzer, J. (1988). Policy perspectives on the problem. In J. G. Looney (Ed.), *Chronic mental illness in children and adolescents* (pp. 53–71). Washington, DC: American Psychiatric Association Press.

Kohlberg, J., & Mayer, R. (1972). Development as the aim of education. *Harvard Educational Review, 42,* 449–496.

Kohlberg, L. (1984). *Essays on moral development.* San Francisco: Harper & Row.

Kohlberg, L., with DeVries, R., Fein, G., Hart, D., Mayer, R., Noam, G., Snarney, J., & Wertsch, J. (1987). *Child psychology and childhood education: A cognitive developmental view.* New York: Longman.

Kohler, F. W., Anthony, L. J., Steigher, S. A., & Hoyson, M. (2001). Teaching social interaction skills in the integrated preschool: An examination of naturalistic tactics. *Topics in Early Childhood Special Education, 21*(3), 93–103, 113.

Kolata, G. (1989, July 19). A new toll of alcohol abuse: The Indians' next generation. *New York Times,* pp. A1, D24.

Kolata, G. (1990, September 16). Why gene therapy is considered scary, but cell therapy isn't. *New York Times,* p. E5.

Kolata, G. (1992a, September 24). Genetic defects detected in embryos just days old. *New York Times,* pp. A1, B10.

Kolata, G. (1992b, January 16). Study reports dyslexia is not unalterable, as experts have been assuming. *New York Times,* p. A18.

Kontos, S., & File, N. (1992). Conditions of employment, job satisfaction, and job commitment among early intervention personnel. *Journal of Early Intervention, 16,* 155–165.

Kozloff, M. A., Helm, D. T., Cutler, B. C., Douglas-Steele, D., & Scampini, L. (1988). Training programs for families of children with autism or other handicaps.

In R. DeV. Peters & R. J. McMahon (Eds.), *Social learning and systems approach to marriage and the family* (pp. 217–250). New York: Brunner/Mazel.

Kozma, I., & Balogh, E. (1995). A brief introduction to conductive education and its application at an early age. *Infants and Young Children, 8*(1), 68–74.

Kreutz, D. (1993). Seating and positioning for the newly injured. *REHAB Management, 6*(1), 67–75.

Kübler-Ross, E. (1969). *On death and dying.* New York: Macmillan.

Kuder, S. J. (1990). Effectiveness of the DISTAR reading program for children with learning disabilities. *Journal of Learning Disabilities, 23*(1), 69–71.

Kyes, K. (1994). Funding for assistive technologies: A conversation with Allan I. Bergman. *REHAB Management,* June/July, 26, 28, 30–31.

LaBlance, G., Steckol, K., & Smith, V. (1994). Stuttering: The role of the classroom teacher. *Teaching Exceptional Children, 26*(2), 10–12.

Ladd, G.W., & Mize, J. (1983). A cognitive-social learning model of social-skill training. *Psychological Review, 90,* 127–157.

Lambert, N., Nihira, K., & Leland, H. (2003). *AAMR Adaptive Behavior Scales—School*. Austin, TX: PRO-ED.

Lange, R. (2004). *The truth about grade level retention and social promotion*. Paper presented at the Truth in Testing Conference, Orlando, FL.

Lantos, J., & Kohrman, A. (1992). Ethical aspects of home care. *Pediatrics, 89,* 920–924.

LaPlante, M., Hendershot, G., and Moss, A. (1992, September 16). Assistive technology devices and home accessibility features: Prevalence, payment, need, and trends. *Advance Data from Vital and Health Statistics, 217*. Hyattsville: National Center for Health Statistics.

LaVor, M., & Harvey, J. (1976). Head Start, Economic Opportunity, Community Partnership Act of 1974. *Exceptional Children, 43,* 227–230.

Law, M., Cadman, D., Rosenbaum, P., Walter, S., Russell, D., & DeMateo, C. (1991). Neurodevelopmental and upper-extremity inhibitive casting for children with cerebral palsy. *Developmental Medicine and Child Neurology, 33,* 379–387.

Law, M., Teplicky, R., King, S., King, G., Kertoy, M., Moning, T., Rosenbaum, P., & Burke-Gaffney, J. (2005). Family-centred service: Moving ideas into practice. *Child: Care, Health & Development*, *31*(6), 633–642.

Lee, V., Burkam, D., Ready, D, Honigman, J., & Meisels, J. (2006). Full-day versus half-day kindergarten: in which program do children learn more? *American Journal of Education, 112*(2), 163–208.

Lerner, J., Lowenthal, B., & Lerner, S. (1995). *Attention deficit disorders: Assessment and teaching.* Pacific Grove, CA: Brooks/Cole.

Levin, J., Perez, M., Lam, I., Chambers, J., & Hebbeler, K. (2004). *Expenditure study*. NEILS Data Report #4. Menlo Park, CA: SRI International. Retrieved from www.sri.com/neils

Levine, M. (2002). *A mind at a time.* New York: Simon & Schuster.

Levine, M. N. (1986). Psychoeducational evaluation of children and adolescents with cerebral palsy. In P. J. Lazarus & S. S. Strichart (Eds.), *Psychoeducational evaluation of children and adolescents with low-incidence handicaps* (pp. 267–284). Orlando, FL: Grune & Stratton.

Linder, T. W. (1993). *Transdisciplinary play-based assessment.* Baltimore: Brookes.

Livingstone, M. S., Rosen, G. D., Drislane, F. W., & Galaburda, A. M. (1991). Physiological and anatomical evidence for a magnocellular defect in developmental dyslexia. *Proceedings of the National Academy of Sciences, 88,* 7943–7947.

Lonigan, C. J., Anthony, J. L., Bloomfield, B. G., Dyer, S. M., & Samwel, C. S. (1999). Effects of two shared-reading interventions on emergent literacy skills of at-risk preschoolers. *Journal of Early Intervention, 22*(4), 306–322.

Lovaas, O. I. (1987). Behavioral treatment and normal educational and intellectual functioning in young autistic children. *Journal of Consulting and Clinical Psychology, 55*(1), 3–9.

Lovaas, O. I. (1989). Interview. *Focus on Autistic Behavior, 4*(4), 1–11.

Lovaas, O. I., Smith, T., & McEachin, J. (1989). Clarifying comments on the young autism study: Reply to Schopler, Short, and Mesibov. *Journal of Consulting and Clinical Psychology, 57*(1), 165–167.

Lozes, M. H. (1988). Bladder and bowel management for children with myelomeningocele. *Infants and Young Children, 1,* 52–62.

Luckasson, R., Borthwick-Duffy, S., Buntinx, W., Coulter, D., Craig, E. M., Reeve, A., et al. (2002). *Mental retardation: Definitions, classification, and systems of support* (10th ed.). Washington, DC: American Association on Mental Retardation.

Luckasson, R., & Reeve, A. (2001). Naming, defining, and classifying in mental retardation. *Mental Retardation, 39*(1), 47–52.

Ludlow, B. L. (1994). Using distance education to prepare early intervention personnel. *Infants and Young Children, 7*(1), 51–59.

Lyon, G. R. (2002, June 6). *Learning disabilities and early intervention strategies: How to reform the special education referral and identification process.* Testimony before the Subcommittee on Education Reform, U.S. House of Representatives. (For copies, contact the Committee on Education and the Workforce, Ford House Office Building, Washington, DC 20515.)

Lyon, G. R., Fletecher, J. M., Shaywitz, S. E., Shaywitz, B. A., Torgesen, J. K., Wood, F. B., et al. (2001). Rethinking learning disabilities. In C. E. Finn, A. J. Rotherham, & C. R. Hokanson (Eds.), *Rethinking special education for a new century* (Chap. 12). Washington, DC: Thomas B. Fordham Foundation and Progressive Policy Institute.

Machado, J. (2007). *Early childhood experiences in language arts: Early literacy* (8th ed.). Clifton Park, NY: Thomson Delmar Learning.

Macy, M., Bricker, D., & Squires, J. (2005). Validity and reliability of a curriculum-based assessment approach to determine eligibility for Part C services. *Journal of Early Intervention, 28*(1), 1–16.

Madden, J. (1993). Psychological adjustment following SCI. *REHAB Management, 6*(2), 67–70.

Mahoney, G., & O'Sullivan, P. (1990). Early intervention practices with families of children with handicaps. *Mental Retardation, 28,* 169–176.

Mahoney, G., O'Sullivan, P., & Fors, S. (1989). The family practices of service providers for young handicapped children. *Infant Mental Health Journal, 10,* 75–83.

Malina, R. (1982). Motor development in the early years. In S. Moore & K. Cooper (Eds.), *The young child: reviews of research* (Vol. 3, pp. 211–229). Washington, DC: National Association for the Education of Young Children.

Malone, F., Canick, J., Ball, R., Sheridan, R., Liu, V., Anupindi, S., Bradley, T., Logan, A., & Kimoff, R. (2005). Continuing medical education. *New England Journal of Medicine, 353*(19), 2097–2100.

Manegold, C. S. (1994, January 26). Special pupils, regular classes, thorny issues. *New York Times,* p. A19.

Marschark, M., Lang, H., & Albertini, J. (2002). *Educating deaf students: From research to practice*. New York: Oxford University Press.

Marston, D., & Deno, S. (1986). *Standard reading passages: Measures for screening and progress monitoring*. Minneapolis: Children Educational Service.

Martin, A. (1988). Screening, early intervention, and remediation: Obscuring children's potential. *Harvard Educational Review, 58*(4), 488–502.

Martin, S. L., Ramey, C. T., & Ramey, S. (1990). The prevention of intellectual impairment in children of impoverished families: Findings of a randomized trial of educational day care. *American Journal of Public Health, 80*(7), 844–847.

Maslow, A. H. (1954). *Motivation and personality.* New York: Harper & Row.

Masse, L., & Barnett, W. (2002). *A cost-benefit analysis of the abecedarian early childhood intervention.* Washington, DC: U.S. Department of Education, National Institute of Early Education Research.

Massoulos, C. G. (1988). *Acceptance and rejection of friendships in peer culture within an early childhood setting: An observational study approach.* Unpublished doctoral dissertation, Ohio State University, Columbus.

McCall, R. (1976). Toward an epigigenetic conception of mental development in the first three years of life. In M. Lewis (Ed.), *Origins of intelligence: Infancy and early childhood.* New York: Plenum.

McCarthy, D. (1972). *McCarthy Scales of Children's Abilities.* San Antonio, TX: Psychological Corporation.

McCormick, J. (1993, January). The enabled computer: Computing for the physically challenged. *Computer Monthly,* 202–203.

McCormick, M., et al. (2006). Early intervention in low birth weight premature infants: Results at 18 years of age for the Infant Health and Development Program. *Pediatrics, 117*(3), 771–780.

McDermott, R. P., & Church, J. (1976). Making sense and feeling good: The ethnography of communication and identity work. *Communication, 2,* 121–142.

McDonald, M. E. (2004). Effects of a treatment package on the creative play behavior of children with autism. *Dissertation Abstracts International, 65,* 03B.

McGinnis, E., & Goldstein, A. P. (2000). *Skillstreaming in early childhood: Teaching prosocial skills to the preschool and kindergarten child.* Champaign, IL: Research Press.

McLean, M., & McCormick, K. (1993). Assessment and evaluation in early intervention. In W. Brown, S. K. Thurman, & L. F. Pearl (Eds.), *Family-centered early intervention with infants and toddlers: Innovative cross-disciplinary approaches.* Baltimore: Brookes.

McLean, M., & Odom, S. (1993). Practices for young children with and without disabilities: A comparison of DEC and NAEYC identified practices. *Topics in Early Childhood Special Education, 13*(3), 274–292.

McLean, M., Wolery, M., & Bailey, D. (2003). *Assessing infants and toddlers with special needs* (3rd ed.). Upper Saddle River, NJ: Merrill/Prentice Hall.

McLoughlin, J. A., & Lewis, R. B. (2001). *Assessing students with special needs* (5th ed.). Upper Saddle River, NJ: Merrill/Prentice Hall.

McNeil, D. (1992). *Hand and mind.* Chicago: University of Chicago Press.

McNeil, J. (1997). *Americans with disabilities: 1994–1995.* U.S. Bureau of the Census, Current Population Reports, P70-61. Washington, DC: U.S. Department of Commerce.

McWilliam, P. J., & Bailey, D. B. (Eds.). (1993). *Working together with children and families: Case studies in early intervention.* Baltimore: Brookes.

Meyer, D., & Vadasy, P. (1996). *Living with a brother or sister with special needs: A book for sibs* (2nd ed.). Seattle: University of Washington Press.

Miller, H. (1997). Prenatal cocaine exposure and mother-infant interaction: Implications for occupational therapy intervention. *American Journal of Occupational Therapy, 51*(2), 119–131.

Miller, P. S. (2006). Toward truly informed decisions about appearance-normalizing surgeries. In E. Parens (Ed.), *Surgically shaping children* (pp. 211–226). Baltimore: Johns Hopkins University Press.

Miller, W. (1989, July). *Obstetrical issues.* Paper presented at conference on "Drugs, Alcohol, Pregnancy and Parenting: An Intervention Model," Spokane, WA.

Minke, K. M., & Scott, M. M. (1993). The development of individualized family service plans: Roles for parents and staff. *Journal of Special Education, 27*(1), 82–106.

Mooney, P., Epstein, M., Ryser, G., & Pierce, C. (2005). Reliability and validity of the parent form of the Behavioral and Emotional Rating Scale—Second edition. *Children & Schools, 27,* 147–156.

Moore, M., Strang, E., Schwartz, M., & Braddock, M. (1988). *Patterns in special education service delivery and cost.* Washington, DC: Decision Resources Corporation.

Moores, D. F. (1982). *Educating the deaf: Psychology, principles, and practices* (2nd ed.). Dallas, TX: Houghton Mifflin.

Moores, D. F. (1991). *Dissemination of a model to create least restrictive environments for deaf students.* Final report, Grant G008720128, Project 84133. Washington, DC: Gallaudet Research Institute, Gallaudet University.

Moores, D. F. (1993). Total inclusion/zero reject models in general education: Implications for deaf children. *American Annals of the Deaf, 138*(3), 251.

Moores, D. F., & Martin, D. S. (Eds.). (2006). *Deaf learners: developments in curriculum and instruction.* Washington, DC: Gallaudet University Press.

Msall, M., DiGaudio, K., & Malone, A. (1991). Health, developmental, and psychosocial aspects of Down syndrome. *Infants and Young Children, 4*(1), 35–43.

Mueller, F. (1992). Telecommunications. *Teaching Exceptional Children, 25*(1), 8–11.

Murray, A. D. (1992). Early intervention program evaluation: Numbers or narratives? *Infants and Young Children, 4*(4), 77–88.

Musick, J. S. (1994). Grandmothers and grandmothers-to-be: Effects on adolescent mothers and adolescent mothering. *Infants and Young Children, 6*(3), 1–9.

Najman, J., Hallam, D., Bor, W., O'Callaghan, M., Williams, G., & Shuttlewood, G. (2005). Predictors of depression in very young children. *Social Psychiatry & Psychiatric Epidemiology, 40*(5), 367–374.

Nancollis, A., Lawrie, B., & Dodd, B. (2005). Phonological awareness intervention and the acquisition of literacy skills in children from deprived social backgrounds. *Language, Speech, and Hearing Services in Schools, 36,* 325–335.

National Center for Educational Statistics. (2005). *Digest of education statistics, 2004.* Retrieved from www.nces.ed.gov

National Clearinghouse for Professions in Special Education. (2003). *Enlarging the pool: How higher education partnerships are recruiting and supporting future special educators from underrepresented groups*. Arlington, VA: Author. Retrieved from www.special-ed-careers.org

National Council on Disability. (1993). *Study on the financing of assistive technology devices and services for individuals with disabilities.* Washington, DC: Author.

National Education Association. (2003). *Status of the American public school teacher, 2000–2001*. Washington, DC: Author (1201 16th Street NW, Washington, DC 20036; www.nea.org).

National Joint Committee on Learning Disabilities. (1988). Letter to NJCLD member organizations. (For copies, contact Learning Disabilities Association of America, 4156 Library Road, Pittsburgh, PA 15234.)

National Reading Panel. (2000). *Report of the national reading panel: Teaching children to read*. Retrieved from www.nichd.nih.gov

Nazzo, J., & Sabo, D. (1991, November). *Screening in audiology: Principles and practices*. Paper presented at the ASHA annual convention, Nashville, TN.

Neisworth, J. T. (1993). Assessment. In Division for Early Childhood (2004), *DEC recommended practices: A comprehensive guide* (pp. 11–16). Denver: Sopris West.

Neuman, S. B., Copple, C., & Bredekamp, S. (2000). *Learning to read and write: Developmentally appropriate practices for young children.* Washington, DC: National Association for the Education of Young Children.

New York State Department of Health. (1999a). *New York State Department of Health clinical practice guideline: The guideline technical report. Autism/pervasive developmental disorders, assessment, and intervention for young children (age 0–3 years).* Publication No. 4217. Albany: Author.

New York State Department of Health. (1999b). *New York State Department of Health clinical practice guideline: The guideline technical report. Communication disorders, assessment, and intervention for young children (age 0–3 years).* (Publication No. 4220). Albany: Author.

Newborg, J., Stock, J. R., Wnek, L., Guidubaldi, J., & Svinicki, J. (1984). *Battelle Developmental Inventory.* Allen, TX: DLM Teaching Resources.

Nickel, R. E. (1992). Disorders of brain development. *Infants and Young Children, 5*(1), 1–11.

Nolan, K., Young, E., Hebert, E., & Wilding, G. (2005). Service coordination for children with complex healthcare needs in an early intervention program. *Infants and Young Children, 18*(2), 161–170.

Noonan, M. J., & Kilgo, J. L. (1987). Transition services for early age individuals with severe mental retardation. In R. N. Ianacone & R. A. Stodden (Eds.), *Transition issues and directions* (pp. 25–37). Reston, VA: Council for Exceptional Children.

O'Connor, R., Harty, K., & Fulmer, D. (2005). Tiers of intervention in kindergarten through third grade. *Journal of Learning Disabilities*, *38*(6), 532–538.

OCR staff memorandum. (1990). *Education for the handicapped law report, 16,* 712. (Now *Individuals with Disabilities Education Law Report.*)

Oddone, A. (1993, Fall). Inclusive classroom applications. *Teaching Exceptional Children,* 74–75.

Odom, S. L., Hanson, M. J., Lieber, J., Marquart, J., Sandall, S., Wolery, R., et al. (2001). The costs of preschool inclusion. *Topics in Early Childhood Special Education, 21*(1), 46–55.

Odom, S. L., McConnell, S. R., Ostrosky, M., Peterson, C., Skellenger, A., Spicuzza, R., et al. (2000). *Play time, social time: Organizing your classroom to build interaction skills.* Minneapolis: University of Minnesota Institute on Community Integration.

Odom, S. L., & McEvoy, M. A. (1990). Mainstreaming at the preschool level: Potential barriers and tasks for the fields. *Topics in Early Childhood Special Education, 10*(2), 48–61.

Olson, H. C. (1994). The effects of prenatal alcohol exposure on child development. *Infants and Young Children, 6*(3), 10–25.

Olson, M. (1987). Early intervention for children with visual impairments. In M. J. Guralnick & F. C. Bennett (Eds.), *The effectiveness of early intervention for at-risk and handicapped children* (pp. 318–321). Orlando, FL: Academic Press.

Oppenheim, J., & McGregor, T. (2002). *The economics of education: Public benefits of high-quality preschool education for low-income children.* Report prepared for The Entergy Corporation (www.democracyandregulation.com).

Ostrosky, M., & Sandall, S. (Eds.). (2001). *Teaching strategies: What to do to support young children's development.* Monograph Series No. 3. Longmont, CO: Sopris West.

Otten, A. (1989, March 8). Parental agony. *Wall Street Journal,* pp. A1, A8.

Overton, S. (2005). *Collaborating with families: A case study approach.* Upper Saddle River, NJ: Merrill/Prentice Hall.

Overton, T. (2006). *Assessing learners with special needs* (5th ed.). Upper Saddle River, NJ: Merrill/Prentice Hall.

Paasche, C., Gorrill, L., & Strom, B. (2003). *Children with special needs in early childhood settings.* Clifton Park, NY: Thomson Delmar Learning.

Page, T. J., & Chew, M. B. (1993). Rethinking TBI. *REHAB Management, 6*(2), 53–64.

Parens, E. (Ed.). (2006). *Surgically shaping children.* Baltimore: Johns Hopkins University Press.

Parens, E., & Asch, A. (Eds.). (2000). *Prenatal testing and disability rights.* Washington, DC: Georgetown University Press.

Parish, S., Cloud, J., Huh, J., & Henning, A. (2005). Child care, disability, and family structure: use and quality in a population-based sample of low-income preschool children. *Children & Youth Services Review, 27*(8), 905–919.

Parrette, H. P., Hendricks, M. D., & Rock, S. L. (1991). Efficacy of therapeutic intervention intensity with infants and young children with cerebral palsy. *Infants and Young Children, 4*(2), 1–19.

Pedhazur, E. J., & Schmelkin, L. P. (1991). *Measurement, design, and analysis: An integrated approach.* Hillsdale, NJ: Erlbaum.

Pennington, F. B., Gilger, J. W., Olson, R. K., & DeFries, J. C. (1992). The external validity of age- versus IQ-discrepancy definitions of reading disability: Lessons from a twin study. *Journal of Learning Disabilities, 25*(9), 562–565.

Perelman, L. (1992). *School's out: Hyperlearning, the new technology, and the end of education.* New York: Morrow.

Perry, D. (1993). *Projecting the costs of early intervention services: Four states' experiences.* Chapel Hill, NC: NEC*TAS.

Piaget, J. (1962). *Play, dreams and imitation in childhood.* New York: Norton.

Piaget, J., & Inhelder, B. (1969). *The psychology of the child.* New York: Basic Books.

Pierangelo, R., & Giuliani, G. (2006a). *Assessment in special education* (2nd ed.). Boston: Allyn & Bacon.

Pierangelo, R., & Giuliani, G. (2006b). *Learning disabilities.* Boston: Pearson.

Polloway, E. A., & Polloway, C. H. (1981). Survival words for disabled readers. *Academic Therapy, 16*(4), 443–448.

Premack, D. (1959). Toward empirical behavior laws. *Psychological Review, 66*(4), 219–233.

Prizant, B., Wetherby, A., Rubin, E., & Laurent, A. (2003). The SCERTS Model. *Infants & Young Children, 16*(4), 296–316.

Rabin, R. (1989). Warnings unheeded: A history of child lead poisoning. *American Journal of Public Health, 79*(12), 1668–1774.

Rall, D. P. (1994, January 24). Test kids' blood for lead. *New York Times,* p. A15.

Ramey, C. T., Bryant, D. M., Wasik, B. H., Sparling, J. J., Fendt, K. H., & LaVange, L. M. (1992). Infant health and development program for low birth weight, premature infants: Program elements, family participation, and child intelligence. *Pediatrics, 3,* 454–465.

Ramey, C. T., & Ramey, S. L. (1992). Effective early intervention. *Mental Retardation, 30*(6), 337–345.

Rapport, M. (1996). Legal guidelines for the delivery of special health care services in schools. *Exceptional Children, 62*(6), 537–549.

Rathbun, A., and West, J. (2004). *From Kindergarten through third grade: Children's beginning school experiences* (NCES 2004-007). U.S. Department of Education, National Center for Education Statistics. Washington, DC: U.S. Government Printing Office.

Rathlev, M. (1994). Universal precautions in early intervention and child care. *Infants and Young Children, 6*(3), 54–64.

Ray, J. (1974). *Ethological studies of behavior in delayed and nondelayed toddlers.* Paper presented at the annual meeting of the American Association on Mental Deficiency, Toronto.

Repetto, J., & Correa, V. (1996). Expanding views on transition. *Exceptional Children, 62*(6), 551–563.

Reynolds, A. (2005). Confirmatory program evaluation: Applications to early childhood interventions. *Teachers College Record, 107*(10), 2401–2425.

Reynolds, A. J., & Temple, J. A. (2005). Priorities for a new century of early childhood programs. *Infants & Young Children, 18*(2), 104–118.

Reynolds, A. J., Temple, J. A., Robertson, D. L., & Mann, E. A. (2002). Age 21 cost-benefit analysis of Title I Chicago Child-Parent Centers. *Educational Evaluation and Policy Analysis, 24*(4), 267–303.

Reynolds, A. J., Temple, J. A., Robertson, D. L., & Mann, E. A. (2001). Long-term effects of an early childhood intervention on educational achievement and juvenile arrest: A 15-year follow-up of low-income children in public schools. *Journal of the American Medical Association, 285*(18), 2339–2346.

Richard, A. (2005). Heeding the call. *Education Week, 25*(7), 23–26.

Roizen, N. (1997). New advancements in medical treatment of young children with Down syndrome: Implications for early intervention. *Infants and Young Children, 9*(4), 36–42.

Romski, M., & Sevcik, R. (2005). Augmentative communication and early intervention: Myths and realities. *Infants and Young Children, 18*(3), 174–185.

Rosen, S., & Granger, M. (1992). Early interventions and school programs. In A. Crocker, H. Cohen, & T. Kastner (Eds.), *HIV infection and developmental disabilities.* Baltimore: Brookes.

Rosenkoetter, S. E. (1992). Guidelines from recent legislation to structure transition planning. *Infants and Young Children, 5*(1), 21–27.

Rosetti, L. (1986a). *High-risk infants: Identification, assessment and intervention.* Boston: Little, Brown.

Rosetti, L. (1986b). Infant assessment. In L. Rosetti (Ed.), *High-risk infants: Identification, assessment and intervention* (pp. 101–138). Boston: College-Hill.

Rosetti, L. (1990a). *Infant-toddler assessment: An interdisciplinary approach.* Baltimore: University Park Press.

Rosetti, L. (1990b). *Rosetti Infant-Toddler Language Scale.* (1990). East Moline, IL: LinguiSystems.

Ross, D. (1985, April). *Social competence in kindergarten: Applications of symbolic interaction theory.* Paper presented at the annual meeting of the American Educational Research Association, Chicago.

Roush, J., Harrison, M., Palsha, S., & Davidson, D. (1992). A national survey of educational preparation programs for early intervention specialists. *American Annals of the Deaf, 137*(5), 425–430.

Royeen, C., DeGangi, G., & Poisson, S. (1992). Development of the individualized family service plan anchor guide. *Infants and Young Children, 5*(2), 57–64.

Sack, K. (1994, June 26). Battle lines drawn over newborn H. I. V. disclosure. *New York Times,* pp. 23, 29.

Salisbury, C., & Vincent, L. J. (1990). Criterion of the next environment and best practices: Mainstreaming and integration 10 years later. *Topics in Early Childhood Special Education, 10*(2), 78–89.

Sandall, S., McLean, M. E., & Smith, B. J. (2000). *DEC recommended practices in early intervention/early childhood special education.* Denver: Division for Early Childhood of the Council for Exceptional Children. (The publication may be ordered at www.sopriswest.com.)

Sandall, S., Schwartz, I., & Joseph, G. (2001). A building blocks model for effective instruction in inclusive early childhood settings. *Young Exceptional Children, 4*(3), 3–9.

Sawyer, R. J., & Zantal-Wiener, K. (1993). Emerging trends in technology for students with disabilities. *Teaching Exceptional Children, 26*(1), 70–76.

Schiller, P. (2003). *The complete resource book for toddlers and twos.* Beltsville, MD: Gryphon House.

Schneider, J., & Chasnoff, I. (1987). Cocaine abuse during pregnancy: Its effects on infant motor development—A clinical perspective. *Topics in Acute Care and Trauma Rehabilitation, 2,* 59–69.

Scholl, G. (Ed.). (1986). *Foundations of education for blind and visually handicapped children and youth: Theory and practice.* New York: American Foundation for the Blind.

Schopler, E., Short, A., & Mesibov, G. (1989). Relation of behavioral treatment to "normal functioning": Comment on Lovaas. *Journal of Consulting and Clinical Psychology, 57*(1), 162–164.

Schrag, J. A. (1990, May 8). Memorandum to state school officers. Unpublished memorandum. Washington, DC: U.S. Department of Education, Office of Special Education Programs.

Schriebman, L. (1988). Parent training as a means of facilitating generalization of autistic children. In R. H. Horner, S. Dunlap, & R. I. Koegel (Eds.), *Generalization and maintenance: Life-style changes in applied settings* (pp. 21–40). Baltimore: Brookes.

Schumacher, R., Ewen, D., Hart, K., & Lombardi, J. (2005). *All together now: State experiences in using community-based child care to provide pre-kindergarten.* Washington, DC: Center for Law and Social Policy (www.clasp.org).

Schumacker, H., Klippel, J., & Robinson, D. (Eds.). (1988). *Primer on the Rheumatic diseases* (9th ed.). Atlanta: Arthritis Foundation.

Schweinhart, L. (2004). *The High/Scope Perry Preschool Study through age 40: Summary, conclusions, and frequently asked questions.* Ypsilanti, MI: High/Scope Press. Retrieved from www.highscope.org

Sciarra, D. (2004). *School counseling: Foundations and contemporary issues.* Pacific Grove, CA: Brooks/Cole.

Setoguchi, Y., & Rosenfelder, R. (1982). *The limb deficient child.* Springfield, IL: Thomas.

Sexton, D., Snyder, P., Wolfe, B., Lobman, M., Stricklin, S., & Akers, P. (1996). Early intervention inservice training strategies: Perceptions and suggestions from the field. *Exceptional Children, 62*(6), 485–495.

Shaer, C. (1997). The infant and young child with spina bifida: Major medical concerns. *Infants and Young Children, 9*(3), 13–25.

Sharav, T., & Schlomo, L. (1986). Stimulation of infants with Down syndrome: Long-term effects. *Mental Retardation, 24,* 81–86.

Shaywitz, S. E., Escobar, M. D., Shaywitz, B. A., Fletcher, J. M., & Makuch, R. (1992). Evidence that dyslexia may represent the lower tail of a normal distribution of reading ability. *New England Journal of Medicine, 326*(3), 145–150.

Shonkoff, J. P., & Hauser-Cram, P. (1987). Early intervention for disabled infants and their families: A quantitative analysis. *Pediatrics, 80*(5), 650–658.

Shonkoff, J., & Meisels, S. (1991). Defining eligibility for services under PL 99–457. *Journal of Early Intervention, 15*(1), 21–25.

Sigman, M., & McGovern, C. (2005). Improvement in cognitive and language skills from preschool to adolescence in autism. *Journal of Autism and Developmental Disorders, 35*(1), 15–23.

Silverstein, R. (1989). A window of opportunity: PL 99–457. In *The intent and spirit of P. L. 99–457: A sourcebook* (pp. A1–A7). Washington, DC: National Center for Clinical Infant Programs.

Simeonsson, R. J., Huntington, G. S., Short, R. J., & Ware, W. (1982). The Carolina record of individual behavior: Characteristics of handicapped children. *Topics in Early Childhood, 2*(2), 43–55.

Skinner, B. F. (1953). *Science and human behavior.* New York: Macmillan.

Skuse, D., Mandy, W., & Scourfield, J. (2005). Measuring autistic traits: heritability, reliability and validity of the Social and Communication Disorders Checklist. *British Journal of Psychiatry, 187,* 568–572.

Slaughter, D. (1983). Early intervention and its effects on maternal and child development. *Monographs of the Society for Research in Child Development, 48,* serial 202.

Smith, A. (1986). Testimony before the Subcommittee on Select Education, July 23. In *House report 99–120* (pp. 123–135). Washington, DC: U.S. Government Printing Office.

Smith, R. (1994). No more child's play. *REHAB Management, 7*(1), 40, 42.

Smith. R., Bale, J., & White, K. (2005). Sensorineural hearing loss in children. *Lancet, 365*, 879–890.

Smith, S. (1991). *Succeeding against the odds: Strategies and insights from the learning disabled.* Rockville, MD: Woodbine House.

Snow, R. E. (1989). Aptitude-treatment interaction as a framework for research on individual differences in learning. In P. L. Ackerman, R. J. Sternberg, & R. Glaser (Eds.), *Learning and individual differences* (pp. 13–59). New York: Freeman.

Socolich, M., et al. (2005 September 22). Evolutionary information for specifying a protein fold. *Nature, 437,* 512–518.

Sontag, J. C., & Schacht, R. (1994). An ethnic comparison of parent participation and information needs in early intervention. *Exceptional Children, 60*(5), 422–433.

Sparling, J. J., & Lewis, I. S. (1979). *Learning games for the first three years: A guide to parent-child play.* New York: Walker.

Sparling, J. J., & Lewis, I. S. (1985). *Partners for learning.* Lewisville, NC: Kaplan.

Sparling, J. J., Lewis, I. S., & Neuwirth, S. (1993). *Early partners.* Lewisville, NC: Kaplan.

Sparrow, S., Balla, D., & Cichetti, D. V. (1984). *Vineland Adaptive Behavior Scales—Expanded form.* Circle Pines, MN: American Guidance Service.

Spina Bifida Association of America. (1997). *Facts about spina bifida.* Retrieved from www.sbaa.org

Stahmer, A., & Carter, C. (2005). An empirical examination of toddler development in inclusive childcare. *Early Child Development & Care, 175*(4), 321–333.

Stahmer, A., & Ingersoll, B. (2004). Inclusive programming for toddlers with autism spectrum disorders: Outcomes from the Children's Toddler School. *Journal of Positive Behavior Interventions, 6*(2), 67–82.

Stoneman, Z. (2005). Siblings of children with disabilities: Research themes. *Mental Retardation, 43*(5), 339–350.

Stoner, J., Bock, S., Thompson, J., Angell, M., Heyl, B., & Crowley, E. (2005). Welcome to our world: Parent perceptions of interactions between parents of young children with ASD and education professionals. *Focus on Autism and Other Developmental Disabilities, 20*(1), 39–50.

Strain, P. S. (1990). LRE for preschool children with handicaps: What we know, what we should be doing. *Journal of Early Intervention, 14,* 291–296.

Strain, P. S., & Hoyson, M. (2000). The need for longitudinal, intensive social skill intervention: LEAP follow-up outcomes for children with autism. *Topics in Early Childhood Special Education, 20*(2), 116–122.

Strain, P. S., Lambert, D. L., Kerr, M. M., Stagg, V., & Lenker, D. (1983). Naturalistic assessment of children's compliance to teacher's requests and consequences for compliance. *Journal of Applied Behavior Analysis, 16,* 2143–2149.

Stuckless, E. R. (1992). Reflections on bilingual, bicultural education for deaf children. *American Annals of the Deaf, 136*(3), 270–272.

Summers, J., Hoffman, L., Marquis, J., Turnbull, A., Poston, D., & Nelson, L. (2005). Measuring the quality of family-professional partnerships in special education services. *Exceptional Children, 72*(1), 65–81.

Summers, J., Poston, D., Turnbull, A., Marquis, J., Hoffman, L., Mannan, H., & Wang, M. (2005). Conceptualizing and measuring family quality of life. *Journal of Intellectual Disability Research, 49*(10), 777–783.

Talan, J. (1990, January 11). How lead destroys lives. *Newsday,* p. 15.

Tallal, P., Stark, R. E., & Mellits, D. E. (1985). Identification of language-impaired children on the basis of rapid perception and production skills. *Brain and Language, 25,* 314–322.

Tarr, J. E., & Barnett, W. S. (2001). A cost analysis of Part C early intervention services in New Jersey. *Journal of Early Intervention, 24*(1), 45–54.

Teller, D. Y., McDonald, M., Preston, K., Sebris, S., & Dobson, V. (1987). Assessment of visual acuity in infants and children: The acuity card procedure. *Developmental Medicine and Child Neurology, 28,* 779–789.

Teplin, S. (1995). Visual impairment in infants and young children. *Infants and Young Children, 8*(1), 18–51.

Thomaidis, L., Kaderoglou, E., Stefou, M., Damianou, S. & Bakoula, C. (2000). Does early intervention work? A controlled trial. *Infants and Young Children, 12*(3), 17–22.

Thomas, J., & Tidmarsh, L. (1997). Hyperactive and disruptive behaviors in very young children: Diagnosis and intervention. *Infants and Young Children, 9*(3), 46–55.

Thorndike, R. L., Hagen, E. P., & Sattler, J. M. (1986). *Stanford-Binet Intelligence Scale: Fourth edition.* Chicago: Riverside.

Timothy W. v. Rochester (NH) School District. (1989). 875 F. 2d 954 (1st Circuit), *cert. denied* 110 S. Ct. 519.

Trohanis, P. (1989). Testimony before the Subcommittee on the Handicapped. In *S. Hrg. 101–287* (pp. 48–73). Washington, DC: U.S. Government Printing Office.

Tumulty, K. (2006). The politics of fat. *Time,* March 27, p. 41.

Turnbull, H. R., et al. (2000). *Free appropriate public education: Law and interpretation* (6th ed.). Denver: Love.

Tynan, W. D., & Nearing, J. (1994). The diagnosis of attention deficit hyperactivity disorder in young children. *Infants and Young Children, 6*(4), 13–20.

U.S. Bureau of the Census. (2005). *Disability and American families.* Retrieved from www.census.gov

U.S. Conference of Mayors. (2005). Resolution 28: Visitability Opportunities for People with Disabilities. Posted at www.concretechange.org

U.S. Congress, House of Representatives. (1988). *Conference report 100-661.* Washington, DC: U.S. Government Printing Office.

U.S. Congress, House of Representatives. (1991). *House report 102–198.* Individuals with Disabilities Education amendments of 1991, Committee on Education and Labor. Washington, DC: U.S. Government Printing Office.

U.S. Department of Education. (1984). *Sixth annual report to Congress on implementation of Public Law 94–142: The Education for All Handicapped Children Act.* Washington, DC: Author.

U.S. Department of Education. (1985). *Seventh annual report to Congress on implementation of Public Law 94–142: The Education for All Handicapped Children Act.* Washington, DC: Author.

U.S. Department of Education. (1992a, October 27). Assistance to states for the Education of Children with Disabilities Program and Preschool Grants for Children with Disabilities: Correction; final rule. *Federal Register,* 48694–48704.

U.S. Department of Education. (1992b, September 29). Assistance to states for the Education of Children with Disabilities Program and Preschool Grants for Children with Disabilities: Final rule. *Federal Register,* 44794–44852.

U.S. Department of Education. (1992c). *Fourteenth annual report to Congress on implementation of the Individuals with Disabilities Education Act.* Washington, DC: Author.

U.S. Department of Education. (1992d, October 30). Notice of policy guidance. *Federal Register, 57*(211), 49274–49276.

U.S. Department of Education. (1993, July 30). Early Intervention Program for Infants and Toddlers with Disabilities: Final rule. *Federal Register,* 40958–40989.

U.S. Department of Education. (1999, March 12). Assistance to states for the Education of Children with Disabilities and the Early Intervention Program for Infants and Toddlers with Disabilities: Final regulation. *Federal Register,* 12405–12672.

U.S. Department of Education. (2000). *Twenty-second annual report to Congress on implementation of the Individuals with Disabilities Education Act.* Washington, DC: Author.

U.S. Department of Education. (2001). *Twenty-third annual report to Congress on implementation of the Individuals with Disabilities Education Act.* Washington, DC: Author.

U.S. Department of Education. (2002). *Twenty-fourth annual report to Congress on implementation of the Individuals with Disabilities Education Act.* Washington, DC: Author.

U.S. Department of Education. (2003). *Twenty-fifth annual report to Congress on implementation of the Individuals with Disabilities Education Act.* Washington, DC: Author.

U.S. Department of Education. (2005). *Twenty-seventh Annual Report to Congress on Implementation of the Individuals with Disabilities Education Act.* Washington, DC: Author. (Tables online at www.ideadata.org.)

U.S. Department of Education. (2006a). Assistance to states for the Education of Children with Disabilities Program and Preschool Grants for Children with Disabilities: Final regulation. *Federal Register,* August 14, 46539–46845.

U.S. Department of Education. (2006b). Early Intervention Program for Infants and Toddlers with Disabilities: Final rule. *Federal Register.*

U.S. Department of Education. (2006c). *Twenty-eighth Annual Report to Congress on Implementation of the Individuals with Disabilities Education Act.* Washington, DC: Author. (Tables online at www.ideadata.org.)

U.S. Department of Health and Human Services, Head Start Bureau. (2005). *Head Start program fact sheet, fiscal year 2004.* Washington, DC: Author.

U.S. Office of Health, Education, and Welfare, Office of Education. (1977). Assistance to states for education of handicapped children: Procedures for evaluating specific learning disabilities. *Federal Register, 41,* 65082–65085.

Vadasy, P., Fewell, R., Greenberg, M., Dermond, N., & Meyer, D. (1986). Follow-up evaluation of the effects of involvement in the fathers program. *Topics in Early Childhood Special Education, 6*(1), 16–31.

Van Riper, C. (1993). *The nature of stuttering* (2nd ed.). Prospect Heights, IL: Waveland.

Vaughn, S. R., Bos, C. S., & Lund, K. A. (1986). . . . But they can do it in my room: Strategies for promoting generalization. *Teaching Exceptional Children, 18,* 176–180.

Vaughn, S. R., Ridley, C. A., & Bullock, D. D. (1984). Interpersonal problem solving skills training with aggressive young children. *Journal of Applied Developmental Psychology, 5,* 213–223.

Verhaaren, P. R., & Connor, F. P. (1981). Physical disabilities. In J. M. Kauffman & D. P. Halloran (Eds.), *Handbook of special education.* Englewood Cliffs, NJ: Prentice Hall.

Viadero, D. (n.d.) Side by side. *Teacher Magazine Reader.*

Vincent, L. J. (1992). Families and early intervention: Diversity and competence. *Journal of Early Intervention, 16,* 166–172.

Vygotsky, L. S. (1978). *Mind in society: The development of higher psychological processes.* Cambridge, MA: Harvard University Press.

Waaland, P. (1990). Pediatric traumatic brain injury. *Special Topic Report.* Richmond: Medical College of Virginia, Rehabilitation Research & Training Center on Severe Traumatic Brain Injury.

Wagner, R., Torgeson, J., & Rashotte, C. (1999). *Comprehensive Test of Phonological Processing*. Austin, TX: PRO-ED.

Waissman, R. (1993). Ethical issues in home care treatment of a chronic illness: Analysis of the notion of responsibility. *Disability Studies Quarterly, 13*(4), 28–32.

Wallis, C. (1994, July 18). Life in overdrive. *Time,* 42–50.

Warfield, M. E. (1995). The cost-effectiveness of home visiting versus group services in early intervention. *Journal of Early Intervention, 19*(2), 130–148.

Warren, D. H. (1984). *Blindness and early childhood development* (2nd ed., rev.). New York: American Foundation for the Blind.

Wasik, B. H., Ramey, C. T., Bryant, D. M., & Sparling, J. J. (1990). A longitudinal study of two early intervention strategies: Project CARE. *Child Development, 61,* 1682–1692.

Wasowicz, L. (1993, June 17). Virtual reality can lend hand to disabled. UPI wire story.

Watson, L. S. (1973). *Child behavior modification: A manual for teachers, nurses and parents.* New York: Pergamon.

Weintraub, F. (1986). Testimony before the Subcommittee on Select Education, July 23. In *House report 99–120* (pp. 23–52, 91–100). Washington, DC: U.S. Government Printing Office.

Weintraub, F. (1989). Testimony before the Subcommittee on the Handicapped, April 3. *Senate report S. Hrg. 101–287* (pp. 13–36). Washington, DC: U.S. Government Printing Office.

Wershing, A. (1994). Making play accessible. *REHAB Management, 7*(1), 123–125.

Wetherby, A., & Prizant, B. (1992). Profiling young children's communicative competence. In S. Warren & J. Reichle (Eds.), *Causes and effects in communication disorders.* Baltimore: Brookes.

White, K. R. (1988). Cost analyses in family support programs. In H. B. Weiss & F. H. Jacobs (Eds.), *Evaluating family programs* (pp. 429–443). New York: Aldine de Gruyter.

White, K. R., Boyce, G., Casto, G., Innocenti, M. S., Taylor, M. J., Goetze, L., & Behl, D. (1994). Comparative evaluations of early intervention alternatives: A response to commentaries by Guralnick and Telzrow. *Early Education and Development, 5*(1), 56–68.

White, K. R., & Casto, G. (1985). An integrative review of efficacy studies with at-risk children: Implications for the handicapped. *Analysis and Intervention in Developmental Disabilities, 5,* 7–31.

White, K. R., Casto, G., Mott, S. E., Barnett, W. S., Pezzino, J., Lowitzer, A. C., et al. (1987). *1986–1987 annual report of the longitudinal studies of the effects and cost of early intervention for handicapped children* (Contract # 800-85-0173). Logan: Early Intervention Research Institute, Utah State University. (ERIC Clearinghouse on Handicapped and Gifted Youth #ED 293–241)

White, K. R., Mastropieri, M. A., & Casto, G. (1984). An analysis of special education early childhood projects approved by the Joint Dissemination Review Panel. *Journal of the Division for Early Childhood, 9,* 11–26.

White, K. R., Taylor, M., & Moss, V. (1992). Does research support claims about the benefits of involving parents in early intervention programs? *Review of Educational Research, 62*(1), 91–125.

Wick, J. (1990). *School Attitude Measure.* Iowa City, IA: American College Testing.

Wiig, E. H., & Semel, E. M. (1984). *Language assessment and intervention for the learning disabled* (2nd ed.). Columbus, OH: Merrill/Prentice Hall.

Will, M. (1986). *Educating children with learning problems: A shared responsibility.* Unpublished document, U.S. Department of Education, Office of Special Education Programs.

Williams, B. (1991). *Testimony before the U.S. House of Representatives Subcommittee on Select Education and Civil Rights.* Santa Fe, NM.

Williams, B. F., & Howard, V. F. (1993). Children exposed to cocaine: Characteristics and implications for research and intervention. *Journal of Early Intervention, 17*(1), 61–72.

Williamson, W. D., & Demmler, G. J. (1992). Congenital infections: Clinical outcome and educational implications. *Infants and Young Children, 4*(4), 1–10.

Wilson, W. M. (1992). The Stanford-Binet: Fourth edition and Form L-M in assessment of young children with mental retardation. *Mental Retardation, 30*(2), 81–84.

Wing, L. (1981). *Early childhood autism: Clinical, educational, and social aspects* (3rd ed.). New York: Pergamon.

Witt, J. C., Elliott, S. N., & Gresham, F. M. (Eds.). (1988). *Handbook of behavior therapy in education.* New York: Plenum.

Wolery, M. (1989). Transitions in early childhood special education: Issues and procedures. *Focus on Exceptional Children, 22*(2), 1–16.

Wolery, M. (1991). Instruction in early childhood special education: "Seeing through a glass darkly . . . knowing in part." *Exceptional Children, 58*(2), 127–135.

Wolery, M. (2001). Embedding time delay procedures in classroom activities. In M. Ostrosky & S. Sandall (Eds.), *Teaching, strategies: What to do to support young children's development.* Longmont, CO: Sopris West.

Wolery, M., Bailey, D., & Sugai, G. (1988). *Effective teaching: Principles and procedures of applied behavior analysis with exceptional students.* Boston: Allyn & Bacon.

Wolery, M., & Gast, D. L. (2000). Classroom research for young children with disabilities: Assumptions that guided the conduct of research. *Topics in Early Childhood Special Education, 20*(1), 49–55.

Wolery, M., Martin, C. G., Schroeder, C., Huffman, K., Venn, M. L., Holcombe, A., et al. (1994). Employment of educators in preschool mainstreaming: A survey of general early educators. *Journal of Early Intervention, 18*(1), 64–77.

Wolery, M., & Sainato, D. (1993). General curriculum and intervention strategies. In Division for Early Childhood (2004), *DEC recommended practices: A comprehensive guide* (pp. 50–67). Denver: Sopris West.

Woodcock, R., McGrew, K., & Mather, N. (2001). *Woodcock-Johnson III.* Itasca, IL: Riverside.

Woolfolk, A. E. (2004). *Educational psychology* (9th ed.). Upper Saddle River, NJ: Prentice Hall.

Wortham, S. (1998). *Early childhood curriculum.* Columbus, OH: Merrill.

Ysseldyke, J., Thurlow, M., & Bruininks, R. (1992). Expected educational outcomes for students with disabilities. *Remedial and Special Education, 13*(6), 19–32.

Zigler, E., Finn-Stevenson, M., & Hall, N. (2004). *The first three years of life and beyond: Brain development and social policy*. New Haven, CT: Yale University Press.

Zigler, E., & Valentine, J. (1979). *Project Head Start: A legacy of the War on Poverty.* New York: Free Press.

Index

Note: page references in **bold** indicate a figure or table

A

Abecedarian Project, 7
Abeson, A., 107
AbleData, 250–251
Academics
increasing emphasis on, 2, 83–84, 90, 94, 95, 150–151, 154–155, 158, 193, 265, 277, 295–296
in Individualized Education Plans, 229–230
in Individualized Family Service Plans, 221
use of technology in teaching, 247–248
See also Curriculum; National Assessment of Education Progress (NAEP); No Child Left Behind Act
Accardo, P.J., 210
Access Board. *See* Architectural and Transportation Barriers Compliance Board (ATBCB)
Accessibility. *See* Environments
Accommodation, 19
places of public accommodation, 125, 126–127
reasonable accommodations, 125, 127
Accountability, 84
See also No Child Left Behind Act
Acoustical Society of America, 310
Adaptability for housing, 133
Adaptations of materials, 163
See also Toys, adaptive
Adaptive Behavior Scales-Schools, 197
Adaptive development, 15–17, 386–387
assessment of, 393–394
developmental delays in, 388
prevalence of disorders in, 387–388
See also individual disorders
Adaptive toys. *See* Toys, adaptive
ADHD. *See* Attention deficit hyperactivity disorders (ADHD)
Administration for Children and Families (ACF), 141
Advance organizer, 175
Adventitious conditions, 330
Affleck, G., 286
African Americans, cultural competence towards, **56,** 58, 202, 373
Age appropriateness, 31, 219
Age at onset, 84–85, 306
Age at start, 84–85
Age ranges, 2–3, **3**
AIDS. *See* HIV/AIDS
Air Carriers Access Act, 134
Allen, D., 286
Allen, K., 25, 156, 400
American Academy of Pediatrics (AAP), 311
"Informed Consent, Parental Permission, and Assent," 294
American Association on Intellectual Disabilities, 353
American Association on Mental Retardation (AAMR), 353
American Institutes for Research (AIR)
NEILS Expenditure Study, 89
American Sign Language (ASL), 170–171, 315, 317, **318**
American Speech-Language-Hearing Association, 311
Americans with Disabilities Act (ADA), 4, 122, 123, 125–128, 245
Title I, 125, 126
Title II, 125, 126
Title III, 125, 126–127
Title IV, 125, 127
Amputation, 334, 343
resources for, 420
Anderson, F.E., 167
Anthony, L., 91
Antia, S., 298, 318
Anti-discrimination policies, 4
Air Carriers Access Act, 134
Americans with Disabilities Act (ADA), 123, 125–128
Fair Housing Amendments Act (FHAA), 133
Rehabilitation Act, 123–125
Telecommunications Act, 134
Television Decoder Circuitry Act, 134
Aphasia, 311
Applied behavior analysis (ABA), 170, 398

Applied verbal analysis (AVA), 398
Appropriateness, 218–219, 230–232, **231**
 age appropriateness, 31, 219
 appropriate behaviors in adaptive development, 386–387, 393–394
 definition of appropriate services, 46–47, 101
Apraxia of speech, 311
Architectural and Transportation Barriers Compliance Board (ATBCB), 182, 185, 310, 338
ARCH National Resource Center for Respite and Crisis Care Services, 140
Ariel, A., 355
Asch, A., 292, 294
Asian Americans, cultural competence towards, **57,** 202
Assessment
 of adaptive development, 393–394
 of children with disabilities, 208–209, **209**
 of children with fragile X syndrome, 356
 of cognitive development, 355–356
 DEC recommended practices for, 201, **201**
 definition of, 190–193
 of families, 207–208, **208,** 209–211, 222, 285
 of hearing, 308–310
 and individualization, 219–220
 of infants and toddlers, **206,** 206–207, 219–220, 222
 of mental retardation, 355
 multidisciplinary approach to, 285
 of physical development, 337–338
 principles of, **191,** 191–192
 of social/emotional development, 372–375, **373**
 of specific learning disabilities, 355–356
 of speech and language, 310–311
 of vision, 311–312
 See also Evaluation; Screening; Testing
Assimilation, 18–19
 See also Inclusion
Assistivetech.net, 250
Assistive Technology Act, 144, 245
Assistive technology devices, 171–172, 244–250
 augmentative and alternative communication technologies, 247, 340
 broadband, 242–243, 249–250
 cell phones, 249
 for children who are blind, 319–320
 for children with cerebral palsy, 333–334
 for children with muscular dystrophy, 342
 defined by IDEA, 245
 e-mail, 246
 instant messaging (IM), 242
 PowerPoint, 248
 speech to text (speech recognition), 242, 245, 246, 298, 321–322
 telemedicine, 249–250
 telepresence, 249
 text to speech (speech synthesis), 248, 321–322, 343, 358, 361
 touch-screen, 242, 245–246, 247
Assistive technology services, 250–252
 environmental control system (ECS), 251
Association for the Fathers Network, 287
Asthma, 330, 341–342
At-risk children, 7, 41, 42, 45, 50
Attention, 18, **19**
Attention deficit hyperactivity disorders (ADHD), 54, 370–372
 ADHD/C (combined type), 370
 ADHD/HI (predominantly hyperactive-impulsive type), 368, 370
 ADHD/I (predominantly inattentive type), 368, 370
 diagnosis of, 374–375
 DSM-IV criteria for, **371**
 medications for, 376, **376**
 prevalence of, 367–368
 resources for, 407, 414–415
 and specific learning disabilities, 368, 372
Attrition, subject. *See* Subject attrition
Audiogram, 309
Augmentative and alternative communication technologies, 247, 340
Autism spectrum disorders, 82, 156, 170, 392–393
 academic performance for children with, 400
 assessment of, 395
 and communication issues, 94
 families of children with, 401
 and inclusion, 91
 intervention for, **398,** 398–400
  applied behavior analysis (ABA), 398
  applied verbal analysis (AVA), 398
  behavior modification, 398–399
  floor time, 398, 399
  SCERTS model, 399
 language development, 386
 prevalence and incidence data, 276, 387, **387–388**
 resources for, 407, 415
Autonomy *versus* shame and doubt, 9
Autosomal dominant inheritance, 306
Autosomal recessive inheritance, 306
Away We Ride, 245–246
Ayers, William, 106

B

Badger, E., 158
Bailey, Donald, 92–93, 182, 208, 282
Bale, J., 309
Bandura, Albert, 19, 396–397
Barlow, J., 344
Barnett, W.S., 89
Baroni, M., 337
Battelle Development Inventory, 195, 205, 355, 394
Bayley Scales of Infant Development II, 200, 204–205, 337, 394

Beach Center Family Quality of Life Scale, 210
Beach Center on Families and Disabilities, 287
Becker MD, 332
Behavior
- appropriate behaviors, 383–394, 386–387
- in the classroom, 156
- social and emotional behavior, 29
- *See also* Adaptive development; Social/emotional development

Behavioral and Emotional Rating Scale (BERS-2), 197
Behavior modification, **10,** 10–11, 19, 169–170, 375, 376, **377,** 377–381, 396, 397, 398–399
- applied behavior analysis (ABA), 170
- cognitive behavior modification, 380, 396, 397

Behl, D., 321
Benefits measured by research, 75–76
Bergman, Allan, 253, 254
Bias in research, 71–72, 80
- *See also* Opinion

Blindness or low vision, children with, 306–308
- assessment of, 311–312
- assistive technology devices for, 319–320
- Braille, 319, 322
- causes of blindness, 307
- families of, 322–323
- intervention for, 318–321
- orientation and mobility specialists, 319, **320**
- prevalence of, 303
- resources for, 415–416

Board of Education, Hendrick Hudson District v. Rowley, 47
Boone, H., 344
Borich, G., 159
Bourland, B., 158
Boyce, G., 85, 329
Braille, 319, 322
Brain injuries. *See* Traumatic brain injuries (TBI)
Brain Injury Association, 328, 334
Brazelton Neonatal Behavioral Assessment Scale, 394
Bredekamp, S., 31
Bricker, Diane, 91, 93, 159, 178, 180, 195
Broadband technology, 242–243, 249–250
Bronfenbrenner, Urie, 9, 93
Brookings Institution, 32
Brown, C.W., 254
Bruner, Jerome, 8, 9, 21
Brunquell, P.J., 391
Bryant, D., 156, 157, 182
Building Standards for Educational Facilities for Handicapped Children (Florida Dept. of Education), 183
Bulletin board system (BBS), 254, 255–256
Bullock, D.D., 397
Bush, George W., 114

C

Call Me Mister program, 58
Campos, J.J., 26
Captions, 256–257, 298
Capute, A.J., 210
Carl, Lisa, 126
Carolina Curriculum, 157
Carolina Record of Individual Behavior, 394
Carta, J.J., 151, 156, 158
Carter, M., 90
Casto, G., 109, 282
CDC. *See* Centers for Disease Control and Prevention
CD-ROM, 257
Cell phones, 249
Center for Accessible Housing, 182–183
Center for Law and Social Policy, 32
Center on Children and Families, 32
Centers for Disease Control and Prevention, 328, 330, 387, 392
Cephalocaudal development, 23
Cerebral palsy (CP), 332–334
- assistive technology devices for children with, 333–334, 343
- physical development, 326–327
- resources for, 407–408, 416
- speech development, 22
- variety of severity, 79

Chandler, L.K., 236
Chapman, J., 181
Chasnoff, I.J., 74
Checklist for Autism in Toddlers, 395
Chicago Longitudinal Study (CLS), **69,** 69–70, 81
Child development
- behavioral approaches, 10–11
- developmental approaches to, 7–10
- diversity of, 12
- domains of development, 13–29, **14, 19, 20** (*See also* Adaptive development; Cognitive development; Communication development; Physical development; Social/emotional development)
- moral development, 10
- sequence of, 12–13

Child find, 63, 193–195, 270
Children with disabilities
- definition of, **44**
- *See also* Infants; Preschool special education; Primary special education; Toddlers

Civil rights. *See* Rights
Clifford, R.M., 182
Cocaine exposure, 74, 389–390
Cochlear implants, 294, 317
Code of Federal Regulations (CFR), 103–104
Cognitive behavior modification, 380, 396, 397
Cognitive development, 14, 17–19, **19**
- accommodation, 19
- assessment of, 355–356
- assimilation, 18–19
- attention, 18, **19**
- developmental delays in, 351, 355
- memory, 19
- perception, 18, **19**
- prevalence of cognitive impairments, 350–351
- processing of information, 18, **19**
- stimulation of, 358–359
- *See also individual cognitive impairments*

Cohen, H., 85
Cole, K., 154, 157, 220
Coleman, L., 78
Communication and Symbolic Behavior Scales (CSBS), 310
Communication development, 15, 19–23, **20**
- definition of, 302–303
- developmental delays, 303–305, **304**
- developmental deviations, 304
- hearing, 20–21, 308–310
- prevalence and incidence data, 303
- speech and language, 21–22, 22, 310–311
- vision, 22–23, 311–312
- *See also* Blindness or low vision, children with; Deaf, children who are; Speech and language impairment (SLI)

Community context, 9
Complaints. *See* Procedural safeguards
Computers. *See* Technology
Concrete operational stage, 8
Conditions, diagnosed. *See* Diagnosed conditions
Conduct disorders, 370
Cone, J.D., 380
Confidentiality. *See* Privacy
Congenital conditions, definition of, 330
- *See also individual conditions*

Congenital cytomegalovirus infection (CMV), 306
Congenital dystrophy, 332
Connors Rating Scales, 374
Consent, family, 196, 225–226
Constitution. *See* United States Constitution
Cooperative learning, 174
Coordination, interagency, 382
Correa, V., 237
Corsello, C., 82, 85, 398
Cost-benefits, 88–90, 213
Cost-effectiveness, 88–90, 213
Costenbader, V., 86
Costs
- of early childhood (EC) education, 31–32
- of early childhood special education, 31–32, 43, 45, 48
- of inclusion, 91

Council for Exceptional Children (CEC), 366
Counseling services for families, 166, 361–362
Cowdery, G., 156
Crack babies. *See* Vulnerable child syndrome (VCS)
Creswell, J.W., 72
Cruickshank, W., 333
Cryer, D., 158
Cukier, A., 385
Culbertson, J.L, 195, 206
Cultural competence, **55–57,** 55–58, 114, 202–203, 373, 393
Cure Autism Now, 392
Curriculum, 93–94
- book resources for, 153
- for children with fragile X syndrome, 361–362
- for children with mental retardation, 359–360
- for children with specific learning disabilities, 360–361
- definition of, 152
- early childhood *vs.* early childhood special education, 156
- for early intervention years, 159–165
- and individualization, 155–156
- for preschool special education, 166–172
- for primary special education, 172–177
- specific curricula, 157–159
  - Carolina Curriculum, 157
  - Early Partners, 157
  - Hawaii Early Learning Profile, 157
  - Learning through Play, 157
  - Portage Guide to Early Education, 157
  - SKI*HI, 157
  - What Works Clearinghouse, 159
- *See also* Academics; Developmentally appropriate practice (DAP); Direct instruction (DI)

Cutler, B.C., 401
Cylert, 376
Cystic fibrosis, 331
- resources for, 416

Cystic Fibrosis Foundation, 331

D

Dale, P., 154, 157, 220
Damasio, A. & H., 18
Davidson, D., 318
DC:03 Casebook, 374
DD act. *See* Developmental Disabilities Assistance and Bill of Rights Act (DD Act)
Deaf, children who are, 8, 84, 297–298, 305–306
- age at onset, 306
- appropriate services, **231,** 231–232
- assessment of, 308–310
- causes of deafness, 306
- developmental delays, 304–305
- families of, 322
- hearing aids, 316
- inclusion issues, 181, 297–298
- intervention for, 314–318
- least restrictive environments, 317–318
- prevalence of, 303
- resources for, 408, 417
- sign language, 170–171, 315, 317, **318**
- SKI*HI, 157
- social/emotional development of, 28
- surgical intervention, 293
  - cochlear implants, 294, 317
- technology for, 321–322
  - speech to text (speech recognition), 242, 245, 246, 298, 321–322
  - text to speech (speech synthesis), 248, 321–322
- telecommunications devices for the deaf (TDDs), 125

television captions, 256, 298
testing of, 197, 200–202
Decoder Circuitry Act, 257
DeGangi, G., 290
Deiner, P., 156
Deitz, S., 312
Delays, developmental. *See* Developmental delays
Demographic Characteristics of Children and Families Entering Early Intervention (NEILS), 50
Demographics
ages of young children in various grades, **264,** 264–265
of children in early childhood special education, 3–4, **4,** 49–53, **50, 51, 53**
errors of measurement, 269
families, 270–272
infants and toddlers served, 272–275, **273**
preschoolers served, 275
prevalence of adaptive development disorders, 387–388
prevalence of cognitive development disorders, 350–351
prevalence of communication development conditions, 303
prevalence of physical development conditions, 328
prevalence of social/emotional development disorders, 367–368
primary-grade children served, 275–277, **276**
socioeconomic status, 269, 270–272
sources for, 269–270
Dent, William, 106
Denver Development Screening Test, 355
Denver II, 195
Depression, childhood, 369–370
Descriptive video service (DVS), 257
Deshler, D., 360, 361
Desk height, 184
Development, child. *See* Child development
Developmental delays, 49, 54, 114, 275
in adaptive development, 388
in cognitive development, 351, 355
in communication development, 303–305, **304**
in physical development, 328–329, 345
in social/emotional development, 368
Developmental deviations, 304
Developmental disabilities, 62, 141–142
Developmental Disabilities Assistance and Bill of Rights Act (DD Act), 62, 141–142, 254
Developmentally appropriate, 8
Developmentally appropriate practice (DAP), 30–31, 151, 154, 219
See also Appropriateness
Developmental plasticity, 7
Deviations, developmental, 304
Dexedrine, 376
Diabetes, 328, 336
resources for, 417
Diagnosed conditions, 50
See also individual conditions
Diagnostic and Statistical Manual of Mental Disorders, 4th ed. (DSM-IV), 370
criteria for ADHD, **371**
Diagnostic Classification of Mental Health and Developmental Disorders of Infancy and Early Childhood, 374
Diamond, K.E., 91
Directed discovery learning, 32, **33,** 177, 360
Direct instruction (DI), 151, 154, 157, 163–164, 172, 220, 359
Directories, 410
Disabilities
definition of for SSI, 136–137
definition of in Americans with Disabilities Act, 125
definition of in DD act, 141–142
definition of in IDEA, 101
definition of in Rehabilitation Act, 124
Disabilities, children with. *See* Primary special education
Disabilities, infants with. *See* Infants
Disabilities, preschoolers with. *See* Preschool special education
Disabilities, toddlers with. *See* Toddlers
Discovery learning, 8, 360
Discrepancy approach, 172–173
Discrimination
genetic discrimination, 292
See also Anti-discrimination policies
Distance learning, 255
DISTAR, 164
Diversity, **55–57,** 55–58, 297
resources for, **60,** 408
See also Cultural competence; *individual cultural groups*
Division for Early Childhood (DEC), 255
recommended practices, 30–31, 154, 201, **201**
Domains of development, 13–15, **14**
See also Adaptive development; Cognitive development; Communication development; Physical development; Social/emotional development
Doors, 183
Double jeopardy, 7, 52
Douglas-Steele, D., 401
Down, John Langdon, 353
Down syndrome, 353–354
hypotonia, 334, 354
prenatal tests for, 291–292, 354
and text to speech (speech synthesis), 358
Drislane, F.W., 356
DSM-IV. See Diagnostic and Statistical Manual of Mental Disorders, 4th ed. (DSM-IV)
Duchenne MD, 331–332, 342
Due process rights. *See* Procedural safeguards
Dunst, Carl, 93, 157, 160
Dwarfs, 292, 293, 294
Dycem, 243
DynaMyte machines, 247, 340
DynaVox machines, 247, 340
Dysautonomia, 327
Dyslexia, 352, 356

E

EAHCA. *See* Education for All Handicapped Children Act (EAHCA)
Early and Periodic Screening Diagnosis and Treatment (EPSDT), 139, 253
Early childhood (EC) education
  costs of, 31–32
  definition of, 6
  educators, 61
  vs. early childhood special education (ECSE), 30–35, 156
Early Childhood Environment Rating Scale (ECERS), 182
Early Childhood Longitudinal Study (ECLS), 83, 270
Early childhood special education (ECSE)
  age ranges, 2–3, **3**
  cost-benefits of, 88–90
  cost-effectiveness of, 88–90
  costs of, 31–32, 43, 45, 48
  definition of, 6
  definition of special education, 45, 101
  educators, 59, **296**
  effectiveness of, 81–84
  mission of, 30–35, 47–48, 264–265, 295–296
  model programs, 48
  population/demographics, 3–4, **4,** 49–53, **50, 51, 53**
  roles and responsibilities, 61–64, 64
  vs. early childhood (EC) education, 30–35, 156
  See also Early intervention; Preschool special education; Primary special education
Early Head Start, 3, 52, 143, 181–182
  See also Head Start
Early intervening services, 151, 173
Early intervention, 7, 40–44, 49–52, **50, 51,** 70
  assessments for, 219–220
  demographics of children served, 272–275, **273**
  direct instruction, 163–164
  effectiveness of, 81–82
  embedding of instruction, 159–163
  individualization of, 219
  legislation for, 109–112
  occupational therapy, 165
  for physical disabilities, 329
  in social/emotional disorders, 375–377
  speech-language pathology, 165
  See also Individualized Family Service Plans (IFSP); Infants; Toddlers
Early Intervention Research Institute, 88
Early Partners curriculum, 157
Early Program for Children with Disabilities (EEPCD), 105–106, 109
  See also Handicapped Children's Early Education Program (HCEEP)
EC. *See* Early childhood (EC) education
Echolalia, 392
ECIA. *See* Education Consolidation and Improvement Act (ECIA)
Ecological inventory, 359
Ecology, 9
ECSE. *See* Early childhood special education (ECSE)
Education Consolidation and Improvement Act (ECIA), 105
Education for All Handicapped Children Act (EAHCA), 101, 107–108
  1983 amendments, 108–109
  1986 amendments, 109–112
Education of the Handicapped Act (EHA), 104, 106–107
EEPCD. *See* Early Program for Children with Disabilities (EEPCD)
EHA. *See* Education of the Handicapped Act (EHA)
Elaboration, 160, 314
Eldredge, N., 298, 318
Elementary and Secondary Education Act (ESEA), 104–105
  1965 amendments, 104, 105
  1970 amendments, 104, 106–107
Elementary educators, 61
Elevators, 183–184
Eligibility for services, 123–124, 206–207
  See also Assessment; Evaluation
E-mail, 246
Embedding of instruction, 93, 151, 155
  in early intervention, 159–163
  phonemic awareness, 155, 168, 314
  phonics instruction, 168–169
  in preschool special education, 166–167, **167**
  in primary special education, 174
Emotional development. *See* Social/emotional development
Emotional disturbance (ED), 54, 369–370
Empowerment of families, 286–287
"Enlarging the Pool," 58
Entitlement program, IDEA as an, 4
Environmental control system (ECS), 251
Environments
  barriers in, 101–102, 124–125
  definition of accessible, 338
  definition of barrier-free, 338
  Early Childhood Environment Rating Scale (ECERS), 182
  importance of, 177
  indoor environments, 182–185, 338, **392**
  Infant Toddler Environment Rating Scale (ITERS), 182
  least restrictive environments, 64, 151, 179–180, 181, 231–232, 317–318
  natural environments, 64, 93–94, 113, 151, 159–163, **161–162,** 178, 181, 225, 231, 317–318
  outdoor environments, 185
  structured environments for social/emotional development, 381
Epilepsy, 391–392
  resources for, 417
Epilepsy Foundation of America, 391

EPSDT. *See* Early and Periodic Screening Diagnosis and Treatment (EPSDT)
Erikson, Erik, 8
Errors of measurement, 269
Escobar, C.M., 321
ESEA. *See* Elementary and Secondary Education Act (ESEA)
Ethics
gene therapy, 292–293
prenatal services, 290–292
resources for, 408–409
surgical interventions, 293–294
Evaluation
definition of, 190–193
evaluation instruments, 204–206
federal requirements, 203–204, **204, 205,** 219–220
and individualization, 219–220
principles of, **191,** 191–192
program evaluation, 211–213
See also Assessment; Screening; Testing
Experiential deprivation, 9, 308, 322, 326, 366, 394
Extinction, 11, 170, 379

F

Facio-scapulo-humeral dystrophy, 332
Fagan, J., 200
Fair Housing Amendments Act (FHAA), 133
Families
assessment of, 207–208, **208,** 209–211, 222, 285
benefits of early childhood special education, 48
of children who are deaf, 322
of children with adaptive disorders, 400–401
of children with autism, 400–401
of children with blindness or low vision, 322–323
of children with cognitive impairments, 362
of children with physical disabilities, 344–346
of children with social/emotional disorders, 382–383
of children with traumatic brain injuries, 345, **345**
communication
impoverishment within, 313, 358, 362
and community context, 9
complaints by (*See* Procedural safeguards)
counseling services, 166, 361–362
and cultural competence, **55–57,** 55–58
demographics of, 270–272
empowerment of, 286–287
family involvement, 32–34, 113
family-centered philosophy, 280, **285,** 285–286
family-focused philosophy, 280, 283–284, **285**
family-friendly philosophy, 280, 283, **283**
fathers, 281, 287
in Individualized Education Plans (IEP), 226–228, **228,** 232–233
in Individualized Family Service Plans (IFSP), 232–233
in prevention of mental retardation, 357
research on, 87
siblings, 287–288
teaming, 280–281, 288–290
traditional approaches, 282, **283**
Family Opportunity Act, 139
family support groups, 287
guardianship, 271–272
Maternal and Child Health Services (MCH), 140
Medicaid, 137–139
as members of multidisciplinary teams, 92–93
parental consent, 196, 225–226
resources for, 408, 417–418
respite care, 140–141, 166, 286
rights of (*See* Rights)
self-defined, 271, 281
Supplementary Security Income (SSI), 135–137
supports for, 43
transition guidance, 236
translation services for, 133
See also Individualized Family Service Plans (IFSP)
Family Education Rights and Privacy Act (FERPA), 107, 129
Family Opportunity Act, 139
Family-Professional Partnership Scales, 88, 210
Family therapists, 60
FAS. *See* Fetal alcohol syndrome (FAS)
Fathers, 281, 287
Federal information sources, 410–412
Federal role, 61–62, 100–103
See also individual laws
Feenan, P., 337
Feinberg, E., 87, 314
Ferrell, K., 312
Fetal alcohol effect (FAE), 389
Fetal alcohol syndrome (FAS), 389
indicators of, **389**
intervention for, **390**
resources for, 419
Fine motor development, 15
First Chance network, 106
See also Handicapped Children's Early Education Program (HCEEP)
Floor time, 398, 399
Florida Department of Education
Building Standards for Educational Facilities for Handicapped Children, 183
Formative evaluation, 211–212
Forness, Steve, 365, 366
Forward funded laws, 111–112
Fowler, S.A., 236
Fragile X syndrome, 354–355
and adaptive development, 394
assessment of children with, 356
curriculum for children with, 361–362
and intensity of intervention, 86
resources for, 419
Fraiberg, Selma, 307–308, 321

Freud, Sigmund, 370
Freund, B., 344, 356, 361, 394
Frith, U., 392–393
Fuchs, Douglas and Lynn, 174
Funding for technology, **252,** 252–254

G

Galaburda, A.M., 356
Gargiulo, R., 156
Garshelis, J.A., 92, 289
Gast, D.L., 166
Generalizability in research, 73–74
Generalization, 166, 377–380
Genetics
- gene therapy, 292–293
- genetic counseling, 362
- genetic discrimination, 292
- resources for, 408–409

Gesell, Arnold, 7
Glass, P., 22, 319
Gliedman, J., 12
- *The Unexpected Minority,* 10

Goldstein, A.P., 179
Goodman, Joan, 158
Goodman, Ken and Yetta, 176
Graham, M., 156, 157, 182
Gray, C., 90
Green, G., 85
Greenfield, J., 393
Gross motor development, 15
Grouping, 174
Guardianship, 271–272
Guided discovery learning, 32, **33,** 176, 360
Guralnick, M., 95, 156, 282, 283, 286

H

Handicapped Children's Early Education Program (HCEEP), 104, 105–106, 109, 110
- *See also* Early Program for Children with Disabilities (EEPCD)

Hanft, B., 87, 91, 314
Harms, T., 158, 182
Harrison, M., 318
Hatton, D.D., 86
Hawaii Early Learning Profile, 157
HCEEP. *See* Handicapped Children's Early Education Program (HCEEP)
Head Start, 52, 142–143
- and age at start, 85
- definition of disability, 62
- founding of, 7, 9
- as a free program, 32
- and inclusion, 91
- lack of special educators, 182
- numbers of children served, 3–4
- safety standards, 184
- transitory effects of, 76
- *See also* Early Head Start

Health and safety. *See* Environments
Hearing, 20–21
- assessment of, 308–310
- *See also* Deaf, children who are

Hearing aids, 316
Hebert, E., 344
Helm, D.T., 401
Hepatitis B (HBV), 30–31
Hierarchy of needs, 11, **12**
Hispanic Americans. *See* Latino Americans
HIV/AIDS, 30–31, 390–391, 395
- resources for, 415

Hobbs, Nicholas
- *Issues in the Classification of Children,* 277

Holahan, A., 86
Horn, Eva, 93, 94, 163, 167
Housing, 133
- *See also* Environments

Howard, J., 85
Howard, V.F., 74
Hoyson, Marilyn, 86, 91, 93
Hubbard, R., 293
Hypotonia, 334, 354

I

IDEA
- 1991 amendments, 112–114, 132–133, 302–303
- 1997 amendments, 114, 278–279, 351
- 2004 amendments, 115
  - changes made by, **116**
  - early intervening services, 115, 151, 173
  - increased emphasis on academics, 7, 83, 90, 94, 95, 150, 154, 155, 158–159, 295
  - Individualized Education Plans, 229
  - Individualized Family Service Plans (IFSP), 221–222
  - specific learning disabilities, 351–352
- as an entitlement program, 4, 42, 70
- definition of assistive technology devices, 245
- eligibility for services, 123
- family involvement, 285
- five domains of development, 13–15, **14**
- informed clinical opinion, 191
- PL numbering, **104**
- terminology in, 101
- testing of children, 198, 199–200

IDEA Part A, 116–117, 250
IDEA Part B, 41–42, 111, 112–113, 117
- ADHD, 372
- appropriateness, 46–47, 230–232, **231**
- assessment, 206, 220
- assistive technology devices and services, 250, 252–253
- autism, 393
- child find, 63, 193–195
- and constitutional amendments, 100
- definition of special education, 45
- emotional disturbance, 369
- evaluation, 203
- family involvement, 282
- funding for, 114
- Individualized Education Plans, 226–232
- labels, 277
- least restrictive environments, 179, 317–318
- local role, 64
- population served by, 3–4, **51,** 272, 275
- preschool special education, 44–47, 52, **53**
- primary special education, 54–55
- privacy, 196
- related services, 44, 45–46

seamless system, 49, 112–113
Section 615 (procedural safeguards), 128–129, **130**
state role in, 63
transition, 234–235
IDEA Part C, 106, 113–114, 117
ADHD, 372
appropriate services, 231–232
assessment, 206–207, 222
assistive technology devices and services, 250, 252–253
child find, 63, 193–195
early intervention, 40–44, 49–52, **50, 51,** 70, 81–82
evaluation, 190, 203–204
family assessment, 208, 222
family involvement, 87–88, 113, 282
federal role, 62
Individualized Family Service Plans (IFSP), 113, 221–225
labeling, 113, 278
lead agency, 63
local role, 64
multidisciplinary teaming, 92
natural environments, 113, 178, 317–318
population served by, 2–4, **51,** 272–275
privacy, 196
seamless system, 49, 112–113
Section 639 (complaints procedure), 129–133, **131**
service coordinator, 134–135, **135**
state role in, 63
transition, 225, **226,** 234–236
IDEA Part D, 114, 117–118, 252
IDEA Part H, 106, 111, 112–114
Identity, separate, 14
IHDP. *See* Infant Health and Development Program (IHDP)
Incidence, 303
Inclusion, 71–72, 90–92, 105, 151, 178, 180–182, 296–297
Independent living centers, 137
Independent Living Resource Utilization (ILRU), 255
Index of Neurobehavioral Dysfunction, 394
Individual appropriateness, 31
Individualization, 218–219
and curriculum, 155–156
in early intervention, 219
and inclusion, 296–297
practical issues, 185–187
related services, 219
using assessment and evaluation findings, 219–220
Individualized Education Plans (IEP), 46, **46,** 62, 64, 124, 155, 156, 177
adaptive development in, 395
appropriateness, 230–232, **231**
date and duration, 230
districtwide assessments, 229–230
educational performance, 228
goals and objectives, 228–229
meetings, 226–228, 288–290
parental participation in, 226–228, **228,** 232–233
preparing, **227**
procedural safeguards, 128
progress reports, 230
services listed in, 229
test accommodations, 193
transition, 230, 234
writing of, 232–233
Individualized Family Service Plans (IFSP), **42,** 42–43, 62, 64, 113, 124, 155, 156, 166, 177, 208
adaptive development in, 395
age at, 273–274, **274**
appropriateness, 230–232
assessment of infants and toddlers, 222
contents of, 223–224
developing, **221**
embedding of instruction, 160
family assessment, 222
family participation in, 232–233, 288–290
federal requirements, 221–222
informed consent, 225–226
multidisciplinary teaming, 92, 223, 288–290
natural environment, 225
other services in, 224, **224**
review of, 223
service coordinator, 225
start date and duration, 225
timing of, 223
transition, 225, **226,** 234
writing of, 232–233
Individuals with Disabilities Education Act. *See* IDEA
Indoor environments, 182–185, 338, **392**
Industry *versus* inferiority, 9
Infant Health and Development Program (IHDP), 86, 357
Infants
adaptive development of, 15
age range, 2–3, **3**
assessment of, **206,** 206–207, **207,** 222
cognitive development of, 17
communication development of, 19–20
curriculum for, 93
definition of, 41–42, **42**
demographics of children served, 3–4, **4,** 272–275, **273**
developmental delays, 49
diagnosed conditions, 50
early intervention, 40–44, 49–52, **50, 51**
embedding of instruction, 159–163
language development of, 21
physical development of, 23, 25–26
social/emotional development of, 27–28
speech, 22
vision, 22–23
See also Early intervention
Infant Toddler Environment Rating Scale (ITERS), 182
Informed clinical opinion, 191
"Informed Consent, Parental Permission, and Assent" (AAP), 294
Ingersoll, B., 91, 399
Initiative *versus* guilt, 9
Instant messaging (IM), 242
Institute of Education Sciences, 77
Insurance, 272
Intensity, research on, 85–87
Intensive care units (ICUs), 234
Interagency coordination, 382
Interdisciplinary services, 48–49

Intervention, early. *See* Early intervention
Ireton, H., 195
Irving Independent School District v. Tatro, 344
Issues in the Classification of Children (Hobbs), 277
I statements, 14

J

Jenkins, J., 157, 220
Job Accommodation Network (JAN), 250–251
Jobs
- child development associate (CDA) paraprofessionals, 61
- early childhood educators, 61
- early childhood special educators, 59
- elementary educators, 61
- psychologists, 60–61
- service coordinators, 59
- social workers, 59
- technology experts, 60–61
- therapists, 60

Johnson, Caroline, 390–391
Johnson, T.E., 236
Journals, 409–410
Jung, L., 289
Juvenile rheumatoid arthritis, 336

K

Kaminski, R., 195
Kaplan-Sanoff, M., 7
Kauerz, K., 297
Kauffman, James, 177
Kauffman Assessment Battery for Children - 2nd Ed. (K-ABC), 205
Keen, D., 399
Keeney, T.J., 345
Keilty, B., 88
Kemp, C., 90
Kemp, David, 309
Kenny, T.J., 195
Kermoian, R., 26
Kidspiration, 248, 361
Kilgo, J., 156
Kindergarten and Elementary Teacher Questionnaires, 374
Kitchen utensils, 243
Knitzer, J., 382
Kohlberg, Lawrence, 10
Kohler, F.W., 91, 94
Kohrman, A., 344
Kozloff, M.A., 401
Kreimeyer, K., 298, 318
Kübler-Ross, Elizabeth, 7
- *On Death and Dying,* 11–12

L

Labeling of children, 30–31, 52, 54, 113, 114, 177, 277–279, **280,** 376
LaBlance, G., 305
Ladd, G.W., 381
Language, 12, 17–18, 21–22
- assessment of, 310–311
- definition of, 20
- phonemic awareness, 22, 155, 168, 175–176, 314
- phonics instruction, 22, 168–169, 175
- pragmatics, 17
- syntax, 21
- used to describe disabilities, 102, 112
- *See also* Communication development; Speech; Speech and language impairment (SLI)

Lantos, J., 344
Latino Americans
- cultural competence towards, **56,** 202, 373

Laws
- explanation of PL numbering, 103–104, **104**
- forward funded, 111–112
- *See also individual laws*

Lawyers and legal advocacy
- resources for, 414

Lead agency, 63
Learning disabilities. *See* Specific learning disabilities
Learning through Play curriculum, 157
Least restrictive environments (LRE), 64, 151, 179–180, 181, 231–232, 317–318
Legislation. *See individual laws*
Lejeune, Jerome, 354
Lennox-Gastaut syndrome, 391
Levin, J., 89
Levine, Mel, 352
Lewis, I.S., 157
Lim, C., 344
Limb-girdle dystrophy, 332
Limb loss. *See* Amputation
Linder, Toni, 206
Literacy
- miscue analysis, 176
- phonemic awareness, 22, 168, 175–176, 314
- phonics instruction, 22, 168–169, 175
- in primary special education, 175–176
- reading instruction, 156
- shared reading, 169
- *See also* Academics

Little People of America, 292, 294
Livingstone, M.S., 356
Living with a Brother or Sister with Special Needs (Meyer and Vadasy), 288
Local role in early childhood special education, 64
Location. *See* Environments
Lonigan, C.J., 169
Lovaas, O.I., 156, 170, 380, 393, 397, 398–399, 400, 401
Low vision. *See* Blindness or low vision, children with
Lyon, G. Reid, 172–173

M

Mahoney, G., 282
Mainstreaming, 180, 399
- *See also* Inclusion; Reverse mainstreaming

Malina, R., 25, 328
Manipulatives, 169, 359
Marotz, L., 25
Martin, Anne, 278
Maslow, Abraham, 7
- hierarchy of needs, 11, **12**
- *Motivation and Personality,* 11

Mastropieri, M.A., 109, 282
Maternal and Child Health Services (MCH), 62, 140
- funding for assistive technology, 254

Mathematics, 169, 176–177
McCarthy Scales of Children's Abilities, 205
McClean, M., 156, 205, 206
McConnell, S.R., 92, 290

McCormick, K., 205, 206
McCormick, M., 70, 86, 357
McDonald, M.E., 399
McEachin, J., 399
McEvoy, M.A., 179
McGinnis, E., 179
McGovern, C., 82–83
McGrade, B., 286
McQueeney, M., 286
McWilliam, P.J., 92–93
Medicaid, 137–139, 253, 271
Medical information, 405–406
Medically fragile, technology-dependent children, 336–337, 344
Medicare Catastrophic Coverage Act, 138
Medications for disorders in social/emotional development, **376**
Meisbov, G., 399
Meisels, S., 219
Memory, 19
Mental illness
 resources for, 420
Mental retardation, 54, 353
 assessment of, 355
 curriculum for children with, 359–360
 prevalence of, 350–351
 prevention of, 356–357
 resources for, 421
 successful intervention for, 358
Metacognition, 352
Metlife, 271–272
Meyer, D., 288
Miller, Paul Steven, 294
Miller, W., 74
Mills, P., 154, 157, 220
Mills v. Board of Education of the District of Columbia, 64
Mind at a Time, A (Levine), 352
Minke, K.M., 92, 122, 233, 289, 290
Minnesota Child Development Inventory, 195
Minnesota Early Child Development Inventory, 195
Minnesota Infant Development Inventory, 195
Minnesota Pre-kindergarten Inventory, 195
Minnesota Preschool Inventory, 195
Miscue analysis, 176
Mize, J., 381
Mnemonics, 361
Modeling behavior, 163, 382, 397
Model programs, 48, 109, 110
Moores, Donald F., 181
Moral development, 10
Morphemes, 22
Moss, V., 282
Motivation and Personality (Maslow), 11
Mounts, L., 195
Mueller, F., 246
Multidisciplinary teaming. *See* Teaming
Multimedia, 257
Multiple sclerosis, prevalence of, 328
Murray, A.D., 213
Muscular dystrophy (MD), 331–332, 342
 resources for, 420
Myotonic dystrophy, 332

N

National Alliance for Autism Research, 392
National Assessment of Education Progress (NAEP), 84, 229–230, 265
National Association for the Deaf (NAD), 294
National Association for the Education of Young Children (NAEYC)
 developmentally appropriate practice, 30–31, 154, 219
 on technology, 246–247
National Center for Culturally Responsive Educational Systems, 58
National Center for Learning Disabilities (NCLD), 255
National Center on Educational Outcomes (NCEO), 193
National Clearinghouse for Professions in Special Education
 "Enlarging the Pool," 58
National Council on Disability (NCD), 244–245
National Cristina Foundation, 254
National Early Intervention Longitudinal Study (NEILS), 49–52, 55, 70, 81–82, 84, 88, 92, 210, 269–270, 272–275, 314
 Demographic Characteristics of Children and Families Entering Early Intervention, 50
 NEILS Expenditure Study, 89
National Easter Seals Society, 254
National Education Association (NEA)
 Status of the American Public School Teacher, 58
National Institute for Early Education Research, 297
National Longitudinal Transition Study - 2, 366
National Multiple Sclerosis Society, 328
National Organization for Rare Disorders, 327
National Task Force on Technology and Disability, 244
Nations Report Card. *See* National Assessment of Education Progress (NAEP)
Native Americans
 cultural competence towards, **57,** 202
 and fetal alcohol syndrome, 389
Natural environments, 64, 93–94, 113, 151, 159–163, **161–162,** 178, 181, 225, 231, 317–318
Naturally Speaking, 246
NEILS. *See* National Early Intervention Longitudinal Study (NEILS)
NEILS Expenditure Study (AIR), 89
Nickel, R.E., 17
No Child Left Behind Act, 2, 7, 35, 47, 71, 77, 83, 90, 94, 95, 98, 114–115, 150, 154, 155, 158, 168, 193, 221–222, 247, 265, 295
Nolan, K, 344
Nondiscrimination. *See* Anti-discrimination policies
Null hypothesis, 72–73
Number sense, 169

O

Obesity, 27, 328
Occupational therapy, 60, 165, 340, 342, 395
 resources for, 420
Odom, S., 91, 156, 179

Office of Special Education Programs (OSEP), 252
Olson, H.C., 389
Olson, M., 321
On Death and Dying (Kübler-Ross), 11–12
Operant conditioning, 10
Opinion
- and research, 76–77
- *See also* Bias

Orientation and mobility specialists, 319, **320**
Orthopedic impairments, 329
Orthoses, 341, 343
O'Sullivan, P., 282
Otoacoustic emission testing, 309
Outdoor environments, 185
Outreach. *See* Child find
Overprotection, 9, 24, 308, 322, 326, 394

P

Palsha, S., 318
Parallel talk, 155, 160, 314
Paraplegia, 335
Parens, E., 292, 294
Parents. *See* Families
Parker, S., 7
Part B. *See* IDEA Part B
Part C. *See* IDEA Part C
Participation, principle of partial, 167
Peabody Development Motor Scales, 337
Peabody Picture Vocabulary Test, 355
Pearl, L.F., 287
PEELS. *See* Pre-Elementary Education Longitudinal Study (PEELS)
Peer group interactions, 381
Peer tutoring, 174
Pennsylvania Association for Retarded Children v. Commonwealth of Pennsylvania, 64
Perception, 18, **19**
Performance cues, 163
Personnel. *See* Jobs
Philosophy of early childhood special education, 30–35
Phonemes, 22
Phonemic awareness, 22, 155, 168, 175–176, 314
Phonics instruction, 22, 168–169, 175
Physical development, 15, 23–27
- assessment of, 337–338
- cephalocaudal development, 23
- descriptions of physical disabilities, **329**
- developmental delays in, 328–329, 345
- fine motor development, 15
- gross motor development, 15
- prevalence data, 328
- proximodistal development, 23
- supports for children with disabilities, 23–24, 25
- working with families, 344–346
- *See also individual physical disabilities*

Physical therapy, 60, 339–340, 342
- resources for, 421

Piaget, Jean, 7–8, 14, 18–19, 47, 156, 350
Picture Exchange Communication System (PECS), 247
Pilkington, K.O., 91
Place. *See* Environments
Places of public accommodation, 125, 126–127
Play, 28
PL numbering, explanation of, 103–104, **104**
Population. *See* Demographics
Portage Guide to Early Education, 157
PowerPoint, 248
Pragmatics, 17, 308
Pre-Elementary Education Longitudinal Study (PEELS), 55, 70, 82–83, 92, 270, 374
PreKNow, 32, 297
Premack principle, 378
Prenatal services, 290–292
- tests for Down syndrome, 291–292, 354

Prenatal Testing and Disability Rights (Parens and Asch), 292
Preoperational stage, 8
Prereferral interventions. *See* Early intervening services
Preschool and Kindergarten Behavior Scales, 374
Preschool Incentive Grant Program, 109, 110
Preschool Performance Profile (5 P's), 88
Preschools
- benefits of, 7, 69–71
- differences between early children education and early childhood special education, 32–35, **33–34**
- *See also* Head Start

Preschool special education, 40–41, 44–47, 52, **53**
- age range, 2–3, **3**
- assessments for, 219–220
- assistive technologies, 171–172
- behavior modification, 169–170
- cost-effectiveness of, 89–90
- curriculum for, 94, 166–172
- demographics of children served, 3–4, **4, 51,** 52, **53,** 275
- differences between early children education and early childhood special education, 32–35, **33–34**
- direct instruction, 172
- effectiveness of, 82
- embedding of instruction, 166–167, **167**
- Individualized Education Program (IEP), 46, **46**
- legislation for, 105–112
- number sense, 169
- phonemic awareness, 168
- phonics instruction, 168–169
- shared reading, 169
- sign language, 170–171

Presentation reinforcement, 10, 170, 379
Pressure sores, 335
Prevalence, 303
- *See also* Demographics

Prevention of cognitive impairments, 356–357
Price, C., 85, 329
Primary special education, 47, 54–55
- advance organizer, 175
- age range, 2–3, **3**
- community-based instruction, 175
- curriculum for, 155–156, 172–177

demographics of children served, 3–4, **4,** 275–277, **276**
effectiveness of, 83–84
embedding of instruction, 174
grouping, 174
instructional methods, **173**
legislation for, 107–108
literacy, 175–176
mathematics, 176–177
response to intervention (RTI), 172–174
science, 176–177
teaching strategies, 174–175
Principle of partial participation, 167
Privacy, 30, 196
of family assessments, 210
Family Education Rights and Privacy Act, 107, 129
protected by IDEA, 128, 132–133
Prizant, Barry, 399
"Problem with an Almost-Perfect World, The," 292
Procedural safeguards
IDEA Part B, 128–129, **130**
IDEA Part C, 129–133, **131**
Processing of information, 18, **19**
Program evaluation, 211–213
Project CARE, 362
Prostheses, 341, 343
Proximodistal development, 23
Psychologists, 60–61
Pullout for related services, 155, 177
Punishment, 11, 170
Push-in for related services, 155, 177

Q

Quadriplegia, 335
Qualitative research, 77–78
Quantitative research, 77–78

R

Ramey, Craig, 7, 357, 362
Ramey, S.L., 357
Ramps, 183
Randomization in research, 75
Rapport, M., 344
Rare disorders, 327
Rathbun, A., 83
Rating scales, 196–197
Reading. *See* Literacy
Reasonable accommodations, 125, 127
Recommendations for Accessibility Standards for Children's Environments (Center for Accessible Housing), 182–183
Recommendations for Accessibility to Serve Physically Handicapped Children in Elementary Schools (ATBCB), 182
Regular education initiative, 180
See also Inclusion
Rehabilitation Act, 4, 102, 123–125, 129, 245, 372
Rehabilitation Engineering Society of North America (RESNA), 251
Reinforcers, 378–380, 396–397
presentation reinforcement, 10, 170, 379
removal reinforcement, 10, 170, 379
vicarious reinforcement, 396
Related services, 44
definitions of, 45–46, 101
individualization of, 219
pullout, 155, 177
push-in, 155, 177
Reliability of research, 76
Removal reinforcement, 10, 170, 379
Repetto, J., 237
Research, 68, 79
age at start, 84–85
bias in, 71–72, 80
on cost-effectiveness and cost-benefits, 88–90
on curriculum, 93–94
on effectiveness of early childhood special education, 81–84
execution of, 75
generalizability, 73–74
on helping children with severe conditions, 92
importance of, 71
on inclusion, 90–92
on intensity, 85–87
long-term effects of, 75–76
null hypothesis, 72–73
and opinion, 76–77
on parental involvement, 87
qualitative research, 77–78
quantitative research, 77–78
randomization in, 75
reliability of, 76
sample size, 79
statistical significance, 73
subject attrition, 74
on target population, 94
on teaming, 92–93
validity of, 76
variables in, 72
within-group differences, 79
See also individual research projects
Respite care, 140–141, 166, 286
resources for, 421
Response to intervention (RTI), 172–174
Retention, grade, 84, 154–155, **264,** 265, 295
Retinopathy of prematurity (ROP), 307
Retrolental fibroplasia, 307
Reverse mainstreaming, 297
Reynolds, Arthur, 68–69
Rheumatoid arthritis, juvenile, 336
Rhode Island Hearing Assessment Project (RIHAP), 309
Ridley, C.A., 397
Rights
Air Carriers Access Act, 134
Americans with Disabilities Act (ADA), 4, 122, 123, 125–128, 245
Fair Housing Amendments Act (FHAA), 133
procedural safeguards in IDEA, 128–133, **130, 131**
Rehabilitation Act, 4, 102, 123–125, 129, 245, 372
Telecommunications Act, 134
Television Decoder Circuitry Act, 134
Risk, children at-. *See* At-risk children
Risk factors for disability, 13
Ritalin, 376
Romski, M, 340
Rosen, G.D., 356
Rosetti, L., 206
Rosetti Infant-Toddler Language Scale, 311
Rosetti Interview Guide, 311
Roth, W., 12
The Unexpected Minority, 10

Roush, J., 318
Rowley, Amy, 231
Royeen, C.B., 290

S

Safety. *See* Environments
Sainato, D., 154, 158
Sample size in research, 79
Sandall, Susan, 93
Sanislaw, H., 85
Saylor, C., 85, 329
Scaffolding, 9
Scampini, L., 401
SCERTS model, 399
SCHIP. *See* State Children's Health Insurance Program (SCHIP)
Schopler, E., 399
Schrag, J.A., 235
Schroeder, M., 337
Science in primary special education, 176–177
Scott, M.M., 92, 122, 233, 289, 290
Screening, 194–195
Seamless system, 48–49, 112–113
  See also Transition
Section 504. *See* Rehabilitation Act
Section 615. *See* IDEA Part B
Section 619. *See* IDEA Part B
Section 636. *See* IDEA Part C
Section 639. *See* IDEA Part C
SEELS. *See* Special Education Elementary Longitudinal Study (SEELS)
Selection error, 79
Self-actualization, 11
Self-help behaviors, 16, 386, 400–401
  See also Adaptive development
Self-talk, 160, 175
Sensorimotor stage, 8
Service coordinators, 59, 134–135, **135,** 225, 284
Sevcik, R., 340
Shaping, 11, 378
Shared reading, 169
Shonkoff, J.P., 219
Short, A., 399
Siblings, 287–288
Siblings Support Project, 288
Sib to Sib newsletter, 288
Sigman, M., 82–83
Signed English, 170–171, 317
Sign language. *See* American Sign Language (ASL)
Silverstein, Robert, 109
Singer, L., 200
SKI*HI curriculum, 157
Skinner, B.F., 10, 19
Smith, Alicia, 110
Smith, R., 309
Smith, T., 399
Smith, V., 305
Snellen Illiterate E chart, 312
Social/emotional development, 15, 16–17, 27–29, 366–367
  assessment of, 372–375, **373**
  early intervention in, 375–377
  interagency coordination for children with disorders in, 382
  medications for disorders in, **376**
  prevalence of disorders, 367–368
  See also individual social/emotional disorders
Social Skills Rating System (SSRS), 197
Social workers, 59
Socio-economic status (SES), 50, 52
  and age at start, 84–85
  and at-risk children, 7
  and communication impoverishment, 358, 362
  demographics, 270–272
  and legislation, 113–114
  and SSI, 137
Southwest Autism Research and Resource Center, 392
Sparkman, C., 85
Sparling, J.J., 157
Special education. *See* Early childhood special education (ECSE)
Special Education Elementary Longitudinal Study (SEELS), 70, 92
  academics, 83–84, 95, 154–155
  ADHD, 54–55, 368
  ages of young children in various grades, **264,** 264–265
  children who are deaf, 306
  communication development, 302, 314
  emotional disorders, 367
  family involvement, 88
Special-needs trusts, 272
Specific learning disabilities, 275–277, 351–353
  and ADHD, 368, 372
  assessment of, 355–356
  curriculum for children with, 360–361
  demographic data, 54
  dyslexia, 352, 356
  prevalence of, 303, 350–351
  resources for, 419
  response to intervention, 172–173
Speech, 22
  assessment of, 310–311
  morphemes, 22
  phonemes, 22
  See also Communication development; Language
Speech and language impairment (SLI), 275–277, 302, 305
  assessment of, 310–311
  intervention for, **313,** 313–314
  prevalence of, 303
  resources for, 422
Speech-language pathology, 60, 165, 310
Speech recognition. *See* Speech to text (speech recognition)
Speech synthesis. *See* Text to speech (speech synthesis)
Speech to text (speech recognition), 242, 245, 246, 298, 321–322
Spina bifida, 332, 342–343
  prevalence of, 328
  resources for, 422
Spina Bifida Association of America (SBAA), 328, 332, 343
Spinal cord injuries (SCI), 335, 341
  prevalence of, 328
  psychological adjustments to, **341**
Squires, J., 195
Stahmer, A., 90, 91, 399
Stairs, 183
Standardized tests. *See* Academics
State Children's Health Insurance Program (SCHIP), 139–140

State implementation grants (SIGs), 106
State role in early childhood special education, 61–62, 63, 100–103
Statistical significance in research, 73
Statistics. *See* Demographics
Status of the American Public School Teacher (NEA), 58
Stay-put provisions, 381
Steckol, K., 305
Steighner, S.A., 91
Stella, M.E., 236
Stimulation of cognitive development, 358–359
Stoner, J., 401
Storage areas, 184
Strain, Philip, 86, 93, 179
Strategic Instruction Model, 360–361
Strategy instruction, 360
Stuttering, 305, 311, 313, **313**
Subject attrition in research, 74
Summative evaluation, 211–212
Supplemental Security Income (SSI), 135–137, 253–254, 271
Support equipment for children with disabilities, 23–24, 25
Surgical interventions, 293–294, 317
Surgically Shaping Children (Parens), 294
Syntax, 21

T

Tallal, Paula, 352, 356
Tarr, J.E., 89
Task analysis, 359
Taylor, M., 282
TDDs. *See* Telecommunications devices for the deaf (TDDs)
Teaching methods
  developmentally appropriate practice, 30–31, 151, 154, 219
  directed discovery learning, 32, **33,** 177, 360
  direct instruction, 151, 154, 157, 163–164, 172, 230, 359
  discovery learning, 8, 360
  guided discovery learning, 32, **33,** 176, 360
Teaming, 92–93, 280–281, 288–290
Technology
  assistive technology devices, 171–172, 244–250
    augmentative and alternative communication technologies, 247, 340
    broadband, 242–243, 249–250
    cell phones, 249
    for children who are blind, 319–320
    for children with cerebral palsy, 333–334
    for children with muscular dystrophy, 342
    in the classroom, 246–248
    e-mail, 246
    instant messaging (IM), 242
    PowerPoint, 248
    speech to text (speech recognition), 242, 245, 246, 298, 321–322
    telemedicine, 249–250
    telepresence, 249
    text to speech (speech synthesis), 248, 321–322, 343, 358, 361
    touch-screen, 242, 245–246, 247
  assistive technology services, 250–252
    environmental control system (ECS), 251
  bulletin board system (BBS), 254, 255–256
  creating a telecommunications capacity, 255–256
  distance learning, 255
  financing options, **252,** 252–254
  information sources, 258–260
  low-tech, 242, 243–244
  multimedia, 257
  resources for, 422
  technology experts, 60–61
  television, 256–257
  use of by ECSE professionals, 254–255
Telecommunications Act, 134
Telecommunications devices for the deaf (TDDs), 125
Telemedicine, 249–250
Telepresence, 249
Teletypewriters (TTYs), 127
Television, 256–257, 298
Television Decoder Circuitry Act, 134
Temple, Judy, 68
Testing, 195
  cultural diversity issues, 202–203
  legal issues, 196–197
  rating scales, 196–197
  test interpretation, 200–202
  variables in children, 197–198
  variables in examiners, 198–199
  variables in instruments, 199–200
  See also Assessment; Screening
Tests, standardized. *See* Academics
Text to speech (speech synthesis), 248, 321–322, 343, 358, 361
Therapists, 60
Thomas, J., 377
Thwing, E., 195
Tidmarsh, L., 377
Time delay, 167
Time-outs, 380–381
Timothy W. v. Rochester School District, 45
Toddlers
  age range, 2–3, **3**
  assessment of, **206,** 206–207, **207**
  communication development of, 19–20
  curriculum for, 93
  definition of, 41–42, **42**
  demographics of children served, 3–4, **4,** 272–275, **273**
  diagnosed conditions, 50
  early intervention, 40–44, 49–52, **50, 51**
  embedding of instruction, 159–163
  I statements, 14
  language development of, 21
  physical development of, 26–27
  self-help behaviors, 16
  social/emotional development of, 28
  See also Early intervention

Toilets, 184
Touch-screen technology, 242, 245–246, 247
Toys, adaptive, 338–339
  adapted toys catalogs, **339**
  resources for, **24**
Transdisciplinary play-based assessment (TPBA), 206
Transition, 34–35
  guidance for parents, 236
  Individualized Family Service Plan (IFSP), 225, **226**
  within Part C, 234
  from Part C to other service programs, 235–236
  from Part C to Part B, 234–235
  from preschool to elementary school, 236–237, **237**
  transition services, 219
  See also Seamless system
Translation services for families, 133
Transportation rights for people with disabilities, 126
Traumatic brain injuries (TBI), 334–335
  families of children with, 345, **345**
  intervention for, 340–341
  prevalence of, 328
  psychological adjustments to, **341**
  resources for, 422
Triangulation, 78
Trusts, special-needs, 272
Trust *versus* mistrust, 9
TTYs. *See* Teletypewriters (TTYs)
Tuthill, P., 337

U

Unexpected Minority, The (Gliedman and Roth), 10
United Cerebral Palsy Association (UCPA), 137, 254
United States Constitution
  Fifth Amendment, 100
  Tenth Amendment, 102
  Fourteenth Amendment, 100, 102
United States Department of Education
  Annual Reports, 94, 269, 387
    7th Annual report, 109–110
    22th Annual Report, 54
    27th Annual Report, 47, 275, 277
    28th Annual Report, 3, 269, 272–273, 275, 303, 350, 368
  Institute of Education Sciences, 77
  regulations, 103–104, 309
Used Equipment Referral Service, 254

V

Vadasy, P., 288
Validity of research, 76
Van Riper, C., 305
Variables in children during testing, 197–198
Variables in examiners during testing, 198–199
Variables in instruments during testing, 199–200
Variables in research, 72
Variety Children's Learning Center (VCLC), **286,** 286–287, 382
Vaughn, S.R., 397
VCS. *See* Vulnerable child syndrome (VCS)
Velcro, 243, 338
Verbal prompts, 163
Vicarious reinforcement, 396
Vineland Adaptive Behavior Scales, 355, 374, 394
Vision, 22–23
  assessment of, 311–312
  See also Blindness or low vision, children with
Visual prompts, 163
Voice-in-a-Box, 247
Voice recognition. *See* Speech to text (speech recognition)
Vulnerable child syndrome (VCS), 74, 389–390, 397–398
Vygotsky, Lev, 9

W

Waissman, Renée, 344
Walking, 12–13, 26
Ward, E., 293
Watson, L.S., 401
Weicker, Lowell, 110
Weintraub, Frederick, 366
Wershing, A., 338
West, J., 83
Wetherby. Amy, 399
What Works Clearinghouse, 159
Wheelchairs, 327, 335
  seating and positioning, **336**
White, K.R., 109, 213, 282, 286, 309, 321
Wietlisbach, S., 290
Wilding, G., 344
Williams, B., 74
Willis, D.J., 206
Wing, L., 392
Winton, P.J., 92–93
Within-group differences in research, 79
Wolery, M., 154, 158, 166, 167, 236
Writing. *See* Literacy

Y

Young, E., 344
Young Autism Project, 398

Z

Zettel, J., 107
Zone of proximal development, 9
Zuckerman, B., 7